ALSO BY YANG JISHENG

Tombstone: The Great Chinese Famine, 1958–1962

THE
WORLD TURNED
UPSIDE DOWN

THE
WORLD TURNED
UPSIDE DOWN

A HISTORY OF THE
CHINESE CULTURAL
REVOLUTION

YANG JISHENG

TRANSLATED FROM THE CHINESE AND EDITED BY

Stacy Mosher and Guo Jian

Farrar, Straus and Giroux
120 Broadway, New York 10271

Printed in the United States of America
Originally published in Chinese in different form in 2016 by Cosmos Books, Hong Kong
English translation published in the United States by Farrar, Straus and Giroux
First American edition, 2021

Library of Congress Cataloging-in-Publication Data
Names: Yang, Jisheng, 1940– author. | Mosher, Stacy, translator. | Guo, Jian,
    1953– translator.
Title: The world turned upside down : a history of the Chinese Cultural Revolution /
    Yang Jisheng ; translated from the Chinese and edited by Stacy Mosher and Guo
    Jian.
Other titles: Tian di fan fu. English | History of the Chinese Cultural Revolution
Description: First American edition. | New York : Farrar, Straus and Giroux, 2020. |
    Originally published in Chinese by Cosmos Books, Hong Kong, 2016. | Includes
    bibliographical references and index. | Summary: "The only complete history of the
    Cultural Revolution by an independent scholar based in mainland China, *The
    World Turned Upside Down* makes a crucial contribution to understanding the
    Cultural Revolution and its lasting influence today" —Provided by publisher.
Identifiers: LCCN 2020039387 | ISBN 9780374293130 (hardback)
Subjects: LCSH: China—History—Cultural Revolution, 1966–1976. | Political
    culture—China—History. | Communism and culture—China.
Classification: LCC DS778.7 .Y3713 2020 | DDC 951.05/6—dc23
LC record available at https://lccn.loc.gov/2020039387

Our books may be purchased in bulk for promotional, educational, or business
use. Please contact your local bookseller or the Macmillan Corporate and
Premium Sales Department at 1-800-221-7945, extension 5442, or by email at
MacmillanSpecialMarkets@macmillan.com.

www.fsgbooks.com
www.twitter.com/fsgbooks • www.facebook.com/fsgbooks

10   9   8   7   6   5   4   3   2   1

CONTENTS

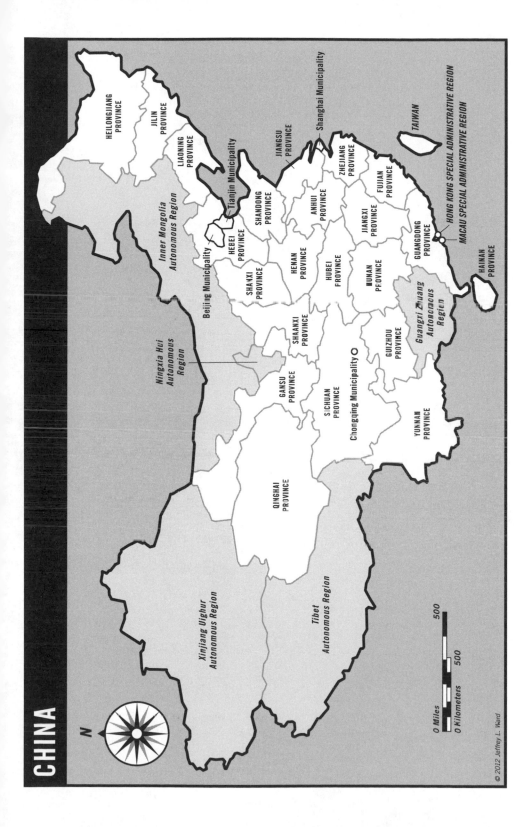

TRANSLATORS' NOTE

Yang Jisheng's *The World Turned Upside Down* arrives with renewed attention to the Cultural Revolution at the fiftieth anniversary of its launch, and as China's president Xi Jinping takes steps to enhance centralized power and to establish a Mao-style cult of personality. The only complete history of the Cultural Revolution by an independent scholar based in mainland China, *The World Turned Upside Down* makes a crucial contribution to understanding the Cultural Revolution and its lasting influence today.

As a major political event and a crucial turning point in the history of the People's Republic of China (PRC), the Great Proletarian Cultural Revolution (1966–1976) marked the heyday as well as the eventual bankruptcy of Mao Zedong's ultra leftist politics. Purportedly to prevent China from departing from its socialist path, Mao mobilized the masses in a battle against what he considered to be the bourgeoisie within the ruling Chinese Communist Party (CCP). This ten-year-long class struggle on a massive scale caused unprecedented damage to traditional culture and to the nation's economy. To a great extent, it was the disaster of the Cultural Revolution that prompted post-Mao Chinese Communist leaders, ahead of their Soviet counterparts, to implement pragmatic economic reforms. Major policies that the post-Mao government has adopted may still be best understood as a reaction to the radical politics of the Cultural Revolution.

The revolution was *cultural* because Mao conceived of it in Marxist terms as a thoroughgoing revolution aimed at eradicating old culture and customs and educating the masses through a series of political campaigns. Mao considered a populace with a revolutionized consciousness to be the best defense against the bourgeoisie taking power over the country. Although Mao's program achieved considerable success in destroying much of traditional culture, the Cultural Revolution also brought about a revival of China's imperial past in the widespread personality cult of Mao and the deification of the leader.

The Cultural Revolution was *political* as well, since the pronounced main task of this movement was to purge "capitalist roaders" in the party leadership and "strengthen the proletarian dictatorship" under Mao. Even though some of the leaders thus named—such as Mao's first chosen successor, President Liu Shaoqi—took an approach less radical than Mao's to China's economic development, all of them were committed Communists and had never designed a program, as charged, to "restore capitalism" in China.

The Cultural Revolution had a far greater impact on the lives of ordinary people and on Chinese society in general than any other political movement in the history of the PRC. Large swaths of the population were demonized and persecuted as political enemies, especially those labeled as "black elements" (landlords, rich peasants, counterrevolutionaries, bad elements, and rightists), along with teachers, scholars, and artists whose work had to do with culture and education. A vast number of them were illegally detained, interrogated, tortured, and even brutally murdered or driven to suicide. The majority of government officials and party cadres were sidelined as capitalist roaders and sent to labor camps to undergo "reform." Enthusiastic urban youths formed Red Guard and rebel organizations and served as Mao's crusading army against the traditional party and state establishment before most of them—seventeen million in total—were likewise sent to the countryside to be "reeducated" by peasants, crippling them for participation in the post–Cultural Revolution era of Reform and Opening. Factional violence among mass organizations throughout the country in 1967 and 1968 resulted in substantial military and civilian casualties that still remain uncounted, except for sporadic provincial and local statistics. According to official estimates, the total number of people affected by campaigns against political enemies amounts to a hundred million, which was one-eighth of China's population at the time. Due to the Cultural Revolution's long-lasting, grave impact on China's economy and national life, it is both officially and popularly referred to as "ten years of chaos."

The post-Mao CCP leadership began in late 1976 to implement concrete measures to reverse Mao's Cultural Revolution policies in all areas. In June 1981, the central leadership adopted the "Resolution on Certain Questions in the History of Our Party Since the Founding of Our Country," an attempt to review Mao's legacy and conclude a highly problematic chapter in the CCP history so that both the party and the nation might be united, leave the past behind, and look ahead. While acknowledging the Cultural Revolution as the cause of "the most severe setback and the heaviest losses the party, the state, and the people had suffered since the founding of the PRC," the resolution nevertheless upheld Mao Zedong Thought as the guiding principle of the CCP, apparently out of concern that a thoroughgoing critique of the Cultural Revolution might put the legitimacy of the entire regime in question. The Cultural Revolution has therefore remained a highly sensitive topic in China, and important Cultural Revolution documents remain classified in Beijing's Central Archives while serious independent studies of the Cultural Revolution such as Yang Jisheng's are invariably censored in mainland China; the Chinese edition of *The World Turned Upside Down* (2016) was published in Hong Kong and cannot be legally sold or circulated in mainland China.

Arriving more than a decade after the publication of official Chinese studies on the subject, such as *A Concise History of the Cultural Revolution* (1996) by Xi Xuan and Jin Chuming, *Turbulent Decade: A History of the Cultural Revolution* (1988) by Yan Jiaqi and Gao Gao, and *Years of Great Turmoil* (1988) by Wang Nianyi, as well as *Mao's Last Revolution* (2006) by Roderick MacFarquhar and Michael Schoenhals, Yang Jisheng's *The World Turned Upside Down* has benefited from many memoirs, local histories, and commentaries published in the intervening years that offer a great deal of additional material and new thinking regarding the Cultural Revolution. Frank Dikotter's recent *The Cultural Revolution: A People's History, 1962–1976* (2016) also takes advantage of more recently unearthed material to offer the thesis that popular passive resistance and noncompliance led to the end of Maoism. Yang Jisheng, on the other hand, posits that the

Cultural Revolution was a triangular game between Mao, the bureaucratic clique, and the rebel faction, and that the bureaucratic clique ultimately won, Mao lost, and the rebel faction bore the consequences of the loss. Yang, who has also written important works on China's Reform and Opening (*The Deng Xiaoping Era: Twenty Years of China's Reform and Opening* [1998] and *Political Struggle During China's Reform Era* [2004]), asserts here that Reform and Opening resulted from the ultimate victory of the bureaucratic clique, of which Deng Xiaoping and other reformers were key members, and that it is therefore essential to understand the mentality and practices of that clique in order to understand China as we know it today.

Yang Jisheng rejects the official version of rebels running amuck and departing from the original trajectory of Mao Zedong Thought, finding instead that Mao fully intended to topple enemies in the bureaucratic clique who stood in the way of his envisioned utopia (already discredited during the Great Leap Forward and the Great Famine) while also forging a "new man" through political campaigns. Mao used the rebel faction to "smash the old state apparatus" but then abandoned the rebels and restored the purged bureaucratic clique to attain "great order" after the nationwide chaos. While most Cultural Revolution histories and popular art and literature demonize the rebel faction, this book describes tragedies created by the bureaucratic clique that far exceeded those created by the rebel faction, in particular among ordinary people.

Official Chinese histories claim that the adverse effects of the Cultural Revolution resulted from its "being made use of by counterrevolutionary cliques," in particular those of Lin Biao and the Gang of Four. This book shows that Lin Biao and Jiang Qing merely supported Mao and that the majority of so-called counterrevolutionary actions were carried out under Mao's leadership to push forward the Cultural Revolution. The book also points out that Liu Shaoqi, depicted in officially influenced histories as a docile victim of the Cultural Revolution, was initially a fully engaged participant in the power struggle at the highest reaches of government, and that Zhou Enlai, typically portrayed in a positive light as opposing the Cultural Revolution and protecting cadres, faithfully assisted Mao throughout the movement.

As the translators of Yang Jisheng's *Tombstone*, we once again faced the task of not only translating but also editing *The World Turned Upside Down* (originally published at a length of eight hundred thousand Chinese characters) to bring it within the acceptable length for publication in English. As with *Tombstone*, we benefited from Mr. Yang's help in first going through the book and making cuts, including the removal of three chapters. In the translation process, our further edits were aimed at highlighting the material that best supports Mr. Yang's thesis, reducing the amount of sometimes bewildering detail, and preserving material that is not replicated in other published works. It is our hope that the version presented here fully reflects Mr. Yang's key points on this complex topic.

The world of translation is notoriously underfunded. We are grateful for the confidence that Farrar, Straus and Giroux has demonstrated in making this English translation of *The World Turned Upside Down* possible. We would also like to thank the Open Society Foundations for their additional and essential support.

AUTHOR'S NOTE

The Chinese writer Wang Meng once said, "Who can explain and furthermore summarize, politically and in terms of schools of thought, the ten-year Cultural Revolution that began in 1966? . . . This is Chinese history, and the Chinese are duty-bound to correctly and unambiguously sum up the Cultural Revolution in all its aspects, not just for China, but for the sake of human history as well."[1] This work that Wang Meng describes has long attracted me, and I hope that my exploration of this complex and dangerous terrain will make a difference.

As a participant in the Cultural Revolution at Tsinghua University in 1966 and 1967, I traveled to a dozen or so cities throughout China for the Great Networking. In January 1968, I became a journalist for the Xinhua News Agency, and over the ensuing years I covered many incidents related to the Cultural Revolution. In both my personal experience and journalistic reporting, however, I "missed the forest for the trees" and lacked a comprehensive and in-depth understanding of this period of history. After I finished writing *Tombstone* in 2007, I turned to researching the Cultural Revolution. Although many general histories of the Cultural Revolution have been published,[2] I decided to offer my experience and understanding of the Cultural Revolution's process for readers' critical judgment.

Researching the Cultural Revolution requires restoring the original features of history by transcending the limitations of that era and of personal interest and feelings and standing on the high ground of human and political civilization. The official version of the Cultural Revolution is limited by its original ideology and political system, which inevitably contradicts historical truth.

On June 27, 1981, the sixth plenum of the Eleventh Central Committee of the Chinese Communist Party (CCP) passed its "Resolution on Certain Questions in the History of Our Party Since the Founding of Our Country,"[3] which became the blueprint for the official history of the Cultural Revolution. This resolution recounted and commented on recent history in accordance with what prevailing political conditions required and allowed and was actually more of a compromise on the political problems faced at that time. Without it, China's great transformation through Reform and Opening over the next thirty years would have been impossible. However, restoring the truth of the Cultural Revolution prohibits historians from taking a middle course and compromising as politicians do.

The resolution preserved the soul of the dictatorial system, and with it the interests of the bureaucratic clique, by upholding Mao Zedong Thought and distinguishing it from the thinking and theories Mao developed after 1956. This utilitarian pruning goes against historical truth and doesn't stand up under scrutiny.

Official Cultural Revolution history also legitimizes the continued rule of the CCP by holding that the Cultural Revolution was "internal disorder, erroneously launched by the leader and made use of by counterrevolutionary cliques,"[4] attempting to push responsibility for the Cultural Revolution onto "the counterrevolutionary cliques of Lin Biao and Jiang Qing" and thereby remedy the crisis of confidence in the CCP. If these two cliques really existed, however, they rose and fell within the party.

The official history of the Cultural Revolution, and the books that have been influenced by it, present Liu Shaoqi as a docile sheep, entirely subject to Mao's whims and finally sent packing down a road of no return. In fact, as a revolutionary who had experienced many battles and years of party infighting, Liu Shaoqi and the bureaucratic clique he represented resisted Mao right from the outset of the Cultural Revolution. After Liu Shaoqi was unseated, there was resistance to the Cultural Revolution faction through the "February Countercurrent" and "February Suppression of Counterrevolutionaries," and from a group represented by Deng Xiaoping, as well as even stronger resistance from the military bureaucratic clique. This series of resistances was not based on right and wrong so much as on opposing interests, and ordinary people bore the brunt of these confrontations. Depicting Liu Shaoqi as a submissive sheep is an attempt to keep the bureaucratic clique from being held responsible for the Cultural Revolution and to cover up the evil conduct of military and government bureaucrats that so devastated masses of ordinary people. Embellishing the image of Zhou Enlai and covering up his complicity with Mao during the Cultural Revolution arises from the same objective.

Official history attempts to exonerate Mao by blaming the evil consequences of the Cultural Revolution on the "counterrevolutionary cliques," but the Gang of Four didn't emerge until August 1973,[5] after most of the veteran cadres had been restored to their posts, and if there was a "Lin Biao clique," it existed from only April 1969 to September 1971. In any case, Lin Biao, Jiang Qing, and their respective groups merely pushed forward the Cultural Revolution under Mao's direction. Jiang Qing said, "I was Chairman Mao's dog, and whomever he told me to bite, I bit." Jiang Qing and Lin Biao were used by Mao, and the most they could do was to make use of the opportunities created by Mao to eliminate some of their opponents.

After the Cultural Revolution was negated, senior party cadres wrote books and articles in which they professed to have adamantly resisted the Cultural Revolution all along. Left unmentioned were the periods when they played along, their persecution of other cadres and oppression of the masses, and their gloating over the misfortunes of their colleagues. Official histories amply cover the persecution of cadres during the Cultural Revolution but barely mention or even distort the repeated bloody suppressions targeting ordinary people, the victims of which outnumber persecuted cadres by many hundredfold. History is written by the victors, and given that the ultimate victor of the Cultural Revolution was the bureaucratic clique, the sufferings of ordinary people have been largely ignored.

The Cultural Revolution was an extremely complex historical process with multiple layers of conflict between multiple forces enmeshed in repeated power struggles and reversals over the course of ten years and a vast geographical space. All kinds of thinking, all types of communities, and all sorts of interest groups repeatedly clashed, but also became interwoven and bound together. The victors at one stage might become the losers at another stage; the people carrying out purges during one period of time might themselves be purged at another juncture. Thinking in black and white with simplified terms of "endorsement" or "negation" makes it impossible to record or comment on this complex historical process.

Any reasonable thesis raised about the Cultural Revolution will be met with an equally reasonable rebuttal; any historical account will be criticized by someone as one-sided, because most of the people who experienced the Cultural Revolution are still alive and well, and their different roles and situations during the Cultural Revolution gave them different perspectives and experiences. The criticisms of these participants are very valuable and push researchers ever closer to historical truth, but this invaluable resource for contemporary history presents its own difficulties.

I'm a latecomer compared with others who have undertaken studies of the Cultural Revolution. Bringing up the rear has its advantages, in that I didn't have to start from scratch and could use the outstanding work of my predecessors as a point of departure. As I've read grand narratives of the overall history of the Cultural Revolution, memoirs by those who experienced it, in-depth research on key topics, histories of the Cultural Revolution in specific localities, and theoretical explorations, these names have become embedded in my memory: Gao Gao, Yan Jiaqi, Wang Nianyi, Xi Xuan, Jin Chunming, Roderick MacFarquhar, Wang Youqin, Zhou Lunzuo, He Shu, Wang Shaoguang, Wang Li, Chen Xiaonong, Wu Faxian, Qiu Huizuo, Li Zuopeng, Xu Jingxian, Nie Yuanzi, Yu Ruxin, Liu Guokai, Xu Youyu, Song Yongyi, Hu Ping, Ding Shu, Guo Jian, Gao Wenqian, Gao Hua, Yin Hongbiao, Han Gang, Xiao Xidong, Ding Dong, Chen Yinan, Bu Weihua, Tang Shaojie, Qian Liqun, Zhang Boshu, Zhu Xueqin, Chen Kuide, Wang Ruoshui, Wang Haiguang, Wang Xizhe, Wang Lixiong, Yang Xiguang, Shu Yun, Ding Kaiwen, Xu Hailiang, Qi Zhi, Sima Qingyang, Zhou Ziren, Hua Xinmin, Alateng Delihai, She Namujila, Jin Guangyao, Jin Dalu, Li Xun, Dong Guoqiang, and Deng Zhenxin, among others. Even more valuable are some scholars who were willing to serve as stepping stones for other researchers as they quietly collected, edited, and sorted historical materials. Fu Sinian[6] said that, in a sense, the study of history is the study of historical material. The editors of works such as *The Chinese Cultural Revolution Database* compiled by Song Yongyi, Ding Shu, Guo Jian, and others; *Chronicle of Events of the Ten-Year Cultural Revolution* compiled by Zhou Liangxiao and his wife, Gu Juying; as well as electronic collections of Cultural Revolution historical materials such as *Remembrance*, *Yesterday*, and the Virtual Museum of the Cultural Revolution[7] have made a profound and indelible contribution. The years I spent researching and writing this book gave me the deepest respect for these forerunners in the field.

Xu Youyu, Ding Dong, Bu Weihua, Yu Ruxin, Li Xun, and Cong Ziwen read the early draft of this book, while He Shu, Cai Wenbin, Xu Hailiang, Wang Haiguang, and Song Yimin read parts of it. They all offered valuable feedback, for which I am deeply grateful.

PREFACE: THE ROAD, THE THEORY, AND THE SYSTEM

In 1966 and the nine years that followed, nearly every person in China became embroiled to some extent in the Cultural Revolution, an experience that left a permanent mark on the lives, fates, and souls of every participant. Even more profound was the movement's effect on China's politics, economy, and society.

Mao Zedong originally expected the Cultural Revolution to last for at most three years. But as it proceeded, many unanticipated situations emerged. Mao never imagined the complete loss of control in August 1967 that would compel him to abandon some of the Cultural Revolution's staunchest supporters. He never imagined the irreconcilable struggle within the military ranks in 1968 would oblige him to cast away another group of allies. He hoped that the Ninth Party Congress would lead to a stage of "struggle-criticism-transformation," never envisioning that a rift between him and Lin Biao would culminate in Lin Biao's shocking escape attempt and death in 1971. Right from the outset, repeated collisions derailed the Cultural Revolution from its initial objectives and left participants stranded. After the Lin Biao incident, Mao hoped to return the Cultural Revolution to its original direction, but by then the movement had lost public support and people had begun fastening their hopeful gazes on Zhou Enlai. That made Zhou the new target of Mao's revolution. One new problem followed another, and new errors were deployed to correct those that had come before. The Cultural Revolution was a ten-year process of feeling for rocks while crossing a river, and may have lasted even longer if Mao hadn't died in 1976.

The Cultural Revolution was like a riptide resulting from the interaction of multiple forces, with each wave of turbulence swallowing up a new batch of victims and creating a new group of "enemies." As the impetus of the Cultural Revolution faltered before growing resistance and the withdrawal of increasing numbers of people to the sidelines, the waves gradually ebbed until the Cultural Revolution failed and was thoroughly repudiated.

With each surge of setbacks and struggles, ordinary people were churned and pummeled in abject misery, while Mao, at a far remove, boldly proclaimed, "Look, the world is turning upside down!"[1] I've used this expression as the title of my book to indicate the extent of this turmoil and suffering.

The roots of the Cultural Revolution have to be sought in the system that existed in the seventeen years before it began, in the prevailing ideology, and in the road Mao maintained at that time.

The Cultural Revolution was a power struggle over the road China should take; power was merely the tool for achieving a political path.

Some researchers believe that the Cultural Revolution was a pure power struggle in which Mao sought to strip Liu Shaoqi of the prestige he'd gained by cleaning up the aftermath of the Great Famine. There's some truth in this view, but it doesn't entirely stand up under analysis. The entire process of the Cultural Revolution was packed with vicious power struggles from the Central Committee down to the grassroots. However, among politicians, power is a tool for realizing political objectives, in this case China's political direction (i.e., "Whither China?"). Mao and Liu had long parted ways on this point, and each had established his own contingent of supporters.

The leadership of the Chinese Communist Party was united on the basic question of taking the socialist road and achieving social justice with a comprehensive plan executed by the regime, but Mao and Liu disagreed on the conditions under which "new democracy" could transition to socialism, and how quickly.

Although Liu Shaoqi, like Mao, put an emphasis on class struggle, the targets of his struggle, i.e., criticism and denunciation, were land-lords, rich peasants, counterrevolutionaries, rightists, corrupt and degenerate grassroots cadres, and intractable intellectuals. Mao was the mastermind of attacks on all types of class enemies, but his main targets were within the party's upper levels, where China's direction was decided. The three-year Great Famine undoubtedly intensified the divisions between Mao and Liu. Unreconciled to the failure of the Three Red Banners, Mao was seeking a new opportunity to establish his utopia of total equality in the political, economic, and cultural spheres. Even if we allow that Mao's intentions were good, socialism, as a form of collectivism, is predicated on the obliteration of the individual and can be achieved only through the evil of coercion. For centuries, socialist ideals had been met with constant rebuff, but rather than recognizing the cause for this in socialism itself, Mao blamed it on "revisionism" and "class enemies."

Combatting and preventing "revisionism" was therefore the chief task of the Cultural Revolution, as Mao tried to clear the way for es-tablishing his utopia. That meant attacking "capitalist roader power-holders" such as Liu Shaoqi, whose attempts to address the problems left over from the Great Famine by giving peasants more autonomy in growing crops and taking a softer line in international affairs were labeled a "counterrevolutionary revisionist line." The path created by Mao had already created hell on earth in the Great Famine era,[2] and the Cultural Revolution that Mao used to clear away obstacles for his envisaged paradise created yet another hell on earth.

The ideology of the political road that Mao chose created a fanatical mass movement that meted out unprecedented brutality to the political underclass and individuals with alternative viewpoints.

The Cultural Revolution was a massive movement that swept up the political underclass[3] at the lower level and attacked the bureau-cratic clique at the upper level. Every work unit, district, and family became embroiled in arguments; married couples fought, fathers and sons became estranged, and the closest of friends parted ways. Mao's main tool for moving the masses, apart from his leadership position and supreme authority, was the ideology in which China's people had been steeped for the past seventeen years through textbooks, newspapers, meetings, and other means. Relentless criticism of nonconformist thinking and watertight imperviousness to outside ideas allowed official ideology to control every individual's brain, guide every person's actions, and monopolize social discourse, creating a group mentality that led people to join movements with enormous political passion. The source of this ideology was Marxism, its sympathy with the oppressed and exploited lending it a moral glamor that inspired tens of millions of people to sacrifice everything for the cause. Ideology became religion, and Mao its high priest. Waving his hand from the gate tower of Tiananmen Square at mass rallies, Mao aroused surges of ardor that dwarfed a papal appearance at the Vatican.

Traditional morality reached its nadir during the Cultural Revolution but was replaced by a different morality that placed group objectives on the highest plane and disregarded all else to achieve them. As Hayek said, "The intensity of the moral emotions behind a movement like that of National Socialism or communism can probably be compared only to those of the great religious movements of history . . . Where there is one common all-overriding end, there is no room for any general morals or rules."[4] The common and all-overriding end was communism.

The root cause of the Cultural Revolution is found in the system of the seventeen years preceding it and not in Mao's individual character alone.

Positioned at the apex of the pyramid of power, Mao inevitably became corrupted by the privileges he enjoyed. But it would be an oversimplification to attribute the Cultural Revolution to Mao's personal qualities. For that reason, this book focuses on Mao's deeds rather than on appraising his personal morals and integrity. The system in place preceding the Cultural Revolution was the fundamental reason that it came about.

The People's Republic of China constructed a Soviet-style power structure on the soil of Chinese imperial autocracy, monopolizing the economy, politics, and ideology. State ownership channeled every person's production and living needs under state planning and allowed the regime to penetrate every pore of society. This tight, harsh system relied almost entirely on a power pyramid of millions of bureaucrats. I adopt "totalitarianism" to denote this system, for lack of a better term.

Wang Ya'nan said, "Bureaucratic politics is a politics of privilege. Under the politics of privilege, political power is not wielded to express the public will or serve the public interest, but rather is wielded in the name of the 'state' or 'citizens' to control and enslave the people in order to achieve the selfish objectives of those in power."[5] Under totalitarianism, privilege became an even more serious problem.

The emperor ruled his people by ruling his officials, and ruling officials was the emperor's greatest challenge. As an old Chinese saying goes, "It is hard to rule the empire; everyone thinks the people are hard to rule, not knowing that the difficulty is not with the people but with the officials." Mao faced the same quandary. Mao was a member of the bureaucratic clique but different from it. He needed bureaucrats to fulfill their duties by implementing his will, but the bureaucrats also had a private side, and they pursued the interests of themselves, their families, and their groups, which were independent of the interests of the supreme ruler. Mao noticed the private side of the bureaucrats steadily swelling and became alarmed by signs that decay was setting in and accelerating.

Although Mao helped create this system, it took on a life of its own. The central government ministries and departments and the local governments were interwoven as in a chain-link fence that confined society, and bureaucrats used this fine-mesh fence to engage in unprecedented suppression of society and ordinary people. In 1958, Mao broke from the Soviet system by transferring power downward from the central government ministries and departments, but the result was chaos. He attempted another power transfer during the Cultural Revolution, but this merely resulted in another cycle of what is known in Chinese politics as "death in centralization, and chaos in release."

Mao's dissatisfaction with this system was multifaceted: The ranking system and bureaucrats' remoteness from the masses conflicted with his inborn populism and the anarchism. He worried that bureaucrats' use of material benefit to muster enthusiasm would lead society into a prevailing materialism, and that privilege and corruption would turn officials into opponents of the people; he naturally knew the old saying "The people are the water that can float the boat or overturn it." Mao therefore declared the "privileged stratum" of the "bureaucratic class" and "academic authorities" to be the new targets of struggle and revolution.

As the Yugoslavian communist Milovan Djilas[6] wrote:

> The Communist revolution, conducted in the name of doing away with classes, has resulted in the most complete authority of any single new class . . . The new class is voracious and insatiable, just as the bourgeoisie was. But it does not have the virtues of frugality and economy that the bourgeoisie had. The new class is as exclusive as the aristocracy but without aristocracy's refinement and proud chivalry . . .
>
> The totalitarian tyranny and control of the new class, which came into being during the revolution, has become the yoke from under which the blood and sweat of all members of society flow.[7]

Djilas pointed out that the power of this class was not based on the riches it possessed but rather on the state-owned assets it controlled, and he predicted that this new class would leave behind "one of the most shameful pages in human history."[8] This new class was the bureaucratic class.

Even so, Mao and Djilas had completely different points of departure and solutions for dealing with this new class.

Djilas stated that one of the main reasons for his disillusionment with communism was Stalinist "tyranny" and "primitive and simplified dogmatic communism," and his ultimate ideal was "democratic socialism." Mao, however, defended Stalin and wanted to establish a utopia that surpassed Stalin's system. He never recognized the fundamental problem, which was the need for a totalitarian system in order to establish a communist utopia.

To solve the problem of bureaucracy, Mao looked to the works of Marx, Engels, and Lenin, which reinforced his views on the dubious nature of the state and its eventual dissolution. Without the power of the state apparatus, there would be no one to manage public affairs, and human beings would engage in mutual annihilation. However, once the state apparatus is established, it becomes a "parasitic excrescence"[9] on society and sprouts an enormous bureaucratic clique. Anarchism endures because the state machine produces class oppression and bureaucratic privilege; the state machinery is indispensable because people dread the destructive power of anarchism. The process of the Cultural Revolution was one of repeated struggle between anarchism and state power. Unfortunately, the state power that prevailed was still that of the bureaucratic clique.

The term "bureaucratic clique" as used in this book is value-neutral. The bureaucrats were administrative executives, but without accountability to the public or a reliable system of checks and balances, they could use their power to suppress and exploit the populace. Only a modern democratic system can prevent bureaucrats from becoming suppressers and exploiters and prevent a "public state" from turning into an oppressive bureaucratic state.

At that time, China's immense totalitarian bureaucratic system created strained relations between officials and the populace (the first tier of strained relations) and also within the bureaucracy itself (the second tier of strained relations). The second tier of strained relations resulted from the cadre appointment system, in which the upper levels decided the fate of the lower levels, and was also related to the formation of factions and "mountain strongholds" in the process of seizing state power. Positioned at the apex of the totalitarian bureaucratic system, Mao regularly used the first tier as a check and balance on the second tier, while using populist slogans to undermine the first tier. Using the power of the masses as a counterweight to the totalitarian bureaucratic system meant encouraging the masses to rebel against the bureaucrats. In the Cultural Revolution, these two tiers of strained relations became interwoven and bound together so that political struggles lost their dividing lines between right and wrong, and participants became a vast herd stampeding around the arena.

Before the Cultural Revolution, struggles against the bureaucratic clique had always been carried out internally, but Mao found that these past methods were as ineffective as performing surgery on oneself. He finally arrived at the method of making himself the direct representative of the lower-class masses in casting off the bureaucratic clique, directly mobilizing and directing the masses to "smash the old state apparatus," "roast" the bureaucracy, and "through nationwide chaos attain great order throughout the land."[10]

In order to mobilize the masses to purge the bureaucratic clique and attain "nationwide chaos," Mao needed rebels, but Mao could not allow a state of anarchy to persist over the long term, and restoring "great order throughout the land" required bureaucracy. The rebels were Mao's left hand, which he needed to attack the bureaucracy; but the bureaucratic clique was Mao's right hand, which he needed to restore order.

During the early stage of the Cultural Revolution, Mao wielded his left hand by encouraging the rebels to attack the bureaucrats and "roast them for a while, but not scorch them"; however, this balance became difficult to maintain once intense conflict arose between officials and the populace.[11] During the latter stage of the Cultural Revolution, Mao brandished his right hand and had the bureaucrats contain the rebels, though he ordered the bureaucrats "not to attack them."[12] But how could the newly reinstated bureaucrats not retaliate against their mortal enemies? The Cultural Revolution was a triangular game between Mao, the rebels, and the bureaucratic clique. The final outcome of this game was that the bureaucratic clique eventually emerged victorious over Mao, and the rebels suffered the consequences of Mao's failure. The rebel faction that served as the stone implement that Mao used to "smash the old state apparatus" and to attack the bureaucratic clique was ultimately crushed to pieces under the ever-grinding wheel of the bureaucratic apparatus.

The great calamities of history bring great compensation, and the factors compensating for the Cultural Revolution are part of its legacy. Yet because China's officials utilized their political power to deflect blame from Mao and the totalitarian system, the bureaucratic clique benefited from the historical compensation while the masses continued to swallow the bitter consequences.

Whether analyzed in terms of ideology, political line, or system, the Cultural Revolution was doomed to fail. Once revolutionary committees were established to "make China red through every hill and vale," the old system was restored without the slightest innovation. When the failed escape attempt by Lin Biao, Mao's most important collaborator in launching the Cultural Revolution, resulted in a massive deterioration in Mao's health, Deng Xiaoping stepped in and engaged in a "general overhaul" that hastened the Cultural Revolution's ultimate defeat; the 1976 "April Fifth Movement" showed that the Cultural Revolution had lost public support and that its failure was a foregone conclusion. Less than a month after Mao's death, the four-member Cultural Revolution leadership (known as the Gang of Four), with Mao's widow at its core, was arrested. The old system that the Cultural Revolution had destroyed was completely restored once the Cultural Revolution ended.

The Cultural Revolution produced millions of unjust cases and unnatural deaths affecting more than one hundred million people to varying degrees.[13] Since most of the official data remains classified, there is no way of ascertaining exactly how many people fell victim to the Cultural Revolution. Even so, what can be unambiguously stated is that it was catastrophic for China in terms of the human toll, immense cultural destruction, and economic loss.

Engels said, "There is no great historical evil without a compensating historical progress,"[14] and the historical compensation for the catastrophic Cultural Revolution is part of its legacy.

First, it destroyed the excellent image of the party and officialdom that the government had molded over the long term, and vanquished blind faith in the party and blind respect for officials. The Cultural Revolution destroyed the myth, which had existed since 1949, and especially since 1957, that the Communist Party was infallible, and replaced slavish submission with suspicion and criticism. In the 1980s, the government summarized this phenomenon as a "crisis of trust," and this distrust of political authority is precisely the condition required for a society of subjects to begin progressing toward a society of citizens.

Second, it destroyed the ideology that had been instilled into the populace for so many years. After the failure of the Cultural Revolution caused its ideological edifice to crumble, the Chinese people cast off the spiritual fetters of the previous decades, and most no longer believed in communism. The government considered this a "crisis of faith," and this breaking of spiritual shackles was the necessary condition for the liberation of the people's thinking.

There was also a crisis of confidence, in which the masses lost confidence in the political and economic systems existing during and prior to the Cultural Revolution. From this arose the demand for systemic reform and the exploration of a new system.

It was precisely what the government perceived as three crises that gave unprecedented dynamism to the thinking of the masses and that allowed ordinary people to begin forming an independent mentality. The April Fifth Movement of 1976, the Xidan Democracy Wall in 1978, and the political protests of 1989 all constituted an emancipation of thought that shattered spiritual fetters, forming the necessary conditions for China's Reform and Opening and subsequent push toward democratization.

Third, savage butchery during the Cultural Revolution exposed "class struggle as guiding principle" as the evil it was. Class struggle harmed not only ordinary people but also the bureaucratic clique, especially members of its top echelon such as Deng Xiaoping. Abandoning class struggle as a guiding principle and implementing a focus on economic construction became a consensus supported by all society.

Fourth, the lawlessness of "dictatorship of the masses" hurt not only ordinary people but also the bureaucracy's top officials. Once bureaucrats were restored to their positions, they began constructing the legal system, which, while falling far short of genuine rule of law, was a least a step in the right direction.

The once glorious ideological edifice was now a pile of rubble, and the impregnable totalitarian system was full of holes. Most of China's people had awakened to the truth, and a batch of rational and ambitious officials was ready to set the locomotive of Reform and Opening rumbling forward. At that point, China entered a critical era of accelerated modernization. This was the historical compensation for the disaster of the Cultural Revolution.

Unfortunately, the ultimate victor in the Cultural Revolution was still the bureaucratic clique, which now wielded the power to investigate and punish those responsible for the Cultural Revolution as well as the power to lead Reform and Opening and apportion its spoils.

Assigning responsibility for the Cultural Revolution determined who filled the cadre ranks during Reform and Opening. Deng Xiaoping emphasized, "Those who followed Lin Biao, Jiang Qing, and their ilk and rose to power through rebelling, those who were infected with a factional mentality, and those who engaged in beating, smashing, and looting must absolutely not be promoted, not even one, and those who are still in leadership positions must be resolutely withdrawn."[15] If Deng Xiaoping's proposed appointment standards were proper and necessary, they were nevertheless applied with a double standard in practice. In the purge of those "three types of people" after the Cultural Revolution, the mainstays of the Red August Terror of 1966 were largely protected, and most were funneled into leadership positions as the next generation of bureaucrats. As for ordinary people, the CCP Central Committee handed down a document[16] demanding that the records of mass organization leaders be taken into account for promotion and overseas assignments, limiting the career prospects of many talented people.

Leading Reform and Opening gave the bureaucratic clique the power to decide what would be changed or not changed, and defending the clique's interests meant limiting reform to the economic sphere. While completely negating the Cultural Revolution, China's new leaders carried forward the entire political system and ideology that had created the Cultural Revolution: one-party dictatorship, highly centralized power, and an overriding emphasis on power. Relying on these political legacies allowed the bureaucratic clique of the Mao era (including their progeny and close friends) to become the new elite of the Reform and Opening era.

The bureaucratic clique's control over allocating the fruits of Reform and Opening disassociated the defrayment of the costs of reform from the allocation of its profits: workers, ordinary civil servants, and intellectuals bore the highest cost of reform and received the least, while the elite syndicates that bore little of the cost were by far the greatest beneficiaries. Members of the first "gilded generation" that went abroad to enhance their prospects came from the elite families, and those who made use of the powerful positions of their elders to enter the market economy and amass billions through business were likewise from these families.

Once officials unseated during the Cultural Revolution were

restored to power, they ignored the lessons of what had given rise to the Cultural Revolution, and apart from ceaseless retaliation against the rebels, they indulged in special privilege and corruption that surpassed pre–Cultural Revolution levels. Compared with the poverty of the PRC's early years, Reform and Opening brought richer material conditions for privilege and corruption; it produced wealthy private entrepreneurs and opportunities for power-money exchange; and the powerful could control and manipulate the market and participate in market competition. Hayek said, "A world in which the wealthy are powerful is still a better world than one in which only the already powerful can acquire wealth."[17] In today's China, it is in fact the powerful who acquire wealth.

The rebels took pride in believing, "In the revolution I gave meritorious service, in the Cultural Revolution I suffered, under reform I have power." But now that Mao lay mute in his crystal sarcophagus, the rebels were cast into the eighteenth circle of hell, and the bureaucrats did everything in their power to obstruct progress toward democracy and to promote the market mechanism. The system established in thirty years of reform is called a "socialist market economy," but essentially it is a "power market economy"[18] in which power controls and manipulates the market. Under the power market economy, large and small power hubs are like so many black holes drawing society's riches into social syndicates closely affiliated with those in power. The fundamental problem with a power market economy is its unfairness; an unfair society cannot be harmonious. Under the power market economy, abuse of power is combined with the malign greed for capital, creating a hotbed for all society's evils. Establishing a system with checks and balances over power and controls over capital is the inevitable demand of all society. Constitutional democracy is this system.

CHRONOLOGY OF THE CULTURAL REVOLUTION

1. FERMENTATION

OCTOBER 1, 1949: The People's Republic of China (PRC) is established.

FEBRUARY 1956: Nikita Khrushchev's "secret speech" criticizes Stalin at the Twentieth National Congress of the Soviet Communist Party.

OCTOBER–NOVEMBER 1956: A democratic revolution in Hungary draws a crackdown by Soviet military intervention.

DECEMBER 29, 1956: Reacting to recent events in the Soviet Union, the Chinese Communist Party (CCP) organ *People's Daily* publishes an editorial defending Stalin and attacking "revisionism."

APRIL 27, 1957: In reaction to discontent expressed through dozens of strikes and demonstrations since September 1956, the CCP launches a rectification campaign and encourages intellectuals to voice their critical views.

JUNE 8, 1957: The launch of the Anti-Rightist Campaign results in 550,000 people being labeled "rightists."

1958–1962: More than thirty million people starve to death during the Great Leap Forward.

JANUARY 11–FEBRUARY 7, 1962: During the Seven Thousand Cadres Conference, the leadership of the CCP becomes divided over the lessons of the Great Famine.

SEPTEMBER 24–27, 1962: At the tenth plenum of the Eighth CCP Central Committee, Mao resurrects class struggle and criticizes efforts by Liu Shaoqi and others to bring the famine situation under control.

SEPTEMBER 6, 1963–JULY 14, 1964: The China-Soviet dispute that began in April 1960 intensifies with China's publication of "Nine Commentaries" critical of Soviet revisionism, signifying the CCP's further move toward ultra-leftist ideology.

SPRING 1963–SUMMER 1966: The Socialist Education Movement is conducted in the cities and in the countryside, and Mao calls for purges of "capitalist roaders" in the government. Mao and Liu Shaoqi clash over the movement's policies and principles.

1964–1965: Mass criticism surges throughout the country as a result of ideological class struggle targeting the cultural and academic sectors. The theory of "continuous revolution under the dictatorship of the proletariat" takes shape as the guiding ideology of the Cultural Revolution.

2. PREPARATION
1965

NOVEMBER 10: Shanghai's *Wenhuibao* publishes Yao Wenyuan's essay "On the New Historical Play *Hai Rui Dismissed from Office*," the blasting fuse in Mao's meticulous plan to launch the Cultural Revolution.

DECEMBER 8–15: During an enlarged meeting of the Politburo Standing Committee, Luo Ruiqing is denounced and subsequently relieved of his position as the chief of General Staff.

1966

FEBRUARY 4: The "February Outline," drafted in line with Beijing mayor Peng Zhen's views, puts ongoing mass criticism under the leadership of the party and limits it to the academic sphere.

MARCH 28–30: Mao, Kang Sheng, and others criticize the February Outline for blurring class boundaries and failing to distinguish between right and wrong.

APRIL 16: An enlarged meeting of the Politburo Standing Committee in Hangzhou discusses Peng Zhen's errors and rescinds the February Outline. Li Xuefeng takes over Peng Zhen's duties in a reorganization of the Beijing municipal party committee on May 10.

3. FORMAL LAUNCH
1966

MAY 16: The May 16 Circular is unanimously passed at an enlarged Politburo meeting.

MAY 25: Nie Yuanzi and others put up a big-character poster at Peking University denouncing university president Lu Ping and others. With Mao's support, the text of the poster is published in the June 2 issue of *People's Daily*.

MAY 28: The Central Cultural Revolution Small Group (CCRSG) is established.

MAY 29: Three members of the Politburo Standing Committee—Liu Shaoqi, Zhou Enlai, and Deng Xiaoping decide to send work groups to *People's Daily* and Peking University. On June 4, the new Beijing municipal party committee dispatches work groups to other college campuses.

4. THE CLIMAX
1966

JULY 18: Mao returns to Beijing and criticizes the work groups, and on July 25 he decides to withdraw them.

JULY 29: The Beijing municipal party committee announces the withdrawal of the work groups at a mass rally for Cultural Revolution with activists from secondary and tertiary schools at the Great Hall of the People. People denounced under the work groups are rehabilitated, and some become leaders of rebel faction mass organizations.

AUGUST 1: Mao writes a letter praising the "revolutionary rebel spirit" of the Red Guards at the Tsinghua University Affiliated Secondary School.

AUGUST 1–12: During the eleventh plenum of the Eighth Central Committee, Mao publishes "Bombard the Headquarters: My Big-Character Poster," which targets Liu Shaoqi. On August 8, the plenum passes the "Resolution Regarding the Great Proletarian Cultural Revolution," subsequently known as the Sixteen Articles. Lin Biao ascends to second place in the hierarchy, and Liu Shaoqi drops to eighth place.

AUGUST 18: Mao carries out the first of seven reviews of a total of more than ten million Red Guards at Tiananmen Square. Red Guards embark on the Great Networking throughout the country, igniting the movement in places where it had not yet begun and launching an assault on the bureaucratic structure.

LATE AUGUST–EARLY SEPTEMBER: Red Guards engage in ransacking homes and smashing the "four olds" in Beijing in a terror-ridden "Red August." Meanwhile, hundreds of "black elements" are slaughtered in Beijing's rural Changping and Daxing Counties.

AUGUST–SEPTEMBER: The bureaucratic clique continues to suppress mass movements throughout the country through "revolutionary committee preparatory committees" and pro-government Red Guards. In some localities, party committees mobilize troops, police, workers, or peasants to attack students. Mao refers to the phenomenon as the "bourgeois reactionary line."

OCTOBER 2: *Red Flag* magazine publishes an editorial calling for a thorough denunciation of the bourgeois reactionary line, followed by a mass pledge rally of more than one hundred thousand people on October 6.

OCTOBER 9–28: A Central Committee work conference denounces the bourgeois reactionary line and the "blood lineage theory" of the earlier Red Guard movement, mobilizing rebel organizations against leading government officials.

1967

JANUARY: During the "January Storm" in Shanghai, worker rebel organizations seize power from the Shanghai municipal party committee. Power seizures spread throughout the country, and "three-in-one combination" leading groups replace the original power structure.

JANUARY 13: The Central Committee issues its "Decision Regarding the People's Liberation Army Supporting the Leftist Revolutionary Masses," which allows the military to dominate the Cultural Revolution at the local level.

MID-FEBRUARY: At two Central Committee briefing sessions convened by Zhou Enlai, Vice-Premiers Tan Zhenlin and Chen Yi and Marshal Ye Jianying stridently criticize the overthrow of veteran cadres; their protest is subsequently referred to as the "February Countercurrent." Support-the-left units in various places suppress rebels as "counterrevolutionaries," resulting in a series of violent incidents.

APRIL 1: A Central Committee document on the problem in Anhui forbids "arbitrarily declaring mass organizations to be counterrevolutionary organizations" and demands the release and rehabilitation of anyone detained or labeled as a counterrevolutionary, further radicalizing the rebel movement.

JULY 20: The "Wuhan Incident." The Million Heroes, a conservative organization supported by the commander of the Wuhan Military Region, Chen Zaidao, detains CCRSG member Wang Li. Chen Zaidao is struck down, followed by a nationwide upsurge in "weeding out the smattering of capitalist roaders within the military."

JULY–AUGUST: Encouraged by the Wuhan Incident, rebels become more active than ever throughout the country, and military and foreign affairs organs come under attack. In an effort to turn the situation around, Mao tosses out the CCRSG members Wang Li, Guan Feng, and Qi Benyu. During his tour of the south from July to September, Mao instructs mass organizations to achieve unity under the principles of the revolution, saying that "the vast majority of cadres are good."

SEPTEMBER 8: *People's Daily* publishes an essay by Yao Wenyuan that includes Mao's attack on the May 16 counterrevolutionary clique. Investigations of the May 16 clique bring a new round of suppression against rebel mass organizations by support-the-left military units throughout the country.

AUGUST 13–OCTOBER 17: A massacre of black elements is carried out in Dao County, Hunan Province, and spreads to other counties in Lingling Prefecture, which records 9,093 unnatural deaths.

NOVEMBER: The Cleansing of the Class Ranks begins, resulting in the victimization of tens of millions of innocent people.

1968

MARCH 24: At a mass rally at the Great Hall of the People, the military leaders Yang Chengwu, Yu Lijin, and Fu Chongbi are dismissed from their positions.

JULY 3: The Central Committee issues its "July 3 Notice" forbidding the obstruction of transport, looting of military convoys, and attacks on PLA organs.

JULY 27–28: Mao sends a thirty-thousand-member Capital Workers Mao

Zedong Thought Propaganda Team to end factional violence at Tsing-hua University. The next day, Mao receives five rebel leaders and withdraws his support for the rebels.

SEPTEMBER 5: The establishment of a revolutionary committee in the Xinjiang Autonomous Region makes China "red through every hill and vale."

OCTOBER 13–31: The twelfth plenum of the Eighth Central Committee permanently expels Liu Shaoqi from the party and dismisses him from all his official positions.

1969

APRIL 1–24: The CCP's Ninth National Congress marks a victory for the rebel faction and the military, and friction develops between Mao and Lin Biao in the process of drafting the political report for the congress. Mao becomes wary of the military's burgeoning power.

1970

JANUARY 31: The Central Committee launches the One Strike and Three Antis campaign, which results in tens of thousands of deaths.

5. MAO SPLITS WITH LIN BIAO
1970

AUGUST 23–SEPTEMBER 6: At the second plenum of the Ninth Central Committee at Lushan, the rivalry between Lin Biao–allied military leaders and key backers of the Cultural Revolution intensifies, and key military leaders carry out self-criticism. A campaign to purge Chen Boda begins after the October 1 National Day celebrations.

NOVEMBER 6: At Mao's suggestion, the Central Committee establishes a Central Organization and Propaganda Group, which is taken over by members of the disbanded CCRSG.

DECEMBER 18: Mao tells the American journalist Edgar Snow that "the 'Four Greats' is annoying!"—generally understood as a criticism of Lin Biao. A transcript of the conversation is printed and distributed to all party members.

DECEMBER 22: The North China Conference reorganizes the Beijing Military Region.

1971

APRIL 15: At a high-level meeting on the campaign to criticize Chen [Boda] and carry out rectification, Lin Biao refuses Mao's implied demand to carry out self-criticism.

AUGUST 15–SEPTEMBER 12: Mao tours the south and targets Lin Biao by innuendo. Lin's son, Lin Liguo, devises an unsuccessful plot to assassinate Mao.

SEPTEMBER 13: Lin Biao dies in a plane crash while attempting to flee China. His wife, Ye Qun, son Lin Liguo, and six others are also killed.

6. DECIDING WHETHER TO DEFEND OR NEGATE THE CULTURAL REVOLUTION

1971

END OF 1971: Zhou Enlai begins measures to correct left-deviation, including sending liberal-minded Wang Ruoshui to *People's Daily*.

1972

MAY 21–JUNE 23: Reflecting Mao's perspective against Zhou Enlai, a reporting meeting on the campaign to criticize Lin and carry out rectification denounces Lin Biao as an ultra-rightist. Zhou Enlai carries out self-criticism on errors allegedly committed during six early line struggles.

OCTOBER 14: *People's Daily* devotes an entire page to articles criticizing anarchism and ultra-leftist tendencies.

DECEMBER 17: Mao criticizes Wang Ruoshui for articles published in *People's Daily* supporting Zhou Enlai's attacks on ultra-leftism. Mao declares the essence of the Lin Biao line to be "ultra-rightist. Revisionist, splittist, scheming and intriguing, betraying the party and the country."

1973

MARCH 10: The Central Committee issues its "Decision Regarding Restoring Comrade Deng Xiaoping's Regular Party Activities and Position as State Council Vice-Premier."

AUGUST 24–28: The Tenth National Congress wholly endorses the political line of the Ninth Congress.

NOVEMBER 21–EARLY DECEMBER: In accordance with Mao's decision, an enlarged Politburo session criticizes "Zhou [Enlai] and Ye [Jianying]'s revisionist line" and "right-deviating capitulationism." Zhou carries out a harsh self-criticism.

DECEMBER 12: At a Politburo meeting, Mao announces his decision to rotate the commanders of China's eight military regions.

1974

JANUARY 25: Mao arranges a mass rally to launch a campaign criticizing Lin Biao and Confucius. Long-marginalized rebels rise up again.

DECEMBER: The Central Committee hands down Mao's "Main Points of a Talk on Theoretical Issues," whose defense of the Cultural Revolution is based on the theory of continuous revolution under the dictatorship of the proletariat.

1975

JANUARY 8–10: During the second plenum of the Tenth Central Committee, Deng Xiaoping attains the highest postings in his career: vice-chairman of the Central Committee and member of the Politburo Standing Committee, as well as vice-chairman of the Central Military Commission and chief of General Staff.

JANUARY 13–17: During the Fourth National People's Congress, Zhou Enlai's report proposes the "Four Modernizations," and Deng Xiaoping is appointed first vice-premier of the State Council. The power balance shifts in favor of the pragmatist faction, and the Cultural Revolution faction retreats to the sidelines.

APRIL 23: Mao writes a memo opposing revisionism, empiricism, and dogmatism, which the pragmatist faction uses to criticize Jiang Qing.

SPRING: Deng Xiaoping launches a general overhaul that leads to attacks on rebel leaders incorporated into the revolutionary committees. Railway transportation and production improve.

AUGUST 14: Based on comments by Mao, the Cultural Revolution faction organizes essays criticizing the classical novel *The Water Margin* and denouncing "capitulators," targeting Zhou Enlai and Deng Xiaoping by insinuation.

AUGUST 13 AND OCTOBER 13: Party leaders at Tsinghua University write letters of complaint against the university party secretary Chi

Qun and the deputy party secretary Xie Jingyi, both trusted by Mao.

NOVEMBER 12: Mao criticizes the letters from Tsinghua, launching a campaign to beat back the right-deviation and case reversal.

1976

JANUARY 8: Zhou Enlai dies.

JANUARY 11: A million Beijing citizens line Chang'an Avenue to pay their respects as Zhou's coffin passes. The Cultural Revolution faction suppresses memorial activities for Zhou.

JANUARY 28: Mao has Hua Guofeng take charge of the Central Committee's routine operations. Deng Xiaoping surrenders all his power as the campaign against right-deviation and case reversal reaches a climax. Rebel leaders become active again.

LATE MARCH–EARLY APRIL: Commemorations of Zhou Enlai during the Qing Ming festival turn into a mass protest movement in Beijing and other major cities.

APRIL 5: With Mao's approval, Beijing authorities send thousands of soldiers, policemen, and militia members to Tiananmen Square to crack down on protesters.

7. THE END OF THE CULTURAL REVOLUTION AND THE BEGINNING OF THE DENG XIAOPING ERA

1976

SEPTEMBER 9: Mao Zedong dies.

OCTOBER 6: Hua Guofeng, Ye Jianying, and other central leaders collaborate in the arrest of Jiang Qing, Zhang Chunqiao, Yao Wenyuan, and Wang Hongwen, known as the Gang of Four.

OCTOBER: Mass arrests of Cultural Revolution radicals occur throughout the country along with a campaign to "uncover, criticize, and investigate," which lasts until 1980.

1977

AUGUST 12: In the political report at the CCP's Eleventh National Congress, Hua Guofeng declares, "The smashing of the Gang of Four symbolizes the victory and conclusion of our country's eleven-year-long Great Proletarian Cultural Revolution."

1978

DECEMBER 18–22: The third plenum of the Eleventh Central Committee shifts the party's core work toward modernization and proposes reforms to the state's centralized economic system.

1979

JANUARY 18–FEBRUARY 22: The first phase of the Theoretical Principles Conference serves as a democratization movement within the party's top leadership, accompanied and enhanced by the Xidan Democracy Wall movement among the general public.

MARCH 30: Deng Xiaoping calls for maintaining the "Four Basic Principles," after which China's economic reforms follow the motto of "Chinese learning for the essence, and Western learning for practical use."

1980–1986

NOVEMBER 1980–JANUARY 1981: Public trials are held for members of the Lin Biao counterrevolutionary clique and the Gang of Four.

1980–1986: A nationwide campaign to investigate "three types of people" results in large numbers of people, mostly former rebels, being registered as undesirables for crimes committed during the Cultural Revolution.

THE
WORLD TURNED
UPSIDE DOWN

1
—

MAJOR EVENTS PRECEDING
THE CULTURAL REVOLUTION

A series of major events occurred before the Cultural Revolution, each the consequence of the one that preceded it. With each event, conflict accumulated until it reached a tipping point that created the even greater event of the Cultural Revolution.

THE ESTABLISHMENT AND SYSTEMIC CHARACTERISTICS OF
THE PEOPLE'S REPUBLIC OF CHINA

After decades of war, Mao Zedong declared the establishment of the Central People's Government of the People's Republic of China (PRC) at a three-hundred-thousand-strong rally at Beijing's Tiananmen Square on the afternoon of October 1, 1949. Instead of becoming a modern nation-state, however, the PRC combined Soviet dictatorship with traditional Chinese despotism and developed the following characteristics during its first seventeen years.

MAXIMIZING CENTRALIZED POLITICAL POWER

The highly centralized pyramidal power structure planted in the cultural soil of traditional Chinese despotism imposed tighter, finer, deeper, and broader suppression on China's society and people than any emperor in history.

As the world's largest cabal, the CCP ensured that the individual submitted to the organization, each level to the level above it, and the entire party to the Central Committee. All party members had to share the same faith in Marxism-Leninism and Mao Zedong Thought and had to worship the same leader: Mao. As the sole ruling party, the CCP imposed this fealty on the general populace as well by penetrating every factory, workshop, and agricultural production team, and every government organ, school, and residents' committee. Although this regime had a constitution, it was basically meaningless.

When the CCP found it impossible to resolve internal differences through consultation, discussion, and the submission of the minority to the majority, with Mao the final arbitrator, it would resort to "line struggle" until one group prevailed as upholder of the "correct line," and the defeated group was declared to hold an "erroneous line" and stepped down.

The CCP maintained power through the military and commanded the military through its Central Military Commission (CMC). Watertight discipline inspection methods controlled the thoughts and actions of every military officer.[1]

As CMC chairman, Mao commanded the gun that commanded the party, and as chairman of the CCP Central Committee, he controlled the entire populace through the bureaucratic system.

MONOPOLIZING THOUGHT AND TRUTH

Newspapers, broadcasting, and news services were all mouthpieces of the CCP Central Committee. Ordinary people were not allowed to learn of events outside China, or any negative news from inside China. Party officials ensured that social science research explained and expounded on official viewpoints and defended official error. Books that diverged from the CCP Central Committee's views were removed from library shelves, and culture and art became the "cogs and screws" of the great revolutionary apparatus, deifying and extolling the Great Leader and creating a simulacrum of peace and prosperity. Repeated political campaigns forced China's greatest minds to relinquish their freedom of thought and independent characters.

Mao was China's sole thinker, and Mao Zedong Thought was the guiding ideology of all China's people. Conditioned to blindly follow directives without understanding the rationale behind them, China's people became politically ignorant.

STATE MONOPOLY OF ECONOMIC RESOURCES AND STRICT CONTROL OF ECONOMIC LIFE

Planned economy was considered a fundamental characteristic of socialism, but it worked only if executive power effectively controlled the economy.[2] Under agricultural collectivization, everything produced by the peasants was purchased and marketed by the state, which managed industry and commerce and controlled all material goods. People relied on state allocation of everything they needed to sustain their lives.

Controlled economy was the economic base of totalitarianism and fertile soil for bureaucratic privilege. Under a highly centralized political and economic system, survival depended on bureaucrats who could arbitrarily allocate state assets and ration the necessities of daily life. A strict household-registration system ensured that the vast majority of China's peasants never ventured far from where they were born. Employees of government organs and state-run enterprises had their housing and all their daily necessities allocated by their work units. Secret dossiers decided the fate of every cadre and worker.

The ruler and the ruled, the oppressors and the oppressed, the deprivers and those who were deprived were locked into an intensely conflictual crosshatch of bureaucratic power. And public resentment, when no longer suppressed, became a powerful force against the bureaucratic clique.

CONFLICT BETWEEN OFFICIALS AND CITIZENS IN A SOCIETY OF PRIVILEGE

Bureaucratic politics is a politics of privilege. By 1956, the wages of the highest-ranking party and government personnel were set at 36.4 times those of the lowest rank.[3] (By way of comparison, the highest wage in the "corrupt" Nationalist government in 1946 was 14.5 times that of the lowest wage.)[4] Officials enjoyed special housing privileges based on rank, as well as household staff, cars, office furnishings, health care, food provisions, and even exclusive summer resorts.[5] Resentment simmered over these material reflections of privilege and caused considerable dissatisfaction in the lower ranks.

At a luxurious Beijing club called Yangfengjiadao, which opened in October 1958, senior central officials enjoyed the attentions of beautiful female performers from the army song-and-dance troupes and waiters, chefs, barbers, and pedicurists brought in from Beijing's top hotels, as well as the protection of personnel from the Ministry of Public Security and the choicest food, even in the middle of the Great Famine. Many provinces, major cities, and even medium-size cities built "imperial tour homes" for Mao (and sometimes also for members of the Politburo Standing Committee) during the Great Famine, and guards ensured that ordinary people kept their distance. In early 1960, when the number of starvation deaths hit its peak, the CCP Central Committee's North China Bureau "studied Chairman Mao's works" at a guesthouse in the famous scenic area of Jinci, where cadres enjoyed chicken, duck, fish, pork, and exotic delicacies at every meal, and went to Taiyuan City to watch plays every evening. Once the Cultural Revolution began, a young provincial cadre named Li Fu, who had attended this "study session," exposed this privileged lifestyle in a big-character poster and became a member of the rebel faction.[6]

Existing on different planes, with different perspectives, and enjoying different access to information likewise engendered mutual misunderstandings and suspicion between officials and ordinary citizens. Recognizing their vulnerability to the roiling populace beneath them, officials suppressed any hint of resistance, intensifying the alienation and opposition.

Striking down all "class enemies" through political campaigns deprived the regime of any checks and balances, and the problem of bureaucratism became even greater and more intractable. Mao then came up with the idea of using a mass movement to remold the bureaucratic system.

THE PROFOUND CRISIS BREWING IN THE YEARS
BEFORE THE CULTURAL REVOLUTION

Under the totalitarian system, it was difficult to peacefully resolve problems of succession and distribution of power, so the system was preserved through suppression of the people and struggle within the bureaucratic clique. The Land Reform movement killed countless landlords,[7] and the Campaign to Suppress Counterrevolutionaries killed at least 710,000 blameless people.[8] Unlike the Soviet Union, China carried out its suppression through mass movements, and "dictatorship of the masses" took shape in the political campaigns before the Cultural Revolution.

Serving as previews to the Cultural Revolution, the 1957 Rectification campaign appealed to the masses to "roast" bureaucrats, while the subsequent Anti-Rightist Campaign suppressed the "rebels" lured out by the rectification and turned more than half a million intellectuals into a political underclass. The Four Cleanups campaign, supposedly targeting capitalist roaders within the party, mainly purged grassroots cadres in the countryside and had no effect on the privileged strata. Every campaign gave bureaucrats an opportunity to attack dissidents, and ultimately resulted only in greater bureaucratic privilege and intensified conflict between officials and ordinary people and within the bureaucracy.

The paramount leader's unchecked power made policy errors inevitable and almost impossible to correct. Repeated policy errors intensified social conflict as well as diverging views and conflicts within the leadership clique.

Succession of paramount power has always been the hardest problem to solve in an autocratic system, and the CCP's succession crisis became increasingly apparent in Mao's growing displeasure with his chosen successor, Liu Shaoqi. At a meeting with Vietnamese leader Ho Chi Minh in Hangzhou on June 10, 1966, Mao said, "One of these days Marx is going to call us over. Who knows if our successor might be a Bernstein, a Kautsky, or a Khrushchev?[9] We have to prepare while there's still time. In short, there are two sides to everything. It's not enough that everyone is yelling 'Long Live!' right now."[10] By saying this, Mao was effectively undermining Liu Shaoqi's status as his successor.

ESTABLISHING MAO'S ABSOLUTE POWER

Although the Cultural Revolution was rooted in the system of those seventeen years, it could not have been launched without Mao's absolute power. The deification of Mao that began in Yan'an continued after the CCP took power through the efforts of central leaders such as Liu Shaoqi, Lin Biao, and Zhou Enlai, aided by social scientists, the cultural community, and educators. The deification and personality cult of Mao reached new heights at the Chengdu Conference in March 1958. Mao observed on March 10:

> There are two kinds of personality cult. One involves appropriate worship of the proper things of Marx, Engels, Lenin and Stalin; these we must worship, forever worship, and never fail to worship . . . The other kind is inappropriate worship, a blind worship without analysis . . . There are two objectives in opposing personality cult: One is opposing improper worship, and the other is opposing the worship of anyone but oneself.[11]

Others responded enthusiastically with pledges of loyalty. In a speech on March 18, Liu Shaoqi proclaimed:

> The Chairman is much wiser than any of us; whether in terms of ideology, standpoint, work style, or methods, we all lag far behind. Our task is to sincerely emulate him, and we should not consider ourselves incapable of doing so. Of course, there are some areas in which we'll find it hard to keep up with the Chairman, such as his rich knowledge of history and theory and his rich experience of revolution, as well as his powerful memory— all of this is beyond our learning.[12]

In January 1962, at the Seven Thousand Cadres Conference, with Mao's prestige considerably undermined by the Great Famine, Lin Biao and Zhou Enlai put even greater emphasis on Mao's personality cult. Lin Biao, who later masterminded the publication of *Quotations of Chairman Mao*, particularly distinguished himself with a fulsome sycophancy that was instrumental in creating Mao's personality cult:

> Mao Zedong Thought is a beacon for humanity and the most
> lethal weapon of world revolution; it is the universal truth that
> applies to the whole world . . . Whoever opposes Chairman Mao
> and opposes Mao Zedong Thought will be punished by the entire
> party, and loathed by the entire country.[13]

On the eve of the Cultural Revolution, Mao possessed absolute power that gave his words precedence over law, policy, and morality. Even those who subsequently killed themselves during the Cultural Revolution often left behind suicide notes declaring their loyalty to Mao.

Mao's works were the Chinese people's bible, and the party called for everyone to read them every day. In 1967 alone, more than 91 million copies of *Selected Works of Mao Zedong* were published, as well as 369 million copies of *Quotations of Chairman Mao*. More than two billion Mao badges were produced by March 1969—an average of three for every Chinese citizen.[14]

Everything Mao said was considered the "highest directive" and was immediately transmitted to the accompaniment of gongs and drums for implementation to the letter. A single mistake in copying down a "highest directive" invited attack as a "current counterrevolutionary." Mao's brain replaced hundreds of millions of brains as people shouted, "Long live Chairman Mao!" at every meeting, and employees of every work unit stood before Mao's portrait to "request instructions" every morning and "report back" every evening.

This deification of the supreme ruler to ensure the public's absolute submission and the unobstructed execution of his decrees was fully in place just before the Cultural Revolution began.

THE GREAT FAMINE AND ITS MORE THAN THIRTY MILLION VICTIMS

From 1958 to 1962, China experienced a famine that resulted in some thirty-six million deaths.[15] The direct cause of the Great Famine was the Three Red Banners, but its fundamental cause was the totalitarian system.

The Three Red Banners were the General Line of Socialist Construction, the Great Leap Forward, and the people's communes. The General Line and Great Leap Forward were meant to spur rapid economic development but exhausted the nation through unrealistic economic targets. The people's communes took agricultural collectivism to an extreme, and when the economic policies failed, the people's communes collapsed and the peasants could do nothing to save themselves.

The policy errors that created the Great Famine continued for years without correction because China had no freedom of the press and no opposition party. Liu Shaoqi was in complete accord with Mao regarding the Three Red Banners in 1958, but Liu was quicker than Mao to perceive the truth and to try to turn policies around, and his faltering commitment to the Three Red Banners greatly displeased Mao. Attempts to trace responsibility for the starvation deaths intensified political infighting at the highest levels of government; and during the Cultural Revolution, Peng Zhen, Yang Shangkun, and Deng Xiaoping were accused of organizing the inspection of official documents to "look for errors and shortcomings of the Center and Mao Zedong."[16]

The Great Famine was at issue in the launch of the Cultural Revolution in the cultural community.[17] Mao claimed that in Yao Wenyuan's "Critique of the New Historical Play *Hai Rui Dismissed from Office*," "the critical point was the dismissal of an official," specifically Peng Dehuai, who had been denounced at the Lushan Conference in an attempt to cover up responsibility for the Great Famine. The Great Famine was also the detonator of the Cultural Revolution in some localities. For example, a big-character poster put up at Zhengzhou University in summer 1996 described the widespread starvation deaths in Xinyang, and referred to Henan's provincial party secretary Wu Zhipu as the "butcher of the people of Henan."[18] The famous economist Yang Xiaokai said, "The complete failure of Mao's economic line in 1958 was the direct historical reason for the eruption of the Cultural Revolution."[19]

The Cultural Revolution was Mao's renewed attempt to create a utopia following the failure of the Three Red Banners that caused the Great Famine.

THE CAMPAIGN AGAINST RIGHT-DEVIATION

After Defense Minister Peng Dehuai submitted a written criticism of the Three Red Banners at the Lushan Conference on July 14, 1959, Mao castigated Peng and others as an "anti-party clique." This was followed by a nationwide campaign against right-deviation during which millions of cadres and party members were denounced.[20] In May 1962, Deng Xiaoping estimated "ten million denounced, and tens of millions of others affected."[21]

At this point, the series of campaigns had sealed everyone's mouth but Mao's, and whatever he said was the highest directive. This not only increased the chance of Mao making mistakes but also contributed to hidden conflict within the party.

THE SEVEN THOUSAND CADRES CONFERENCE

While Liu Shaoqi kept in lockstep with Mao in 1958, his views changed after an inspection visit to his home village in 1961, and he began singing a different tune from Mao's at the Seven Thousand Cadres Conference in 1962.

The ninth plenum of the Eighth Central Committee in January 1961 had formally adopted the guiding principle of "adjustment, consolidation, replenishment, and enhancement" as a means of resolving the serious problems caused by the Great Leap Forward, but differences of opinion prevented thorough implementation, and the economic situation remained dire. Toward the end of 1961, the Central Committee decided to unify thinking throughout the bureaucracy by convening a large-scale conference, which came to be known as the Seven Thousand Cadres Conference. Liu Shaoqi and Deng Xiaoping were put in charge of drafting the report for the conference, which Liu felt should reflect the Politburo's responsibility for the shortcomings of the past four years and blame the tardy correction of errors on a lack of democracy in the party.[22]

Discussion of Liu's report at the conference quickly focused on the Three Red Banners as a possible cause of policy errors during the

Great Leap Forward.[23] Mao proposed a new twenty-one-member report-drafting committee led by Liu Shaoqi and including Zhou Enlai, Chen Yun, Deng Xiaoping, Peng Zhen, Chen Boda, and other senior leaders, but the committee could not agree on who was responsible for the shortcomings and errors of the past few years. Peng Zhen and Deng Xiaoping pointed out that Mao was not infallible and had never claimed to be. Peng said, "If we cannot discuss Chairman Mao's one percent or one-tenth of one percent of error, it will have a bad effect on our party. Do we want the provinces and cities to bear all the responsibility? It won't benefit those below or teach any lessons. Everyone should be called to his own account, from Chairman Mao to every party branch secretary."[24] Peng would pay for these remarks during the Cultural Revolution, when he was purged as a leader of an anti-party clique in 1966.

For the present, Zhou Enlai responded by defending Mao:

> The Chairman discovered problems early and was prepared, and the errors were ours. He can't fight back the raging tide all on his own. The entire party needs to be of one heart and mind and to strengthen centralization and unity, obey our Helmsman and obey the Central Committee, with the Central Committee listening to Chairman Mao."[25]

After Chen Boda backed up Zhou's remarks, Peng Zhen quickly explained, "What I mean is that it's not good if we can criticize everyone but Chairman Mao."[26]

Mao endorsed the direction of the second draft of the report that came out on January 22, and it was adopted by an enlarged meeting of the Politburo on January 25. Mao and the other Standing Committee members also approved Liu Shaoqi's outline of his oral presentation of the report, but in fact Mao was displeased with several points that Liu raised, in particular the negative effects of the Great Leap Forward, the predominant contribution of human error to the problems, a larger percentage of errors relative to accomplishments, the Central Committee and Politburo's responsibility for the errors, and the need for the Three Red Banners to be tested in practice.[27]

After the meeting, Liu Shaoqi told others, "The errors of the Great

Leap Forward were serious, and this is the first time we've summarized the experience. Every year from now on we need to look back and summarize it again." He also referred to the cannibalism that had occurred during the Great Famine, saying, "This will be memorialized as a decree in which the emperor admits his crimes against the people."[28]

Mao no doubt heard about what Liu said. Years later, in February 1967, he told the Albanian delegation head Beqir Balluku that he had anticipated revisionism at the Seven Thousand Cadres Conference and had predicted that China would eventually "change color." "Those remarks were never published, but at that time I already saw the problem."[29]

Strong reaction to Liu's report led to the conference being extended. On January 29, Lin Biao absolved Mao of responsibility for the famine and attributed it to "an exceptionally serious and sustained but localized natural disaster." He observed, "I feel deeply that we manage our work better when Chairman Mao's thinking is put into practice without a hitch and when there is no interference with Mao Zedong Thought. When Chairman Mao's opinions aren't respected or encounter major interference, problems arise."[30]

Mao later had the edited version of Lin Biao's speech sent to Tian Jiaying and Luo Ruiqing with the memo, "Read this through. It's an excellent and meaty essay that's a joy to read."[31] During the Cultural Revolution, Jiang Qing revealed that during the Seven Thousand Cadres Conference, Mao was "holding back a belly full of rage" and that it was only Lin Biao's speech at the conference that had "made him feel grateful."[32]

In his own speech on January 30, Mao did not allude directly to the Great Famine but spoke at length on the importance of "democratic centralism" and on the correctness of the Three Red Banners.[33]

From beginning to end, the Seven Thousand Cadres Conference defended the Three Red Banners and prevented a reversal of the Lushan Conference. This displeased grassroots cadres, who voiced many sharp comments while discussing the resolutions of the conference. During discussions in the Gansu group, a cadre from the provincial party school said, "In the past I felt Gansu's problems were serious, but now I know how pervasive the problems were. It will take more than thirty or fifty years to recover from the losses in Gansu, Henan, Shandong, Anhui, and other provinces." A comrade in the provincial finance and trade office said, "The problems of these last few years have been so widespread and protracted, it can't be said that there are no problems with the Central Committee's leading ideology." Someone directly targeted Mao: "The Chairman may have made subjectivist errors in his later years, like Stalin did."[34]

Reading similar briefing papers from every province must have made Mao sense a terrifying force that could imperil his position if he didn't effectively counter it.

The Seven Thousand Cadres Conference revealed serious divisions within the party's top leadership between those who thoroughly endorsed the Three Red Banners and those who maintained doubts. Mao saw clearly who was an enemy and who was a friend, and this "first question of revolution" formed the basis for whom he would rely on and whom he would strike down when the Cultural Revolution began four years later.

After the conference adjourned on February 7, Mao withdrew to Wuhan while Liu Shaoqi, Zhou Enlai, and Deng Xiaoping manned the "front line" in Beijing. Liu Shaoqi took full charge of the Central Committee's party and government leadership work, but Mao continued to observe him from the sidelines.

THE TENTH PLENUM OF THE EIGHTH CENTRAL COMMITTEE

After the Seven Thousand Cadres Conference, an even grimmer view of the situation was presented at an enlarged meeting of the Politburo Standing Committee held on February 21, 1962, in Zhongnanhai's Xilou (Western Pavilion) conference room. Liu Shaoqi said, "What's to fear about revealing the situation's true colors? Painting it black can make people pessimistic, but it can also spur people to courageously struggle against adversity . . . We don't need routine measures but rather emergency measures to readjust the economy."[35]

Mao objected to painting a uniformly bleak picture when Liu Shaoqi, Zhou Enlai, and Deng Xiaoping flew to Wuhan to report to him on March 16, but Liu continued to describe the grim economy as a threat to political stability at a Central Committee work conference in May.[36] Plagued with anxiety that this bleak assessment would lead to the negation of the Three Red Banners, Mao went to Shanghai, Shandong, Hangzhou, Wuhan, and other places to consult the views of leading cadres, who affirmed that things were improving. Of course, in provinces where millions had starved to death, the situation could only have improved since 1960, but Mao saw this as a sign that provincial party secretaries supported him.

Acting on Liu Shaoqi's guiding principle of "adequate retrenchment" and also based on Chen Yun's suggestions, the Xilou Conference and May Conference adopted measures to put the national economy on a more balanced, sustainable, and stable footing.[37] With the support of Vice-Premier Deng Zihui, by mid-1962 more than 20 percent of production teams nationwide were implementing assignment of agricultural output to households, with implementation reaching 80 percent in Anhui and exceeding 70 percent in parts of Gansu, Zhejiang, and Sichuan.[38] Deng Xiaoping said, "In regions where peasants are suffering hardship, adopt all kinds of methods. Anhui comrades have a good reason for saying, 'It doesn't matter whether a cat is black or yellow; as long as it catches mice it's a good cat.'"[39] But household production quotas ran contrary to Communist Party ideals, and Mao found them intolerable.

On July 8, 1962, Mao summoned Liu Shaoqi, Zhou Enlai, Deng Xiaoping, Chen Boda, and Tian Jianying for a meeting, during which he explicitly expressed his disagreement with these agricultural reforms. He called Liu Shaoqi in again on July 10 and berated him for failing to "keep things under control." Mao was releasing resentment that had been building up for a long time, but Liu, although taken by surprise, was just as eager to get the issue off his chest: "History will record the role you and I played in the starvation of so many people, and the cannibalism will also be memorialized!"

Mao said, "The Three Red Banners have been refuted, land is being divided up, and you did nothing? What will happen after I die?"[40]

Adding to Mao's anxiety was a decision by the Seven Thousand Cadres Conference to screen and rehabilitate party members and cadres who had been wrongfully denounced in recent years; now Peng

Dehuai was mounting a spirited plea in his own defense. Another source of vexation were the measures proposed by Wang Jiaxiang, head of the Central Committee's International Liaison Department, to reduce tensions with foreign countries, in particular by avoiding an open rupture with the Soviet Union, assuming a milder attitude toward the United States, trying to break the current deadlock in Sino-Indian relations through negotiation, and "being practical and realistic" in assisting revolutions in other countries.[41] Mao saw both the agricultural and diplomatic compromises as part of a "program of capitalist restoration."

The Seven Thousand Cadres Conference and the events immediately following it signaled to Mao that the Central Committee under Liu Shaoqi's leadership was increasingly diverging from his line in economics, politics, and domestic and foreign policy. Most alarming to Mao was when Liu on March 17, 1962, told the Public Security Ministry to summarize the lessons of beating deaths and abuse of the innocent over the past few years. Liu said, "If the living don't uncover it, the next generation will uncover it after we're dead."[42] Liu's words made Mao think of Khrushchev's exposure and criticism of Stalin.

As estrangement from Mao within the party converged with the social undercurrent, Mao sensed the buildup of a powerful force hostile to him. As a lifelong proponent of "struggle philosophy," he was ready to launch a new battle at any moment. The tenth plenum of the Eighth Central Committee gave him this opportunity.

The formal plenum, held in Beijing, lasted only four days, from September 24 to 27, 1962, but the preparatory meetings ran from August 26 to September 23 and were preceded by a Central Committee work conference at Beidaihe from July 25 to August 24 that set the tone for the plenum. On August 6, Mao suddenly gave a speech on "class, situation, and contradictions" without prior notice,[43] and he continued to interject his views during committee meetings, turning the theme of the conference toward criticism of the "wind of gloom" (hei'an feng), the "go-alone" or "individual farming wind" (dan'gan feng), and the "verdict-reversal wind" (fan'an feng). On August 15, he complained about people who "beat the drum for individual farming, encourage gloom and talk about shortcomings and errors, but they have no enthusiasm for talking about the bright spots and achievements or about collective economy."[44] Mao's comments brought some people back to the fold, and Liu Shaoqi felt obliged to offer explanations and self-criticism regarding the May Conference. After Mao and others denounced Deng Zihui for encouraging assignment of production quotas to households, Deng was removed as head of the Central Committee's Rural Work Department and relegated to the nominal position of deputy director of the State Planning Commission.[45]

The focus of criticism of the verdict-reversal wind was Peng Dehuai, whose letters in his own defense were treated as a renewed attack on the party. Speeches condemning Peng continued right up to the end of the plenum. Huang Kecheng, Zhang Wentian, and others were also forced to undergo self-criticism, and the Central Committee organized a team headed by He Long to investigate Peng, Huang, and Zhang.[46]

While criticism of Peng Dehuai continued, another controversy over "verdict reversal" revolved around the novel *Liu Zhidan*, which was alleged to be a vehicle promoting Gao Gang, a senior official who had killed himself in 1954 after being accused of involvement in an anti-party clique. During a meeting on September 8, Kang Sheng[47] observed, "The central question is why Gao Gang is being promoted at just this time."

Escalation of the issue lent ammunition to criticism of the verdict-reversal wind,[48] and Gao Gang's former associates Xi Zhongxun, Jia Tuofu, and Liu Jingfan were declared members of an anti-party clique. While Mao was speaking at the Central Committee's tenth plenum on September 24, Kang Sheng passed him a note that said, "Using a novel to carry out anti-Party activities is a great invention." Mao read out this note, and added, "Anyone who wants to overturn a regime needs to first create public opinion and carry out ideological work. Whether revolutionary or counterrevolutionary, that's how it's done."[49] On September 27, the plenum decided to establish a special investigation committee headed by Kang Sheng to examine the cases of Xi Zhongxun, Jia Tuofu, and Liu Jingfan.[50]

The crux of the Beidaihe Conference was Mao's remarks on class struggle. According to Marxist tenets, class was supposed to be an economic category—a person's relations to the means of production. By 1957, China's Land Reform movement had seized all land from landlords and rich peasants, and industry and commerce had undergone socialist transformation, so how could people be divided into classes? Mao had finessed the issue in 1958 when he said, "There are two kinds of elimination of class: The easier one is eliminating the economic exploiting class, and we can now say it's been wiped out; the harder one is eliminating political and ideological classes, and these have not been eliminated, as we discovered during last year's rectification."[51] A philosophy professor at the Central Party School, Ai Siqi, called this pernicious concept a "new stage in the development of Marxism."[52]

Now, during the Beidaihe Conference, Mao made further pronouncements on the subject, which were ultimately expressed in the bulletin of the tenth plenum:

> Throughout the entire history of the proletarian revolution and dictatorship of the proletariat, and in the entire historical period of the transition from capitalism to communism (this period requires several decades or even more), there exists a class struggle between the proletarian and capitalist classes and a struggle between the two roads, socialism and capitalism. The overthrown reactionary ruling class has not resigned itself to its demise and is still scheming for restoration to power. At the same time, society retains some capitalistic influence and the force of custom from the old society, as well as a tendency toward spontaneous capitalism among a portion of small producers. For that reason, some among the people have still not undergone socialist transformation; their numbers are not many, only a few percentage points, but once they have the opportunity, they intend to depart from the socialist road and follow the capitalist road. Under these circumstances, class struggle is unavoidable. Marxism-Leninism expounded on this historical pattern early on, and we must absolutely not forget it. This class struggle is complex, tortuous, varying in intensity, and sometimes fierce. This class struggle will inevitably be reflected within the Party. The influence of foreign imperialism and domestic capitalism are the social roots of revisionist thinking arising within the Party. While carrying out struggle

against class enemies at home and abroad, we must at all times be wary and resolute in opposing all opportunistic ideological tendencies within the Party.[53]

Mao called for "talking of it every year, every month, every day . . . so we'll have a more sober awareness of this problem, and a Marxist-Leninist itinerary."

The Great Famine undoubtedly undermined Mao's prestige and threatened the legitimacy of CCP rule. The Seven Thousand Cadres Conference put Mao at a disadvantage, and after stewing over it for two years, Mao turned the political situation around by wielding the magic weapon of class struggle at the tenth plenum of the Eighth Central Committee.

Mao's comments on class struggle became grist for the theory of "continuous revolution under the dictatorship of the proletariat," the theory of the Great Proletarian Cultural Revolution.

Once the bugle call of class struggle sounded, the party organization at all levels seized on it as a matter of priority and sought out "the new trend in class struggle." As class struggle became a major topic in all kinds of publications and meetings, the Socialist Education Movement was launched.

THE SOCIALIST EDUCATION MOVEMENT

The "rectification of work styles and cooperatives" that took place after the Great Famine was the prelude to the Socialist Education Movement, or Four Cleanups campaign.

The Central Committee divided the people's communes into three categories, with category 3 as the most problematic, and composing up to one-third of the total.[54] Mao noted in a memo on November 15, 1960, that problems developed "where the democratic revolution has not yet been completed and feudalistic influence creates great mischief, where there is greater hostility to socialism, and where socialist relations of production and productivity have been sabotaged."[55]

There were indeed hooligans among China's rural grassroots

cadres who abused their power and rode roughshod over ordinary people, but in most cases it was the faithful execution of the Central Committee's policies that harmed peasants the most, and the over-zealous inflicted even greater damage. Using class struggle to ana-lyze the problem, however, Mao and others claimed that those causing the harm were class enemies who continued to exist because demo-cratic revolution had not been thorough enough. The rectification of work styles and cooperatives was therefore a "remedial lesson in dem-ocratic revolution."

The rectification of work styles and cooperatives was a massive purge carried out on rural cadres. For example, the campaign in Hebei Province from winter 1960 to spring 1961 exposed errors committed by 174,575 cadres, 13.9 percent of all cadres in the province. An esti-mated 37,412, or 2.98 percent, were disciplined. During the campaign, production teams where the "Five Evil Winds" of bureaucratic mal-practice[56] had raged the fiercest were said to have been taken over by "black elements,"[57] "degenerate elements," or "incorrigible bureau-crats," and cadres who had committed Five Wind errors were rounded up into "training courses" carried out by the county or commune—in fact, denunciation. According to incomplete statistics from April 1961, 6,763 cadres throughout the province were "assembled for training."[58]

From February 11 to 28, 1963, the CCP Central Committee held a meeting in Beijing mainly to discuss the socialist education being car-ried out in the countryside. Because this campaign aimed to "clean up accounts, inventory, financial affairs, and work points," it was referred to as the Four Cleanups (*siqing*) campaign.

The Central Committee drafted three documents to guide the cam-paign, each presenting a grimmer assessment of the situation of class struggle than the one before, and the last of which redefined the Four Cleanups as political, economic, ideological, and organizational cleans-ings and expanded it to urban areas as well. An immense contingent of Four Cleanups work teams were dispatched throughout the country, and some university students and military cadres were recruited into the teams.

No examination of the Four Cleanups can overlook Wang Guang-mei's report "The Taoyuan Experience." The Taoyuan production bri-gade of Luwangzhuang Commune in Hebei's Funing County was originally designated a category 1 brigade (the best kind). In accordance with Liu Shaoqi's suggestion, his wife, Wang Guangmei, went to that brigade incognito to gain experience as deputy leader of the Four Cleanups work team. The team acted as if on a secret mission in enemy-occupied territory, establishing contacts and asking people about their hardships. Wang Guangmei was commended for discovering that the Taoyuan party branch was "basically not communist" and a "counterrevolutionary double-faced regime," and that the party branch secretary was a "bad element who had squeezed into the party" and a "Kuomintang element."[59]

On the ascendance after the Great Leap Forward, Liu Shaoqi became overconfident. From June until August, he took Wang Guangmei on a nationwide tour to describe her experience in Taoyuan, and in many other places people listened to tape recordings of her report.[60] On August 1, Liu himself gave a major speech to the heads of the central organs at Beijing's Great Hall of the People, which led senior leaders to grumble that he was promoting his own wife. Liu also observed that it was not necessary to "be dogmatic regarding Chairman Mao's works." According to one observer, after the speech, "Jiang Qing went crying to Chairman Mao, saying, 'After Stalin died, Khrushchev made a secret speech, and now you aren't even dead and someone is making an open speech.'"[61]

After Liu Shaoqi criticized the Guizhou provincial first secretary Zhou Lin during a talk in Kunming on August 24, 1964, Zhou and other provincial party leaders were rounded up and replaced during power seizures in October and November. Many cadres were suspended or discharged, some were expelled from the party and removed from all their positions, and some were imprisoned.[62]

Under Liu Shaoqi's leadership of the cleanup work, 77,560 cadres and ordinary people died, while 5,327,350 were purged. The campaign ferreted out 5,760 anti-party, anti-socialist cliques; 276,256 people were labeled and punished as enemies; and another 558,220 people were also labeled as enemies but received lenient treatment for "contradictions among the people."[63] A reexamination of these cases in December 1978 found that the vast majority were completely unjustified.

Wang Guangmei's writings thirty-five years later suggest that Mao had to take a share of the blame, because he took a keen interest in "The Taoyuan Experience" and promoted it throughout the country.[64] But Liu Shaoqi certainly initiated interest in the report and pushed for its formal approval by the Central Committee before Mao wrote his August 27 memo recommending that the report be printed and distributed.[65]

Launched soon after the Great Famine, the Four Cleanups campaign gave the peasantry an opportunity to vent their disgust and loathing for grassroots cadres who had shown disregard for human life during the famine. The Four Cleanups campaign encouraged peasants to speak of their misery in the "Old Society" and their present happiness in the "New Society." But instead, commune members talked of their suffering during the Great Famine, choking back sobs as they described how cadres had beaten them and allowed their families to starve. A single cry from a commune member was all it took to have any cadres present pulled onto the stage and beaten and kicked. Terrified and filled with despair, many rural cadres killed themselves.[66]

As the campaign progressed, the divisions between Mao and Liu Shaoqi finally came to the surface. Wang Guangmei and Liu Yuan describe how Liu engaged in an open wrangle with Mao during a Central Committee work conference held from December 15, 1964, to January 14, 1965, to discuss the Four Cleanups.

Liu Shaoqi stated that the main contradiction was between the "four cleans" and the "four not-cleans," and its nature was the "intersection of a contradiction among the people with a contradiction between the enemy and us."

Mao Zedong said that the landlords and rich peasants were the backstage operators and the "unclean" cadres their frontmen. The unclean cadres were the ones in power, and the poor and lower-middle peasants wouldn't be satisfied with attacking only landlords and rich peasants. It was essential to target cadres and to mobilize the masses to rectify the party.

Liu Shaoqi said that all kinds of contradictions had come together during the "Four Cleanups" campaign, and the situation was complicated. It was better to use facts as a starting point and to resolve contradictions as they were discovered rather than elevating all of them to contradictions between the enemy and us.

Mao became agitated and said, "This movement of ours is called the Socialist Education Movement, not some kind of 'four cleans' or 'four not-cleans' or some kind of intersection of multiple contradictions—who says there's an intersection? . . . This is a socialist education movement, and its main focus is to rectify the faction of capitalist roaders who have gained power within the Party!"

Liu Shaoqi stood his ground and said, as if seeking advice, "I still don't understand much about this 'faction.' Individual capitalist roaders exist, but the capitalist class has died out, so how can there be a faction? A faction implies numerous people, and contradictions between the enemy and us are not all that prevalent. Where do we find capitalist roaders in the Coal Ministry or Metallurgy Ministry?"

Without thinking, Mao blurted out, "Zhang Linzhi is one!"

Liu Shaoqi did not pursue the matter, because under those circumstances, once Mao Zedong mentioned a name, that person would be struck down.[67]

Mao took this dispute very seriously. Several days later, December 26, was Mao's seventy-first birthday, and he used his own funds to host a dinner at the Great Hall of the People. Mao sat at a table with several model workers and scientists, with the other central government leaders at another table. Mao was usually ebullient at such events, but this time his demeanor was solemn.[68] Mao said, "The Socialist Education Movement has just begun, so how is it that someone is getting so cocky? I don't have a work experience assignment, so I don't have the right to speak, but I'm going to speak anyway, and if I'm wrong everyone can criticize me." He went on to criticize phrases such as the "four cleans" and "four uncleans" and the "intersection of contradictions inside and outside the Party" as not Marxist. He also censured some central organs as being run as "independent kingdoms" and spoke of the danger of revisionism within the party.[69] He repeated his allegations of separate socialist and capitalist factions within the party and the formation of "independent kingdoms" while presiding over the Central Committee work conference on December 27.[70]

On the afternoon of December 28, Mao gave a long speech during which he emphasized that the nature of the Four Cleanups campaign was a contradiction between socialism and capitalism, and the focus was on purging capitalist roaders. He then read out several articles from the Constitution of the Chinese Communist Party and the Constitution of the People's Republic of China, and asked, "Are we considered citizens of the People's Republic of China? If we are, then do we have freedom of speech? Do we allow other people to speak?"[71] Before the meeting, Deng Xiaoping had thought it was just a routine reporting meeting called by the Central Committee Secretariat, and he'd told Mao, "If you're busy, you don't have to attend," but Mao thought Deng was trying to keep him from attending the meeting. He also believed that Liu Shaoqi was depriving him of his constitutional right to speak.

The work conference adjourned on December 28, and the provincial party secretaries attending it all returned to their home provinces. Tao Zhu's wife, Zeng Zhi, recalls that after the conference, Jiang Qing invited her to a small auditorium of the Great Hall of the People to watch a performance of *The Red Lantern*. Before the performance began, Mao asked Tao Zhu, "Have you finished the meeting? Did you adjourn it without my being there? Someone's shitting on my head! Even if I've retreated to the rear line, I can still have a say!" Mao also asked Tao Zhu, "Has everyone who attended the meeting left already?" Tao Zhu said, "Some have." Mao said firmly, "Tell those who have left to hurry back!" So the provincial party secretaries were all called back, and the work conference resumed again after New Year's Day 1965.[72]

Wang Guangmei and Liu Yuan write in their book, "Mao Zedong could not tolerate even the slightest challenge to his authority. A discussion between equals implied a scorning of his authority, and even the smallest contradiction could send him into a rage. He told Liu Shaoqi, 'Who do you think you are? All I have to do is lift a finger and you're finished!'"[73]

In a conversation with the American journalist Edgar Snow in 1970, Mao confirmed that he had decided to strike down Liu Shaoqi during the discussions on the Four Cleanups in January 1965.[74] Likewise, he told the leader of an overseas Communist Party on January 17, 1967, "There's a party within our party—you didn't know this before. On the surface it looks like everyone gets along, but in fact the infighting is fierce . . . Without this Cultural Revolution, we'd be in trouble."[75] On February 3, 1967, Mao told a foreign guest that in the past "we'd carried out some struggles within the cultural community and in the villages and factories—that was the Socialist Education Movement . . . But that didn't solve the problem; we weren't able to find an open, comprehensive, and bottom-up method to mobilize the broad masses to expose our dark side."[76] The form required was a widespread mobilization of the masses to launch comprehensive class struggle.

After the Central Committee work conference agreed to expand the Four Cleanups to the urban areas in January 1965, Mao did little more to promote the campaign, which he felt would be ineffective in preventing a capitalist restoration. In May 1965, Mao climbed Jinggang Mountain once more and wrote his poem "Jinggang Mountain to the tune of *Ci Nian Nu Jiao*":

> *I still recall the flames of war,*
> *Escaping death as if the night before.*
> *Only lofty sentiment remains,*
> *A glowing moon or thundering storm*
> *Above the plains.*
> *At cock's first crow,*
> *Myriad monsters are no more.*[77]

After the Cultural Revolution began on May 16, 1966, the Four Cleanups campaign was merged into it. The Four Cleanups had exposed the split between Mao and Liu and intensified the conflict between them, and as will be seen later, its iteration at Peking University became the trigger point for the Cultural Revolution.

THE SINO-SOVIET DEBATE: IDEOLOGICAL MOBILIZATION AGAINST REVISIONISM

At the same time that the tenth plenum resurrected class struggle, it launched criticism against "revisionism." Revisionism emerged as early as the 1890s, when Eduard Bernstein, an executor of Friedrich Engels's will, revised Marxist theory in line with the developing situation. In *Revisionism Within the Socialist Democratic Party*, Bernstein held that revisionism was an ideological standpoint that "engaged in criticism against socialist theory or its interpretations,"[78] indicating that "revisionism" carried no negative connotation at that time. After the Second Communist International followed this line of thought in criticizing Russia's October Revolution and the system it established, Lenin criticized the Second International, and "revisionism" became a derogatory term.

The CCP's criticism of revisionism could be said to have started in 1956, when China was facing the crucial question of whether to continue class struggle after the elimination of economic classes. Stalin had provided an answer for that question in 1936, when socialist public ownership of the means of production was established in the Soviet Union's national economy. Stalin declared that the exploiting class had been eliminated and that "Soviet society was composed of two amicable classes, workers and peasants."[79] However, when China found itself in a similar situation in the late 1950s, Mao took a different approach and developed the theory of continuous revolution under the dictatorship of the proletariat.

Mao took his new approach to class struggle as the Soviet Union was implementing revisionism through a reassessment of Stalin. As the Communist Party of the Soviet Union (CPSU) wrapped up its twentieth national congress in February 1956, Khrushchev delivered a secret speech, "Regarding Personality Cult and Its Consequences," which thoroughly exposed Stalin's errors. In mid-March, Mao commented that this report "indicates that the Soviet Union, the CPSU, and Stalin are not infallible. This shatters superstition so we no longer have to copy the Soviet Union wholesale in all things, and it facilitates opposing dogmatism. On the other hand, the secret report has serious errors in both content and method, mainly in that wholesale negation of Stalin is inappropriate."[80] On April 5, 1956, *People's Daily* published an essay by its editorial department that had been vetted and revised by Mao and then discussed and passed at an enlarged Politburo meeting. The essay "Regarding the Historical Experience of the Dictatorship of the Proletariat" fully endorsed Stalin's accomplishments and analyzed the errors of his last years. A follow-up published on December 29 emphasized the necessity of "affirming and defending his correct aspects" while criticizing Stalin's errors.

Mao explicitly raised the question of opposing revisionism in a February 1957 speech, "On the Correct Handling of Contradictions Among the People."

In April 1960, the CCP Central Committee acknowledged the ninetieth anniversary of Lenin's birth by arranging for the publication of three essays defending Leninism. These essays expounded on the CCP's positions on major theoretical issues such as peaceful coexistence, peaceful transition, socialist revolution, war and peace, and the nature of imperialism.

In separate talks in the latter half of May with the secretary-general of North Korea's Labor Party, Kim Il-sung, and with the chairman of Denmark's Communist Party, Knud Jespersen, Mao stated outright that the CCP did not agree with peaceful coexistence or peaceful transition, and he criticized the Communist Parties of the Soviet Union and Eastern Europe for abandoning the class standpoint. He even went so far as to criticize Khrushchev by name.

These strident criticisms of the Soviet government and Khrushchev did not pass unnoticed. In June 1960, Peng Zhen led a CCP delegation attending the Conference of Communist and Workers' Parties of Socialist Countries in Bucharest. Prior to the conference, on June 21, the Soviet delegation suddenly issued a notice that the Soviet government had sent to the CCP Central Committee, and during the conference Khrushchev himself came forward to criticize CCP policies. From this point forward, the CCP Central Committee became even firmer in its opposition to revisionism. In October 1961, the CPSU's twenty-second congress adopted a program that comprehensively and systematically proposed theories and policies such as "peaceful transition," "peaceful coexistence," and "peaceful competition." In his keynote speech, Khrushchev openly criticized Albania for its refusal to endorse the CPSU's standpoints, but his real target was the CCP. The CCP delegation head Zhou Enlai returned to China early in protest after pointedly leading the delegation to place a wreath on Stalin's grave. The CCP Central Committee considered the CPSU's draft program and twenty-second congress symbols of the systemization of "modern revisionist" standpoints that had usurped control of the CPSU and caused the Soviet Union to change colors.

Under Mao's renewed emphasis on class struggle, "revisionism,"

"right-deviating opportunism," and "capitalist restoration" became in-
terlinked concepts. Mao called Peng Dehuai a revisionist and eventually placed the same cap on Liu Shaoqi's head. From the 1960s onward,
Mao treated fighting revisionism as a crucial political task.

To ensure victory in the war against revisionism, the CCP Central
Committee established the Central Committee Leading Group to
Counter Revisionism, headed by Deng Xiaoping. The group spent
the months of September 1963 to March 1964 hunkered down at
the Diaoyutai Guesthouse writing a total of nine essays criticizing
"Khrushchev revisionism." Known as the "Nine Commentaries," the
essays were published in *People's Daily* and *Red Flag* and read out
in a strident and bellicose tone over the Central People's Broadcasting
Station.

One of the "Nine Commentaries," titled "Regarding Khrushchev's
Bogus Communism and Its Lessons for World History," included a
large portion personally rewritten by Mao that exposed how the Soviet
Union's "privileged stratum" had "turned its prerogative of serving the
people into a prerogative of ruling the masses, and used their power
to allocate the means of production and means of livelihood for the
selfish gain of their own clique . . . [They] used their privileged position to engage in graft, corruption, and bribe-taking, and to turn public property to private use." This segment showed Mao's anxiety over
the situation in China.

The "Nine Commentaries" raised anti-revisionism to a new height
and pushed the CCP's ideology and itinerary far left. The persistent
Stalinism of Mao and his colleagues drove China into a blind alley and
led to the disastrous Cultural Revolution.

Stalin's death in 1953 had given Mao hopes of becoming the
leader of the International Communist Movement. He suspended his
commitment to new democracy and picked up the pace of progress
toward socialism, while also attempting economic construction
through the Great Leap Forward in hopes of overtaking the Soviet
Union. Even after the Great Leap Forward failed, he wouldn't give
up. The seventh of the "Nine Commentaries," an open letter to the
CPSU vetted by Mao and published on February 4, 1964, stated:
"Since the CPSU leaders have embarked on the road of revisionism

and splittism, they have naturally lost their status as the heads of the International Communist Movement . . . The front-ranking status Engels and Lenin spoke of is not fixed and constant, but can be transferred as conditions change." A 1967 essay commemorating the fiftieth anniversary of the October Revolution even more explicitly stated: "In the early years of the twentieth century, the hub of revolution shifted to Russia and engendered Leninism. After that, the hub of world revolution gradually shifted to China and engendered Mao Zedong Thought."[81] Making China the "hub of world revolution" and the leader of the International Communist Movement required preventing the restoration of capitalism in China and making China the prototype of "pure" socialism. This is what the Cultural Revolution strove to accomplish.

REVOLUTIONARY MASS CRITICISM THROUGHOUT THE COUNTRY

During the tenth plenum of the Eighth Central Committee, Mao had said, "Anyone who wants to overturn a regime needs to first create public opinion and carry out ideological work." In a speech to the philosophy and social sciences department of the Chinese Academy of Sciences on October 26, 1963, Zhou Yang[82] systematically laid out the task of opposing modern revisionism in the ideological sphere. In July 1964, the Central Committee established the five member Cultural Revolution Small Group to lead criticism in the cultural and academic domains. Peng Zhen[83] was chairman and Lu Dingyi[84] was vice-chairman, with the remaining members consisting of Kang Sheng, Zhou Yang, and Wu Lengxi.[85]

The Central Committee called on party committees and departments at all levels to place even greater emphasis on class struggle in the ideological realm, and every trade and profession held revolutionary mass criticisms. Newspapers, broadcasts, meetings, and classes were full of the militant rhetoric of mass criticism.

Philosophy circles criticized the "two combined into one" standpoint of Yang Xianzhen, vice-president of the Central Party School. In a November 1963 teaching document, Yang had written, "The unity of opposites, two sides to everything, and two combined into one all mean the same thing." "Two sides to everything" could be used to express two parts of a unified thing, and also to express that "a unified thing is composed of two opposites."[86] Mao described the "two combined into one" concept as revisionism and class compromise during a Central Committee work conference on June 8, 1964, and in the months that followed at least five hundred articles criticizing Yang Xianzhen's essay were published in *Guangming Daily*, *Red Flag*, *People's Daily*, and other major publications throughout China.[87] A report by the Central Party School's party committee in March 1965 declared Yang a "spokesman for the bourgeoisie within the party, part of Peng Dehuai's gang, and a little Khrushchev." Yang subsequently spent eight years in prison, and philosophers Sun Dingguo and Li Ming committed suicide. More than 150 people were denounced at the Central Party School, with innumerable members of the general public also implicated.[88]

Economic circles launched criticism against the economist Sun Ye-fang, who had summarized the lessons of the failure of the Great Leap Forward to analyze problems in the economic management system and economic policies. Sun's call for enterprises to keep accurate accounts, take profit seriously, and focus on economic results was criticized as revisionism.

In history circles, criticism was launched against the bourgeois "historicism" of the Peking University history professor Jian Bozan, who opposed a one-sided emphasis on "theory-driven history" and advocated that historical research should reach conclusions consistent with Marxism based on large amounts of historical material. Equally objectionable was Jian's observation that "after every major rebellion, the new ruler restored feudal order by making concessions to the peasants to some degree . . . This is what pushed forward China's progress." This "concessionist policy" "fundamentally distorted Chairman Mao's theory on the historical role of China's peasant wars."[89]

In literary and arts circles, revolutionary mass criticism had occurred in periodic surges since the 1951 criticism of the film *The Story of Wu Xun*. The new round of criticism was sparked by two of Mao's memos on reports by the Propaganda Department's literature and arts section. On December 12, 1963, Mao wrote, "The economic foundation has already changed for socialism, but the arts departments that serve as part of the superstructure for this foundation remain a major problem to this day . . . Many Communist Party members enthusiastically advocate feudalist and bourgeois art and not socialist art—isn't that absurd?"[90] The second memo, on June 27, 1964, stated that China's literature and arts associations and most of the publications they controlled had failed to execute the party's policies and had "arrived at the brink of revisionism.[91]

Around the time of these two memos, criticism targeted the leaders of the Ministry of Culture and of key cultural organizations, including Qi Yanming, Xia Yan, Tian Han, Yang Hansheng, and Shao Quanlin.[92] Many literary works were also criticized, along with certain viewpoints on literature and art, such as "writing about people who are neither heroic nor advanced" and seeing "no harm in ghost stories."

While listening to a report in November 1964, Mao said, "If the entire Ministry of Culture isn't in our hands, how much of it is? Twenty percent? Thirty percent? Or maybe half? Is most of it out of our hands? It looks to me as if at least half of it is. The Ministry of Culture has collapsed."[93] This may be why the Cultural Revolution used the cultural sector as its breakthrough point.

Mao's wife, Jiang Qing, played a crucial role in mass criticism in the literary and arts circles. In a speech at a national symposium of performers convened by Zhou Enlai on June 23, 1964, Jiang told workers in the literature and arts fields to "carefully orient themselves": "Everything on stage these days is about emperors, generals, and ministers, gifted scholars and beautiful ladies—all that feudal and bourgeois stuff. That's not going to protect our economic base, but will sabotage it instead." On June 26, Mao wrote a memo on Jiang Qing's speech: "Well said."[94] Jiang Qing described herself as the "sentinel" of the ideological realm, and this was true; she was always monitoring the ideological domain on Mao's behalf, and whenever she detected something new that went against Mao's thinking, she would report it to Mao and launch a criticism. In order to clear the "feudal and bourgeois stuff" from the stage, Jiang Qing personally organized, participated in, and created modernized "model" Peking operas such as *The Red Lantern*, *Raid on the White Tiger Regiment*, and *The Red Detachment of Women*. Referred to as the standard-bearer of culture, Jiang Qing was Mao's most devoted supporter during the Cultural Revolution.

2
—
LIGHTING THE FUSE

On November 10, 1965, the Shanghai newspaper *Wenhui Bao* published Yao Wenyuan's essay "A Critique of the New Historical Play *Hai Rui Dismissed from Office*." With so much mass criticism going on, no one took any notice at the time, but this essay became the blasting fuse for the Cultural Revolution, and the author of the play, Wu Han, who had leveled baseless accusations against Zhang Bojun and Luo Longji during the 1957 Anti-Rightist Campaign,[1] became its first victim.

The frontline leaders of the CCP Central Committee had kept this essay secret during the entire drafting process until it was published eight months later; even the Central Committee Secretariat, Politburo, and Propaganda Department knew nothing about it. The essay had been the brainchild of Mao,[2] and its impetus was the Great Famine. Back during the seventh plenum of the Eighth Central Committee in April 1959, Mao had proposed learning from the famous Ming official Hai Rui and had suggested finding historians to write essays on the subject.[3] Mao may have become nostalgic for Hai Rui's integrity and courage because no one had dared to tell him the truth about the Great Leap Forward, or because the bureaucracy had descended into abuse and indulgence, but he never reckoned on Peng Dehuai becoming a modern Hai Rui by implicating the Three Red Banners at the Lushan Conference. Mao said there was a difference between a "leftist Hai Rui" and a "rightist Hai Rui," and he criticized Peng as the latter type.[4]

As a leading Ming historian within the party, Wu Han used Marxism to interpret history and used history as a politically charged allusion to the present. Prior to the establishment of the PRC, Wu Han's works had castigated the founding Ming emperor, Zhu Yuan-zhang, as a stand-in for Chiang Kai-shek, but after the PRC was established, Wu's book *Zhu Yuanzhang* served as a paean of praise to Mao. This double standard is typical of intellectuals who rise to fame under a totalitarian government. At Mao's request, Wu Han published the essay "Hai Rui Scolds the Emperor" under the pen name Liu Mianzhi in *People's Daily* in June 1959. When Wu published another essay in *People's Daily* in September 1959 after Peng Dehuai came under criticism, Hu Qiaomu took the precaution of adding a paragraph condemning right-deviation to remove any suggestion of sympathy for Peng Dehuai.[5] Soon after that, Wu Han began writing the script for *Hai Rui Dismissed from Office* at the request of the famous Peking opera performer Ma Lianliang. The opera was performed for the first time in Beijing in January 1961. After the tenth plenum of the Eighth Central Committee in September 1962, the hypervigilant Jiang Qing and Kang Sheng decided that this play was "related to the Lushan Conference" and that it implicitly endorsed "assigning output quotas to households" and the ongoing verdict-reversal wind. Mao took their views seriously and instructed Jiang Qing to find a hit man to denounce the play.

Jiang went to Shanghai with this mission in February 1965. At the recommendation of the secretary of the municipal party committee secretariat, Zhang Chunqiao, Jiang entrusted the essay to Yao Wenyuan, who was on the editorial committee of *Liberation Daily* (*Jiefang Ribao*) as well as a key official responsible for publications, literature, and arts in the East China Bureau. Zhang Chunqiao recruited a history instructor from Fudan University, Zhu Yongjia, to compile preparatory material. (It was not until the essay reached its sixth revision that Zhu realized it was being written as a criticism of Wu Han.) Yao Wenyuan spent eight months writing the essay, and Mao personally vetted and approved the tenth revision[6] after reading the essay three times.[7] Meanwhile, during a Central Committee work conference in September 1965, Mao signaled his intentions to Peng Zhen by asking him if it was acceptable to criticize Wu Han.[8] Peng Zhen replied that Wu Han had some problems that could be criticized, but stopped short of saying that Wu himself could be criticized.

After Yao Wenyuan's essay was published in *Wenhui Bao* on November 10, it was reprinted in Shanghai's *Liberation Daily* on November 12, then in various regional newspapers under the East China Bureau, and finally in *People's Daily* on November 30. Peng Dehuai was infuriated when he read the essay on December 4, having just arrived in Sichuan on Mao's orders to help oversee development of the defense industry there.[9]

Now Mao closely watched the response from Beijing.

PENG ZHEN, MAINSTAY OF LIU SHAOQI'S STRONGHOLD

Mao's main objective in criticizing Wu Han was to prevent a verdict reversal on Peng Dehuai and continue the class struggle he had launched at the tenth plenum of the Eighth Central Committee. His specific objective was to bait Peng Zhen. At that time, Peng Zhen was a Politburo member and a secretary of the Central Committee Secretariat, as well as being First Party Secretary and mayor of Beijing. While not a member of the Politburo Standing Committee, he often attended its meetings. At the Secretariat, he was in charge of the National People's Congress standing committee, public security, and political and legal work.

Mao focused on Peng Zhen because Peng had directly pursued Mao's accountability for the Great Famine during the Seven Thousand Cadres Conference and, even more critically, was a mainstay of Liu Shaoqi's political stronghold. Peng Zhen and Liu Shaoqi went back a long way; when Liu was appointed secretary of the North China Bureau in 1936, Peng was head of the bureau's organization department, making Peng second only to Liu in the "white" (Kuomintang-controlled) areas. On March 23, 1938, the Central Committee Politburo held a standing committee meeting to discuss problems in the party's work in northern China, and Mao recommended that Liu Shaoqi continue to direct the bureau's work from within the Central Committee. Liu sent Peng Zhen to be the bureau's representative in the Jin-Cha-Ji

(Shanxi-Chahar-Hebei) border region, teaming up with Nie Rongzhen to direct the party's operations there and in the cities of Beiping and Tianjin. Former bureau members took on leadership roles in northern base areas and formed a core group around Liu Shaoqi with Peng Zhen as its backbone.

Liu Shaoqi's willingness to criticize Wang Ming[10] made him essential to Mao in his battle against the Comintern faction, and as Liu Shaoqi's right-hand man, Peng Zhen also enjoyed Mao's trust. When Mao became director of the Central Party School in March 1943, Peng Zhen effectively ran the school as deputy director, and he used his position to render distinguished service to Mao during the Yan'an Rectification Movement, while also enhancing his own status and strengthening Liu Shaoqi's power base. In July 1943, An Ziwen, an old subordinate of Liu Shaoqi's and Peng Zhen's during their North China Bureau days, was transferred to the party school and became Peng Zhen's right-hand man. Peng Zhen was promoted to director of the Central Committee Organization Department in 1944. Preparations for the Seventh National Party Congress, held in Yan'an from April 23 to June 11, 1945, gave Peng Zhen and An Ziwen an opportunity to arrange positions for other former North China Bureau cadres and helped Liu form a major stronghold within the CCP.

Peng Zhen headed the white area delegation at the Seventh Party Congress, during which Mao designated Liu Shaoqi the "representative of the correct line in the white areas," and Liu Shaoqi and others saw to it that the Seventh Congress established Mao Zedong Thought as the party's leading ideology. The congress confirmed Mao, Zhu De, Liu Shaoqi, Zhou Enlai, and Ren Bishi as secretaries of the Central Committee and Mao as Central Committee chairman; while Liu Shaoqi was listed in third place, he was actually second in power.

After the People's Republic of China was established, Liu Shaoqi's stronghold was fortified by members of the "sixty-one traitors clique," which included Bo Yibo, Liu Lantao, An Ziwen, Yang Xianzhen, Liao Luyan, Xu Zirong, and Wang Qimei. Liu Shaoqi had gained the allegiance of this group after being sent to Tianjin covertly in January 1935 to manage the work of the North China Bureau. The head of the bureau's organization department, Ke Qingshi, suggested addressing the overwhelmingly urgent shortage of cadres by allowing a group of

CCP cadres being held in a Beiping Kuomintang (KMT) prison to sign an anti-communist declaration the enemy required for their release. Liu agreed with Ke's suggestion and reported it to the Central Committee, and with the agreement of the Central Committee's main leader at the time, Zhang Wentian, these cadres began signing the statement as required and leaving prison in September 1936. Among the original sixty-one prisoners, forty-one were still alive by the time of the Cultural Revolution, and twenty-two held leadership positions at the provincial level or above. In a speech on June 20, 1967, Yang Chengwu said spitefully, "These people meet for dinner and take a group photo every year."[11]

Liu Shaoqi's status as successor to Mao allowed his confederates to occupy key positions in the party leadership and expand their power. In April and May 1953, An Ziwen drafted a list of candidates for the Politburo, which included Bo Yibo but not Lin Biao, apparently because Lin had been on medical leave for three years and his leadership of the South Central Bureau was actually being carried out by Deng Zihui. Somehow that list reached Mao's hands, and he was very displeased. During a top-level meeting he demanded to know what gave the vice-director of the Organization Department the authority to draw up this kind of list. An Ziwen carried out self-criticism on the spot. Mao said, "The matter ends here, and it's not to be disclosed to anyone else." Gao Gang, who at that time was still in Mao's good graces, felt that Liu Shaoqi must be behind it, and sensing Mao's displeasure with Liu, he disobeyed Mao's order and spoke of the name list in conversations with a number of leading cadres as a pretext for attacking Liu.[12]

Gao Gang had personal reasons for undermining Liu Shaoqi's power base, which threatened his own stronghold within the party. Previously secretary of the Northeast Bureau, Gao Gang had been transferred to Beijing in 1952 around the same time as four other bureau secretaries: the South Central Bureau deputy secretary Deng Zihui (in charge of actual operations under Secretary Lin Biao), Southwest Bureau secretary Deng Xiaoping, Northwest Bureau deputy secretary Xi Zhongxun (under Secretary Peng Dehuai), and East China Bureau secretary Rao Shushi. Gao Gang was ranked the highest among them, and some speculated that Mao was preparing to make

Gao his successor in place of Liu Shaoqi, given their shared views on agricultural collectivization and other key issues.

Repeating Mao's criticism of Liu in private conversations, Gao complained to other leading cadres about Liu's advocacy of the 1940s CCP policy proposal for new democracy, his defense of private business,[13] and his approach to rural matters, including his objection to expelling party members purely on the grounds of rich peasant status. Gao subsequently said in his self-criticism, "My political views regarding Liu Shaoqi weren't my own, but what I heard someone else say." That "someone else" was Mao, who had at one point entrusted Gao Gang with examining the records of the KMT and Japanese puppet governments to see how Liu Shaoqi had behaved while under arrest in the Northeast in 1929. But by the end of 1953, Mao had begun to regard Gao as more dangerous than Liu: Liu had taken the initiative to undergo self-criticism while Gao Gang refused, and Gao had longstanding connections within the military and a power base in the Northeast, which Liu did not. Furthermore, Gao Gang telling others what Mao was saying in private put Mao in an embarrassing position. After repeatedly weighing the situation, Mao decided to get rid of Gao[14] and implicated the Central Committee Organization Department director Rao Shushi as part of a "Gao-Rao League." Having lost Mao's support, Gao Gang killed himself in 1954.

The Gao-Rao incident only exacerbated resentment of Liu Shaoqi within the party. In spring 1962, Lin Biao told Gao Gang's wife, Li Liqun, "Gao Gang wasn't the only one in the party who objected to Liu Shaoqi; in the Northeast there was me, Wang Heshou, He Kaifeng, Chen Yun, Li Fuchun, and Chen Zhengren. In Beijing, it was Chairman Mao who first objected to Liu Shaoqi and was dissatisfied with his conduct and work, and he even has doubts about Liu Shaoqi's history."[15]

Gao Gang's secretary, Zhao Jialiang, said that Mao began taking Liu down in 1953, and this makes sense to me. Why else would Mao have Gao Gang look into the KMT and puppet regime dossiers; why else tell Gao Gang that he was going to have Liu moved out?[16] By 1965, Mao had resolved to purge Liu Shaoqi, but that required first breaking his arm, so Peng Zhen came under attack.

Mao was also anxious about the close relationship between Peng

Zhen, He Long, and Luo Ruiqing. Peng Zhen had become friends with He Long in Yan'an, and the two had remained in close contact since arriving in Beijing. He Long liked to go fishing and often sent fish to Peng Zhen. Peng Zhen, for his part, dropped in on He Long when he had time and looked after He Long's wife, Xue Ming, who worked in the Beijing municipal party committee's propaganda department. Luo Ruiqing worked closely with Peng Zhen as director of the Beijing Municipal Public Security Bureau, as minister of public security and as the PLA's chief of General Staff. He almost always accompanied Peng Zhen in watching parade rehearsals before National Day.[17]

Some scholars insist that Mao must have trusted Peng Zhen, given his key position as head of the Cultural Revolution Five-Member Small Group (hereafter Group of Five). But a key posting didn't necessarily imply trust; Mao had Liu Shaoqi preside over the May 1966 enlarged Politburo conference that passed the May 16 Circular, even though he clearly didn't trust Liu at that time.

PENG ZHEN'S RESISTANCE

Soon after Yao Wenyuan's essay was published, the publisher of *Beijing Daily*, Fan Jin, and the head of the *People's Daily* theoretical section, Sha Ying, telephoned Shanghai's *Wenhui Bao* to ask about Yao Wenyuan's background but received no direct response. Instead, *Wenhui Bao*'s chief correspondent in Beijing asked Fan Jin to arrange a follow-up in *Beijing Daily*. Requesting instructions from the Beijing municipal party committee propaganda department, Fan Jin was told, "Just talk about the weather. Ha ha ha!"[18]

When Mao noticed that the essay wasn't being reprinted in Beijing, he went to Shanghai on November 17 and had the essay printed into a separate pamphlet to be sold throughout the country. On November 24, the Shanghai Xinhua Book Store sent urgent telegrams to its branch stores soliciting orders and received positive replies from most places. The Beijing branch finally agreed to order some copies on November 29.[19]

On November 26, Peng Zhen told the Beijing party committee that the Wu Han issue was not one of a conflict between the "enemy and us" and that a clear boundary had to be drawn.[20] After Zhao Enlai stepped in under Mao's orders, Peng Zhen held a meeting at the Great Hall of the People on November 28 to discuss the issue of Beijing newspapers reprinting Yao's essay. The secretary of the Beijing municipal party committee, Deng Tuo, attended the meeting along with the vice-director of the Central Committee Propaganda Department, Zhou Yang, among others. Deng Tuo told Peng Zhen, "Wu Han is very anxious because he knows there's something behind this criticism." Peng Zhen said, "It doesn't matter whether there's something behind it or not. What matters is the truth, and all people are equal before the truth."[21]

It was the Shanghai party secretary Chen Pixian who broke the deadlock on November 25 by telling Luo Ruiqing the background of the essay and having him pass it on to Zhou Enlai. *People's Liberation Army Daily* reprinted the article under orders from Luo Ruiqing on November 29, and Zhao Enlai ordered *People's Daily* to reprint it the next day.[22] After stalling for eighteen days, *People's Daily* reprinted Yao's essay in its "Academic Research" section. Under orders from Peng Zhen, the newspaper wrote an editorial note that discussed Yao's criticism of *Hai Rui Dismissed from Office* as an academic issue and emphasized that "freedom to criticize is permitted, and so is freedom to counter-criticize." The last paragraph of the editor's note, added by Zhou Enlai, quoted Mao in stating the need to engage in struggle against anti-Marxist toxins.[23]

On December 12, *Beijing Daily* and *Frontline (Qianxian)* magazine both published an article by Deng Tuo under the pen name Xiang Yangsheng titled "On *Hai Rui Dismissed from Office* and the 'Theory of Moral Legacy,'" which reduced the play from a political issue to an "academic" issue. The article was written under Peng Zhen's direction, and Peng Zhen revised it before it was finalized by the Beijing municipal party committee secretariat.[24]

In a conversation with Chen Boda, Ai Siqi, Guan Feng, and others on December 21, Mao praised Yao Wenyuan's essay with reservations: "It names names and has really shaken up the theatrical, historical, and philosophical circles, but it still didn't hit the vital part. The crucial point is the 'official dismissed from office.' Emperor Jiajing dismissed Hai Rui, and in 1959 we dismissed Peng Dehuai. Peng Dehuai is 'Hai Rui.'"[25] Mao repeated these views the next day in a conversation with Peng Zhen, Kang Sheng, Yang Chengwu, and others, but Peng Zhen said that no organizational relationship had been found between Wu Han and Peng Dehuai. The next day, Mao summoned Peng Zhen and said, "Reach a political verdict on the Wu Han problem in two months."[26] At a meeting of the Beijing municipal party committee soon after that, Peng Zhen said, "You need to make self-criticism about your errors; stand firm on what's right, insist on the truth, but correct your errors." He was clearly signaling support for Wu Han.[27]

On December 26 and 27, the Shanghai municipal party committee reported to Peng Zhen that Yao Wenyuan's essay had been published in accordance with Chairman Mao's instructions at a Central Committee work conference in September. Without taking a stand, Peng Zhen said that there were two sides to Yao's essay and that the Wu Han issue had to be discussed as an academic issue. Peng Zhen also said, "During the democratic revolution period and the Anti-Rightist campaign, Wu Han was a leftist. Deng Tuo is a leftist, and his essay under the pen name Xiang Yangsheng was written at my instruction." Mao took careful note of these instances of resistance.

Peng Zhen was experienced enough to have known that Mao supported Yao Wenyuan's essay. Even if Peng initially resisted in ignorance, once Mao said that the "crucial point" of *Hai Rui Dismissed from Office* was the "official dismissed from office," Peng Zhen's insistence that criticism of the play should be limited to the academic sphere was a challenge to Mao. Today Peng Zhen's resistance looks correct and politically courageous. Did he have Liu Shaoqi's support? No written materials have verified this so far.

The February Outline that Peng Zhen and others organized showed that Peng Zhen swallowed Mao's bait.

THE FEBRUARY OUTLINE

After Mao specified the key point in *Hai Rui Dismissed from Office*, the number of critical articles surged. In mid-January 1966, the

Central Committee Propaganda Department received two essays from Guan Feng, an editor at *Red Flag*, and Qi Benyu, head of the magazine's history group. Since the essays raised the issue to a "higher plane of principle," the Propaganda Department referred them to the Group of Five.

Mao had suggested establishing this group in July 1964 to lead mass criticism in the cultural sector, so it naturally took on criticism of *Hai Rui Dismissed from Office*. Peng Zhen was head of the group, and the other members were Lu Dingyi (director of the Propaganda Department), Kang Sheng (chairman of the Central Committee's Theoretical Committee), Zhou Yang (vice-director of the Propaganda Department), and Wu Lengxi (director of the Xinhua News Agency and publisher of *People's Daily*). At an enlarged meeting on February 3, 1966, the group criticized Guan Feng and Qi Benyu as leftists, and Peng Zhen emphasized that neither Wu Han nor the play had any connection to Peng Dehuai and that the issue was purely academic. In accordance with Peng Zhen's views, Xu Liqun and Yao Zhen (both vice-directors of the Propaganda Department) drafted a report that came to be known as the "February Outline" at Diaoyutai on February 4. The outline said that discussion "should not be limited to the political issue but should touch on various issues of academic theory for ample discussion." Some understood this as an attempt to play down the political aspect. The outline also called for "seeking truth from facts, maintaining the principle of all people being equal before the truth, and convincing by reason rather than arbitrarily overwhelming people like a scholar-tyrant." This last point was clearly aimed at Yao Wenyuan.[28]

On February 5, Liu Shaoqi presided over a discussion of the draft February Outline by members of the Politburo Standing Committee who were in Beijing at the time. Peng revised the outline after this discussion, and it was approved by the Standing Committee and cabled to Mao in Wuhan on February 7.[29]

Peng Zhen, Lu Dingyi, Kang Sheng, Wu Lengxi, Xu Liqun, Hu Sheng, Tian Jiaying, and others flew to Wuhan on the morning of February 8 and were taken straight to Mao's residence on East Lake. After meeting with Mao, Xu Liqun had word sent to Yao Zhen in Beijing that the outline had been approved without a hitch,[30] but subsequently the appendix to the May 16 Circular said that Mao neither opposed nor endorsed the February Outline.[31] Mao subsequently criticized Xu Liqun, who admitted that he had failed to catch Mao's drift at the meeting. This was typical of Mao, who at every crucial juncture of political struggle was ambiguous in conversations with his political opponents.

After the reporting meeting in Wuhan, Peng Zhen wrote a memo on behalf of the Central Committee without submitting it to Mao for his approval. Peng then telephoned the Politburo Standing Committee and said that the outline had been approved by Mao and should be distributed to the entire party as soon as possible. A few days later, Peng Zhen told the Shanghai municipal party committee that the February Outline had been discussed by the Politburo Standing Committee and that Mao had approved it, that the issue had been resolved, and that there was no need to discuss it with them. On Peng Zhen's instructions, Hu Sheng told Zhang Chunqiao on February 13 that Mao said that Wu Han was not to be referred to as anti-party and anti-socialist, and that no connection was to be made with the Lushan Conference.[32] The February Outline was distributed to the entire party as a Central Committee document under Deng Xiaoping's signature on February 12.

On March 11, 1966, the director of the Shanghai municipal party committee propaganda department, Yang Yongzhi, telephoned Xu Liqun and asked who exactly the February Outline was targeting and who was being referred to as "loftist." Representing Peng Zhen, Xu replied that it targeted "Ah Q and other scrofulous types," and he demanded to know why Shanghai had published Yao's essay without prior notice. Where was the municipal party committee's sense of party spirit?[33] After learning of this telephone call, Zhang Chunqiao said it proved that "the Central Committee Propaganda Department and the Beijing municipal party committee oppose Yao Wenyuan's essay, and that the February Outline targets Yao Wenyuan's essay and Chairman Mao."[34] It made Mao all the more determined to strike down Peng Zhen.

MAO GOES ON THE COUNTERATTACK

After observing the resistance of Peng Zhen and the others, Mao at the end of March told Kang Sheng that the Beijing municipal party committee and Central Committee Propaganda Department were shielding evildoers and must be disbanded, and that Peng Zhen should stop protecting evildoers and apologize to Shanghai. Shortly after that, Mao told Kang Sheng, Zhao Yimin, Wei Wenbo, Jiang Qing, Zhang Chunqiao, and others that the February Outline had blurred class boundaries and failed to distinguish right from wrong. Why didn't the Propaganda Department demand prior notice when Wu Han was publishing reactionary articles, and then expect prior notice of Yao Wenyuan's essay? Mao said that spiking leftist articles while shielding anti-party intellectuals was an act of "scholastic tyranny." The Propaganda Department had become Yama's Palace, and it was time to "strike down the King of Hell and liberate the little demons!" Mao said, "I've always advocated calling for local rebellions whenever Central Committee organs act badly. All the localities should produce more Monkey Kings to create an uproar in the celestial palace. During last year's September Conference, I asked comrades from all over China, 'What would you do if the Central Committee embarked on revisionism?' It's very possible, and very dangerous." Mao called for support for the left and the establishment of a force to carry out a great cultural revolution.[35]

While in Handan, Hubei Province, on April 2, Zhou Enlai wrote a letter to Mao saying that he completely agreed that the Group of Five's outline was in error and that he was preparing to call a meeting of the Secretariat to discuss Mao's directive.[36] Over the next few days, Kang Sheng authorized *Guangming Daily*, *People's Daily*, and *Red Flag* to publish essays by Qi Benyu, Guan Feng, and Lin Jie that Peng Zhen and Xu Liqun had been withholding for more than two months.

Called back to Beijing on urgent notice, Deng Xiaoping presided over a meeting of the Central Committee Secretariat from April 9 to 12, during which Peng Zhen declared that he had never opposed and would never oppose Chairman Mao. Kang Sheng and Chen Boda proceeded to criticize Peng Zhen's erroneous line, and Zhou Enlai and Deng Xiaoping agreed, while still referring to Peng as "Comrade." The meeting resolved to (1) draft a notice that thoroughly repudiated and rescinded the Group of Five's February Outline; and (2) submit names for a Cultural Revolution document-drafting group to be approved by Mao and the Politburo Standing Committee. This group eventually became the Central Cultural Revolution Small Group (CCRSG).[37]

On April 16, *Beijing Daily* dedicated three pages to criticism of Deng Tuo, Liao Mosha, and Wu Han, with an editorial comment by the municipal party committee's official organ *Frontline*. The municipal party committee thought it could settle the matter by hanging Deng Tuo and the others out to dry, but its editorial was omitted when the Xinhua News Agency and Central People's Broadcasting Station aired the criticisms that same day.

From April 16 to 24, Mao presided over an enlarged meeting of the Politburo Standing Committee in Hangzhou, which discussed Peng Zhen's errors, rescinded the February Outline, disbanded the Group of Five, and established the Central Cultural Revolution Small Group. The main drafter of the February Outline, Xu Liqun, was criticized by Mao and subsequently jailed for eight years. Mao said, "I don't believe that it's only Wu Han's problem . . . it exists in the imperial court and in every region and province . . . There was talk in Wuhan of purging leftists, but I disagreed."[38] Mao was referring here to Peng Zhen arranging for dossiers to be compiled on Guan Feng and Qi Benyu in February and March 1966.[39]

Peng Zhen had been refused an audience with Mao upon arriving in Hangzhou, and sensing that something major was going to happen, none of the six regional secretaries dared to be seen with him. After the meeting, the Central Committee had Li Xuefeng and Song Renqiong accompany Peng Zhen on his flight back to Beijing; in effect, he was being sent back under escort. The three of them sat facing each other without talking.[40] In the CCP, only political and class relationships existed, and once Mao decided someone was politically untrustworthy, everyone else would cut off relations with him and even kick him while he was down.

After attending the Hangzhou Conference, Yang Chengwu told Qiu Huizuo that Mao complained of being kept in the dark while away from Beijing: "Carrying out a cultural revolution was a major matter, but they made resolutions and issued directives without telling me anything about it. Everyone needs to consider what the problem is here." Yang told Qiu, "Lao Qiu, there's going to be a counterattack,"[41] meaning against Liu Shaoqi and Peng Zhen.

Mao continued to criticize Peng Zhen in conversations with Chen Boda and Kang Sheng in Hangzhou on April 28. Mao said, "Peng Zhen was remolding the party according to his worldview, but things moved in the opposite direction, and he engineered his own downfall. We have to thoroughly attack his errors. Class struggle can't be shifted by human will."[42]

On May 10, the Central Committee decided to reorganize the Beijing municipal party committee and have Li Xuefeng take over Peng Zhen's responsibilities there. At an enlarged Politburo meeting on the afternoon of May 11, the indignant Peng Zhen demanded, "Who was the first to cry out, 'Long live'?" Liu Shaoqi immediately put an end to the commotion,[43] and soon afterward the Central Committee notified Peng Zhen that he was not to attend any more enlarged Politburo meetings.

Liu Shaoqi had been on an official visit to Southeast Asia with Chen Yi while Mao was purging his right-hand man in April, and he planned to carry out an inspection visit of the border region when he returned to Kunming from Rangoon, Burma, on April 19. Instead, the CCP Central Committee General Office notified him to go directly to Hangzhou for the enlarged Politburo Standing Committee meeting. The moment Liu arrived in Hangzhou, Zhou Enlai told him what had been going on, and Liu realized that he was helpless to resist Mao's purge of Peng Zhen.

At the same time that Peng Zhen and the others were writing their February Outline, Jiang Qing was in Shanghai overseeing the drafting of another document, the "Summary of the Symposium Convened by Comrade Jiang Qing at the Behest of Comrade Lin Biao on the Work of Literature and Arts in the Armed Forces." Mao had Chen Boda make a special trip to Shanghai to help Zhang Chunqiao revise this "February Summary." Diametrically opposed to the February Outline, the summary said, "Since the country's founding, the literary and arts circles have basically failed to execute Chairman Mao's cultural line . . . and have imposed dictatorship over us with an anti-party, anti-socialist reactionary line antithetical to Mao Zedong Thought." The summary called for "resolutely carrying out a socialist revolution on the cultural battlefront and thoroughly vanquishing the reactionary line." Like Yao Wenyuan's essay, the summary was Mao's idea. Mao personally vetted and revised the drafts written by Chen Boda, Zhang Chunqiao, Liu Zhijian, Chen Yading, and others, and provided a title that put Lin Biao's imprimatur on the document. On March 19, Jiang Qing requested Lin Biao's approval, and Lin gave the summary a high appraisal in letters to several vice-chairmen of the Central Military Commission.

The summary was distributed to the county and regimental levels as Central Committee Document No. 211 [1966] on April 10, 1966, with an editorial comment rewritten under Zhou Enlai's direction to emphasize that the summary had been "personally revised by Chairman Mao three times."[44] The summary was a call for cultural revolution issued by the "proletarian headquarters headed by Chairman Mao" and backed by the military.

Fire-and-brimstone editorials in major newspapers over the following weeks raised the curtain on the Cultural Revolution.

Although Mao remained in the south, Lin Biao's and Zhou Enlai's support gave him remote control over the enlarged Politburo meeting that began in Beijing on May 4. At that meeting, Peng Zhen, Luo Ruiqing, Lu Dingyi, and Yang Shankun were laid out on the sacrificial altar.

3

REMOVING OBSTRUCTIONS

By the time Peng Zhen was denounced at the enlarged Politburo Standing Committee meeting in April 1966, Yang Shangkun and Luo Ruiqing had already been dealt with.

On November 10, 1965, the day that Yao Wenyuan's essay criticizing *Hai Rui Dismissed from Office* was first published, Yang Shangkun was removed from his position as head of the Central Committee General Office, ostensibly to serve as secretary of the Guangdong provincial party committee secretariat, but in fact to be investigated. On May 24, 1966, the Central Committee issued its "Explanation of the Errors and Problems of Comrade Lu Dingyi and Comrade Yang Shangkun" (Central Committee Document No. 277 [1966]), which accused Yang of unauthorized installation of a listening device to monitor Mao's conversations,[1] providing others with unauthorized access to top-secret documents, and having "an extremely abnormal relationship with Luo Ruiqing and others and actively participating in antiparty activities."

The head of the Central Committee General Office was in charge of the Central Guard Regiment, and was responsible for Mao's safety and the management of his daily needs. Replacing Yang Shangkun with the more trustworthy Wang Dongxing was therefore essential preparation for launching the Cultural Revolution. Yang Shangkun's problem wasn't his relationship with Peng Dehuai, but rather his relationship with Liu Shaoqi and Deng Xiaoping. In a speech on May 21, 1966, Zhou Enlai said, "Peng Dehuai overturned the commode on the mountaintop, spreading his stench far and wide and arousing public indignation . . . Yang Shangkun cannot be compared with those three; he doesn't have enough stamina on his own, but can only clutch at their legs." The legs Zhou referred to were Liu's and Deng's.[2] Luo Ruiqing effectively controlled the military and was also on good terms with Liu and Deng, so Mao went after him first.

THE FALL OF LUO RUIQING

Luo Ruiqing was one of the ten Senior Generals of the People's Liberation Army (PLA),[3] and Mao had given him a nickname, which he did for only his favorite subordinates. Mao called Luo Ruiqing Changzi, "Tall Man," while Ke Qingshi was "Big-Nose Ke," Tan Zhenlin was "Boss Tan," etc. It was Mao's genial and humorous way of treating these men as equals. Mao had appointed Luo to important postings such as minister of public security, secretary of the Central Committee Secretariat, secretary of the Central Military Commission, vice-premier of the State Council, vice-minister of defense, and head of the Defense Industry Office. Mao wielded Luo Ruiqing like a sword in his hand to suppress counterrevolutionaries, oppose the Hu Feng clique,* and manufacture countless cases of injustice. In December 1965 that sword landed on Luo's own neck.

Luo Ruiqing also had a deep relationship with Lin Biao. When Lin became commander of the Fourth Red Army in 1930, Luo was political commissar of the Forty-First Division. When Lin was appointed commander of the First Army Group, Luo headed the army group's security bureau. When Lin was director of the Red Army University in Yan'an, Luo was the provost. After the 1959 Lushan Conference, Lin Biao took charge of the Central Military Commission (CMC) in place of Peng Dehuai, and he nominated Luo, who had left the armed forces ten years earlier, to replace Huang Kecheng as chief of General Staff.

---

* Hu Feng was a writer and theorist who openly opposed Mao's politicization of art and literature. As a result, he was arrested as a counterrevolutionary in 1955, and anyone associated with him was also persecuted. He was finally released in 1979. —Trans.

Luo had also been with the First Front Red Army, which was Mao's "personal asset," and the cadres of which now dominated the CMC. Why would a senior cadre who enjoyed so much trust from Mao and Lin be struck down?

Wu Faxian believes that Lin Biao raised the issues relating to Luo's downfall, while Mao made the decision and took the necessary action.[4] In his first three or so years as chief of General Staff, Luo worked well with Lin Biao and effectively managed the work of the CMC.[5] In autumn 1962, Lin Biao requested sick leave for severe relapses from old war injuries, and responsibility for the CMC's work fell to his second-in-command, He Long. From then on, He Long and Luo Ruiqing ran the armed forces as a team, while Luo's former close relationship with Lin Biao began to unravel.

Qiu Huizuo believes that Lin and Luo had a good relationship, but that Lin wasn't a detail man, especially as his health declined, and that Luo finally gave up and turned toward He Long. Seeing Luo drifting away from him, Lin complained, "You're the Chief of General Staff and I'm still your superior. I have to know what you're doing—I'm accountable to the Central Committee for the military's operations."[6]

The struggle against Luo Ruiqing within the military was related to the army's power bases. The first of these power bases was the First Front Red Army, formed of the army led by Zhu De and Chen Yi in the 1927 Nanchang Uprising and which then converged with Mao at Jinggang Mountain, and in which Lin Biao became the backbone in subsequent battles. The second was the Second Front Red Army, established in the western Hunan, western Hubei-Hunan, and Honghu revolutionary base areas and led by He Long. And the third was the Fourth Front Red Army, established by Zhang Guotao and Xu Xiangqian in the E-Yu-Wan (Hubei-Henan-Anhui) revolutionary base area. Zhang Guotao was purged during the Yan'an period, and the Fourth Army's influence had waned after substantial losses suffered during the westward march, but it still had several cadres. During the War of Resistance against Japan, the main force of the three Red Armies was reorganized into three divisions of the Eighth Route Army led by Lin Biao, He Long, and Liu Bocheng, and the New Fourth Army commanded by Chen Yi. During the civil war between the Communists and the Nationalists, these became the four armies of the People's Liberation

Army: the First Field Army under Peng Dehuai, the Second Field Army under Liu Bocheng, the Third Field Army under Chen Yi and Su Yu, and the Fourth Field Army under Lin Biao.

After the CMC was reorganized in 1959, Mao remained chairman, and Lin Biao, He Long, and Nie Rongzhen were the vice-chairmen, indicating the control the former First Front and Second Front armies exerted within the military. On the eve of the Cultural Revolution, He Long's Second Front Army was the real rival to Lin Biao's camp. After Peng Dehuai was unseated and one of the senior generals, Xu Haidong, became ill, He Long absorbed the "homeless" from their Third and Fifteenth Army Groups. He Long's close relationships with certain top leaders such as Deng Xiaoping also allowed him to carry considerable weight in the party's internal struggle.

Luo Ruiqing's drift away from Lin Biao and toward He Long split the military into two camps: one headed by He Long and Luo Ruiqing, and the second by Lin Biao and the other veteran marshals. "Camp consciousness" was very intense in the military's upper echelons. Usually the camps coexisted peacefully, but ruptures would form at crucial junctures. Luo Ruiqing's transfer of loyalty from the First Front Army to the Second Front Army offended not only Lin Biao but also other marshals. "Liu Bocheng, Chen Yi, Luo Ronghuan, Nie Rongzhen, Ye Jianying, and other marshals supported Lin Biao, leaving He Long very isolated within the Central Military Commission."[7] This naturally made things difficult for Luo as well.

Ye Jianying's and Nie Rongzhen's resentment of Luo Ruiqing was also rooted in work-related factors. At the end of 1963, having engaged in study and firsthand observation, Ye Jianying wrote a report recommending that the CMC promote the teaching methods used by Guo Xingfu in the Nanjing Military Region. Mao endorsed and praised this report. At the end of January 1964, Luo Ruiqing represented the CMC in convening a military training conference that launched the use of Guo Xingfu's training methods throughout the military. Ye Jianying did not attend this conference, and the military's upper echelons felt that Luo Ruiqing was stealing Ye Jianying's thunder.[8] Then, at the end of 1964, He Long and Luo Ruiqing presented a large-scale competition of military skills, demonstrating the improvement of the army under their leadership. Lin Biao, Ye Jianying, and Nie Rongzhen watched coldly from the sidelines. This competition eventually led to Luo Ruiqing's being accused of opposing "giving prominence to politics."[9] Added to all this, Luo Ruiqing's supervision of the defense industry overlapped with Nie Rongzhen's management of the State Commission of Science for National Defense, making conflict inevitable, especially when Luo failed to show Nie proper deference.

In June 1965, Ye Jianying summoned the General Logistics Department head Qiu Huizuo to discuss the Luo Ruiqing problem. Ye had just seen Lin Biao and told him that Mao had said of Luo: "I say Tall Man Luo is prickly, and you're getting poked. I wonder if Comrade Lin Biao has been poked yet." Ye said that Lin had complained: "Tall Man has changed. Maybe becoming a senior official with all that power has turned him into a full-fledged bureaucrat. When he first became chief of General Staff, he knew his place, but now he's lording it over everyone as if he were commander in chief. He looks down on me and Marshal Nie, not to mention Marshal Liu, Marshal Xu, and you." Ye and Qiu agreed that they needed to get others on board and keep them from joining the Luo-He alliance, especially as He Long had been successfully pulling in Lin Biao allies such as Xiao Hua, Liang Biye, and Wu Kehua.[10] The conversation indicates that Mao must have discussed the Luo Ruiqing problem with Ye by June 1965.

Luo Ruiqing's "prickly" and domineering personality was bound to cause conflict, but the real problem was an imbalance in the distribution of power. In 1965, Luo held thirteen key positions, and the documents that formed a small mountain on his desk every day required four secretaries to manage.[11] While Luo Ruiqing attended to numerous affairs of state, some marshals and senior generals had nothing to do. Furthermore, Luo Ruiqing had general oversight while veteran marshals were responsible only for departmental operations (Ye Jianying was in charge of military training, Nie Rongzhen of defense research, Xu Xiangqian of the militia). Internal friction of this type is hard to avoid under a totalitarian government, when the first-in-command distributes power among those he trusts.

Mao was less worried about the grousing of top-ranking military leaders than he was about Luo Ruiqing's tilt toward He Long, Liu Shaoqi, and Deng Xiaoping. Luo Ruiqing began drawing close to Liu Shaoqi from 1962 onward. When Liu Shaoqi presided over the

Third National People's Congress in January 1965, Luo was added as vice-chairman of the National Defense Council, and Liu promised that Luo would succeed the ailing Lin Biao. All this aroused Mao's suspicions (chapter 4 of this book will go into Mao's uneasiness with He Long). By 1965, Mao was ready to unseat Liu Shaoqi, but that required the backing of the military, which was controlled by Liu's cronies He Long and Luo Ruiqing. The infighting among the military leaders gave Mao a perfect opportunity to eliminate obstructions in the upper echelons. When Ye Jianying went to see Lin Biao in August 1965, he said, "Today the Chairman called me in. You no longer have to deal with the Luo Ruiqing matter; the Central Committee will resolve it."[12]

In autumn 1965, at Mao's behest, Liu Biao and Ye Jianying began informing ranking military officers of the Luo Ruiqing problem. Ye Jianying told them: "Luo Ruiqing is banking on Marshal Lin's poor health to rise in the ranks. Whiskers [He Long] always likes to create his own clique. Luo helped him pull in Marshal Lin's old subordinates. The Chairman put Marshal Lin in charge of the armed forces, but Marshal Lin delegated his responsibilities because of his poor health, and now such a major problem has arisen!" Ye emphasized that Mao had told him to inform the others of this issue.[13]

At the beginning of December 1965, Lin Biao's wife, Ye Qun, went to see Mao in Hangzhou and informed on Luo Ruiqing. Shortly after that, an enlarged Politburo Standing Committee meeting was held in Shanghai under Mao's direction from December 8 to 15.[14] The sixty-one attendees included thirty-four high ranking military officers. Liu Shaoqi, Zhou Enlai, and Deng Xiaoping ran the meeting, along with Xiao Hua and Liu Zhijian, who, with several other military leaders, had reported to Mao on the Luo Ruiqing problem before the meeting.

Ye Qun was the first to speak at the meeting: "Tall Man Luo opposes giving prominence to politics. He talked nonsense like saying that since prominence had to be given to politics and also military matters, they must be equally important. That's eclecticism." She accused Luo of using Lin Biao's illness as an excuse to undermine his authority, ranting on and on for hours.[15]

Luo Ruiqing was on an inspection visit in Yunnan at the time. On the evening of the third day of the conference, Zhou Enlai told Wu Faxian to send an aircraft with the most dependable flight crew to pick up Luo Ruiqing in Kunming and bring him back to Shanghai. He instructed Wu to personally ensure that the aircraft didn't head west, which Wu Faxian understood to mean that Luo might try to flee to India or Burma. Zhou Enlai also said that Luo's flight could be met only by Wu and two others: Chen Pixian, the representative host; and Xie Fuzhi, the minister of Public Security. No one else was to be told of Luo's arrival in Shanghai.[16] Wu Faxian told the pilot, Shi Niantang, that he was being given several handguns. "If anything unusual happens during the flight, you should obey the Central Committee. You'll need to monitor [the passengers'] movements."[17]

When Luo Ruiqing arrived in Shanghai, he was put under house arrest in a compound at No. 618 Jianguo West Road, where Zhou Enlai and Deng Xiaoping were waiting for him. Zhou and Deng told Luo that he was accused of opposing and shutting out Lin Biao, refusing to give prominence to politics, and making demands on the party. Luo Ruiqing countered that his work had been assigned by the Central Committee and Chairman Mao, and he insisted that he had told Lin Biao everything he was supposed to. Zhou and Deng said there were also other things they could investigate: "You're on bad terms with some others." Luo Ruiqing mournfully repeated the phrase "on bad terms!" over and over again.[18] Luo was kept under watch by guards from Beijing's Central Guard Regiment and wasn't allowed to attend the Shanghai Conference. Zhou Enlai refused Luo's request to meet with Mao and Lin Biao to defend himself.[19]

Recognizing his disadvantaged position, He Long disparaged Luo to everyone he saw at the conference. He said, "That damned son-of-a-bitch Tall Man! He used the Ministry of Public Security's ways to serve his own purposes in the Party and the military! He's despicable!" Ye Jianying roared, "Get rid of the fiend and liberate the marshals!" He also said, "Of course none of you likes being pigeonholed, but at least you have jobs to do, and he has to show you a little courtesy in order to make things work. He doesn't show *us* any courtesy at all. He looks down on people like me!"[20]

Once the Shanghai Conference ended, Luo was replaced with Yang Chengwu as chief of staff. Ye Jianying was promoted to CMC vice-chairman and soon afterward also became its secretary-general.

On March 4, 1966, the Central Committee held a denunciation meeting for Luo Ruiqing at Beijing's Jingxi Guesthouse, attended by ninety-five military leaders. Mao assigned Deng Xiaoping, Peng Zhen, and Ye Jianying with running the meeting, but Deng went off to inspect defense industry constructions in the western provinces after putting in an appearance on the first day, and the meeting was actually managed by Ye Jianying. In her book, Luo Ruiqing's daughter describes the scene as Luo entered the conference hall on the afternoon of March 4: "After months without seeing him, the conference attendees, who'd once been my father's closest comrades, had turned into strangers or enemies. Everyone's face had completely changed, and apart from denouncing Luo Ruiqing for opposing the party and Chairman Mao, they showed that they'd cut off all relations with him. No one at the meeting greeted him or said a word to him, and all looked at Luo Ruiqing with hostility in their eyes."[21] The meeting lasted thirty-five days, with attendees leaping at the chance to speak. There were eighty-six texts of speeches made individually or jointly.

Qiu Huizuo recalls Ye Jianying, Xie Fuzhi, Xiao Hua, Yang Chengwu, and Liu Zhijian among those who charged the enemy lines. Carrying special weight were Xiao Hua's denunciation and Yang Chengwu's repeated systematic exposure, as well as Ye Jianying's summing-up speech. Once a close confederate of Luo's, Xiao Hua denounced him with all his might. When someone is purged in a totalitarian government, it's usually members of his inner circle who deal the fatal blows, because they know the most and are in the best position to sell out their friends in exchange for the trust of those at the top. When Luo Ruiqing was purged, those accused of being his trusted lieutenants provided written exposés of the inner workings of Luo's "small coterie." Ye Jianying provided Luo with this material, along with revelations by Lieutenant General Liang Biye, the deputy director of the PLA's General Political Department and a key member of Luo's inner circle. Luo spent all night reading the material in an agitated state.[22]

On the morning of March 18, Luo attempted suicide by leaping out a window, but he survived with shattered legs. He had left a suicide note for his wife, Hao Zhiping:

Zhiping: I haven't told you about the meeting, in observation of the rules . . .

Farewell. Tell the children to always obey the party and Chairman Mao!

Our party is forever glorious, correct, and great, and you must continue to reform yourselves and continue revolution forever![23]

The denunciations of Luo Ruiqing continued while he was in the hospital.

When news of Luo's failed suicide attempt reached the Politburo meeting in Hangzhou (see below), Mao asked, "Why did he jump?" and then added, "He's a good-for-nothing!" Liu Shaoqi said, "If you're going to jump out a window, you should do it right and go headfirst, but he jumped feetfirst. He was determined to resist the party." Deng Xiaoping said, "Tall Man Luo jumped like a popsicle." Ye Jianying recited a rhyme quoting well-known sad farewells.

The "Report on the Question of Comrade Luo Ruiqing's Errors," produced by a Central Committee work group led by Ye Jianying, was issued as Central Committee Document No. 268 [1966] on May 16. It accused Luo of being hostile to Mao Zedong Thought; promoting a bourgeois military line, and in particular, opposing giving prominence to politics; practicing arbitrary behavior and attempting to establish an independent kingdom; having poor character and a persistent exploiting-class standpoint; openly demanding positions of power; forcing Comrade Lin Biao to step aside; and plotting to usurp military power and oppose the party.

The real problem, however, was that Mao needed to oust Luo Ruiqing to keep the military under firm control so that he could purge Liu Shaoqi.

THE FALL OF LU DINGYI

Lu Dingyi was an alternate Politburo member, a secretary of the Central Committee Secretariat, director of the Central Committee Propaganda Department, State Council vice-premier, and minister of culture. The trigger for his fall from power was an anonymous letter written by his wife, Yan Weibing.

At a session of the enlarged Politburo meeting in May 1966, a document was placed on the table of each attendee, written in Lin Biao's hand with Chinese characters as large as a walnut:

> I hereby testify: (1) When I married Ye Qun, she was a pure virgin, and she has been chaste throughout our marriage; (2) Ye Qun never had a love affair with Wang Shiwei; (3) Tiger [Laohu] and Beany [Doudou] are the blood offspring of myself and Ye Qun; (4) Everything in Yan Weibing's counterrevolutionary letter is rumor-mongering.
> Lin Biao, May 14, 1966[24]

Marshal Nie Rongzhen picked up Lin Biao's letter and angrily demanded, "Why has this been circulated? Take it back!" The document was quickly withdrawn.

Why would Lin Biao, with his formidable title and powerful position as defense minister, have written such a document?

Yan Weibing wrote dozens of letters from 1960 to January 1966. One of them was in the form of doggerel, sent on January 26, 1966, to the Shanghai mayor and deputy party secretary Cao Diqiu to be passed on to Lin Biao. The letter stated: "Hug one slut, give birth to two bastards. Rise three ranks in office, afraid of the light four seasons of the year. Five facial features askew and eyebrows upside-down, stunned out of six senses but still in power. Opium smoke streaming from seven orifices, last eight hairs plucked from the head. Racking one's brain like a nine-headed bird, Yama placing recruitment notices on ten temples." Almost all the other anonymous letters were sent to wherever the family was living at the time, and most tried to sow discord by saying that Beany (Lin Liheng) wasn't Ye Qun's daughter and that she looked like Liu Shaoqi. Lin Biao's secretary, Zhang Yunsheng, saw a photocopy of a letter saying that Ye Qun was "Wang Shiwei's mistress" and "feudal nobility with modern privileges."[25] Yan's letters disturbed Lin Biao's family, and for a period of time Beany didn't believe that Ye Qun was her mother, leading to repeated quarrels. Ye Qun requested testimonials to her innocence from all and sundry, even former grooms and bodyguards, seriously disrupting the household. The Central Committee took the case seriously, and the Ministry of Public Security organized an investigation under the personal direction of Liu Shaoqi, Zhou Enlai, and Peng Zhen.

In early February 1966, Peng Zhen confronted Lu Dingyi with a stack of Yan Weibing's anonymous letters and said, "Lin Biao is the party's vice-chairman, and sending anonymous letters to him is being treated as a political issue. Many of the letters are written under the name Wang Guang-X and were sent from a nursery run by Wang Guangmei's mother, so they're naturally being regarded as an attempt to sow discord within the Central Committee [Politburo] Standing Committee. Quite a few of the letters have been written on postcards, which makes them the equivalent of openly distributed leaflets." Lu told Peng he had no idea that Yan Weibing was sending anonymous letters.[26] Yan was arrested on April 28, 1966.

The Biography of Lu Dingyi states that Yan Weibing had developed a dislike of Ye Qun during the Yan'an Rectification Movement because of things she'd heard about how Ye Qun had joined the party, as well as Ye's domineering attitude after marrying Lin Biao and her mistreatment of the daughter of Lin's former wife. Lu Dingyi summed up the situation to his biographer: "Yan Weibing wrote those anonymous letters because she was mentally ill and couldn't control herself."[27]

While Yan Weibing was being investigated, Zhou Enlai advised Lu Dingyi to leave town for a while—the longer the better. Lu Dingyi went south on March 6 but was called back to be denounced at an enlarged Politburo meeting on May 8.[28]

At the meeting, Lu Dingyi made self-criticism, admitting that it seemed unbelievable that he could have lived with Yan Weibing for twenty-five years without knowing about her letters, but insisting on his innocence. "Yan Weibing is now at the Ministry of Public Security, so please ask her. If I knew anything about her letters before reading the Ministry of Public Security files, please treat me like a chief conspirator and accomplice of counterrevolution and punish me more harshly." In reply to Lin Biao's grilling, Lu said, "Isn't it quite common for husbands not to know what their wives are up to?" Lin Biao said, "I'm itching to shoot you right here and now!"[29] He went on, "I've always had a liking for some intellectuals, and I've been especially fond of you, Lu Dingyi. So why do you engage in this kind of mischief? What's your intention?" When Lu Dingyi said he really didn't know about the letters, Lin Biao smacked the table and said, "How can you not know when you're in bed fucking every day?"[30] The denunciation turned farcical as Zhou Enlai hurled a tea mug in Lu Dingyi's direction, and Yang Chengwu shook his fist under Lu's face and said, "This is the dictatorship of the proletariat!"[31]

After the denunciation meeting, the Politburo Standing Committee decided to disqualify Lu from attending further meetings. When Li Xuefeng delivered the news, Lu shouted, "Comrade Xuefeng, I'm only engaged in Communism, and I hope to see Communism!"[32]

Attributing Lu Dingyi's fall to his wife alone is an oversimplification, however. Lu Dingyi had been in charge of ideological work since the founding of the PRC. He played an important role in organizing ideological campaigns, including those against the intellectuals Hu Shi and Hu Feng, but he fell out of favor with Mao from the early 1960s onward. As noted earlier, Mao had written memos expressing sharp criticism of the intellectual and artistic communities in 1963 and 1964, and Jiang Qing's February Summary had accused the literature and arts community of being "dominated by an anti-party, anti-socialist reactionary line." These departments were under Lu Dingyi's leadership, as was the educational community, which by then had also incurred Mao's displeasure. Mao's irritation increased when Lu Dingyi took the side of Peng Zhen and other Beijing party officials in balking at the publication of Yao Wenyuan's criticism of *Hai Rui Dismissed from Office* in November 1965. In his remarks at the enlarged Politburo Standing Committee meeting held in Hangzhou from March 17 to 20, 1966, Mao stated that the academic and educational communities were under the effective control of bourgeois intellectuals, and he warned that the Propaganda Department "must not turn into the Rural Work Department," which he had ordered disbanded because of Deng Zihui's support of assigning output quotas to households.

In a May 21 speech criticizing Lu Dingyi, Zhou Enlai declared that the Yan Weibing incident exposed Lu Dingyi's opposition to giving prominence to politics, to Mao Zedong Thought, and to the study of Chairman Mao's works by workers, peasants, and soldiers: "They came out to oppose Comrade Lin Biao because Comrade Lin Biao was the first to promote Mao Zedong Thought, raised it the highest, gave it the freest rein, used it the most effectively, and put in the greatest effort . . . After Peng Dehuai was dismissed from office in 1959, Lu's wife spent six years writing anonymous letters. There was a pattern, which was that the most letters were written when the greatest prominence was given to politics, and they used open postcards for publicity."[33]

In the CCP's political campaigns, thoroughly striking down someone required honing in on a fundamental issue. Lu Dingyi came from a well-off bureaucratic family in Wuxi, graduated from Nanyang University, and then joined the revolution as a student in 1925. Returning to Nanjing from northern Shaanxi in 1937 to be treated for an illness, Lu accepted an inheritance of over 2,000 yuan, handing over 1,000 yuan to the Communist Party's Nanjing office as party membership dues; giving another 1,000 yuan to the family of his former wife, who had sacrificed herself in the revolution, to help them locate a lost daughter; and keeping the remaining few hundred yuan for his own medical expenses. Communist Party members weren't allowed to receive an inheritance from an exploiting family, so Lu Dingyi was harshly punished as an alien-class element.

Lu Dingyi was put under isolation and investigation and subjected to interrogation under cruel torture: "The interrogators rushed forward and tightened his handcuffs and twisted his ears, and Lu couldn't keep from issuing blood-curdling screams of pain . . . Every interrogation left Lu with a swollen face, ears, and hands, and streaming with blood." His excessively tight handcuffs "dug into his flesh, and his wrists began to fester."[34] Lu Dingyi was sent to Qincheng Prison in April 1968 without undergoing trial. As punishment for writing an appeal, "Lu was put in handcuffs again, and was not allowed to loosen them even to eat, sleep, or use the toilet. Only during his semi-monthly shower were they taken off, and half an hour later, when his shower was finished, they were put back on. The handcuffs rubbed his wrists raw, creating searing pain. He stuffed his sleeves inside the cuffs, but they even rubbed through the sleeves, streaking them with dark red blood."[35] Lu Dingyi had been thoroughly demonized, so any amount of abuse was justified. The popular slogans "Heroically pursue the routed foe" and "Beat the dog that's fallen in the water" encouraged persecutors with the sense that justice was on their side.

Lu Dingyi was expelled from the party as an alien-class element and anti-party element on November 2, 1975. By then, Lin Biao and Chen Boda had fallen from power, and the Cultural Revolution was a spent force. It is mystifying that at a time when many veteran cadres were being released, the Central Committee imposed even harsher punishment on Lu Dingyi.

An article published in 2006 states that "an influential person in the Central Committee" gave three directives regarding Lu's case. The first was in July 1966: "It is said that while Lu Dingyi was in the Soviet Union, the Soviet revisionists gave him 10,000 rubles. It's possible that they will engage him in illicit relations with a foreign country in future." The second was in February 1976: Lu Dingyi "wants to defend himself, but you can criticize him. He demands to be released from prison, but ignore him for now." The last time was on October 18, 1978: "Chairman Mao gave the order to release him and be done with it, but he refused to come out. He said that he wouldn't come out without a verdict, and that he would stay in prison until he wore out the floor. If so, he will end up in America on the other side of the world."[36] Given the situation after the Cultural Revolution, this "influential person in the Central Committee" had to have been a revered elder of the proletarian revolution. On December 2, 1978, more than two years after the arrest of the Gang of Four, Lu Dingyi regained his freedom after thirteen years in prison.

THE PURGE OF PENG, LUO, LU, AND YANG

The enlarged Politburo meeting in Beijing in May 1966 designated "Peng, Luo, Lu, and Yang" as the "Four Big Clans," borrowing the designation applied to the Kuomintang's "Chiang, Soong, Kung, and Chen,"[37] a synonym for "abject evil" in the Communist Party's dictionary. In a speech on May 21, Zhou Enlai described the purge of Peng, Luo, Lu, and Yang as the latest step in a process to ensure that "revisionism cannot prevail and so that revisionism doesn't emerge in our country." Liu Shaoqi said, "Peeling away those anti-party, anti-socialist elements is a good method. If they're not peeled off, they'll gain power and topple us and change the policies."[38]

On May 22, 1966, the Politburo unanimously passed a resolution that formally revoked all official postings of Peng Zhen, Luo Ruiqing, Lu Dingyi, and Yang Shangkun. After that, the Central Committee on May 24 issued the "Explanation Regarding the Errors and Problems of Comrade Lu Dingyi and Comrade Yang Shangkun," designating them an "anti-party clique." The May 1966 enlarged Politburo meeting also decided to establish an investigation group headed by Zhou Enlai to form four committees to investigate Peng, Luo, Lu, and Yang.

Rather than say that the downfall of Peng, Luo, Lu, and Yang was part of the Cultural Revolution, it would be more accurate to say that it was crucial preparation for Mao's comprehensive launch of the Cultural Revolution. Eliminating those four people made Mao feel safer; he had left Beijing on November 12, 1965, and didn't return until July 18, 1966, even for the extremely important enlarged Politburo meeting in May. Even after Peng, Luo, Lu, and Yang were unseated, Mao didn't let his guard down. When reorganizing the Beijing municipal party committee, he had military reinforcements sent to the garrison in Beijing. When speaking of a coup d'état on May 18, Lin Biao said, "Chairman Mao has mustered and organized troops, and the army and public security apparatus have made arrangements." Mao also prompted Zhou Enlai to establish a "capital work group" to guarantee the safety of the capital.

Meanwhile, Peng, Luo, Lu, and Yang were sent to the chopping block of class struggle. From the night of December 3 to the morning of December 4, 1966, many officials at the rank of vice-minister and above, including Peng Zhen, Liu Ren, Wan Li, Xia Yan, and Tian Han, were detained and spirited away to unknown locations. The organizers of the arrest operation had scouted out the usual movements of the targets and prepared vehicles accordingly. They communicated through the confidential red telephones of high-ranking cadres, and everyone involved in the operation wore army coats. Only later was it learned that the arrests were carried out by Red Guards from four arts academies, led by Ye Jianying's daughter, Ye Xiangzhen.[39] Ye

Xiangzhen led two vehicles full of Red Guards to Peng Zhen's residence at No. 7 Taijichang, where they forced their way in, seized Peng from his bed, and then concealed him in the main hall of the Central Philharmonic. When Zhou Enlai learned what had happened, he persuaded Ye Xiangzhen to hand Peng over in return for facilitating a "mass rally to struggle Peng, Luo, Lu, and Yang."[40] While receiving mass organization representatives from the Central Academy of Drama, Beijing Film Academy, and two other schools on December 4, Zhou Enlai described the operation as "revolutionary and very successful." But he added, "It's impossible for it not to have flaws. I ask you all to consider how you can cooperate with the Central Committee." Ye Xiangzhen set the precedent for arbitrary abduction of leading cadres by the masses during the Cultural Revolution.

Zhou Enlai had the army lock Peng Zhen up in the headquarters of the Wukesong Garrison Command, then authorized several Beijing mass organizations to hold a denunciation rally at the Beijing Workers' Sports Stadium on December 12, 1966. Huge banners proclaimed, "Rally to pledge our lives to defending Chairman Mao and struggling against the Peng, Luo, Lu, Yang counterrevolutionary revisionist clique." More than thirty-six thousand people took part in the rally, singing Mao quotations set to music as well as a new song titled "We Will Fight to the Death Against Whoever Opposes Chairman Mao!" The rally also brought in many other leading cadres as secondary targets of struggle. All were made to stand bent at the waist with their arms raised in back of them in the posture known as "flying the jet" while their heads were yanked upward by their hair. Luo Ruiqing, crippled by his failed suicide bid, was hauled to the rally in a bamboo basket.

This rally set an example for the entire country. During the Cultural Revolution, especially after criticism of the bourgeois reactionary line, leading cadres might preside over a meeting one day and be seized and struggled the next. Some veteran cadres were abducted without knowing why. They and their families lived in a state of constant terror.

4

—

THE MAY CONFERENCE: FORMAL LAUNCH OF THE CULTURAL REVOLUTION

The enlarged Politburo meeting held in Beijing from May 4 to 26, 1966, was attended by seventy-six people, including Politburo members, alternate members, and heads of relevant departments.[1] Apart from denouncing Peng Zhen, Luo Ruiqing, Lu Dingyi, and Yang Shangkun, and launching a special investigation into their "conspiratorial anti-party clique," the May Conference formed the Central Cultural Revolution Small Group (CCRSG) and passed the Central Committee's May 16 Circular, which effectively launched the Cultural Revolution.

Mao managed the May Conference by remote control,[2] but Liu Shaoqi, Zhou Enlai, and Ye Jianying took turns presiding. During the first four days, Kang Sheng circulated Mao's remarks on Peng Zhen, Lu Dingyi, and the others and described the drafting of the May 16 Circular, emphasizing that Mao had amended it seven times and pointing out which words and paragraphs Mao had personally added; Zhang Chunqiao described the "struggle between the two lines" that had erupted on the cultural battlefront since the publication of Yao Wenyuan's essay criticizing *Hai Rui Dismissed from Office*; Xiao Hua explained Luo Ruiqing's problems; and Chen Boda gave a long talk denouncing Peng Zhen. These first four days set the stage for Mao's intentions to be carried out during the rest of the conference.

Mao's personality cult was ignited at this conference. Lin Biao said, "Everything Chairman Mao says is truth, and one sentence of his is better than ten thousand by any of us," and "Anyone who dares to make a secret report after his death like Khrushchev did must be a careerist and utter scoundrel who deserves to be assailed by the entire party and loathed by the entire country."[3] Zhou Enlai said, "Chairman Mao is our leader today and forever. Lack of loyalty in our later years would negate our entire revolutionary careers."[4]

THE MAY 16 CIRCULAR PASSED UNANIMOUSLY

With Liu Shaoqi presiding, the enlarged Politburo meeting on May 16 unanimously passed what came to be known as the May 16 Circular.

Although issued in the name of the Central Committee, the circular thoroughly reflected Mao's thinking. One of the drafters, Wang Li, recalls that in March 1966, Kang Sheng and Zhao Yimin went to Hangzhou to report to Mao on problems in the International Communist Movement. (Wei Wenbo also took part, and Jiang Qing sat in at the meeting.) Mao angrily overturned the Central Committee's decision to attend the twenty-third congress of the Communist Party of the Soviet Union, as well as cursing the February Outline and berating Peng Zhen, the Beijing municipal party committee, Wu Han, the Propaganda Department, and the material they'd collected about leftists. After Kang Sheng returned to Beijing, Deng Xiaoping called a meeting to communicate Mao's views, and Wang Li was told to draft a circular to the entire party rescinding the February Outline. Wang Li came up with a single sentence revoking the report outline by the Group of Five, but Mao insisted on stating the report's substantive problems.

On April 16, Jiang Qing arranged for the establishment of a drafting committee headed by Chen Boda and consisting of Kang Sheng, Jiang Qing, Zhang Chunqiao, Wu Lengxi, Wang Li, Yin Da, Chen Yading, Guan Feng, Qi Benyu, and Mu Xin. Since Chen Boda and Kang Sheng were attending the enlarged Politburo meeting in Hangzhou in April, Jiang Qing effectively ran the committee in a building behind the Jinjiang Hotel in Shanghai,[5] with Zhang Chunqiao serving as secretary-general. Wang Renzhong's notes of Mao's criticisms of the February Outline during the enlarged Politburo meeting served as the foundation for the May 16 Circular,[6] and each draft was sent to

Mao in Hangzhou for his further input.[7] When the circular was discussed at the May Conference, Chen Boda and Kang Sheng insisted
on leaving every word unchanged.

Fewer than five thousand words long, the May 16 Circular mainly
criticized the February Outline as "opposing carrying out the socialist
resolution to the end, opposing the cultural revolution line of the party
Central Committee led by Comrade Mao Zedong, attacking the proletarian left, protecting the bourgeois right, and forging propaganda for
a bourgeois restoration. This outline reflects bourgeois thinking
within the party and is revisionist through and through." It claimed
that bourgeois representatives had infiltrated the Central Committee
and its organs and that "equality before the truth" did not exist in the
struggle to the death to enforce the dictatorship of the proletariat over
the bourgeoisie; construction was impossible without destruction, and
all erroneous thinking, "poisonous weeds, ox demons, and snake spirits" must be thoroughly criticized, especially the "anti-party, anti-
socialist academic authorities" who had taken over the country's
cultural sphere. Even more alarmingly, it claimed that the party, government, military, and cultural sphere had been infiltrated by "counterrevolutionary revisionists" who would seize power when the time
was ripe. "We have already discerned some of these people, while others remain undetected. Some enjoy our trust and are being groomed
as our successors, like Khrushchev, and they are sleeping beside us.
Party committees at all levels must pay full attention to this."

Several months later it became clear that the person "like Khrushchev" was Liu Shaoqi, but Jiang Qing's confidential secretary Yan
Changgui says that at the time the May 16 Circular was passed, even
Kang Sheng and Zhang Chunqiao believed that the person being referred to was Peng Zhen.

Kang Sheng reportedly drafted the appendix to the May 16 Circular, the "Chronicle of the Struggle Between the Two Roads on the
Cultural Front from September 1965 to May 1966," which, despite its
intense political tone, may still serve as an important reference for
studying this period of history. The May 16 Circular was issued on
May 19 as Central Committee Document No. 267 [1966] to the entire
party down to the county level. It was finally published in newspapers
one year later, on May 16, 1967.

OUSTING HE LONG TO PREVENT A COUP D'ÉTAT

When criticizing Peng, Luo, Lu, and Yang on May 18, Lin Biao emphasized the possibility of a coup d'état,[8] which had become an obsession for
Mao.[9] Xiao Hua observed: "Last year after the Shanghai Conference, the
Chairman asked Comrade Xu Shiyou, what would you do if there was a
coup d'état in Beijing? The Chairman said, revisionism has emerged not
only in culture, but also in the party, government, and military, especially in the party and military. That's the greatest danger."[10]

Mao had been in a state of high alert since the "bloodless coup
d'état" in the Soviet Union on October 14, 1964, that forced Khrushchev from power. Mao's bodyguard Chen Changjiang recalled: "One
time we were very tense. Chairman Mao couldn't sleep and walked to
the door and asked me, 'Are you sentries all armed? We have to be on
guard against bad people!' I told the Chairman, 'We're armed not only
with handguns, but even with assault rifles and machine guns and
plenty of bullets. A few dozen of us can hold off one or two hundred
people.' The Chairman nodded, satisfied."[11]

Shortly after the coup in the Soviet Union, Zhou Enlai had led a
delegation to Moscow to mark the forty-seventh anniversary of the
October Revolution. At a reception hosted by the Soviet government
on the night of November 7, the Soviet defense minister Rodion Malinovsky said to He Long, "We've gotten rid of Khrushchev now, so you
should follow our example and unseat Mao Zedong. Then we can rec-
oncile." He Long immediately reported the comment to Zhou Enlai,
who asked Khrushchev's successor, Leonid Brezhnev, about it. Brezhnev dismissed Malinovsky's comment as "a slip of the tongue after
drinking," but Zhou Enlai suggested that it seemed more like "in vino
veritas" and issued a formal protest.[12] He knew full well that Mao was
terrified of being toppled as divisions deepened within the party.

Since the Communist Party of the Soviet Union had unseated
Khrushchev with the support of the military, Mao was especially wary
of a military coup in Beijing. Plotting within the upper echelons is the
most common method for toppling the leader of a highly centralized
political system, and as a military man, Mao knew that He Long
would be in the best position to carry out a coup. Malinovsky's comment sealed He Long's fate.

He Long had made a crucial contribution to the Communist revolution since surrendering his army to the Communists when the Kuomintang split with the CCP in 1927. As standard-bearer for the Second Front Red Army, He Long was not altogether submissive to Mao. In the 1950s, the Central Committee eliminated the Southwest Military Region, which He Long commanded with Deng Xiaoping as political commissar, and He Long was transferred to Beijing to oversee athletics. He grumbled, "Why eliminate a military region? The Central Committee and Chairman Mao must be afraid we'll revolt!"[13] Even so, He Long's Second Front Red Army remained largely intact after the First Front Red Army, Second Front Red Army, and Fourth Front Red Army factions had all been crippled by repeated line struggle. He Long was both powerful and sociable, which fueled suspicions of "empire building," and the National Defense Sports Club under the National Sports Committee that He Long managed came to be referred to as a "counterrevolutionary underground army that would become the vanguard of a counterrevolutionary coup when the time was ripe."[14]

The fall of He Long was set in motion during a meeting of the Central Military Commission standing committee after the eleventh plenum of the Eighth Central Committee and before the October 1966 Central Committee Work Conference. Only He Long was absent from the meeting. On Mao's instructions, Lin Biao and Zhou Enlai briefed their respective associates on the He Long problem, after which Ye Jianying presided over a denunciation of He Long.

Chen Yi and Nie Rongzhen's speeches were particularly strident, and even Liu Bocheng, who usually said little, made critical comments. Ye Jianying instructed those in attendance to keep the proceedings confidential, but some military leaders told others of the suspicions against He Long.[15] Meanwhile, Ye Jianying informally briefed military leaders about the problem on two occasions around that time.[16]

The issue came to a head in spring 1968, when Li Zhonggong contacted Zhou Enlai about "begging surrender letters" that He Long had supposedly written to Chiang Kai-shek after the failed Nanchang Uprising in 1927. By the time of the Cultural Revolution, Li Zhonggong had become an adviser to the State Council and a member of the Chinese Kuomintang Revolutionary Committee's standing committee, but at the time of the letters, he was considered Chiang Kai-shek's "trusted lieutenant." A descendent of Li Zhonggong explains that Li wrote to Zhou Enlai on March 29, 1968, offering to provide him with two letters of surrender that He Long had asked Li to forward to Chiang back in 1929. Li never passed the letters to Chiang, but he called them "ironclad evidence of this great traitor's betrayal of the party."[17]

Mao condemned He Long in his closing speech for the twelfth plenum of the Eight Central Committee on October 31, 1968: "In the past it was said that He Long should be criticized but also protected because he represents the Second Front Red Army. Now it looks like we may not be able to protect him, because we previously didn't know what he'd done." It would have been possible to give He Long the benefit of the doubt by seeing the letters as a tactic to alleviate the Kuomintang's military suppression and allow the revolutionary ranks to grow, but in any case, the letters turned out to be fake.

Years later, on December 21, 1973, Mao told members of the CMC, "I think we went wrong with Comrade He Long, and I have to take responsibility."[18] By then, steps were being taken to rehabilitate He Long and others,[19] and in September 1974 the letters provided by Li Zhonggong were declared forgeries. The failure to carry out an appraisal of the letters back in spring 1968 was blamed on Lin Bao and the Gang of Four. In June 1978, the State Council's Adviser's Office determined that Li Zhonggong should be harshly punished, but given his advanced age, he would instead be placed under supervision. Li Zhonggong, by then ninety-two years old and seriously ill, died before his family could inform him of this decision.

He Long's fall was clearly connected to Mao's obsession with a possible coup d'état. In his remarks on May 18, 1966, Lin Biao highlighted Mao's concern, observing, "Recently there have been many strange matters, strange phenomena, that we should take note of. It's possible that there will be a counterrevolutionary coup d'état . . . In the past few months, Chairman Mao has taken particular care to prevent a counterrevolutionary coup d'état, to prevent them from capturing our vital positions and broadcasting stations." He then enumerated hair-raising coups in ancient and modern China and overseas. Zhou Enlai and Liu Shaoqi echoed Lin Biao's warnings in the following days, and Lin Biao's speech was subsequently issued as a Central Party document following Mao's vetting.

Kang Sheng later spoke of a "February Mutiny" in a speech at Beijing Normal University on July 27, 1966. He claimed that "Peng Zhen's big reactionary gang" had prepared for a coup by sending battalions of troops to Peking University and Renmin University of China.[20] Lin Biao's close associate General Li Zuopeng revived this allegation in February 1967, attributing the planned coup to He Long.[21] The truth, revealed during the trials of the "counterrevolutionary cliques" of Lin Biao and Jiang Qing in 1980, turned out to be much more innocuous: The CMC had decided in February 1966 to organize a regiment under the Beijing Garrison Command to strengthen local armed forces by training militias, maintaining public order, and other such tasks. Since barracks were lacking, accommodation for the regiment was arranged in vacant housing at the universities.[22]

On May 15, 1966, in accordance with the spirit of Mao's directive to "defend the capital," Zhou Enlai and Ye Jianying jointly submitted a report to Mao and the Politburo Standing Committee that suggested organizing a Capital Work Group (CWG) to strengthen Beijing's security, with Ye Jianying as chairman and Yang Chengwu and Xie Fuzhi as vice-chairmen,[23] and directly accountable to Zhou Enlai, who, in turn, was directly accountable to Mao. Mao approved the CWG's plan on May 29,[24] and at dawn on June 1, 1966, residents of Beijing's western suburbs awoke to the roar of tanks and motor vehicles as columns of PLA soldiers began moving in. By daybreak, troops were stationed in Nanyuan, Changxindian, Qinghe, and other districts.

On June 3, Zhou Enlai presided over a meeting of cadres of the Beijing Garrison Command at the Jingxi Guesthouse, during which Yang Chengwu read out the CMC's orders putting Zhou, the CWG, and Ye Jianying in charge of adjusting and enlarging the garrison.[25] Zhang Min, who attended the meeting, recalls: "What left the deepest impression on me was Marshal He Long. He arrived fairly early and sat down on a sofa in the lounge behind the auditorium's stage, looking reticent and heavy-hearted and completely different from before. I felt his color wasn't very good, his face wan and thin as if he'd recently been seriously ill. There was no sign of the garrulous and jolly man he'd once been."[26]

Inspections and security measures were put in place for the

Central People's Broadcasting Station, television station, state communications hubs, and other organs that would most easily come under attack in a coup d'état. Surveys were also carried out on airports, reservoirs, power plants, prisons, and other important installations. The telegram office building at Xidan was immediately declared a military restricted zone because Mao's residence could be seen from its windows with binoculars.

Once Mao felt that the CWG's coup-prevention arrangements had made Beijing safe, he returned to the city on July 18. After the eleventh plenum of the Eighth Central Committee, Mao was in complete control of the situation and could no longer allow this kind of superorgan to exist, so the CWG's office was closed in February 1967, and its work was handed over to the chief of General Staff's war department. It was at this point that the CWG chairman Ye Jianying was accused of being a main force in the "February Countercurrent."[27]

THE ESTABLISHMENT OF THE CENTRAL CULTURAL REVOLUTION SMALL GROUP

The Central Cultural Revolution Small Group was formally established on May 28, 1966. Mao appointed Chen Boda[28] to serve as chairman and Kang Sheng[29] as adviser. (Tao Zhu was appointed adviser on August 2, but he was struck down in January 1967.) Jiang Qing, Wang Renzhong, Liu Zhijian,[30] and Zhang Chunqiao were vice-chairs, and the other members were Xie Tangzhong, Yin Da, Wang Li, Guan Feng, Qi Benyu, Mu Xin, and Yao Wenyuan. Although under the direct leadership of the Politburo Standing Committee, the CCRSG was in fact a special organ under the direct leadership of Mao, who put the CCRSG in command of the Cultural Revolution. Chen Boda was chairman in name only; Jiang Qing made the decisions after passing them by Zhou Enlai, and actually began chairing the CCRSG in September 1966 when Chen Boda went on sick leave.

The CCRSG met in Shanghai on June 20, and by the time Mao returned to Beijing on July 18, Jiang Qing was already there establishing administrative support for the CCRSG at No. 16 Diaoyutai as well as an information-gathering apparatus to publish *Express* (*Kuaibao*). More than a hundred political and ideological cadres helped the CCRSG monitor the progress of the Cultural Revolution in their capacity as journalists for *Red Flag*, *PLA Daily*, *People's Daily*, and *Guangming Daily*. Jiang also established a system of enlarged briefing meetings (*pengtouhui*) that included other government and military leaders. All members of the CCRSG were to meet every afternoon at three o'clock, with Zhou Enlai and Tao Zhu also attending. Later, these meetings typically ended with the CCRSG going to a work unit to take part in a mass rally and give speeches supporting the rebels.[31]

Eventually, members of the CCRSG were struck down one by one, leaving only Chen Boda, Kang Sheng, Jiang Qing, Zhang Chunqiao, and Yao Wenyuan. Beginning in February 1967, the Central Committee's day-to-day work was handled through the CCRSG briefing meetings, with Zhou Enlai presiding.[32] The briefing meetings made decisions on all major issues in the Cultural Revolution, and all their documents were signed by Zhou. As the State Council premier, Zhou had previously dealt only with matters of state, but after the denunciation of Luo Ruiqing and the enlarged Politburo meeting in May 1966, Zhou Enlai also took part in military and party matters, forming a tight-knit team with Lin Biao and Ye Jianying.

MAO'S UTOPIA: THE MAY 7 DIRECTIVE AND "THE PRINCIPLES OF THE PARIS COMMUNE"

The May 16 Circular represented the destruction of the system that had existed for seventeen years. Mao's intention was to construct a utopia to replace it, using the economic and social systems laid out in the May 7 Directive and the political system in "The Principles of the Paris Commune."

Mao's May 7 Directive was a memo he wrote to Lin Biao in 1966 on the PLA General Logistics Department's "Report on Advancing Further on the Army's Agricultural and Sideline Production." In it, he laid out his concept of the "Communist new man":

As long as there are no world wars going on, the army should serve as a big school. Even if there's a Third World War, it can still serve as this kind of big school. Apart from waging war, it can do all kinds of work. Isn't that what we did in the anti-Japanese resistance base areas during the eight years of the Second World War? In this big school, people need to learn politics, military affairs, and culture. They can also engage in agriculture and sideline occupations and operate small factories to produce some of the goods they need as well as products for equal value exchange with the state, etc. They can also engage in mass work, participating in the Socialist Education Four Cleanups Movement in the factories and villages. When the Socialist Education Movement is finished, they can do mass work whenever they like so that soldiers and civilians are permanently integrated; and they should also take part in the cultural revolutionary struggle against the bourgeoisie. In this way, military study, military agriculture, military labor, and military-civilian relations can all be combined. Of course, deployment must be appropriate, and there should be primary and secondary occupations, i.e., each military unit engaging in one or two of agriculture, labor, or civilian work, but not all of three at the same time. In this way, our millions of troops can have a tremendous impact.

Similarly, workers, peasants, students, commercial employees, and staff of state and party organs should integrate military, political, cultural, and agricultural work into their main focus of activity. Mao observed, "None of this is particularly new or innovative, and many people have been doing it for years already, but it has not yet become general practice. The army has been doing this for decades, but now it is necessary to develop it further."[33]

The Central Committee issued the May 7 Directive on May 15 and called for its gradual implementation throughout the party as "an extremely important document of historical significance, and an epochal development in Marxism-Leninism." On August 1, *People's Daily* published the main content of the May 7 Directive with an editorial stating that the directive would greatly enhance people's proletarian consciousness and accelerate the revolutionizing of people's thinking; gradually shrink the three distinctions[34] and promote the integration of intellectuals with working people, while also intellectualizing laborers; bring about the arming of the entire nation and form an ocean of civilian fighters; and turn seven hundred million people into critics of the old world and builders and guardians of a new world in a great school of Mao Zedong Thought and of communism.

Mao's conceptualization of the political system followed the principles of the Paris Commune.[35] In *The Civil War in France*, Marx wrote that the Commune's first decree was "suppression of the standing army, and the substitution for it of the armed people." Marx went on to describe the election by universal suffrage of municipal councilors, the majority of whom would be "working men, or acknowledged representatives of the working class," and who would combine executive, legislative, and judicial powers. The police force would not be a political agent, but rather "the responsible, and at all times revocable, agent of the Commune," as would all other branches of the administration. Public servants would be paid a workman's wage. In short, the Commune was "essentially a working class government, the product of the struggle of the producing against the appropriating class," and would achieve "the economical emancipation of labor" by providing cheap government through elimination of "the two greatest sources of expenditure: the standing army and state functionarism."[36] Engels likewise condemned the traditional state as "nothing but a machine for the oppression of one class by another" and lauded the Paris Commune as the "Dictatorship of the Proletariat."[37]

How to make officials into public servants rather than overlords has been a quandary from ancient times to the present, and all over the world. Like Marx, Mao believed that this problem could be solved by replacing the state with "communes," a term that he particularly loved. Although his attempt to establish people's communes in 1958 met with failure, he wanted to continue exploring the idea through the Cultural Revolution. After the Cultural Revolution caused government organs to collapse, Mao had Wang Li telephone Shanghai and Heilongjiang, the first two places to topple their governments, and told them to adopt the form of people's communes.[38]

The principles of the Paris Commune, the "May 7 Road," and the ancient Chinese concept of the "Great Harmony" (*Datong*) constituted Mao's utopian blueprint: (1) Eliminate the social division of labor, eliminate the difference between physical and mental labor, and implement "comprehensive development of the individual"; (2) eliminate the production and trade of commodities and establish a self-sufficient natural economy, thereby eradicating exploitation and achieving social equality; (3) implement a rationing system and eliminate scaled wages,[39] and in distribution, oppose material incentives and maintain politics in command; (4) do not separate the party from government, and combine legislative, executive, and judicial powers; (5) choose commune representatives through general elections and make them subject to recall at any time; (6) eliminate the standing army and replace it with armed civilians; and (7) implement local self-government.

Achieving these objectives required fundamentally remolding human nature by "fighting selfishness and criticizing revisionism" and launching a "great revolution that touched people's souls." All people had to be remolded into "Communist new men" free of selfish motives. Aware that he could not achieve this aspiration during his lifetime, Mao proposed a cultural revolution that would be repeated every seven or eight years to bring his ideals to fruition.

The May 7 Road that Mao imagined was finally implemented in the form of a multitude of May 7 cadre schools established throughout the country. Large numbers of intellectuals and cadres who fell out of favor were sent to these places, which became "lands of exile," "labor camps," and venues for investigating the May 16 clique. As for the Paris Commune, it was tried in Shanghai but came to nothing. The old bureaucratic apparatus was merely replaced by a new bureaucratic apparatus.

Mao imagined eliminating division of labor in society, but the trend of social development is for division of labor to become ever finer; he imagined a society with no commodity exchange, but a society with a high degree of division of labor requires commodity exchange to supply everyone's needs; he imagined a society with equal distribution, but without distribution incentives, society becomes stagnant and unproductive. Combining executive, legislative, and judicial functions eliminates the balance of powers, and the Cultural Revolution proved that replacing security forces with the dictatorship of the masses results in lawlessness and mass persecution. Mao envisaged being able to recall public servants at will, but that would require an ultrapowerful individual higher than the public organs. Clearly, what Mao imagined was a totalitarian society ruled by a superpowerful individual and with no rule of law. However sincere Mao's utopian vision, it was his coercive imposition of these systemically flawed theories that brought so much disaster on China.

"CHINA'S FIRST MARXIST-LENINIST BIG-CHARACTER POSTER"

Nie Yuanzi was a member of the Peking University party committee and party branch secretary of the school's Philosophy Department. On May 25, 1966, Nie Yuanzi, Song Yixiu, Xia Jianzhi, Yang Keming, Zhao Zhengyi, Gao Yunpeng, and Li Xingchen put up a big-character poster against the university's leadership,[40] saying that while the rest of the country was roiling with the Cultural Revolution, the university was "holding back, cold, cheerless, and stagnant, and the intense revolutionary demands of numerous teachers and students are being suppressed." It went on:

> [Song Shuo said] that the movement now urgently needs to strengthen its leadership, and is asking school party organizations to strengthen their leadership and hold their positions . . . The masses have risen up and need to be guided onto the correct path . . . This ideological battle is a serious class struggle, and anti-party, anti-socialist speech must be thoroughly refuted from a theoretical standpoint. Persist in talking reason, and use whatever methods facilitate refutation . . . If the masses indignantly demand to hold a mass rally, don't stifle them, but guide them to hold small-scale meetings to study documents and write small-character posters.

The big-character poster then rebutted each of Song Shuo's viewpoints, ending with the appeal: "This is the time for all revolutionary intellectuals to fight!"[41]

That same night, the Peking University party committee held a meeting to criticize the poster and organized a counterattack in the form of a thousand big-character posters and besieging the writers with debate.

The poster had its roots in the Socialist Education Movement (Four Cleanups) at Peking University.

In July 1964, Zhang Panshi, vice-director of the Central Committee Propaganda Department, led a ten-member group to the university for an investigation. During the group's inquiries, Nie Yuanzi expressed unfavorable views of Lu Ping and the university party committee. After Zhang Pangshi's investigation committee wrote a report giving an excessively grim appraisal of class struggle at the university, Zhang led a 210-member "socialist education work team" to Peking University in November. The work team pushed aside the university party committee, mobilized the masses, and relied on leftists such as Nie Yuanzi to launch class struggle. At a mass rally on November 12, members of the work team criticized the university party secretary Lu Ping and the deputy secretaries Peng Peiyun and Xie Daoyuan by name, and a week later, their report accused the university party committee of taking the capitalist road. Over the next two months, people were attacked mercilessly in every work unit, and the university devolved into chaos.

However, the university leaders gained the support of the deputy party secretary of the work team, Chang Xiping (party secretary of Shanghai's East China Normal University), as well as Peng Zhen and the Propaganda Department's leaders, emboldening Lu Ping and Peng Peiyun to begin openly criticizing the work team in late January 1965.

Lu Dingyi attempted to break the deadlock during a February 20 meeting with ten Propaganda Department work teams when he observed that Lu Ping was a good person who had made mistakes. This judgment was repeated during a Central Committee Secretariat meeting led by Deng Xiaoping on March 3. Lu Ping, Peng Peiyun, and another deputy secretary, Ge Hua, were added to the socialist education work team's leadership group, and when Zhang Panshi objected, he was criticized by Deng Xiaoping and Peng Zhen on March 30.

On April 29, Lu Dingyi replaced Zhang Panshi with the Propaganda Department's deputy director, Xu Liqun, and added Chang

Xiping to the work team's leadership committee. After Peng Zhen voiced support for Lu Ping in a talk to the work team and university cadres on June 29, the work team surrendered the dossiers compiled at the outset of the Socialist Education Movement. Over the ensuing months, Lu Ping and the others retaliated against Nie Yuanzi and other leftists and activists and assigned them to socialist education work teams in the countryside. Objecting strongly to this treatment, Nie petitioned the Central Committee and wrote letters to Mao and Liu Shaoqi.[42]

The Central Committee's May 16 Circular hit the university like a bolt from the blue, and the judgments against Peng Zhen, Luo Ruiqing, Lu Dingyi, and Yang Shangkun also left everyone thunderstruck. Nie Yuanzi was sleepless for several nights, pondering how those who were now being criticized were the very people who had suppressed Nie and her cohort. She called together the Philosophy Department's deputy party secretary, Zhao Zhengyi, along with the activist instructors Song Yixiu, Yang Keming, Gao Yunpeng, and Xia Jianzhi so that they could discuss the situation and write a report to Mao and Liu Shaoqi. Yang Keming said, "Why bother with a report? Let's write a big-character poster!"[43]

Despite Nie's insistence in her memoirs that she and her six cosigners were the only ones involved in conceiving and writing of the poster, an inside track cannot be entirely ruled out. In early 1966, Kang Sheng's wife, Cao Yi'ou, had gone to Peking University as head of a small information-gathering group that included Zhang Enci, formerly a teacher in the university's Philosophy Department. Cao Yi'ou had advised Nie Yuanzi against going to the countryside on the socialist education work team because the problem at Peking University was going to be resolved. Now Nie telephoned Zhang Enci and asked him to sound Cao out on the big-character poster. Cao Yi'ou subsequently received Nie Yuanzi and Yang Keming in the parlor of the Xiyi Guest-house[44] and said that the May 16 Circular authorized big-character posters. Nie later said that she asked Cao Yi'ou only about the party's principles and that they didn't discuss the specific content of the poster. On the night the poster appeared, Nie Yuanzi telephoned Zhang Enci and asked how the Central Committee felt about the controversy the poster had caused. About an hour later, Zhang Enci came to Yang Keming's home, where all seven signers of the poster were waiting, and said that the party leadership wanted the text of the poster copied and delivered to the CCRSG and the Central Committee.

After reading the poster, Mao, still in Hangzhou, wrote a memo on June 1: "Comrades Kang Shen and Boda: This text can be broadcast in full by the Xinhua News Agency and published in all of the country's newspapers. It is essential. The smashing of that reactionary fortress, Peking University, can now begin. Please handle as you see fit."[45] Mao also telephoned Kang Sheng and Chen Boda and declared the big-character poster a manifesto of the Beijing Commune of the 1960s, and even more meaningful than the Paris Commune. At 8:30 p.m. on June 1, the Central People's Broadcasting Station aired the entire text of Nie Yuanzi's big-character poster, along with Mao's praise of it as "China's first Marxist-Leninist big-character poster." Soon after that came an article by a *People's Daily* commentator stating, "Anyone who opposes Chairman Mao, Mao Zedong Thought, and the directives of Chairman Mao and the Party Central Committee, no matter what flag they carry and no matter how high their position or how long-standing their qualifications, in fact represents the interests of the overthrown exploiting class, and all China's people will rise up against them and strike them down, utterly destroying their reactionary gang, reactionary organizations, and reactionary laws and regulations." The broadcast of the poster's content and the *People's Daily* commentary far exceeded Nie Yuanzi's expectations.

Zhang Chengxian (at that time the secretary of the Hebei provincial party committee secretariat) went to Peking University that night with a hastily assembled work group to lead the Cultural Revolution, and the university became a template for the Cultural Revolution from that day forward as waves of people poured in to read its big-character posters. On June 3, the Xinhua News Agency issued two pieces of shocking news: the Central Committee's decision to reorganize the Beijing municipal party committee and the new municipal party committee's decision to reorganize the Peking University party committee. Following massive broadcast and newspaper coverage of the "first Marxist-Leninist big-character poster," the party committees of all China's universities came under attack. Intense conflict broke out between forces opposing and defending university party committees, and university campuses were blanketed with big-character posters.

On June 9, Liu Shaoqi, Zhou Enlai, and Deng Xiaoping flew to Hangzhou and asked Mao to return to Beijing to take charge of the Central Committee's work. Mao declined, and at an enlarged session of the Politburo Standing Committee, he said, "Regarding the Cultural Revolution, we have to stand back and not be afraid of the chaos; feel free to mobilize the masses and do it in a big way. That's how we'll expose all the ox demons and snake spirits. It may not be necessary to send work groups, and don't worry about the rightists causing trouble. A big-character poster at Peking University lit the fuse of the Cultural Revolution, and no one can suppress this revolutionary storm . . . A large group of activists has emerged during this movement; rely on these people to see the Cultural Revolution through to the end."[46]

Following transmission of the May 16 Circular and the broadcast of Nie Yuanzi's big-character poster, the Cultural Revolution spread like wildfire. Terrified of being engulfed in the conflagration, the bureaucratic clique that occupied the leading positions throughout China tossed out officials in charge of literature and arts or those with whom they had differences, and large numbers of prominent intellectuals became the first victims of the Cultural Revolution's initial stage. While Liu Shaoqi was in charge of the Central Committee's work from June to August, the Central Committee endorsed, signed, and issued more than a dozen documents listing nearly two hundred key cadres, and more than fifty university presidents were struck down. The Propaganda Department's statistics state that 174 people were denounced by name in publications throughout China from May 8 to August 10, but the actual number was much higher. A number of famous educators, scientists, writers, and artists died of physical abuse or committed suicide during this time.

5

—

LIU SHAOQI'S ANTI-RIGHTIST MOVEMENT

Mao lit the fuse of the Cultural Revolution through the unusual measures of publishing Yao Wenyuan's essay, handing down the May 16 Circular, supporting the big-character posters of Nie Yuanzi and others, and using newspapers to manufacture public opinion. For their part, Liu Shaoqi and Deng Xiaoping, then in charge of the Central Committee's day-to-day operations, used the CCP's conventional method of dispatching work groups to each work unit to suppress and stamp out the fire of the Cultural Revolution.[1]

On May 29, Liu Shaoqi, Zhou Enlai, and Deng Xiaoping convened a meeting of the relevant Central Committee departments to look into problems with the movement. They decided to send a work group headed by Chen Boda to *People's Daily*[2] and another group headed by a secretary of the Hebei provincial party committee secretariat, Zhang Chengxian, to Peking University. On June 4, the newly reorganized Beijing municipal party committee followed suit by dispatching nearly ten thousand people in work groups to various schools and work units.[3] Ostensibly, the main task of the work groups was to lead the Cultural Revolution, but their real task was to seize rightists.

THE CULTURAL REVOLUTION AT TSINGHUA UNIVERSITY

Tsinghua University was a classic case in the Cultural Revolution.[4] Liu Shaoqi sent his wife, Wang Guangmei, to control the work group and direct the Cultural Revolution there. Mao personally wrote a letter to the Tsinghua University Affiliated Secondary School supporting its Red Guard rebellion, and he sent Zhou Enlai to Tsinghua University to monitor the Cultural Revolution.

As soon as Nie Yuanzi's poster was broadcast on June 1, the big-character poster plastered every wall at Tsinghua University as well as temporary walls around the auditorium, sports ground, and main roads. The first posters were written with ink brushes on white paper, but old newspaper was used later when paper stock ran low. Posters exposed and denounced members of the university party committee, individual instructors, or the Beijing municipal party committee and the Peng-Luo-Lu-Yang clique. Some posters exposed the privileges of senior cadres or suggested that the university president Jiang Nanxiang was a revisionist rather than a Marxist.

The Tsinghua party committee constantly emphasized that Tsinghua was different from Peking University, hoping in this way to stifle criticism from teachers and students. Someone put up a big-character poster about the 1957 anti-rightist movement as a warning to opponents of the party committee, but on June 4, a poster by seven students from the Automated Control Department targeted the university party committee, and when Liu Shaoqi's daughter Liu Tao signed her name, it began to draw serious attention. On June 5, Liu Tao, He Pengfei (He Long's son), and five other children of senior cadres put up a poster imperiously stating, "The Tsinghua party committees should adopt a positive attitude toward leading the Cultural Revolution."

Children of senior cadres were especially active at Tsinghua at that time, and they also engaged in secret activities. At one small covert meeting, Li Jingquan's son, Li Lifeng, declared the Tsinghua University party committee revisionist and Jiang Nanxiang a reactionary, and Liu Tao stated that the Central Committee wanted Tsinghua's leftist organizations to rise up.[5] They probably reflected the views of their parents at a time when senior leaders were tossing out university party secretaries in order to both resist Mao and protect themselves.

On June 9, a 513-member work group led by the vice-chairman of the State Economic Commission, Ye Lin, seized power over Tsinghua University, and soon after that Jiang Nanxiang was relieved of his post. This immediately released the pressure on students and teachers, whose unruliness drew renewed pressure from the work group. The mathematics and mechanics students Wang Tiecheng and Liu Quan and the chemical engineering students Liu Caitang and Kuai Dafu then challenged the authority of the work group, which responded by organizing a poster campaign in its defense.

Liu Shaoqi and Wang Guangmei both went to Tsinghua to read the posters. Later that month, and under Wang's direction, the university work group labeled Kuai Dafu and other opponents as counterrevolutionaries and deprived them of their personal freedom. After a debate organized by the work group on June 24 unexpectedly turned to Kuai Dafu's advantage, Liu Shaoqi told his daughter Liu Tao that Kuai Dafu had to be made an example of and his faction marginalized and denounced in order to reinforce the status of the work group.[6] Kuai Dafu was constrained and barred from putting up big-character posters, and posters denouncing him blanketed the campus as he was repeatedly subjected to denunciation rallies. Bearing up with great fortitude under this immense pressure, Kuai wrote, "The policy of high pressure is in itself an expression of weakness. However, I once again state that it is having zero effect on me! They'll never get me to admit to being a counterrevolutionary! Even if they take me to the gallows, I will declare myself a revolutionary, a steadfast revolutionary to the end!"[7]

"Kuai factionalists" in every department were put under isolation and examination, and more than seven hundred people were labeled counterrevolutionaries. A young teacher in the automatic control engineering department, Shi Mingyuan, was driven to suicide. Such were the calamitous consequences of Wang Guangmei's applying her Taoyuan experience at Tsinghua University.

ANTI-RIGHTISTS CAMPAIGNS BY WORK GROUPS
AT OTHER BEIJING UNIVERSITIES

Some work groups joined with school party branches to suppress students who exposed school leaders, even those officially labeled "reactionaries." The work groups also cracked down on responses to grandiloquent appeals in *People's Daily*, *PLA Daily*, and *Red Flag* for students to rise up in rebellion.

On June 3, Liu Shaoqi convened an enlarged meeting of the Politburo Standing Committee that formulated eight rules forbidding students from posting big-character posters off campus, obstructing work or classes with meetings, holding public processions, allowing foreigners to observe or take part, harassing people in their homes, revealing confidential information, assaulting people, or demeaning people. The newly appointed first secretary of the Beijing municipal party committee, Li Xuefeng, agreed that the rules would make things easier,[8] but the rules were meant to preserve order, and Mao wanted to create disorder and "through great chaos achieve great order."

When Mao advocated giving the Cultural Revolution free rein at the enlarged meeting of the Politburo Standing Committee in Hangzhou in June, he also suggested delaying admissions to universities for half a year and allowing for some disorder and fighting before sending in work groups.[9]

The opposite tack was taken back in Beijing, however, where Liu Shaoqi and Deng Xiaoping convened two enlarged meetings of the Politburo Standing Committee in June to decide on how to deal with the campaign. Suggestions raised by Deng Xiaoping regarding the work groups' tactics resulted in "the phenomenon of anarchy being contained" for a time. At a third meeting, on June 28, Liu and Deng proposed that the movement proceed in stages and called for concrete policies to maintain control of the situation.[10] Years later, Deng Xiaoping's daughter Mao Mao (Deng Rong) wrote, "Their methods fundamentally contradicted Mao Zedong's thinking."[11]

When ten young teachers and some students at the Central Institute of Finance and Economics organized a mass rally on June 10 to expose problems with the institute's leadership and criticize the work group sent by the Ministry of Commerce, the institute's party committee and work group labeled it a "frenzied counterrevolutionary attack" and immediately organized struggle rallies where the teachers were forced to admit to an "anti-party program."[12] An assembly at the Beijing Foreign Language Institute on June 13 was likewise labeled a "counterrevolutionary rally," and an attempt to drive out the work group was labeled a "Little Hungarian Incident."[13] Protesters at the Beijing Geological Institute and Beijing Normal University were also denounced as rightists and accused of taking the side of the "ox demons and snake spirits."[14]

At a work conference of the new Beijing municipal party committee on June 23, First Secretary Li Xuefeng proclaimed the current situation excellent, and quoting Mao, he called for continued effort against troublemakers of all stripes. (Li later claimed that he was "basically expressing Liu Shaoqi's views in this speech, and just changed the tone a little.")[15] The Universities Committee of the Beijing municipal cultural and education apparatus responded by making a preliminary categorization for twenty-four colleges and universities: 31,877 people (32 percent of the total) were labeled leftists, 57,235 (57.9 percent) were labeled centrists, and 10,211 (10.1 percent) were labeled rightists. The work groups went further, designating 90 percent of the party committees and more than 60 percent of the research department heads as problematic and subject to denunciation and dismissal.

LIU'S AND DENG'S NEW ANTI-RIGHTIST STRUGGLE

Since Mao considered a purge of "those in power" the focus of the Cultural Revolution, it was natural for those in power at the time to resist the Cultural Revolution. Official histories have praised veteran officials' resistance, but in fact it was a form of self-defense. Diverting the spearhead of attack, officials launched a top-down mass assault on "class enemies" and "rightists." Never guessing that their conventional methods put them in diametrical opposition to Mao's out-of-bounds strategy, the Central Committee under Liu and Deng and regional and provincial party leaders effectively created a second anti-rightist movement, but one even more wide-ranging and virulent.

On June 11, Liu and Deng directed that a new anti-rightist struggle be carried out in Beijing under the leadership of the work groups and that students should be attacked as rightists in accordance with their actual numbers, without constraints.[16] In comments accompanying his transmission of situation reports on the Cultural Revolution from the South Central Bureau and Northwest Bureau on June 23, Liu Shaoqi wrote: "When the ox demons and snake spirits emerge from their dens to attack us, we shouldn't rush our counterattack; we must tell the leftists, brace ourselves, stand up to it, and demonstrate our ability to take the heat in our leadership. Once the large share of ox demons and snake spirits have been exposed, that is the time to organize a counterattack." As for those graduating from secondary school, "with the permission of municipal-level party committees, they can be denounced and labeled."[17] What Liu and Deng called rightists were those who opposed the party committees and work groups, but these were the people Mao called leftists, and they were the activists in the Cultural Revolution.

The South Central Bureau report that was the subject of Liu Shaoqi's comment called for identifying 1 percent of secondary and tertiary students as rightists, which would amount to 150,000 people. The proportion of rightists among teachers would be even higher. Even before Liu Shaoqi wrote his memo on those reports, quite a few senior officials wanted to use the 1957 methods against the masses. As early as April, Wang Renzhong, the second secretary of the South Central Bureau and first party secretary of Hubei Province, described the Cultural Revolution as a combination of the Four Cleanups and the Anti-Rightist Campaign and said, "One of the results of the Cultural Revolution will be to ferret out five to ten percent of anti-party, anti-socialist, anti–Mao Zedong Thought intellectuals as the new rightists."[18] Similarly, Tao Zhu directed that the movement target rightists and "anti-party, anti-socialist elements among the teachers and staff."[19] Given a grand total of 16.43 million teachers and students in 1965, Wang Renzhong's quota would have resulted in 821,500 to 1.643 million people being labeled rightists, far exceeding the number of people labeled rightists in 1957.

Liu Shaoqi gained a pretext for a major roundup of rightists at Peking University when turmoil in the university's chemistry, biology,

Asian languages, Western languages, Chinese, and radio departments resulted in more than sixty people being denounced, humiliated, and physically abused on the morning of June 18. The university's work group that night sent the Central Committee its *Peking University Cultural Revolution Bulletin,* no. 9, which described the incident as counterrevolutionary and stated, "Mainly it was scoundrels intentionally causing trouble, but it may also have been an organized, planned, conspiratorial action." Liu Shaoqi issued this bulletin in the name of the Central Committee the next day, adding the comment: "The Central Committee feels that the Peking University work group's handling of the turmoil was correct and timely. If such phenomena occur in other work units, they can use the measures at Peking University as a reference." From then on, work groups applied even greater pressure to students and designated radical mass activity as counterrevolutionary incidents.

On June 28, Wang Renzhong drafted a situation report on the Cultural Revolution that emphasized sending in work groups and rounding up rightists and especially focusing on leaders.[20] Wang repeated these views to the Hubei provincial party committee on July 3, and advocated "seizing hold of the root and digging it out from top to bottom," and "ferreting out the worst rightist students and denouncing them collectively."[21] Li Jingquan, who at that time was a member of the Politburo Standing Committee and secretary of the Central Committee's Southwest Bureau, publicly declared, "This time we need to nab 200,000 rightists."[22]

Liu Shaoqi focused on the work group at the Beijing Normal University No. 1 Affiliated Secondary School, where his daughter Liu Pingping was a first-year student. Nearly 90 percent of the school's cadres were labeled "ox demons and snake spirits" and "reactionaries," while 77 percent of its head teachers were denounced, attacked, and forced to undergo "labor reform," while some were viciously tortured.[23] Disturbed by the work group's methods, the students Chen Yongkang and He Fangfang on June 20 put up a big-character poster accusing it of directional and line errors. That same day, Liu Shaoqi received Gou Deyuan and three other members of the work group and encouraged them to "use the conflict to win over the majority and isolate the minority, crushing them one by one."[24] The work group organized three mass denunciation rallies against Chen Yongkang, He Fangfang, and other students from June 24 to 30, and more than 150 of the school's 1,000 teachers and students were designated as "counterrevolutionaries" or "fake leftists and genuine rightists."[25]

While hearing a report on the Cultural Revolution in Beijing's secondary schools on July 13, Liu Shaoqi suggested that cadres and teachers be divided into four categories: Those in category 1 could retain their positions; those in category 2 had to undergo criticism and self-criticism; those in category 3 had to be criticized, and some would be dismissed; while those in category 4 were to be the major targets of criticism.[26] Later, under political pressure, Deng Xiaoping's daughter Deng Rong said that Deng imposed similar categories on cadres and students at the Beijing Normal University Affiliated Girls' Secondary School, where she was a student.[27]

Once this process started in Beijing, secondary and primary schools throughout the country put teachers in "training courses" to be investigated and criticized. Their experience was similar to the 1957 anti-rightist movement, and the number of victims is inestimable. The work groups of some Central Committee ministries and commissions also "tossed out" cadres with intellectual backgrounds as targets of criticism.

RIGHTISTS TARGETED THROUGHOUT CHINA

Under the anti-rightist directives of the top leadership, anti-rightist campaigns spread through China like wildfire.

In June, some 240,000 big-character posters were pasted up on Nanjing's nineteen tertiary institutions, and more than 5,700 intellectuals were criticized by name.[28] Another report shows that up to June 20, posters at forty-seven secondary schools denounced 1,626 teachers or staff (about one in four) as "ox demons and snake spirits."[29] Under the direction of the work group at Wuhan University, 232 of the university's 1,242 cadres and instructors were labeled "reactionaries," along with 108 of the cadres leading party branches or teaching and research sections. In four party branches, all the rank-and-file cadres were labeled reactionaries or sidelined.[30]

At the Wuhan Institute of Hydraulic and Electric Engineering, students were categorized as leftists, centrists, or rightist. The rightists, composed of around 250 students or 8 percent of the total, were made targets of attack, and the work group lured critics into the open by encouraging teachers and students to write big-character posters about the party committee. On June 13, 1966, the party branch secretary of the irrigation and water conservancy department held a meeting of leftist students to assess the movement. One of the students attending this meeting, Guo Mingzheng, wondered how students could be assessed as leftist when the campaign had just begun, and he and other students wrote a big-character poster that caused a furor among the students. The institute's work group and party committee immediately organized a counterattack; workers in the benefits department and machine factory wrote big-character posters with titles such as "The Workers Have Spoken,"[31] which were broadcast repeatedly over the radio, and Guo Mingzheng was denounced as a "rumor monger" who was "sabotaging the Cultural Revolution." On July 15, the entire school launched a campaign to expose and denounce rightists, and those who had written big-character posters about the party committee lost their personal freedom. Guo Mingzheng was arrested on July 17, teachers Zhang Tingying and Luo Shoulin killed themselves, and a student was driven insane.[32]

The campaign continued to accumulate victims: 383 designated rightists at the Central China Engineering Institute; 62 students denounced at Wuhan Medical School; more than 300 denounced at Central China Normal School; 23 denounced at the Wuhan Postal and Telecommunications Institute; 200 out of 1,400 students denounced at the Wuhan Institute of Water Transportation Engineering; 18 arrested and more than 30 denounced at the Building Engineering School. The provincial party committee homed in on top schools such as Wuhan University and Hubei University and exposed a series of "counterrevolutionary incidents" involving teachers and students.[33]

On the night of June 1, 1966, a first-year student in the Chinese department of Henan's Zhengzhou University, Wang Xianghai, and thirteen other students put up a big-character poster criticizing the university party committee for stifling the mass movement. The university's party secretary, Wang Peiyu, immediately organized a counterattack, and at least 174 people were labeled counterrevolutionaries. After Wang Xianghai leaped to his depth from a window in the early hours of June 6, the school sent people to hold a denunciation rally at Wang's home village.

After the vice-governor of Shaanxi Province, Yan Kelun, led a work group of several hundred people to Xi'an Jiaotong University on June 3, 1966, the students Li Shiying and Liu Weina put up posters and banners against the work group, and Yan Kelun was besieged and debated by several hundred students in what came to be known as the June 6 Counterrevolutionary Incident. Subjected to struggle for three days straight as a counterrevolutionary, Li Shiying took an overdose of sleeping pills and was saved from death only by being rushed to the hospital.[34] Liu Weina was paraded through the streets with a pair of shoes hanging around her neck,[35] and a student named Wang Yongting leaped to her death. The work group sent a cable to Wang's parents accusing her of "sabotaging the Cultural Revolution at our school."

In Guizhou Province, big-character posters at Guiyang Teachers' Institute criticized the provincial party committee; and some secondary school students, supported by college students, staged a rebellion at *Guizhou Daily* on June 6. The provincial party committee quickly designated the action a "counterrevolutionary incident" and sent out 147 work groups, leading to attacks on more than half the students at Guizhou University and more than 273 people at the Guiyang Medical Institute being accused of involvement in the June 6 incident. More than 7,200 people throughout the province were labeled counterrevolutionaries, and by July 10, 189 people had been driven to suicide, 107 of them succeeding.[36]

MAO OPPOSES THE WORK GROUPS

During the Central Committee meetings on July 13, 19, and 22, arguments erupted over whether to withdraw the work groups. Deng Xiaoping's daughter Mao Mao writes:

Chen Boda, representing the Central Cultural Revolution Small Group, said the work groups were suppressing democracy and throwing cold water on the masses, and he called for them to be withdrawn. Liu Shaoqi angrily rebutted him and got into an argument with Kang Sheng. Known for steadiness, Deng Xiaoping couldn't hold back, and he leaped to his feet, pointed at Chen Boda, and said, "You say we're afraid of the masses—why don't you go out in front and give it a try!" And he bluntly declared, "I don't agree to withdrawing the work groups!" At the meeting, the first-line leaders of the Central Committee were in diametrical opposition to the CCRSG in their thoughts and speech, and the fighting became white-hot.[37]

Li Xuefeng, who was personally involved in this dispute, recalls:

Liu Shaoqi sharply criticized the CCRSG, saying, "What you're doing is actually inciting the masses to struggle against the masses. This isn't the way to do things. We have the reports here." Kang Sheng retorted, "Comrade Shaoqi, we have reports, too." Chen Boda and Deng Xiaoping began arguing. The meeting had just begun when Jiang Qing came tiptoeing in without greeting Shaoqi, who was presiding over the meeting . . . Shaoqi and Deng Xiaoping were too agitated to notice that anyone had come in.[38]

Chen Boda recalls:

The antagonism between the masses and the work groups that had been sent to the schools had become an enormous problem. My suggestion to withdraw the work groups was rejected by Comrade Shaoqi and Comrade Xiaoping, but they did so without putting it to the meeting for discussion . . . If we didn't withdraw the work groups, we'd be going back to the situation of the anti-rightist campaign in 1957.[39]

Wang Li recalls that Chen Boda received a call from Shanghai (i.e., Mao) in late June disagreeing with the old work organs dispatching work groups. That was why Chen Boda suggested withdrawing the work groups and argued with Deng Xiaoping.[40]

On July 16, the seventy-three-year-old Mao swam in the Yangtze River in Wuhan to reassure the nation of his robust health. This marked his shift from remote control of events from the back line to direct control on the front line, and Mao returned to Beijing on July 18. Liu Shaoqi and Deng Xiaoping had no idea that he'd returned, but Kang Sheng, Chen Boda, and Jiang Qing immediately went to see him. When Liu Shaoqi heard of Mao's return, he also went to see him but was turned away at the door.[41] After Chen Boda and Deng Xiaoping's argument about the work group problem, they went to Mao for instructions on July 19, and Mao decided to withdraw the work groups.[42] On July 23, Mao heard a report by Li Xuefeng and Wu De regarding the situation of the Cultural Revolution in Beijing. Tao Zhu, Kang Sheng, and others were also present, but Liu Shaoqi and Deng Xiaoping were not.[43] Mao said, "I've thought it over for a week, and I feel the movement is being carried out in a cold and lifeless fashion in Beijing. I feel dispatching the work groups was wrong. What role are the work groups playing now? They're just an impediment."[44]

After Mao's criticism of the work groups, Kuai Dafu was released on July 20, and on July 22 the CCRSG members Wang Li and Guan Feng went to Tsinghua to ask his views on the work group. On July 30, Zhou Enlai had two groups of Tsinghua students come to a meeting room in the Great Hall of the People for a talk.[45] In the early hours of the next morning, he went to Tsinghua University to talk with Kuai Dafu alone for three hours; and at Zhou's request, Kuai brought Liu Quan, Liu Caitang, and Shen Taiping for a three-hour conversation that evening with Zhou, the Shandong provincial party secretary Tan Qilong, and the Jiangsu provincial party secretary Jiang Weiqing.[46] Mao used the material that Zhou Enlai obtained from Kuai Dafu as key evidence in his counterattack against Liu Shaoqi.

Regarding Peking University's June 18 incident, Mao had declared the incident revolutionary before knowing about bulletin no. 9, and when he returned to Beijing and read the bulletin and Liu Shaoqi's memo, he flew into a rage. Mao berated Liu Shaoqi and also Kang Sheng for not giving him the bulletin earlier.[47]

After Mao decided to withdraw the work groups, the new Beijing municipal party committee issued its "Resolution Regarding With-drawing the Work Groups from All Universities" on July 28 and de-cided to hold a mass rally the next night. That afternoon, Mao called in the CCRSG and suggested that "people holding alternative views," such as Kuai Dafu, could also attend the rally.[48]

The mass rally was held at the Great Hall of the People. Li Xuefeng represented the Beijing municipal party committee in announcing the decision to withdraw the work groups, and Deng Xiaoping, Zhou En-lai, and Liu Shaoqi gave speeches. Liu Shaoqi said, "As to how to carry out the Great Proletarian Cultural Revolution, you aren't very clear and don't know very much. If you ask me how to carry out the revolu-tion, I have to tell you very honestly that I also don't know, and I don't think others in the Central Committee know, either." He also said, "The Central Committee decided to send in the work groups; the Cen-tral Committee agreed to it. Now the work groups don't meet the needs of the Great Proletarian Cultural Revolution, and the Central Com-mittee has decided to withdraw them." He told the students that they could decide whether the work groups should leave right away or after hearing the views and criticisms of the students.

After Liu Shaoqi spoke, Mao stepped forward without warning. Deng Rong, who attended this rally, writes:

> With the air of a peerless colossus, he waved again and again to all who were present. The assembly hall immediately boiled with excitement, and some people were so astonished and agi-tated that they began shouting, and tears ran down their faces. In order to see Chairman Mao, people in the back stood on chairs and tables, shouting at the top of their voices, "Long live Chairman Mao!" The extremely inhibited and depressing atmo-sphere at the beginning of the meeting instantly turned into a sea of jubilation.[49]

As the cheering continued nonstop, Zhou Enlai led everyone in singing "Sailing the Ocean Relies on the Helmsman." As soon as Kuai Dafu returned to school, he wrote a big-character poster titled "I Saw Chairman Mao," which was aimed at the work group: "You called me a counterrevolutionary, but I've seen Chairman Mao!"

By liberating the multitudes labeled "rightists" by Liu Shaoqi, Mao gained the undying support of the masses. Beijing's rebel faction was the first to regain its footing, and when rebels in other localities heard the news from Beijing, some broke out of their jails and went to Beijing to lodge complaints. These newly liberated activists became the nucleus of opposition against the bureaucratic clique, and some became leaders of rebel faction mass organizations. When Mao referred to Liu Shaoqi's attack on rightists as a "bourgeois reactionary line," these people denounced the bourgeois reactionary line even more fervently, and the momentum of the rebel movement continued to build. Meanwhile, the government-backed Red Guards, who had followed Liu Shaoqi in purging the masses, fell from power.

6

MAJOR INCIDENTS DURING THE ELEVENTH PLENUM

Before the eleventh plenum of the Eighth Central Committee, Qiu Huizuo sat in on a long conversation between Huang Yongsheng and Tao Zhu in Huang's quarters in the Jingxi Guesthouse. Tao Zhu said, "Our party has more than one central committee now . . . Chairman Mao has said several times, What should we do if revisionism emerges in the Central Committee? A short time ago, the Chairman talked about the problem of a two-headed snake. The Chairman said, 'As the name implies, a two-headed snake has two heads, one going east and the other going west, so it can never go in any one direction. Can we tolerate this?'" Just before he left, Tao Zhu said to Huang, "Be sure to wear a mask so you don't catch the flu. If you catch the flu, you lose your sense of smell and go to the wrong door." Ye Jianying also told Qiu Huizuo what Mao had said about the two-headed snake after the rally to denounce Luo Ruiqing in 1966.[1]

Qiu, who attended the eleventh plenum, recalls, "The plenum declared that the Cultural Revolution launched by Liu Shaoqi and Deng Xiaoping was bankrupt, and the Great Proletarian Cultural Revolution that put Chairman Mao in opposition to Liu and Deng had been launched."[2] Here Qiu states that there were two Cultural Revolutions: He believed that the February Outline and the attack on rightists were Liu's and Deng's Cultural Revolution, and that the eleventh plenum raised the curtain on Mao's Cultural Revolution.

On the eve of the plenum, Mao decided to remove Liu Shaoqi as his successor. At that time, Lin Biao wasn't in Beijing, so Zhou Enlai took care of day-to-day operations and approved Central Committee documents. Mao returned to the front line at the eleventh plenum,[3] and the "two-headed snake" became a "one-headed snake."

This plenum was originally scheduled for July 21, 1966, but on July 17, Mao sent Deng Xiaoping a cable from Shanghai saying that he was coming back to run the meeting and that it should by no means be held until he returned. As a result, the notice for the plenum was not sent out until July 24.[4]

Held in Beijing from August 1 to 12, the eleventh plenum was attended by 141 members and alternate members of the Central Committee and 48 nonvoting representatives. Deng Xiaoping announced that the agenda would include a resolution on the Great Proletarian Cultural Revolution, approving measures the Central Committee had taken on domestic and international issues, and formally approving the personnel changes decided at the May enlarged Politburo meeting. Reporting on major steps the Central Committee had taken on domestic and international issues since the tenth plenum, Liu Shaoqi said, "Beijing's Cultural Revolution had some errors, especially on the issue of the work groups, and I take the main responsibility for that." Mao interrupted by criticizing the work groups for "playing the role of repressing and obstructing the masses," and said, "More than ninety percent of the work groups did every bad thing possible."[5]

Mao continued to condemn the work groups while presiding over an enlarged meeting of the Politburo Standing Committee on August 4. He said, "The best that can be said is that it was a problem of orientation; in fact it was an orientation problem, a line problem, a line error, and opposing Marxism . . . It was repression and terror, and this terror came from the Central Committee."[6] Pointing at Liu, he denounced him for "doing a fine job of carrying out dictatorship in Beijing!" Liu Shaoqi met Mao's criticism head-on: "Then I'll leave office. I'm not afraid to do that, nor am I afraid of the other five possibilities."[7] Mao said, "We have ox demons and snake spirits among us," and he canceled the plenum session scheduled for that day.[8] At a meeting of the South Central Group that afternoon, Liu Shaoqi negated his approval of bulletin no. 9 on the June 18 incident, but defended rounding up rightists: "The rightists are causing trouble now and are trying to seize power, but don't worry: If you let them lead for a while, won't that give you a clearer view for catching counterrevolutionaries?"[9] That evening, Zhou Enlai, Dong Biwu, Deng Xiaoping, Li Fuchun, Chen Boda, Li Xuefeng, Tao Zhu, Wang Renzhong, and members of the CCRSG went to Tsinghua University's eastern sports ground for a mass rally of nearly twenty thousand teachers and students, during which the work group head, Ye Lin, made a self-criticism acknowledging the work group's directional and line errors. At 1:00 a.m., Zhou Enlai gave a long speech, declaring, "Today marks the birth of a new Tsinghua University."

After a meeting with Mao on August 5, Zhou Enlai telephoned Liu Shaoqi and suggested that he maintain a low profile.[10] Liu had just met a delegation from Zambia; it was probably the last meeting he had with foreign visitors.

MAO "BOMBARDS THE HEADQUARTERS"

The most notable incident during this plenum was Mao personally writing a big-character poster targeting Liu Shaoqi. Everyone was shocked to see the head of the ruling clique write a poster about his second-in-command, especially one so strongly worded:

> *Bombard the Headquarters: My Big-Character Poster*
>
> The country's first Marxist-Leninist big-character poster and the commentary by the *People's Daily* commentator were excellent! I ask comrades to reread this big-character poster and this commentary. However, in the fifty-plus days since, certain leading comrades, from the Central Committee to the localities, have been acting in exactly the opposite way. Taking a reactionary bourgeois standpoint, they have carried out bourgeois dictatorship and repressed the proletariat's stirring and dynamic Cultural Revolution movement. They have confounded right and wrong and black and white, besieged the revolutionary faction, suppressed alternative viewpoints, and carried out white terror. They have complacently inflated the prestige of the bourgeoisie while snuffing out proletarian aspirations. How venomous they

are! Given the 1962 right-deviation and the 1964 erroneous tendency to be left in form but right in essence, shouldn't this pro-
voke deep thought?

Mao Zedong

August 5, 1966

Mao drafted his big-character poster in pencil along the margin of
the June 2, 1966, *Beijing Daily*, after which his secretary, Xu Yefu,
copied it down and, after a few edits from Mao, it was printed and
distributed to the plenum delegates on August 7 and then to the
county level as a Central Committee document on August 17. One year
later, on August 5, 1967, it was published in *People's Daily*. Mao said,
"Over the past two months they've attacked me, and I'm fighting back."
He also said, "During this time, it was the CCRSG that was correct,
not the Central Committee."[11]

The "1962 right-deviation" that the poster mentioned referred to
the remedial measures Liu Shaoqi had agreed to after the Great Famine. The "1964 erroneous tendency" referred to Liu Shaoqi's guiding
principles during the Four Cleanups movement, especially as manifested in the Taoyuan experience.

Red Guards rapidly distributed the poster throughout the country,
and the "bombarding" of various party and government organs at the
central, provincial, and municipal level surged from then on.

The memoirs of Qiu Huizuo and Wu Faxian both emphasize Zhou
Enlai's role in promoting Mao's big-character poster during the plenum. Wu Faxian recalls Zhou saying, "Liu Shaoqi can no longer be in
charge of the Central Committee's work, because he has disappointed
the Chairman's hopes. The Central Committee has now decided to
bring Comrade Lin Biao to Beijing to take over from Liu Shaoqi."[12]

LIN BIAO BECOMES MAO'S SUCCESSOR

Lin Biao was convalescing in Dalian and didn't plan to return to Beijing until the National Day celebrations in October,[13] but one week into

the eleventh plenum, Mao told Lin to put in an appearance to accept a new position. Lin Biao tried to plead illness, but Mao said, "For routine meetings [during the plenum], you can send Ye Qun as your representative."[14] At Mao's repeated insistence, Lin Biao arrived in Beijing on the evening of August 6 and went straight to the Great Hall of the People.

One of the key tasks of this plenum was to restructure the central leading organs. On August 6, Zhou Enlai met with Mao to discuss the reorganization, and after drafting a list of leaders based on that discussion, he reported it to Mao and Lin Biao. While vetting the list, Mao adjusted the order of names for the Politburo Standing Committee, moving Tao Zhu up from seventh place to fourth place, right behind Zhou Enlai.[15] As surprised as many others by his ascent, Tao Zhu immediately asked Mao to move his name farther down the list, but Mao replied, "The list has been set and it's not going to be changed."[16]

Lin Biao presided on the last day of the plenum, August 12, when the elections took place. Tao Zhu, Chen Boda, Kang Sheng, Xu Xiangqian, Nie Rongzhen, and Ye Jianying were added to the Politburo in a by-election, while all eleven nominees to the Politburo Standing Committee were elected. Four were elected unanimously: Mao, Lin Biao, Deng Xiaoping, and Kang Sheng. Zhou Enlai, Tao Zhu, and Chen Boda lacked just one vote (possibly because they didn't vote for themselves). The others were all voted in by a simple majority.[17] In the Standing Committee's rankings, Liu Shaoqi dropped from second place to eighth, and Lin Biao rose from sixth place to second. There was no re-election for chairman or vice-chairmen at this plenum, but in documents issued after the plenum, former Central Committee vice-chairmen Liu Shaoqi, Zhou Enlai, Zhu De, and Chen Yun were no longer mentioned, while Lin Biao was referred to as vice-chairman. In practical terms, the plenum confirmed Lin Biao's status as Mao's successor, and others in the top leadership responded with a surge of adulation.

Ye Jianying described Lin as "tested by forty years of revolutionary struggle" and "a great statesman and strategist, with a high degree of leadership skill that makes him the best successor to Chairman Mao."[18] Ye also repeatedly stressed Lin Biao's health and relative youth: "We must not only publicize Mao Zedong Thought, but must also publicize Chairman Mao and Comrade Lin Biao's health to all of China and the whole world. It has enormous political significance!"[19] Zhou Enlai said that while everyone makes mistakes, the sole standard for appraising a person was his attitude toward Mao. "To have never committed a line error or opposed Chairman Mao is called 'consistent correctness,' and Comrade Lin Biao represents consistent correctness among the party's senior cadres. He deserves the title of Chairman Mao's close comrade-in-arms."[20]

Lin Biao presided over several meetings of the eleventh plenum as the party's second-in-command, but Zhou Enlai took over the day-to-day operations of the Central Committee from August 24 onward. Apart from his poor health, Lin Biao may have noticed Mao putting constraints on him: Ye Jianying had become general secretary of the Central Military Commission at the beginning of the year, and during the eleventh plenum, Mao promoted Ye, Xu Xiangqian, Nie Rongzhen, and others to the Politburo. Lin Biao's residence in Maojiawan had previously been guarded by the security office of the Central Military Commission General Office, but after the eleventh plenum, the security team was bolstered by the 8341 Unit under Wang Dongxing's direct command, with a deputy chief of staff personally stationed there. Lin Biao must have sensed that Mao distrusted him and therefore involved himself in matters of state as little as possible.

Although Mao returned to controlling front-line operations after the eleventh plenum, neither he nor Lin Biao was interested in dealing with concrete matters, so Zhou Enlai became indispensable. His authority expanded from being State Council premier to taking full charge of party, government, and military operations. Long-term contact with Zhou Enlai led Qiu Huizuo to conclude that Zhou "was a steadfast supporter and powerful executor of Chairman Mao's Cultural Revolution."[21] Qiu also wrote, "Zhou Enlai more than once heartily urged all of us to support the Cultural Revolution; otherwise it would be impossible to maintain our integrity in our last years, and our personal revolutionary histories would be wiped out in one stroke."[22]

THE "SIXTEEN ARTICLES"

The "Sixteen Articles" is a nickname for the "Resolution of the CCP Central Committee Concerning the Great Proletarian Cultural Revolution." After the May 16 Circular was issued, Mao told Chen Boda to draft some rules and guidelines for the movement. Chen Boda went to work on it with Wang Li, Guan Feng, Yin Da, and Mu Xin in Diaoyutai in early June, and Mao, still in Shanghai, was in regular communication with the drafting committee, amending the draft more than twenty times. After returning to Beijing and reading the draft, Mao found it generally acceptable but too long,[23] so he told Tao Zhu, Wang Renzhong, and Zhang Pinghua to take over revising it. After discussion with Zhou Enlai, Tao Zhu removed references to "black gangs" and the "black line" and some other derogatory terms and added some delimiting phrases. What the plenum passed on August 8, 1966, was the thirty-first draft, vetted and approved by Mao on August 7.[24]

The "Sixteen Articles" can be summarized as follows:

Article 1: The Cultural Revolution was a "great revolution that touched people's souls, and a new and deeper, more wide-ranging stage in the development of our country's socialist revolution." The present tasks were to struggle against and defeat "capitalist roader power-holders," denounce bourgeois reactionary academic authorities and bourgeois ideology, and reform education, culture, and all superstructure to facilitate consolidation and development of the socialist system. (This was subsequently referred to as "struggle, denounce, reform.")

Article 2: "The vast number of workers, peasants, and soldiers, revolutionary intellectuals, and revolutionary cadres are the principal force of this Cultural Revolution." Revolutionary youths were "courageous pathbreakers" with "audacity and wisdom." The main resistance to the movement came from capitalist roaders within the party and old conventional forces without.

Article 3: The various levels of the party's leadership shouldn't be afraid to freely mobilize the masses. Suppression of the mass movement was blamed on "capitalist roaders who are terrified that the masses will expose them."

Article 4: Trust the masses and allow the mass movement to use the "four bigs"[25] to increase their competence, clearly distinguish right from wrong, and distinguish the enemy from us.

Article 5: Execute the party's class line. Rely on leftists, isolate the most reactionary rightists, win over the centrists, and through the movement achieve unity among at least 95 percent of the cadres and masses.

Article 6: Correctly handle contradictions among the people. Debate must involve stating facts, speaking rationally, and convincing people by reason. Fight with words, not with violence.

Article 7: Beware of those who attempt to label the revolutionary masses as counterrevolutionary. "It is not permissible on any pretext to incite the masses to denounce the masses, or to incite students to denounce students."

Article 8: Good cadres made up the majority, and while denouncing the minority of anti-party, anti-socialist rightists, it was necessary to "give them a way out and allow them to make a fresh start."

Article 9: The Cultural Revolution Small Group, Cultural Revolution Committee, and Cultural Revolution Congress were "the best new organizational forms for the masses to educate themselves under the leadership of the Communist Party . . . They are appropriate not only for schools and government organs, but also for factories and mines, residential neighborhoods, and villages."

Article 10: Reform the old educational system. "It is essential to thoroughly change the phenomenon of bourgeois intellectuals dominating our schools." Apart from schoolwork, students needed to learn industrial production and undergo military training and should take part in denouncing the bourgeoisie at all times.

Article 11: Criticism was to be organized against bourgeois representative figures who had infiltrated the party and bourgeois reactionary academic authorities. Party committee approval was required before criticizing someone by name in the newspaper.

Article 12: Policies toward scientists, technicians, and ordinary working personnel.

Article 13: Coordination with the urban and rural Socialist Education Movement.

Article 14: Fully mobilize the masses to seize revolution and push production. "Seeing the Cultural Revolution as contradictory to production development is an incorrect view."

Article 15: The Cultural Revolution and Socialist Education Movement in the army must be carried out under the direction of the Central Military Commission and PLA's General Political Department.

Article 16: Mao Zedong Thought was the guide of action for the Cultural Revolution.

The Sixteen Articles were hailed throughout the country with gongs and drums and parades in the streets. However, many concepts in the Sixteen Articles lacked legal definitions, making them impossible to implement in practice and creating confusion and chaos.

For example, the Sixteen Articles said that "good and relatively good cadres make up the majority," but millions of cadres were investigated, denounced, detained, or implicated, including 75 percent of all cadres at the level of state organ deputy director or provincial vice-governor or above.[26] Although the focus of the movement was to purge capitalist roaders, there was no clear standard for determining what a capitalist roader was.

Likewise, the Sixteen Articles said that care should be taken to "rigorously distinguish between anti-party, anti-socialist rightists and those who endorsed the party and socialism but have said or done something wrong or have written some bad essays." But there was no clear legal demarcation between these two groups, so distinguished intellectuals also came under attack. The number of persecuted intellectuals vastly outnumbered the leading cadres who were persecuted.

In yet another example, the Sixteen Articles encouraged debate between different viewpoints and advocated strengthening unanimity over the general direction rather than endless wrangling over details. In actuality, divergent views coalesced into mutually antagonistic mass organizations, each believing that they alone upheld Mao Zedong Thought. Endless factional fighting led to large-scale violence.

The Sixteen Articles called for elections in accordance with the principles of the Paris Commune, but in reality, members of revolutionary committees were chosen through internal discussions managed by the military. Not a single revolutionary committee was formed through election.

The central theme of the Sixteen Articles was to support rebellion by the masses, effectively abandoning the long-standing tradition of political campaigns led by party committees at various levels. It was what Mao meant by "achieving great order across the land through massive chaos throughout the land."

People who had been forcibly suppressed for seventeen years could now express their wills through the "four bigs." Some activists (at the time referred to as "rebels") vigorously attacked the detested bureaucratic system, not only persecuting many innocent cadres but also ultimately becoming victims themselves.

MAO SUPPORTS THE RED GUARD REBELLION

On August 1, Mao wrote a letter of support to the Red Guards of the Tsinghua University Affiliated Secondary School (Tsinghua Secondary), sparking a Red Guard movement that swept the nation.

The words "Red Guards" were originally a signature on a big-character poster. At first, people signed their actual names to big-character posters, and people who agreed with the views in the poster would add their names. Eventually "battle groups" were established among like-minded people who joined in writing big-character posters, gathering news about the movement and studying its direction. A battle group needed a name, and fashionable political expressions commonly served this purpose. In May 1966, Zhang Chengzhi and some other students at Tsinghua Secondary adopted the name Red Guards (originally Red Bodyguards) to signify that they were Chairman Mao's revolutionary defenders.

The Red Guards originated in secondary schools, and their first rebellion was against the education system.

China's education system, largely transplanted from the Soviet Union seventeen years earlier, afflicted its students with excessive degree requirements (most universities required five years to graduate, while Tsinghua required six) and burdensome coursework that bred passivity and stifled creativity. The autodidact Mao naturally perceived the flaws of this system and proposed shortening the number of years of schooling and revolutionizing education, holding that schools were dominated by bourgeois intellectuals. In a conversation with his nephew, Mao Yuanxin, on July 7, 1964, he emphasized, "Class struggle must be one of your main subjects . . . If someone doesn't even know about class struggle, how can he be a college graduate?" The Ministry of Higher Education's nationwide dissemination of the "Summary of Chairman Mao's Conversation with Mao Yuanxin" in November that year provided the content and direction for the revolution in education.

Secondary students were at the prime age for challenging the status quo, and Mao's educational ideology provided them with ammunition. The children of ranking cadres, being the most well-informed, were naturally the most daring. One student from that time recalls the situation at the Beijing No. 4 Secondary School:

> The most disruptive students were mainly children of high-ranking cadres in the third-year class. They felt there was class struggle in the school, that some teachers with bad family backgrounds focused on cultivating students with similar bad backgrounds while excluding the offspring of revolutionaries, and that they encouraged emphasis on nonpolitical academic matters. So the Four Cleanups should be carried out in the schools, along with class struggle.[27]

The Seven Thousand Cadres Conference in early 1962 had introduced more flexible policies regarding culture, education, and technology, and some talented students with "bad" family backgrounds were able to enter Tsinghua University in 1962 and 1963. Some key secondary schools also admitted students from "bad" family backgrounds (mainly students whose parents were classified as capitalists or high-level intellectuals), and a clear demarcation arose between the offspring of ranking cadres and students from intellectual families. Cadre offspring claimed the superiority of their family backgrounds, while those with undesirable family backgrounds focused on their academic accomplishments. Teachers inevitably favored students with good academic performance.

After 1963, class struggle heated up and the class line evolved toward "exclusive emphasis on class origin." In June 1965, a modest campus upheaval occurred in Beijing's No. 4, No. 6, and No. 8 secondary schools, referred to as the "4-6-8 student strike." The main participants were cadre offspring, many of them the sons and daughters of central government leaders. They wrote a "letter of advice" to the Central Committee that stridently accused school administrators of neglecting the class line and teachers of favoring students from bourgeois families, and complained of oppression of cadre offspring.[28] One teacher at the Beijing No. 4 Secondary School recalls: "They felt that China's future should be theirs, that they had 'red roots,' the deepest feelings for Chairman Mao, and the strongest sense of duty toward the revolution."[29] Some students raised the slogan "Better red with an F than white with an A."

At Tsinghua Secondary and other secondary schools, the mutual antagonism between senior cadre offspring and intellectual and bourgeois offspring steadily intensified. When the school administration turned a physical fight between students into a "class line" issue of "beating cadre offspring," students from intellectual families became indignant. Each side put up uncompromising big-character posters that filled half the school cafeteria. One student from an intellectual family recalls, "The offspring of 'revolutionary cadres' and 'revolutionary military officers' . . . were always scowling at me. They had an irreconcilable 'class' relationship with 'landlord bourgeois progeny' and 'revisionist sprouts' like me." At that time, Tsinghua Secondary had established a college-preparatory class with educational materials compiled and taught by Tsinghua University professors. Being admitted to the preparatory class was a stepping stone for admission to Tsinghua University. Admission hinged chiefly on academic performance, and many cadre offspring didn't get in. This became one of the crimes for which principal Wan Bangru was denounced during the Cultural Revolution.[30]

An essay by the "Red Flag" battle group of the Peking University Affiliated Secondary School early in the Cultural Revolution expressed the mentality of senior cadre offspring: "Our parents spilled their blood and sacrificed their lives for the revolution, but their descendants have been relegated to third class, not even as good as those bourgeois whelps."[31] A big-character poster at Tsinghua Secondary said, "Anyone who isn't the offspring of a worker, peasant, or revolutionary cadre is going to be called in for a talk with us, and they'll have to shrink before us!"[32]

In early May 1966, some privileged students from Tsinghua Secondary went on an excursion to the Jietai Temple in Beijing's Western Hills and discussed their objections to the bourgeois educational line of the school party branch.[33] On the night of May 28, 1966, they decided to produce a wall newspaper (i.e., articles pasted up on a wall or bulletin board) and adopted the name Red Guards, used by Zhang Chengzhi and others. Within days, Central People's Broadcasting Station read out the big-character poster put up by Nie Yuanzi and the others on June 1, and the very next day, this Tsinghua Secondary group issued an open challenge to the school's leaders by putting up their big-character poster titled "Pledging Our Lives to Defending the Dictatorship of the Proletariat, Pledging Our Lives to Defending Mao Zedong Thought," signed with the name "Red Guards." The poster started out by clearly stating their family backgrounds and standpoint: "We, the descendants of the proletarian revolution, infinitely and ardently love, believe in, and worship Mao Zedong Thought. We harbor hatred to our very bones for all words and actions that oppose Mao Zedong Thought." They pledged to fight "until we have pulled out the reactionary banner, routed the reactionary gangs, smashed the reactionary storefronts to smithereens, and eliminated all black platforms!" The name Red Guards was followed by more than one hundred signatures. On June 8, more than three hundred students from other schools went to Tsinghua Secondary to support the Red Guard with their own posters, also signed "Red Guards."[34]

On June 21, the school held a mass rally for all teachers and students to elect a twenty-one-member revolutionary committee, which was dominated by core members of the Red Guards and the offspring of senior cadres. Soon after that, the Youth League official Hu Keshi passed on Liu Shaoqi and Deng Xiaoping's instructions to "resume classes and make revolution" and "absorb the Red Guards," so the school's work group announced that it was establishing a new Communist Youth League committee to replace the Red Guards. This sparked a conflict between the work group and the Red Guards. On June 23, the Communist Youth League Central Committee's official newspaper, *China Youth Daily*, published an editorial emphasizing that leftists had to submit to the work group and unite with the majority, but the Red Guards countered the next day with posters hailing the "revolutionary

rebel spirit of the proletariat." On July 13, Liu Shaoqi directed Hu
Keshi: "We have to use party and youth league organizations to replace the spontaneous organizations students are running. It's imper-
missible to operate secret organizations and secret activities outside
of the party and youth league."[35] The authorities refused to acknowledge the legitimacy of the Red Guards but couldn't prevent them
from growing.

The glorious revolutionary records of their elders and their privileged living conditions gave these youngsters an incomparable sense of
superiority. They constantly declared: "The country is ours, the world
is ours. If we don't speak, who will? If we don't act, who will?" What
they wanted to say was incisively and vividly expressed by the Tsinghua Secondary Red Guards: They wanted to smash the "four olds."

Their poster on June 24, 1966, titled "Long Live the Revolutionary
Rebel Spirit of the Proletariat," said:

> Revolution is rebellion, and the soul of Mao Zedong Thought is
> rebellion . . . We need to relentlessly work toward the word
> "rebellion": dare to think, dare to speak, dare to do, dare to
> charge, dare to carry out revolution—in short, dare to rebel.
>
> . . . Revisionism has dominated the schools for seventeen
> years; if we don't oppose it now, how long will it continue?
>
> . . . We need a strong smell of gunpowder. Bangalore torpe-
> does, hand grenades, thrown in together for a great battle! "Hu-
> man feelings" can go to hell!
>
> . . . You say we're too presumptuous? That's just what we
> want . . . Revolutionaries take responsibility for the world, so
> how can they not be presumptuous?[36]

A July 4 poster continuing this theme explicitly stated the target
of their struggle:

> Have all the old thinking, old culture, old customs, and old hab-
> its engendering revisionism been completely eliminated? No!
> Have all the black lines and black gangs in all places and all
> work units been eliminated? No! Does eliminating black lines
> and gangs now mean that no new black lines or gangs will

emerge in the future? No! Have imperialism, modern revisionism, and all reactionaries been eliminated? No! No!! No!!!

The poster emphasized, "We only allow leftists to rebel, and not
rightists! If you dare to rebel, we will immediately suppress it!"[37]

And a third poster on July 27 drew a dividing line between revolutionary and counterrevolutionary rebellion:

> Are you revolutionaries? Then you must welcome revolutionary
> rebellion and endorse revolutionary rebellion to the bitter end!
> Are you counterrevolutionaries? Then proceeding from class in-
> stinct you are certain to berate rebellion, oppose rebellion, resist
> rebellion, and suppress rebellion.[38]

The militant writing style and radical language of these three
short texts echoed the extremist thinking instilled by Mao and the
Central Committee since the tenth plenum of the Eighth Central
Committee. At a mass rally of Haidian District secondary students
at the Beijing Exhibition Hall on July 28, two core members of the
Tsinghua Secondary Red Guards tore out the first two texts from
their notebooks (the third text was not in the notebooks) and handed
them to Jiang Qing, who was attending the rally, along with a note
asking Chairman Mao to read them to see if they were reactionary.[39]
Mao found that they were exactly what he'd hoped for. On July 31, he
wrote (dictated) a letter to the Tsinghua Secondary Red Guards: "I
express my ardent support for you . . . My revolutionary comrades-in-
arms and I all have the same attitude. Whether in Beijing or in the
entire country, all those who take the same revolutionary approach
as you do in the Cultural Revolution will have our enthusiastic support."[40] Mao's letter asked them to unify with all those who could be
brought into unity, and to provide a way out to those who made mistakes. It was issued to the party's upper echelon as a document of the
eleventh plenum.

Mao's letter not only supported the Red Guard rebellion but also
endorsed the Red Guards as a mass organization. Although China's
constitution guaranteed freedom of association, this was the closest
anyone had come to enjoying this freedom in the seventeen years since

the PRC was founded. During the Cultural Revolution, similar mass organizations sprang up like bamboo shoots after rain.

Mao's letter remained an internal party document at this point, and the Red Guards had not yet gained wide renown. All this changed when Mao reviewed the Red Guards at Tiananmen Square on August 18 and received Red Guard leaders in the gate tower. After that, the Red Guard movement surged throughout the country.

7

—

THE RED GUARDS AND RED AUGUST

Mao's letter expressing support for the Tsinghua Secondary Red Guards provided a powerful impetus for the Red Guard movement. Wielding his status as supremo leader to further utilize these ignorant and dauntless young people, Mao repeatedly appeared at mass rallies for Red Guards from all over the country, creating a nationwide upsurge in the movement. Other bureaucrats used the Red Guard movement to brutally persecute intellectuals and members of the political underclass. The fifty-day assault on rightists by the work groups and the Red Guard movement consisted of successive rounds of organized persecution by those in power, and a genuine rebel faction had yet to emerge. During the second round of persecution, from July to September 1966, many famous cultural figures were driven to suicide or beaten to death, and politically problematic families were expelled from the cities.

MAO RECEIVES THE RED GUARDS

On August 18, 1966, a one-million-strong rally was held at Tiananmen Square to "celebrate the Great Proletarian Cultural Revolution." Sleepless the night before, Mao arrived at the Tiananmen gate tower at four o'clock that morning in military dress. When other central leaders arrived and saw Mao's attire, they rushed home to change. Lin

Biao, arriving in a light gray gabardine Sun Yat-sen suit, sent someone home to fetch his army uniform.[1]

As the celebration began at 7:30 a.m. amid the strains of "The East Is Red," Mao and Lin Biao stepped out to the gate tower's white-marble railings and waved at the crowd in the square. Shouts of "Long live Chairman Mao!" rang out, and multitudes of Little Red Books rose and swayed like a red tide.

After rousing speeches by Lin Biao and Zhou Enlai, hundreds of thousands of secondary-school Red Guards, who were amassed on Chang'an Avenue, poured through Tiananmen Square to be reviewed by Mao. The march slowed to a crawl in front of the gate tower as necks craned for a glimpse of Mao, and some marching in front doubled back for a second look, creating a vast whirlpool. At Mao's suggestion, 1,500 students squeezed into the gate tower,[2] and streaming with sweat, Mao shook hands with them one by one. Wang Dongxing said that Mao's hand became so swollen from the hand-shaking that he was unable to write for days afterward.[3] A student from the Beijing Normal University Affiliated Girls' Secondary School, Song Binbin, tied a Red Guard armband around Mao's upper arm, leading to the now famous exchange in which he told her that she should change her name from Binbin, meaning "refined and gentle," to Yaowu, meaning "militant." His words "be militant" became a "highest directive" that spread throughout the country, and Mao's acceptance of the armband turned August 18 into a Red Guard holiday and propelled the movement throughout the country.

After receiving the Red Guards on August 18, Mao received them again on August 31, September 15, October 1, October 18, November 3, November 10–11, and November 25–26, involving a total of twelve million people.

These mass receptions were marked by complications. Before Mao was scheduled to receive the Red Guards on September 15, he suddenly fell ill; bedridden with fever, he arranged for Lin Biao to take his place if necessary. He recovered just enough to attend the rally.

On October 1, Red Guards surrounded Mao's car at the corner of West Chang'an Avenue and Nanchang Street. As Mao became engulfed in a sea of humanity, Lin Biao climbed out of the car and shouted, "I am the minister of defense. Let our car through so we can attend the gala at Tiananmen!" When Red Guards crowded even more densely around the car, the security forces deployed a mobile-force regiment to forcibly extricate Mao from the encirclement.

On November 25, Mao stood in the biting cold and wind for four hours to review 650,000 Red Guards at Tiananmen Square. The next day, as Mao was returning by car from Xijiao Airport after reviewing the last batch of 1.85 million Red Guards, road obstructions required a detour to Yuquan (Jade Spring) Hill, where Mao rested for a while. But when he tried once more to return to Zhongnanhai, his car was surrounded again, and his security detail had to half carry him back up the hill on foot. Efforts to disperse the crowds resulted in a small bridge collapsing, with several people killed and many more injured in the ensuing stampede.

The rallies at Tiananmen Square brought traffic to a standstill on Beijing's main thoroughfares, and crowding on the square was so severe that truckloads of discarded shoes and dozens of broken wristwatches had to be hauled away each time.

With millions of Red Guards arriving in Beijing from all over China, Zhou Enlai had to mobilize all the city's resources to provide them with food, lodging, and transportation. The need for six thousand vehicles to transport Red Guards on November 10 required bringing in one thousand vehicles from the army and navy and from the Shenyang, Beijing, and Jinan Military Regions.

Mao insisted on reviewing the Red Guards because he believed it would send them home inspired to ignite the mass movement throughout the country. Mao also said that the Soviet Union had gone revisionist in part because few of its people had personal contact with Lenin. Allowing more young people to see Mao would prevent China from turning revisionist after he died.[4]

During the time that Mao was reviewing the Red Guards, they were also allowed to travel all over China for the Great Networking. A CCP Central Committee notice issued on September 5, 1966, stipulated that those involved in the networking would be allowed to travel free of charge on trains and that "state finance would pay" for their living expenses. With classes suspended, secondary and college students set off to network with others all over the country. At the outset, Red Guards from Beijing went to other parts of the country to "fan the flames" by supporting rebels, who were still in the minority then, and attacking local leaders who were suppressing them. Later on, students from other parts of China began arriving in Beijing to learn from the experience there, to petition, and to catch a glimpse of Mao. Tens of millions of young people took this priceless opportunity to tour their country while they attacked the bureaucratic system. Trains were filled beyond capacity, with even aisles and bathrooms crammed with people. To alleviate the enormous burden on the transportation system, the Central Committee began encouraging people to travel by foot on what they call the "Long March." Large groups of young people made pilgrimages to Yan'an, Mao's birthplace at Shaoshan, and other revolutionary meccas. Each destination set up Long March reception centers and provided free lodging. Although the Central Committee issued a notice to end the networking in March 1967, it continued until free transport, lodging, and food were cut off at the end of 1967.

THE RISING STORM OF "BLOOD LINEAGE THEORY"

The Chinese Communist Party put great emphasis on family background, considering it a major factor in a person's political attitude. When cadres were called to account after the Great Famine, the disaster was attributed in part to the fact that some county party secretaries had married into "landlord families." Zhou Enlai criticized his own "feudal bureaucratic" family background on many public occasions and used it to explain his political attitude and need for remolding. Of course, under normal circumstances, the party's policy was that "a person was not to be judged by family background alone; an individual's political performance deserved greater emphasis." There was no clear standard for "political performance," however, which was left to the judgment of work unit leaders. At the outset of the Cultural Revolution, some Red Guard offspring of senior cadres criticized the emphasis on political performance as part of Peng Zhen's "revisionist class line."

With class struggle heating up after the tenth plenum of the Eighth Central Committee, the class line evolved from "exclusive emphasis on class origin" to "blood lineage theory." People classified as landlords, rich peasants, counterrevolutionaries, bad elements, rightists, and later capitalists were regarded as "black elements," and they and their children became a political underclass. Correspondingly, the "red elements" were revolutionary army officials, revolutionary cadres, revolutionary martyrs, workers, and poor and lower-middle-class peasants. Workers and poor peasants were "the reliables," while the families of revolutionary army and civilian cadres were most honored; their offspring were a charmed class who considered themselves the natural successors of revolution.

As the Red Guard movement surged, blood lineage theory ran wild. A big-character poster by Qi Xiangdong at Tsinghua Secondary stated: "We must rebel and seize power; we must organize class ranks to carry out revolution, we must play up the class line, that is, class origin!" A big-character poster by the Red Flag battle group of the Peking University Affiliated Secondary School (PU Secondary) stated:

> Some people disparage us as "born red." Sons of bitches, your insult is the highest honor to us. You're right—our fathers were such, so our great name is "Born Red" . . . We are of pure proletarian lineage; we are the progeny of genuine revolutionaries! And you, born and raised in an environment of counterrevolutionaries and rightists, have spent your days at home receiving the education of a motley mix . . . We bear the heavy burden of revolution; government power will be passed down to us! This is the greatest power that Chairman Mao gives us, and whoever opposes us will be subjected to dictatorship and execution![5]

On July 1, 1966, the PU Secondary Red Flags commemorated the founding of the Communist Party. A participant recalls: "We were all cadre offspring and all dressed in khaki army uniforms. The rally inspired Red Terror . . . The strains of the self-composed 'Ode to Rebellion' soared to the heavens. It truly pumped up the aspirations of the offspring of workers, peasants, and cadres, and punctured the dignity of offspring of the exploiting classes."[6] The group's self-composed "Ode to Rebellion" called for "taking up pens as swords and guns" against the "reactionary gang," and proclaimed, "Whoever dares to say the party is not good, we'll send him straight to the King of Hell! Kill! Kill! Kill! Hey!"

The great wind of blood lineage theory swept from the secondary schools to the universities, and a couplet began making the rounds among the Red Guards: "The son of a hero is a good fellow, the son of a reactionary is a bastard," with a horizontal scroll between them that read, "It is basically like this." It became a source of great controversy among students.

On August 12, a student from the Beijing Industrial University (BIU), Tan Lifu (son of the deputy chief procurator of the Supreme People's Procuratorate, Tan Zhengwen, and head of a Cultural Revolution group at the university), joined with several others in signing and posting a big-character poster titled "Speaking of the Couplet." It discussed the rationale behind blood lineage theory and proposed that the couplet be "comprehensively" and "strategically" implemented as the party's class line, "refining it into policy and elevating it to legal writ." At a university debate on August 20, Tan declared his endorsement of the work groups, which he said brought "the sunlight of the party and of Mao Zedong Thought to BIU." Tan Lifu was very eloquent, and his remarks were constantly punctuated by fervent applause: "When the son of a poor peasant who has risen up discusses land reform with the son of a denounced landlord, how will they share the same state of mind?! [*wild applause*] Comrades, this is what is called 'class branding' . . . Struggle demands unity—first we struggle you, seven or eight times, until you forsake your families and remold your thinking, and that's when we have unity [*applause*]."[7] Cadre offspring disseminated Tan's speech throughout the country, and it added fuel to the flames ignited by the blood-lineage couplet.

Impelled by the blood lineage theory, some cadre offspring donned faded army uniforms and brass-buckled belts and went around searching for class enemies. Students from bad family backgrounds were denounced and beaten. In some localities, people boarding trains and buses were forced to declare their family backgrounds, and hotel guests and hospital patients received different treatment depending on their class background.

On August 4, Red Guards in a second-year class at the BNU Affiliated Girls' School ordered ten students from "black category" families to stand in front of the classroom roped together by their necks. Ten Red Guards from "red category" families sat in chairs looking fearsome, while students who belonged to neither category had to sit on the floor. The

Red Guards ordered the black-category students to "frankly confess" their "reactionary thinking" and the "crimes" of their parents, and to repeat three times "I am a son of a bitch. I'm a bastard. I deserve to die." Then they punched the students and poured black ink over them.

At the Beijing No. 101 Secondary School, Red Guards ordered black-category students to enter through a smaller door called the "dog hole." A third-year student named Wu Fangfang became mentally deranged after she was beaten for tearing up a portrait of Mao (the truth was that she had picked up a Mao portrait that had blown into the street). At PU Secondary, a first-year student named Wan Hong was horrifically beaten and then forced to spend the night on a balcony in the pouring rain. A second-year student named Ning Zhiping at the Affiliated Secondary School of Renmin University of China lost his ear after Red Guard beatings. At Tsinghua Secondary, a second-year student named Guo Lanhui poisoned herself to death when the school's Red Guards announced that a rally would be held to "help her." At the Taipingqiao Secondary School in Xicheng District, a fifteen-year-old student was beaten to death after saying, "Chairman Mao didn't come from a red category family, either."[8]

Blood lineage theory was able to gain so much traction because these Red Guards wanted to inherit the country their fathers had conquered and the privileges their fathers enjoyed. Although blood lineage theory died out after a time, this demand for inherited status never changed; in the Reform and Opening period, some who had advocated blood lineage theory became senior officials, and others became millionaires, enjoying the greatest benefit of every policy and systemic reform.

TSINGHUA'S AUGUST 24 INCIDENT

Around August 20, Mao's "Bombard the Headquarters" began circulating among the Tsinghua students, and posters calling for "bombarding" Liu Shaoqi began appearing on August 23 and 24. The university's Cultural Revolution Committee Provisional Preparatory Group[9] saw this as a rightist resurgence, and the Red Guard leader He Pengfei took coercive measures.

On the afternoon of August 24, the Red Guards of twelve secondary schools gathered at Tsinghua Secondary for a rally at which He Pengfei called for "defending the party Central Committee to the death." The Red Guards then marched onto the university campus and ordered all posters opposing central leaders to be torn down by six o'clock. Students who objected were paraded in front of the auditorium and lashed with belts. By seven o'clock, all the posters had been removed and replaced by the slogan "Only leftists can rebel, and rightists aren't allowed to stage an overthrow." The quarters of the "battle group" members who had written the posters about Liu Shaoqi were also ransacked.

In the meantime, under He Pengfei's command, Red Guards knocked down the university's symbolic second gate and ransacked the homes of "black gang elements"[10] and members of black categories, beating their occupants. They ordered cadres of mid-level rank and above to clear away the stones and bricks from the ruined second gate, flogging those who moved too slowly and savagely beating those who collapsed under their burdens.

The scale and brutality of this incident far surpassed that of the June 18 incident at Peking University. The university's deputy party secretary, Liu Bing, recalls his experience as a beating victim:

> They blindfolded me and then several of them seized my arms, pressed my head down, and forced me to walk forward while flogging my back with belts . . . Then I was taken to a room . . . and told to kneel, and when they removed my blindfold I found I was in the lecture theater. All of the university's party general branch secretaries, party committee secretaries and deputy secretaries, administrators, and department heads were kneeling in line on the floor. As dawn broke, they moved us to the science building and then to the biology building . . . They pushed us to the ground and beat us with cudgels, then forced us to beat each other, and those who refused to take part were smacked in the face or beaten on the back with cudgels.[11]

Luo Zhengqi, who was head of the university party committee's propaganda department before the Cultural Revolution, recorded his experience:

On the night of August 24 . . . several people dragged Youth League secretary Zhang Mujin to the interrogation room, and as I tried to watch, someone whipped me: "Don't look!" I heard the sound of harsh beating from the interrogation room and Zhang Mujin's moans. After a while, a student came out of the interrogation room and yelled, "Zhang Mujin tried to escape the dictatorship of the masses, but we caught him, and now he'll have to crawl out of the interrogation room . . ." After that, noise burst out at the southern end of the corridor: Several people holding belts and cudgels were ordering party committee office director He Jieren and propaganda department deputy director Lin Tai to beat each other. I heard someone shout, "Harder! Harder!" . . . I was extremely distressed. Were these our students? How could this be happening? Then someone suddenly yelled from the interrogation room, "He Pengfei is coming for an inspection!" Several people ran out of the interrogation room to the stairway to meet him. We were lying on the cement floor. "Quick, get up! Kneel in place with your heads down and hands behind your back! Your heads should be fifteen centimeters from the floor and no more than twenty centimeters. Hurry up!" We'd just gotten ourselves "arranged" when He Pengfei arrived. I had time to steal a glance, and found he closely resembled Marshall He Long, wearing heavy leather shoes and holding a belt. It looked like the people in the interrogation room were reporting something to him. He Pengfei walked over, and seeing that I had allowed my head to rest on the ground, he stomped on my head with his leather shoe and said sternly, "No heads on the floor!" A wound on my head started bleeding heavily . . . I was taken to the biology building. I hadn't been allowed to eat or drink anything since being forced to move the rubble from the second gate, and I was desperately hungry and thirsty. At that point, several of the "revolutionary masses" escorted several "black gang elements" to the staff canteen to get something to eat . . . The "black gang elements" lined up, and a student stood in front of them admonishing them: "If you want to eat, then listen up: You have to say 'The stinking black gang bastard son of a bitch XXX thanks Chairman Mao for this food.' Did you hear me? Try it now." The first was Professor Qian Weichang, and after he spoke this humiliating sentence, the student shouted, "You have to add 'major rightist' as well. Say it again!" Mr. Qian repeated the sentence, grabbed some food and stood in place . . . I was next, and I was able to get by without adding anything else . . . In the afternoon there was something new. A student named Ma Nan came to the biology building with two "adjuncts" to interrogate us. We heard this Ma Nan was the descendent of a military man, and he was nicknamed "General Ma Nan" and went around ransacking people's homes. The first to be taken out was Qian Weichang . . . After a while, Qian Weichang came back, and I saw that his back had been whipped until it was thoroughly bruised and bleeding—it was a horrible sight . . . Finally somewhere down the line they called me, and I walked into the interrogation room. Ma Nan had a cigarette hanging out of his mouth, his legs resting on the table, looking like a complete army thug, with a big fellow standing wide-eyed by his side.[12]

The Red Guard rampage continued the next day.

Tsinghua's August 24 incident shows how the secondary school Red Guards went from rebelling against school leaders, teachers, and work groups to protecting Liu Shaoqi and their parents once they were denounced. These teenagers could hardly be expected to understand the shift of attack and were bound to be influenced by their parents' views of the situation.

On the eve of May Day 1967, the Tsinghua Jinggang Mountain Red Guard Headquarters led by Kuai Dafu erected a huge statue of Mao where Tsinghua's second gate had been destroyed. At Kuai Dafu's request, Lin Biao wrote the inscription engraved on the statue's pedestal: "Long live the Great Teacher, Great Leader, Great Commander in Chief, and Great Helmsman Chairman Mao! Long life! Long long life!" *People's Daily* and other newspapers reported, "The never-setting Red Sun has risen over the Tsinghua campus." This was the first of tens of thousands of Mao statues erected in the public spaces of every city and town in China during the Cultural Revolution.

THE SMASHING OF THE "FOUR OLDS"

The programmatic document of the Cultural Revolution, the Sixteen Articles, stated: "Although the capitalist class has been overthrown, they intend to use the old thinking, old culture, old customs, and old habits of the exploiting classes to corrupt the masses, conquer popular sentiment, and attempt to restore their old order. The proletariat, conversely, must repulse the frontal assault of all the bourgeoisie's challenges in the ideological sphere, and use the proletariat's own new thinking, new culture, new customs, and new habits to change the entire face of society." After Mao's review of the Red Guards on August 18 increased their ranks exponentially, mobs of Red Guards took to the streets to smash the "four olds."

"Exotic clothing" or "bourgeois" hairstyles became intolerable; Red Guards would chop permanent curls into a lopsided "yin-yang" haircut on the spot.[13] A couplet hanging in the streets of Tianjin proclaimed, "Merciless scissors destroy your skinny trouser legs," and "Hair clippers want revolution and will shave your hooligan haircut." The horizontal scroll between them read, "Foster the proletarian, eliminate the bourgeois."

On August 19, Beijing Red Guards destroyed the sign for the famous Quanjude (perfection, unity, and virtue) Roasted Duck Restaurant and replaced it with "Beijing Duck Restaurant," and put images of Mao in place of the landscape paintings decorating the restaurant's dining room, hallways, and staff quarters. A sign over the entrance for foreigners quoted Mao: "People of the world unite to defeat the American invaders and their running dogs!"

The Red Guards demanded the removal of any words that sounded "feudal, bourgeois, or revisionist" and replaced them with revolutionary words. Some people changed personal names denoting flowers, jade, gold, or jewels into popular phrases such as Weidong (defend [Mao Ze]dong), Yongge (eternal revolution), or Fanxiu (anti-revisionist). The names of shops, streets, and squares in Beijing and other cities became East Is Red Avenue or Anti-Imperialist Road. Wangfujing (Prince's Well) Avenue became Prevent Revisionism Road. Xiehe (Union) Hospital, founded with foreign money, became Anti-Imperialist Hospital. The Red Guards claimed to be destroying "thousands of years' worth of feudal and capitalist decay, the reactionary toxins of imperialism and revisionism, and outmoded customs and habits diffusing the stench of rot."[14]

Red Guards sorted through the merchandise in bookstores and handicraft shops, and rampaged through temples, parks, and museums, destroying vast quantities of cultural items, including priceless artifacts.

Minister of Public Security Xie Fuzhi approved an infantile demand by the Red Guards that traffic police replace their batons with *Quotations of Chairman Mao*, claiming that only Mao Zedong Thought could point people in the correct direction. Zhou Enlai managed to talk the Red Guards out of their demand to change traffic lights because red was the symbol of revolution and should not be the color for obstructing progress. He and the commander of the Beijing Military Region, Zheng Weishan, were also able to convince the Red Guards to abandon their demand to march from west to east (i.e., away from capitalism) when being reviewed by Mao at Tiananmen Square, pointing out that reversing the direction would require Red Guards to salute Mao with their left hands and force Mao to look right rather than left from the gate tower.[15]

Smashing the four olds involved ransacking homes on a massive scale. Red Guards forced people to hand over any gold or silver in their possession and to transfer any property they owned to the state. More than half a million private homes were confiscated in Beijing,[16] and property totaling 1.24 million square meters was confiscated in Shanghai.[17]

According to incomplete figures, in August and September 1966, Red Guards ransacked 114,000 homes in Beijing[18] and confiscated 3,222 kilos of gold, 10,788 kilos of silver, 55,459,900 yuan in cash, and 613,600 cultural objects and jade carvings.[19] Mountains of other items, from pianos to Simmons mattresses, from high heels to nylon stockings, filled the sports grounds of athletic stadiums.[20] Some 157,700 homes were ransacked in Shanghai—6.5 percent of the city's 2.41 million households, and 8.2 percent within the city limits.[21] At least 21,000 homes were ransacked in Wuhan, and 112 people were driven to suicide, 62 of them succeeding, while 32 others died of torture.[22]

Red Guards ordered the democratic parties disbanded, denounced some of their leaders, and shut down their offices. Statistics show that more than a third of the leading democratic party members living in

Beijing, totaling more than a hundred, were subjected to struggle or had their homes ransacked.[23]

On August 23, the Central Committee's official newspaper, *People's Daily*, published a front-page story with the headline "Red Guards Fiercely Attack Bourgeois Customs and Habits" and the subtitle "The Wave of the Great Proletarian Cultural Revolution Rolls Through the Streets of the Capital; the Great Revolutionary Masses Most Ardently and Most Resolutely Support the Revolutionary Rebel Spirit of the Red Guard Young Militants." This was accompanied by two front-page editorials titled "Well Done!" and "Workers and Peasants Must Resolutely Support the Revolutionary Students." With this endorsement, others joined the Red Guards in smashing the four olds. Religion came under attack, and temples, churches, and cultural heritage sites were destroyed. At some temples, monks joined the rebellion and took park in the destruction. Nearly 5,000 of Beijing's 6,843 registered cultural relics and historical sites were destroyed, most of them in August and September 1966.[24] The 5,884 scrolls of canonical Buddhist writings held in the Baima Temple[25] were incinerated, and the temple and tomb of Confucius in the sage's hometown of Qufu, Shandong Province, were destroyed.

HOMES FILLED WITH GRIEF

One of the responsibilities of the Capital Work Group (CWG) established on May 15, 1966, was to deploy neighborhood committees and police to screen the population and search for firearms and ammunition in private hands.[26]

Screening the population involved expelling "problematic" residents from the capital in a process referred to as "repatriation"—forcing people to return to their ancestral villages, a campaign that destroyed countless lives and families. The first batch of repatriations soon after the CWG was established sent black elements (landlords, rich peasants, counterrevolutionaries, bad elements, and rightists) to Xinjiang and other remote localities. Neighborhood committees and police stations handled the actual repatriation, but the screening process was handled by Red Guards, who swarmed through the streets, ransacking homes and terrorizing people with sometimes fatal results.[27] Official histories of the Cultural Revolution acknowledge that in the period prior to October 14, 1966, some 397,400 "ox demons and snake spirits" were expelled from the cities to the countryside. In Beijing alone, 85,198 people were driven back to their ancestral villages, while 1,772 were beaten to death and 33,695 homes were ransacked.[28] The actual number of victims is almost certainly greater. In Tianjin, 41,571 people were expelled,[29] and in Jinan, 7,400 households totaling 22,197 people were forced back to the countryside.[30] Deprived of homes or land for growing crops, these exiles faced a dire situation.

Most people were expelled under escort by Red Guards with only their most basic belongings. The waiting rooms and platforms of the Beijing train stations "were packed with people on their knees awaiting repatriation, some of them forced to wear dunce caps of various shapes and some with bandaged wounds."[31]

Minister of Public Security Xie Fuzhi required the public security apparatus to actively assist the Red Guards' campaign. Neighborhood committees and police stations provided the Red Guards with information on which homes to ransack and which families to expel. CWG head Ye Jianying said, "The Red Guards solved many major and difficult problems that had been troubling us for years. Some ultra-reactionary fellows had been berating our party and Chairman Mao on a daily basis for more than a decade, and everyone knew who they were and thoroughly hated them, but no one dared to move against them. This time the young militants beat them to death. Maybe it violated some policies, but the greater benefit was that it cleared away scoundrels—cleared away the rubbish in our society."[32]

At the height of the smashing of the four olds, Wu De, second secretary of the new Beijing municipal party committee, reported to Mao on problems that had emerged in the campaign in hopes that Mao would calm things down a little. Mao said, "No one's done anything about several dynasties' worth of defunct remnants in Beijing. Now the 'smashing of the four olds' has dealt with it, and that's good."[33] Wang Li, however, says that Mao felt the central leadership was being sidetracked from targeting the capitalist roaders in power, and he was displeased with the propaganda head Tao Zhu when *People's Daily* and the Xinhua News Agency published reports extolling the Red Guards for taking to the streets, smashing signs, and changing the names of roads.[34] The fact remains that he never did anything to stop it.

Commentaries praising the smashing of the four olds in *People's Daily* on August 29 and in *Red Flag* on September 17 fueled the Red Guard movement even more.

THE RED TERROR ESCALATES[35]

As mass violence and bloodshed escalated, on August 6 some of the more rational Red Guards distributed an "urgent letter of appeal" proposing that "the genuine leftists in each school unite and take action to rigorously prevent beatings, hooligan behavior, and damage to state property" and "mercilessly force bastards who intentionally violate party policy out of the Red Guards, Red Flags, and other genuine leftist organizations." But the appeal fell on deaf ears, and the Red Terror continued to surge.[36]

Red Guards from the red categories physically assaulted "reactionaries" and "sons of bitches" in the schools as well as "little hooligans" and black elements in the wider society, rampaging through the streets in their old army uniforms and brass-buckled belts. That August, the Red Terror that the Red Guards had created in Beijing spread through the rest of the country. Red Guards forced "targets of dictatorship" to sing: "I'm an ox demon and snake spirit, I'm a criminal among the people. I'm guilty, I deserved to die, I'm guilty, I deserved to die. The people should smash me to pieces, smash me to pieces . . ." Those whose performance failed to meet the Red Guards' standards of perfect pitch and appropriately mournful demeanor were beaten senseless with belt buckles.

At a mass rally at Beijing Workers' Stadium on August 13, "little hooligans" were physically assaulted as the vice-chairman of the Central Cultural Revolution Small Group, Wang Renzhong, looked on. The rally demonstrated to the public that the stipulation in the Sixteen Articles to "fight with words, not with violence" was worth no more than the paper it was written on, as the vice-principal of the

Peking University Affiliated Secondary School, Liu Meide, was forced to crawl around the sports ground, had filth shoved into her mouth, and then was made to kneel on a table that was kicked out from under her. Liu was pregnant at the time, and her child died soon after birth.

By then, the Red Guards had claimed their first fatality; on August 5, the vice-principal of the Beijing Normal University Affiliated Girls' Secondary School, Bian Zhongyun, was beaten to death by students, while the vice-principals Hu Zhitao and Liu Zhiping and the head teachers Mei Shumin and Wang Yubing were tortured for more than three hours with nail-spiked boards and scalding water. More deaths followed at other schools.

The torments and fatalities became even worse after Mao reviewed the Red Guards on August 18 and urged them to "be militant," and the violence spread to other work units. At the Beijing Municipal Federation of Cultural Circles, more than forty elderly writers and cadres were forced to stand in the federation's courtyard under the broiling sun with placards around their necks proclaiming them "black gang members" while Red Guards flogged them with belt buckles. The "ox demons and snake spirits" were then taken to the Imperial College Confucius Temple and forced to kneel in a circle around a bonfire of Peking Opera costumes and props while Red Guards beat them over the head with wooden swords.[37] One of the victims, Lao She, a venerated author and vice-chairman of the National Federation of Cultural Circles, drowned himself the next day.

Red Guard violence gave rise to two instances of resistance on August 25. Li Wenbo, a resident of Chongwen District, stabbed a Red Guard from the No. 15 Girls' Secondary School who arrived at his home for a second day of ransacking and physical abuse, then leaped to his death from an upstairs window. Li was posthumously sentenced to death, and his wife, Liu Wenxiu, was executed.[38] On the same day, Cao Binhai, a third-year student at the Beijing Normal University Affiliated No. 2 Secondary School, stabbed one of the Red Guard classmates who had come to ransack his home. The Beijing Municipal Public Security Bureau arrested Cao, while the Red Guards took his mother, Fan Ximan, back to the school and beat her to death. Cao Binhai became mentally deranged after this incident.

The party's top leaders quickly sided with the Red Guards. At a

Red Guard assembly on August 26, Zhou Enlai said, "Yesterday some of our Red Guards were wounded by scoundrels. We are deeply grieved by this and are trying to think of how to help you." After attending a Central Committee meeting that same day, Public Security Minister Xie Fuzhi told the Public Security Bureau, "We have to protect the Red Guards. Counterrevolutionaries killed Red Guards so we have to resolutely suppress counterrevolutionaries . . . When Red Guards beat undesirables, we can't say it's wrong, even if they kill them." Around two weeks later, Zhou Enlai told Red Guards that Li Wenbo's resistance was "a reactionary capitalist assaulting Red Guards."[39]

Official condemnation of the two incidents further aroused the class fury of Red Guards, and fatal beatings rose exponentially from August 26 to September 1. On August 28, Red Guards in Beijing's Xicheng District killed five members of Huang Duanwu's family after an alleged attempt to "transfer assets" (consisting of records, music scores, perfume, and a fake pearl necklace that Huang's wife wanted to hand over to her work unit), and the discovery of a bullet shell that Huang Duanwu had picked up as a boy. The victims included Huang, his sister, their mother, another female relative, and a male servant who was accused of having a landlord background.[40]

The bulk of Beijing's Red Guard killings occurred during this period, and the city's crematorium was so overburdened at the end of August that bodies were stacked and incinerated together. Even at that, the crematorium couldn't keep up and resorted to heaping ice on the bodies until they could be burned.

The brutality of these adolescents (many of them girls) was the result of long-term official brainwashing through newspapers, radio, meetings, classes, and cultural activities that demonized "class enemies" and primed "red elements" to become a savage mob the minute any new political movement was launched.

THE XICHENG PICKETS AND THE UNITED ACTION COMMITTEE

As the Red Terror became increasingly horrific in late August, the Red Guards of several secondary schools in Xicheng District united to form the Xicheng Branch of the Capital Red Guard Pickets (Xicheng Pickets for short), which subsequently grew to include forty to fifty schools. The Xicheng Pickets reportedly intended to curb arbitrary violence by Red Guards, and while some historians feel that they "played a role in controlling the chaos" and that "their historical contribution cannot be overlooked,"[41] others say that they merely perpetuated the Red Terror. The actual situation can by analyzed on the basis of the tasks they assigned to themselves at their founding, the content of their initial "proclamation," their actions, and the direction of the Red Terror after their establishment.

Upon their establishment, the Xicheng Pickets declared themselves "a revolutionary rebel contingent and a tool of the dictatorship of the proletariat." They were empowered to "rescind all propaganda material and prohibitions inconsistent with Mao Zedong Thought"; inspect the Red Guards of every school, organ, factory, and work unit and "detain bogus Red Guards and hooligans"; and "temporarily perform security functions for key state organs and major thoroughfares prior to the establishment of pickets in other districts." Their targets of suppression included not only the usual black elements but also, for the first time, the bourgeoisie and their offspring. Their responsibilities, self-conferred rather than lawfully endowed, did not include the prevention of beating, smashing, looting, detaining, or killing.

Ye Jianying and many other veteran cadres supported the establishment and activities of the Xicheng Pickets, and Zhou Enlai sent the State Council's secretary-general and deputy secretary-general to direct their activities and resolve any issues with housing, transportation, printing facilities, and so on.[42] The saying within the Capital Work Group was that "only Red Guards can control the Red Guards."[43]

The Xicheng Pickets issued ten "general orders" in a little more than one month after they were established. These included orders that Mao's works, badges, and portraits be sold in large quantities in Xinhua Bookstores; that foreign visitors be well treated and encouraged to light the fire of world revolution with Mao's ideas; that investigation, home ransacking, and struggling of black elements be carried out under the combined power of the Red Guards, the local police, and the neighborhood committees; and that senior cadres and their homes be protected. Although earlier orders repeatedly called for "fighting with words, not violence," one of the later ones declared, "Our revolutionary masses and Red Guards, out of deep-seated hatred toward class enemies, ransack your homes and beat you and make you wear tall hats and force you to march through the streets and force you back to your ancestral homes for reform through labor. We feel there's nothing wrong with any of this!" These ten general orders reflected the domineering and privileged thinking of cadre offspring. Repeated emphasis on protecting senior cadres showed the immense importance the Xicheng Pickets placed on safeguarding their own families.

After the establishment of the Xicheng Pickets on August 25, the Red Terror intensified because of the Li Wenbo and Cao Binhai incidents, reaching a peak on September 1, when 228 people were beaten to death in a single day.[44] The surge in violence coincided with the launch of the Xicheng Pickets, and the fatalities were greatest in Xicheng District, where the pickets were most active—totaling 333 deaths, more than the next three districts put together.[45]

Wang Youqin, who has spent years researching the abuses of the Cultural Revolution, produced a graph[46] (below) showing that the establishment of the Xicheng Pickets did nothing to prevent the violence but rather perpetuated the Red Terror in Beijing.

The Xicheng Pickets were the "military police" of the Red Guards; their power was unlimited, and their guiding ideologies were blood lineage theory and class dictatorship; in certain respects they were

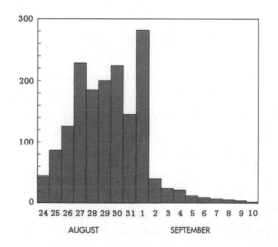

even more brutal than other Red Guards, as can be seen from the example of the Beijing No. 6 Secondary School.

The Xicheng Pickets used No. 6 as their own "labor reform camp," inflicting horrifying and sometimes fatal brutality against other students. The "labor reform camp" had a watchtower with a gun turret, lookout holes, an alarm bell, and air guns, topped by a revolving searchlight. Sentries posted around the clock closely monitored all who passed inside and outside the school. The wall facing the gate was emblazoned with words written in red paint: "Long Live the Red Terror!" More than fifty people were viciously beaten at the school, and at one point, a lashing whip, screams of pain, and fiendish laughter could be heard on a daily basis.

All the "inmates," male and female, were squeezed into a room of about one hundred square feet. They were not allowed to talk to one another, open their eyes at bedtime, roll over, or snore, and they had to line up for permission to use the toilet. The Red Guards inflicted all kinds of torture on them, including something called "flying the homemade airplane," which involved several people grabbing the victim by his arms and legs like a battering ram, tossing him about a yard into the air, and then letting him crash onto the concrete floor. During the torture sessions, the Red Guards said, "This is fighting with words, not violence," or "This is a combination of words and violence, the highest form." They made their victims recite Mao quotes for hours at a time, sometimes while kneeling on stool legs and wearing a tall hat. Anyone who made a mistake had to start from the beginning.

After a nineteen-year-old student from a "small proprietor" family, Wang Guanghua, went on the Great Networking without obtaining permission from the Red Guards, Xicheng Picket members locked him up and beat him to death, then sent him to the crematorium. Several days later, the Red Guards demanded twenty-eight yuan from Wang's mother for the cremation fee and threatened to exterminate the whole family if she told anyone of the incident.

An eighty-six-year-old retired handyman, Xu Peitian, who still lived at the school, was ferreted out by the Red Guards because his father had owned a rickshaw business. The Red Guards made him crawl around the sports ground carrying worn-out shoes in his mouth, and then pushed him into a urinal and urinated on him. On

October 3 they beat him and doused him with boiling water, forced him to sing and dance and eat excrement, and then hung him with a nylon rope. They dumped his body in the school's backyard and left it exposed for three days.[47]

The Xicheng Pickets soon fell out of favor. Jiang Qing and Chen Boda criticized them at a "national mass pledge rally for the revolutionary faction in Beijing to defend Chairman Mao's revolutionary line and seize new victories" at the Beijing Workers' Stadium on December 17. Zhou Enlai said, "Some secondary schoolkids, a smattering of Picket members, committed illegal acts and violated Central Committee stipulations by doing some bad things . . . Having proven impenitent and unreformed after our repeated education, they have been arrested for education and reform . . . The Red Guard Pickets . . . have sullied the picket name. I propose that the Red Guards at all schools abolish the name of Pickets."[48] After Zhou Enlai proposed the abolishment of the Xicheng Pickets at a mass rally on December 27, newspapers referred to them as a reactionary organization, and the leader, Kong Dan, was arrested.

A new organization emerged at the end of 1966 called the United Action Committee (UAC) of the Capital Red Guards, which combined some key members of the Dongcheng Pickets, Xicheng Pickets, and Haidian Pickets into one group. Initiated by the Haidian Pickets, the UAC defined its mission as opposing "the new form of bourgeois reactionary line" (i.e., attacks on veteran cadres and their families). The UAC came into being on December 5, 1966, when the Beijing Engineering Institute–affiliated secondary school student Zou Jianping and others climbed the city wall at Xizhimen and painted an enormous slogan proclaiming, "The CCRSG is forcing us to revolt, we have no choice!" Other slogans stating, "United Action Committee sounds the death knell of the CCRSG!" and "Resolutely defend the revolution's veteran cadres!" appeared at Tiananmen and Wangfujing Avenue.[49]

The UAC marked Mao's birthday at the theater of the Beijing Exhibition Hall on December 26 with a "mass pledge rally to overcome selfishness and foster public spirit." Slogans shouted at this rally[50] accused "certain people in the CCRSG" of "opposing Mao Zedong Thought." The UAC called for the offspring of revolutionary soldiers and cadres to unite and for all work units and departments to be placed under the leadership of the Central Military Commission: "Silence is death! Fight to survive!"

At the end of December 1966 or the beginning of 1967, in the poster area of the Peking University Triangle, I was among a large group of students standing three-deep to silently read a very long big-character poster. One sentence on the poster has remained with me through all the decades since: "Resolutely smash the left-deviating opportunistic road of the two chairmen and several members of the CCP Central Committee." The "two chairmen" were clearly Mao and Lin Biao, and the "several members" clearly referred to members of the CCRSG. On closer inspection, I found that this daring notice had been posted by the UAC. I'd heard of a UAC organization among secondary school students but had never guessed they would be so bold. Recently someone posted the entire notice online, and I saw that it also called for "abolishing all autocratic systems," which was truly groundbreaking at that time. The demons Mao had released had ultimately turned against him! This was probably the first time Mao confronted a force opposing the Cultural Revolution, and may have been the earliest call to "abolish all autocratic systems," coming three years before Lin Liguo's Project 571 outline.[51] It is worth noting that the UAC notice and Project 571 outline were both issued by the offspring of top officials, indicating a powerful force opposing autocracy in the highest reaches of the autocratic system.

Opinions were not unanimous within the UAC, however, as a letter written by a UAC member in April 1967 shows:[52]

> Scoundrels and Bastards of the Jinggang Mountain Corps of the Peking University Affiliated Secondary School:
>
> Don't enjoy your fucking rabble-rousing too much today, and watch out for your asses' heads in the future. Don't go crazy, you whelps—just wait and see! Twenty years from now, the world will belong to us cadre offspring, and you'll have to stand aside! You'll pay for the blood and hate you've inflicted on us. Little bastards, don't be happy too soon!
>
> Whether you're genuinely active or faking it, the heavy burden of revolution will never fall on your shoulders. The world is

ours! The country is ours! Society is ours! Whelps, carefully consider your escape route!

. . . Cadre offspring will be in control!

The world is ours!

—Your grandfathers at the Beijing No. 101 Secondary School—the Old Red Guards

What the letter said about "twenty years from now, the world will belong to us" turned out to be true. The truth is that as long as the Communist Party remains in power, the offspring of officials will inevitably assume power in a hereditary system.

Not long after the UAC was established, Mao said, "These Red Guards were revolutionary in the summer but no longer so in the winter."[53] Organizations like the UAC also existed in Xi'an, Shenyang, and other places under names such as Red Terror Fighting Force, Red Posterity, and so on. All had cadre offspring as their core members, and their objective was to protect veteran cadres and oppose the CCRSG and rebel faction. They were part of what came to be known as the "Black Wind in December."

In late December 1966 and early January 1967, the UAC carried out a series of attacks on the Ministry of Public Security, yelling slogans such as "Fry Jiang Qing" and "Long Live Liu Shaoqi." In mid-January 1967, the UAC was designated a reactionary organization. Mao said, "We can't let their leaders operate freely; we need to round them up and put them through education and reform."[54] In late January 1967, under orders from the CCRSG, the rebel organizations of Beijing's tertiary institutions and of some factories, assisted by the public security organs, mounted a surprise attack on the UAC headquarters at PU Secondary, arresting more than a hundred core leaders and members there and in some other schools. The UAC was formally banned as a "counterrevolutionary organization" just two months after its founding.

When central leaders such as Nie Rongzhen criticized the arrest of senior cadres' offspring, it contributed to the "February Countercurrent" among the old marshals.[55] After hearing the views of senior military cadres, Mao decided to release the arrested UAC members, later saying, "I agreed with arresting them, and I agreed with releasing them."[56] The released UAC members were received on April 22, 1967, by Zhou Enlai, Jiang Qing, and members of the CCRSG. Jiang Qing told them, "Today it was the Chairman who decided to let you go home. You've been behaving well. Now go home and continue studying and taking part in the Cultural Revolution; take the right side and no longer the wrong side." She presented each of them with a book, and all the young people cheered and thanked Chairman Mao and Auntie Jiang Qing.[57]

In early 1967, the Old Red Guards led by the offspring of senior cadres fell from power. Their movement lasted less than five months, from when Mao expressed his support of the Red Guards at Tsinghua Secondary until the UAC leaders were arrested. It was these Old Red Guards who victimized teachers, intellectuals, black elements, and their offspring and destroyed many cultural and historical objects. The Peng-Luo-Lu-Yang clique and those connected with them were implicated during this time, but other senior cadres continued to hold power, and power struggle formed the background of this disastrous movement. The Old Red Guards experienced the ruin of their families and being sent down to the countryside, joined the military from 1967 onward, or later entered college as "worker-peasant-soldier" students. Gradually abandoning their blood lineage theory and political fanaticism, they became a key political force controlling China in the 1980s, 1990s, and the new century.

8

—

DENOUNCING THE BOURGEOIS REACTIONARY LINE

Following the eleventh plenum of the Eighth Central Committee, mass organizations throughout the country "bombarded" leading party organs at all levels, as Mao had hoped. Even so, "the party's leadership" was a major and insurmountable political principle of many years' standing, and the concept of the party leading through the party committees had been deeply impressed on the popular mind since the 1957 Anti-Rightist Campaign. After seventeen years of the formidable bureaucratic hierarchical structure extending its roots and branches in all directions, the intense assaults of the rebel masses and equally virulent backlash of the bureaucrats created "incidents" throughout the country. The various rebel forces were still at a disadvantage in this round, as the bureaucratic apparatus used all the power in its possession to adapt to the situation and suppress the rebel faction.

BUREAUCRATS PROTECT THEMSELVES BY SUPPRESSING REBELLION

From May to December 1966, party committee leaders at the provincial, municipal, prefectural, and county levels repeatedly changed the approach they took toward the Cultural Revolution's mass movements: At the outset, they tossed out intellectuals and dissenting cadres (typically those in charge of culture and education) for the masses to denounce while following the guiding ideology of Liu Shaoqi and Deng

Xiaoping by sending work groups into the schools and cultural work units to attack rightists and suppress rebels. When Mao harshly criticized the work groups in July and August, the party leaders withdrew the work groups. In August and September, party committee leaders changed tack by controlling mass movements through official "Cultural Revolution leading groups" and fostering conservative mass organizations to counter rebel mass organizations.

BEIJING

After the work groups withdrew from the universities, the newly reconstituted Beijing municipal party committee continued to control the movement through liaison officers, observers, inspectors, and consultants. The new municipal party committee's use of the conservative faction gave it the opportunity to manipulate elections through Cultural Revolution committees and preparatory committees and other leading groups that shifted the focus of attack from the work groups to "black gangs." Students labeled as "counterrevolutionaries" during the work group period remained in custody, and colleges and universities operated "labor reform teams" made up of mid-level cadres and professors.

SHANGHAI

Mayor Cao Diqiu arranged investigations into the backgrounds of Red Guards arriving from Beijing for the Great Networking, then sent incriminating material back to Beijing in hopes that work-unit party organizations would punish "scoundrels" who had come south. The Shanghai municipal party committee organized cadres, workers, and students to attack Red Guards from Beijing[1] while also arranging for "activists studying the works of Chairman Mao" and "five-good workers"[2] to send cables to the Central Committee and Mao extolling the virtues and accomplishments of the municipal party committee.[3] As part of its effort against the local rebel faction, the municipal party committee established a citywide Red Guard organization under the deputy director of its organization department, Zhang Wenbao, on August 23. Most of the leaders of the official Red Guard headquarters were the sons and daughters of Shanghai's party, government, and military leaders.[4]

GUANGXI[5]

Two days after the work group withdrew from Guangxi Normal College in Guilin on August 5, the authorities sent thousands of workers and peasants to the college to besiege and attack the dominant rebel faction in what came to be known as the August 7 Incident. In the latter half of the month, the first secretary of the Guangxi Zhuang Autonomous Region party committee and first political commissar of the Guangxi Military Region, Wei Guoqing, sent five companies of soldiers from the PLA's 141st Division to Guilin, telling bureau and department heads that "Guilin's 'majority faction' is being manipulated by rightists."

This was followed by the shocking September 9 Incident, in which the party committee sent conservative mass organizations to attack local rebel faction members and Red Guards from Beijing who were holding a sit-in and hunger strike at the autonomous region party committee offices in Nanning.

GUIZHOU[6]

On September 5, 1966, Beijing Red Guards joined more than three thousand local tertiary and secondary students for a denunciation rally and sit-in outside the provincial party committee offices in Guiyang. The provincial security bureau sent more than one hundred "official organ Red Guards" to protect the building, and the provincial Cultural Revolution leading group organized a parade of 120,000 cadres, workers, and city residents on the pretext of publicizing the Sixteen Articles. These official forces surrounded and split up the protesters, denouncing them in shifts around the clock until September 8. The provincial first secretary Jia Qiyun took further measures against the rebel faction with the establishment of the Guiyang College Red Guard Headquarters on September 8, an officially sponsored Red Guard Pickets brigade on September 28, and a Workers' Pickets Liaison Station, headed by the main leaders of the provincial federation of trade unions, on October 15. The officially sponsored Red Guards and the Workers' Pickets besieged Red Guards from Beijing as soon as they stepped off the train.

HUNAN[7]

After Mao reviewed the Red Guards on August 18, the offspring of senior cadres in Changsha organized the Red Regime Defense Force, which vowed to "defend the party and municipal party committees and the Communist red land to the death" and attack all sons-of-bitches, rightists, and "black devils" (class enemies) of various kinds. The municipal party secretary Kong Anmin imitated Mao by personally receiving the Red Guards in military uniform.[8] When the rebel Red Guards of Hunan University held a protest at the municipal party committee offices on August 19, the municipal party committee defended itself through a rival organization made up of party and youth league members from the factories, who beat up the university rebels in what came to be known as the August 19 Incident.

As the situation in Hunan spun out of control, the Central Committee appointed Zhang Pinghua, who had recently become deputy director of the Central Committee's Propaganda Department, to serve as first secretary of the Hunan provincial party committee. Unsure of what to do upon arriving in Hunan, Zhang Pinghua sent Hua Guofeng[9] to Beijing in early September, and Hua learned that the Central Committee was inclined toward organizing a counterattack.[10] When a rebel-supporting cadre was ousted from the Xiangtan Electrical Machinery Factory, Zhang Pinghua duly took the first opportunity to organize a province-wide attack on "black devils"—who were allegedly attacking the party—on September 24.

Given the anti-rightist proclivities of bureaucrats, the campaign rapidly netted large numbers of black devils. Rebel-supporting workers and cadres were jailed and subjected to struggle by their work units, with some of them driven to suicide. The provincial second secretary Wang Yanchun observed, "Originally it wasn't clear what the Cultural Revolution movement was all about, but now it's clear—it means seizing people!" Worrying that things were getting out of hand, Zhang Pinghua gave a talk on September 28 that subtly called for the campaign to end, but the bureaucrats were all fired up and had no intention of stopping.

HUBEI[11]

After the eleventh plenum, two large batches of Beijing students arrived in Wuhan for the Great Networking. One batch consisted of secondary school students, led by Song Binbin, now known as Song Yaowu, and had been sent by Wang Renzhong to protect the provincial party committee, so they enjoyed a warm reception. The other group, composed of students from Renmin University of China led by Zhao Guilin, had come to support the rebel faction and attack the provincial party committee, so the provincial party committee organized conservative-faction Red Guards to attack and drive them out.

The Hubei and Wuhan party committees established the Wuhan Area College Red Guards Headquarters at Wuhan University on September 12 to defend the provincial party committee. Leaders of the provincial party committee and Wuhan Military Region arrived in thirty jeeps to review the Red Guards in an awe-inspiring display to intimidate rebel students from the north.

During a mass rally convened by the provincial party committee at the Hongshan Assembly Hall on September 15, provincial governor Zhang Tixue "represented the thirty million people of Hubei" in denouncing Zhao Guilin and the "small handful of students coming south." Zhang Tixue said, "The skies have the ominous nine-headed bird, but the earth has Hubei fellows. I'm a Hubei fellow, and you can't push me around! You want to rebel against me? Kiss my balls!"

SICHUAN[12]

During the first half of August 1966, the Sichuan provincial party committee arranged for the Cultural Revolution leading groups and Cultural Revolution committee preparatory committees at the various colleges and universities to launch a unified campaign against students and teachers who had been designated political enemies. The Chengdu Institute of Technology ferreted out more than a quarter of the institute's teachers, which, when added to politically problematic teachers who had been secretly placed under control by the authorities, reached a total of more than four hundred people. These teachers had to labor every day with yin-yang haircuts, painted faces, and placards hanging around their necks while being forced to sing the "ox demon and snake spirit song." Similar things were done at the other tertiary institutions.[13]

A directive from provincial first secretary Li Jingquan stated: "Revolutionary cadres and workers, peasants, and soldiers are only able to speak through their children, so we need to organize workers and peasants to send their children to join the Red Guards." He compared it to "the peasants sending their children to join the army during the Revolutionary War." In many places, officially sponsored Red Guards became the main force for suppressing rebel students.

NANJING

With the backing of the Jiangsu provincial party committee, Nanjing established the Nanjing Factory and Mining Enterprise Workers' Red Guardians to oppose recently established rebel mass organizations.[14] The core members of the Workers' Red Guardians were party and youth league members, grassroots cadres, model workers, and political activists from the various factories and mines, and their expenses were covered by the provincial party committee.[15] When the rebel faction attacked the main leaders of the provincial and municipal party committees from the latter half of November until mid-December, the Workers' Red Guardians and officially sponsored student Red Guards diverted the attack to official scapegoats such as the former party secretary and president of Nanjing University, Kuang Yaming.

After the eleventh plenum of the Eighth Central Committee, rebel organizations came under attack throughout the country, and party committees throughout the country mobilized the army and police and organized workers and peasants to head off rebel student attacks. The PLA's General Staff Department and General Political Department countered this trend on August 21 with "provisions absolutely forbidding the use of troops to carry out armed suppression of the revolutionary student movement," for which the Central Commission issued a formal consent on August 22. These measures failed to turn the situation around.

On September 7, Mao wrote a comment on the "Situation Report on Changsha, Qingdao, Xi'an, and Other Places," noting that all these places had organized workers and peasants to oppose the students. "It seems appropriate for the Central Committee to issue a directive forbidding the localities from doing this, and then write an editorial advising workers and peasants not to interfere with the student movement."[16] On September 11, the Central Committee issued a directive forbidding the incitement and organization of workers, peasants, and residents to oppose the students.[17] On that same day, *People's Daily* published an editorial titled "The Worker and Peasant Masses and Revolutionary Students Unite Under the Banner of Mao Zedong Thought."

MAO PROPOSES DENOUNCING THE BOURGEOIS REACTIONARY LINE

In an effort to mobilize the masses to carry out cultural revolution, Mao issued a new appeal to denounce the bourgeois reactionary line, which essentially was attempts by party committees at all levels to resist rebellion, block further progress of the Cultural Revolution, and suppress the rebel masses.

Wang Li recalls that Zhou Enlai at one point questioned the appropriateness of Mao's formulation: "In the past, line problems have always been referred to as left- or right-deviating, but never reactionary." Mao used English to explain that the original term "counterrevolutionary line" (*fangeming luxian*) had later been changed to "antirevolutionary line" (*fandui geming luxian*), and finally the term "reactionary line" (*fandong luxian*) seemed best. Zhou said, "Now I understand."[18]

On October 1, 1966, the thirteenth issue of *Red Flag* magazine had an editorial titled "Advancing on the Great Path of Mao Zedong Thought," which described the Sixteen Articles as "the product of struggle between the two lines, and the product of the victory of the proletarian revolutionary line represented by Chairman Mao over the bourgeois reactionary line." The editorial specifically stated: "Whether or not to denounce the bourgeois reactionary line is the key to whether or not the Sixteen Articles of the Cultural Revolution can be implemented and executed, and whether or not it is possible to properly carry out widespread struggle, criticism, and reform. Eclecticism is not an option at this point."

Mao believed that the main targets should be people who, following the withdrawal of the work groups, were resisting the mass movement, controlling the masses, and preventing rebellion by inciting the masses against each other and organizing some of the masses as protection. Denouncing the bourgeois reactionary line therefore involved examining both the "fifty days" (i.e., the period of the work groups) and the "two months" (i.e., August and September following the eleventh plenum).[19] Since the eleventh plenum, the Central Committee's work had been managed by Zhou Enlai, and under him by Tao Zhu, so Zhou and Tao were bound to be held responsible for the bourgeois reactionary line that had supposedly emerged during this time. Mao placed the main blame on Tao Zhu, and Tao was struck down three months later.

Denouncing the bourgeois reactionary line also raised the question of whether every political movement since the founding of the PRC had involved the masses being persecuted by the bourgeois reactionary line, and gave rise to radical rebel factions that even negated the PRC's first seventeen years.

Denunciation of the bourgeois reactionary line helped fuel the rise of the Capital College Red Guards Revolutionary Rebel Headquarters (known as the Third Command Post), established on September 6. The Third Command Post, which combined rebel organizations from multiple colleges and universities, was organized by the rebel organization East Is Red at the Beijing Geological Institute and led by its students Zhu Chengzhao, Wang Dabin, and others. The deep background of the Third Command Post is suggested by the fact that Mao's daughter Li Na had gone to the Beijing Geological Institute several times in August and September on behalf of the Central Cultural Revolution Small Group to gain an understanding of the situation there and to establish ties with Zhu and Wang.[20] The Third Command Post had enormous influence over the rebel faction throughout the country, and it assisted many rebels who came to Beijing to file petitions after being labeled "counterrevolutionaries" by their local bureaucracies. Through its "liaison stations" in every province, the Third Command Post played a major role in attacks on the bourgeois reactionary line as well as power seizures in various places.

The Third Command Post held a mass rally of more than one hundred thousand "revolutionary teachers and students" to "fiercely open fire on the bourgeois reactionary line" at the Beijing Workers' Stadium on October 6. Chen Boda presided over the rally, which was also attended by Zhou Enlai, Jiang Qing, Kang Sheng, Tao Zhu, Zhang Chunqiao, and other members of the CCRSG. After delivering the first speech in support of the rebel faction, Jiang Qing had Zhang Chunqiao read out the Central Military Commission's "Urgent Directive Regarding the Great Proletarian Revolution in the Military Academies," which emphasized the importance of the four bigs and repeated the prohibition against inciting students against other students. People who had been initially labeled as counterrevolutionaries or other types of political enemies by party committees and work groups were to be rehabilitated and have their reputations publicly restored, and their self-criticisms and "black dossiers" destroyed.

Zhou Enlai elaborated that this "urgent directive" applied to non-military tertiary and secondary schools as well. Those attending the rally included rebel faction members from all over the country who had been labeled "counterrevolutionaries" and "rightists," and who had risked their lives to break out of work unit jails and submit petitions in Beijing, some of them written in blood. Zhou Enlai called on local party committees "not to persecute, unlawfully detain, or torture" rebels when they returned to their localities, but rather to "ensure their personal safety" and "continue to pay their wages."[21]

The resulting campaign began by rehabilitating people who had been labeled as counterrevolutionaries and rightists at the first stage of the movement, and public indignation over the exposure of cabinets full of black dossiers expanded the ranks of the rebel faction.[22] Newly liberated rebels enthusiastically responded to Mao's appeal by aiming their spearhead of struggle at those in power who had suppressed them, and they subjected large numbers of officials to unprecedented suffering.

THE OCTOBER CENTRAL COMMITTEE WORK CONFERENCE

A CCP Central Committee work conference convened from October 9 to 28, 1966, focused mainly on denouncing the bourgeois reactionary line and eliminating obstructions to the Cultural Revolution. Rebel faction leaders from some localities were invited to address the conference, which was attended by leaders of provincial-level party committees, State Council ministries and commissions, and headquarters and military branches under the Central Military Commission.

Why was this conference still necessary once Liu Shaoqi had been sidelined and the work groups withdrawn? Wang Li says it was a matter of shifting the focus of criticism from the fifty days before the eleventh plenum to the two months after the eleventh plenum:

> Chairman Mao felt that the struggle between the two lines continued after the eleventh plenum . . . After the work groups withdrew, if there were still old organizations left intact, or old apparatuses, old discipline, and old methods but just in different form, this was still not acceptable . . . Chairman Mao felt that during this period there was no support for people who had steadfastly endorsed the revolutionary line and had been labeled counterrevolutionaries, some of whom were genuine revolutionary rebels.[23]

Mao felt that the main spearhead had yet to be aimed at the capitalist roaders,[24] and that the Central Committee work conference needed to take further action to mobilize the masses against leading cadres at every level.

Mao explained his thinking to Chen Boda before the meeting, and Chen wrote it up in a report titled *The Two Lines in the Great Proletarian Cultural Revolution*,[25] which he delivered as the keynote report of the conference on October 16. The report analyzed the new manifestations of the bourgeois reactionary line and criticized local moves to label the rebel faction as counterrevolutionary. It criticized blood lineage theory and demanded, "Why should it be inevitable for the offspring of senior cadres to hold power? Is their blood really that noble? . . . It would be best to allow the offspring of workers and peasants and of ordinary cadres to take charge." The report called on cadres at all levels to banish their fears and freely mobilize the masses.

Mao evaluated this report as "very good" in an October 24 memo. He requested "adding in the phrase 'seize revolution and push production' somewhere" and directed that the report be printed into booklets and distributed to each party branch and Red Guard team.[26]

Tao Zhu's secretary Ma Encheng, who helped compile brief reports on the conference, says that most of the cadres in attendance were flummoxed by Chen Boda's heavy-handedness, and some resented the attacks by the rebel faction. Tianjin's Second Party Secretary, Zhao Wucheng, complained in his speech that First Secretary Wan Xiaotang had died of a heart attack under Red Guard persecution, but this only led to Zhao becoming a key target of criticism in his group. Other group meetings aimed virulent criticism at leaders of the Northwest Bureau, Southwest Bureau, Northeast Bureau, South Central Bureau, and Fujian Province in the East China Region, employing overblown political rhetoric.[27]

Reports on the suppression of the rebel faction were printed and distributed, and on October 23, Liu Shaoqi and Deng Xiaoping carried out self-criticism before the full conference.

Liu Shaoqi wrote his self-criticism on September 14 and then wrote a letter to Mao expressing his willingness to serve as "a model of error" for the benefit of the party, the people, and the Cultural Revolution.[28] Mao wrote a memo on Liu's self-criticism that day: "Basically it's written very well and very seriously; the second half is especially good."[29] In the second half that Mao referred to, Liu criticized himself not only for the "fifty days" but also for right-deviation in 1962 and "left in form and right in reality" errors in 1964.[30] Liu's October 23 self-criticism was more than ten thousand words long, and according to Wang Li, it was printed and distributed to the whole party.[31] Liu admitted that "[I] regarded some normal and unavoidable shortcomings that emerged in the mass movement as an 'anti-party, anti-proletarian dictatorship' 'countercurrent.' As a result I reached an incorrect conclusion that made me adopt a reactionary bourgeois standpoint and implement a bourgeois line."[32]

Deng Xiaoping's self-criticism acknowledged that the serious error of sending in the work groups put him "on the side that opposed the mass revolution" and "on the side of the reactionary bourgeoisie." He described the Cultural Revolution as "a mighty movement to promote the proletarian and eliminate the bourgeois, to ensure that our country never changes color, and to avoid the peril of revisionism and the restoration of capitalism. This is a mighty and pioneering undertaking . . . [and] has immensely profound and epochal significance, not only for China, but for the world." He also praised Lin Biao as Mao's successor: "It is he who has raised high the banner of Mao Zedong Thought, and has raised it the highest, learned it the best, and used it most vividly . . . Someone like me who has committed errors should conscientiously learn from Comrade Lin Biao."[33]

On October 24, the group meetings launched criticism of Liu Shaoqi, with attendees vying to prove their loyalty to Mao and their revolutionary character.

In his speech to the full conference on October 25, Mao remarked, "I'm the one who lit the flame of the Cultural Revolution. It was done in a rush, in just a few months . . . there was misunderstanding and resistance; that's understandable and natural." He comforted and encouraged the cadres: "If you took the wrong line, just correct it. Who wants to strike you down? I don't want to strike you down, and I don't think the Red Guards necessarily want to strike you down."[34]

The conference issued Chen Boda's report and published Mao's August 5 "Bombard the Headquarters: My Big-Character Poster," which became an ideological tool for further mobilizing the masses.

THE CONSEQUENCES OF CRITICIZING THE BOURGEOIS REACTIONARY LINE

After the Central Committee work conference drew to a close, mass student rallies to denounce the bourgeois reactionary line pushed the rebel movement to a new high throughout the country. Launched in schools in October, this round of struggle then spread to government organs, businesses, and enterprise work units, reaching its climax from mid-November to the end of the year. Although the Sixteen Articles called for freely mobilizing the masses, this didn't happen until

Mao criticized the bourgeois reactionary line and obstructionist party leaders were denounced.

The denunciation of the bourgeois reactionary line was a major turning point in the Cultural Revolution, and was largely responsible for the sudden rise of the genuine rebel faction. The term "genuine rebel faction" refers to those who aimed their attacks at the privileged strata and who were labeled rightists and counterrevolutionaries under the party committees and work groups at the outset of the Cultural Revolution. Although they'd regained their freedom after the eleventh plenum of the Eighth Central Committee, it was only after the denunciation of the bourgeois reactionary line in October 1966 that rebel mass organizations were truly able to emerge from the shadows and mount the political stage. The rebels said, "Chairman Mao has given us his backing, and we will fight for Chairman Mao!" This made them even more dauntless, as well as drew them closer to the CCRSG.

Before the denunciation of the bourgeois reactionary line, bureaucrats at all levels wielded all the power within their grasp to point the spearhead of struggle toward the rebel masses. Now the rebels responded to Mao's appeal by fiercely attacking bureaucrats and imperiling their families. The officially sponsored conservative mass organizations that had been used against the rebel faction fell into complete disarray, but once this opposition disappeared, rebel mass organizations began to split and fight among themselves.

If Mao's reviews of the Red Guards after the eleventh plenum caused large numbers of secondary students to employ red terror in "smashing of the four olds," this time the Central Committee work conference inspired more mature college students and workers to take extreme measures against the bureaucratic system. The eleventh plenum made waves on school campuses, but the turbulence stirred up by the work conference swept across the entire country.

Although trans-sectoral organizations were not yet allowed, students denouncing the bourgeois reactionary line went to the factories, and a small number of daring young workers joined up with them. The flames of the Cultural Revolution began to spread from the schools to government organs, factories, and villages, and those who had been labeled as counterrevolutionaries during the first phase were even fiercer in their attacks on those in power. Upper-level military bureaucrats had been active in striking down the "Peng-Luo-Lu-Yang clique" and even more enthusiastic in denouncing the "reactionary academic authorities," but these new attacks on the entire bureaucracy displeased them, and they began brewing a counterattack.

While departing a Central Committee conference of regional, provincial, and municipal first secretaries on October 27, Ye Jianying recited a poem he had just composed, wondering how many more officials would be dismissed. "Majestic were those of yore on the battlefield! / So pitiable now at the hands of young warriors . . ." Marshal Chen Yi subsequently pronounced it "an ingeniously excellent poem." Gu Mu noted that the poem reflected "further lack of understanding and a resolve to fight another battle." The other battle Gu Mu referred to was the 1967 "February resistance."[35]

The denunciation of the bourgeois reactionary line totally paralyzed the party and government, creating the conditions for the January power seizure.

9

—

THE RISE, ACTIONS, AND DEMISE OF
MASS ORGANIZATIONS

Once Mao allowed China's people to enjoy the freedom of association enshrined in the constitution, mass organizations proliferated. At first these organizations were confined to individual work units, but eventually they began to span work units and professions to become large-scale organizations that demolished the bureaucratic structure and the old order, bringing about the "great chaos under heaven" that Mao desired. While permitting the establishment of trans-sectoral mass organizations, Mao prohibited national-level organizations in order to prevent resistance to the central government. Once Mao had released the mass organization genie from its bottle, however, he could only do so much to keep it in submission. This tool for achieving "great chaos under heaven" eventually obstructed the process of achieving "great order across the land." At that point, Mao was obliged to condone the iron-fisted bureaucrats who upheld and restored order; the mass organizations Mao had once supported were suppressed, and their leaders became sacrificial lambs in the process.

To mobilize the Cultural Revolution, Mao allowed these new mass organizations to publish their own newspapers and magazines, resulting in more than five thousand Red Guard periodicals (some estimates claim more than eight thousand).[1] Tsinghua University's *Jinggang Mountain* had an airmail edition and printing plants in several cities throughout the country, and accepted mail subscriptions, but even individuals could print and distribute leaflets. With students and even some teachers and workers allowed to travel around the country for the Great Networking, the Chinese enjoyed a brief period of something like genuine democracy and freedom.

THE RED GUARDS AND THE REBEL FACTION

It is difficult for people who didn't experience the Cultural Revolution to understand the relationship between the Red Guards and rebels. "Red Guards" was a general term referring to all mass organizations. Generally speaking, there were two major factions among these mass organizations: the rebel faction and the conservative faction. (There was also a neutral "bystander" [xiaoyao] group made up of the unaligned. Very small at first, the bystander crowd grew as the movement progressed.) A given city might have multiple Red Guard organizations belonging to a single faction. The rebel faction could also contain smaller factions, but all responded to Mao's call to rise up in rebellion against the bureaucratic targets specified by Mao. In short, the rebel faction aimed its attacks upward against capitalist roaders within the party, while the "royalist" conservative faction allied itself with those in power and aimed its attacks downward against mass opposition to party committees and work groups (Zhou Enlai decided that this faction should be referred to as "conservative" rather than "royalist"). The rebel faction started out as the minority faction but gained popularity and increased its ranks as the movement progressed. Eventually, one mass organization might oppose a certain leading cadre but protect another, while another mass organization would do just the opposite. For this reason it could be said that apart from the officially sponsored Red Guards (which largely disbanded and disappeared at the end of 1966), everyone who joined a mass organization belonged to the rebel faction, and the groups were differentiated by no more than their specific targets. To demonstrate their revolutionary character, both the more radical and the more conservative rebel factions excluded and attacked black elements and preserved the "purity" of their ranks as much as possible. However, the conservative faction was "purer."

The Red Guards that first emerged were rebels; the Red Guards of the Tsinghua University Affiliated Secondary School gained Mao's support by shouting the slogan "To rebel is justified." These Old Red Guards rebelled against the school leadership and teachers, and against the four olds. Strictly speaking, however, a rebellion is carried out by those below against those above—the weak against the strong—but the Old Red Guards were typically the offspring of officials whose status was higher than that of school leaders and teachers, and they also benefited from inside information. A genuine rebellion requires taking a political risk, but the Old Red Guards, with their privileged backing, had little to fear from attacking teachers or the four olds. When the situation of the Cultural Revolution changed and the parents of these Red Guards were attacked as capitalist roaders, the Old Red Guards openly protected the cadres and attacked the rebel faction, and in that way became a "conservative faction" in name as well as practice, however they might disavow the label.

The evolution of the rebel and conservative factions is exemplified by the Red Guards at Tsinghua University. After Kuai Dafu was labeled as a counterrevolutionary by the work group sent in by Liu Shaoqi, some relatively moderate students established "combat groups" and wrote big-character posters criticizing the work group. However, even after Kuai was rehabilitated, these mass organizations were afraid to accept him, which shows the lingering influence of the work group. While still in charge, the work group engineered the establishment of a Tsinghua University Cultural Revolution Leading Group Provisional Preparatory Committee led by, among others, He Long's son, He Pengfei; Liu Shaoqi's daughter Liu Tao; Li Jingquan's son, Li Lifeng; and Qiao Guanhua's son, Qiao Zonghuai. Teachers and students who opposed the work group referred to it as a "fake provisional preparatory committee."

On August 7, the provisional preparatory committee proposed shifting the focus of criticism from the work group to the black gang. This "August 7 Proposal"[2] clearly had a deeper intention to protect Wang Guangmei and Liu Shaoqi. Students who opposed the work group responded on August 8 by organizing an "8-8 network" that rejected the August 7 Proposal. This, in turn, was countered on August 9 by an "8-9 network" organized by Liu Jufen[3] and other supporters of the provisional preparatory committee at the suggestion of

Wang Guangmei. This split Tsinghua University into an 8-8 faction, which criticized the work group, and an 8-9 faction, which criticized university president Jiang Nanxiang and enjoyed majority control. After Mao reviewed the Red Guards at Tiananmen Square on August 18, the "8-9 network" transformed overnight into the Tsinghua University Red Guards (TU Red Guards), while the 8-8 faction eventually became the Mao Zedong Thought Red Guards (MZT Red Guards). The MZT Red Guards remained greatly overshadowed by the majority TU Red Guards, but gained great inspiration from "Ode to the Minority," written by a student in the Automated Control Department, Sun Yinji (who later changed his name to Sun Nutao—"raging billows").

Because the TU Red Guards opposed only the university party committee and not the work group or Liu Shaoqi, they became the conservative faction. That made the MZT Red Guards the rebel faction, but they were still unwilling to accept Kuai Dafu, so Kuai decided to establish his own organization. The Tsinghua Jinggang Mountain Corps consisted of Kuai Dafu and a few dozen others whom the work group designated as counterrevolutionaries or "Kuai-type persons." This organization aimed to denounce the bourgeois reactionary line of the work group, denounce the TU Red Guards, and thoroughly rehabilitate Kuai-type persons. He Pengfei prohibited the group from broadcasting its founding manifesto over the university radio station, but the Jinggang Mountain Corps rose to prominence after *Red Flag* published an editorial proposing criticism of the bourgeois reactionary line on October 1, and Zhou Enlai and Central Cultural Revolution Small Group leaders spoke at the October 6 mass rally organized by the Third Command Post.

The Third Command Post was one of three loosely organized city-wide organizations established by Beijing's colleges and universities in late August and early September 1966. The Capital College Red Guards Headquarters (known as the First Command Post) was established on August 27, 1966, with twenty-nine mass organizations from twenty-seven tertiary institutions taking part. Led by Wang Yanqun, the daughter of Mao's chief bodyguard, Wang Dongxing, the First Command Post was a coalition of conservative Red Guards, which disbanded at the end of the year. The Capital College Red Guards General Headquarters (known as the Second Command Post) was established on September 5. Provisionally headed by Zhou Tai'an, son of the navy deputy commander Zhou Xihan, it included both rebel and conservative Red Guard groups and didn't engage in any major activities. The Capital College Red Guards Revolutionary Rebel Headquarters (the Third Command Post), established on September 6, included Tsinghua's MZT Red Guards and was headed by Zhu Chengzhao from the Beijing Geological Institute. The Third Command Post was a rebel organization, and most of its members were students who had been attacked under the bourgeois reactionary line.

After early summer 1967, Beijing's rebel faction college Red Guard organizations realigned around a "heaven faction," named for the "aeronautical" element in its core constituent, the Beijing Aeronautical Engineering Institute Red Flag; and an "earth faction," named for the "geological" element in its core constituent, the Beijing Geological Institute Red Guards. There were no real differences in principle between the heaven and earth factions, while differences of opinion existed among the members of each of them. Likewise, there were no major skirmishes between the two factions, but they sometimes engaged in petty tactics against each other.

THE RANKS OF THE REBEL FACTION AND THEIR POLITICAL DEMANDS

After the Cultural Revolution, "rebel faction" became a synonym for "evil," and the rebels were blamed for everything bad that happened during the Cultural Revolution. But it wasn't rebels who labeled multitudes of students, teachers, workers, and ordinary cadres as "rightists" or "reactionary devils" from May to August 1966. It wasn't rebels who ransacked homes, beat people to death, expelled hordes of people from the cities, and persecuted prominent cultural figures to death in August and September 1966. The horrific massacres of black elements in Beijing's Daxing County and Hunan's Dao County and the appalling purge of the Inner Mongolian People's Revolutionary Party had nothing to do with the rebel faction. It wasn't rebels who tortured and persecuted multitudes of innocent people in the Cleansing of the Class Ranks,[4] the One Strike and Three Antis campaign, or the investigation of the May 16 clique, nor was it rebels who killed pioneering thinkers such as Yu Luoke, Zhang Zhixin, Shi Yunfeng, and Wang Shenyou. All this mass persecution was decided on and organized by the people in power.

This is not to say that the rebel faction was innocent of all wrongdoing in the Cultural Revolution. It served as the main force for Mao to create "great chaos under heaven," and bore a heavy responsibility for the destruction of Chinese culture and outstanding traditions. In attacking the bureaucratic system, it ruthlessly persecuted many good cadres. Innocent people became victims during armed conflicts among rebel mass organizations. The rebel faction impelled Mao's utopian vision forward and served as the vanguard for his ultra-leftist line. If what the rebel faction (and Mao) advocated had prevailed, China would have regressed even further from modernization than it did.

Zhou Enlai had a saying concerning the Cultural Revolution's factions: "Those who insist on and defend the Chairman's line are of course leftist, while those who vacillate are of course middle-of-the-roaders, and the rightists are the relatively conservative faction."[5] According to Zhou Enlai, the rebel faction was leftist. The rebel faction rose through the repeated encouragement of Mao, the Central Committee, and some central leaders.

The Sixteen Articles prevented party committees from attacking the rebel masses, while giving the masses the freedom and confidence to rebel, and the higher the rank of the leader denounced, the more revolutionary the critic was considered to be. Tao Zhu, an adviser to the Central Cultural Revolution Small Group, said, "All of Zhongnanhai, including me, can be opposed; only our party's central committee and Chairman Mao cannot be opposed, along with our Comrade Lin Biao."[6]

The rebel faction emerged in Beijing during the eleventh plenum of the Eighth Central Committee, but in most major cities further from the political center it appeared from August to October 1966, as indicated by the names of organizations such as Chongqing's August 15, Chengdu's August 26, and Liaoning's August 31. In medium-size and small cities it didn't surface until November or December, and in the factories it emerged after the bourgeois reactionary line was denounced in October. It could be said that the denunciation of the bourgeois reactionary line spawned or even compelled the birth of most rebel faction organizations.

Students divided into conservative and rebel factions based on the political criteria of class struggle. One portion of students had good family backgrounds, pursued political advancement, and allied themselves with party organizations, thereby gaining the party's trust and its favorable consequences; another portion came from politically disadvantaged families, maintained their distance from party organizations, avoided political movements, and were considered politically backward. Of course, advantage and disadvantage were relative and could change in the course of any political movement; students in the advantaged group might come to be regarded as undesirables if their parents were purged.

Those in the advantaged group enjoyed better career prospects as well as the privilege of attacking others without being attacked themselves. As beneficiaries of the system that existed before the Cultural Revolution, they naturally defended and endorsed that system and its bureaucratic clique. People in the disadvantaged group suffered inferior jobs and living conditions and routinely came under attack during political campaigns. Long repressed by officials, they naturally felt great satisfaction at seeing those officials struck down.

Other factors also determined which faction a person fell into. A person could take a conservative position out of fear, after observing the persecution of critics in previous political campaigns; out of a deep veneration for revolutionary leading cadres instilled by years of propaganda; or from being overcautious and timid by nature. That's why the rebel faction was initially the minority. But as the movement progressed, some of these people became bolder, and exposure of the malpractices of bureaucrats swelled the ranks of the rebel faction. The conservative faction didn't oppose the Cultural Revolution; it opposed only overturning the existing order and denigrating officials who had been esteemed for so many years.

The rebel faction particularly appealed to naive young people who believed Chairman Mao and the Central Committee and responded to their calls to rebel, and to people who were "intellectually active" and didn't respect the leaders. People scarred by unfair treatment in a previous political campaign might also feel compelled to join the rebel faction.

The frontmen of the rebel faction typically came from privileged backgrounds. They were eloquent, liked taking a stand, and spoke out against injustice. At the outset of the movement, those in power labeled them "little Deng Tuos," "neo-rightists," and "counterrevolutionaries," and gave them outlaw status, but their "red roots and straight shoots" protected them from serious opposition. In an environment that tracked political lineage for three generations, only those from the best families could survive as leaders of the rebel faction. Many were independent thinkers who dared to put their words into action, and their opposition to the existing order was what Mao most needed to create "great chaos under heaven." When it came time to establish "great order under heaven," however, they were ruthlessly sacrificed.

Factionalism by those in power created rebels. Before the work group entered the Wuhan Institute of Hydraulic and Electrical Engineering, the institute's party committee divided teachers and students into leftists, who could be relied on; centrists, who might be brought on board; and rightists, who were to be targets of attack. Students and teachers persecuted for objecting to this practice eventually became the rebel faction.[7] A similar situation arose at the Chongqing Jiangling Machine Factory in November 1966, when the technician Gao De'an discovered a list categorizing staff according to their political reliability on the desk of the technical department's party secretary. Gao De'an, Li Musen, and others in the "undesirable" categories established the Dagger Combat Group, which led the machine factory's staff in a revolt demanding the destruction of all such lists. Gao De'an subsequently became "top man" for the Defense Industry Jinggang Mountain Jiangling Corps.[8]

In the wider society, long-suppressed black elements sympathized with and supported the rebel faction, but rebel faction organizations didn't dare accept them for fear of being accused of "impure ranks." Some courageous rightists, such as the author Bai Hua,[9] nevertheless publicly supported the rebel faction.

Deciding which faction to join depended on observing the situation, judging the direction in which things were headed, and then making the most advantageous or least harmful choice in a process known as "falling in." There was no way to guarantee making the right choice. Chairman Mao's "highest directives," Central Committee documents, and the speeches of central leaders could be interpreted differently to support different sides, and the choice of factions often depended largely on circumstances. Social status and personal connections were important factors; people tended to join factions along with their friends and avoided factions whose members included people they disliked.

The rebel faction ostensibly opposed those in power who had departed from Chairman Mao's revolutionary line, but the radical wing went further to negate the entire first seventeen years of the regime. What they objected to was not the autocratic deprivation of basic human rights, or economic controls that reduced people to poverty, but rather the bourgeoisie's reactionary leadership during that time. Opposing Mao, the Communist Party, or the political demands of the socialist system would have been the most monstrous of crimes, deserving of death, and only a tiny minority dared go that far.

The mainstream rebels therefore made demands consistent with the Central Committee's October work conference—exposing the bourgeois reactionary line of those in power and the work groups, rehabilitating people who had been labeled political enemies, encouraging the masses to rebel, and destroying conservative faction organizations. But those who went further wanted to pursue the culpability of local leaders in the Great Famine, and a minority wanted to overturn the existing bureaucratic class and establish a new society along the lines of the Paris Commune.

As members of both the conservative and rebel factions vied to display their revolutionary bona fides, some provincial and municipal leaders became targets of both factions and were marched through the streets in dunce caps and subjected to a range of physical torments. Reactionary academic authorities and black elements were also brought out as secondary targets. These "revolutionary competitions" were the main cause of the extremist acts that occurred during the Cultural Revolution.

DIVISION AND FACTIONAL STRUGGLE WITHIN THE REBEL FACTION

After conservative faction mass organizations collapsed at the end of 1966 and rebel faction mass organizations became the mainstream, Mao envisaged the rebel organizations coming together to create a new "great order out of great chaos." Instead, the ideology of class struggle, a penchant for power struggle, the spirit of individual heroism, and egotistical desire for power came to the fore. Without a guiding ideology of democracy and rule of law or a rational objective of systemic innovation, a rebel faction organization that attained power became a dictatorial "king of the hill," and factional struggle developed among rebel groups with an intensity and brutality that far surpassed earlier struggles between conservative and rebel factions.

In spring 1967, some provincial and municipal party committees and local army garrisons took advantage of the February Countercurrent to resurrect the defeated conservative faction (in some smaller cities, the conservative faction had never fallen) and join in the factional struggle. This created an even more chaotic situation in which rebel organizations fought with each other and also with conservative organizations.

Although all groups claimed to be responding to Mao's call to rebel, conflicts developed over differing views on major issues or on certain leading cadres, as well as over the allocation of power in the January power seizure. Support-the-left troops also took different sides, with a field army supporting one faction and a provincial military district supporting the other, and this made factional struggle even more violent and protracted.

Nanjing serves as a perfect example.

As a key university, Nanjing University was the main conduit for spreading the "seeds of fire" of the Cultural Revolution throughout the region. After the broadcast of Nie Yuanzi's big-character poster, the party secretary and president of Nanjing University, Kuang Yaming, was struck down on June 2. As the movement progressed, three types of Red Guards emerged at Nanjing University: the Nanjing University Red Rebel Force (NU Red Rebels), the Nanjing University August 27 Revolutionary Network (NU August 27), and the Nanjing University Red Banner Combat Team (NU Red Banner). NU Red Banner, which criticized Kuang Yaming and supported the work group, was part of a conservative coalition and collapsed with the denunciation of the bourgeois reactionary line, along with larger officially sponsored conservative organizations such as Nanjing Red Guard Headquarters and the Nanjing Workers Red Guardians.

The surviving NU Red Rebels and NU August 27 teamed up with workers to establish trans-sectoral rebel organizations in the wider society. The NU Red Rebels were the initiators and core force behind the radical Jiangsu Province Red Rebel Headquarters (Provincial Red Headquarters), established on November 1, 1966. The Provincial Red Headquarters had the largest power base in Nanjing and incorporated many subsidiary organizations, the most combat-effective of which were the Provincial Red Headquarters College Headquarters and the Jiangsu Province Workers' Red Rebel General Headquarters (Provincial Workers' Headquarters, for short), a citywide workers' rebel organization established in mid-November with the approval of Zhou Enlai.

Another major power base of the Nanjing rebel faction was Nanjing August 27, which was established on December 20 through the efforts of NU August 27. Nanjing August 27 included some workers and peasants but was mainly composed of teachers and students from secondary schools and colleges, and it was more politically moderate than the Provincial Red Headquarters.

Spurred on by Shanghai's "January revolution," the heads of Nanjing's various power bases held a joint conference from January 22 to 25, 1967, to discuss seizing power. At the meeting, a conflict developed between the Provincial Red Headquarters and Nanjing August 27, and the latter threatened to withdraw along with some other smaller power bases. But the Provincial Red Headquarters disregarded the boycott and continued organizing other radical forces to launch the "January 26 power seizure." After the Nanjing Military Region expressed its support, the "power seizure committee," composed chiefly of the Provincial Red Headquarters and its supporters, declared that it had taken control of the city. The excluded Nanjing August 27 and its supporters quickly disputed that pronouncement, resulting in the Nanjing area rebel faction splitting into two camps. The Provincial Red Headquarters camp proclaimed the January 26 power seizure "excellent," while the Nanjing August 27 camp called it "bullshit," so a sustained factional struggle developed between the "excellent faction" and the "bullshit faction."[10]

These kinds of struggles between power bases arose in localities throughout China. On top of that, the same rebel faction organization might split into several suborganizations, each forming its own new power base, and factional struggle between them became a pervasive phenomenon.

Why did rebel faction organizations splinter? My personal experience at Tsinghua University serves as an example.

As noted earlier, by the end of September 1966, Tsinghua University had three student organizations: the TU Red Guards led by Liu Tao, He Pengfei, and other offspring of senior cadres; the MZT Red Guards; and the Jinggang Mountain Corps, led by Kuai Dafu. After the bourgeois reactionary line came under attack, the conservative TU Red Guards were disbanded at the end of 1966. The two remaining organizations both belonged to the rebel faction, but the Jinggang Mountains Corps was more radical. With Jiang Qing's persuasion and urging, on December 19, 1966, the two groups united to form the Tsinghua University Jinggang Mountain Corps, and the group headquarters led by Kuai Dafu became the highest leadership organ at the university.

Uniting the two organizations did not erase the divergent views of their respective memberships, however; a splinter group, formed on April 14, 1967, soon became the Jinggang Mountain 4-14 Headquarters. The Corps and 4-14 disagreed over how to handle cadres and in their views on the PRC's first seventeen years. The Corps held that the educational line of the seventeen years was revisionist and represented the bourgeoisie's dictatorship over the proletariat, and that the old Tsinghua must therefore be "thoroughly smashed"; while 4-14 held that the seventeen years were marked mainly by accomplishments and that a complete overthrow was absolutely unacceptable.

Mao supported Kuai Dafu and disliked 4-14, while both sides clearly sensed Zhou Enlai's undeclared sympathy for 4-14. The Corps faction wanted to leverage its advantage to merge the two factions into a revolutionary committee under its leadership, but 4-14 wouldn't accept the Corps faction's conditions, dooming the merger and the revolutionary committee.

As hostility between the two factions intensified, Kuai Dafu followed the example of Nie Yuanzi's use of armed force against her opponents at Peking University. The sustained battles between the two groups from April 23 to July 27, 1968, became known as the One-Hundred-Day Armed Conflict and resulted in the deaths of eleven students. On July 27, 1968, Mao dispatched a thirty-thousand-strong Capital Workers and PLA Mao Zedong Thought Propaganda Team to Tsinghua University to end the fighting, and both mass organizations were disbanded.

The splintering of rebel organizations throughout the country was even more complex than at Tsinghua mainly for the following reasons: (1) divergent political views regarding the PRC's first seventeen years that emerged as the movement progressed; (2) struggles for power and status in the midst of coalition building and power seizure; and (3) the backing of different groups by support-the-left troops and veteran cadres, which exacerbated splits and factional struggle among mass organizations.

Power bases that emerged from original organizations or from splits within an organization could merge with other power bases, fight with them, or unite and then fight with them, always with covert or open manipulation and meddling by senior military officials or veteran cadres from different factions and with differing viewpoints. Factional battles between mass organizations were linked to factionalism within the Communist Party.

In early 1967, the military directly intervened in the Cultural Revolution in various localities, and a large share of support-the-left troops supported the conservative faction, or even helped resurrect it from a state of collapse. Military support resulted in the use of modern weaponry in large-scale battles.

May 1968 saw the issuance of Mao's newest directive: "A faction is the wing of a class."[11] This raised the fighting between various mass organizations to the level of class warfare, even though each faction considered itself to be part of the proletarian class and its opponent to be part of the bourgeois class.

MAO PARTS WITH THE REBEL FACTION

Mao didn't part ways with the rebel faction until 1968, but for the sake of narrative clarity, we'll deal with that episode here. By 1968, the "great chaos under heaven" had been going on for two years, and Mao felt an urgent need to restore order through "the grand alliance," the "three-in-one combination," and the establishment of revolutionary committees.[12] Reinstated bureaucrats and some military bureaucrats in charge of support-the-left units used the restoration of order as a pretext to suppress the rebel faction, which resisted its marginalization, sometimes with extreme measures. In Guangxi, the rebel organization 4-22 commandeered weapons meant to aid Vietnam in order to fight the Guangxi Alliance Command Post, which was armed by the local support-the-left unit. The Central Committee responded with a stern "7-3 Notice" aimed at the rebel faction in Guangxi and the rest of China. This was followed by a "7-24 Notice" aimed at the rebel faction in Shaanxi and other parts of China, demanding that "every mass organization, group, and individual must resolutely, thoroughly, and sincerely execute the '7-3 Notice' personally approved by the Great Leader Chairman Mao and may not defy it."

The rebel faction had started out as Mao's "rock" to throw at the bureaucrats, but now it had become a stumbling block to implementing "great order under heaven" and an opponent to the revolutionary committees of the "newborn regime." As the "proletarian headquarters" in Beijing joined reinstated bureaucrats and support-the-left troops in suppressing the rebel faction, rebel leaders from various provinces congregated at the Beijing Aeronautical Engineering Institute on July 17, 1968, to decide on a countermove. Kuai Dafu listened awhile and then left. The Central Committee designated it a "black meeting." While receiving leaders of mass organizations from both factions and military cadres from Guangxi at the Great Hall of the People on July 25, 1968, key officials from the proletarian headquarters, including Zhou Enlai, Chen Boda, Kang Sheng, Yao Wenyuan, Xie Fuzhi, Huang Yongsheng, Wu Faxian, and Wen Yucheng, bluntly and sternly censured the rebels and demanded the details of the black meeting.

Mao had lost all patience with the rebel faction. The "7-3 Notice," the "7-24 Notice," and the harsh criticism by key officials of the proletarian headquarters showed that Mao was ready to slice through the Gordian knot in dealing with the problem of mass organizations. Military control and beefed-up work groups were the most effective method.

That is how Mao came to send the thirty-thousand-strong Capital Workers and PLA Mao Zedong Thought Propaganda Team to Tsinghua University on July 27, 1968, to end the fighting and take full control over the university, putting an end to both factions of mass organizations. This "management takeover unit" was composed of personnel from the Central Security Unit 8341 and workers from factories such as the Beijing Textile Industrial Complex and Xinhua Printing Plant, where the 8341 Unit had carried out support-the-left work. The surprise attack on Tsinghua University marked Mao's abandonment of his strategy of using the rebel faction.

While receiving the "five great leaders" of Beijing's rebel faction on July 28 immediately after the Tsinghua crackdown, Mao warned: "Some say, 'The Guangxi Notice only applies to Guangxi and not to us here,' or that the Shaanxi Notice only applies to Shaanxi. Let's issue a nationwide notice here and now: Anyone who persists with violations, fights the PLA, snatches military supplies, sabotages transportation, kills people, or commits arson is guilty of a crime. If a minority of people can't be dissuaded, they are bandits and Kuomintang and must be encircled and suppressed, and if they continue to stubbornly resist, they will be annihilated." After this, some recalcitrant rebel factions in various localities were actually encircled and suppressed like bandits, and the attack on Guangxi's 4-22 group resulted in one hundred thousand people being massacred. The truth was that 4-22's opponent, the Guangxi Alliance Command Post, was just as extremist but enjoyed the support of the army and veteran cadres.

Han Aijing records that after Mao ended his meeting with the "five great rebel faction leaders" on July 28, and the rebels were shaking hands with Lin Biao, Zhou Enlai, Jiang Qing, and other central leaders, Mao returned to the room:

> Chairman Mao walked over and said, "I left, but I was worried that you would turn around and attack Kuai Dafu, so I came back." Chairman Mao said to the central leaders who were

present, "You mustn't turn around and attack Kuai Dafu again; you mustn't attack them again." Chairman Mao spoke for a little while, and then we shook hands with him again, reluctant to part from him.

This meeting marked the end of the rebel faction and showed Mao's conflicted feelings. During the meeting, Mao repeatedly expressed his support for these radicals and repeatedly criticized the moderate 4-14 rebel faction group. What displeased him most was the essay "The 4-14 Mindset Will Prevail," which seemed to imply that "those who conquer the country cannot rule the country." Mao wasn't referring here to the Communist Party, which after all was firmly established, but rather to the rebel faction, which he wanted to rule after conquering the country. Instead, he had to restore order through the rule of bureaucrats, who were certain to victimize the rebels.

During that audience on July 28, both Mao and the rebel leaders wept—the rebel leaders over being marginalized, and Mao because of his conflicted feelings toward the rebel faction.

The fact was that student rebels had waned in influence even before the Mao Zedong Thought Propaganda Teams entered the schools. Secondary school students had been sent "up the mountains and down to the countryside," and college students had been sent to PLA farms for "reeducation." When the Capital Workers and PLA Mao Zedong Thought Propaganda Team entered Tsinghua University, the student rebel faction had been active for only twenty months.

Article 4 of the Chinese Communist Party Central Committee Decree issued on August 28, 1969, stated: "All revolutionary mass organizations must resolutely execute the directives of the Great Leader Chairman Mao, and implement the revolutionary grand alliance according to apparatus, profession, department, and work unit. All trans-sectoral mass organizations must immediately disband. The establishment of other power bases or regrouping of contingents is illegal and will be forcibly disbanded."[13] This ended the freedom of association Mao had granted, and mass organizations withdrew from the political stage.

Given that the rebel faction was active in wider society for less than three years, it cannot be considered to have played the main role in the "ten years of turbulence." Yet, the rebel faction continued to come under attack in the subsequent One Strike and Three Antis campaign, the "one criticism and three investigations" campaign, the investigation of the May 16 clique, the Cleansing of the Class Ranks, and other political campaigns.

The rebels and the bureaucrats were all subjects of Mao's dynasty, and Mao commanded a portion of his subjects (the rebels) to attack another portion (the bureaucrats). Afterward, the emperor was still the same, and the imperial court was still the same, and the doctrine remained the same, and the bureaucrats continued to extol the "brilliance of the honored one" and maintain the original doctrine while taking revenge against the rebels who had attacked them under orders from that honored one.

In October 1976, a campaign was launched in every province and city to "expose, denounce, and investigate" the Gang of Four's black operators and black henchmen and to screen the activities of their alleged followers and people who had engaged in "beating, smashing, and looting." This evolved into a new campaign, described in chapter 27, in which multitudes of ordinary people who had joined the rebel faction were persecuted.

During the Cultural Revolution, the conservative faction demonstrated an ability to defend the existing order and the authority of the leaders, which suited it to reestablishing a new order after the Cultural Revolution. In the 1980s, some conservative faction leaders became celebrated senior officials, and no one made them accountable for their errors during the Cultural Revolution, even those who had slaughtered ordinary people while defending the interests of the bureaucracy.

A leader of a workers' rebel faction in Hubei, Hu Houmin, addressed this double standard while on trial on July 4, 1982: "It's unacceptable for one faction of victims to obtain a just and reasonable assessment and all kinds of generous considerations, while victims from another faction have not received just and reasonable assessments and are still shouldering all kinds of criminal charges . . . Isn't everyone supposed to be equal before the law? . . . I'm willing to take responsibility for the damage the rebel faction committed against the other side, so who's going to take responsibility for the harm inflicted on our side?" He detailed the political campaigns that had resulted in multitudes of people being denounced, jailed, wounded, and crippled, then asked, "Who should be made accountable, and how?"

10

THE "WORKERS COMMAND POST" AND SHANGHAI'S "JANUARY STORM"

As rebel mass organizations proliferated and spread with the denunciation of the bourgeois reactionary line, Mao hosted an intimate dinner to mark his seventy-third birthday on December 26, 1966. At the dinner, Mao noted that China's revolutionary movements had always begun with students and then spread to workers, peasants, and revolutionary intellectuals before achieving any results; that was an objective law. The May Fourth Movement had progressed in this way, and the Cultural Revolution was doing the same. While offering a toast, he said, "To all-out class struggle throughout the country!"[1]

WORKER REBELS TAKE THE STAGE

Prior to the Cultural Revolution, a person spent his or her entire working life at a single work unit. A unified work assignment resulted in stable employment but didn't allow workers to choose their occupation or place of work. In the urban areas, "Everyone had a job and enough to eat," but five people did the work of three while three people ate as much as five. One-third of those employed in any given factory were superfluous.

The state's unified system set and adjusted wages, which were paid out of the state treasury from the profits that enterprises were required to turn over to the state. There was no relationship between wages and economic performance. An eight-grade wage scale was adjusted nationwide every few years, with only a portion of workers allowed to advance to the next grade. From 1963 onward, wages were virtually frozen at a very low level. Worker households had almost no assets and were "proletarian" in fact as well as name. Employment, remuneration, and social security were implemented through the work unit, and leaving the work unit meant losing all security.

A person could work for decades without ever enjoying a decent home. In 1950, living quarters in Tianjin allotted an average of 3.8 square meters per person; by 1972, that average had dropped to 3 square meters. It was common for three generations to share a home measuring little more than 10 square meters.[2] Working environments were also atrocious; workers spent their days surrounded by toxic substances, and diseases associated with lead, benzene, and mercury poisoning were common, as was silicosis.

Factory managers, while earning only about three times as much as workers, enjoyed the significant advantages of superior living quarters, health care, the provision of scarce commodities, and better education and work opportunities for their children. The leadership status of workers extolled in political theory and news media was a matter of pride, but brought little benefit in terms of social wealth or a say in the workplace.

These conditions kept the working class relatively stable and disinclined to revolt. But poverty and inferior social status put workers into profound conflict with the bureaucratic clique, and once encouraged to rebel, they became a formidable force.

After the Cultural Revolution was launched, debate was intense among the top leaders over whether to allow workers to rebel.

On July 2, 1966, while Liu Shaoqi was still in charge, the Central Committee issued a notice regarding the effect that the Cultural Revolution was having on production and required that it be combined with the Four Cleanups movement. This notice stifled rebellion among the workers, and Mao, still away from Beijing at the time, was very displeased.[3]

At Mao's direction, soon after the Central Committee's October work conference, Chen Boda and Wang Li drafted "Twelve Directives on the Cultural Revolution in the Factories (draft)."[4] The Twelve

Directives came under harsh criticism by leaders on the industrial and communications front line at a seminar convened by the State Construction Commission chairman Gu Mu and the oil minister Yu Qiuli on November 16, 1966. Soundly endorsing the accomplishments of the industrial and communications sector over the past seventeen years, speakers at the seminar warned against the wholesale approach that the Cultural Revolution was taking in the culture and education fields and called for implementation in phases and without united rebel organizations among the workers.[5] The seminar produced its own "Fifteen Articles" ("Certain Stipulations on Carrying Out the Cultural Revolution in Industrial and Communications Enterprises"), which fundamentally negated the Twelve Directives.

At a Politburo meeting on December 4, Gu Mu emphasized that the industrial and communications sectors were faithful to Mao Zedong Thought and unthreatened by a "reactionary line," that their employee ranks enjoyed solidly proletarian leadership, and that it was essential for production and party work within these enterprises to remain uninterrupted. The Central Cultural Revolution Small Group launched into virulent criticism of Gu Mu's report. Wang Li accused Gu Mu of "a purely capitalist roader viewpoint," while Kang Sheng insisted, "The main problem causing a country to become revisionist is in the economic base, not in the culture and education departments."

In his remarks on December 6, Lin Biao thoroughly negated the Fifteen Articles and called for "actively pushing this revolution throughout the country and allowing it to sweep through and permoate every sector, and consciously expanding it, deepening it, and keeping it going." He also said, "Cadres have been in power for all these years, and they've done themselves credit and made great achievements, but if people aren't allowed to mention their shortcomings, degeneration is inevitable. It's essential to mobilize the masses to give them a good dose of criticism at this time! We must ensure that neither the bourgeois power-holders nor the proletarian power-holders get a good night's sleep!"[6]

By this time (due to the Anting Incident in Shanghai, described below), Tao Zhu knew that Mao supported trans-sectoral workers' organizations but still helped draft the Fifteen Articles that were diametrically contrary to Mao's views. Mao believed that Tao Zhu was maintaining the views that prevailed when Liu and Deng were in control. The criticisms aimed at the Fifteen Articles and Gu Mu during the December Politburo meeting therefore applied to Tao Zhu as well,[7] and Tao Zhu's fall from power was related to the issue of the industrial and communications sectors' engagement in the Cultural Revolution.

At the eleventh plenum of the Eighth Central Committee, Tao Zhu was listed fourth, after Mao, Lin Biao, and Zhou Enlai, as a member of the Politburo Standing Committee. He had taken some extremist stands, such as allowing big-character posters to be put up in the streets and saying that everyone but Mao and Lin was subject to suspicion and overthrow, but he insisted on mass organizations submitting to the leadership of party committees in the Cultural Revolution, and his role as "royalist" and "flame-snuffer" put him at loggerheads with Mao. Under Mao's instructions, Zhou Enlai presided over a meeting during which Tao Zhu was denounced as "China's biggest royalist" and "an agent of the Liu-Deng line," and Jiang Qing and Chen Boda called for Tao Zhu's overthrow at a mass rally on January 4.

On January 8, 1967, Mao observed: "The departments that Tao Zhu led have all collapsed. None of them was essential for revolution. The Ministry of Education couldn't handle it, the Ministry of Culture couldn't handle it, we couldn't handle it, but as soon as the Red Guards appeared, they could handle it. We didn't solve the problem of Tao Zhu, but the Red Guards rose up and solved it."[8] Mao also blamed Tao Zhu for an incident in which the Xinhua News Agency replaced Chen Yi's head with Deng Xiaoping's in a photo before it was published. The "head-switching incident" occurred because Deng was a member of the Politburo Standing Committee and Chen Yi wasn't, and members of the standing committee were supposed to be included in all published photographs. Tao Zhu was also labeled a traitor because of a document written by his elder brother, a senior Kuomintang military official, which described Tao Zhu's behavior while in a KMT prison.[9]

After Tao Zhu was struck down, some Central Committee elders objected to unseating a member of the Politburo Standing Committee without discussing the issue. Mao made a show of responding to these views at an enlarged meeting of the Politburo Standing Committee on February 10, where he criticized Chen Boda and Jiang Qing and said that Chen was "one standing committee member striking down another standing committee member."

A Politburo meeting on December 9, 1966, with Mao in attendance and Zhou Enlai presiding, passed Chen Boda's new draft of the Twelve Directives, titled "The CCP Central Committee's Ten Provisions on Seizing Revolution and Pushing Production" (known as the Industrial Ten Provisions, Central Committee Document No. 603 [1966]). This document proposed "maintaining eight-hour production" and "after-hours revolution," but it emphasized that factories could engage in the four bigs and that they should denounce the bourgeois reactionary line. It also stated that workers "had the right to form revolutionary organizations" and "could establish revolutionary ties in their own cities during their spare time" and that students were allowed to establish ties with workers.[10]

At his seventy-third birthday dinner on December 26, Mao said, "The participation of workers and peasants in the Cultural Revolution is an irresistible historical tide, and anyone who tries to obstruct it will be swept away by this historical tide. This is the essence of my dispute with Tao Zhu."[11]

All restrictions lifted, the Cultural Revolution was launched in the factories.

Factories were production units, and anyone in control of a factory, unless an absolute simpleton, had to emphasize production, even after the rebel faction took over from party organizations. In December 1966, disgusted with the factional fighting going on at Tsinghua University, several classmates and I organized the Red Apprentice Combat Group and lived at the Beijing Woolen Mill for one month. We spent half of every day laboring in the workshop and the other half observing the Cultural Revolution in the factory. The head of the rebel faction in this factory, surnamed Hong, had been a doctor in the factory clinic and initially had been labeled a counterrevolutionary, but after the bourgeois reactionary line was denounced, he became the factory's manager. He kept production going as normal, but eliminating some of the factory's regulations and excluding intellectuals did undermine the factory's management and technical work.

Some workers attacked as counterrevolutionaries and neo-rightists for supporting student rebels before it was allowed now became leaders of the workers' movement. The worker rebel faction was far more effective and sustained than the student rebel faction, and its social influence was enormous. Of the Red Guards who joined the Central Committee during the Ninth Party Congress, only Fudan's Chen Ganfeng[12] and Peking University's Nie Yuanzi came from the universities, while more than twenty were workers (some of them designated by the higher authorities and not members of the rebel faction).

THE ANTING INCIDENT

The Politburo's discussions and directives on worker rebel organizations in December 1966 have to be understood against the background of events in Shanghai immediately before then.

The first batch of big-character posters began appearing in Shanghai's factories in June and July 1966, most of them criticizing factory party committees and Four Cleanups work teams. "Combat groups" of various kinds also emerged.

On November 6, a sculpture student from the Beijing Academy of Fine Arts, Bao Pao (formerly Bao Changjia), chaired a meeting of more than thirty people from seventeen Shanghai factories at the Shanghai liaison station for the Capital Third Command Post in Jing'an District. Those in attendance included Wang Hongwen, Pan Guoping, Ye Changming, Dai Zuxiang, Chen Ada, Huang Jinhai, Fan Guodong, and Cen Qilin. After complaining of how factories had labeled rebel workers as counterrevolutionaries, the workers decided to establish a citywide workers' organization called the Shanghai Workers Revolutionary Rebel General Headquarters, or Workers Command Post (WCP), and then chose a leader from five candidates. Pan Guoping impressed the others as being dynamic and eloquent and having a true rebel spirit, but Wang Hongwen came from a poor peasant family, was a Communist Party member, and had fought in the Korean War. Considered more solid and reliable, Wang was ultimately elected.[13]

After the Workers Command Post was established, its legality became the main concern. The regulations at that time did not allow workers to establish trans-sectoral organizations, making anyone who joined the organization liable to attack. On November 9, the WCP held a mass rally at the Shanghai Culture Square to declare itself formally established and demanded that Mayor Cao Diqiu attend and acknowledge it as a "legal organization." Cao declined under the Shanghai municipal party committee's policy of "no attendance, no acknowledgment, and no support," and members of conservative mass organizations charged up to the rostrum to disrupt the rally. WCP members went to the municipal party committee offices demanding an audience with Cao Diqiu, and after ignoring them for hours, the municipal party committee finally told them to gather at the Shanghai Exhibition Center, where the chairman of the Shanghai Municipal Federation of Trade Unions, Zhang Qi, explained the Central Committee's policy against establishing trans-sectoral organizations. By this time it was past midnight and raining, and the workers had gone all day without eating; now they feared they would be persecuted after returning to their factories. In the confusion, someone shouted through a loudspeaker, "We need to go to Beijing and see Chairman Mao!" Sun Fuxiang from the No. 3 Bicycle Factory then used the loudspeaker to broadcast a fabricated "great news item" that Zhou Enlai had sent a cable saying, "If Cao Diqiu won't see you, I will!"[14] People took it seriously, and Wang Hongwen and others organized a group to go to Beijing to submit a complaint. This is one of many examples of the important role false rumors played in the development of mass incidents.

A group of WCP members immediately proceeded to Shanghai's northern train station, with a group led by Pan Guoping boarding a Red Guard train from Shanghai to Beijing, and Wang Hongwen leading another group onto the Beijing-bound no. 602 train. Pan Guoping's train was intercepted in Nanjing, and no. 602 was stopped at Anting Station. Shivering in the cold and rain, the workers lay down on the train tracks, disrupting train service on the Shanghai–Nanjing line for more than thirty-one hours.[15] This is what came to be known as the Anting Incident.

The Shanghai–Nanjing line being a major transport artery, the Shanghai municipal party committee quickly reported its suspension to the Central Committee. Zhou Enlai called a brief meeting of the Central Committee, which decided to have Chen Boda draft two cables. The first cable directed the East China Bureau to hold fast and refuse to acknowledge the legality of the WCP or the train-blocking as a revolutionary act, while the second cable was sent to the Shanghai worker rebels. Meanwhile, the Central Committee sent Zhang Chunqiao to Shanghai on a military aircraft on the night of November 11, with Chen Boda instructing him, "Go to the masses first and keep them from coming to Beijing, and solve the problem on the spot."[16]

By the time Zhang Chunqiao arrived in Anting at midnight, the situation was chaotic, and a municipal party cadre had to locate Pan Guoping, Bao Pao, Wang Hongwen, and several other workers so that Zhang Chunqiao could begin negotiating with them. Service had been restored on the Shanghai–Nanjing line, so the negotiations centered on getting the workers to return to Shanghai. Zhang started out with a show of strength, describing their actions as a counterrevolutionary incident: "Under the Central Committee's previous stipulations, sabotaging transport links alone would have qualified for a death sentence. Tonight's discussion is over whether or not you return to Shanghai, and anything else can be discussed further in Shanghai." Wang Hongwen and Pan Guoping were duly intimidated, and sensing an opportunity to back out of a perilous situation, they agreed to mobilize the others to return to Shanghai on the conditions that the Central Committee acknowledge the WCP as a revolutionary rebel organization, that their action be acknowledged as a revolutionary act, and that the municipal party committee bear the blame for this incident.

Pan Guoping then located two trucks at a nearby factory, fitted them with loudspeakers, and drove them to the coal-loading stack where the workers were gathered. Zhang Chunqiao, Wang Hongwen, and Pan Guoping stood on the trucks in the pouring rain as Wang and Pan ordered everyone back to Shanghai. There were catcalls from the workers, who felt betrayed. Zhang Chunqiao took over at that point, saying, "Comrade workers, the Great Leader Chairman Mao has sent me to call on you!" The crowd seethed with emotion, and cries of "Long live Chairman Mao!" rang out for a very long time. Zhang Chunqiao kept talking for nearly an hour and ended by telling everyone to return to Shanghai. Bao Pao and other Red Guards criticized Zhang Chunqiao for not supporting the workers, and the workers spent hours complaining of persecution at the hands of the local authorities.

Zhang's tone softened, and he promised to report to the Central Committee and Chairman Mao that the Shanghai municipal party committee had executed a bourgeois reactionary line. However, he still refused to acknowledge the Anting Incident as a revolutionary incident, or the WCP as a revolutionary rebel organization, merely saying that this could be discussed further after returning to Shanghai.

By this time, Zhang Chunqiao and the workers had been standing in the rain for thirteen hours with nothing to eat or drink. On Zhang's instructions, Wang Hongwen picked up his megaphone and announced that the WCP had decided that everyone should return to Shanghai to resolve the issue. Zhang Chunqiao then said, "Chairman Mao sent me to Shanghai to solve this problem. I will certainly take care of the Anting Incident, and I won't go back to Beijing until it's settled!" At noon, the National No. 17 Cotton Mill sent vehicles to pick up the workers, and with Wang Hongwen in the lead, everyone returned to Shanghai.

With the legality of the WCP still at issue, the workers were afraid they'd be accused of being counterrevolutionaries once they returned to Shanghai. Huang Jinhai led his group of workers straight to Shanghai Culture Square, and the others joined them there, demanding to see Zhang Chunqiao.[17] Upon learning that Zhang wanted to meet with the workers, the Shanghai municipal party committee called a meeting, which Zhang Chunqiao attended, and decided that it would not acknowledge citywide trans-sectoral organizations or acknowledge the Anting Incident as a revolutionary act.

The weather was bitter cold on November 13. Huang Jinhai assigned workers' pickets to maintain order among the workers gathered at Culture Square. Zhang Chunqiao arrived at 2:30 p.m. and began negotiating with Pan Guoping and Wang Hongwen in a small vestibule of the theater at the square.

The WCP wanted Zhang to sign off on five points: (1) acknowledging the Workers Command Post as a revolutionary and legal organization; (2) acknowledging the November 9 mass rally and attempt to petition Beijing as revolutionary acts; (3) making the East China Bureau and the Shanghai municipal party committee bear full responsibility for the consequences of this action; (4) making Cao Diqiu deliver a public self-criticism; and (5) facilitating the work of the WCP from now on.

Zhang Chunqiao kept making telephone calls from another room, always coming back with an anxious look on his face.[18] Finally he stopped making calls, and after pacing back and forth in the empty room for a while, he returned to the negotiations looking as if he'd reached a decision. On the point about the workers attempting to petition Beijing, he added the sentence, "If this situation arises again, you should send a small number of representatives." He then signed the paper: "Zhang Chunqiao, November 13, 1966, in Shanghai."[19]

On the evening of November 13, Zhang Chunqiao telephoned Chen Boda and reported his negotiation of the Five-Point Agreement and his understanding of the issue. Right after Zhang Chunqiao ended his call, Shanghai party chief Chen Pixian telephoned Chen Boda, wrathfully criticizing Zhang for flouting law and discipline by signing the agreement.[20]

On November 16 at 3:00 p.m., Mao called an enlarged meeting of the Politburo Standing Committee and said that the WCP conformed to the constitutional provisions on "freedom of association." Regarding Zhang Chunqiao's signing of the Five-Point Agreement without first requesting instructions from the Central Committee, Mao said, "It is permissible to act first and report afterward. Facts should always come before concepts."[21]

Mao placed the greatest importance on Beijing and Shanghai. In Beijing he supported the student Red Guards, and in Shanghai he supported the worker rebel organizations. Given the emblematic status of Shanghai's factory workers, Mao's legitimizing of the trans-sectoral WCP set an example for the entire country. From then on, trans-sectoral organizations sprang up all over the country and took the leading role in the Cultural Revolution.

As rebel workers established citywide organizations, the conservative faction followed suit. The Shanghai Workers Red Guardians (WRG), established on December 6, at one point reached a membership of eighty thousand.

The WRG immediately clashed with the WCP, starting with the *Liberation Daily* Incident on December 1. The Shanghai College Red Guards Revolutionary Committee (known as the Red Revolutionary Committee, or RRC for short) published an article in its official newspaper, *Red Guard War Communiqué*, accusing *Liberation Daily* of being "the faithful instrument of the Shanghai municipal party committee in promoting the bourgeois reactionary line" and demanding that *Liberation Daily* jointly deliver the *Communiqué* as a form of "disinfectant." On instructions from the municipal party committee, *Liberation Daily*'s leaders refused the demand, whereupon the RRC marched into the newspaper's office and forced it to suspend publication. A large group of WRG members responded by launching a protest nearby, shouting, "We want to read *Liberation Daily*!" A standoff ensued between a thousand rebel students inside the newspaper office and more than ten thousand workers outside the building. On December 4, the WCP sent a team to support the RRC, and after eight days and nights of fighting, the Shanghai municipal party committee finally acknowledged the demands of the RRC on December 8.

On December 23, the WRG held a mass rally at People's Square and relentlessly pestered Mayor Cao Diqiu until he signed off on eight demands opposing the WCP. The WCP responded with a mass denunciation rally at the square and forced Cao to nullify the paper he'd signed for the WRG. The enraged WRG sent a huge mob to surround the municipal party committee offices in Kangping Road, and by the afternoon of December 28, tens of thousands of people had joined a massive standoff between the two groups, blocking traffic in all directions.

Zhang Chunqiao's wife, Wen Jing, was one of a handful of people who remained in the Kangping Road compound, and she told Zhang of the situation that night. Zhang told Wen, "Ask Xu Jingxian to tell Shanghai's rebel organizations not to allow the WRG to snatch away the fruit of victory!"

Xu Jingxian, formerly party branch secretary of the municipal party committee's writing group, had on December 18 led a rebellion and established the Municipal Party Committee Organ Revolutionary Rebel Liaison Station, setting off a bomb in the core of the municipal party committee.[22] Like the WCP, the Rebel Liaison Station played a critical role in Shanghai, which was a bellwether for the entire country in the Cultural Revolution.

After Wen Jing passed Zhang Chunqiao's message to Xu Jingxian, the WCP launched an assault on the WRG in the early hours of December 30, and the WRG finally surrendered. Ninety-one people were injured, but none severely, and no one was killed.[23] Six big sacks of armbands were surrendered, along with hundreds of boxes of cookies. At 7:00 a.m., nearly twenty thousand WRG members lined up in six groups in the surrounding streets, where they received a scolding and were sent home.

THE "LETTER TO ALL RESIDENTS OF SHANGHAI" AND THE "URGENT NOTICE"

The WRG could hardly accept defeat so easily. On December 31, 1966, they replicated the WCP's Anting Incident by sending a force of twenty thousand to Shanghai's northern train station in an attempt to pile onto a Beijing-bound train. They were intercepted at the train station and diverted to Kunshan, but a dispatcher in the Shanghai Railway Branch Office, Wang Yuxi, was a leader of the WRG, and he convinced most of the dispatch officers to desert their posts, once again suspending service on the Shanghai–Nanjing line.

At midnight on December 31, 1967, Zhou Enlai telephoned Chen Pixian and told him to end his sick leave and return to the front line, arrest Wang Yuxi, and restore service on the Shanghai–Nanjing line as quickly as possible.[24] In the early hours of January 1, Zhang Chunqiao telephoned Xu Jingxian from Beijing and informed him of the serious situation on the railway, demanding that service be restored immediately and telling him of Zhou Enlai's phone call to Chen Pixian. Zhang told Xu, "It's possible that Chen Pixian no longer has any say-so, and I'm telephoning you so you can pass on the Central Committee's views at the meeting and persuade people to act accordingly."[25]

In accordance with Zhou Enlai's views, the Shanghai municipal party committee called a meeting, which Chen Pixian attended in his military uniform (he was first political commissar of the Shanghai Garrison Command). He passed on Zhou Enlai's directive, noting that twenty-six trains had been suspended, tens of thousands of passengers had been waylaid en route without food or water, some sixty freight trains had been disrupted, and Shanghai had only a week's supply of grain in storage: "We need to discuss how we're going to turn this situation around."[26]

Upon learning of the serious situation, the rebel faction leaders simply blamed the municipal party committee for inciting the masses against each other. Given that Chen Pixian had proven as ineffectual as Zhang Chunqiao had expected, Xu Jingxian launched into a scathing attack on Chen for refusing to acknowledge the rebel workers, and blaming him for the Kangping Road and Kunshan incidents. He then recommended that in accordance with instructions from the Central Cultural Revolution Small Group, rebel organizations should draft a joint statement appealing for the entire city to target the municipal party committee, in particular Chen Pixian and Cao Diqiu, and welcoming WRG members to return to their posts. Several student Red Guards set about drafting the statement, which Chen Pixian signed. *Wenhui Bao* was tasked with printing off two hundred thousand copies for citywide distribution, while Xu Jingxian and Wang Hongwen set off for Kunshan to deal with the WRG.[27] The "Letter to All Residents of Shanghai," subsequently published in the January 5 issue of *Wenhui Bao* and signed by twelve mass organizations headed by the WCP, accused capitalist roaders of "inciting a large group of their hoodwinked Worker Red Guardians" to "sabotage production and transportation in order to achieve their objective of sabotaging the Great Proletarian Cultural Revolution," and called on all workers to seize revolution and push production.

Meanwhile, on January 3, the rebel organization inside *Wenhui Bao* published a "Letter to Readers" on January 4 proclaiming that it had seized power. The same happened at *Liberation Daily*, with the rebel faction announcing on January 6 that the newspaper was no longer the official organ of the Shanghai municipal party committee.

On January 8, Mao called in Chen Boda, Kang Sheng, Jiang Qing, Wang Li, Guan Feng, Qi Benyu, Tang Pingzhu, Hu Chi, and others for a meeting. While speaking of the power seizure at the two Shanghai newspapers, Mao said: "Power seizures at two newspapers is a national issue, and we must support their rebellion. This is one class toppling another—it's a major revolution. These two newspapers stepping forward is sure to affect East China and the entire country."[28] He added, "They think we can't do without them, but don't you believe it!"[29] Mao also said that the "Letter to All Residents of Shanghai" was an essay of rare excellence that "talked about problems in Shanghai that are also national problems."[30] *People's Daily* reprinted the letter on January 9, with an editorial note quoting most of Mao's January 8 remarks.

Also on January 9, *Liberation Daily* and *Wenhui Bao* published the "Urgent Notice" along the same lines signed by thirty-two rebel organizations led by the WCP. The notice additionally called for freezing the revolving funds of all enterprises and institutions beyond what was necessary to cover production outlay, wages, Cultural Revolution expenses, operational expenses, and other legitimate expenses; wage adjustments, supplements, and benefits, were to be handled at a later stage. This demand targeted the "economism wind" (*jingjizhuyi feng*), which began in late 1966 or early 1967, when temporary workers, contract workers, apprentices, and other groups on society's lower rungs took advantage of the Cultural Revolution to try to improve their status through rebel organizations, forcing supervisors or even municipal-level leaders to sign agreements that resulted in massive bank withdrawals. Rebel leaders agreed to issue the "Urgent Notice" after Wang Hongwen and other WCP leaders reported this to Zhang Chunqiao and Yao Wenyuan as an urgent problem and demanded that the practice be halted. The CCP Central Committee, State Council, Central Military Commission, and CCRSG sent a congratulatory telegram on January 11 endorsing the "Urgent Notice."

The "Letter to All Shanghai Residents" and the "Urgent Notice" greatly enhanced the reputation of the WCP and other Shanghai rebel organizations and set the stage for them to seize power over the entire city. At a broadcast rally on January 22 for people who had come to Beijing from other localities, Zhou Enlai drew thunderous applause as he described the "Letter to All Shanghai Residents" and the "Urgent Notice" as marking a new stage in the Cultural Revolution, in which proletarian revolutionaries would unite the revolutionary masses to snatch back the party, government, and economic power usurped by bourgeois elements: "Only when the revolutionary masses have seized power will it be possible to denounce the smattering of capitalist roaders until they are struck down, thoroughly discredited, and destroyed."[31]

SHANGHAI'S "JANUARY STORM"

On January 2, 1967, the WCP and more than twenty other rebel organizations began preparing for a mass rally to denounce the leaders of the municipal party committee on January 6. Zhang Chunqiao and Yao Wenyuan arrived in Shanghai on January 4, with Zhang telling Xu Jingxian and others that the CCRSG had sent them to "stand with you." The next day, Zhang and Yao told the leaders of the WCP, "The most important issue at present is to gain control of key departments, including the ports, railways, power plants, waterworks, coal and gas, telephones, etc."[32]

On the day of the mass rally, the weather was hazy, and snow was trampled into slush as multitudes gathered at People's Square (it was subsequently announced that one hundred thousand attended). Chen Pixian, Cao Diqiu, Wei Wenbo, Han Zheyi, Ma Tianshui, Wang Yiping, Yang Xiguang, Wang Shaoyong, Liang Guobin, and other leaders of the East China Bureau and Shanghai municipal party committee were led to the stage to be denounced, while hundreds of bureau-level cadres served as secondary targets. Wang Hongwen delivered a speech (revised multiple times by Zhang Chunqiao) that "exposed the heinous crimes of the Shanghai municipal party committee in aiming their gun muzzle at the proletarian headquarters." Finally, a female Red Guard from Beijing represented the masses in reading out the rally's three general orders:

General order number 1: Cao Diqiu was to be removed as Shanghai's party secretary and mayor and handed over to the rebels for supervised labor. General order number 2: Chen Pixian was to acknowledge manipulating Cao Diqiu and the Shanghai municipal party committee to oppose Chairman Mao, resist the party Central Committee, and sabotage the Great Proletarian Cultural Revolution. General order number 3: The rally organizers would reorganize the Shanghai municipal party committee under instructions from the Central Committee.

The general orders treated Chen Pixian and Cao Diqiu differently because Mao had issued a "highest directive" that Chen could be "roasted a little, but not burnt to a crisp." The Central Committee had originally intended for Chen Pixian to come out and work, but Chen told Zhang Chunqiao that would be very difficult under the prevailing circumstances.[33] Chen's overthrow was by then a fait accompli.

Zhang Chunqiao and Yao Wenyuan watched the broadcast of the mass rally from the comfort of their guesthouse. Afterward, Zhang told Xu Jingxian, "With the weather so cold and the ground so slippery, standing there for hours without moving really takes discipline. It's amazing!"[34] Zhang had Xu made fifteen copies of all the speeches' texts, notices, and cables from the mass rally and sent them to the CCP Central Committee General Office.

Under the planning of Zhang Chunqiao, Yao Wenyuan, and others, the Shanghai Seize Revolution and Push Production Command Post was established on January 8 to take control of Shanghai's railways, ports, post and telecommunications, factories, and mines. The Great Proletarian Cultural Revolution Security Committee was also established to replace Shanghai's public security authorities, and the Rebel Organization Liaison Station replaced the Shanghai municipal party committee.

Other rebel organizations could hardly let the WCP reap all the benefit of the power seizure, and opposition soon emerged through the second most influential rebel organization, the Shanghai College Red Guards Revolutionary Committee. On the night of January 24, the RRC organized more than a dozen Red Guard groups to snatch the official seals of party and government organs, then issued a notice declaring that it had taken control of Shanghai.[35] When Zhang Chunqiao and Yao Wenyuan criticized their action, Red Guards under the RRC kidnapped Xu Jingxian on January 27, expecting him to provide them with information they could use to attack Zhang Chunqiao. The RRC also organized a mass rally against Zhang and Yao on the night of January 29, with further plans for a protest march the next day. Zhang and Yao sent an emergency report to the CCRSG, which on Mao's instructions immediately issued an "extra-urgent cable" criticizing the RRC for aiming the spearhead of struggle at Zhang Chunqiao, Yao Wenyuan, and the CCRSG rather than at the bourgeois reactionary line and capitalist roaders represented by Chen Pixian and Cao Diqiu.

With the entire propaganda apparatus mobilized against it, the RRC released Xu Jingxian and canceled its mass rally and parade and soon collapsed. Zhang Chunqiao, Yao Wenyuan, et al. retaliated against 2,500 of the young students involved, with more than two hundred placed under isolation and investigation, and more than four hundred obliged to attend study sessions. Five people were driven to suicide, six went insane, and many were disabled by beatings.[36]

EXPLORING NEW FORMS FOR THE STATE APPARATUS

The events in Shanghai were followed with great interest back in Beijing. At an enlarged meeting of the Politburo Standing Committee on January 16, Mao observed, "In the past, the armed forces contended for state power, but now it's the workers and peasants themselves contending for state power with the help of the military." He nevertheless delineated the limits of this takeover: "Taking control is very good, but only of administration and not of professional work; people should keep doing their original jobs, and we'll just handle the supervision."[37] However, the boundary disintegrated as the movement to seize power proceeded.

Having energetically endorsed the seizure of power in Shanghai, Mao had the Central People's Broadcasting Station air the congratulatory cable on the "Urgent Notice." On January 16, *People's Daily* published a *Red Flag* editorial that summarized the "Shanghai experience" as proletarian revolutionaries uniting and seizing power from of capitalist roaders within the party and "a revolution in which the proletariat eliminates the bourgeoisie," and credited Mao with "adopting yet another great strategic measure that will propel the Great Proletarian Cultural Revolution in a new leap throughout the country."

People's Daily followed up on January 22 with an editorial personally vetted by Mao that extolled developments in Shanghai as "an immense pioneering undertaking in the International Communist Movement, and a major event unequaled in human history." The editorial stated, "Power is everything. Without power, there is nothing. Come together in unity and seize power! Seize power! Seize power!"

On January 31, 1967, *People's Daily* published in advance *Red*

Flag's February 3 editorial, which abjured reformism and peaceful transition in favor of "thoroughly smashing it to pieces . . . and creating a new organizational form of state apparatus under dictatorship of the proletariat."

Thoroughly destroying the old state apparatus and creating it anew was a principle derived from the Paris Commune, and the victors in the Shanghai power seizure accordingly declared the establishment of a Shanghai People's Commune at a million-strong mass rally on February 5, 1967.[38]

This was in line with Mao's utopian vision of a three-in-one regime that included representatives from mass organizations, leftist party officials, and rebel-supporting army personnel, and Mao had Wang Li telephone Shanghai and Heilongjiang to tell them to adopt the people's commune as their form of governance.[39] However, Mao soon had second thoughts about what would be entailed in eradicating the separation of party from government and legislative from executive powers, and in uniting public security, procuratorial, and judicial functions under the "dictatorship of the masses." On February 12, Mao recalled Zhang Chunqiao and Yao Wenyuan to Beijing. After expressing his approval of their work in Shanghai, Mao said that establishing a People's Commune would involve issues in the entire state system, including amendment of the constitution and diplomatic recognition. Mao said it would be better to call Shanghai's governing body a revolutionary committee instead.[40]

In accordance with Mao's views, the Shanghai Revolutionary Committee was established on February 23. Establishing a three-in-one revolutionary committee in place of a commune was a compromise of Mao's idealism in the face of hard reality, but he didn't abandon his concept of a new regime.

At the outset, the new governing organs had a flavor of nearness to the masses. Representatives on the revolutionary committees continued to draw wages from their original work units and had no special privileges. When Wang Hongwen subsequently became vice-chairman of the Central Committee, he still drew his wages from Shanghai. When Wu Guixian became vice-premier of the State Council, she continued to draw the same wages she had always been paid from her factory in Xi'an. Leaders attending State Council meetings had to pay for their own tea. Cadres who joined the three-in-one leadership ranks were under the supervision of the masses, and weren't allowed to "walk the old road in new shoes."

In the administrative structure, mergers reduced the number of organs and staff. Prior to the Cultural Revolution, the Tianjin municipal party committee and government had more than one thousand cadres, but the new apparatus had only two hundred, a goodly portion of whom came from the military. The 80 percent of staff who were downsized were sent to labor at May 7 cadre schools.[41]

Class A state organs also cut staff down to the bone. The State Council's original ninety ministries and commissions were reduced to twenty-seven in June 1970, and more than 80 percent of the staff were cut, from 53,784 to just 9,710.[42]

Every level of the leadership structure was referred to as a "group," and there were no directors, only group chairs. The result was "big groups encapsulating small groups, all equal in power." Boundaries and responsibilities were unclear, and management at all levels was chaotic. Furthermore, the newly established revolutionary committees didn't employ modern management concepts of minimizing malpractice through systemic and legal checks and balances; it remained an essentially omnipotent governance body. Duties and responsibilities did not change and still had to be handled by someone. From 1970 onward, the original government organs were gradually restored, and by 1972, the government structure was even more bloated than before It could be said that establishment of the revolutionary committees marked the gradual return of the old government. People who believed in the principles of the Paris Commune found this intolerable, and in many places the rebel faction launched campaigns against this "reversion to the past."

Representatives of the masses in the various revolutionary committees (typically the leaders of relatively moderate rebel factions) were from the outset not allowed to control the most important departments of authority. Some managed to fulfill the role of opposition faction by "locking horns" within the committees or by organizing mass pressure outside the committees, only to be expelled on pretexts such as "eliminating factionalism," or investigated and imprisoned as "May 16 elements."[43] The mass representatives who submitted to those in authority became genuine bureaucrats.

For the time being, however, the appeals by Mao and the Central Committee caused the power-seizure movement to genuinely "sweep through the entire country with overwhelming and overpowering force." It was what Mao spoke of as a "full-scale class struggle," in which leading cadres were denounced across the board and suffered unprecedented devastation.

11

THE "FEBRUARY COUNTERCURRENT" AND THE "FEBRUARY SUPPRESSION OF COUNTERREVOLUTIONARIES"

The January power seizure paralyzed the bureaucracy at every level as the party's organized activities ceased and rebels created chaos throughout the country. The revolutionary old guard responded by mounting a resistance that was soon denounced as a "February Countercurrent" and was accompanied by a new round of military suppression against rebels throughout the country. This latter campaign, which came to be known as the "February Suppression of Counterrevolutionaries," began in February 1967 and lasted into the summer.

THE RESISTANCE OF THE REVOLUTIONARY OLD GUARD

According to Qiu Huizuo:

> When the rebels turned their spearhead toward us, senior cadres spontaneously rose up in resistance. Some advocated production and business as a pretext to oppose revolution; some engaged in purely academic criticism to "beat a dead tiger"; some let the masses run amok and allowed the situation to run its course while they sat by and watched; some organized model workers and party and Youth League mainstays to take part in the four bigs; the bolder tried to create difficulties for the rebels

while secretly recording their activities so they could be purged later. I belonged to that last category.[1]

Members of the revolutionary old guard regularly met to discuss the situation. Ye Jianying hosted the marshals in his home; frequent guests included Nie Rongzhen, who lived nearby in the Western Hills, and Chen Yi. Chen Yi and Ye Jianying were both great gastronomes, and the air force was constantly bringing Ye pangolin, fruit fox, snakes, and turtles from the south. Members of the old guard who weren't in the military gathered at the home of Li Fuchun. Li became a member of the Politburo Standing Committee in the eleventh plenum of the Eighth Central Committee, and he and his wife, Cai Chang, were friends of Mao's, so members of the old guard hoped he could relay their views to Mao.[2]

Their dissatisfaction developed into actual resistance against the Central Cultural Revolution Small Group at a meeting of the Central Military Commission Standing Committee in January 1967 and at Central Committee briefing sessions on February 11 and 16. The marshals and vice-premiers didn't risk openly criticizing the CCRSG, however; instead, they took advantage of Mao's capricious criticism of Chen Boda and Jiang Qing for striking down Tao Zhu. At an enlarged meeting of the Politburo Standing Committee on February 10, Mao castigated Jiang for "high aims but limited abilities, great ambition but little talent," and accused her of withholding information from him.[3]

Emboldened by Mao's criticism, several old marshals crossed swords with Jiang Qing and Chen Boda at enlarged meetings of the CMC Standing Committee held in the Jingxi Guesthouse on January 19 and 20. At one of these meetings, Jiang and Chen criticized the head of the General Political Department, Xiao Hua, as a "bourgeois politician" and said the department was trying to upstage the CCRSG, while the military in general was refusing to actively engage in the four bigs. When they ordered Xiao Hua to carry out self-criticism at a rally of one hundred thousand people at the Workers' Stadium that night, Ye Jianying and Nie Rongzhen withdrew from the meeting in protest.

Zhou Enlai said that Xiao could only make a self-criticism at a rally under his orders, and went with Ye Jianying to report the matter to Mao, effectively preventing the rally from taking place. That night, however, the military's rebel faction ransacked Xiao Hua's home, and Xiao fled out the back door and sought refuge in Ye Jianying's home. At the CMC Standing Committee meeting the next day, high-ranking military officers who were aware of Mao's intention to protect Xiao criticized the CCRSG. When Jiang Qing demanded to know where Xiao Hua had gone into hiding, Ye Jianying pounded on the table and said, "If giving shelter is a crime, I'll bear the blame!" He went on to criticize the CCRSG: "Anyone who tries to cause chaos in the military ranks will face dire consequences!" Ye pounded the table so violently that he fractured the metacarpal bones in his right hand. This incident became known as the "Commotion in the Jingxi Guesthouse."[4]

After the meeting, Ye Jianying reported to Lin Biao on Jiang Qing's and Chen Boda's attacks on the military and made an impassioned appeal to stabilize the military ranks. Mao received military leaders on January 22, asking them to side with the left, while at the same time patiently listening to their complaints of political victimization and agreeing that the army needed to be stabilized.

At a Central Committee briefing session convened by Zhou Enlai at Huairen Hall on February 11, Ye Jianying reprimanded Kang Sheng, Chen Boda, and Zhang Chunqiao, saying, "You've thrown the party and the government into confusion, you've thrown the factories and the villages into confusion, and that's still not enough! Now you want to throw the army into confusion as well! What exactly are you trying to do?" Marshal Xu Xiangqian pounded the table and said, "The army is the pillar of the dictatorship of the proletariat! If you send the army into disarray, are you going to do without that pillar?" Nie Rongzhen was particularly angry about the arrest of Red Guards from the United Action Committee, and said, "You can't go striking a man down and then seize and struggle his children and pull the whole family into it. This brutal persecution of veteran cadres is kicking a man when he's down! It's pure malice!"[5]

Zhou Enlai convened another briefing session at Huairen Hall on February 16 to discuss "seizing revolution and pushing production." Before the meeting started, Tan Zhenlin asked Zhang Chunqiao, "Why won't you allow Chen Pixian[6] to come to Beijing?" Zhang said,

"When we go back, we'll discuss it with the masses." Tan Zhenlin said, "Yes the masses, the masses, always the masses—isn't the party supposed to be leading them? Your aim is to get rid of all the veteran cadres—you're attacking them one by one. After forty years of revolution, their families are being destroyed and their wives and children dispersed. The children of cadres are being made into political victims . . . This is the most brutal struggle in the history of the party. It's worse than anything that's ever happened before . . . I've never wept in my life, but now I've wept three times." Li Xiannian said, "I've also wept several times." Tan Zhenlin became more agitated as he spoke: "I'm sorry I ever joined the revolution. I should never have joined the party. I'm sorry I've lived this long. I'm finished! Chop off my head, send me to prison, expel me from the party—I'll keep fighting to the end!" Chen Yi said, "Didn't Stalin hand over power to Khrushchev, who carried out revisionism once he was in power?" He observed that people such as Liu Shaoqi and Peng Zhen who had been active participants in the Yan'an Rectification Movement were now energetically opposing Mao Zedong Thought, and that people who were active in the Cultural Revolution would change in the future as well. Li Xiannian said, "How can the United Action Committee be a reactionary organization? Can seventeen- or eighteen-year-old kids be counterrevolutionaries?" This kept going until Zhou Enlai finally adjourned the meeting seven o'clock that night.[7]

This was what came to be known as the "Commotion in Huairen Hall."

After the meeting, Wang Li, Zhang Chunqiao, and Yao Wenyuan immediately wrote up a record of the event, which Wang Li then drafted into minutes that were amended by Chen Boda and Zhou Enlai. At a point where Chen Yi mentioned political persecution in Yan'an, Zhou added, "It was right for me to make self-criticism and to be punished. I was wrong, and I've never objected to the criticism at that time."[8]

After Zhang Chunqiao, Wang Li, and Yao Wenyuan told Jiang Qing what had happened, Jiang Qing said they should immediately inform Chairman Mao. Around ten o'clock that night, the three of them went to report to Mao on the meeting.

In the early hours of February 19, Mao called a meeting attended

by Zhou Enlai, Ye Qun (representing Lin Biao), Kang Sheng, Li Fu-
chun, Ye Jianying, Li Xiannian, and Xie Fuzhi. Kang Sheng was the
only member of the CCRSG who attended, and he took detailed notes.
Mao lost his temper at the meeting, saying, "I'll be leaving soon, and
Lin Biao as well! Chen Boda and Jiang Qing will be executed! Kang
Sheng can be sent into military servitude and the Central Cultural
Revolution Small Group will be reorganized. Let them take over—
Chen Yi can be director, and Tan Zhenlin and Xu Xiangqian can be
the deputy directors, and they can get Yu Qiuli and traitors like Bo
Yibo and An Ziwen to serve as group members. If they need more
manpower, they can get Wang Ming and Zhang Guotao to come back.
And if they're worried that's still not enough, they can invite the U.S.
and the Soviet Union as well!" Mao recommended that the Politburo
resolve the matter, and it was decided then and there to hold a "life
meeting"[9] for Chen Yi, Tan Zhenlin, and Xu Xiangqian and to have
them "take leave to carry out self-criticism." Mao said that the CCRSG
was executing the spirit of the eleventh plenum of the Eighth Central
Committee and at least 97 percent correct. "I will resolutely oppose
whoever opposes the CCRSG! You want to negate the Cultural Revolution? Impossible!"[10] After returning to the CCRSG, Kang Sheng
said, "In all the years I've been with the Chairman, I've never seen
him lose his temper this way."[11]

After learning of Mao's views later that day, Chen Yi realized how
serious the problem had become, and he went that night to see Zhou
Enlai. He also wrote a letter to Mao asking for an opportunity to explain things to his face, but Mao refused to see him, saying that Chen
Yi had "constantly made mistakes" and "would not easily change."[12]

This resistance by the party veterans came to be called the "February Countercurrent." Mao knew very well that in order to stage a
counterattack, he needed to ensure Lin Biao's reliability. The night
before the meeting where he flew into a rage, Mao suddenly called Ye
Qun to his quarters in Zhongnanhai for a talk and ranted, "Chen Yi,
Tan Zhenlin, Li Fuchun, Xu Xiangqian, Nie Rongzhen, Ye Jianying,
and Li Xiannian are all opposing the Cultural Revolution. They're not
listening to me or going along with me anymore . . . If the PLA doesn't
follow me, the three of us should go south, organize another PLA, as-
cend Jinggang Mountain again, and make a new start." Ye Qun

immediately said that Lin Biao would follow Chairman Mao to the death. Mollified, Mao instructed Ye Qun to attend meetings of the Central Committee Standing Committee and enlarged CCRSG briefing meetings on Lin Biao's behalf.[13]

After venting his rage at the meeting, Mao had Zhou Enlai preside over a "Politburo democratic life meeting" at Huairen Hall from February 25 to March 18, 1967, during which members of the CCRSG gave impassioned speeches. Kang Sheng said, "Chairman Mao's rage is the rage of the proletariat. This is the most serious anti-Party incident since the eleventh plenum. It's a preview of a coup d'état—a preview of the restoration of capitalism." Jiang Qing said that the party elders had engaged in a "bourgeois restorationist countercurrent." Each of the veteran cadres had to make an in-depth self-criticism.

Meanwhile, Qi Benyu and some other CCRSG members informed college rebel leaders in Beijing of the "capitalist restorationist countercurrent," and soon the streets were plastered with slogans proclaiming, "Down with Tan Zhenlin!" and "Resolutely Retaliate Against the 'February Countercurrent'!" Rebels in some other localities followed suit.

The denunciations at the Politburo democratic life meetings thoroughly routed the veteran cadres who had opposed the CCRSG. The briefing sessions of the Politburo Standing Committee that Zhou Enlai had held to handle the routine operations of the party, government, and army were suspended and replaced with enlarged CCRSG briefing meetings. Mao had Zhou Enlai preside over these meetings, but as Jiang Qing took an increasingly important role on the political stage, the CCRSG effectively replaced both the Politburo and the Central Committee Secretariat.

Falling out with so many veteran cadres was hardly a good thing, however, and as tough as Mao was, he was adept at the tactic of putting on pressure and then releasing it, and he took the initiative to approach each of the party veterans in the latter half of April 1967. He referred to the opinions they'd expressed regarding the Cultural Revolution as mere grousing, and said that what they'd done was all open and aboveboard, not scheming. Mao laughingly asked Tan Zhenlin, "Boss Tan, are you still mad? I'm not. Let's reach a gentleman's agreement not to curse each other."[14] On May Day, Zhou Enlai took advantage of Mao's more appeasing attitude to have the party veterans put in an appearance at Tiananmen gate tower. At the same time, worried that they might again cause a fuss, Zhou wrote a letter addressed to Chen Yi, Tan Zhenlin, Li Xiannian, Hu Qiuli, Gu Mu, and Li Fuchun, warning them not to get a "mistaken impression" from the May Day get-together and "head down a blind alley" by carrying out "retaliatiory attacks." He said, "You would completely lose the trust of the people and the Party, and it would be no great matter for the Party or the revolution. This reflects class struggle within the Party, and will be a profound lesson for the revolutionary young soldiers."[15]

As Zhou Enlai predicted, Mao didn't let the party elders off, and they were again called to account for the February Countercurrent at the twelfth plenum of the Eighth Central Committee in 1968. This will be covered in more detail later.

THE FEBRUARY SUPPRESSION OF COUNTERREVOLUTIONARIES

While the February Countercurrent was confined to conference rooms, the February Suppression of Counterrevolutionaries was a bloody suppression of the rebel faction. The suppression lasted from February until it was brought under control by the Central Committee's "Resolution Regarding the Anhui Problem" on April 1, 1967,[16] and didn't come to a complete halt until the "July 20 Incident" in Wuhan.

On January 23, 1967, the Central Committee ordered the army to carry out a policy of supporting the left, but some mass organizations felt suppressed rather than supported and began organizing attacks on the military. In mid-February, Mao issued a memo on how to handle these attacks, the gist of which was that rightist mass organizations should be dealt with through persuasion and retreat; if the masses pushed these concessions too far, the troops were allowed to open fire to protect themselves, but could only suppress core leaders. Lin Biao had his secretary Zhang Yunsheng send this memo to the CMC's secretary-general, Ye Jianying, who promptly passed it along at an enlarged CMC meeting as a sign that "the Chairman placed extreme importance on the stability of the armed forces."[17] The military leaders took this as permission to open fire on whoever attacked them.

The suppression of rebel factions occurred under two scenarios: The first was suppression carried out by government and military bureaucrats opposed to the Cultural Revolution, with the cooperation of conservative mass organizations, and followed the thinking of the February Countercurrent. The second was suppression carried out by support-the-left troops and certain rebel groups against other rebel groups that were seen as opposing the revolutionary committees (or the revolutionary committee preparatory committees), and the thinking behind it had nothing in common with the February Countercurrent. The February 23 Incident in Qinghai belonged to the first type of suppression, while the suppression in Guizhou belonged to the second type. The nationwide suppression from February to May 1967 was even harsher than the suppression of counterrevolutionaries in the early 1950s. During these few months, millions of rebel faction members were detained throughout the country. Following are descriptions of some of the anti-rebel campaigns.

THE FEBRUARY 23 INCIDENT IN QINGHAI

On June 3, 1966, *Qinghai Daily* published an editorial that reprised the gist of Mao's speech to the enlarged meeting of the Politburo Standing Committee in Hangzhou in mid-April calling for the masses to rise up in rebellion. The publisher of *Qinghai Daily*, Cheng Guangyuan, and the editorial's drafter, Chen Yi, ended up being attacked as the "Cheng-Chen anti-party clique" because of this editorial, but by then the fire of rebellion had been ignited in Qinghai. The counterattack by the conservative faction was also intense. By August, Qinghai's mass organizations were divided into two main factions: One was the Qinghai Province August 18 Revolutionary Rebel Headquarters (8-18), and the other was the conservative faction consisting of the Red Guard Headquarters, Poor and Lower-Middle Peasant Red Guards, and Mao Zedong Thought Defense Force. A series of violent confrontations occurred between these two large factions of mass organizations.

After the CCP Central Committee issued its resolution for the military to support the leftist revolutionary masses, the standing committee of the Qinghai provincial military district under commander Liu

Xianquan on January 23 decided to support the 8-18 faction and reported this decision to the higher levels. However, the majority of cadres in the military district, including Zhao Yongfu, the deputy commander, did not accept this decision. They quickly formed the Headquarters (later renamed Command Post) of the Qinghai Province Military District Office Revolutionary Rebel Masses and demanded nullification of the decision to support the 8-18 faction. Around nine o'clock that night, they seized Liu Xianquan, stripping him of his cap and collar insignia, detaining and beating him, and ransacking his home.[18]

The political commissar of the Lanzhou Military Region, Xian Henghan, considered Zhao Yongfu's attack on Liu Xianquan "a completely extra-organizational action, and very serious in nature." At that time, Xian Henghan was in charge of support-the-left work in Gansu, Qinghai, Ningxia, and Shaanxi.

On January 25, Zhao Yongfu became the effective top leader in Qinghai Province with the support of Zhang Xiaochuan, deputy director of the PLA General Logistics Department's Qinghai-Tibet administrative office. Meanwhile, the 8-18 faction seized the official seals of the provincial party committee and people's committee on January 29, but its only real power was its control of *Qinghai Daily*, which became the hub of the province's rebel organizations and a major headache for Zhao Yongfu. Zhao repeatedly demanded that the Lanzhou Military Region put the newspaper under military control, to no avail.

On February 3, Zhao Yongfu mobilized more than 250 battle-ready vehicles from the PLA garrison at Qinghai's capital, Xining, and carried out a military demonstration to "support the revolutionary factions and suppress counterrevolutionaries." Zhao and the Xining Garrison Command followed up on February 14 with a report stating that *Qinghai Daily*, "under the control of a smattering of people with ulterior motives, has distorted facts, created rumors and transmitted false reports. It has been resolved to impose military control on *Qinghai Daily*, effective immediately." Red Guards from more than twenty schools swarmed into *Qinghai Daily*'s compound to "defend the newspaper." The army surrounded the newspaper offices and demanded the withdrawal of 8-18 and other rebel faction organizations. This was met with refusal, and a nine-day standoff ensued.

Eventually, martial law was imposed on Xining on the morning of February 23. The Xining Garrison Command issued a general order banning 8-18 and warning that continued unlawful activities would be dealt with severely. Troops of the provincial military district laid siege to the newspaper compound and blocked the highway between Xining and Lanzhou. Violence resulted, and by early afternoon, 169 people were dead and 178 wounded.

Responding to Zhao's claim that troops had fired in self-defense on an "armed rebellion" by 8-18, a CMC leader telephoned Zhao Yongfu later that evening, saying, "Splendid battle! . . . The CMC supports you," and urged Zhao to round up the "remnants of the counterrevolutionaries." Zhao later told people that "Vice-Chairman Lin [Biao]" had called him,[19] but in fact it was Ye Jianying who called, as confirmed by the *Chronology of Ye Jianying*.

After this February 23 incident, the provincial military district carried out a mass "arrest, attack, struggle, and ransack" campaign against 8-18. Liu Xianquan said that "10,157 people were detained, arrested, or placed under guard or house arrest, with 4,131 of them formally arrested. The masses were subjected to all kinds of torture in the process of 'extort, confess, believe,'[20] and not only the principal suspects were beaten, bound and had their homes ransacked, but also family members and children."[21]

In early March, the General Political Department of PLA headquarters ordered Liu Xianquan, Zhang Jianglin (deputy commander of the Qinghai Provincial Military District), and Zhao Yongfu to Beijing for a meeting of military cadres. Liu and Zhang were brought to Beijing under escort. It appears that the CMC accepted Zhao Yongfu's description of "suppressing a counterrevolutionary rebellion" and supported him.

Soon afterward, the CCRSG received many letters and petitions from Red Guards who had returned from Qinghai. There were also letters of complaint, some written in blood, from parents of Beijing students tearfully reporting that their children had gone to Qinghai for the Great Networking and now they didn't know if they were dead or alive.

On March 11, Mao and Lin Biao each issued memos demanding an investigation into the Qinghai matter. With Zhou Enlai's direct involvement, a conclusion was soon drawn and recorded in a document jointly issued by the CCP Central Committee, State Council, CMC, and CCRSG, which Zhou announced on the evening of March 29 to mass organization representatives in the Anhui Hall of the Great Hall of the People. The document declared Zhao Yongfu's actions a "counterrevolutionary coup d'état" and a "brutal armed suppression of the Xining 8-18 group and other revolutionary mass organizations." It stated: "Zhao Yongfu gave false reports about the military situation to deceive the Central Committee and hoodwink the masses by saying that 8-18 and the other revolutionary mass organization had a large number of weapons and opened fire first, which was utterly unfounded."[22]

The CMC issued an order granting the provincial military district commander and party secretary, Liu Xianquan, full responsibility for handling the Qinghai issue with the help of leading comrades from the Lanzhou Military Region. The dead and wounded revolutionary masses had their reputations fully restored, and compensation was paid to comfort the bereaved, along with medical treatment for the wounded. All revolutionary masses arrested were immediately released, and those labeled counterrevolutionaries were rehabilitated.

Ten years later, Ye Jianying sent two directives to the Lanzhou Military Region political commissar and Gansu provincial party chief Xian Henghan, demanding Zhao Yongfu's release from prison. Xian resisted and was later labeled a representative of the Gang of Four in Gansu, while Zhao was eventually released and granted an advisory position in the Beijing Military Region.[23]

SICHUAN'S SUPPRESSION OF COUNTERREVOLUTIONARIES

The Chengdu Military Region supported the conservative Industrial Army, and as a result, it came under violent opposition by the rebel faction's Chengdu Workers Rebel Corps and Sichuan University August 26 Combat Unit, which carried out a sit-in protest in front of the military region headquarters, followed by actual attacks. On February 17, Ye Jianying signed and issued an open letter from the CMC criticizing the two rebel organizations and warning their leaders of serious consequences if they continued to incite the masses against the military and attack military organs. The Chengdu Military Region dispatched helicopters to air-drop leaflets of Ye Jianying's "February 17 Open Letter" throughout Sichuan Province, as well as imposing martial law and sending out heavily armed and manned military vehicles to round up the instigators, but the rebel organizations refused to retreat.

With the enthusiastic cooperation of the conservative Industrial Army, the Chengdu Military Region and local judicial, procuratorial, and public security organs staged a joint action during which a large number of leaders and mainstays of the Chengdu Workers Rebel Corps were arrested. Designated a counterrevolutionary organization and attacked at every level, the group collapsed in mid-March. The Sichuan University August 26 Combat Unit survived, but its leaders and key members were arrested, and the rest of its members were required to acknowledge their error, inform against their "bad leaders," and identify their "backstage supporters." Other associated rebel organizations were implicated, with 1,100 groups banned and more than 80,000 leaders and core members arrested, including more than 33,000 in Chengdu alone.[24]

As the scope of attack gradually expanded, Chengdu's prisons overflowed, and temples were commandeered to hold detainees.[25] Believing reported estimates on the number of people arrested, Mao said at the twelfth plenum of the Eighth Central Committee, "Who told you to carry out the February Countercurrent and arrest 100,000 people? You wrongly arrested people and then released them. Has the problem been resolved? Hasn't everyone been released?" Zhang Guohua interjected, "There are still five hundred left, and they're all criminals." Mao continued, "So you released 95,000 people. Doesn't the fact that you released them prove that you were wrong?"[26]

The February Suppression in Chongqing involved part of the rebel faction (August 15) suppressing another part of the rebel faction (Rebel to the End). After the Cultural Revolution, the Chongqing Municipal Public Security Bureau Historical Gazetteer Office reported that 2,253 people were arrested and that twenty-four mass organizations were banned as counterrevolutionary or illegal organizations.[27] The figure provided by the rebel faction mass organizations was much larger.

On February 22, 1967, the Sichuan Wan County Military Subdistrict announced that the rebel faction organization Main Force was a counterrevolutionary organization and that the Red Flag group was a counterrevolutionary gang, and it repeatedly broadcast notices of martial law being imposed in certain sectors. Students took to the streets in protest, and workers, cadres, and ordinary citizens soon joined their ranks. The army attacked Zhenyuan Hall (originally a church), where Main Force was based, and began strafing it with bullets, shooting five people dead on the spot. When an enraged mob poured into Zhenyuan Hall to grab the bodies, the military opened fire, and another eighteen people were killed on the spot, along with a passerby struck by a stray bullet, bringing the total death toll to twenty-four. The rebel masses staged a protest march, carrying eighteen of the bodies around the city. This incident became known as the Wan County February 22 Counterrevolutionary Suppression Incident. The military region subsequently staged another roundup of dozens of rebel faction leaders, who were escorted to their work units to be struggled.[28]

SUPPRESSION OF COUNTERREVOLUTIONARIES IN OTHER PROVINCES

Hubei: On March 21, the Wuhan Military Region issued a notice that banned Wuhan's largest workers' rebel organization, the Wuhan Workers Rebel General Headquarters, as a counterrevolutionary organization. Conservative organizations that had fallen from power rapidly revived, the most influential of them being Red Soldiers, which was supported by all levels of the armed forces and composed of people's armed militias. The military region also established "provincial and municipal offices to seize revolution and push production" (known as "seize offices"), which were used by leading cadres who supported the military region's viewpoints to suppress the rebel faction.[29]

Fujian: On February 11, two hundred thousand soldiers and civilians in Fuzhou staged a "pledge rally against renewed resurgence of the bourgeois reactionary line." During the rally, the commander of the Fuzhou Military Region, Han Xianchu, denounced a rebel faction attack on the military region headquarters as "a counterrevolutionary countercurrent." At a mass rally on March 9, leaders of the rebel organizations Red September 2 and Fujian Province Teachers and Staff Red Guards were publicly arrested, and the Fujian Province Military Control Commission ordered the disbanding of some rebel faction mass organizations. According to the Military Control Commission's figures, more than two thousand people were subsequently arrested or detained, and more than eighty mass organizations were disbanded.[30]

Guizhou: From February to March 1967, 218 revolutionary mass organizations with a total of 520,000 members were labeled "reactionary organizations," and more than 2,000 people were imprisoned. The February Suppression of Counterrevolutionaries in Guizhou[31] took place after the provincial revolutionary committee was established, and was actually executed by the CCRSG. It targeted those who rebelled against the new power establishment, including rebel organizations without representatives in the revolutionary committee (radical rebel faction organizations were excluded for obstructing the "grand alliance" and the "three-in-one combination") and those who were represented but felt that their representatives were sidelined. This situation became even more common in the various provinces in 1968.

Hunan: In Hunan, it was mainly two large rebel organizations, the Workers' Alliance and Xiang River Storm, that were suppressed. Most of their members were workers, especially industrial workers who were employed in large factories and enjoyed strength in numbers. At the beginning of February, the Hunan Military District sent up a report calling Xiang River Storm a "conservative" organization and charging it with various violent and destructive actions. Chen Boda issued a memo in February declaring Xiang River Storm a reactionary organization and instructing the Hunan Military District to arrest its leaders. An estimated one hundred thousand people were detained throughout the province at this time.

Henan: Henan's three factions were the February 7 Commune, and the opposing Henan Rebel Headquarters and Ten Big Headquarters. In early March 1967, the Henan provincial military district declared the February 7 Commune an "illegal organization" and detained thousands of people. The First Army, stationed in Kaifeng, also opened fire on protesters. On March 8, Henan's security apparatus set up a "registration station" at Zhengzhou University and ordered more than two hundred members of the Zhengzhou University Alliance Committee (which shared the standpoints of the February 7 Commune) to turn themselves in and produce an acceptable self-criticism within forty-eight hours. The Alliance Committee was declared an illegal organization, and more than forty of its members were jailed.[32]

Nanjing: Nanjing Military Region commander Xu Shiyou sent in tanks to suppress the rebel faction. Xu took an even tougher approach to rebels within the military; in military region organs and among troops stationed in the city and its surrounding provinces, twenty-two people were arrested and eight were discharged, while 475 were placed under watch or under isolation for introspection. Ten rebel organizations were banned in Nanjing, and more than 330 rebel leaders were jailed.[33]

Jilin: Military aircraft scattered leaflets condemning the rebel Changchun Commune and forcing its members to raise the white flag and "admit their error and request punishment." Three rebel groups were denounced and forced to disband.

Guangdong: The Guangzhou Military Region arrested 450 leaders of mass organizations in Guangzhou and another 238 outside the city limits. Another 508 mass organization leaders were arrested in the week before the Guangzhou International Trade Fair in March.[34]

Throughout the country, jailed rebels sang out, "Lift your eyes to the Big Dipper and think of Mao Zedong," waiting for Beijing to rescue them from their misery.

THE COUNTERATTACK AGAINST THE FEBRUARY COUNTERCURRENT

The CCRSG and rebel faction reacted strongly to the military and bureaucratic suppression of the rebel faction throughout China. Rebels in Beijing convened a "Mass Pledge Rally to Smash the Bourgeois Restorationist Countercurrent," and Tan Zhenlin became their first target. On March 11, nearly one hundred mass organizations, led mainly by the Capital Red Guards Congress and rebel factions in the agriculture and forestry division,[35] united to form the Capital Liaison Station to Thoroughly Rout the Tan Zhenlin Top-Down Bourgeois

Restoration. That afternoon, the Jinggang Mountain group at Beijing Normal University and more than thirty other organizations gathered in front of the Agricultural Ministry for the "Mass Pledge Rally to Pluck Out Tan." Tan was denounced at a rally of thirteen thousand people from 178 work units on the campus of the Beijing Agricultural University on March 16 and at a rally of revolutionary rebel organizations of agricultural and forestry division on March 19. Other party veterans, including Chen Yi, Ye Jianying, Li Fuchun, Li Xiannian, Xu Xiangqian, and Nie Rongzhen, were denounced in a street demonstration on March 14 drawing around one hundred thousand people from more than fifty educational institutions.

Facing the conservative faction's challenge to the Cultural Revolution and the intense reaction from the CCRSG and the rebel faction, Mao began putting pressure on the conservative faction and supporting the rebel faction. On Mao's instructions, the Central Committee issued a document on April 1 regarding problems in Anhui Province but intended for broader application.[36] The document stated that mass organizations could not be arbitrarily declared counterrevolutionary organizations and that people labeled counterrevolutionaries merely for storming military headquarters, criticizing the army, or for having alternative views regarding local power seizures must be released and rehabilitated. On April 2, 1967, *People's Daily* published an editorial criticizing a countercurrent that attacked the shortcomings and errors of revolutionary young militants and totally negated their generally correct orientation. On April 6, the CMC issued the "Ten-Point Order" prohibiting arbitrary arrests, labeling, and banning. "No action is to be taken against the masses, whether on the left, right or center, who have attacked military organizations in the past."

These signals buoyed up the rebel faction throughout China; rebels fervently exchanged information on the situation in Beijing and carried out demonstrations large and small. The slogan "Thoroughly smash the counterrevolutionary restorationist countercurrent" was painted everywhere, while local variants of "Down with Tan Zhenlin" were heard throughout China. Rebel faction organizations that had been undermined staged a comeback. In Chengdu, the long-dormant downtown area was energized by spontaneous debates that often went on deep into the night. The number and vigor of rebel supporters among the masses increased noticeably.[37]

After the counterattack against the February Countercurrent, the Central Committee's mainstream approach to problems in various localities was to support the rebel faction and suppress the conservative faction, facilitating a "big alliance" made up largely of the rebel faction. For example, the Central Committee's May 7 ten-point decision on handling the Sichuan problem explicitly declared that the Industrial Army was a conservative organization, that the Chengdu Military Region had committed "directional and line errors" in the early stage of its operations, and that Li Jingquan was Sichuan's biggest capitalist roader. This decision also reorganized the Chengdu Military Region, appointing Zhang Guohua as the military region's political commissar and Liang Xingchu as regional commander.

At the end of 1966, Mao estimated that the Cultural Revolution could be concluded by the end of 1967. When the power seizures began in January 1967, Mao said, "Let's see how things look in February, March, and April this year, and look at the results this time next year or maybe a little later."[38] After Mao endorsed a "classroom-based schoolwide alliance" at the Tianjin Yan'an Secondary School, *People's Daily* on March 7, 1967, published an editorial calling on teachers and students to return to school to "rectify thinking, rectify work styles, rectify organization, and achieve the proletarian revolutionary grand alliance." The Central Committee also handed down a document requiring students to return to their schools by March 20. Mao sent the PLA to carry out phased military training in colleges, secondary schools, and primary schools. The Central Committee also required trans-sectoral mass organizations throughout China to form grand alliances based on work units and departments. All this indicated that the Cultural Revolution was moving into a closing phase. However, the 1967 February Countercurrent and the retaliation against it caused a major setback in the course of the Cultural Revolution that Mao had never anticipated.

Retaliation against the February Countercurrent resulted in another wave of rebellion that made it basically impossible to "resume classes and make revolution" and disband trans-sectoral and trans-work-unit mass organizations. The rebel factions that rose up again in the fight to counter the February Countercurrent rapidly expanded in scale, and their horizontal straddling was even greater than it had been before. At the same time, the Great Networking movement also experienced a resurgence. Rebel students went down to the factories and the countryside, pouring into the suburbs and outer counties to help prop up and revive rebel faction organizations.[39] The result was that rather than drawing to a close, the Cultural Revolution actually expanded even further and deeper.

Even more crucially, the CCP Central Committee's guiding ideology of forming a "grand alliance" with the rebel faction as its main part, followed by the establishment of tripartite revolutionary committees, was strenuously resisted by the conservative faction and some support-the-left military units, and the rebel factions also experienced internal division and reorganization. The conflict between conservative and rebel factions and between different groups within the rebel faction became protracted and increasingly intense. Mao's intention to "see how things look in February, March, and April this year, and look at the results this time next year" proved illusory.

12

THE ARMED FORCES AND THE "THREE SUPPORTS AND TWO MILITARIES"

Once Mao's desire to smash the old state apparatus created anarchy, rescuing the situation required relying on the country's remaining organized force, the army. With Lin Biao in command, Mao could trust the armed forces.

In democratic countries, the army is for national defense and maintains neutrality in political disputes. In China, the army is the tool of the Communist Party for seizing and maintaining political power, making it the most sensitive piece in a power struggle. During the Cultural Revolution, the darkness of power struggle loomed like a malign nimbus in the military's highest reaches, rife with conspiracy, hypocrisy, deceit, and brutality, and as a result, the "three supports and two militaries" policy made the Cultural Revolution even more complex and vicious.

An army draws vitality from war, and peace is the worst corrosive. With few military engagements after the Korean War, the military bureaucracy's corruption became even more serious, blatant, and barbarous than that of its civilian counterpart as senior military officers sated their ambition with vice. Since the corruption seldom seeped outside of the military's self-contained system, Mao tolerated it as long as the military remained obedient to him.

The May 16 Circular brought "bourgeois representative personages" in the army within the purview of Cultural Revolution struggle. Defining these personages as those who failed to execute his political line, Mao encouraged the rebel faction to oppose the "bourgeois reactionary line" in the military, while prohibiting the destruction of "our Great Wall, the army."

REBELLION AND ITS SUPPRESSION WITHIN THE MILITARY

As the Central Military Commission's first vice-chairman and defense minister, Lin Biao wanted the military to remain stable and not devolve into chaos like the local governments had. He therefore opposed military involvement in the Cultural Revolution at the local level.[1]

At the outset of the Cultural Revolution, the General Political Department (GPD) of the People's Liberation Army stipulated that military academies, military science research units, and military cultural troupes, as noncombat departments, were focal points for the Cultural Revolution. The GPD had each unit "sound out the ranks" to discover and compile dossiers on "targets of revolution,"[2] taking advantage of Liu Shaoqi's guideline against rightists to attack those who had criticized the army leadership. After Liu and Deng Xiaoping fell from power, these purge targets rebelled and demanded the launch of the four bigs and the destruction of black dossiers.

At an enlarged meeting of the CMC standing committee in May 1966, Ye Jianying, who had just been named a member of the Central Committee Secretariat and secretary-general of the CMC, relayed Lin Biao's general principle for the military: There would be no four bigs but rather education by positive example. And while carrying out revolution, it was also necessary to maintain combat effectiveness and enhance combat readiness; the military was not to intervene in the Cultural Revolution at the local level. Ye Jianying and Nie Rongzhen both opposed the four bigs. At one meeting of the CMC standing committee, Ye Jianying said, "People are organizing some kind of rebel shock brigades and saying, 'The Chairman commended Nie Yuanzi, so why can't the army have a Nie Yuanzi?' How can this thinking be tolerated?" Nie Rongzhen interposed, "Military cadres are not allowed to rebel, and we'll cut off anyone who does."[3]

On June 14, 1966, the CMC issued a document stipulating that within the army, the Cultural Revolution was to be carried out on only a limited basis in internal propaganda and cultural departments. On September 3, 1966, the CMC, in the name of the PLA's GPD, issued a directive forbidding students of military academies from organizing Red Guards or engaging in the Great Networking. All this reflected the will of the military leadership and Mao's desire to stabilize the military, but it was fundamentally contrary to the May 16 Circular and Mao's determination to "oppose revisionism." The denunciation of the bourgeois revolutionary line gave military academy students an opportunity to rebel.

The editorial in issue no. 13 of *Red Flag* forced the CMC and General Political Department to toe the line by requiring denunciation of the bourgeois reactionary line in order to implement the Sixteen Articles. On October 5, 1966, the CCP Central Committee endorsed and transmitted the "CMC and GPD's Urgent Directive Regarding the Great Proletarian Cultural Revolution in the Military Academies" (Central Committee Document No. 515 [1966]). The urgent directive called for the elimination of all restrictions fettering the mass movement in the military academies, the promotion of the four bigs, and the rehabilitation of anyone declared counterrevolutionaries, rightist, or anti-party elements.

There are differing views on how the urgent directive came about. Qiu Huizuo believes that Liu Zhijian and other members of the PLA Cultural Revolution Small Group were behind it, and that the marshals were powerless to block it.[4] Others say that Lin Biao decided on it after his daughter, Lin Liheng, showed him material compiled on a rebel leader at the Second Military Medical University.[5]

Once the urgent directive was handed down, the rebel wave of military academy students burst through the dike. Students in military uniforms besieged Beijing's military headquarters and the leading organs of armies and military branches, and military cadres who had forbidden the four bigs and suppressed the rebel faction were attacked as executors of the "bourgeois reactionary line." Classes at more than one hundred military academies were paralyzed, much to Mao's glee.[6]

The urgent directive stipulated that the army and military academies were not to intervene in the Cultural Revolution at the local level, but local rebel organizations still launched assaults on the military's leading organs. There were two reasons for this: One was that the army took care of important files on behalf of the provincial party committees, and the rebels suspected that these included black dossiers on them. The second was that some military units sheltered capitalist roaders evading denunciation by the masses.

In order to allow central leading military organs to resume normal operations, Lin Biao authorized a mass rally at Beijing Workers' Stadium on November 13, 1966, to mobilize students from military academies outside Beijing to return to their schools. Chen Yi warned the rebels: "Line struggle can lead to great achievements but also to great errors . . . Someone will say, 'Oh! Commander Chen, today at the stadium you poured cold water on the movement!' It's not good to pour cold water, but when people get too hotheaded, a good rubdown with cold towels is in order." Ye Jianying said, "We're keeping one eye shut and one eye open. By shutting one eye we're letting it go as much as possible, but we still have one eye open, and that eye sees everything very clearly." The rebels resented these criticisms, and as murmurs rumbled, Xiao Hua and Liu Zhijian declared the rally ended and escorted the veteran marshals from the scene. Chen Yi and Ye Jianying fought back against the criticism of rebels at another mass rally for military academy students on November 29.[7]

The Central Cultural Revolution Small Group responded by organizing a rally for nonmilitary rebel students to denounce Chen Yi, Ye Jianying, and other military leaders. When Chen and Ye failed to attend, the rally was canceled, but by then the students had spent all day at the stadium with no food, and they vented their rage with big-character posters all over the city calling for Chen and Ye to be struck down. On December 31, 1966, the CCRSG held a meeting of two thousand people at the Jingxi Guesthouse and called on Ye Jianying to make a self-criticism.[8] Before Ye could finish, students began to denounce him vehemently. When Mao demanded an investigation into the incident, the CCRSG pushed all the blame on Liu Zhijian, who had presided over the meeting. On January 4, 1967, Liu was criticized by Jiang Qing and dismissed from his positions as chairman of the PLA Cultural Revolution Small Group and vice-director of the GPD, and he was imprisoned soon after that.[9] Lin Biao declared Xu Xiangqian chairman of the PLA Cultural Revolution Small Group, with Jiang Qing as adviser and the air force political commissar Yu Lijin and the navy deputy political commissar Wang Hongkun serving as vice-chairmen. Ye Jianying was still in charge of the CMC's day-to-day operations.

Becoming adviser to the PLA Cultural Revolution Small Group satisfied Jiang Qing's desire for involvement in the military. At the first meeting after Xu Xiangqian took charge, Xu stated three guiding principles for the small group: First, have no fear of chaos; second, thoroughly denounce the Liu-Deng bourgeois reactionary line; third, veteran cadres need not fear the masses and should engage in revolution on their own initiative. This was fully consistent with Mao's thinking and of course with Jiang Qing's as well. Apart from these three principles, Xu called for learning from the local rebels: "Paranoia of the masses is the main thing now, and if this illness isn't cured, the Cultural Revolution cannot be successful!" He criticized Xiao Hua as a coward for fearing the masses. Xu's remarks greatly displeased the senior military officers who were present.

In the first half of January 1967, Mao authorized an enlarged conference of the CMC at Beijing's Jingxi Guesthouse. Lin Biao entrusted Ye Jianying with managing the conference, which lasted three months. One of its objectives was to place leading military cadres under protection in Beijing and prevent them from being subjected to struggle in their localities, and the second was to study how the military could engage in the Cultural Revolution. Military leaders attending the conference were extremely unhappy at being denounced by the masses. After eight leaders in the Nanjing Military Region had been denounced and forced to kneel, Commander Xu Shiyou had started drinking heavily and had fled to the Dabie Mountains and threatened to shoot anyone who tried to seize him. The commander of the Fuzhou Military Region, Han Xianchu, said that rebels from the Capital Third Command Post running amok in Fuzhou made it impossible to carry out war preparedness: "If this happens again, I'll go into the mountains and become a guerrilla fighter!"[10] Ye Jianying had attendees visit Qiu Huizuo, who had been rescued after being beaten, and everyone was incensed, with some insisting that Ye Jianying report this to Mao.

Qiu Huizuo deserves sympathy for being nearly beaten to death, but there was a reason that the masses attacked him. As soon as the Cultural Revolution began, Qiu targeted the political commissar Li

Jukui and other leaders of the General Logistics Department (GLD), and twenty-two cadres at the army level or above had been denounced by the end of 1966. When the bourgeois reactionary line came under attack, the spearhead of struggle shifted to Qiu Huizuo.[11] On January 12, 1967, personnel from the GLD political department put up a big-character poster accusing Qiu of misconduct and had people testify to his sexual abuse and vindictiveness, inflaming public indignation. Qiu was denounced and tortured at denunciation rallies and then locked up on January 24 by students from the Second Military Medical University. He was released only after his wife, Hu Min, appealed to Lin Biao's wife, Ye Qun, and Lin Biao and Chen Boda intervened.[12]

After returning to work at the GLD at the end of March 1967, Qiu began taking revenge on those who had persecuted him. He told the department's special case officers to resolutely attack the "counterrevolutionary attitude" of their targets and to interrogate them nonstop until they confessed: "The hearts of special case group members must be ruthless; the struggling must be ruthless. This is the dictatorship of the proletariat! Softheartedness is right-deviating opportunism."[13] The deputy director of the GLD's Armaments Department, Liang Bing, was physically devastated by twenty-three kinds of torture, and twelve of his friends and relatives were pulled down with him, resulting in four deaths.[14] Qiu manufactured twenty-nine bogus cases of major and minor cliques involving more than 700 people in GLD agencies, and established seven secret jails for special investigations that resulted in 143 GLD personnel being killed or driven to suicide and more than 3,200 cadres and personnel being put under "focused investigations" that implicated tens of thousands of their friends and relatives. After the Ninth Party Congress appointed Qiu to the Politburo, Qiu methodically dealt with all those in the GLD apparatus who had opposed him: 1,005 cadres were demoted and sent to labor in factories, stables, farms, and storehouses; 3,302 cadres were banished to the department's May 7 cadre school in Ningxia's Helan Mountain; 4,738 cadres were demobilized; and 147 were transferred to the production-construction corps in Xinjiang.[15]

As the military's leading organs came under attack and some military leaders were seized and struggled in the latter half of January 1967, Lin Biao called in Ye Jianying, Xu Xiangqian, Nie Rongzhen,

and Yang Chengwu for an urgent meeting and said, "It's very dangerous for this to continue in the military. We need to come up with a
directive." Lin Biao then dictated a seven-point CMC order to his secretary, and the military leaders present all agreed to it. However,
when the order was discussed at an enlarged CMC meeting, Jiang
Qing and other members of the CCRSG rejected it. Lin Biao went with
Xu Xiangqian to see Mao, who agreed to the seven points and added
an eighth: "Strengthen education of offspring." Clearly, Mao was targeting the offspring of senior cadres who had organized the United
Action Committee of the Capital Red Guards. Mao then wrote a memo
on the document: "These eight clauses are very good; issue as written."
Lin Biao said, "Chairman, for signing this document, may you live
forever!"[16]

On January 28, 1967, the CMC formally promulgated the Central
Military Commission Order (known as the CMC Eight-Point Order),
which stipulated that dictatorship was to be resolutely imposed on
proven counterrevolutionary organizations and elements, and that the
military's war-preparedness and secret apparatus should be exempt
from attack and networking. While circulating the Eight-Point Order
at an enlarged CMC meeting on January 29, Ye Jianying noted, "Anyone creating trouble in the military ranks will not come to a good end!"
When more than three hundred members of the Inner Mongolia Military District's security battalion came to Beijing demanding the four
bigs, Ye Jianying mustered troops to round them up for training and
remolding, after which most of them were discharged and sent home.[17]
Military leaders throughout the country used the Eight-Point Order
to suppress the rebel faction, with some provincial military districts
opening fire on rebels. The Eight-Point Order became the policy basis
for the February Suppression of Counterrevolutionaries. Of course,
Mao and the CCRSG weren't about to allow this suppression of rebels
to go on for long, and the Central Committee's April 1 "Resolution
Regarding the Anhui Problem" (discussed in the previous chapter)
turned things around by demanding the release and rehabilitation of
anyone targeted as a revolutionary for criticizing the military and
other power-holders. This was followed on April 6 by the Ten-Point
Order, which negated the Eight-Point Order and brought about a resurgence of the rebel faction. Within the military, however, there was

resistance to the Ten-Point Order, with Wuhan Military Region commander Chen Zaidao stating bluntly that he would "not execute the Ten-Point Order, not implement it, and not discuss it."[18]

As can be seen above, the military's attitude toward the rebel faction followed a zigzag course: The CMC's "Urgent Directive" on October 5, 1966, supported the rebel faction. The CMC Eight-Point Order of January 28, 1967, suppressed the rebel faction. The CMC Ten-Point Order of April 6, 1967, once again supported the rebel faction. This zigzag reflected Mao's conflicted attitude: He wanted the military to support the rebel faction, but he also wanted to keep the military stable. Whenever the zigzag moved left, a large number of leading cadres came under attack; whenever it moved right, the rebel faction was suppressed.

Around this time, the "Prairie Fire Fighting Force" of the Beijing Military Region song-and-dance troupe was organizing joint rehearsals for the song-and-dance ensembles of the navy, air force, engineering corps, artillery, and other military units and performed several times at the Beijing Military Region auditorium. Mass organizations in the military that shared the views of these military units also joined together, forming the Old Three Forces[19] faction (also known as the Three Forces Revolutionary faction). This faction supported the CMC Eight-Point Order and the work of the party committees and opposed chaos in the military. It endorsed Wu Faxian in the air force, Li Zuopeng in the navy, and Qiu Huizuo in the General Logistics Department. This gave rise to an opposing New Three Forces faction, which advocated rebellion within the military and endorsed the "Resolution Regarding the Anhui Problem" and the CMC Ten-Point Order. This faction gained the support of the CCRSG and rebel organizations at Tsinghua University and the Beijing Aeronautical Engineering Institute.

The latest move in April 1967 gave the New Three Forces the upper hand and put the Old Three Forces at a disadvantage. The rebel faction was strongest in the artillery, PLA Academy of Art, Logistics Institute, navy, air force, Beijing Military Region Song-and-Dance Troupe, Second Artillery Song-and-Dance Troupe, and other units with a large number of intellectuals. They denounced the bourgeois

THE ARMED FORCES AND THE "THREE SUPPORTS AND TWO MILITARIES" | 213

reactionary line and seized and struggled leading cadres in the various units. Military leaders and the Old Three Forces needed to reverse the rebel faction's advantage.

THE MAY 13 INCIDENT

A beautiful woman is credited with reversing the conservative faction's disadvantaged situation. The woman's name was Liu Suyuan, and she was an opera singer in the Air Force Political Department Song-and-Dance Troupe. She had developed a special relationship with Mao when she began dancing at Zhongnanhai in 1958 at the age of eighteen, and regular visits gave her opportunities to speak with him. At that time, the Air Force Political Department Song-and-Dance Troupe was split into two factions, one of which endorsed the air force commander Wu Faxian and the political commissar Yu Lijin, and the other of which opposed them. Liu Suyuan belonged to the conservative faction, and after the CMC issued its Ten-Point Order, her faction was reduced to five members who were constantly attacked by the other faction. Liu went weeping to Mao and asked, "What attitude should we take to Wu Faxian?" Mao replied, "Wu Faxian can be bombarded and scorched but cannot be struck down." Liu's faction began resolutely supporting Wu Faxian and soon leveraged Mao's attitude to become the majority faction, with Liu now known as Commander Liu.[20] The Air Force Political Department Song-and-Dance Troupe became a key force within the Old Three Forces.

Liu Suyuan told Mao that the various song-and-dance troupes of the Beijing military units wanted to team up for a performance celebrating the twenty-fifth anniversary of the publication of Mao's *Talks at the Yan'an Forum on Literature and Art*. Mao suggested that she speak with Lin Biao's wife, Ye Qun, and told his secretary, Xu Yefu, to instruct Ye Qun to support the performance. Lin Biao viewed this new development as an opportunity to stabilize the military through the conservative faction, so Ye Qun quickly arranged to see Liu Suyuan and other faction members and said, "Comrade Lin Biao shares your views. Don't worry about being considered conservative. You should boldly support whoever is in the proletarian headquarters and be the royalist faction of the revolution!"[21]

Ignorant of Mao's support, the New Three Forces organized a contingent to sabotage the Old Three Forces performance on May 13 at the Beijing Exhibition Hall. To prevent disruption of the performance, a group of senior military leaders gathered nearby and had the garrison command send two companies of soldiers to prevent any violence. Li Zuopeng states in his memoirs that the security measures allowed the New Three Forces performances to go ahead successfully, with only a few dozen people injured in a minor skirmish.[22] However, someone from the New Three Forces recalls, "Our people were already on the stage brandishing the banner of occupying the central elevation; the orchestra pit was empty, and some of the larger musical instruments had been carelessly abandoned there." The group then realized that they were surrounded by troops and charged out of the encirclement. An announcement over the loudspeaker proclaimed: "Vice-Chairman Lin's office has telephoned and said that it was wrong to mount an assault on the performance to commemorate Chairman Mao's *Talks at the Yan'an Forum on Literature and Art* and promote Mao Zedong Thought! Vice-Chairman Lin supports the performance!"[23] After the attackers were ordered to withdraw, the Old Three Forces resumed their performance.

Liu Suyuan was with Mao while the Old Three Forces and New Three Forces battled it out at the exhibition hall. Liu told Mao, "The revolutionary faction was victorious." Mao said, "What are you so happy about? After a while the rebel faction will be on top again." Qiu Huizuo says, "Mao supported Liu Suyuan, and fortunately Liu was in the revolutionary faction. If Liu had been in the rebel faction, Mao would still have supported her."[24]

During the Old Three Forces performance, Zhou Enlai, Chen Boda, Xiao Hua, Zhang Xiuchuan, and others were at the Great Hall of the People talking with mass organization leaders. Xiao Hua felt it would be better for the two factions to hold a joint performance; if one faction was performing and the other was kept outside, violence was inevitable. Unaware of Mao's and Lin's attitude, Zhou Enlai was still trying to convince the heads of the two factions to perform together. When Liu Suyuan rushed to the assembly hall and told the Premier that Mao supported her side, Zhou ordered the rebel faction not to burst in on the performance venue. At that time, the Great Hall of the People was in chaos, and the Premier had to stand on a chair and shout, "Don't burst in on the performance! If you do, you're attacking Chairman Mao's revolutionary line!" Zhou told Chen Boda and Xiao Hua to go to the venue to prevent the attack.[25] This young performer, relying on her charms, was able to walk into core political venues such as Zhongnanhai and the Great Hall of the People, and the State Council premier Zhou Enlai had to do what she told him—nothing like that could have happened even during the imperial era, but it happened under Communist Party rule.

Their successful performance lent new momentum to the Three Forces Revolutionary Faction, and on May 14 they took to the streets with big-character posters and slogans, followed by a celebratory rally on May 16, which the CCRSG felt obliged to send Qi Benyu to attend to express support.[26] The faction staged a lengthy performance at Tiananmen Square on May 23; and at another performance in the small auditorium of the Great Hall of the People on June 9, central leaders showed their backing for the Old Three Forces by mounting the stage to have their pictures taken with the performers.

After the May 13 performance, the military bureaucrats put immense pressure on the rebel faction within the military, and rebel groups disbanded one by one. The Central Military Commission Administrative Group (CMCAG), headed by Huang Yongsheng, carried out administrative restructuring of the military units where the rebel faction was strongest and employed special methods where restructuring was inappropriate. For example, Shanghai's Second Military Medical University was one of the key work units where rebels seized power during the January Storm, but Shanghai was the rebel faction's turf, so it was impossible to restructure the university. The CMCAG therefore used "relieving the garrison" as a pretext for moving the school to Xi'an, where it was then restructured.[27] "Restructuring" involved purging and attacking the rebel faction. The May 13 Incident therefore served Lin Biao's purpose of stabilizing the armed forces, while also allowing Huang, Wu, Li, and Qiu to overwhelm the rebel faction and strengthen the CMCAG.

The Cultural Revolution historian Wang Nianyi explains the victory of the Old Three Forces over the New Three Forces from a different angle: In reaction to wholesale power seizures, nearly all military regions supported conservative organizations in their support-the-left work, and were therefore considered to have committed "line errors." At that time, the "proletarian headquarters" made a secret decision to rely on Lin Biao and his old subordinates such as Wu Faxian, Li Zuopeng, and Qiu Huizuo to stabilize the situation within Beijing's military ranks. This would achieve their objective of stabilizing the entire military, and then the entire country. Implementation of this policy began on May 13, 1967, after which the Three Forces Proletarian Revolutionary Faction eliminated its opposition (which was supported by the CCRSG and which opposed Wu Faxian, Li Zuopeng, and Qiu Huizuo). From then on, Wu, Li, and Qiu gained control over the PLA's General Political Department, General Logistics Department, air force, and navy, and the situation inside Beijing's military establishment quickly stabilized.[28] The CMCAG—dominated by Huang, Wu, Li, and Qiu and controlled by Lin Biao—replaced the CMC Standing Committee in handling the daily operations of the CMC and controlling the army, navy, and air force. This was how the Lin Biao clique eventually came into being.

The "proletarian headquarters" Wang Nianyi speaks of must of course include Mao at its core. Since Mao made the "secret decision" to rely on Lin Biao and his cohort to stabilize the military in Beijing, then Liu Suyuan's request for Mao to support her faction simply coincided with this decision, and Mao wasn't supporting her conservative faction purely because of his special relationship with her. Liu Suyuan was just a pawn Mao used to implement that policy decision. One of the leaders of the performance disruption subsequently realized, "Mao Zedong knew in advance that the Three Forces would have this joint performance and that the opposition would launch an assault on it, so he directed a female member of the song-and-dance troupe to go see Ye Qun."[29]

THE "THREE SUPPORTS AND TWO MILITARIES": THE ARMY DOMINATES THE CULTURAL REVOLUTION

When the rebel faction in Anhui Province held a mass rally to seize power from the provincial party secretary Li Baohua in January 1967, it demanded that the army provide security at the scene. The Nanjing Military Region sent a report requesting instructions from the CMC. On January 21, Mao wrote a memo on the report instructing Lin Biao to issue a new order for the PLA to support the leftist masses: "That should be done from now on whenever any genuine revolutionary faction requests the support or assistance of the army. The so-called 'nonintervention' is bogus; they've been involved for a long time." Lin Biao immediately took action, and the next day, an enlarged CMC meeting passed the "Resolution Regarding the PLA Resolutely Supporting the Revolutionary Leftist Masses" (Central Committee Document No. 27 [1967]).

The resolution nullified all previous directives barring military intervention in the Cultural Revolution at the local level and stated that the army should send troops to any genuine proletarian revolutionary leftist faction requesting help. At the same time, it said, the armed forces should resolutely suppress counterrevolutionary elements and should fight back against any violent action. Furthermore, the military should not harbor capitalist roaders and stubborn adherents to the bourgeois reactionary line represented by Liu Shaoqi and Deng Xiaoping, but should undergo education on the proletarian revolutionary line represented by Chairman Mao.

Document No. 27 (1967) was apparently intended to provide military protection to power seizures by rebels in all localities, but it provided no definition of what constituted "proletarian revolutionary leftist faction," "counterrevolutionary elements," "capitalist roaders," or "stubborn adherents to the bourgeois reactionary line." This ambiguity gave the army leeway to decide whom to support, since both the rebel and conservative factions referred to themselves as the "proletarian revolutionary leftist faction" and demanded the army's assistance in suppressing their opponents.

On Mao's instructions, the CMC on March 19 issued its "Resolution Regarding Concentrating Strength to Execute the Task of

Supporting the Left, Supporting Farming, Supporting Industrial Production, Military Control, and Military Training." This resolution, known as the "Three Supports and Two Militaries," aimed to maintain social stability with the immediate participation of "one-third, one-half, or even two-thirds of personnel."

From February 1967 to the end of 1969, the PLA deployed 2.8 million personnel to this task. Nine of China's provinces and twenty-five of its major cities implemented military control, and the military took full control over dozens of prefectures and hundreds of counties. Other localities implemented partial military control; more than 80 percent of revolutionary committees at the county level or above were chaired by military cadres, and in Yunnan and Hubei the proportion reached 97 percent.[30] Some central government ministries and commissions also implemented military control, including the Railways Ministry, Communications Ministry, Ministry of Post and Telecommunications, the Xinhua News Agency, Central People's Broadcasting, and various defense industry organs. The "Three Supports and Two Militaries" operation continued for more than five years until the CCP Central Committee and CMC jointly issued a document to end it in August 1972.

The "Three Supports and Two Militaries" policy made the army the dominant force in the Cultural Revolution, entrusted with the mission of promoting the "grand alliance and three-in-one combination,"[31] ensuring a stable power seizure and social stability, and facilitating the establishment of revolutionary committees.

The army embodied order and relied on discipline and obedience to maintain combat-effectiveness, so forcing the army to support rebels who sabotaged order was no easy matter. Furthermore, Mao wanted rebels to "scorch" the bureaucratic clique, but military leaders were the core and most corrupt portion of that clique. The fact was that most senior officers and rank and file resented the rebel faction. Marshals such as Ye Jianying and Chen Yi and members of the CMCAG maintained a conservative stance, and the CMCAG member specifically responsible for the "Three Supports and Two Militaries," Qiu Huizuo, particularly loathed the rebel faction after suffering their physical abuse. That meant that the military almost always supported the conservatives and suppressed the rebel faction, especially units under provincial military districts, which maintained close relations with local bureaucrats.

Mao made it clear that he intended the military to support the rebel faction. In an exceptional case, after the Twenty-First Army was transferred from Shanxi to Shaanxi, Commander Hu Wei invited the leader of the Xi'an Jiaotong University rebel faction, Li Shiying, to army headquarters to hear his views and to demonstrate support. Mao considered this very important, and when the April 21, 1967, edition of the CCRSG-edited *Express* (*Kuaibao*) reported on this matter, he wrote a memo directing Lin Biao and Enlai to print and distribute the article at an enlarged CMC meeting. "This is the right thing for the army to be doing. I hope the entire army will adopt such methods." This made Hu Wei a star in the support-the-left campaign for a time.[32]

Given the key role of military bureaucrats in the bureaucratic faction, Mao's desire for them to support rebels in order to purge the bureaucratic faction was paradoxical to say the least. Mao had a conflicted attitude toward the military bureaucratic clique: He criticized their resistance toward the Cultural Revolution but also protected them and exempted them from attack. The criticism was hollow, but the protection was real. There was an irreconcilable conflict between the bureaucratic faction and the Cultural Revolutionary forces, and as the restoration of social order weakened the Cultural Revolutionary forces and bolstered the strength of the military bureaucratic clique, conflict with Mao became inevitable.

THE YANG-YU-FU INCIDENT

The military's participation in the Cultural Revolution was marked by an incident that reflected no struggle between lines or viewpoints, but only the treachery, filth, darkness, and brutality of struggle within the military. It involved the General Staff acting chief Yang Chengwu, the air force political commissar Yu Lijin, and the Beijing Garrison commander Fu Chongbi, who were struck down together on March 24, 1968.

On September 23, 1967, Yang Chengwu, Li Zuopeng, and Yu Lijin returned to Beijing with Mao from an inspection of the Yangtze River region. At an enlarged CCRSG briefing meeting that day, Zhou Enlai announced that the Central Military Commission Four-Member Small Group[33] had been changed into the Central Military Commission Administrative Group (CMCAG), consisting of Yang Chengwu, Wu Faxian, Ye Qun, Qiu Huizuo, and Zhang Xiuchuan, and with Yang as chairman and Wu as vice-chairman. Yang and Wu were also members of the enlarged CCRSG briefing meetings.[34] The CMCAG was tasked with leading the Cultural Revolution in the military, strengthening war preparedness, controlling day-to-day operations, and organizing the military's "Three Supports and Two Militaries" work.

After Luo Ruiqing was unseated, Yang Chengwu became one of the core military leaders under Lin Biao, along with Ye Jianying and Xiao Hua. Ye Jianying was ten years older than Lin Biao, while Xiao Hua suffered from liver disease, so Yang Chengwu was tacitly regarded as Lin Biao's successor. Yang energetically curried favor with Mao, Lin Biao, and Jiang Qing, but some of his flattery proved counterproductive.

In winter 1967, Yang Chengwu published an essay titled "Vigorously Foster the Absolute Authority of the Great Commander-in-Chief Chairman Mao and of Mao Zedong Thought—Thoroughly Expose and Criticize the Heinous Crimes of Luo Ruiqing in Opposing Chairman Mao and Mao Zedong Thought." This had originally been written by the General Staff criticism group, but Yang took it over and had it revised multiple times, saying that its publication would unite the thinking of the entire party, military, and populace. A few days after the essay was published, Mao said, "I've only read the title of this essay, and it already contains errors—it's metaphysical!" Mao then issued a directive: "The phrase 'absolute authority' is inappropriate; there has never been a single absolute authority. All authority is relative, and absolute things exist only among relative things . . . The phrase 'vigorously foster' is also inappropriate. Authority or prestige can only be established naturally through struggle and practice and cannot be established artificially; prestige established in this way is certain to collapse."[35]

In another incident, Yang Chengwu personally took charge of compiling the *Outline of Party History*, and the first draft fully affirmed the status of Mao as leader, Lin Biao as successor, and Jiang Qing as "standard-bearer" of the Cultural Revolution. Zhou Enlai's name appeared, but not prominently, and other leaders were not named at all.[36] However, Yang had the draft destroyed around February 1968, apparently after getting wind of some new development.

Overconfident of having gained Jiang Qing's trust, Yang sometimes got carried away and played the Jiang Qing card in dealing with Lin Biao. Wounded, Lin Biao said, "Once you've lost friendship, nothing is left."[37] But the two didn't become completely estranged, as demonstrated by Yang's laudatory essay titled "Army Group Commander Lin Biao Taught Me to Be a Division Commander."

Qiu Huizuo believes that by that straddling the boats of Lin Biao and Jiang Qing, Yang Chengwu ultimately ended up in the water.[38]

Yang's fall was triggered by a minor matter regarding his eldest daughter, Yang Yi. Employed at *Air Force Daily*, Yang Yi became romantically involved with Yu Lijin's secretary, Shan Shichong, leading Shan's wife to raise a commotion in the air force leadership and involving Wu Faxian.[39] According to Wu Faxian, this scandal eventually made Lin Biao suspect that Yang Chengwu and Yu Lijin might be allied against Wu for total control of the air force.[40] It so happened that at this time, Nanjing Military Region commander Xu Shiyou provided Mao with a recently discovered file from the Nationalist era indicating that Yu Lijin had turned traitor after being taken prisoner by Nationalist troops in 1941. This was enough to destroy Yu Lijin's reputation, and Yang Chengwu was despondent.

Qiu Huizuo says that in mid-March 1968, Lin Biao tried to settle the matter between Wu Faxian and Yang Chengwu, and failing that, he sent Ye Qun to report the matter to Mao. After calling four meetings to hear detailed reports, Mao felt that there was no choice but to take down Yang Chengwu. During the reporting, Jiang Qing discovered that Yang had been presumptuously banking on her support, so she reversed her previous position and insisted that Yang be struck down.[41]

However, according to Chen Hong, the deputy director of the organization department of the political department of the PLA General Staff, Yang Chengwu's downfall mainly hinged on a file on Jiang Qing's activities in Shanghai in the 1930s. In her youth, Jiang Qing had been an actress while also taking part in revolutionary activities.

She had joined the CCP in 1933 but had lost contact with it after being briefly jailed for participating in anti-Japanese protests in late 1934, and there were rumors of scandalous behavior connected with her acting career. Jiang arrived in Yan'an in mid-July 1937, had her party membership restored in October, and eventually married Mao in November 1938. The party's top leadership had divided opinions about the marriage, given Jiang Qing's controversial past. Years later, in March 1954, Jiang Qing received an anonymous letter that said, "Jiang Qing, your history is degenerate, and a report has been sent to the Central Committee Organization Department." After years of investigation, the Shanghai Public Security Bureau finally determined in 1961 that the letter had been written by Zhu Ming, the wife of Lin Boqu, a Politburo member and vice-chair of the Standing Committee of the National People's Congress. Zhu Ming immediately killed herself. Later Jiang Qing learned that the file relating to this investigation was in Shanghai. In April 1967, Jiang Qing, Ye Qun, Qi Benyu, and Yang Chengwu arranged for Chen Hong to go to Shanghai with Wang Yumin and two others to examine the black dossier. After locating the box of files, Chen Hong telephoned Yang Chengwu to report the mission accomplished and took a night flight back to Beijing after being warned by Yang to keep the matter confidential.

Once the box of files was in Beijing, Yang Chengwu said that Jiang Qing wanted the group to look at the material, but not to let anyone else touch it, and then report to the Central Committee. After vetting the material, Chen Hong and Wang Yumin wrote a report recommending that the matter be handled by special investigators from the Ministry of Public Security. Jiang Qing was angry and told Lin Biao that saving that material was persecuting her, so Lin Biao told Yang to have a new report written and then to destroy the files.

After more than a week, Yang Chengwu called Chen Hong and Wang Yumin to his office again and said, "The report has been sent over and Jiang Qing has read it. She says the case has been solved, the perpetrator, Zhu Ming, has killed herself, and there's no need to preserve the files." In accordance with Yang's verbal directions, the report written by Chen Hong and Wang Yumin was submitted to the Central Committee on July 7. After reading it, Lin Biao wrote a memo on it in red pencil: "Xie Fuzhi, Yang Chengwu, Wang Dongxing, and Guan

Feng are jointly responsible for destroying [the files]," and he sent the report to Zhou Enlai. Zhou added the memo: "Destroy them along with the files stored in the Beijing Library and the packet of material sent over by Wu (Faxian) and Fu (Chongbi)," then passed it along to Mao. But Yang Chengwu and Wang Dongxing were accompanying Mao on his inspection of the Yangtze region, and Guan Feng was arrested in August, so the destruction of the files was delayed.

When Yang Chengwu returned to Beijing with Mao on September 23, Xie Fuzhi told him that Jiang Qing had flown into a rage multiple times, claiming that Yang was out to get her.[42] Yang reported the situation to Zhou Enlai and asked him how to deal with it. Zhou directed Xie, Yang, and Wang Dongxing to oversee the destruction of the files. Wang Yumin delivered the files to Wang Dongxing's office, and after the documents were checked against the catalog of contents, Xie lit a fire and Wang Yumin fed each document into the flames while the other three watched. Xie, Yang, and Wang Dongxing then signed their names to a report on the process. From then on, Jiang Qing repeatedly accused Yang of compiling a black dossier on her.[43]

Since Yang had been in charge of the process from beginning to end, Jiang Qing apparently misconstrued his motives, and this became the impetus for his downfall. Chen Hong was also imprisoned for six years.

In the early hours of March 23, Wu Faxian received a telephone call from the Central Committee General Office telling him to attend a meeting with Mao at the Great Hall of the People. When Wu arrived, the meeting had already begun. The participants included Mao, Lin Biao, Zhou Enlai, Chen Boda, Kang Sheng, Jiang Qing, Zhang Chunqiao, Yao Wenyuan, Xie Fuzhi, Ye Qun, and Wang Dongxing. Mao told Wu, "I know about your issue with Yang Chengwu, and you are right and Yang Chengwu is wrong." After a while, Mao asked Lin Biao, "Who's going to become chief of General Staff?" From this Wu knew that they'd already decided to unseat Yang Chengwu. Lin Biao recommended the commander of the Guangzhou Military Region, Huang Yongsheng, and Mao agreed. As to how to deal with Yu Lijin, Mao said, "Xu Shiyou's file was sent to me early on, and it says Yu Lijin is a traitor. Since that's the case, arrest him." Jiang Qing then noted that the Beijing Garrison Command was a critical post, and Fu Chongbi had a close relationship with Yang Chengwu, so a transfer was advisable. Mao agreed, and it was decided that Fu Chongbi would be transferred to the Shenyang Military Region as deputy commander and would be replaced by the deputy commander of the Guangzhou Military Region, Wen Yucheng. After these personnel issues were sorted out, Mao told Lin Biao, "We'll leave the rest to Zhou Enlai to handle. The two of us can withdraw and rest." After Mao and Lin left, Zhou continued the meeting and made specific arrangements in line with their views.[44]

At a mass rally for military cadres held at the Great Hall of the People on the night of March 24, 1968, Yang Chengwu was dismissed from his position as chief of General Staff, Yu Lijin was arrested, and Fu Chongbi was relieved of his command of the Beijing Garrison. Lin Biao gave a speech that he had discussed with Mao in advance, and which focused on opposing factionalism and double-dealing, and on the philosophical issue of the relative and the absolute.[45] Lin said, "Recently there has been collusion between Yang Chengwu and Yu Lijin to seize leadership of the Air Force from Wu Faxian . . . Yang Chengwu and Fu Chongbi colluded to strike down Xie Fuzhi . . . Yang's personal ambition was to push aside Xu Shiyou, Han Xianchu, and Huang Yongsheng and the people above and below them." Lin Biao also lavished praise on Jiang Qing as an "outstanding comrade."[46]

Zhou Enlai followed Lin Biao's example by extolling Jiang Qing as a "proletarian warrior" while denigrating Yang Chengwu's "empire building" and "double-dealing."[47] He drew parallels between the actions of Yang, Yu, and Fu and the earlier February Countercurrent, possibly because Yang and Fu were closely associated with Nie Rongzhen, and Yu Lijin had been a subordinate of Chen Yi's. Jiang Qing, Chen Boda, Kang Sheng, and others also took their turns giving speeches. Then Mao suddenly appeared at the rostrum and the entire hall rang with cries of "Long live Chairman Mao!" and choruses of "Sailing the Ocean Depends on the Helmsman."

In fact, even before the March 24 rally, Yang Chengwu's home had been searched and his documents sealed up.[48] Around 10:00 a.m. on the twenty-third, Lin Biao and Zhou Enlai and designated attendees of the enlarged CCRSG briefing meeting talked with Yang Chengwu. Lin gave Yang a preview of what was in store and said that arrangements had been made for him and his family to leave Beijing and move into the guesthouse at Donghu, Wuhan, where he could rest and reflect on his actions.[49] Zhou Enlai brought Huang Yongsheng and Yang Chengwu together in the Great Hall of the People on March 23 to announce that Huang would replace Yang as chief of General Staff.[50]

As for Fu Chongbi, it appears he was struck down because of his close relationship with Yang Chengwu when they were military leaders in north China in the 1940s.[51] Li Zuopeng recalls that on March 5, Jiang Qing tasked Fu Chongbi with searching for a handwritten manuscript by Lu Xun that had gone missing. After locating the manuscript, Fu and his secretary rushed to Jiang Qing's home at Diaoyutai (where the CCRSG office was located) to report the successful mission. Fu's secretary was so nervous that he tripped on a carpet in the reception room, sending his briefcase crashing into Jiang Qing and giving her a fright. This was construed as the major crime of "storming the CCRSG."[52]

On the afternoon of March 27, a mass rally of one hundred thousand people was held at the Beijing Workers' Stadium to "thoroughly smash the resurgence of the February Countercurrent and score a comprehensive victory for the Great Proletarian Cultural Revolution." Zhou Enlai first read out the decisions regarding Yang, Yu, and Fu, after which Jiang Qing, Kang Sheng, Chen Boda, and Zhou Enlai gave speeches. Zhou once again praised Jiang Qing profusely and elaborated on her revolutionary history. Lin Biao and Zhou Enlai's extravagant praise of Jiang Qing while striking down Yang Chengwu suggests that Jiang Qing's historical file was the main reason for Yang's downfall.

On March 25, the CMC Administrative Group was reorganized, with Huang Yongsheng (chief of General Staff and commander of the Guangzhou Military Region) as group head and Wu Faxian (deputy chief of General Staff and air force commander) as deputy head. The other members were Ye Qun (head of Lin Biao's office, member of the standing committee of the CMC general office party committee), Li Zuopeng (first political commissar of the navy, and from September 1968 onward deputy chief of General Staff), and Qiu Huizuo (director of the General Logistics Department, and from September 1968 onward also deputy chief of General Staff). When receiving Huang Yongsheng and the others along with Lin Biao on March 28, Mao said that the CMCAG would take over the role of the CMC standing committee, with Lin Biao in charge.[53] The CMCAG was now the most powerful organization in the armed forces. But extremes breed reversals, and this development planted the seeds for an incident that would occur during the second plenum of the Ninth Central Committee.

13

"RED THROUGH EVERY HILL AND VALE"

Mao originally envisioned that after smashing the old regime with "great chaos under heaven," he could establish a "new revolutionary regime" under the "three-in-one combination" of revolutionary masses' representatives, revolutionary cadres, and military representatives, and that this new regime would then use the process of "struggle, criticize, and reform" to bring about "great order under heaven" in about three years. Making Mao's vision a reality proved much more complicated, however.

THE DIFFICULT BIRTH OF THE REVOLUTIONARY COMMITTEES

Mao faced two quandaries. One was the resistance of the civilian and military bureaucratic clique, and the second was the undermining of Mao's "strategic vision" by the "factionalism" of the unruly rebels. On the first point, Mao refused to compromise on principle, but he wavered on tactics. His attitude toward the revolutionary elders involved in the February Countercurrent was to stand firm on the Cultural Revolution while allowing individuals back into the fold in order to keep the vast bureaucratic apparatus operating while trying to fix it. Regarding mass organizations, Mao started out firmly on the side of the rebel faction but then began to emphasize, "There is no fundamental conflict of interest within the worker class . . . even less is there a reason for splitting into two irreconcilable factions"; he called for "analyzing the rebel faction, which is not all good."

In a conversation with Zhou Enlai, Wang Li, Xie Fuzhi, Chen Zaidao, and Zhong Hanhua on the evening of July 18, 1967, Mao said, "Why not arm the workers and students? I think we should arm them." On July 21, Jiang Qing said that the rebel faction needed to engage in "verbal attack and armed defense." On August 4, Mao wrote Jiang Qing a letter in which he said that at least 75 percent of military cadres supported the right, and therefore the crucial issue was to arm the left.[1] After the slogan of "Arm the left" was raised, violence escalated from fists and clubs to bullets. In the first half of August 1967, large-scale armed conflicts broke out in Nanjing, Changchun, Shenyang, Chongqing, Changsha, and other major cities.

These armed conflicts initially occurred between the conservative and rebel factions, but then progressed to divisions within the rebel faction. Thousands of large-scale armed conflicts throughout the country resulted in the deaths of more than a hundred thousand people. According to incomplete figures, as of September 1969, mass organizations had seized 1,844,216 weapons, and 2,131,036 weapons were reclaimed from them. These included 10,266 pieces of heavy artillery seized and 14,828 recovered, and 442 million rounds of ammunition seized and more than 340 million rounds recovered; 390,642 artillery shells seized and 294,259 shells recovered; and 2,719,545 hand grenades seized and 2,734,381 recovered.[2] The number of armaments recovered was sometimes larger because the number seized didn't account for weapons that went "missing" from military ordnance factories; Mao candidly admitted that the army had given people these weapons. Mao had called for arming the left, and the army usually decided that the left was conservative faction organizations.

After Wuhan's July 20 Incident showed Mao the peril of suppressing the army, he tilted the balance in favor of the armed forces against the rebel faction. First came Mao's criticism of the phrase "rooting out the smattering within the army," then came the ousting of Wang Li, Guan Feng, and Qi Benyu, radical but relatively powerless members of the CCRSG. Mao's tilting of the balance encouraged a resurgence of conservative forces and their military supporters throughout the country.

Students had gradually withdrawn from the political stage with the end of the Great Networking in late 1967, sending secondary school students "up the mountains and down to the countryside" and college students to "reeducation" on PLA-run farms, and dispatching Worker Mao Zedong Thought Propaganda Teams to schools in late July 1968. Now the trouble came from worker rebel faction organizations.

Mao refused to recognize any power seizure that wasn't carried out under a "grand alliance," but unifying the various power bases raised the problem of allocating power, while each rebel organization held fast to its own views, preventing the movement from proceeding in the direction that Mao intended. This kind of "bourgeois and petty bourgeois factionalism" was condemned in the 1968 New Year's Day editorial jointly issued by the *People's Daily*, *PLA Daily*, and *Red Flag*, but the military bureaucrats simply used "factionalism" as a pretext to suppress the rebel faction, while the CCRSG held that "proletarian factionalism" was essential. This instrumentalization of factionalism only intensified "factional struggle."

The central leadership still carried enough authority to resolve intractable local conflicts by summoning representatives of the "military, cadres, and masses" to undergo "study classes" in Beijing guesthouses. Some provinces sent as many as one thousand to two thousand people to these classes, which consisted of one to eight months of closed-door discussion, debate, and negotiation. Central leaders weighed in periodically to bring about an agreement for a grand alliance and three-in-one combination that inevitably sidestepped major issues and differed substantially from what Mao had proposed at the outset of the Cultural Revolution. Zhou Enlai played a key role in these study classes, with the additional participation of CCRSG members before the Ninth Party Congress and Politburo leaders after the Ninth Congress. Localities that couldn't even reach a watered-down agreement were placed under military control.

By 1968, the "great chaos under heaven" had been going on for nearly three years, and Mao wanted revolutionary committees established in all provinces as soon as possible. At that point, no one cared if the new regime conformed to the principles of the Paris Commune; "whatever was tossed into the basket was a vegetable," and Mao simply had to accept whatever Zhou Enlai managed to pull together.

The relationship between the rebel faction and the military and civilian bureaucratic cliques followed roughly the same pattern throughout the country, with the masses rebelling against the bureaucratic clique, followed by the bureaucratic clique's suppression of the rebels, and Mao alternatively playing the two sides off each other until he died and the rebel faction was vanquished forever. Mainstream public opinion has blamed all the evils of the Cultural Revolution on the rebel faction, but the vast majority of victims died while the rebel faction was suppressed under the new order of military and administrative bureaucratic control. The rebel faction was indeed savage and cruel when it had the upper hand, but these periods covered only two years of the Cultural Revolution, and those who suppressed the rebels during the other eight years were even more savage, while the rebels were more brutally purged after the Cultural Revolution. The number of rebel faction victims and the degree of their persecution vastly outweighed those of the power-holders and royalist faction, but they became the scapegoats of the Cultural Revolution.

The Cultural Revolution began by criticizing everything and calling for destroying the old order. Then those who destroyed the old order developed splits and began fighting one another in a repetitive process in which the different sides took turns enjoying the upper hand and losing power, being honored and imprisoned, and purging and being purged. This process was accompanied by alliances and mergers between various subfactions, waves of turmoil and stability, the shifting of mainstream ideology from revolutionary to conservative, and reversals of values that made what was right today wrong tomorrow. Finally the revolutionary tide completely subsided, and a new phase of history began.

The narrative above tracks the general development line of the movement, but the situation varied widely in each province, making a categorized analysis difficult.

Provincial-level revolutionary committees were established in the following chronological order:

PROVINCE/ MUNICIPALITY	REVOLUTIONARY COMMITTEE ESTABLISHED	REVOLUTIONARY COMMITTEE LEADER(S)
1967		
Heilongjiang	January 31 (Central Committee authorized March 20)	Pan Fusheng
Shandong	February 3 (name changed Feb. 23)	Wang Xiaoyu
Shanghai	February 5 (name changed Feb. 23)	Zhang Chunqiao
Guizhou	February 13	Li Zaihan
Shanxi	March 18	Liu Geping
Beijing	April 20	Xie Fuzhi
Qinghai	August 12	Liu Xianquan
Inner Mongolia	November 1	Teng Haiqing
Tianjin	December 6	Jie Xuegong
1968		
Jiangxi	January 5	Cheng Shiqing
Gansu	January 24	Xian Henghan
Henan	January 27	Liu Jianxun
Hebei	February 3	Li Xuefeng
Hubei	February 5	Zeng Siyu
Guangdong	February 21	Huang Yongsheng
Jilin	March 6	Wang Huaixiang
Zhejiang	March 24	Nan Ping
Hunan	April 8	Li Yuan
Ningxia	April 10	Kang Jianmin

Anhui	April 18	Li Desheng
Shaanxi	May 1	Li Ruishan
Liaoning	May 10	Chen Xilian
Sichuan	May 31	Zhang Guohua
Yunnan	August 13	Tan Furen
Fujian	August 14	Han Xianchu
Guangxi	August 26	Wei Guoqing
Tibet	September 5	Zeng Yongya
Xinjiang	September 5	Long Shujin

Beginning with the Shanghai power seizure on January 6, 1967, Chinese society was embroiled in twenty months of constant upheaval until the last of the twenty-nine provinces, municipalities, and autonomous regions established their revolutionary committees on September 5, 1968. The government celebrated this as the achievement of China becoming "red through every hill and vale."

Among these twenty-nine revolutionary committees, only eight (Heilongjiang, Shandong, Shanghai, Shanxi, Tianjin, Henan, Hebei, and Shaanxi) had local cadres as their chairmen, while the other twenty-one chairmen were all military men. These first revolutionary committee chairmen also became Central Committee members or alternative members during the Ninth Party Congress.

"RESTORATION" AND "ANTI-RESTORATION"

The military-dominated "newborn red regime" could claim no systemic innovation, provided no checks and balances against bureaucratism, and did nothing to solve the government's functional problems. It did, however, reduce staffing and pull in some rebel faction leaders. A new atmosphere prevailed initially, but not for long. Mass representatives were either bureaucratized or eventually marginalized as most of the veteran cadres incorporated into the revolutionary committees "walked the old road in new shoes." Rebels saw this as a restoration of old power organs and operational methods further manifested in a gradual expansion of executive power and privilege. The expansion of office space was a case in point. For some years before the Cultural Revolution, Tianjin was the capital of Hebei Province, but in 1966 it reverted to a municipality under the direct jurisdiction of the central government, while the provincial government moved to Baoding (and subsequently to Shijiazhuang). By 1972, the Tianjin municipal party committee and revolutionary committee's leading organs and subordinate departments occupied a total of 82,500 square meters of office space, which was 26,000 square meters more than all the space occupied by the Hebei provincial party committee, provincial government, municipal party committee, and municipal departments before the Cultural Revolution. The revival and burgeoning of bureaucratic privilege also helped the children of officials avoid becoming "sent-down youths" and instead be admitted to college through the "back door."

With military and civilian bureaucrats resuming their old ways, the rebel faction launched anti-restoration campaigns in Shandong, Hubei, Gansu, Fujian, Jiangsu, Shanxi, Heilongjiang, and other places. The campaign in Shandong was launched by the chairman of the provincial revolutionary committee, Wang Xiaoyu.

Wang Xiaoyu had joined the CCP in June 1938 and became deputy chief procurator of Shandong Province in April 1954. Wang was demoted to running a cotton mill after he objected to four subordinates being designated rightists during the 1957 Anti-Rightist Campaign, but after a reexamination of his case, he was appointed deputy mayor of Qingdao in 1965. When the Red Guards began moves against the Qingdao municipal party committee in August 1966, Wang publicly expressed support for them. Mao endorsed Wang's actions in a memo on September 7, and when Shandong established its revolutionary committee on February 3, 1967, Wang was appointed its chairman. With Mao's approval, Wang was also named first political commissar of the military region in May. However, his sympathy with rebels in Shandong and with the radical faction of the leadership in Beijing soon put him in conflict with local military leaders. Under Wang's leadership, the Shandong provincial revolutionary committee launched a campaign at the end of 1968 to oppose the "pernicious trend toward reversing the verdict on the 'February Countercurrent' and toward restoration of the old ways," known for short as the anti-restoration campaign.

The anti-restoration campaign in Shandong did several things:

- It sent a worker propaganda team from Shandong's largest worker rebel faction organization, the Workers Command Post, to seize power over the provincial revolutionary committee's production headquarters, which was led by military men and had absorbed several veteran cadres from the old provincial administration, and which Wang Xiaoyu and others felt had become an independent stronghold against the revolutionary committee.
- A worker propaganda team took over the provincial revolutionary committee's data group, which Wang and others believed was compiling black dossiers to sideline rebel faction members.
- Worker organizations took over leadership of military units that had carried out the four bigs.
- The "verbal attack and armed defense general headquarters" seized control of police stations in December 1968 and January 1969, alleging that they were "compiling black dossiers on leaders of the provincial and municipal revolutionary committees."
- At the height of the anti-restoration campaign, 40 percent of the province's county and municipal revolutionary committees were toppled or reorganized by worker propaganda teams. In Liaocheng Prefecture, 90 percent of the grassroots revolutionary committees were reorganized or rebuilt from scratch.

Wang Xiaoyu's campaign infuriated the high-ranking military officers, who repeatedly complained about him to the central leadership and attacked him during the Ninth Party Congress. Mao continued to defend Wang, however, and told Jinan Military Region commander Yang Dezhi to "bring about unity." Even so, Mao couldn't afford to offend the numerous generals who opposed Wang, including Huang Yongsheng in the CMC Administrative Group. The central leadership gradually relieved Wang Xiaoyu of his official positions from November 1969 to March 1971, with Yang Dezhi taking over as chairman of the Shandong provincial revolutionary committee and head of the provincial party committee's core leading group. Almost all the power organs and key production departments came under the control of military men, leading some people to describe Shandong as a "military regime."

The situation in Heilongjiang followed a similar pattern. Pan Fusheng, who had come under attack as a member of the "Pan, Yang, Wang right-deviating anti-party clique" in Henan in 1958, was rehabilitated in 1962, and in January 1966 he became first party secretary of Heilongjiang Province and first political commissar of the provincial military district. After supporting the province's rebel faction in August 1966, Pan became chairman of China's first provincial revolutionary committee on January 31, 1967, and on May 10, 1967, Mao appointed him political commissar of the Shenyan Military Region (which had jurisdiction over Heilongjiang Province). In 1968, Pan carried out an anti-restoration campaign that resulted in the dismissal of many leading cadres from the revolutionary committees; reportedly, 29,091 cadres at the level of production brigade and above were seized and denounced, and more than fifty thousand people were implicated as accessories.[3] Having offended a large number of officials as well as violating Mao's strategic plan to "move toward great order," Pan was dismissed from all his positions in 1971 and replaced as revolutionary committee chairman by Wang Jiadao, a military man.

Since there was no systemic innovation, moving from "great chaos to great order" meant restoring the old pre–Cultural Revolution order and effectively negating the Cultural Revolution, but opposing this restoration contradicted Mao's objective of "moving toward great order." Conflicted, Mao initially encouraged the anti-restoration campaign through the October 14, 1968, *Red Flag* editorial, but when the campaign attacked the "newborn red regime," he said, "Opposing restoration is in fact restoration."[4] Zhou Enlai said, "Some places are still carrying on and still wanting to seize power, but whose power are you seizing? Isn't it seizing power from the proletariat?"[5] The rebel faction opposing restoration was suppressed in the name of "defending the newborn red regime."

After Lin Biao died while attempting to flee China in the 1971 "9-13 Incident," the military clique he'd led fell from power, and leaders of provincial revolutionary committees who were associated with Lin were unseated. As the 1970s began, Mao further undermined the military's control over the localities by switching around the commanders of the eight major military regions. Some military cadres in the revolutionary committees were returned to the ranks or demobilized, while rebel faction leaders in the revolutionary committees were marginalized. This left only the cadres who had been integrated into the revolutionary committees, allowing bureaucrats to assume control of governments at the provincial level and below, as before the Cultural Revolution.

Establishing revolutionary committees ultimately restored the state apparatus that existed during the PRC's first seventeen years while inflicting the torment of blood and fire on the general populace in the process. The red that stained "every hill and vale" at that time was the blood of ordinary people, in particular of the rebel faction, as can be seen in the narratives that follow.

HUBEI: TURBULENCE ON THE YANGTZE

Hubei's location along the middle reaches of the Yangtze River made it a transit hub in all directions. Mao had always shown a keen interest in the political situation in its capital, Wuhan, and the Cultural Revolution's progress there can be considered a classic case.

PROTECTING THE PROVINCIAL PARTY COMMITTEE AND ATTACKING RIGHTISTS

At the initial stage of the Cultural Revolution, the Hubei provincial party committee tossed out a batch of college administrators and "bourgeois reactionary academic authorities" while also attacking "rightists" among the students and teachers. This was followed in July 1966 by the ferreting out of "reactionaries" in Wuhan's factories, government organs, schools, and hospitals, and black elements came under renewed attack.[6]

As the Red Terror swept through the city in August, more than 400 people were arrested for "resisting and sabotaging the Cultural Revolution," including 159 secondary students,[7] and many people drowned themselves.

From August 1966 onward, the Capital Red Guards arrived from Beijing to fan the flames in Wuhan and bombard the Hubei provincial party committee; the city reportedly received four million students from other places by December 22.[8] The provincial party committee mobilized its own officially sponsored Red Guards to attack "a smattering of the students coming south." The rise and fall of this campaign sealed the fates of Tao Zhu and Wang Renzhong, both of whom remained in lockstep with Mao's arrangements in Beijing while doing their utmost to suppress the rebel faction in the south-central region. When Mao accused Tao Zhu of being a "double-dealer," he was probably referring to this situation. Although Tao and Wang fell from power when the bourgeois reactionary line was denounced, their anti-rightist mentality continued to heavily influence cadres and the masses in Hubei.

THE RISE OF THE REBEL FACTION

After the central leadership proposed denouncing the bourgeois reactionary line in early October 1966, Wuhan's rebel faction experienced a resurgence, and Wang Renzhong wrote a self-criticism acknowledging directional and line errors committed by the Hubei provincial party committee.

In the latter half of October 1966, the citywide Mao Zedong Thought Red Guards (part of the rebel faction) discussed establishing a unified command post but were unable to reach a consensus on positions in the organization. As a result, some school representatives withdrew and set up their own umbrella organizations, in particular the New Faction, with Zhang Liguo as one of its leaders, and the Mao Zedong Thought Red Guards Wuhan Region Revolutionary Rebel Headquarters (the Second Command Post), headed by Yang Daoyuan.

On October 11, 1966, worker rebel faction organizations throughout the city formally established a Mao Zedong Thought Fighting
Force Wuhan Regional Workers' Headquarters (the Workers' Headquarters), headed by Zhu Hongxia and Hu Houmin. Sensing luke-
warm support from the provincial party committee leaders Zhang
Tixue and Zhao Xiu, hundreds of members of the Workers' Headquarters swarmed onto a Beijing-bound train, intending to file a
complaint against the provincial party committee. This was at the
same time that Shanghai workers were hunkered down at Anting,
and Chen Boda had sent a cable to the workers in Shanghai per-
suading them to "make the minor principle subordinate to the major
principle." The Wuhan workers pasted a poster on the western gate
of Zhongnanhai demanding to know whether the "major principle"
was revolution or production. "We feel that Chan Boda reversed the
major and the minor, and this is inconsistent with Mao Zedong
Thought."[9]

The Wuhan Area Workers' Rebel Headquarters (Workers' Rebel
Headquarters) was established on December 8 (some say November
10) with Wu Yanjin as leader. On December 12, the Wuhan Steel Company rebel faction established the Mao Zedong Thought 9-13 Combat
Force (9-13 for short, named after Mao's inspection of the steel plant
on September 13, 1958), with Li Xiangyu as leader.

On November 16, the Second Command Post and other rebel faction organizations and Red Guards from Beijing marched to *Hubei
Daily*, where they demanded a reorganization of the editorial department and ordered the presses stopped. The next day, the provincial
party committee told Red Guards from the first unified command post
to protect the party newspaper and drive out the rebel Red Guards,
resulting in bloodshed. On November 18, Zhang Tixue acknowledged
the rebel faction's "revolutionary action."

In early December, with the support of the Wuhan municipal party
committee, some staff held a meeting at the Wuhan Machine Tool
Factory advocating the establishment of the citywide Revolutionary
Staff Federation,[10] which rapidly developed into a conservative workers' organization with four hundred thousand members. The Revolutionary Staff Federation defended the provincial party committee,

demanded that the Workers' Headquarters be disbanded, and opposed students going to the factories to establish ties.

At the beginning of January 1967, hundreds of thousands of Wuhan students and workers held two denunciation rallies against Wang Renzhong at the Xinhua Road Stadium, with Zhang Tixue, Zhang Xiu, and other provincial and municipal leaders serving as secondary targets of criticism. The rebel faction took control of schools, government organs, and factories throughout the city, bringing operations to a standstill.

THE POWER SEIZURE ABORTED, THE REBEL FACTION SPLITS INTO THE "FRAGRANT FLOWER" AND "POISONOUS WEED" SUBFACTIONS

On the morning of January 26, 1967, student and worker rebel leaders held a power seizure preparatory meeting at Hubei University but failed to reach a consensus on the leadership of the revolutionary committee. That afternoon, the Workers' Headquarters declared the seizure of power over the municipal and provincial party committees, but in the meantime, the Second Command Post had snatched the official seals from the provincial party committee, while the Workers' Rebel Headquarters had snatched the official seals from the Wuhan municipal party committee. As a result, the power seizure fell through.

The failure of the January 26 power seizure intensified the conflicts among the rebel faction organizations. After big character posters accused the Workers' Headquarters, the Second Command Post, and other organizations of revisionism and impurity, twelve radical rebel organizations jointly published the "February 8 Statement" in *Changjiang* (Yangtze) *Daily*, which they controlled, accusing their rivals of "right-deviating opportunism" and of being "Trotskyites," and calling for utter chaos throughout the city. The Workers' Headquarters, 9-13, Second Command Post, and other organizations considered the article a "big fragrant flower," while the Workers' Rebel Headquarters and New Faction pronounced it a "big poisonous weed." This split the rebel faction into the "fragrant flower" and "poisonous weed" subfactions.

THE MILITARY SUPPRESSES THE REBEL FACTION

On February 18, the Wuhan Military Region issued a "stern announce-ment" (the "February 18 Statement") condemning the February 8 State-ment as "a meticulous plot by a smattering of people with ulterior motives to create division and instigate fighting among the masses and divert the spearhead of struggle." On February 22, Zhu Hongxia, Hu Houmin, and Yang Daoyuan responded with a diametrically opposite viewpoint pub-lished at length in *Changjiang Daily*, and tens of thousands of members of the "fragrant flower" subfaction marched through the streets protest-ing the February 18 Statement. On the afternoon of February 23, the military region deployed more than seventy vehicles carrying more than three thousand fully armed soldiers to parade through the streets yelling out, "The February 8 Statement is a big poisonous weed!" while innumer-able copies of the February 18 statement were dropped from airplanes.

On March 4, *Hubei Daily*, controlled by the poisonous weed New Faction, published an editorial criticizing the military's suppression of the rebel faction, and the military considered this essay another big poisonous weed.

On March 6, the Wuhan People's Armed Forces Seize Revolution and Push Production Office (known as the Seize Office) was estab-lished. Composed of representatives of the military, civilian cadres, and the masses, the Seize Office took up the work originally carried out by the provincial government. On March 15, the Wuhan Military Region held a cadre rally during which military region leaders such as Chen Zaidao, Zhong Hanhua, and Han Dongshan harshly criticized the rebel faction. The rebel faction referred to the military-dominated Seize Office as a "military regime."

A joint operation by the military and police to implement the CMC's Eight-Point Order on the night of March 17 resulted in the arrest of more than five hundred members of the Workers' Headquar-ters, which was then banned as a counterrevolutionary organization. This revitalized the conservative faction, with organizations such as the Staff Federation, once in disarray, rapidly resurrected under var-ious pretexts. The most influential of these, the Red Militia, went zooming around in trucks, armed and helmeted,[11] as a show of force.

Facing immense pressure from the military, the rebel faction's fragrant flower and poisonous weed subfactions reunited for a protest march on March 27, during which they demanded, "Ferret out the military's Old Tan and reverse the verdict on the Workers' Headquarters!"[12] The New Faction and Workers' Rebel Headquarters attacked the military region headquarters on April 11, and on May 1, the fragrant flower and poisonous weed subfactions jointly staged massive protests throughout the Greater Wuhan area. In the face of united resistance by Wuhan's rebel faction, the armed forces supported several dozen conservative faction organizations in establishing an umbrella organization called the Million Heroes, which rapidly grew from 920,000 members to 1.29 million. The group moved to an office in the Wuhan municipal party committee compound on June 4, with more than a hundred veteran municipal party committee cadres putting in an appearance as a show of support.[13]

On June 4, the Wuhan armed forces announced that "ox demons and snake spirits were swarming out, making waves, and taking advantage of circumstances," after which the Million Heroes intensified armed attacks on the rebel faction, resulting in a series of violent incidents in which more than a hundred rebels were killed or injured in less than a month.[14]

The rebel faction responded to this immense pressure by adding the word "Steel" to the names of some of its organizations, and the Three Steels joined with other rebel organizations known as the Three News to organize regular protest marches of hundreds of thousands of people. The famous poet Bai Hua, who was in active military service at that time, voiced his support for the rebel faction by distributing a suite of poems titled "Leaflets Distributed in the Face of Iron Spears," which were copied onto big-character posters throughout Greater Wuhan. The writer Yao Xueyin likewise wrote a poem distributed in mimeographed booklets that compared the Wuhan Military Region's suppression of the rebels to the KMT's crackdown on Communists in Hunan in 1927.

The Central Party School professor Wang Haiguang observes that in Beijing the Cultural Revolution was driven by students, while in Shanghai it was driven by workers and in Wuhan by a combination of students and workers.[15] One more feature should be added: The rare phenomenon of Wuhan's rebel faction splitting into the fragrant flower and poisonous weed subfactions and then uniting again to resist suppression.

After Mao and Zhou Enlai arrived in Wuhan on July 14, Zhou summoned Xie Fuzhi, Yu Lijin, and Wang Li, who were in the southwest dealing with problems in Kunming, Chengdu, and Guiyang. Mao took personal command of the Wuhan problem by explicitly supporting the rebel faction, referring to the Million Heroes as a conservative organization, and accusing the Wuhan Military Region of line errors. Mao and Zhou's attitudes met with intense resistance from the armed forces and Million Heroes, resulting in the July 20 Incident that caused a nationwide sensation as the "Wuhan mutiny" (the details of this incident will be described in the next chapter). This incident resulted in the ousting of the leaders of the Wuhan Military Region and the bloody annihilation of the conservative faction at the hands of the rebel faction, which put up banners proclaiming, "Dawn has broken, liberation is here!" Shaken by the July 20 Incident, Mao felt compelled to modify his wholesale support for the rebel faction.

THE ALLIANCE OF THE STEEL FACTION AND THE NEW FACTION

After the July 20 Incident, the central leadership appointed Zeng Siyu (formerly deputy commander of the Shenyang Military Region) to replace Chen Zaidao as commander of the Wuhan Military Region, and Zeng became a top power-holder in Hubei and Wuhan, along with other new appointees: the political commissar Liu Feng (formerly deputy commander of the Wuhan Military Region air force), the Fifteenth Airborne Army commander Fang Ming, and the political commissar Zhang Chunqing.

The July 20 Incident gave the rebel faction the upper hand, but with the conservative faction greatly weakened and external pressure largely removed, conflicts between the Steel Faction and the New Faction resurfaced. Cashing in on its new renown, the Steelworkers' Headquarters wanted to form a grand alliance of all Wuhan's rebel organizations under its banner, but the New Faction resented having put its neck on the line and getting no thanks from Zhu Hongxia apart from an overture to absorb it.

While accompanying some foreign guests to Wuhan on October 8, 1967, Zhou Enlai found time to receive representatives of Wuhan's various mass organizations. Zhou said, "If I say there should be a grand alliance led by the Steel Faction, the New Faction will be unhappy, and if I say there should be a grand alliance led by the New Faction, the Steel Faction will be unhappy. I think neither should lead; why not establish a revolutionary workers' representative assembly instead?" Everyone fervently applauded this suggestion, and Zhou said, "Then it's settled—form this alliance, and we'll all be happy."[16]

Under Zhou Enlai's prompting, the Wuhan rebel faction prepared to establish representative assemblies for workers, peasants, and Red Guards, and after several meetings with military cadres, they finally reached an agreement to form a grand alliance. The Wuhan Municipal Revolutionary Committee was formally established on January 20, 1968, with the Fifteenth Airborne Army commander Fang Ming as chairman. Among the eight vice-chairs, three were military men and three were cadres, and the Steel Faction and New Faction were each represented by one worker. Among the twenty-seven standing committee members, five were from the military, five were cadres, and the rest were mass representatives from the Steel Faction and New Faction. The Hubei provincial revolutionary committee was established on February 5, 1968, with the military region commander Zeng Siyu as chairman, and Liu Feng and Zhang Tixue appointed vice-chairmen, along with several rebel faction leaders. *People's Daily* published editorials celebrating both occasions.

The majority of mass organization representatives recruited into the revolutionary committees had no real power; Zhu Hongxia was vice-chairman of the provincial revolutionary committee, but his actual posting was as commander in chief of the Hubei Province Flood-Prevention Headquarters. Li Xiangyu, although vice-chairman of the municipal revolutionary committee, was officially chairman of the Wuhan Municipal Patriotic Health Campaign Committee; and another vice-chairman, Wu Yanjin, was head of the Wuhan Municipal Repair and Recycle Office. The student leaders Zhang Liguo and Yang

Daoyuan were ostensibly vice-chairmen of the provincial revolutionary committee, but their actual postings were as chairmen of the revolutionary committees of the Central China Engineering Institute and Wuhan Surveying and Mapping Institute, respectively, and after the Worker Propaganda Teams entered the universities in autumn 1968, both were sent back for "reeducation."

RESTORATION AND ANTI-RESTORATION

After the revolutionary committees were established, they shifted to the pattern of struggle, criticize, and reform. According to the Sixteen Articles, this meant struggling against capitalist roaders, criticizing bourgeois reactionary academic authorities, and reforming education, literature, and art. But in Wuhan this process was applied to the rebel faction. This was because pre–Cultural Revolution bureaucratic forces continued to dominate the revolutionary committees, and the military leaders shared their viewpoints. Of course it didn't help that the rebels were so violent and unruly.

Many work units took advantage of the Cleansing of the Class Ranks in 1968 to isolate rebel faction members for "special investigation," and many work units rebelled against the rebel faction and seized power from those who had seized power.[17]

On April 10, 1969, a big-character poster signed by Zhu Hongxia, Li Xiangyu, and Wu Yanjin was pasted on the water tower in Wuhan's city center. Titled "When Humanity Is Liberated, I Am Liberated: Shedding Hot Blood for the People," it proclaimed the opposition of "restoration," defined as the targeting and marginalization of rebels. This big-character poster was rapidly copied by hand and mimeograph and distributed throughout Greater Wuhan, and the rebel faction responded with anti-restoration pledge rallies, including one in Hankou on April 27 that drew more than one hundred thousand participants.

The campaign occurred just as the CCP was holding its Ninth Party Congress. On the morning of April 29, the central leadership invited the rebel leaders Zhu Hongxia, Li Xiangyu, Wu Yanjin, Yang Daoyuan, and Zhang Liguo to Beijing to resolve the problems in Wuhan. Several more meetings were held with Hu Houmin and other representatives in the provincial and municipal revolutionary committees in May. During these meetings, central leaders harshly criticized the anti-restoration campaign. Kang Sheng said, "The situation is excellent now; how is it a restoration of the old ways?"[18] On the night of May 27, Zhou Enlai transmitted a Central Committee document[19] that accused the anti-restoration campaign of "placing the three representative assemblies, primarily the Workers' Representative Assembly, above all else. This defies Chairman Mao's instructions regarding the revolutionary grand alliance, revolutionary three-in-one combination, and centralized leadership." The anti-restoration campaign languished from then on, but antagonism between the rebel faction and the revolutionary committees continued.

THE BEI-JUE-YANG CASE

As the grand alliance and three-in-one combination reinstated cadres who had been struck down, and rebel faction leaders wrangled over positions on the revolutionary committees, many people lost direction and joined the "aloof faction," while those who continued to harbor idealistic feelings began to consider some deep-seated issues: What was the point of participating so enthusiastically in the Cultural Revolution? How would the Cultural Revolution continue? In which direction was China going? In August 1967, Mao stimulated young people's reflections by saying, "The real hope is with those who have the ability to ponder problems without seeking the limelight. The people who are causing such a big fuss now are sure to be a flash in the pan."[20] In the Mao era, ordinary people were allowed to read only the works of Mao, Marx, and Lenin, so these became sources for social criticism in a "new thought trend" (xinsichao). Many of the resulting essays were eloquent and incisive, but it was inevitable that a trend toward heterodox thinking would develop according to its own logic and break through the boundaries of Mao Zedong Thought to become its antithesis. After the revolutionary committees were established, the "new thought trend" expressed young people's dissatisfaction with the Cultural Revolution, targeting the CCRSG, Lin Biao, Zhou Enlai, and even Mao and the entire social system. The Bei-Jue-Yang group that emerged in Wuhan was an example of this.

On November 7, 1967, a dozen or so students from the Central

China Engineering Institute, led by Lu Li'an and Feng Tianai, established the Big Dipper Society and pasted its founding manifesto on the Hankou water tower democracy wall. The manifesto ended with the words "Big Dipper, Big Dipper, who will decide the destiny of China and the world over the coming decades?" In late December they organized a liaison station to "resolutely carry out the Great Proletarian Cultural Revolution to the end," as a result of which they came to be known as the Resolute Faction. The authorities eventually referred to them as Bei-Jue-Yang, the Chinese characters standing for "Big Dipper," "resolute," and Yangtze, referring to the *Yangtze Review*, a journal they published. They never numbered as many as thirty members and had no power, but their thinking was very penetrating, with "uninhibited essays, eloquent argumentation, untrammeled spirit, and righteous sentiments that were once legendary in Greater Wuhan."[21] Their radical viewpoints—publicly criticizing the revolutionary committees and military region, calling for armed battle, and criticizing Zhou Enlai and Zhang Chunqiao—went too far for the Steel Faction's and New Faction's leaders, and some rebels criticized their thinking as "ultra-leftist."

Perceiving the danger of this thought trend, the CCP Central Committee on September 27 issued its "Directive on the Wuhan Problem,"[22] which referred to Bei-Jue-Yang as a "hodgepodge of traitors, spies, and counterrevolutionaries operating under false pretenses and plotting behind the scenes." The directive accused Bei-Jue-Yang of "engaging in a counterrevolutionary restoration of the old order," demanded the closure of *Yangtze Review* as "a reactionary publication," and called for "massive opposition to anarchism."

The document's baseless framing of these young people shows the Central Committee's urgent need to stabilize the revolutionary committees. After the July 20 Incident, the Central Committee used iron-fisted military officers such as Zeng Siyu and Liu Feng to investigate Bei-Jue-Yang on the pretext of cleansing the class ranks, and to ruthlessly crush the rebel faction in the name of investigating the "May 16 conspiratorial clique."[23] On May 17, 1968, Lu Li'an was seized by the New Faction and then held for eleven years without trial before finally being released without charge in 1979. Feng Tianai also spent ten years in prison. By the time the Hubei investigations ended in late

1973, a total of 33,659 people had been investigated in connection with May 16 and Bei-Jue-Yang;[24] some sources claim that 600,000 people were purged.[25]

On November 5, 1969, Wuhan sent 1,319 major and minor leaders of the Steel Faction and New Faction and other relevant individuals to Beijing, where they were held at the Air Force Academy for "Mao Zedong Thought study classes" run by the Central Committee (another 1,600 people joined them midway). According to Chen Boda's instructions, they had to confess the errors and crimes they'd committed during the Cultural Revolution and thoroughly expose and criticize Bei-Jue-Yang, May 16, and rebel faction leaders. Liu Wantai from the Steelworkers' Headquarters, Zhang Pengcheng from Steel 9-13, and Wang Jinming from the Workers' Rebel Headquarters were designated "current counterrevolutionaries," denounced by the entire study class and escorted back to Wuhan under arrest. Later Hu Houmin, Yang Daoyuan, and Li Xiangyu were also imprisoned. When the study classes ended at the end of June 1970, the participants were sent back to their original work units to undergo investigation and mass criticism.

After 1971's 9-13 Incident, the Wuhan Military Region's political commissar, Liu Feng, was expelled from the party as a die-hard follower of Lin Biao's. Military region commander Zeng Siyu was declared only a "marginal member" of the Lin Biao clique and continued working in Hubei. On January 6, 1973, military representatives of Wuhan's "Three Supports and Two Militaries" returned to their units. A reorganization of the military region leadership in December 1973 resulted in Zeng Siyu switching places with the Jinan Military Region commander Yang Dezhi, and Zhao Xinchu became chairman of the Hubei Provincial Revolutionary Committee.

The rebel faction revived for a time after one hundred thousand soldiers and civilians took part in a mass mobilization rally to "criticize Lin Biao and Confucius" on January 28, 1974. Hu Houmin, Li Xiangyu, and other rebel leaders were released on March 2 and resumed their postings in the provincial and municipal revolutionary committees; Hu Houmin was "boosted" to vice-chairman of the provincial federation of trade unions.

When Deng Xiaoping engaged in economic improvement and

"general overhaul" in 1975, rebel faction leaders were sent to the country-side for "tempering," but they became active again during the subsequent campaign to "criticize Deng and beat back against the right-deviating case-reversal trend." The Gang of Four was arrested in Beijing on October 6, 1976, and on December 28, Hubei's Gang of Four, Xia Bangyin, Zhu Hongxia, Hu Houmin, and Zhang Liguo were also arrested. Xia Bangyin, a former Hanyang steelworker appointed to the Ninth and Tenth Central Committees, was imprisoned for thirteen years. Zhu Hongxia was sentenced to fifteen years, and Zhang Liguo to thirteen years. Hu Houmin, also sentenced to thirteen years, died in prison. Other rebel faction leaders also received lengthy prison terms. The leader of the Second Command Post, Yang Daoyuan, was imprisoned for twelve years, after which he went into business, only to be imprisoned for another fifteen years for accepting 30,000 yuan as a middleman in a corruption case. Ren Aisheng, a former member of the Hubei provincial party committee who had staunchly supported the rebel faction, was also imprisoned in the later stage of the Cultural Revolution.

GUIZHOU: ENDLESS THUNDER[26]

Guizhou was the fourth province (after Heilongjiang, Shanghai, and Shanxi) to carry out the "red through every hill and vale" campaign. *People's Daily* hailed the January 25, 1967, power seizure in Guizhou with a February 1 editorial titled "Spring Thunder in the Southwest," but the thunder continued rumbling nonstop in Guizhou after the revolutionary committee was established on February 13, 1967.

FROM THE "6-6 INCIDENT" TO THE ESTABLISHMENT OF THE REVOLUTIONARY COMMITTEES

The Four Cleanups movement in Guizhou adhered to Liu Shaoqi's thinking and the "Taoyuan experience," holding that "Guizhou was already rotten" and that "Guiyang City was a duplicitous counterrevolutionary regime." After the Four Cleanups movement, the provincial first secretary, Zhou Lin, was ousted and replaced by Li Dazhang, but after Mao ordered the recall of the Four Cleanups work teams in January 1965, Zhou Lin was appointed secretary of the Southwest Bureau secretariat, and Jia Qiyun replaced Li Dazhang as provincial first secretary. In May 1966, the provincial party committee, under Jia Qiyun, tossed out Wang Xiaochuan, a provincial party committee standing committee member and provincial propaganda department head who had been denounced during the Four Cleanups campaign, making him the first victim of the Cultural Revolution in Guizhou.

On June 6, 1966, *Guizhou Daily* devoted a three-page essay and an editorial to attacking Wang Xiaochuan under the subheadings "Anti-Party," "Anti-Socialist," and "Anti–Mao Zedong Thought." Hypervigilant students at Guiyang's No. 5 Secondary School interpreted the subheadings as reactionary slogans, setting off mass criticism of the newspaper and the provincial party committee. The provincial party committee retaliated on June 8 by labeling the protests a "counterrevolutionary incident," and sent 130 cadres in seven work groups and one observation group to eight universities and colleges. According to incomplete statistics, more than 7,200 people throughout the province were denounced, imprisoned, and sent to labor reform as "counterrevolutionaries," and 189 people attempted suicide (107 successful) in the Guiyang area by July 10.[27]

The Guiyang Medical School, which seized and denounced nearly 16 percent of its students and staff following the "6-6 Incident," became a Cultural Revolution experimental unit for the provincial first secretary Jia Qiyuan. Adhering to Mao's directive, Jia rehabilitated the students and teachers who had been labeled as counterrevolutionaries, and some became core members of an officially sponsored Red Guard organization established at the school on August 22. This Red Guard organization naturally endorsed the provincial party committee and opposed the medical school party committee. Students and teachers who supported the school's party committee then established an alliance with students from Beijing on the Great Networking and began bombarding the provincial party committee on August 27. The provincial party committee retaliated with mass attacks against the rebels, which only inspired more rebellion. After Mao reviewed the Red Guards for the third time on September 15, a host of new student

Red Guard organizations sprang up in Guizhou commemorating the date in their names.

Gradually, various student and worker groups formed umbrella alliances against or in support of the provincial party committee. The provincial first secretary, Jia Qiyun, and the deputy political commissar of the provincial military district, Li Zaihan, who was also a member of the provincial Cultural Revolution leading group, were instrumental in the formation of groups and alliances that defended the provincial party committee against the rebel faction.

The rebel faction formed its first "grand alliance" at the end of November, and soon afterward enjoyed a turn of events in its favor. During a traffic accident in Guiyang on December 3, a vehicle driven by members of the conservative faction killed two rebel workers. Li Zaihan agreed to a three-day citywide work stoppage and street protests to mourn the deaths, and he and Jia Qiyun sent a floral wreath to the memorial ceremony as well as delivered eulogies in which they acknowledged the deceased as martyrs. Afterward, the rebels escorted a cowering Jia Qiyun back to the provincial capital in a grand procession, and Li Zaihan was hailed for joining with the worker rebel leader Li Tienai in opposing the provincial party committee.

The "two-Li" alliance was fleeting, however; on December 5, worker rebels seized a large amount of black dossier material from *Guizhou Daily*, which Li Tienai claimed contained "ironclad" evidence that Li Zaihan was "even worse than Jia Qiyun." This raised Li Zaihan's guard, and on December 27 he told Li Tienai to hand over leadership of the rebel alliance to another rebel leader, Xu Yingnian. Li Tienai refused and in short order established a new rebel alliance, while also going to Beijing in January 1967 to agitate against Li Zaihan.

Back in Guiyang, Li Zaihan bolstered his alliance and then sent a cable to the PLA's General Political Department and to the CCRSG on January 20, accusing Li Tienai's alliance of shifting its spearhead of struggle toward the military and of "kidnapping soldiers and seizing weapons and ammunition." The CCRSG immediately had Li Tienai arrested and escorted back to Guiyang, where he subsequently spent fifteen years behind bars. Heads of other worker mass organizations were also arrested and their headquarters disbanded.

On January 21, Mao wrote a memo to Zhou Enlai on Li Zaihan's cable, suggesting that Li Zaihan, "certain revolutionary cadres," and "reliable mass revolutionary rebel faction leaders" should be brought to Beijing to hash out a resolution. "This can be done for each province and city. Resolve one at a time."[28]

Zhou Enlai responded on January 24 by flying a twelve-member delegation from Guizhou to Beijing, including Li Zaihan and the provincial military district commander He Guangyu. Central leaders received the delegation five times over the next five days.

Meanwhile, on January 25, rebels in Guizhou seized power and established the Guizhou Province Proletarian Revolutionary Rebel General Headquarters. Early the next morning, however, military and public security forces raided rebel alliance strongholds and arrested more than a hundred people, and members of the conservative alliance likewise carried out attacks on rebel-controlled work units, claiming a string of victories.

When Commander He Guangyu updated central leaders on these developments during their third meeting on January 28, Jiang Qing said, "Li Tienai is a hooligan! He wants to be king of the southwest. We don't know what's going on, but we decided to arrest him based on Comrade Li Zaihan's grasp of the situation and his cables." However, she denied that the rebel alliance was a counterrevolutionary organization: "This cannot be said of the broad masses. The main leaders have already been arrested." On February 13, the Mao Zedong Thought Guizhou Province Revolutionary Committee was established with Li Zaihan as chairman.

THE RED REGIME'S OPPOSITION FACTION

Li Zaihan summed up the experience of power seizure in Guizhou as "seizing above and sweeping below, hitting out in both directions," by which he meant that power had been seized from Guizhou provincial first secretary Jia Qiyun at the top, and Li Tienai and other ox demons and snake spirits had been swept out below, while attacking and disbanding radicals on both the left and the right.

According to incomplete figures, this strategy resulted in 218 mass organizations with a total of 520,000 members being labeled as "reactionary organizations" in February and March 1967, and more than

2,000 people being imprisoned. Unlike other localities, Guizhou's "February Campaign to Suppress Counterrevolutionaries" was carried out by the province's newly established revolutionary committee.

The suppression inevitably drew a counterattack, to which Li Zaihan responded with a second round of suppression.

After the Guizhou Province Revolutionary Committee was established, Li Zaihan decided to convene a representative assembly of Guizhou's Red Guards and reorganize the Red Guards from top to bottom, but this only resulted in more conflicts and protests, and the formation of two new factions, one supporting and the other opposing the representative assembly.

The representative assembly ended on April 20 with the selection of forty-five committee members and a nine-member standing committee, all members of the supporting faction, which exacerbated the antagonism between the two factions. Opposition to the representative assembly coalesced into a larger faction opposing the provincial revolutionary committee, named the 4-11 Faction for a mass rally held on April 11. Li Zaihan responded with a crackdown, and anyone who shared the viewpoints of the 4-11 was ejected from the provincial revolutionary committee and its departments and from Red Guard organizations in tertiary and secondary schools.

At the same time, Li Zaihan deployed massive manpower to forcibly establish supportive revolutionary committees at Guiyang Medical School, Guiyang Normal School, and Guizhou University in May and June. These three revolutionary committees were energetically promoted in *New Guizhou Daily* and became models for establishing revolutionary committees in every work unit, county, and city in the province.

Nevertheless, the 4-11 Faction drew increasing support among Guiyang's students and workers. To "defend the red regime," Li Zaihan organized a special fighting organization, the Guizhou 8-18 Corps, to attack the 4-11 Faction multiple times from April to August. More than sixty thousand students, workers, and cadres affiliated with 4-11 fled to Beijing and other major cities, where they exposed Li Zaihan's military suppression.

The suppression of 4-11 facilitated the establishment of revolutionary committees in all the province's eighty-five counties and cities by

April 14, 1968, but the majority were controlled by one faction and were therefore unstable.

LI ZAIHAN STEPS DOWN, LAN YINONG TAKES CHARGE

Around November 18, 1968, the support-the-left PLA unit stationed in Guizhou was replaced by one that had been stationed in Yunnan and which had a different perspective regarding its mission. This led to a resurgence of the 4-11 Faction, which resumed its battle against Li Zaihan. The situation in Guizhou became increasingly complex.

On February 24, 1969, the central leadership held a meeting to solve the problems in Guizhou. Then, following a March 27 directive that called for "continuing to strengthen and develop the existing revolutionary grand alliance and revolutionary three-in-one combination" and "persistently supporting the Guizhou Province Revolutionary Committee and endorsing the newborn red regime," Li Zaihan released imprisoned 4-11 leaders and disbanded the violent Guizhou 8-18 Corps. However, Li then used a July 23, 1969, notice by the Central Committee targeting the rebel faction in Shanxi as a rationale for once again attacking 4-11 strongholds. Mass violence at Guiyang's Zhilin'an Square on July 29 resulted in fifty-four deaths and more than one hundred people injured.

An investigative report by Xinhua journalists in the latter half of August 1969 led Zhou Enlai to call eighty-seven provincial and prefectural leaders from Guizhou to Beijing for study classes to solve the problems in Guizhou. In a report to Mao on September 24, Zhou Enlai, Chen Boda, and Kang Sheng blamed Li Zaihan's guiding ideology for a long-term factional split in the provincial military district that had prevented resolution of the problem. On October 26, the Central Committee issued Document No. 71 (1969) stating that Li Zaihan, "after seizing power, became big-headed and gradually sank into bourgeois factionalism and engaged in double-dealing, whipped up an 'independent kingdom' to oppose the central leadership and suppress the masses, and deviated from Chairman Mao's revolutionary line." This document announced that the Kunming Military Region deputy political commissar Lan Yinong would simultaneously serve as first political commissar of the Guizhou Province Military District, while the

Forty-Third Army commander Zhang Rongsen would lead the military's support-the-left work in the province.

During another round of study classes from November 1969 to April 1970, the leaders of both of Guizhou's factions carried out self-criticism and urged all mass organizations to form a grand alliance, and 4-11 voluntarily disbanded. In the second half of May, leading organs in Guizhou underwent restructuring with the approval of the central leadership. Lan Yinong was appointed chairman of the provincial revolutionary committee, with Zhang Rongsen as its first vice-chairman. Nine former 4-11 members joined the committee, with one becoming a vice-chair and two appointed to the standing committee. Li Zaihan was dismissed from all his civilian and military positions.

During the rectification movement after Lin Biao's downfall, Lan Yinong said he would not "betray a friend for personal benefit" and took a passive approach to the campaign. On September 3, 1972, thirteen Guizhou officials, including Lan Yinong and Zhang Rongsen, were summoned to Beijing to report on the anti-Lin campaign in Guizhou. On September 15, the Central Committee issued Document No. 38 (1972) regarding Guizhou Province, which stated, "Comrades Lan Yinong and Zhang Rongsen have taken the side of the Lin Biao anti-party clique and have committed directional line error and the error of factionalism. Comrade Lan Yinong's error is especially grave." Lan was sent to the countryside for manual labor.

On September 16, 1972, Lu Ruilin became chairman of a work group to resolve the Guizhou problem, and a year later he became first secretary of the Guizhou provincial party committee and chairman of the provincial revolutionary committee.

CHONGQING, SICHUAN PROVINCE: AN INCESSANT BARRAGE[29]

Chongqing is the economic hub of the upper reaches of the Yangtze River, and the largest industrial and commercial city and land and water transport hub in southwestern China. During the War of Resistance against Japan, after Nanjing fell, Chongqing became China's secondary capital. On the eve of the Cultural Revolution, Chongqing was a municipality under the direct jurisdiction of Sichuan Province, with eight districts and three counties and a total population of more than four million, making it one of China's eight major cities.

At the outset of the Cultural Revolution, the Chongqing municipal party committee followed Beijing's example by rooting out black gangs. On June 21, Zheng Siqun, party secretary and president of Chongqing University, was denounced as a black gang member in *Chongqing Daily*. The municipal party committee dispatched a work group of more than two hundred people to the university, and 90 percent of its top two levels of administrators were sidelined and denounced. The July 1, 1966, issue of *Red Flag* magazine published an essay by the CCRSG member Mu Xin[30] that resurrected a decades-old literary dispute in which Chongqing's current first secretary and mayor, Ren Baige, had been tangentially involved. This resulted in Ren Baige falling from power and being replaced by a member of the provincial party committee secretariat, Lu Dadong.

CONSERVATIVE FACTION, REBEL FACTION

The efforts of the municipal party committee and of the first secretary of the Southwest Bureau, Li Jingquan, resulted in the formation of four massive, officially sponsored umbrella groups among students, workers, and cultural personnel that the rebel faction referred to as the "Royalist Four Armies." These conservative organizations focused on smashing the four olds, and according to statistics from the Chongqing Municipal Public Security Bureau, 13,160 "ox demon and snake spirit" homes were ransacked throughout the city.

Chongqing's rebel faction originated at Chongqing University. Unlike those in other places, the university's rebel faction didn't oppose the school leadership but rather protested the unjust treatment of the university president Zheng Siqun. Zheng had studied in Japan early on, and after joining the CCP he had reached the level of a seventh-class cadre, enjoying enormous prestige among his students. But at the outset of the Cultural Revolution, he was formally denounced by the municipal party committee and repeatedly attacked by teachers and students. After Zheng cut his throat with half a razor blade on August 2, the university work group called a mass rally to posthumously denounce him and expel him from the party. A student from the department of electrical engineering, Zhou Ziren, put up a big-character poster demanding a reexamination of Zheng's case, and this soon led to the establishment of a rebel organization opposing the municipal party committee. Similar rebel organizations then proliferated at other tertiary institutions, and a student rebel umbrella group was established on September 29.

By then the authors of the popular revolutionary novel *Red Cliff*, Luo Guangbin and Yang Yiyan, had established a rebel group for cultural personnel, which carried out the first rebel power seizure in Chongqing. At the end of September, student rebel organizations helped with the formation of the first worker rebel faction organization, under the leadership of Huang Lian, a demobilized soldier.

Chongqing's earliest rebels were attacked and paraded through the streets, but at the height of the campaign against the bourgeois reactionary line in October, rebel faction organizations rose up to denounce power-holders at every level and demanded rehabilitation of those who had been labeled counterrevolutionaries.

The participation of six hundred of Chongqing's rebel workers in Mao's sixth review of the Red Guards in Beijing on November 3 lent enormous momentum to Chongqing's rebel mass organizations and allowed them to claim equal status with the Royalist Four Armies.

When one of the officially sponsored groups held a "mass pledge rally to expose and criticize the bourgeois reactionary line of the Southwest Bureau and provincial and municipal party committees" on December 4, 1966, the rebel faction designated this a "fake criticism and actual cover-up plot" and attacked the rally venue, resulting in hundreds of injuries and rumors of deaths in what came to be known as the December 4 Incident.

As criticism of the bourgeois reactionary line progressed, many rebel organizations joined to create the enormous 8-15 Faction. The Fifty-Fourth Army, which had supported the conservative faction at the outset of the Cultural Revolution, switched its allegiance to the 8-15 Faction once the bourgeois reactionary line was denounced and the central leadership handed down its order to support the left. By then, Chongqing's conservative faction had already disintegrated.

POWER SEIZURE SPLITS THE REBEL FACTION

After the January 1967 power seizure, splits developed between the dominant 8-15 Faction and other rebel groups.

The 8-15 coalition in late January 1967 declared that it had seized power over all Chongqing's party and government organs and formed a Chongqing Proletarian Revolutionary Rebel Alliance Committee Preparatory Committee (Revolutionary Alliance) led by representatives of the Fifty-Fourth Army. On February 1, more than fifty rebel mass organizations sent a joint cable to Beijing claiming that the January 24 power seizure was bogus. Using the slogan "Smash the Revolutionary Alliance," these organizations came to be known as the Smash Faction. Despite their protest, the Revolutionary Alliance was declared formally established on February 8, with the deputy director of the Fifty-Fourth Army's political department, Liu Runquan, as chairman. This exacerbated the antagonism between the 8-15 Faction and the Smash Faction.

Without a grand alliance, the central leadership refused to acknowledge the January power seizure in Chongqing. Nevertheless, the Revolutionary Alliance considered itself the newborn red regime, and its members drew on the instruments of dictatorship to suppress the Smash Faction as counterrevolutionary, rightist, and illegal, and to subject its members to ransacking, arrest, and torture. Huang Lian and others were imprisoned, and one of the *Red Cliff* authors, Luo Guangbin, was driven to suicide. From February 24 to March 18, 36 reactionary organizations were banned, and 82 were destroyed by 8-15 mass organizations, while 146 disbanded of their own accord. The Chongqing Public Security Bureau's historical annals office subsequently reported that during the February Suppression of Counterrevolutionaries, 2,253 people were arrested, and twenty-four mass organizations were banned as counterrevolutionary or illegal organizations.

THE DENUNCIATION OF THE FEBRUARY COUNTERCURRENT
AND THE RISE OF "REBEL TO THE END"

On April 1, 1967, the Central Committee handed down its "Decision Regarding the Anhui Problem and Appendix," which was followed on

April 6 by the CMC's Ten-Point Order. The two authoritative documents, combined with denunciation of the February Countercurrent, led to the rapid resurgence of banned mass organizations, and people who had been attacked began organizing rallies and marches against the February Countercurrent and calling for the smashing of "the illegal Revolutionary Alliance."

After Huang Lian and other imprisoned leaders of the Smash Faction were released, they accompanied the chief of staff of the Fifty-Fourth Army, Geng Zhigang, to Beijing for meetings on how to solve the Sichuan problem. Following their return, a Smash Faction student organization called Chongqing Red Guard Rebel to the End Headquarters was established in May.

On May 16, 1967, with Mao's approval, the Central Committee issued Document No. 159 (1967) (known in Chongqing as the Red Five Articles), which held that Chongqing's support-the-left troops, while making "notable achievements," had erred by "supporting one side and suppressing another side, supporting the public security departments in their wrongful arrest of revolutionary masses, and labeling one group of revolutionary masses as 'counterrevolutionaries.'" The document demanded rehabilitation of mass organizations and individuals and authorized the immediate establishment of the Chongqing Revolutionary Committee Preparatory Committee with the deputy political commissar of the Fifty-Fourth Army, Lan Yinong, as chairman and the deputy commander, Bai Bin, as vice-chairman. However, the document evaded the subject of the Revolutionary Alliance, which was the bone of contention between the two factions.

On May 17, the Smash Faction organized a huge rally and march endorsing the Red Five Articles and hailing the "death of the Revolutionary Alliance," countered on May 18 by an 8-15 Faction march to "defend the Revolutionary Alliance to the death." After the leaders of the Fifty-Fourth Army convinced the 8-15 Faction that the Chongqing Revolutionary Committee Preparatory Committee was just another name for the Revolutionary Alliance, the faction publicly endorsed the Red Five Articles. The Smash Faction, however, refused to recognize the Preparatory Committee because of its favoritism toward 8-15.

In mid-July 1967, Liu Jieting, vice-chairman of the Sichuan Province Revolutionary Committee Preparatory Committee, which supported the Smash Faction, recommended that the faction change its name to Rebel to the End. So 8-15 and Rebel to the End then became the two major factional alignments in Chongqing.

CIVIL WAR

On June 5, 1967, a factional battle broke out at the Southwest Normal College in Beibei District, and members of the 8-15 and Rebel to the End Factions went to the college to render aid to their respective allies. As a "full-scale civil war" developed between the two factions, professional fighting and command organizations emerged, including the 8-15 Faction's 301 Guerrilla Corps (in charge of fights outside of the college) and 301 Army (for fighting and security on campus), and the Rebel to the End Faction's Fighting Tiger Regiment and Huangshan Garrison Command Headquarters. Battles between the two sides occurred almost daily in Chongqing in July and August 1967, veiling the city in smoke and imposing relentless terror on its residents.

On July 14, the Central Committee representatives Xie Fuzhi and Wang Li, who were passing through Chongqing, received representatives of both factions at the Chongqing Garrison Command Headquarters and demanded an end to the fighting. The Sichuan Province Revolutionary Committee Preparatory Committee's chairman, Zhang Guohua, and vice-chairman, Liu Jieting, issued an order to cease all hostilities. The opposing factions within Chongqing's defense industry signed a fourteen-point cease-fire agreement and then held a "unity rally," but both sides scrapped the agreement almost immediately, and the fighting resumed.

Factional fighting groups seized armaments factories and distributed massive amounts of weapons and ammunition. As a base area for China's munitions industry, Chongqing provided an endless supply of weapons for the fighting.

After a napalm attack by an 8-15 Faction combat group destroyed eighteen homes in a residential area on July 31, personnel from the PLA Chongqing Garrison Command Headquarters engaged in cease-fire and rescue operations, only to come under attack themselves, with two killed and ten injured. The fighting continued and intensified, with hundreds of casualties among the fighters and residents, and massive financial losses due to the destruction of property.

Most of the young people taking part in the fighting were college and secondary school students and young workers. Years of education in class struggle and revolutionary heroism had filled them with a fervor that made them willing to sacrifice their lives to "defend Chairman Mao's revolutionary line."

On August 23, the CCRSG Administrative Group issued an extra-urgent cable, vetted and approved by Zhou Enlai, ordering an immediate end to the fighting in Chongqing. The two sides were ordered to immediately reach a cease-fire agreement and ensure that it was actually executed. On that same day, a Rebel to the End shelling caused a massive fire at an air-compressor factory controlled by 8-15. Before retreating, the 8-15 combat team executed five Rebel to the End prisoners, including a pregnant woman. The fighting continued unabated until September 5, when the Central Committee handed down its "9-5 Order"[31] and the two factions negotiated a cease-fire at the Garrison Command from September 8 to 9. After that, the fighting began to taper off, and on September 11, more than two thousand Rebel to the End refugees who had withdrawn to Chengdu returned to Chongqing by train.

Then factional conflict resurfaced at Chongqing University in late December. Liang Xingchu, who was vice-chairman of the Sichuan Province Revolutionary Committee Preparatory Committee and commander of the Chengdu Military Region, endorsed one group, while another vice-chairman of the preparatory committee, Liu Jieting, expressed his support for the other. With senior military and civilian leaders supporting different factions, the nearly extinguished hostilities flared up again. On December 30, Rebel to the End sent more than ten thousand people to attack the Chongqing Revolutionary Committee Preparatory Committee, and numerous people were wounded in the ensuing battle.

On January 8, 1968, 250,000 Rebel to the End members held a rally at the municipal stadium to denounce the Southwest Bureau leader Li Jingquan and provincial first secretary Liao Zhigao. On the way to the rally, 8-15 Faction members attacked people, and six were killed in a gun battle during a parade after the rally. The next day,

8-15 members attacked and drove off Rebel to the End members who had returned to Chongqing University to "resume classes and make revolution."

On March 15, Zhou Enlai and other central leaders received leading military and civilian cadres from Sichuan and criticized attacks on two leaders of the Sichuan Province Revolutionary Committee Preparatory Committee, Liu Jieting and Zhang Xiting. Chengdu's rebel faction was split into two opposing groups like Chongqing's, and in both cities, one subfaction (including 8-15) opposed Liu Jieting and Zhang Xiting, while the other subfaction (including Rebel to the End) opposed Liang Xingchu. Zhou Enlai said that attacking Liu Jieting and Zhang Xiting was attempting to restore the old order under Liu Shaoqi and Deng Xiaoping, and he communicated Mao's support for Rebel to the End. Rebel to the End used this "3-15 Directive" to rebuild its prestige, but 8-15 wasn't ready to admit defeat, and conflicts between them escalated during the remainder of March and into April.

On April 27, Zhou Enlai and other central leaders once again received Sichuan's civilian and military leaders, but this time criticized Rebel to the End's opposition to the Chengdu Military Region deputy political commissar Xie Jiaxiang and commander Liang Xingchu. Telling the Fifty-Fourth Army to get some backbone, Zhou Enlai said, "There can be no more chaos in Chongqing." Zhou ordered the leaders of the Sichuan Province Revolutionary Committee Preparatory Committee, including Zhang Guohua, Liang Xingchu, Liu Jieting, and Zhang Xiting, to come to Beijing posthaste for Mao Zedong Thought study classes. He also demanded that Chongqing's two factions immediately stop seizing arms and return the arms they had taken, or be dealt with in accordance with law. Zhou followed up on April 29 with a phone call to Zhang Guohua demanding severe punishment for further factional violence. Zhang Guohua and the other provincial leaders relayed these instructions to ten representatives from each faction who were attending the Beijing study courses and demanded their immediate implementation.

Fighting continued nevertheless in June and July. On July 16, Chongqing's 8-15 Faction and allied combat groups intercepted and looted a military train transporting arms and ammunition to aid

Vietnam. After learning of this, Zhou Enlai sent an urgent cable to Zhang Guohua, calling this a counterrevolutionary political incident and demanding that all the arms be recovered.

After Worker Mao Zedong Thought Propaganda Teams entered schools at the end of July and student rebel faction Red Guards withdrew from the political stage, mass organizations were no longer able to sustain themselves. The Fifty-Fourth Army was transferred from Chongqing to Yunnan, and the fighting gradually dwindled. On August 22, the first group of more than 4,500 Rebel to the End members who had fled to Chengdu returned to Chongqing, and thousands of other "refugees" returned to the city each day thereafter.

On September 23, the Chongqing Municipal Revolutionary Committee and Garrison Command ordered all mass organizations and individuals to unconditionally surrender all their weapons, ammunition, and transport vehicles; demolish all battle fortifications and strongholds; and disband all specialized fighting units by October 15. A mass pledge rally on October 15 declared the mass organizations of both factions disbanded, and armed factional conflict basically ended in Chongqing and its surrounding districts.

According to the *Chongqing Public Security Chronicle (1949–1997)*, a June 5, 1971, investigative report by a provincial work group found that "during twenty-two relatively major battles and killing incidents during the Cultural Revolution, 878 rebel faction perpetrators killed 1,737 people on the grounds of being 'traitors,' 'prisoners of war,' or 'spies' (among them fourteen black elements)."[32] These were people killed after being captured, so the number of people killed during the battles in Chongqing must be much larger. Another source gives a conservative estimate of at least three thousand people killed in battle, and at least ten thousand wounded.[33] The fighting destroyed buildings and machinery, and disruptions of transport and production resulted in incalculable economic losses.

14

THE WUHAN INCIDENT AND MAO'S STRATEGIC SHIFT

When the military responded to Mao's directive to support the left by supporting the conservative faction, Mao felt a need to adjust the direction of support-the-left efforts. He decided to start with the Wuhan Military Region; effecting a turnaround in the transportation hub of central China would not only solve the problem in the Central Plains provinces but would also serve as a model for the rest of the country. Mao was so full of confidence that he planned to take a swim in the Yangtze River after the problem was resolved, never imagining that the sensational July 20 Incident would break out while he was in Wuhan.

THE CENTRAL LEADERSHIP SETS THE DIRECTION FOR THE WUHAN PROBLEM

The central leadership had decided to deal with Wuhan's intense factional violence by summoning the leaders of the Wuhan Military Region and of mass organizations to Beijing for discussions. On July 10, however, Zhou Enlai informed the military region commander Chen Zaidao that Mao had decided to go to Wuhan to deal with the issue personally. By then, Mao and Zhou had decided to handle Wuhan in the same way they had handled Henan and Hunan: They would support the rebel faction, disband conservative faction organizations, and then incorporate members of those conservative organizations into a grand alliance with the rebel faction at its core.

Implementing this plan required first dealing with Wuhan's military forces; military leaders who admitted their error would be allowed to remain in control.

Mao arrived in Wuhan by train on the evening of July 14 with Yang Chengwu, Zheng Weishan, and Wang Dongxing and stayed at the special villa for top leaders at the East Lake Guesthouse. Zhou Enlai had already flown in that morning with navy commander Li Zuopeng (who was to accompany Mao on his swim in the Yangtze)[1] and was staying at another of the guesthouse's special villas. Zhou and Li had been met at the airport by Wuhan air force deputy commander Liu Feng and the political commissar Xiao Qian; Chen Zaidao, although military region commander, had been kept out of the loop, and he was greatly displeased.[2]

Xie Fuzhi, Wang Li, and Yu Lijin had gone to the southwest with student Red Guards from the Beijing Aeronautical Engineering Institute as part of a Central Committee investigation group to deal with problems in Kunming, Chengdu, and Guiyang. When Zhou Enlai summoned them to Wuhan, however, it was not only to provide an update on the situation in the southwest. Mao's main concern was that Xie Fuzhi had once been political commissar of some of the troops stationed in Wuhan—the Airborne Fifteenth Army, made up of units previously commanded by Chen Geng.

Having arrived in Wuhan in advance, Zhou Enlai took the precaution of changing all the staff at the East Lake Guesthouse to ensure Mao's safety. The original staff were mostly members of the Million Heroes, and Zhou replaced them with members of the rival faction. Some of the replaced staff later joined the Million Heroes in charging into the guesthouse villa where Xie Fuzhi was staying and questioning him, as will be described later. For now it should simply be noted that the security arrangements reflected the bias of the central leadership in favor of one faction over the other.[3] Furthermore, Zhou Enlai replaced the 8201 Independent Division with personnel from Beijing's Central Guard Regiment. The 8201 unit's political commissar, Cai Bingchen, grumbled about this slight for days afterward.

On July 16, Mao called a meeting to hear Zhou Enlai's report on the progress of the Cultural Revolution in the Wuhan area. Yang Chengwu, Wang Dongxing, Xie Fuzhi, Yu Lijin, Wang Li, and Li

Zuopeng attended the meeting. After hearing Zhou's report, Mao called for rehabilitating the Wuhan Workers' Headquarters and releasing Zhu Hongxia and other arrested rebel faction heads: "The Wuhan Military Region should support both factions and not plant its buttocks on the side of the Million Heroes. Wuhan's two factions need to reach an agreement and announce an alliance." He also said, "The military has made mistakes; it needs to promptly acknowledge and correct them."[4]

On the morning of July 17, Mao heard a report from Xie Fuzhi and Wang Li on the situation in Yunnan and Sichuan and studied the problem in the Wuhan area. Mao said that the Wuhan Military Region needed to draft and issue a public statement outlining its achievements in supporting the workers and peasants and its errors in supporting the left. He repeated his order to rehabilitate members of the Workers' Headquarters and release detained rebel leaders, saying that it should be done that day or the next. If Chen Zaidao admitted his errors, he wouldn't be unseated.[5] In the afternoon, Zhou Enlai and others called a meeting to hear situational reports from leaders of the Wuhan Military Region and of support-the-left units at the division level and above. Some military cadres reported the "ten great crimes" of the Workers' Headquarters and the "ten great virtues" of the Million Heroes, but the central leaders interrupted them and reminded the military leaders to adhere to the struggle between the two lines, grasp the essence of the issue, and enhance their line consciousness.[6]

During meetings on the seventeenth and eighteenth, Zhou continued to urge military leaders to acknowledge and correct their errors in their support-the-left work: "Acknowledging your errors and writing self-criticisms will protect you." Chen Zaidao still couldn't see his way around it, and antagonism between the central leaders and Wuhan military leaders made it impossible to solve any problems during these meetings.[7]

In his summary remarks to Wuhan military leaders on the afternoon of July 18, Zhou Enlai blamed the military region's missteps for pitting mass organizations against each other and causing the Workers' Headquarters to disband. He repeated the demand for the military region's leaders to acknowledge their directional line error and release and rehabilitate targeted groups and individuals, in particular recognizing the Three Steels and Three News as revolutionary mass organizations, and called for a grand alliance with these groups at its core; no mass organizations were to be banned but rather should be won over through education, and the central leadership would assist in mending the conflict between the conservative Million Heroes and the rebel Workers' Headquarters. These suggestions came to be known in Wuhan as the Four-Point Directive. Zhou also told the military region to ensure that peasants didn't come to the city to wage struggle, and to educate the troops as well as give mass organizations a better understanding of the PLA's actions. The military region was to correct its errors and execute the Chairman's pronouncements, whether these were understood or not.[8] Yang Chengwu carried this outline between Zhou and Mao, and affirms that Mao authorized it.[9]

Unaware until then that Mao was in Wuhan, Chen Zaidao was upset when he heard Zhou Enlai's summary report, and he provided Zhou with the material that the military region had collected on the Workers' Headquarters, demanding a further investigation. Chen said that it was impossible to accept the Three Steels and Three News. Pointing out that Mao had said that the majority should be trusted, Chen said that the majority of cadres, soldiers, and members of the public supported the Million Heroes. Slapping the table, Chen said, "Whiskers Zhou, what gives you the right?" Pointing at Zhou's speech notes, he said, "I'll only execute what you've said in your speech if Chairman Mao has put his signature on it." Zhou also lost his temper and slapped the table, saying, "Don't think we don't know how to deal with you!"[10]

On the evening of eighteenth, Zhou Enlai took Chen Zaidao and the military region's political commissar, Zhong Hanhua, to the East Lake Guesthouse to see Mao; Xie Fuzhi, Yang Chengwu, Wang Dongxing, Yu Lijin, Wang Li, and Li Zuopeng were also in attendance. Mao told Chen and Zhong that the military region needed to work on the Million Heroes and bring them around quickly so that they wouldn't be at a disadvantage. Mao also told Chen and Zhong that their support-the-left work erred in being one-sided and that they should carry out self-criticism and correct the directional line errors, and then work with Zhou Enlai to make the masses endorse Chen. Chen and Zhong expressed their acceptance of the central leadership's handling of the Wuhan problem and said that they would do their part to convince the troops. At the end of the conversation, Mao saw Chen Zaidao to the corridor and told several guesthouse staff, "Don't try to strike down your commander anymore!"[11]

Before Zhou Enlai flew back to Beijing just before midnight,[12] he emphasized that the Wuhan air force had to guarantee Mao's safety. Fu Chuanzuo was Wuhan's air force commander, but because someone said he was "He Long's man," Zhou Enlai decided to put the deputy commander Liu Feng and political commissar Xiao Qian in charge.

WUHAN RESISTS BEIJING

Before the central leaders arrived in Wuhan, the military region standing committee had called a meeting of the heads of all major work units on July 9 and 10 to affirm that there had been no directional line error, that there would be no verdict reversal on the Workers' Headquarters, and that the Million Heroes was a revolutionary mass organization.[13] The subsequent arrival of so many VIPs to resolve the problems in Wuhan aroused intense interest among the mass organizations of both factions. Late at night on July 14, Wang Li, Xie Fuzhi, and others went to Hubei University to read big-character posters and disclosed some of the central leaders' thinking to the people who crowded around them. The news spread rapidly, and the rebel faction painted numerous slogans welcoming these views. When lights in the East Lake Guesthouse signaled the arrival of the central leaders, the loudspeakers at every school blasted out the tune "Chairman Mao Sent His Men Here," unaware that Mao himself had also come. It was difficult to keep secrets during the Cultural Revolution, and Beijing's principles for resolving the Wuhan problem inevitably leaked out while the central leaders were holding their meetings with military region leaders. On July 16, the Million Heroes posted banners all over the streets of Wuhan saying, "No investigation, no say," "Oppose the imperial envoy," and "Strongly demand that Xie Fuzhi and Wang Li join us workers and peasants."

After Zhou Enlai left Wuhan on the night of the eighteenth, his remarks on that day were made public through two channels.

The first channel was the military. Zhou had repeatedly told military leaders that he didn't want his remarks communicated to the lower levels, but political commissar Zhong Hanhua authorized the 8201 Independent Division to pass them along.[14] The 8201 unit's political commissar, Cai Bingchen, informed military region personnel that central leaders had listened to reports on three days and delivered speeches on one day, noting, "But the Premier and Wang Li seemed unwilling to hear our reports. When Commissar Zhong was giving his report, he would say one sentence and then the Premier would ask him something, and when Commissar Zhong didn't know how to answer, all he could do was place his report outline aside and make self-criticism." Cai said that Wang Li excused attacks on the military by the Three News and Second Command Post and "turned the Million Heroes' merits into defects." These words provoked intense resentment, but Cai and the 8201 unit's commander, Niu Huailong, said, "Don't tell others that it was the Premier who said these things," intimating that the spearhead should be aimed toward Wang Li. Cai and Niu went on to falsely accuse Wang Li of a personal bias toward the Second Command Post and of being a former member of the Kuomintang.[15]

The second channel of information was Wang Li and Xie Fuzhi, who, after seeing Zhou Enlai off at the airport, went straight to the Wuhan Hydraulic and Electrical Engineering Institute, where worker and student rebels were "taking refuge." Wang Li expressed his support and hopes for Wuhan's rebels, saying that the general direction of the military region's support-the-left work was incorrect, the Workers' Headquarters had to be rehabilitated, the Three Steels and Three News were revolutionary leftists, and the Million Heroes was a conservative organization.[16] The next day, Wuhan's rebel faction broadcast the Four-Point Directive throughout the city. This aroused intense resentment among the Million Heroes and PLA rank and file, and posters and banners condemning Wang Li went up all over the city.[17]

The Wuhan military was clearly acting strategically by blaming Wang Li rather than opposing the central leadership for its handling of the Wuhan problem.

THE ACTIONS OF THE MILLION HEROES AND THE 8201
INDEPENDENT DIVISION

On July 19, Chen Zaidao and Zhong Hanhua compliantly acknowledged their error and drafted and mimeographed a notice while also
preparing to release rebel faction heads. Meanwhile, that afternoon,
the Wuhan Military Region convened an enlarged standing committee meeting for cadres at the division commander level and above,
during which Xie Fuzhi communicated Zhou Enlai's remarks on the
previous day. Wang Li spoke on theoretical problems in the Cultural
Revolution, and of Chen Zaidao and Zhong Hanhua's self-criticisms.
The commander of the 8201 Independent Division, Niu Huailong,
asked to speak but was prevented, and political commissar Cai Bingchen stormed out of the meeting with Niu at his heels. After they returned to the division's war department at the foot of Hong Mountain,
Niu pounded the table, tossed chairs, and yelled in frustration in front
of his subordinates. In the hours that followed, division personnel besieged the military region compound, demanding to see Wang Li and
Xie Fuzhi.[18] They were soon joined by some thirteen thousand members of the Million Heroes, who established a "command post to root
out Wang Li" in the Wuhan Railway Bureau office across from the
Wuhan Military Region headquarters.[19]

Two days earlier, someone in the military region had told a Million
Heroes leader that Mao was at the East Lake Guesthouse.[20] Now some
members of the Million Heroes' decided to tell Mao their views face-
to-face. In the early hours of July 20, fourteen Heroes who worked for
the Wuhan Municipal Public Security Bureau drove a vehicle through
the northern gate of the guesthouse, shouting that they wanted to see
Xie Fuzhi and Wang Li. When the head of the military region's security section, Wang Zhenying, tried to intercept the group, they took out
a letter of introduction from a military representative in the Wuchang
District Public Security Bureau and stubbornly said, "If we're not received by dawn, thousands will come! . . . Vice-Premier Xie Fuzhi is
our ultimate superior and we want to see him." Wang Zhenying immediately reported to the Central Guard Regiment, and Wang Dongxing
told a functionary of the Central Cultural Revolution Small Group,
Zhang Gencheng,[21] to hurry to the north gate. Wang Zhenying also

telephoned Zhong Hanhua and told his secretary that Zhong had to do something right away; Zhong was asleep by then, so Wang asked the military region to send in the Twenty-Ninth Division (i.e., the 8199 Unit). Meanwhile, Zhang Gencheng told the Heroes that they and other mass organization representatives would be received in the afternoon and that they should leave for now, but the group forced its way inside. Around 3:00 a.m., the Twenty-Ninth Division rushed over with a platoon of soldiers and some officers to subdue the intruders. The leader of the group of Heroes told the 8201 Unit guards, "They don't trust you and have sent another unit instead."[22]

The Horticulture Army under the Million Heroes, instructed to control the guesthouse's waterways and docks, burst in through the guesthouse's western and northern gates, after which another large group of Heroes, armed with spears and daggers and wearing safety helmets, arrived at the guesthouse in five vehicles. After subduing the sentries, the group surrounded the rooms where Xie and Wang were staying and demanded to see them. Xie came out and said, "I am Xie Fuzhi. Where are you from? Why are you here? Do you want to kidnap us? We've prepared to see your representatives this afternoon. What you're doing now is very wrong." Some of the invaders acknowledged their error and withdrew, but five or six people continued to make trouble.

At 5:10 a.m., twenty-one vehicles from the 8201 unit, six propaganda trucks, three jeeps, and one sedan entered the guesthouse compound, shortly after which forty-one armored vehicles from Million Heroes and three fire engines manned by Wuhan Public Security also roared in. Soldiers from the Independent Division leveled their submachine guns at Xie and Wang as others charged into Wang Li's room and rummaged through his drawers and cupboards. A soldier struck Chen Zaidao with his rifle butt, and falling to the ground, Chen yelled, "I'm Chen Zaidao, not Wang Li!" One of the unit's section heads quickly yelled, "That's our Commander Chen, not Wang Li! Don't beat him!" and they picked Chen Zaidao up off the ground. That was around 6:00 a.m. Learning of the incident, the military region section chief Wang Zhenying and Zhang Zhaojian from the 8199 Unit went over to where the Million Heroes were beating people on the lawn, and Zhang Zhaojian's ribs were broken when he attempted to intervene. Students from the Beijing Aeronautical Engineering Institute who had accompanied Xie Fuzhi and the others to Wuhan were beaten until they fell to the ground. Wang Li was loaded into a vehicle, while the CCRSG functionary Zhang Gencheng and two of the students were taken away by the Independent Division soldiers and Million Heroes members. Spotting division commander Niu Huailong, Wang Zhenying asked him to step forward and stop the soldiers. Niu looked into the vehicle where Wang Li was being held and said carelessly, "Don't be so rough, will you? Why do you need to be so rough? Put away the machine guns!" Then he turned and left.[23]

Tension was rife at the villa where Mao was staying; there were rumors that someone had been discovered swimming across the lake with a knife gripped in his mouth. Wang Dongxing told Mao's confidential personnel Xie Jingyi and Fan Yimin, "Always have matches in your hands so you can burn the secret codes if necessary, and throw the cipher machine out the window and into the lake." The leaders told their staff (including a Xinhua photographer) to carry wooden clubs to protect themselves.[24]

Zhang Gencheng recalls that after he was captured by the Independent Division, he heard a leader of the division's political department come in and ask, "What's with that guy?" Cai asked back, "Which guy?" "The swimmer, the old guy." Zhang Gencheng knew they were referring to Mao, and his heart sank as he thought, "Isn't this a revolt?"[25]

Wang Li was taken to the military region compound, where he had to pass through a phalanx of people wearing wicker helmets and carrying spears. Inside a room, Wang Li was beaten, and his wristwatch and pen were taken. The political commissar Zhong Hanhua kowtowed to the masses from the rostrum and begged, "Wang Li is Chairman Mao's man, you have to let him go!"[26] In the morning, personnel from the Independent Division and Million Heroes attacked Wang Li from all sides. One picked up a microphone, looked at a piece of paper, and began interrogating Wang about the Four-Point Directive and what he had been doing in Wuhan, but then the scene devolved into chaos. Wang Li, hands bound, was pushed onto a second-floor balcony and forced to once again declare his stand on the Wuhan problem.[27]

After 10:00 a.m., armed conservative faction soldiers and civilians marched in the streets in a procession that included 396 vehicles of various kinds mounted with machine guns. The vehicles drove up to Hubei University, where an Independent Division officer fired off rounds while members of the Million Heroes charged yelling into the school. Three people were badly injured, and one was killed. Fire engine sirens created an atmosphere of abject terror while loudspeakers on propaganda vehicles blasted slogans: "Down with Xie Fuzhi, hang Wang Li, execute Yu Lijin!" "Weed out the smattering of scoundrels in the Central Cultural Revolution Small Group!" "Stomp flat the Workers' Headquarters, suppress the counterrevolutionaries!" "Our Million Heroes cross the great Yangtze, sweeping away all ox demons and snake spirits!"

Over the following days, the Million Heroes besieged and attacked a dozen or so work units and detained more than two hundred rebel faction students and teachers at Hubei University. They laid siege to Wuhan Steel on the twentieth, and more than a hundred trucks and a dozen fire engines surrounded schools and factories, where more than a hundred people were seized.[28]

On the morning of the twenty-first, the Million Heroes held a power-seizure mobilization rally to discuss how to press their advantage to seize power from the provincial and municipal party committees. They organized manpower to control land and water transport so Wang Li couldn't escape to Beijing and the central leaders would be forced to solve the Wuhan problem on the spot, and they planned to issue notices and telegrams nationwide to gain outside support.[29]

By then, the Million Heroes completely controlled Wuhan's telecommunications system. They inspected all reports on the situation of the Cultural Revolution in Wuhan that the Hubei branch of the Xinhua News Agency sent to headquarters, and they maintained surveillance over the Xinhua office.[30]

THE CENTRAL LEADERSHIP'S RESPONSE

Back in Beijing, Zhou was holding an enlarged CCRSG briefing meeting on the morning of July 20 when an urgent telephone call from

Yang Chengwu informed him of the turmoil in Wuhan. Zhou decided to fly back to Wuhan and in the meantime told Yang to be prepared to transfer Mao to a safe location at a moment's notice. Before Zhou left Beijing, the CCRSG decided to jointly issue a document with the Central Committee stating that the Wuhan Military Region had made directional line errors in its support-the-left work and must change its stand. The document would also require all military branches and headquarters under the CMC to publicly express support for Wuhan's rebel faction, and to convince their Wuhan-based units to do likewise. Wu Faxian telephoned Fu Chuanzuo, Xiao Qian, and Liu Feng at the Wuhan air force and told them to comply with Beijing's decision.[31] Wuhan-based air force and naval personnel were to be deployed to stabilize the situation.

Distressed at the threat to Mao's personal safety, Jiang Qing begged Lin Biao to go to Wuhan with Ye Qun to protect Mao. Instead, Lin Biao, assisted by Qi Benyu, Chen Boda, and Guan Feng, wrote a note with Jiang Qing's signature advising Mao to leave Wuhan immediately, and at four in the afternoon, Qiu Huizuo was summoned to the Great Hall of the People, where Ye Qun informed him of the situation and told him to fly to Wuhan immediately and deliver Jiang Qing's note to Mao.[32] Lin Biao also tasked Qiu with reporting to Mao on the situation throughout the country and advising that Mao shift to a different location of his own choosing—"The Chairman's safety is the party's safety—tell him I said that." Lin prepared for the possibility that Wuhan might devolve into utter chaos and that Chen Zaidao might defy orders, in which case Qiu was to find a way to tell Zhou Enlai to sit tight in Wuchang and await assistance. "If you can't get close to the Premier, establish a command post at Wangjiadun Airport and maintain close contact with Beijing. The Wuhan Military Region's Twenty-Ninth Division and airborne troops are prepared for battle." He added, "Tell Yang Chengwu, Yu Lijin, and Li Zuopeng to protect the Chairman's safety at any price, and avoid bloodshed." Qiu's plane landed at Wuhan's Wangjiadun Airport around 11:00 p.m. that same day,[33] along with a medical team from the PLA Hospital.

Somehow Zhou Enlai's itinerary became known as he was on his way to Wuhan on the afternoon of July 20, and more than a hundred armed soldiers from the Independent Division and members of the

Million Heroes descended on Wuhan's Wangjiadun Airport in trucks, yelling, "We want to see Premier Zhou! We want to file a complaint with Premier Zhou!"[34] Zhang Zuoliang, a doctor accompanying Zhou Enlai, recalls, "When the aircraft began circling over Wangjiadun Airport, we could see black masses of people and fluttering red banners. At that point, the pilot came over and spoke to Zhou, and the aircraft gained altitude and flew in a different direction, and ten minutes or so later we landed at Shanpo Airport. It was around five o'clock by then. A little while later, we flew back to Wangjiadun Airport. To reduce visibility, we waited until after dark, and Zhou Enlai put on street clothes and dark glasses, and the Air Force escorted him and his small group in two jeeps to the East Lake Guesthouse." As soon as he arrived, Zhou arranged for Mao to be removed to safety, and an air force special forces unit escorted him to a special train waiting on the Hankou Airport branch line.

Zhou had instructed Qiu Huizuo to wait at Wangjiadun Airport for further orders, and at 3:00 a.m. on July 21, Yang Chengwu came to the airport and told Qiu, "We succeeded! Come with me." Qiu accompanied Yang in his Volga sedan to Mao's train. Mao immediately asked, "Is your General Logistics Department still obeying you? The Cultural Revolution is a great method; good people and bad people all act their parts." Qiu gave Mao Jiang Qing's letter and passed along Lin Biao's cautionary words.[35] Up to then, Mao had not expressed any opinion on whether or not he should leave Wuhan, but after reading the letter, he seemed to sense the gravity of the situation and said, "Prepare an aircraft. I'm leaving Wuhan." Mao, Liu Feng, Yang Chengwu, and Li Zuopeng took a Wuhan air force sedan to the airport under the protection of the Central Guard Regiment. Yang Chengwu asked if he should arrange for a chartered flight or an air force jet, and Mao said, "Both." When it was about time for takeoff, Mao told Yang Chengwu, "We'll take the Air Force jet." The pilot asked, "Which direction are we going?" Mao said, "Just take off first!" Once the jet was in the air and circling over Wuhan, Mao said, "Fly east to Shanghai."[36] The Central Committee had previously stipulated that for safety's sake, Mao should normally not travel by airplane, but this time there was no choice.

Mao's aircraft landed in Shanghai at 11:00 a.m. on July 21. The flight team deputy commander Pan Jingyin, who handled this mission, was the same pilot who later flew the aircraft that crashed in Mongolia with Lin Biao aboard on September 13, 1971.[37]

Still in Wuhan dealing with the July 20 Incident, Zhou Enlai stayed in the same guesthouse villa as Li Zuopeng, but the two of them switched rooms, and Li turned the lights on and off according to Zhou's normal habits in order to mislead anyone watching from outside. On the morning of the twenty-first, Zhou received Chen Zaidao again with Li Zuopeng present. Zhou told Chen to bring Wang Li back, but Chen claimed he couldn't find him. Infuriated, Zhou slapped the table, stood up, and yelled, "What kind of attitude is that? Don't think it's enough to have the Million Heroes supporting you. Who are the Million Heroes? If the entire country learns of your decision to oppose the central leadership, threaten Chairman Mao's safety, and seize a member of the CCRSG, you'll have eight hundred million people opposing you. Now, which do you think is more powerful, eight hundred million people or the Million Heroes? If you're going to take this attitude, get out of here and go to Beijing!" Chen Zaidao bowed his head and left.[38]

While Zhou Enlai was frantically searching for Wang Li, the Independent Division handed Wang Li over to the Twenty-Ninth Division, where the Wuhan air force deputy commander Liu Feng found him, safe and sound except for an injured leg from a fall while he was being transferred. Liu Feng then moved Wang Li to a secure location with the air force. He rescued Wang Li because Wu Faxian had told him in advance not to obey the Wuhan Military Region.[39] That afternoon, Liu informed Zhou Enlai of Wang Li's whereabouts, and the overjoyed Zhou praised Liu Feng for his extraordinary service.[40]

Late that night, Zhou Enlai directed Li Zuopeng and Liu Feng to take Wang Li to the Shanpo Military Airport. They arrived at Shanpo at 3:00 a.m. on July 22, and Zhou Enlai, Xie Fuzhi, and their entourage arrived soon after. Zhou Enlai came straight upstairs and yelled, "Where's Wang Li?" Rushing into the room, he gripped Wang Li's hand and embraced him over and over again, saying emotionally, "We support Comrade Wang Li! We support Comrade Wang Li!" Wang Li recalls that Zhou actually shed tears. Zhou then held a meeting to make arrangements to stabilize the situation in Wuhan, including the deployment of troops.

On the afternoon of the twenty-second, Zhou Enlai saw Wang Li and Xie Fuzhi onto an airplane, after which Zhou and Li Zuopeng took off in a chartered plane. Upon reaching Beijing, Zhou had Wang Li's aircraft circle in the air so that he and Li Zuopeng could land at Beijing's Xijiao Airport first and receive Wang Li there.[41] At least ten thousand people had gathered at the airport to offer Wang Li a boisterous hero's welcome.[42] Wearing an ill-fitting air force cadre's uniform and hobbling from his earlier mishap, Wang Li was propped up by Zhou Enlai and Jiang Qing as he accepted the enthusiastic welcome of the crowd.[43]

When the Central People's Broadcasting Station reported Xie and Wang's return to Beijing in the early hours of July 23, Greater Wuhan immediately erupted. Over the next few days, rebel faction members and ordinary people emerged from hiding to spread the news, and the streets were plastered with posters proclaiming, "Dawn has broken!" and "Liberation!"

On July 25, a mass rally of three hundred thousand people (some say a million) was held at Beijing's Tiananmen Square to welcome the Central Committee delegation back to Beijing. Lin Biao, Zhou Enlai, and other central leaders all put in an appearance at the gate tower, with Wang Li positioned in the place of honor in his wheelchair. Wang Li protested his high-profile reception, but Lin Biao and Jiang Qing told Wang, "This isn't for you; it's for the Chairman."[44]

With Mao's approval, the Wuhan Military Region issued an announcement on July 26 describing the July 20 Incident as "a flagrantly traitorous action to oppose our Great Leader Chairman Mao, Chairman Mao's proletarian revolutionary line, the party Central Committee, the Central Military Commission, and the Central Cultural Revolution Small Group." Expressing support for the Steels and News and other rebel groups, and reiterating that the military region had committed directional and line errors in its support-the-left work, the announcement declared, "Chen Zaidao cannot evade responsibility for his crimes; we resolutely draw a clear distinction from Chen Zaidao and resolutely strike him down." A cable issued in the name of the Central Committee endorsed the announcement, and the two documents were issued together as Central Committee Document No. 227 (1967).

Lin Biao and Zhou Enlai had arranged for Chen Zaidao and Zhong

Hanhua to be brought to Beijing on July 24, and they were denounced at an informal enlarged meeting of the Politburo Standing Committee at the Jingxi Guesthouse on July 26. Zhou Enlai accused Chen of "engaging in rebellious activity against Chairman Mao and the party," and Wu Faxian, Liu Feng, and others tore off Chen's and Zhong's insignia and made them stand in the painful "jet formation" while Wu slapped Chen in the face.[45]

Chen and Zhong were dismissed from their official positions on July 27, and Zeng Siyu became commander of the Wuhan Military Region, with Liu Feng as political commissar. The rebel faction now enjoyed the political advantage in Wuhan, and the Million Heroes dispersed, with some of its members suffering retribution in their work units. According to official figures, 600 Heroes were beaten to death, 64,000 were seriously injured, and 184,000 suffered minor injuries.[46]

LOSS OF CONTROL IN AUGUST, AND MAO'S STRATEGIC SHIFT

Mao had proposed "arming the left" on July 18 while still in Wuhan. After he arrived in Shanghai, the Workers' General Headquarters under Wang Hongwen deployed more than one hundred thousand people armed with clubs, spears, and wooden training guns in trucks, forklifts, and fire engines to violently suppress the opposing Shanghai Diesel Factory Revolutionary Rebel Alliance Headquarters on August 4. That night, Mao took an inspection tour of the Bund in a Soviet-manufactured armored sedan and saw "verbal attack and armed defense combatants" from the Workers' General Headquarters with spears and clubs in their hands. He also watched a documentary broadcast on Shanghai Television showing the attack on the Shanghai Diesel Alliance Headquarters and commended the heroism of the people who scaled the fire engine ladders. Noticing how much Mao enjoyed the documentary, Zhang Chunqiao took the opportunity to ask Mao for advice on "how to rebuild the Shanghai militia." Mao answered, "Arm a hundred thousand Shanghai workers." Zhang asked, "Can we issue firearms to them?" Mao replied, "Give each worker a club."[47] But he quickly agreed to supplying rebels with guns.

It was on that same day that Mao wrote his letter to Jiang Qing saying he wanted to arm the left and speaking of "dictatorship of the masses." After Jiang Qing read this letter out loud during an enlarged Politburo Standing Committee meeting convened by Lin Biao,[48] Mao's order to arm the left was rapidly executed throughout the country. The chairman of the Sichuan Province Revolutionary Committee Preparatory Committee and political commissar of the Chengdu Military Region, Zhang Guohua, said in a speech, "Arming the left is Chairman Mao's great strategic plan. Sichuan has already armed the tested revolutionary leftist faction in several places, including Wan County, Fuling, and Luzhou."[49]

Once the military began arming the faction it trusted, the other faction was naturally displeased and seized weapons, and violence escalated as mass organizations throughout the country received the message to engage in "verbal attack and armed defense."

Since most support-the-left efforts benefited the conservative faction, the rebel faction found itself under military suppression in many places, and after Wuhan's July 20 Incident, rebels all over China began attacking military units that supported the conservative faction. Military regions at all levels began deluging Beijing with urgent missives and telegrams reporting efforts to "weed out local Chen Zaidaos."[50]

Attacks on the military that the Cultural Revolution depended on presented an intractable problem. If the military became paralyzed like local governments, the situation would become untenable, and the military was already making its deep discontent apparent. Although a political strongman, Mao still had to maintain a power equilibrium that kept him on top, even at the expense of sacrificing extremists who were loyal to him, and regardless of how much support he might have expressed for them in the past. Once he'd calmed down after the July 20 Incident, he decided to change the strategy of the Cultural Revolution.

During this period, events on the diplomatic front also spun out of control. The Foreign Ministry was Zhou Enlai's domain, and when the ministry's Revolutionary Rebel Liaison Station was established, Zhou supported it. This rebel faction adhered to the principle of "leading the movement and supervising operations" set by Zhou and approved by

Mao, and had not seized power over the ministry's official business (exceeding its authority only in some operational tasks such as sending unauthorized cables).

This changed after the Wuhan Incident. Wang Li had been in the limelight since his return from Wuhan, and it swelled his head. On August 7, he reached out to the Foreign Ministry's rebel faction and said, "Chairman Mao and the Premier wanted me to come over and ask how things are going in the Foreign Ministry . . . The movement is facing obstruction in the Foreign Ministry. Diplomacy is intimidating and is considered a specialist field. But what's so hard about it? I think managing problems within the Red Guards is actually a lot more complicated. Can't Red Guards carry out diplomacy?" Asking how much power the rebel faction had imposed over the Foreign Ministry's operations, Wang observed, "You need power in order to have prestige."[51]

After this conversation, the Foreign Ministry's rebel faction seized control over the political department and sent dozens of cables to China's overseas embassies, some of which used the phrase "Down with Liu [Shaoqi], Deng [Xiaoping], and Chen [Yi]!" Mao had hoped that the rebel faction would put some pressure on Chen Yi but not strike him down. However, Wang Li's remarks intensified opposition to Chen Yi, culminating in a mass denunciation rally in the Great Hall of the People on August 11.

Realizing that he had to regain control of the situation, Mao decided to toss out some relatively powerless civilians as scapegoats, including Wang Li, Guan Feng, and Qi Benyu. His pretext was the essay "The Proletariat Must Firmly Grasp the Barrel of the Gun," published in the August 1, 1967, edition of *Red Flag*, which stated, "It is necessary to expose the smattering of capitalist roaders in the military and denounce them until they are thoroughly discredited politically and ideologically." The essay had been edited by Guan Feng and approved for publication by Chen Boda. Mao harshly criticized the editorial, stating that the formulation of "a smattering of capitalist roaders within the military" was not strategic and that he wanted his "Great Wall" back.[52] His Great Wall was the PLA. On August 12, Mao's directive was transmitted to Beijing.[53]

By then, young students who felt that diplomacy was too soft on imperialists, revisionists, and reactionaries had engaged in actions that caused disputes with nearly thirty of the forty-odd countries with which China had established diplomatic relations,[54] culminating in an arson attack on the British mission in Beijing on August 22. In the early hours of August 25, Zhou Enlai had a one-on-one meeting with Yang Chengwu, who was serving as Mao's liaison, to discuss his concerns about a critical situation that he felt had spun out of control since Wang Li's August 7 remarks. Zhou said, "If things continue this way, it will be disastrous. I'm worried that there will be a chain reaction. Right now the central leaders cannot be allowed to waver, and the PLA's prestige cannot be shaken!" Zhou had Yang Chengwu fly immediately to Shanghai to report to Mao on the "August 7 remarks" and related matters.[55] This came at a decisive moment for Mao, and he told Yang Chengwu, "Wang Li and Guan Feng are bad people who are sabotaging the Cultural Revolution. Only report to the Premier—they are to be arrested and cannot remain in the CCRSG. Report this to the Premier alone, and he'll take care of it. Deal with Wang and Guan first and keep an eye on Qi for now."[56] Mao wrote a memo on Wang Li's remarks, describing them as "huge, huge, huge poisonous weeds."[57]

Yang flew back to Beijing at noon on August 26 and reported Mao's decision to Zhou Enlai. Zhou lost no time, convening an informal top-level meeting attended by Chen Boda, Kang Sheng, Jiang Qing, and others that same night. Zhou announced an "important policy decision by Chairman Mao" and then read out Mao's directive word for word as recorded by Yang Chengwu.[58] After that, Wang Li and Guan Feng were put under isolation and investigation. Yan Changgui recalls, "After the Premier left, Jiang Qing began sobbing . . . Jiang Qing was deeply saddened by Wang Li and Guan Feng being put under investigation."[59] Qi Benyu was similarly handled in January the next year and spent eight of the Cultural Revolution's ten years in prison. When amnesty was declared in 1975, Mao made a point of excluding "Chen Boda, Wang, Guan, and Qi." After the October 1976 coup d'état, Qi Benyu was sentenced to eighteen years in prison.

The British author Han Suyin, who had a personal relationship with Zhou Enlai and his wife, Deng Yingchao, wrote, "Zhou purged Wang, Guan, and Qi from the Cultural Revolution Small Group and did it cleanly, crippling Madame Mao's power."[60] Mentioning Zhou but not Mao makes sense; at the critical juncture, Zhou advised Mao through Yang Chengwu and eliminated the radical wing of the CCRSG, dulling the spearhead of the Cultural Revolution. This was a positive move of "eliminating bad courtiers from the emperor's side."

After Wang, Guan, and Qi were removed from power, Zhou told the Beijing Municipal Revolutionary Committee chairman Xie Fuzhi and vice-chairman Wu De and the Beijing Garrison commander Fu Chongbi to purge anyone associated with Wang, Guan, and Qi from the city's leading organs. Some 150 people were subsequently purged, including many in the municipal revolutionary committee and the Chinese Academy of Sciences' Department of Philosophy and Social Sciences.[61]

In the space of one month, Wang Li descended from heaven to hell as part of Mao's changing strategy for the Cultural Revolution. Even the Great Helmsman had to steer his boat according to how the wind blew; sailing against the headwind could overturn the boat. Mao seemed capricious, but in fact he had his difficulties. When Wang Hairong[62] sounded out Mao on the Wang Li matter around this time, Mao responded with a quote from the Tang poet Luo Yin: "A hero must bend to the forces of heaven and earth."[63]

The shift in strategy for the Cultural Revolution was announced by several CCRSG leaders at an enlarged meeting of the Beijing Municipal Revolutionary Committee standing committee on September 1. Reversing her usual support for the rebel faction, Jiang Qing said, "I think Beijing should set an example on struggle, criticize, and reform and on the grand alliance by carrying out these tasks in each work unit. Otherwise, how long will the Cultural Revolution have to go on? . . . Don't be afraid that others will accuse you of right-deviation . . . You need to resolutely oppose reactionary anarchism." She criticized the rebels for "pointing the spearhead of struggle" at the military instead of at Liu, Deng, and Tao, and of "creating chaos in our military and destroying our own Great Wall . . . Even if our veteran military cadres have said and done some things wrong, whenever there's a war, they've courageously followed Chairman Mao." Chen Boda emphasized that Jiang was speaking for the CCRSG and the Central Committee. Zhou Enlai finally summarized the meeting into a few points: (1) The Great Proletarian Cultural Revolution had been handled well on the national level over the past year; the second year should be dedicated to striving for victory, and the third year to winding things down. (2) Most of the military's high-ranking officials were good; it was necessary to support the PLA and not destroy the Great Wall. (3) The masses visiting Beijing should be mobilized to go home, and violent battles should end. (4) The Great Networking should end, and those still at large should immediately return to their units. (5) Every unit needed to accomplish the grand alliance and three-in-one combination within that year. (6) It was necessary to seize revolution and push production, with production as the ultimate result. (7) Students who should have graduated in 1966 were to be treated as graduates starting on September 1.

When Kang Sheng, Li Fuchun, Jiang Qing, Li Tianyou, Yao Wenyuan, and others received mass representatives from Anhui on the evening of September 5, Kang Sheng and Jiang Qing emphasized the importance of supporting the PLA and surmounting anarchy and factionalism, and reiterated the Central Committee's June 6 Notice[64] and the "Appeal Regarding the Launch of a Campaign to Support the Army and Cherish the People," issued on August 25.

Mao worried about long-term division emerging in China. At Shanghai's Hongqiao Guesthouse on September 9, he told Yang Chengwu, Zhang Chunqiao, and Yu Lijin, "At this point of the Cultural Revolution, I foresee two possibilities: One is that it will proceed with even greater success, while the other is that the country will become split into two irreconcilable sides, as in Nanjing, Wuxi, and Beijing. If the country is split into two major factions and cannot be united, will we have a repeat of the 1911 Xinhai Revolution, which brought chaos and long-term division to the country? Do you think that might happen?"[65]

Mao left Shanghai on September 16 and spoke with provincial leaders in Hangzhou, Nanchang, Changsha, Wuhan, and Zhengzhou as he passed through those cities on his way back to Beijing. After he returned to Beijing, the Central Committee issued "Chairman Mao's Important Directives upon Inspecting Northern, Central, and Eastern China," which started out by affirming, "The situation is not just good but excellent, and better than ever before." It then appealed to all mass organizations to form a grand alliance, saying, "Under the dictatorship of the proletariat, there is no reason for the working class to split into two irreconcilable factions." Mao also said that the vast majority of cadres were good; that treating cadres correctly was crucial for forming the new three-in-one combination power organs and carrying out the revolutionary grand alliance and the process of struggle, criticize, and reform in every work unit. Rebel faction leaders and Red Guards needed to be told how easy it was to make mistakes at this time.[66] In contrast to the relentless radicalism of the May 16 Circular and "My First Big-Character Poster," Mao's remarks on his southern tour showed a shift in emphasis toward "great order under heaven" after the chaos of the July 20 Incident.

Soon after Mao's return, on September 26, 1967, the CMC Administrative Group asked him to receive representatives of a military study class. Mao began the meeting by loudly asking, "Did Chen Zaidao come?" Chen quickly stood up and replied, "Chairman, I'm here!" Mao waved and nodded at him and said, "Good! Good! I'm glad you came! It's good that you've been studying. Don't lose heart. Continue the revolution."[67] The man who had rendered outstanding service in the July 20 Incident had by then been taken prisoner, while the chief instigator of the incident had become a guest of honor, all within two months' time!

Several years later, Chen Zaidao and Zhong Hanhua were appointed to key positions. While Jiang Qing was in Guangzhou convalescing in spring 1972,[68] she gave a speech at a conference of Guangzhou cadres during which she mentioned the July 20 Incident: "We made mistakes. It was Wang, Guan, and Qi's fault." Zhong Hanhua, by then deputy political commissar of the Guangzhou Military Region, was deeply moved by Jiang Qing's words.[69]

15

THE BAFFLING "MAY 16" INVESTIGATION

The campaign to investigate the May 16 conspiratorial clique lasted the longest and racked up the greatest number of victims in the Cultural Revolution. Beginning in August 1967 and reaching its peak from 1970 to 1971, it was suspended in 1972 but remained unresolved until 1976. By then, countless people had been investigated, and more than one hundred thousand died as a result.[1] Much about this campaign remains a mystery, but one thing is clear: It was a campaign in which officials persecuted ordinary citizens. As the authorities rounded up the rebel faction's most extreme elements, countless innocent people came to grief.

THE CAUSE: RADICAL TROUBLEMAKERS

Zhou Enlai supported the rebel faction as Mao intended, but he also took measures to quell its radical elements, and the military's suppression of the rebel faction in spring and summer 1967 caused many deaths. Since Liu and Deng had already fallen from power, the rebels considered Zhou Enlai to be the conservative faction's new backer within the central leadership. The programmatic document of the Cultural Revolution, the May 16 Circular, had weeded out Liu Shaoqi in 1966, and some young people believed that its publication one year later was meant to weed out other important officials.

Some radical rebels believed that after Liu Shaoqi's fall, the main conflict was between the "new cultural revolution" and the "old government," and that Zhou Enlai was the "backstage supporter" of the February Countercurrent. Zhang Jianqi and others established the May 16 Corps at the Beijing Iron and Steel Institute, and on June 2, Zhang posted "An Open Letter to Premier Zhou," which asked Zhou twenty-three questions.[2] Zhou also came under attack from the June 16 Combat Group, led by Liu Lingkai at the Beijing Foreign Languages Institute. For all their militaristic names, both were very small groups of students. At the end of June, these student opponents of Zhou Enlai organized the Capital May 16 Red Guard Corps, which held its first representative assembly at the Beijing Foreign Languages Institute and drafted a resolution that included the following passage:

> Zhou Enlai is an operative of the Liu-Deng Headquarters, China's biggest counterrevolutionary double-dealer, and one of China's worst traitors, revisionists, and right-deviating opportunists . . . He is China's second Khrushchev, a careerist who relentlessly strives to sow chaos and usurp leadership over the party, the military, and the government in order to pluck the fruits of victory of the Great Proletarian Cultural Revolution. We in the Capital May 16 Red Guard Corps swear to engage in a fight to the death against the counterrevolutionary clique led by Zhou Enlai and with Tan Zhenlin, Li Xiannian, Chen Yi, Yu Qiuli, and Gu Mu as its key operatives![3]

On August 8, the May 16 Corps distributed leaflets in various districts and universities, including one attacking Zhou Enlai and the People's Liberation Army as part of a "struggle between the two lines in the military." The next day, leaflets, banners, and posters throughout Beijing accused Zhou Enlai of betraying the May 16 Circular and the Cultural Revolution.[4] Even so, many rebel faction organizations criticized and boycotted the campaign. According to a contemporary news report, "On August 26, more than 1,000 proletarian revolutionary faction units from the capital and other parts of the country staged a mass rally at the Iron and Steel Institute to 'Thoroughly smash the reactionary Capital May 16 Corps.'" Zhang Jianqi and four other May 16 leaders were denounced at the rally.[5]

Rallies were followed by the arrest of some May 16 Corps leaders and sympathetic cadres in central government agencies in August and September 1967. An investigative group under the CCRSG soon afterward reported, "'May 16' is a small organization with few members and has been thoroughly destroyed and no longer exists." On September 10, Xie Fuzhi, vice-premier and minister of public security told a delegation of secondary school Red Guards that the membership of the May 16 Corps "didn't exceed fifty people, and the genuinely bad among them numbered no more than a dozen; they might have had the backing of capitalist roaders." A Beijing Red Guard rally of some one hundred thousand people on September 12 celebrated the crushing of the May 16 elements.[6]

By October 1967, the May 16 Corps was effectively defunct. The investigation of the group should have ended there, but in fact it had just begun.

ESCALATION: A STRATEGIC PLAN TO TURN THE SITUATION AROUND

Mao considered ending the Cultural Revolution in 1968, but in summer and autumn 1967, the situation spun completely out of control. Rebel attacks on the military following Wuhan's July 20 Incident were creating chaos in the military ranks, and in many places violence was escalating into armed battles. Resistance to the grand alliance under the revolutionary committees was shaking the stability of the "newborn red regime." Rebels created international incidents that disrupted Beijing's diplomatic relations, and masses of Red Guards besieged Zhongnanhai with demands that Liu Shaoqi be brought out and denounced. The genie of "justified rebellion" that Mao had released from the bottle had become more than he himself could subdue.

Mao had responded to Wuhan's July 20 Incident by shifting the focus of the Cultural Revolution from the bureaucratic clique to "evildoers" within the rebel faction, and from suppressing the conservative faction to restraining the rebel faction, starting with the ouster of

Wang Li, Guan Feng, and Qi Benyu and attacks on rebel leaders who supported their views. Now the investigation of the May 16 clique was meant to tighten the thumbscrews on the rebel faction, put the genie back into the bottle, and end the chaos. Mao said that it was necessary to "take precautions against 'black hands' and 'counterrevolutionaries' who incite ultra-leftist behavior" and end the Cultural Revolution by the following spring. He agreed with Zhou Enlai that the situation had to be stabilized as soon as possible.[7]

During this time, the Beijing municipal authorities submitted a report regarding Beijing Normal University, which said, "Some rebel faction members are evildoers and may be 'May 16' elements." Next to this sentence, Mao wrote the memo, "That's good," and he criticized the Beijing municipal party committee for not arresting May 16 members.[8] What he meant was that the way to clean up the rebel faction was to arrest May 16 elements—the supposed "'black hands' and 'counterrevolutionaries' who incite ultra-leftist behavior."

Yet, once again Mao lost control of the situation. Military units antagonistic to the rebel faction, officials who had been persecuted by rebels at the outset of the Cultural Revolution, and the new elite in the revolutionary committees immediately grasped this opportunity to deal with the rebel faction. Mass organizations also used the pretext of seizing May 16 elements among rival groups.

Key members of the proletarian headquarters took note of Mao's strategic shift and began singing the same tune. In speeches on August 11, 1967, Chen Boda and Jiang Qing referred to the May 16 Corps as a secret conspiratorial organization targeting Zhou Enlai and effectively also the central leadership: "Some people want to shake the center from two sides, 'left' and 'right.'"[9] In a speech to the Beijing Municipal Revolutionary Committee standing committee on September 1, Jiang Qing called for rebel faction members to undergo "struggle, criticism, and reform" in their own work units, demanded trust in the military, and accused May 16 elements of "using an ultra-leftist guise to create chaos."[10] While receiving a delegation from mass organizations in Anhui Province on September 5, Jiang Qing said that the May 16 clique "uses the ideological instability of young people. The people actually behind it are very evil."

An essay published under Yao Wenyuan's name on September 8,

1967, stated that Tao Zhu's two volumes of essays, *Ideals, Sentiment, and Spiritual Life* and *Ideology, Emotion, and Elegance*, were companion volumes to Liu Shaoqi's "reactionary 'Self-cultivation.'"[11] The essay might have gone unnoticed if not for a passage that aroused great concern:

> This counterrevolutionary organization [May 16] has two objectives: One is to sabotage and split the party central leadership led by our Great Leader Chairman Mao; the other is to sabotage and split the main pillar of the dictatorship of the proletariat— the great Chinese People's Liberation Army. Afraid of making itself known to the public, this counterrevolutionary organization has hidden underground in Beijing for the past few months. Most of its members and leaders remain unknown at present; they simply send people out in the depths of night to paste up and distribute leaflets and write slogans. The vast masses are now investigating and studying these people, and all will soon become clear.

The last two sentences of this paragraph had been added by Mao himself when he vetted the essay, which he revised three times.[12] It reflected his need to protect Zhou Enlai and the PLA in order to continue the Cultural Revolution.

Mao's appeal launched a bloody suppression of the May 16 counterrevolutionary conspiratorial clique throughout the country.

HIGH POINTS IN THE INVESTIGATION OF THE MAY 16 CLIQUE

THE FIRST CLIMAX: AUGUST–OCTOBER 1967

In the latter half of August, the Yan'an Commune, a mass organization at the Beijing Iron and Steel Institute, seized the May 16 Corps student leaders Li Fang, Zhang Jianqi, and others. The group's "backstage supporters" were arrested as well, beginning with a vice-minister-level cadre in the Foreign Ministry, Chen Jiakang,[13] and Wang Huande from the ministry's confidential bureau in early

September. Arrests in the Foreign Ministry were made with Zhou Enlai's approval.

Mu Xin (CCRSG member and chief editor of *Guangming Daily*), Lin Jie (editor of *Red Flag*), Zhou Jingfang (standing committee member and secretary-general of the Beijing Municipal Revolutionary Committee), Zhao Yiya (chief editor of *PLA Daily*), and leftists in the Philosophy and Social Sciences Department of the Chinese Academy of Sciences (known as the Academic Department) such as Pan Zinian, Wu Chuanqi, and Lin Yushi were also imprisoned as "backstage supporters" of the May 16 clique.

During an urgent meeting on the May 16 problem on October 26, the Central Military Commission Administrative Group declared, "We must go without eating or sleeping to root out these counterrevolutionaries! We cannot die easy if we don't uproot them!" The investigation of the clique in the military targeted opponents of the CMCAG's Huang, Wu, Ye, Li, and Qiu who had come to the fore on May 13, 1967.[14]

After this first climax in the campaign against the May 16 clique, there seemed to be no major moves for several months. Then, on March 27, 1968, a mass rally to "thoroughly smash a new counterattack by the 'February Countercurrent'" was held at the Beijing Workers' Stadium to denounce Yang Chengwu, Yu Lijin, and Fu Chongbi as backstage supporters of the May 16 clique, and their associates were also put under investigation.

On July 28, 1968, Mao sent worker and PLA propaganda teams to work units where intellectuals were concentrated, and some of the hard-core rebels who launched "anti-restoration" campaigns[15] in some provinces and cities were also labeled May 16 elements. At the end of 1968, the CCP Central Committee established a special leading group to investigate the May 16 clique, with Chen Boda as chairman and Xie Fuzhi and Wu Faxian as members.

From 1968 to 1969, the investigation of the May 16 clique was carried out in an on-again, off-again fashion in some work units but without significant momentum in society at large, possibly because this so-called counterrevolutionary conspiratorial organization didn't really exist.

THE SECOND CLIMAX: DEFENDING THE RED REGIME

As rebel resistance continued to threaten the stability of the revolutionary committees, the central leadership, determined to restore order after the Ninth National Party Congress in April 1969, responded with a new upsurge in investigations against the May 16 clique. In a speech on the evening of September 20, 1969, Zhou Enlai accused some people of using "May 16" tactics in an attempt to "seize the power of the proletariat." He observed, "When we previously dealt with and uprooted 'May 16,' we emphasized four points: First, don't broaden the scope; second, don't let the old conservatives take advantage of the situation to make a comeback; third, differentiate between leaders and their followers; and fourth, promote the grand alliance. These four points were necessary at the time . . . but resulted in holding back, and central agencies haven't carried out the campaign deeply and thoroughly enough!"[16]

In a speech to the Ministry of Education, Ministry of Culture, and Academic Department on October 29, 1969, Vice-Premier and Public Security Minister Xie Fuzhi called for mobilizing the masses and carrying out a campaign to thoroughly cleanse the class ranks, and especially to investigate the May 16 clique.

When Zhou Enlai, Kang Sheng, and Jiang Qing received a delegation of PLA propaganda teams from the central apparatus and various cultural and education organs on January 24, 1970, Zhou Enlai said that investigations had determined that "May 16" had existed before the publication of the May 16 Circular in 1967 and required further exposure and criticism. He identified two strongholds for the group: "The larger one has the CAS Philosophy and Social Sciences Department as its hub, and also includes the divisions of foreign affairs, politics and law, agriculture and forestry, industry and communications, culture, education, propaganda, ethnic minorities, and the united front. In the military, the main force is the field armies and the 'New Three Armies' faction . . . There are also small May 16 cliques composed mainly of students in the colleges and universities." Kang Sheng said that the main question was how May 16 backers in the central government had conspired to usurp power over confidential and important matters. Jiang Qing said, "This May 16 counterrevolutionary conspiratorial clique used one-way contact; they didn't tell their parents or their children, but carried out secret activities."[17]

THE THIRD CLIMAX: THE MARCH 27 NOTICE

On March 27, 1970, the Central Committee issued its "Notice Regarding the Investigation of the May 16 Counterrevolutionary Conspiratorial Clique" (Central Committee Document No. 20 [1970], commonly known as the March 27 Notice), which Zhao Enlai took charge of drafting. The document prohibited broadening the scope of the investigation, which had labeled upward of one out of every seven people in some work units as May 16 elements: "Clean out these counterrevolutionaries, call the organizations by their names, and designate their actual character; don't refer to everything as 'May 16.'"

The March 27 Notice stated that May 16 clique membership should no longer be investigated, mainly because it was impossible to track down when someone had joined an organization that didn't exist. Half a year later, Zhou Enlai went a step further by saying, "Anyone involved in a conspiracy is May 16 . . . It doesn't matter whether the organization is called 'May 16' or whether a membership form was filled out; what matters is their counterrevolutionary activities . . . The weight should be on criminal acts."[18] This effectively enlarged the scope of investigation to include anyone taking part in certain activities and gave more leeway to work units where investigations had produced meager results. On November 20, 1970, Zhou Enlai said, "This time, it has to be taken to completion, no matter what."[19]

On February 8, 1971, the Central Committee issued its "Decision Regarding the Establishment of the May 16 Special Investigation Joint Group" (Central Committee Document No. 13 [1971], commonly known as the February 8 Decision). The fifteen-member investigation group was headed by Wu De, with Li Zhen as vice-chairman, and with Yang Junsheng, Huang Zuozhen, and Yu Sang among its members. This document stipulated, "Since it is necessary to prevent expansion but also to avoid all coming to naught, it is essential to focus on ascertaining individual criminal acts committed by the May 16 counterrevolutionary conspiratorial clique rather than starting off with sweeping investigations of organizational relationships and whether or not a form was filled out."

A member of the Red Flag Combat Group at the Beijing Foreign Languages Institute, Zhang Hanzhi, wrote a letter to Mao saying that the chairman of the Beijing Municipal Revolutionary Committee, Xie Fuzhi, and the navy's support-the-left personnel were supporting a faction at the institute that opposed the Premier. Directed by Mao to deal with the problem, Zhou Enlai sent the Central Guard Regiment to take over the institute's support-the-left work while stepping up purges of May 16 elements.[20]

Members of the public in Beijing informed on more than fifty thousand people and implicated around fifteen thousand; more than seven hundred key targets were reported from below, and three thousand people were sent to study classes that required them to sleep on the premises.[21]

The shift in focus from participation in a May 16 organization to "criminal acts" resulted in the identification and investigation of multiple "incidents" in each locality and the continual expansion of the scope of investigation. In August 1967, only two criminal activities were attributed to the May 16 clique: opposing the PLA and opposing the proletarian headquarters. After the Ninth Party Congress, opposing the revolutionary committees was added as a crime. By 1971, the criminal acts of the May 16 clique included nearly every action carried out by the rebel faction during the Cultural Revolution.

The focus of the investigations was to root out "backstage supporters" of the "May 16 counterrevolutionary conspiratorial clique." At first these supporters were identified as Wang Li, Guan Feng, and Qi Benyu, but then Yang Chengwu, Yu Lijin, and Fu Chongbi were added to the list, and the March 27 Notice included Xiao Hua as well. Chen Boda joined their ranks after being struck down during the second plenum of the Ninth CCP Central Committee in 1970. In every province, veteran cadres whose views diverged from those of power-wielding military and administrative bureaucrats were also labeled May 16 supporters. In a bizarre twist, Lin Biao was included among the backstage supporters of the May 16 clique after he died attempting to flee from China in September 1971, even though criticizing Lin Biao was initially considered a major crime of the May 16 clique and the very definition of a May 16 element.

Adding to the intrigue was an incident on October 22, 1973, when Li Zhen, the deputy head of the May 16 Special Investigation Joint Group, head of the CCP Public Security Ministry Core Group, and chairman of the ministry's revolutionary committee, was found dead inside an underground thermodynamics conduit in the Public Security Ministry's compound. At first homicide was suspected, but then Li Zhen was determined to have "commit[ed] suicide to escape punishment." Given that Li Zhen occupied key positions and reported directly to Zhou Enlai, it was unclear what crime he might have been attempting to escape punishment for, nor was any allegation ever made public.

It should be noted that Zhou Enlai knew very well that the May 16 organization no longer existed anywhere in China, but as the leader of the efforts against the alleged group, Zhou never admitted this or acknowledged his error.

THE INVESTIGATION IN THE FOREIGN MINISTRY

The investigation in the Foreign Ministry was of particular interest to Mao, and Zhou Enlai controlled its every detail from beginning to end. The Foreign Ministry's investigation of the clique served as a model for other work units throughout the country.[22]

At the outset of the Cultural Revolution, under the direction of Minister Chen Yi, the ministry party committee led by Vice-Minister Ji Pengfei carried out a campaign to "sweep out ox demons and snake spirits from the Foreign Ministry," labeling some senior and junior cadres as "anti-party, anti-socialist elements" and arranging for them to be subjected to brutal struggle by the masses. When the bourgeois reactionary line was denounced, the rebel faction confiscated eight gunnysacks of files that the party committee had compiled against cadres and ordinary people.

On December 20, 1966, more than two hundred ministry personnel established a rebel faction organization called the Foreign

Ministry Revolutionary Rebel Liaison Station. The ministry party committee tried to disband it, but when Zhou Enlai said a few days later that revolutionary mass organizations could be established in foreign affairs units, the Liaison Station's membership burgeoned to more than 1,700 out of just over 2,200 staff.

When the Liaison Station decided to seize power from the party committee on January 18, 1967, Zhou Enlai and Chen Yi voiced their support and cheered the rebel faction's success. However, Zhou Enlai explicitly stipulated that the power seizure related only to leading the Cultural Revolution and supervising the ministry's daily activities, and that the central leadership retained diplomatic authority.

After Chen's Yi's outburst at Huairen Hall on February 16, some people in the Foreign Ministry's rebel faction called for Chen Yi to be struck down as part of the campaign against the February Counter-current. Mao wanted the rebels to only "scorch" Chen, however, so Chen was simply denounced and continued to act as minister of foreign affairs. Aware of Mao's intentions, Zhou Enlai publicly supported Chen Yi at the time, so the rebels became displeased with Zhou and began targeting him as well.

In the latter half of May, the leader of the Liaison Station, Wang Zhongqi, and a few others put up big-character posters against Zhou Enlai using names such as May 16 Combat Group. Upon learning of it, Mao ordered the CCRSG to put a stop to it. The ministry's Wang Hairong and Tang Wensheng submitted a report to Mao about a trend toward attacking the Premier within the ministry and also in wider society. Mao responded with a memo stating, "Ultra-leftist viewpoints are wrong."[23] The Liaison Station collapsed after Zhou Enlai sent down instructions in October 1967 that some people in its core group were directly or indirectly connected with the May 16 clique.

Zhou Enlai directed the Foreign Ministry to focus on its campaign against the May 16 clique in 1968. When Chen Boda expressed concern over expansion of the scope of the campaign, Zhou warned him against dashing cold water on the mass movement. In fact, the campaign at the Foreign Ministry did go too far, as exemplified by the purge of Yao Dengshan, a high-ranking diplomat sent to Qingcheng Prison on a nine-year sentence as a top May 16 element.[24] A veteran cadre who had joined the party in 1936, Yao had been appointed attaché to the Chinese embassy in Indonesia in March 1966. During anti-Chinese riots following Suharto's military coup d'état against the Sukarno regime and bloody crackdown on the Indonesian Communist Party, a mob laid siege to the Chinese embassy and cut off supplies of food and water to the compound. The Chinese ambassador was recalled to China, and Yao Dengshan, serving as interim chargé d'affaires, drew praise from Mao for leading embassy personnel in battling the mob. After being expelled by the Indonesian government, Yao and other embassy staff were enthusiastically welcomed at the Beijing airport on April 30, 1967, by Zhou Enlai and other central leaders. Yao was invited to the Tiananmen gate tower to view a fireworks display on the evening of May 1, and a photo of Yao with Mao published in *People's Daily* the next day made Yao famous overnight as a "warrior of red diplomacy." Once back in Beijing, however, Yao became embroiled in struggles within the Foreign Ministry and took the side of the rebel faction's Liaison Station, serving as adviser to its core group. The result was Zhou Enlai labeling him a May 16 counterrevolutionary element.

Zhou Enlai personally mobilized investigations against the May 16 clique inside the Foreign Ministry and advised leaders and core members of the Liaison Station to set an example by confessing. The news section's Cheng Shousan and Huang Anguo responded by admitting to heading the May 16 organization in the ministry and offered up one hundred other names. Zhou also drew a "candid confession" (subsequently retracted) from the veteran cadre Lin Zhaonan.[25]

The investigation of May 16 elements in central government agencies was for a long time carried out in May 7 cadre schools, and extraction of confessions under torture meant that most people at the cadre schools became suspected May 16 elements.[26] One of those suspects in autumn 1968 was Zhu Genhua, a cartoonist with the Foreign Ministry's subordinate World Knowledge Publishing House. Zhu was initially locked in a dark room around the clock and was not even allowed out to use the restroom. In 1969, he was sent to the ministry's May 7 cadre school in You County, Hunan Province, while his wife and children were sent to the countryside in Gansu. The family was not reunited until ten years later. Apart from hard labor, around-the-clock interrogation was routine, and Zhu was repeatedly beaten. At a mass

rally at the cadre school on May 5, 1970, Zhu was forced to wear a
"May 16 counterrevolutionary element" dunce cap and had his arms
twisted so severely that he became permanently disabled.[27] The May
16 clique investigation also led to the suicide of Tang Xianyao of the
Soviet Union and Europe section and Peng Ning, a young teacher at
the Foreign Affairs Institute.[28]

According to verdicts delivered in 1972, the Foreign Ministry's investigation of the May 16 clique reaped "brilliant results": 20 people
were officially designated May 16 counterrevolutionary elements, 31 were
handled as a "contradiction between the enemy and us"; 80-odd were
disciplined for May 16 problems; and more than 170 were determined
to have committed serious errors, and 1,408 to have committed routine errors—bringing the grand total to more than 1,700 people. This
was more than half of all Foreign Ministry personnel.[29]

THE INVESTIGATION IN THE AGRICULTURE AND FORESTRY DIVISION

After Tan Zhenlin was named a key leader of the February Countercurrent, college Red Guards went to the agriculture and forestry division[30] looking for "bombshells" to use against Tan. What they discovered
was that Qin Hualong, a revered political commissar of the Shanghai Garrison Command who subsequently became director of the
Central Committee's agriculture and forestry political department,
had been denounced as a counterrevolutionary at Tan Zhenlin's
bidding. Now that Tan had been discredited, the Red Guards insisted
on Qin's rehabilitation, and when the conservative Yan'an Commune
in the State Council's agriculture office opposed rehabilitating Qin,
the rebel faction interpreted this as effectively protecting Tan. Zhou
Enlai's suggestion that the mass organizations reach a consensus
through debate only incurred the wrath of the rebel faction.

On May 16, 1967, Red Guards from Beijing Agricultural University announced the establishment of the Agricultural University East
Is Red Commune May 16 Corps, with a manifesto declaring a "resolute counterattack against the February Countercurrent" and calling
for "rehabilitation and verdict reversal for General Qin Hualong."

When the manifesto immediately came under criticism as an indirect attack on Zhou Enlai, the group put up a big-character poster admitting error and disbanded, but its brief existence proved disastrous for all involved.

At a representative assembly of Capital Red Guards in early September 1967, Kang Sheng and Jiang Qing accused Qin Hualong of being a backstage supporter of the May 16 counterrevolutionaries and of involvement with a Xinjiang renegade clique, and later that month, with Zhou Enlai's authorization, Qin was turned over to the Beijing Garrison.[31]

From September 1969 onward, cadres from the agricultural and forestry division were sent down to May 7 cadre schools in Hubei, Jiangxi, and Henan and underwent investigation for involvement in the May 16 clique. Qin Hualong was sent to Qincheng Prison as a backstage supporter of the clique, and cadres who supported him were put under isolation and investigation and tortured into confessing their criminal acts as core members of the clique. At a mass rally just after New Year's Day in 1970, military representatives at the cadre schools announced the arrest of Wu Wenping, propaganda head of the Central Committee's agriculture and forestry political department, as a core member of the May 16 clique. Several other key department officials were denounced along with Qin Hualong's secretary, Xu Renjun, who confessed after being tortured for seventy-two hours nonstop. Some cadres who couldn't bare the humiliation hanged themselves or leaped to their deaths.[32]

After Lin Biao's death in September 1971, the May 16 special case group suddenly called a meeting of the people being investigated and announced, "The backer of your May 16 counterrevolutionary clique, Lin Biao, is finished!" The investigation targets just gaped at one another, not knowing whether to laugh or cry, and the investigation continued. Finally in 1974, the Shayang Labor Reform Farm that served as a May 7 cadre school for the agriculture and forestry division was disbanded, and the targets of five years of investigation were allowed to rejoin their families in Beijing, but without formal verdicts. Eventually the political situation changed, and the investigation targets demanded clarification of what the May 16 clique actually was, as well as redress for Qin Hualong and Wu Wenping, who remained in prison.

At one point, investigation targets Xu Renjun and Liu Zibing went together to talk to an old colleague, Liu Chuanxin, who by then was chief of the Beijing Municipal Public Security Bureau. Liu was sympathetic, but pointed to a mountain of files on his desk and said, "Just look at that—I've seized many May 16 elements in Beijing and sent them to prison, and there's a stack of files that I still don't know what to do with!" He added sorrowfully, "While I seized May 16 elements here, my wife was seized as a May 16 element in Jiangsu, and she's still being detained and interrogated! I can't even tell you what the May 16 Clique is!"[33] After the Cultural Revolution ended, Liu Chuanxin was investigated for his role in suppressing the 1976 April Fifth Democracy Movement and other activities connected with the Gang of Four. He killed himself on May 19, 1977.

THE INVESTIGATION IN THE FOOD MINISTRY[34]

In the Food Ministry, a bogus case against a "May 16 conspiratorial clique" resulted in the purging of 123 alleged May 16 elements, or one out of every six cadres. Two people were persecuted to death in the course of brutal investigations.[35]

On February 5, 1970, a clerk at the ministry's party committee office, Chen Qizhen, was placed in isolation and under investigation by a five-member group. Subjected to constant physical abuse and deprived of basic dignity, he finally confessed to participating in May 16 activities after hearing a recording of another alleged clique member who fabricated remarks by Chen. When the investigation group demanded more details, however, Chen retracted his confession, as a result of which he was slapped so hard that a blood vessel in his temple burst and blood poured down his face. The next day, the investigation group brought over two of Chen's good friends, who told him, "There's no use resisting; it's every man for himself. Just find a way out!" Seeing that so many others couldn't bear up under the pressure, Chen created a credible confession and admitted his guilt at a mass rally on February 16, 1971. This resulted in improved treatment: He was allowed to write to his family and eat in the canteen with other members of the study class; he could buy things at the commissary and didn't have to ask permission to use the washroom. But he still wasn't allowed contact with the outside world.

Other investigation targets were treated much the same, with some suffering lost teeth and broken bones. Some described their travails at a symposium for thirty-six victims held at the cadre school in January 1974. In an article published in *Yanhuang Chunqiu* in 2010, Liao Zhunan described how he was tortured, deprived of sleep, and interrogated nonstop: "They drew a chalk circle about the size of a pot cover and made me stand in the middle of it for sixteen hours straight, from morning until night, only allowing me a few minutes to use the restroom, and I even had to stand while I ate. Finally I passed out, and they dashed cold water on me to wake me up, then kicked me viciously and ordered me to stand up immediately."

In 1973, a verdict was reached: "Following investigation, no May 16 counterrevolutionary organization was found in the Food Ministry, nor were any May 16 elements discovered."

INVESTIGATIONS IN OTHER CENTRAL ORGANS

The Academic Department was a key unit in the investigation of the May 16 clique. Political campaigns in the Academic Department had been led since June 1966 by a work group headed by the director of the State Council's culture and education office, Zhang Jichun, and Academic Department leftists such as Wu Chuanqi, Lin Yushi,[36] and Pan Zinian.[37] Pan became head of the Academic Department's Cultural Revolution committee, while Wu was one of its leading members. Because they were associated with Guan Feng and actively participated in the rebel faction, they eventually became targets of the investigation of the May 16 clique, along with the leaders of rival rebel organizations. More than half the personnel in the Academic Department were labeled May 16 elements, and around ten people died of unnatural causes.[38]

At the CAS's Physics Institute, more than a hundred people were labeled May 16 counterrevolutionaries in the greatest case of injustice since the institute's establishment.[39]

The Ministry of Health was another investigation focal point. The ministry's rebel faction held a meeting on March 10, 1967, to criticize the ministry's urban focus and the special medical privileges central leaders enjoyed. At a reception for the ministry's mass organization representatives toward the end of the year, Zhou Enlai accused the meeting organizers of attacking the proletarian headquarters and revealing internal information,[40] and Vice-Premier Li Xiannian said that those involved with the May 16 clique were secret agents. A famous medical expert and official doctor of the central leaders, Ye Xinqing, was labeled a May 16 element after Zhou Enlai disparaged him as a quack.[41]

Four members of the Central Philharmonic Orchestra committed suicide after being framed and tortured, and concertmaster Yang Bingsun and chorus member Wang Peng were sentenced to lengthy prison terms as counterrevolutionaries. Two Philharmonic rebel faction organizations were almost totally annihilated, and their core members were labeled May 16 elements. Zhang Yunqing, a composer and lead performer in the symphony *Shajiabang*, was labeled a May 16 element. Nearly one hundred suspects were sent to a May 7 cadre school for reform through labor.[42]

INVESTIGATIONS OF THE MAY 16 CLIQUE IN THE PROVINCES

On instructions from Beijing, investigation campaigns were launched throughout the country. In Guangxi, for instance, the autonomous region's leading group to investigate the May 16 clique arranged for more than four thousand people to join investigation-leading groups in the prefectures and cities. The investigation process unearthed sixty-eight alleged cases involving some one thousand cadres and ordinary citizens. Large numbers of people had their homes searched and ransacked; some were interrogated under torture, bound, and beaten; and some were persecuted to the point where they went insane, died, or killed themselves.[43]

Investigations varied among the different provinces, but in all cases, opposing the military, the grand alliance, or the revolutionary committees (or preparatory committees) was considered a criminal act of the May 16 clique. The suppressors were support-the-left military units or revolutionary committees, while the victims were radicals within the rebel faction and large numbers of innocent people. In some places the investigations overlapped with the Cleansing of the Class Ranks and the One Strike and Three Antis campaigns. Each faction used investigation of the May 16 clique as an opportunity to attack its opponents, and various political powers within the military and civilian bureaucratic cliques used factionalism among the mass organizations to suppress their own political opponents. The investigations resulted in overcrowded prisons and countless deaths.

The investigation of the May 16 clique in Jiangsu provides a glimpse of the situation. After the July 20 Incident in Wuhan, rebel groups attacked the leadership organs of the Nanjing Military Region with the intention of weeding out Commander Xu Shiyou. Under Mao's adamant protection, Xu was appointed chairman of the Jiangsu Province Revolutionary Committee on March 23, 1968, and to the Politburo during the Ninth National Party Congress in 1969. Given Xu's position, his rebel faction opponents stood accused not only of opposing the military but also of the May 16 crime of attempting to split the proletarian headquarters.

Xu Shiyou went after his opponents with a vengeance. At one meeting he said, "The main work in Jiangsu is the 'two digs'—digging out coal and digging out May 16!" He then raised his fist and bellowed, "Both are digging out black things!" Xu had responded to Mao's call to mine coal in the south with a wasteful and futile mass campaign, but his attack on May 16 elements achieved rich yields.

Xu Shiyou and others maintained that May 16 organizations were deeply entrenched and engaged in clandestine activities throughout Jiangsu, and that they were highly reactionary and dangerous. Based on this judgment, the entire province engaged in an all-out war to annihilate the May 16 clique.

Second Special Case Offices (referred to as "Second Offices," or in Nanjing as the "320 Office") composed of support-the-left military personnel were established at the provincial, prefectural, municipal, and county levels to unify administration of the investigative work. Xu Shiyou entrusted a senior support-the-left officer in the provincial party committee, Wu Dasheng, with sole oversight of the provincial Second Office, which came up with a list of thirty-one offenses qualifying people as May 16 elements.

When the commanders of eight major military regions were transferred at the end of 1973, Xu Shiyou was sent to Guangdong, and Peng Chong took charge of the Jiangsu party committee's work. In spring 1975, Peng disclosed that 130,000 people were designated May 16 elements in Jiangsu's investigations, not counting those in Xuzhou Prefecture.[44] Peng's statement was supported by subsequently published official figures, which also stated that more than 57,000 people confessed under torture. Information compiled from the province's various municipal and county courts found that more than 2,000 people died during the May 16 investigations, and that an even larger number of people were injured. Other sources state that more than 6,000 people died or became physically handicapped or mentally deranged while being investigated or imprisoned.[45] The Jiangsu Province Policy Implementation Office concluded that the campaign to investigate and excavate the May 16 clique caused twenty times more harm than the 1957 Anti-Rightist Campaign.[46]

The number of victims at some work units targeted as "focal points" of the investigation is shocking. For example, at the Nanjing Electron Tube Factory, more than 2,700 of some 3,800 cadres and staff were investigated; 1,266 were designated May 16 elements, and 7 died while being interrogated under torture.[47] At the Nanjing Municipal Public Works Construction Company, more than 1,200 people were investigated, around 60 percent of all cadres and staff, and 894 were designated May 16 elements.[48]

After more than four months of investigation beginning in April 1970, Nanjing University locked up 108 May 16 elements, named 248 others, and produced a roster of 1,154 suspects. Twenty-one of those implicated took their own lives.[49] The university achieved its impressive results by interrogating people under torture around the clock, sometimes for thirteen days straight. The wife of an elderly staff member of the university's sports office was summarily executed at a mass rally after being identified as the author of an anonymous letter to the provincial party mouthpiece *New China Daily* expressing her objections to the May 16 investigations.[50]

Chi Mingtang, a member of the provincial revolutionary committee's core group who was in charge of the investigations at Nanjing University, had joined the revolution in 1938, but when a subordinate under investigation reported that Chi himself was a May 16 element, he was placed under isolation and investigation in October 1971 and imprisoned soon afterward. After this "breakthrough," the provincial Second Office determined that 72 percent of provincial-level leading cadres, 38 percent of bureau and department leading cadres, and 41 percent of prefectural and municipal leading cadres were implicated in May 16 crimes.[51]

Wu Dasheng and two other key officials in Jiangsu's support-the-left military units were also fingered by someone at Nanjing University who had been labeled a core May 16 member.[52] Although Wu Dasheng emerged unscathed, one of the others remained under a cloud of suspicion, and the third was wrongfully investigated.

Military cadres weren't exempt, either. A 1975 investigative report by a provincial party committee investigation and research group found that the provincial Second Office had compiled files on 298 military cadres, including 84 at the army level or above. Eleven army-level leading cadres were implicated in the Nanjing Military Region alone.[53]

Twenty-five of the forty-five members of the provincial revolutionary committee standing committee were labeled May 16 elements, including eight support-the-left military cadres. Apart from Wu Dasheng, Yang Guangli, and Jiang Kesan, all were investigated as May 16 suspects, including the provincial party chief Peng Chong.[54]

The province's May 7 cadre school became a de facto labor camp for May 16 elements. By the end of 1971, more than 1,600 of the 3,000 people at the cadre school were named in investigations of May 16 crimes, and another 400 were listed on the suspect roster.[55] Under isolation and subjected to interrogation around the clock, some broke down and confessed to May 16–related activities, only to be relentlessly pursued and attacked until they also implicated "confederates," causing the number of investigation targets to snowball. In order to "round up the whole gang and not let any slip through the net," the cadre school pushed investigation targets to inform on investigating personnel. This opportunity to take revenge on persecutors resulted in an utter melee.

Nanjing City was designated a major May 16 base camp. Over the course of more than three years, investigation teams in every sector and at every level carried out more than 3,900 denunciation and study classes of various kinds with more than 200,000 individual participations, and more than 1,200 rallies were staged throughout the city. By the end of 1972, more than 20,000 people had been labeled May 16 elements, and more than 300 had been persecuted to death; in the municipal commerce sector alone, 33 people committed suicide.[56] According to a popular doggerel in Nanjing, "Every family has a May 16 member, if not a relative then a friend."

Liu Zhong, a former member of the municipal party committee secretariat, was denied timely medical treatment for cancer, no doubt contributing to his early demise. When the former deputy mayor Fang Zhen refused to confess to being a backstage supporter of the May 16 clique, he was plied with liquor in hopes that he would "vomit out the truth when drunk." A former municipal leading cadre who confessed under torture to being a backstage supporter of the May 16 clique wasn't let off until she implicated another three hundred May 16 members.[57]

The deputy director of the Nanjing Song-and-Dance Troupe, Li Xiangzhi, had taken a leading role in the troupe's rebel faction at the outset of the Cultural Revolution and had put up a big-character poster objecting to the practice of making female performers dance with senior cadres. May 16 investigators latched onto some ravings she uttered after being politically victimized, and she was executed as a counterrevolutionary in September 1971.[58]

Other places in Jiangsu followed Nanjing's example. In Yancheng Prefecture, for instance, six of the thirteen former members of the prefectural party committee standing committee were labeled May 16 elements, and another four were put on the suspect roster; more than half of eighty-four mid-level cadres were labeled May 16 elements, as were nearly two-thirds of the five hundred security cadres and police officers in the prefectural public-security, procuratorial, and judicial organs.[59] Xuzhou purged more than six thousand people in its campaign against the May 16 clique.[60]

16

THE CLEANSING OF THE CLASS RANKS

The Cleansing of the Class Ranks (CCR) was a major component of the Cultural Revolution. Mao said, "The cleansing of the class ranks must target traitors, spies, inveterate capitalist roaders, counterrevolutionaries, and unreformed landlords, rich peasants, bad elements, and rightists."[1] The CCR was a ruthless and violent purge by the regime directed mainly at the political underclass and old functionaries of the Kuomintang regime who had managed to survive previous political campaigns. The CCR's full-fledged launch occurred in 1968, just as Mao demanded a grand alliance and the rebuilding of a new order as soon as possible. Members of mass organizations who had undesirable family backgrounds, or those from good backgrounds who obstructed the restoration of order, also became victims of the CCR.

THE GUIDING IDEOLOGY AND LEGAL BASIS FOR THE CLEANSING OF THE CLASS RANKS

On January 30, 1967, Mao wrote a memo on Tan Zhenlin's report regarding the situation in the State Council's agricultural division: "A minority of counterrevolutionaries, rightists, and degenerates have infiltrated the party, government, army, civilians, schools, factories, villages, and businesses. It's very fortunate that these people have all jumped out during this campaign. The revolutionary masses should earnestly investigate and thoroughly criticize them, and then deal with each of them according to the seriousness of the case. Please take note of this problem."[2] The leaders of work units at all levels responded to this memo by scrutinizing their staff and those who had served during the Republican period through the lens of class struggle.

By then, Mao had directed the Central Committee to issue a document on January 13 titled "Several Provisions Regarding Enhancing Public Security Work in the Great Proletarian Cultural Revolution," subsequently known as the "Public Security Six Provisions." Among the stipulations, article 2 criminalized thought and speech that "attacked and vilified" Mao and Lin Biao, and in practice also Zhou Enlai, Jiang Qing, Kang Sheng, and other leaders of the proletarian headquarters, while article 4 expanded the targets of dictatorship to include twenty-one categories of people and their family members. This evil law served as the legal basis for the Cleansing of the Class Ranks that followed.

Trial campaigns were held in various provinces from November 1967 to April 1968. Shortly after an outspoken critic of the CCP, Lin Zhao, was executed in Shanghai on April 29, 1968, the CCR campaign was launched nationwide.

A directive by Mao issued in spring 1968 provided a theoretical basis for the CCR by defining the Cultural Revolution as "a continuation of the long-term fight between the broad revolutionary masses and the Kuomintang reactionaries under the Chinese Communist Party and its leadership, and a continuation of the struggle between the proletariat and the bourgeoisie."[3]

In October 1968, at the height of the CCR, Mao explained the campaign to the head of a visiting Albanian delegation, Beqir Balluku:

> A failed class will still struggle, so we never speak of final victory. Even after decades, we cannot speak of it or lose our vigilance. Those people still exist; that class still exists; the mainland has dregs of the Kuomintang. Some have drilled into our central leadership organs or into local leadership organs. This time we're cleaning them out one by one . . . This time has brought quite a major clean-up to the party, government, army, and civilians; they're cleansing and exposing themselves. If

we're talking about seven hundred million people, and one out of a thousand are bad, this indicates that the contradiction between the enemy and us is serious . . . We'll probably continue cleansing the class ranks and purging the party for half a year to a year. That will keep things quiet for a while, ten years to twenty years.[4]

The bulletin issued by the twelfth plenum of the Eighth CCP Central Committee on October 31, 1968, stated: "It is essential to continue earnestly cleansing the class ranks in the factories, people's communes, government organs, schools, all enterprises and state-run institutions, and neighborhoods, and to unearth the smattering of counterrevolutionaries concealed in mass organizations."

THE POLICY TEMPLATE FOR THE CCR

On February 21, 1968, military control personnel sent by the Central Security Unit 8341 Unit entered the Xinhua Printing Factory to "fight the enemy." The summary of this experience, issued nationwide as Central Document No. 74 (1968) at Mao's suggestion, led to an upsurge in the CCR throughout the country. The document particularly emphasized the need to take note of policy: "Their basic method was to freely mobilize the masses, rigorously differentiate between the two kinds of contradictions, firmly grasp the direction of struggle, bring people into unity as much as possible, muster all positive factors, and isolate and ruthlessly attack the smattering of class enemies to the greatest extent possible."

Despite what the document and central leaders said about policy, the campaign's attacks rapidly widened in scope and became increasingly brutal. Long imbued in the ideology of class struggle, leaders at all levels and core activists in political campaigns saw class enemies everywhere they looked. It was better to commit a policy error by seizing too many people than to commit a standpoint error by seizing too few. Under the totalitarian system, the pandering of the lower levels ensured that the original intentions of the higher levels were magnified at each step downward, so that purges always transcended the original boundaries. Furthermore, in localities and work units where a grand alliance had not been achieved, factions sought to undermine each other by seizing "evildoers" who had "infiltrated" the opposing faction, and to insulate themselves from criticism by taking the initiative to "cleanse" their own class ranks of the "tiny minority of scoundrels."

The February 7th Locomotive Factory (originally called the Changxindian Locomotive Factory) was one of the "six factories and two schools" held up as "Chairman Mao's test sites" during the Cultural Revolution[5] because their PLA Mao Zedong Thought Propaganda Teams had been sent in by the Central Guard Regiment. At the first plenum of the Ninth CCP Central Committee on April 25, 1969, Mao said, "The leadership of a substantial majority of factories is not in the hands of genuine Marxists or worker masses . . . For example, the February 7th Factory . . . is a large factory with eight thousand workers and tens of thousands of family members. In the past, the Kuomintang had nine district headquarters and the Three People's Principles Youth League had three organizations, along with eight secret agent organizations." On May 27, 1969, the Beijing Municipal Revolutionary Committee handed down a report that made the February 7th Locomotive Factory a national template for executing the policy of cleansing the class ranks. At that time, the experience of the February 7th Locomotive Factory was seen as rectifying left-deviation and emphasizing policy, but all that really meant was that some of the people falsely identified as counterrevolutionaries weren't formally labeled as such. Even so, 215 people were named traitors, secret agents, incorrigible capitalist roaders, and counterrevolutionaries of various kinds, and nearly a third of the 155 middle- and upper-ranking cadres were categorized as incorrigible capitalist roaders or historical counterrevolutionaries. Many cases were based on testimony extorted through torture. More than twenty elderly party members and workers were driven to suicide. During the CCR, the factory's staff didn't dare talk to or visit one another, as all were living in a state of Red Terror.

A reexamination carried out seven years later, in 1975, found that 203 of the 215 counterrevolutionary cases were groundless while only one of the cadre cases warranted further investigation. A 1978 policy implementation initiative discredited much of the information in the influential 1969 report.[6]

The example set by the February 7th Factory had a baneful effect on Beijing's general population in 1968. The Beijing Municipal Revolutionary Committee's September 2 report to the Central Committee, "Current Situation of the Cleansing of the Class Ranks," stated: "As of August 28, 68,123 evildoers of various kinds have been uncovered throughout the city, including 2,827 traitors, 3,721 secret agents, 2,688 incorrigible capitalist roaders, 7,942 current counterrevolutionaries, 24,161 unreformed black elements, 151 reactionary academic authorities, 1,855 reactionary capitalists, 2,284 scoundrels infiltrating mass organizations, 10,819 newly unearthed black elements, and 11,675 others."[7] The persecutions continued to snowball, and a new situation report by the Beijing municipal party committee on March 9, 1969, stated that "as of the end of February, 99,000 people have been uncovered throughout the city." Incomplete figures indicate that by February 20, 15,000 cases had been concluded, with more than half classified as "contradictions between the enemy and us."[8]

In accordance with Mao's highest directive that "dictatorship is dictatorship of the masses,"[9] all localities organized mass dictatorship teams. In Anhui Province, membership of such organizations burgeoned to 1.1 million by spring 1969 and spread to every corner of the province. Taking no notice of laws, the mass dictatorship teams arbitrarily imposed dictatorship on more than 1.5 million people in three years (including 430,000 "scoundrels" newly unearthed during the CCR). The victims were denounced, beaten, and tortured, and more than 180,000 were subjected to protracted unlawful imprisonment. More than 50,000 were still in custody on June 7, 1971, when the provincial revolutionary committee announced the disbanding of the mass dictatorship organizations.[10]

To prevent "class enemies" from slipping through the net, work units mimicked the campaign models of the "six factories and two schools" by establishing special case groups composed of their most politically reliable and historically untarnished personnel. The provinces and cities also organized specialized teams to scour old government files for information on employees of the pre-1949 regime and

report their names to their current work units. Jiangsu Province organized thousands of personnel for this purpose, compiling file cards
on more than 8,000 organizations and 420,000 individuals, and dossiers on 1,110 individuals.[11] Anyone with a file card became a target of
the CCR. In Sichuan, droves of investigators wrote up 160,000 file
cards that included allegations against 800 traitors, 3,000 secret
agents, and 108,000 counterrevolutionaries.[12]

TENS OF MILLIONS OF VICTIMS

Following research using a large quantity of county gazetteers, the
Chinese American scholar Ding Shu concluded that in the typical Chinese county, more than ten thousand people were seized and struggled
and more than a hundred people died due to the Cleansing of the Class
Ranks.[13] Ding Shu estimates that a total of thirty million people were
subjected to struggle nationwide during the CCR and that half a million died.[14] Andrew Walder and Su Yang, pulling together information
from more than 1,500 post–Cultural Revolution county gazetteers to
analyze the movement in the rural areas, estimate that 36 million
people were persecuted and that between 750,000 and 1.5 million people
were killed and a similar number of people were permanently injured.[15] Official histories of the Cultural Revolution acknowledge that
millions of bogus cases were fabricated during the CCR, implicating
some 100 million targets, associates, and family members.[16]

In one example, after the Anhui revolutionary committee was established, more than 430,000 "evildoers" were identified throughout
the province by the end of 1968 and denounced, beaten, and tortured
in a multitude of ways. Among them, 188,225 were locked up by official organs of dictatorship at the county level and above, with 4,646 of
those people driven to suicide and 1,074 beaten to death while in custody. Another 359 subsequently died as a result of their beatings. In
Huoqiu County alone, 90 people were killed by beating, live burial, or
drowning from May to September 1968, and 445 killed themselves.[17]

In Shanghai, according to incomplete statistics, the municipal special case office handled at least 965 major cases and at least 731 major

clique cases, investigating 169,405 people, among whom 5,449 were persecuted to death. Most of the city's important cultural figures came under attack and investigation.[18] The municipal revolutionary committee's progress report to the Central Committee in September 1968 stated that "142,453 traitors, secret agents, incorrigible capitalist roaders, and unreformed landlords, rich peasants, counterrevolutionaries, bad elements, and rightists have been identified, including 53,344 named in the past and 89,109 new cases. Another 8,893 current counterrevolutionaries were also uncovered."[19]

In Jiangsu, where the CCR continued until 1970, the provincial revolutionary committee reported to the Ministry of State Security in November 1971 that more than 83,190 counterrevolutionaries had been uncovered,[20] and a much larger number implicated. In Gaoyou County alone, 13,326 people were investigated from 1968 to 1969.[21] Jiangsu's Wujin County Revolutionary Committee used the slogan "category twenty-four red typhoon" to lock up 108 "ox demons and snake spirits," and seized and struggled more than 14,600 people.[22] Zhejiang Province locked up hundreds of thousands of people during the CCR, and 9,198 were persecuted to death.[23] In some cases, entire villages were classified as counterrevolutionary or bandit villages.

Guangdong Province persecuted 253,200 "class enemies" from 1968 to February 1969, and by March 1970 had uncovered 20,291 "political cliques" and seized and struggled 63,297 major targets. The city of Guangzhou ran 28,261 study classes with nearly 2.17 million participants to cleanse the class ranks from July to October 1968, and by November had uncovered 28,738 "class enemies" and people with "serious problems," some of whom were persecuted to death.[24] An opinion paper drafted by the provincial revolutionary committee resulted in persecution and bias against returned overseas Chinese and people with family members living outside mainland China. In Taishan County, more than 4,000 cadres were forced to fill out forms stating they had "severed their overseas relations," and in Foshan, more than half of 15,000 overseas Chinese households were reclassified as landlords or rich peasants and had their homes ransacked and their bank accounts frozen.[25]

The campaign in Guangxi's Nanning Prefecture resulted in 78,746 people being seized and struggled and 17,372 being persecuted to death.[26] Shaanxi denounced, investigated, and locked up more than 400,000 people, purged more than 62,000 cadres and ordinary civilians, and added more than 50,000 households to the blacklist of landlords or rich peasants, with some people suffering unnatural deaths as a result.[27] Gansu Province locked up more than 300,000 cadres and civilians,[28] and in Dingbian County alone, 3,091 "class enemies" and 15 "reactionary organizations" were identified as a result of confessions obtained through torture.[29] In Shandong Province, 113,605 people were purged in what were almost all demonstrably fraudulent cases.[30] By the end of November 1968, more than 100,000 people had been investigated and suspected of being class enemies in Heilongjiang Province, and more than 4,100 of them had died of unnatural causes.[31] By September 1968, Jilin Province had uncovered 90,090 "class enemies" and 560 counterrevolutionary secret agent groups with 12,464 members.[32] The persecution of thousands of innocent people in the Changchun area resulted in 1,929 unnatural deaths, including 184 people beaten or tortured to death and 1,745 committing suicide.[33] In Liaoning Province, more than 20,000 people died unnatural deaths from 1968 to early 1969.[34]

Jiangxi's CCR was carried out with an additional local initiative called "Three Investigates" (investigate traitors, spies, and current counterrevolutionaries). This movement, combined with the subsequent One Strike and Three Antis campaign, targeted more than 900,000 people, manufactured at least 4,102 bogus cases, wrongfully labeled more than 171,000 people as counterrevolutionaries, and caused more than 20,000 unnatural deaths.[35] An engineer for the provincial Department of Water and Power who was under investigation killed himself in a particularly horrific fashion. Standing in the corridor of his office building, he sliced open his abdomen with a kitchen knife, pulled out his entrails, and proceeded to cut them into pieces as he said, "Look, everyone, am I red or black inside?" Another man who was being denounced went to the restroom and pounded a nail into his head.[36] According to statistics from Jiangxi's public security departments, from September 12 to October 19, 1968, mass dictatorship committees in fourteen communes (towns) murdered 202 alleged counterrevolutionaries ages nine to eighty-one years old with spears and other sharp implements. Yichun Prefecture's CCR and One Strike and Three Antis campaigns resulted in wrongful cases against 644 "counterrevolutionary cliques," 3,384 counterrevolutionaries, and 9,973 "black elements," with 7,709 households mislabeled as "class enemies," 39,002 homes illegally ransacked, 4,512 people "sentenced by the masses," 4,378 people driven to suicide, and 217 crippled by beatings.[37]

Yunnan's CCR campaign, which lasted from December 1968 to the end of 1969, resulted in 237,310 people being purged and at least 6,769 "counterrevolutionaries" imprisoned.[38] The province's CCR campaign was combined with a process of "drawing the line and falling in," resulting from earlier factional conflict, with members of one faction becoming the main targets of the CCR. In a notorious example in Yunnan Province, a factional conflict that led to the fall of a member of the CCP's Yunnan Province secretariat, Zhao Jianmin, caused the investigation of more than 1.38 million people and more than 17,000 unnatural deaths during the CCR. In Yuxi Prefecture, 1,089 people were killed or driven to suicide, and in the city of Kunming, more than half a million people were persecuted, and 1,486 died.[39] In Qiaojia County, the executioners of peasant Zhou Mingtai disemboweled him and removed his brain from his skull, and one of them sliced off Zhou's sex organs, cooked them, and ate them.[40]

Tan Furen, political commissar of the Kunming Military Region and chairman of the Yunnan provincial revolutionary committee, claimed that 900,000 people had not yet been classified under land reform, so in early 1969, 83,687 people were sent to minority regions in the province's hinterland to carry out a "second land reform." People were assigned to a class based on faction: Those associated with the wrong faction were designated as landlords and rich peasants. Statistics from a portion of counties show that 7,605 poor or lower-middle peasant households were "upgraded" as landlords or rich peasants, and 30,620 homes were ransacked.[41]

The CCR brought another round of ransacking throughout the country, ordered by revolutionary committees on the grounds that the 1966 smashing of the four olds hadn't been thorough enough. After more than a year, almost no gold or silver remained in private hands.

VARIOUS SOCIAL GROUPS UNDER ATTACK

Intellectuals were among the main targets of the CCR, and the universities became disaster zones. At Tsinghua University, 1,228 out of 6,000 teachers and staff were investigated during the CCR,[42] with 16 unnatural deaths. When the Capital Workers and PLA Mao Zedong Thought Propaganda Team stationed itself in Peking University in August 1968, it said, "PU is packed with sons-of-bitches." (Mao had once said that Peking University was "a small temple wracked with evil winds and a shallow pond with many tortoises"—"tortoise" being another word for "son-of-a-bitch.") More than 900 people at the university—22.5 percent of all teachers and administrators—became major investigation targets, and 23 people were persecuted to death.[43]

At the Beijing units of the Chinese Academy of Sciences, the physicist Zhang Zongsui, geophysicist Zhao Jiuzhang, zoologist Liu Chongle, and other famous scientists were persecuted to death. Of the academy's 9,279 Beijing-based staff, 881 were placed under isolation and investigation, and 102 were classified under "contradictions between the enemy and us." Among 180 senior research fellows, 107 were investigated, with 83 reduced to a living allowance of only 6 percent of their original pay.[44]

At the academy's Shanghai research branches, more than 600 people were accused of being secret agents, more than 200 were put under isolation and investigation, 2 were beaten to death, 10 were permanently crippled, and 4 committed suicide, including the scientist Lei Hongshu, who had returned to China from America in 1949. Another 9 people attempted suicide but survived.[45]

At the academy's Changchun branch, 166 scholars at the Optics Precision Machinery Research Institute and 110 at the Applied Chemistry Research Institute were labeled secret agents. Thirteen at the Optics Institute were driven to suicide.[46]

A research fellow at the academy's Dalian Institute of Chemical Physics, Xiao Guangyan, had made important contributions to China's petroleum industry after returning to China in 1950 out of patriotic fervor. On October 5, 1968, Xiao was thrown into an "ox pen" and his home was ransacked. After Xiao was found dead of an overdose of sleeping pills on the morning of December 11, the Worker Propaganda

Team put up a large banner proclaiming, "Exceptionally good news" and notified the entire academy of its decision to "advance on the crest of victory and dig deep for all class enemies." Investigation of an alleged "301 special agent clique" involving Xiao Guangyan implicated twenty-six people in eleven work units.

At the time that Xiao overdosed, his wife, Zhen Suhui, was undergoing labor reform at the Yingchengzi labor farm. That afternoon, someone from the institute's propaganda team called her in and told her, "The counterrevolutionary secret agent Xiao Guangyan committed suicide to escape punishment for a contradiction between the enemy and us. You have to continue confessing." Zhen Suhui calmly requested two days' leave to look after her fourteen-year-old daughter, Luoluo, whom she hadn't seen for many days, and who had been left to fend for herself since her parents were detained. It appears that mother and daughter came to an understanding over the hard choices left to them. Luoluo gave a photo to her classmate with a message written on the back: "In eternal memory." Zhen Suhui and Luoluo prepared and ate several dumplings, and a few days later, they were discovered dead, wrapped in each other's arms.[47]

Other suicide victims in the science community included Rao Yutai, a founder of modern physics in China; Dong Tiebao, an expert in mechanics and computational mathematics and a pioneer in China's research into computing systems and fracture mechanics; Zhao Jiuzhang, a renowned meteorologist and expert in space physics; and twenty Class A fellows of the CAS, including the mathematician Xiong Qinglai, entomologist Liu Chongle, mycologist Deng Shuqun, and chemical engineering and metallurgy expert Ye Zhupei.

Scholars in the humanities likewise committed suicide following harrowing persecution. They included the renowned author Li Guangtian and the famous translator Fu Lei and his wife, Zhu Meifu.

The Twenty-Third Installation Engineering Company (originally called the 103 Company), which made an outstanding contribution to China's first atomic bomb, detained an increasing number of staff as the CCR progressed. A military representative said at a mass dictatorship rally: "Someone said we've detained too many people! How is it too many? Chairman Mao has taught us, we need to unify two ninety-five percents and leave two five percents, which added together is ten percent. We have to make arrests based on a ten percent ratio!"[48] At that time, this engineering facility was responsible for constructing the country's largest atomic energy reactor, the 801 Project. The company's third engineering division had more than 1,500 staff, so according to the 10 percent ratio, that meant detaining more than 150, which would affect advancement on the project. Even so, the ox pen continued to grow as more than 150 people were detained. At that time, the military representative said, "The people detained so far are just the little shrimp floating on the surface. The big fish are still deep underwater and we have to keep trying to catch them!" The entire factory became embroiled in battles on June 29 and August 23, 1967. Right afterward, the USSR's radio broadcast to China reported a huge battle at China's largest atomic installation. Concluding that this information must have been leaked by Soviet agents within the ranks, the military representatives carried out a massive dragnet, and technical personnel who had studied in the Soviet Union all became suspects. Eventually the circle of suspicion expanded to transistor radio hobbyists, and the number of detainees exceeded 170. A reexamination of the cases years later found that all the accusations were completely groundless.[49]

One of China's leading authorities on physics, Ye Qisun, already seventy years old during the CCR, was imprisoned because of a groundless case against a former student. When interrogated, he said just one thing: "I am a scientist, I am honest, I don't lie." By the time he was released, he was already seriously ill and incontinent, his legs so swollen that he could hardly stand, and his body bent into a ninety-degree angle.

In county seats where there were no universities, primary and secondary school teachers became the main targets of the CCR. Two-thirds of the teachers in Jiangxi's Chongyi County were purged after a group investigation.[50] In Guangdong's Heping County, 38.5 percent of the teachers were investigated,[51] and a total of 38,000 people were seized and struggled, of whom more than 750 were seriously injured and 249 suffered unnatural deaths.[52]

China's literary and art circles were a prime focus of the CCR. Yan Fengying, a beloved performer of Anhui's Huangmei opera, was

targeted as a "bourgeois reactionary authority" and repeatedly denounced along with her husband and two young children. Determined
to end her suffering, Yan took an overdose of sleeping pills and wrote
a suicide note. Her husband, Wang Guanya, discovered her while she
was still alive and tried to obtain emergency treatment. Instead, the
military representative Liu Wanquan and others held a denunciation
meeting around Yan's bed until she fell into a coma. Deprived of timely
treatment, Yan died early the next morning at the age of thirty-seven.
Liu Wanquan demanded an autopsy, alleging that Yan had killed herself on the instructions of a foreign espionage agency and that she had
a radio transmitter and camera in her bowels. On Liu's orders, the
doctor stripped Yan Fengying while Liu Wanquan watched and cut
her open, spreading her internal organs on the operating table, but all
that was found were the partially digested sleeping tablets. Standing
beside the desecrated corpse, Liu Wanquan declared, "Yan Fengying,
I never saw you perform on the stage or in film, but today I've seen the
real you."[53]

In some long-established enterprises, elderly workers who had
joined before 1949 were also investigated as a rule. The Gansu Yumen Oil Depot had been one of China's main petroleum companies
while the KMT was in power. During the CCR, all employees eighteen or older when the CCP took control in 1949 had to be screened.
In autumn 1968, the company's revolutionary committee began a
large-scale investigation of "secret agent organizations" at the oil
depot, torturing an elderly technician, Zhu Youqing, into confessing
the existence of a spy ring. The oil depot's former deputy party secretary, Nie Hongxin, was brought back and interrogated nonstop for
seventeen days and nights until he named 247 secret agents. The
result was that ten cadres and eight workers were persecuted to
death, hundreds were tortured, and thousands of family members
were implicated. Since China's oil industry originated in Yumen, the
false-spy case had a serious impact on the country's other oil fields
during the CCR.[54]

MAJOR CASES OF INJUSTICE INVOLVING LARGE NUMBERS OF PEOPLE

Mao had planned for 1968 to be the crucial year during which the "great chaos" would segue into the "great order," and the grand alliance managed by support-the-left units further marginalized the rebel faction to this end. When uncooperative rebel faction members became an obstruction to the grand alliance, some localities manufactured bogus cases of "counterrevolutionary cliques" as a means of eliminating them. Central leaders cooperated with local officials in creating some of these unjust cases.

THE ANTI-COMMUNIST NATIONAL SALVATION CORPS GUANGXI BRANCH

In the early hours of July 25, 1968, central leaders receiving representatives of Guangxi's conservative and rebel factions in the Eastern Parlor of the Great Hall of the People harshly criticized Guangxi's 4-22 mass organization and asked about sensationalist rumors regarding an Anti-Communist National Salvation Corps (ACNSC). Zhou Enlai said, "There must be a black hand behind all of the counterrevolutionary crimes that have occurred in Guangxi. There's an Anti-Communist National Salvation Corps in Guangzhou, and you have a branch in Guangxi." Kang Sheng said, "Some Banner Faction leaders in Guangdong have become leaders of the Anti-Communist National Salvation Corps, and you may have this problem as well."

Central leaders' interest in the ACNSC was spurred by a May 17 report by the Guangxi revolutionary committee preparatory committee and Guangxi Military District titled "Breaking the Case of the Chiang Bandit's 'Republic of China Anti-Communist National Salvation Corps Guangxi Branch.'" The report claimed that the "counterrevolutionary organization," formed on February 3 that year, was active in Nanning City and four prefectures and had grown into a membership of two thousand "bandits" organized into brigades and squadrons. The ACNSC allegedly used factional conflict to infiltrate mass organizations and gain funding and weapons through looting and fighting. It was said to be headquartered in an area controlled by the 4-22 faction and using the faction's stronghold as a liaison station to make contact with overseas Chinese in Vietnam.

In the 1950s and 1960s there had actually been a Republic of China Anti-Communist National Salvation Corps Guangxi Branch Tenth Brigade that had organized rebellions, but local law enforcement organs had dealt with it at the time. Now this dead case was being revived as an excuse for suppressing the 4-22 faction.

Guangxi's revolutionary committee preparatory committee and military district had already mobilized the masses against the ACNSC in May and June, resulting in tens of thousands of people being brutally denounced, with numerous fatalities and serious injuries.[55] In Hechi Prefecture, for example, 7,864 people were killed or driven to suicide, and in Qinzhou Prefecture's seven counties and cities, 10,420 people were killed, driven to suicide, or disappeared.[56] After Zhou Enlai and Kang Sheng's July 25 remarks, hundreds of thousands of people were locked up and sentenced throughout Guangxi, and people caught up in the allegations numbered in the millions, with tens of thousands beaten to death or executed. The victims weren't rehabilitated until an investigation into the aftermath of the Cultural Revolution was carried out in 1983 and completed in 1984.[57]

THE PURGE OF THE INNER MONGOLIAN PEOPLE'S REVOLUTIONARY PARTY

On May 21, 1966, the Central Committee called a meeting of the North China Bureau at Beijing's Qianmen Hotel, with 146 party, military, and government leaders from Inner Mongolia attending. At this meeting, the Inner Mongolian party leader, Ulanhu, was designated an "anti-party, anti-socialist, anti–Mao Zedong Thought element" and was accused of the errors of "sabotaging the unity of the Motherland, engaging in nationalist separatism and establishing an independent kingdom, and revisionism." The Central Committee stripped Ulanhu of all his official positions on August 16 and imprisoned him in Beijing. After the North China Bureau conference, the Central Committee downgraded the Inner Mongolia Military Region to a provincial military district with Teng Haiqing, deputy commander of the Beijing

Military Region, as acting commander. Teng Haiqing immediately imposed military control over the autonomous region's public security apparatus, and on November 1, 1967, the Inner Mongolian Autonomous Region Revolutionary Committee was established, with Teng Haiqing as chairman.

The main thread running through the Cultural Revolution in Inner Mongolia was the issue of "national separatism," and that was likewise the main theme of the CCR campaign launched in November 1967 to "root out the Ulanhu reactionary line and eradicate Ulanhu's bad influence" ("root out and eradicate" for short), and more specifically, to purge the "anti-party traitorous Inner Mongolian People's Revolutionary Party" (IMPRP), of which Ulanhu was the alleged ringleader.[58] But this was a misapprehension. At the North China Bureau conference, Ulanhu had admitted that there were separatists in Inner Mongolia, but he averred that he was not one of them and that he was rounding up a two-hundred-member separatist group called the IMPRP. The truth was that Ulanhu had arrested members of the IMPRP before the Cultural Revolution.[59]

The IMPRP had been established in October 1925 as a branch of the Communist International. The group was anti-imperialist, antifeudalist, and anti-Han-chauvinist. When Chiang Kai-shek purged the Communists from the KMT in 1927, the IMPRP split into two groups, one of which sought refuge with the KMT and the other of which continued under the leadership of the Comintern. After Japan surrendered, leaders of the IMPRP such as Hafenga, Boyanmandu, and Temuerba issued a declaration that Inner Mongolia should be led by the IMPRP and join the People's Republic of Mongolia in hopes of "fairly and thoroughly resolving the problems between the Mongolian and Han peoples with the revolutionary close guidance of the allied nation of China." After their overtures to Outer Mongolia were rebuffed, Hafenga and the others turned toward independence with the Eastern Mongolian People's Autonomous Government. In March 1946, Ulanhu met with Boyanmandu, Hefenga, and Temuerba in Chifeng as a representative of the CCP Central Committee to negotiate this issue, which resulted in Hafenga and the others abandoning their call for independence. The IMPRP no longer existed after May 1947.

In the early 1960s, a history teacher at Inner Mongolia University who had been transferred from inland and was ignorant of Inner Mongolia's revolutionary history concluded on the basis of historical materials that the heads of the original IMPRP had infiltrated the Communist Party and seized control of Inner Mongolia. He secretly reported this "enemy situation" to the university's party secretary, Guo Yiqing. Around the same time, on February 6, 1963, public security postal inspectors discovered an anonymous letter from the Inner Mongolian People's Revolutionary Party Second Congress to the president of the People's Republic of Mongolia, Yumjaagiin Tsedenbal, requesting unification with Outer Mongolia. The case was never cracked.[60] In May 1965, Guo Yiqing repeatedly sent secret reports to the autonomous region party committee regarding the IMPRP, and once Teng Haiqing became chairman of the revolutionary committee in 1967, Guo Yiqing told him of the "long history of the IMPRP's separatist activities."[61] By then, the North China Bureau conference had manufactured the Ulanhu Anti-Party Traitorous Clique, so Teng Haiqing believed Guo Yiqing. Another key player in the purge was an ethnic Mongolian named Ulanbagan (born Baoyin Dalai), who was the vice-chairman of the Inner Mongolian Federation of Cultural Circles and author of the novel *Prairie Fire*. In September 1967, he established the Inner Mongolia Liaison Station to Root Out Traitorous Cliques, which specifically targeted the IMPRP.

In July 1968, the Inner Mongolia revolutionary committee, led by Teng Haiqing, determined that the IMRPR was a "reactionary organization hidden in the Inner Mongolian region and engaged in national separatism" and that it was the "secret group of Ulanhu." "New IMPRP elements" at Inner Mongolia University and in the military region's political department were tortured into confessing, and in October members of the "New IMPRP" were ordered to register and surrender.

Teng Haiqing accused Ulanhu of heading an immense cabal that had infiltrated the revolutionary committee and seized power in the autonomous region, and a campaign was launched to root out New IMPRP members. Almost all the ethnic Mongolian cadres in the western regions had been unseated after the North China Bureau conference, and some Han cadres had also been denounced, but they had been released after the campaign against the bourgeois reactionary line, and some of them, such as Wang Zaitian (at that time deputy party secretary of Inner Mongolia and vice-chairman of the autonomous region's government) and Tegusi (at that time deputy director of the autonomous region's propaganda department), had been "integrated" into the revolutionary committee. Now they became the first targets of the "root out and eradicate" campaign. The campaign had an even more devastating effect on ordinary ethnic Mongolian cadres and on personnel in the cultural and education sectors.

As the campaign progressed, the scope of attack expanded, and opinions began to diverge within the core group of the revolutionary committee. One core group member, Gao Jinming, who had denounced Ulanhu's national separatism at the May 1966 North China Bureau conference, now said, "This is Han chauvinism, but it can't be said that the campaign is purging Mongolians . . . We can't keep rooting them out, or it will come right back to us." Gao's views were treated as right-deviating opportunism, and he was subjected to mass denunciation. The "uproot and eradicate" campaign became more extensive and brutal, even after more than one hundred thousand of the two million ethnic Mongolians in Inner Mongolia had been rooted out. Almost every home had a counterrevolutionary, even among ordinary workers, farmers, and herders, and many Han cadres and workers who had lived in Inner Mongolia for a long time were also targeted.[62] Confessions were extracted through a wide array of grisly tortures.[63] The chairman of the Ulanqab league party committee, Bilig Tumen, had each of his teeth pulled out with pliers and his tongue and nose cut off before he finally died. The secretary of Baiyinebo commune in the Siziwang Banner, Aoribuzhamusu, and his wife were cut with razors, after which salt was rubbed into their wounds and red-hot branding irons applied. After husband and wife were tortured to death, their five-month-old child died of starvation. When the wife of the Darhan Muminggan United Banner party secretary Bao Guoliang was labeled a member of the IMPRP, her torturers used a rope to create a fistula between her anus and vagina.[64]

In the Yikezhao League, 150,000 people, or more than one-fifth of the population, were labeled as New IMPRP members, leading to the deaths of 1,260 and the permanent debilitation of 2,322.[65] In Tuke commune, 926 out of 2,961 people were rooted out—71 percent of the adults—while another 270 were "suspects." Forty-nine died, and 270 were seriously injured. Women were forced to confess by being stripped naked and having their bellies burned with red-hot wet willow branches until their intestines were exposed, at which point the willows were applied to their genitals. People were flogged with whips laced with wire until their spinal columns were laid bare. Their festering wounds were left untreated and putrefied until they died.[66] Thousands of activists involved in the "root out and eradicate" campaign were promoted to important positions,[67] which further inspired the torturers and led to even more deaths and injuries.

There are three versions of the number of people killed or injured during the campaign against the IMPRP. According to official statistics published after the Cultural Revolution, 346,000 people were jailed, 16,222 were persecuted to death, and 81,808 were permanently disabled.[68] An ethnic Mongolian scholar in exile overseas, Bahe, says that 800,000 were jailed, 500,000 were disabled, and 50,000 were persecuted to death. *History of the Inner Mongolian Autonomous Region*, edited by a semi-official academic body, Inner Mongolia University, states that 27,900 people were persecuted to death and more than 120,000 were permanently disabled, but it doesn't provide figures on the number incarcerated. Scholars believe this third view comes closest to reality and hold that 20,000 to 30,000 died, 120,000 were disabled, and 500,000 were jailed.[69]

In spring 1969, Mao declared, "The cleansing of the class ranks has been over-magnified in Inner Mongolia." On April 19 (during the Ninth Party Congress), Teng Haiqing, Wu Tao, and Li Shude carried out self-criticism before the Central Committee. On May 19, Teng and others presented the Central Committee with a document that labeled the campaign to root out the IMPRP as "left-deviating" and demanded its immediate termination along with the release and rehabilitation of all detainees except "a small number against whom there is evidence supporting major suspicion on the IMPRP issue." On May 22, 1969, the Central Committee approved and circulated this document with a memo requiring "promptly correcting the error of over-magnification . . . and implementing policy." Mao added the memo saying, "Act accordingly."[70]

A stalemate between two views persisted after this May 22 memo.

One view, held by Teng Haiqing and his supporters, was that rooting out the IMPRP was necessary and had merely gone too far; the other was that the New IMPRP was pure fiction and that the campaign against it was completely wrong. Rebel faction mass organizations had acted rather passively in the campaign while trying to hold down conservative faction organizations, so Teng Haiqing had called on conservative mass organizations to rise up and kick aside the "fake foreign devils" who were stifling their revolution and bring new results to the "root out and eliminate" campaign. As a result, conservatives were some of the most brutal executors of the campaign and were targeted along with Teng after the May 22 memo was handed down. The armed forces, however, supported the pro-Teng group, resulting in a stalemate.

On December 19, 1969, with Mao's approval, Inner Mongolia was put under military control by the Beijing Military Region, and a frontline command post led by Commander Zheng Weishan was installed in Hohhot. Zheng believed that the "root out and eliminate" campaign had gone too far but was not completely wrong, and his favoritism toward campaign activists was reflected in cadre appointments. During the 1974 Campaign to Criticize Lin Biao and Confucius, the anti-Teng faction denounced the military control commission, so that what had originally been a struggle between the "root out and eliminate faction" and the "anti-Teng faction" became a struggle between those who endorsed and opposed military control.[71]

After Lin Biao's death on September 13, 1971, Zheng Weishan came under investigation for his relationship with Lin Biao and was transferred out of Inner Mongolia. He was replaced by the deputy commander of the Beijing Military Region, You Taizhong, who, like his two predecessors, continued to treat national separatism as a major problem and was lenient toward those who had been active in rooting out the IMPRP. After You Taizhong was transferred out in October 1978, his successor in Inner Mongolia, Wang Duo, was put in charge of investigating people and incidents connected with the Gang of Four, which in Inner Mongolia mainly meant investigating the campaign against the IMPRP. Wang endorsed the conservative faction for supporting the party, so many people who had committed multiple crimes during the campaign against the IMPRP came under protection.[72]

UNJUST CASES AGAINST BOGUS CLIQUES IN MANY LOCALITIES

Wrongful cases against fictitious cliques abounded during the CCR.

In the Guangxi, more than seven hundred personnel from revolutionary committee special case groups spent three years in a full-scale investigation of CCP members who had worked underground during the Republican era, creating many unjust, false, and erroneous cases. Similarly, in Guangdong, many former CCP underground organizations were referred to as secret agent organizations, traitor party branches, and KMT branches, and more than seven thousand people were locked up and denounced, with tens of thousands of friends and family members implicated.

In Tianjin and Hebei Provinces, investigation of an alleged "Shenze County Traitor Clique" implicated more than thirty thousand innocent people.[73] The deputy director of the Central Committee's Organization Department, Li Chuli, who had led a CCP branch in eastern Hebei during the Republican period, was now labeled a traitor, and the former CCP branch was declared a "KMT organization." More than eighty thousand people were implicated, and three thousand died of unnatural causes.[74]

In Liaoning's Lingyuan County, a single case against a fictitious "KMT anti-communist national salvation corps" targeted 913 people, of whom 25 died and 51 were permanently disabled.[75] An investigation against an "anti-communist national salvation army Beijing underground guerrilla army" in Beijing's Miyun County framed more than a hundred people, with seven persecuted to death.[76]

In Zaozhuang, Shandong Province, 11,720 people were locked up in connection with a bogus anti-party rebellion counterrevolutionary incident, and 10,659 were harshly beaten, with 2,425 suffering long-term injuries, 692 permanently disabled, and 94 persecuted to death. In the province's Linyi Prefecture, more than 40,000 people were detained and beaten as members of a "Maling Mountain guerrilla force bandit clique"; more than 9,000 became permanently disabled, and 569 died.[77]

In Anhui's Dongzhi County, 58 counterrevolutionary cliques with 3,564 members were targeted during the CCR, and 37 people were persecuted to death in what were subsequently determined to be completely bogus cases. Lingbi County became a giant prison as half the population was forced to take part in study classes as a result of investigations into a bogus "secret agent network"; 120 people died, and 146 were permanently disabled. The Anhui Provincial Revolutionary Committee held up Lingbi County as a model for other counties with a special exhibit in Hefei in early 1970.[78]

17

THE ONE STRIKE AND THREE ANTIS CAMPAIGN

The One Strike and Three Antis (OSTA) campaign originated with three Central Party documents: the January 31, 1970, "Directive to Strike Against Destructive Counterrevolutionary Activities" (Central Committee Document No. 3 [1970], known as the "One Strike"); and the "Anti-Graft and Embezzlement and Anti-Speculation and Profiteering Directive" (Central Committee Document No. 5 [1970]) and "Anti-Extravagance and Waste Notice" (Central Committee Document No. 6 [1970]), both issued on February 5, 1970, and referred to as the "Three Antis." Those who experienced the campaign found that the emphasis was on the One Strike.

The One Strike aimed at suppressing political dissidents within the Cultural Revolution movement. While most victims of the Cleansing of the Class Ranks belonged to the political underclass, the main victims of the One Strike were thinkers who challenged mainstream ideology through "speech crimes" and "thought crimes." Of the fifty-five "criminals" declared by the Beijing Municipal Public Security, Procuratorial, and Judicial Military Commission on February 11, 1970, apart from a handful of people found guilty of murder, the vast majority had been convicted of being "ideologically reactionary" or "disseminating counterrevolutionary speech." This shows that the OSTA was a political movement that the totalitarian government launched on a massive scale to stifle thought and speech.

The OSTA began in early 1970, reached its peak that autumn, and basically ended in November (although somewhat later in a few localities). One expert on the Cultural Revolution, Wang Nianyi, holds that more than 1.84 million "traitors," "secret agents," and "counter-revolutionaries" were rooted out from February to November 1970; that at least 284,800 were arrested; and that tens of thousands were killed.[1] Another researcher, Wang Rui, estimates 20,000 to 30,000 fatalities,[2] while the American Chinese scholar Ding Shu puts the number killed at 100,000;[3] a death toll of tens of thousands is generally accepted.

The investigation of the May 16 clique (August 1967 to 1972), the Cleansing of the Class Ranks (early 1968 to early 1970), and the One Strike and Three Antis (early to late 1970) were all campaigns in which power-holders suppressed the masses. There was overlap between the three campaigns, and in some places there were periods when all three were carried out at once. This makes it difficult to isolate the number of victims of the OSTA campaign. I estimate that the three campaigns combined resulted in more than two million deaths by unnatural causes, twenty times the number of such deaths among cadres during the entire Cultural Revolution.

THE BEGINNING OF THE ONE STRIKE AND THREE ANTIS CAMPAIGN

On January 30, 1970, Zhou Enlai delivered an amended version of the "Directive to Strike Against Destructive Counterrevolutionary Activities" to Mao and Lin Biao. Mao wrote a memo stating, "Act accordingly."

There is no evidence that Mao ordered the drafting of the One Strike document as he did for the Public Security Six Provisions. Currently available material indicates that the One Strike was Zhou Enlai's initiative to counter "sabotage of war preparations by a smattering of counterrevolutionaries"[4] and that he delivered this document to Mao as a "finished product."

Zhou might have seen three reasons for this document. The first was strained Sino-Soviet relations, and the nationwide implementation of what a New Year newspaper editorial termed Mao's "great strategic principle of 'preparing for war and natural disaster for the sake of the people.'" Harsh repression was required to prevent domestic "counterrevolutionaries" from becoming "agents planted by the imperialists and revisionists." The second reason was to preserve social stability. At that time, revolutionary committees had been established throughout the country, the Ninth Party Congress had been going on for more than half a year, and the marginalized rebel faction was agitating against a "restoration" of the old power structure, prompting a crackdown on counterrevolutionaries. The third reason was that opposition to the Cultural Revolution was emerging in society as its problems became increasingly apparent. Expressions of doubt and criticism were increasing steadily.

The One Strike document emphasized, "It is necessary to resolutely attack the various destructive activities of the counterrevolutionaries with steadiness, precision, and ruthlessness . . . We must resolutely kill those insufferably arrogant counterrevolutionaries, whose crimes are so innumerable that killing them is the only way to appease public indignation." The document called for "propaganda and mobilization on a grand scale, extensively, and in depth," and required public discussion of all sentencings and executions as well as public trials and immediate public executions as "the only way to gratify the people and intimidate the enemy." The document delegated the power of execution to the provincial revolutionary committees, which were to report all executions to Beijing.

Chronology of Zhou Enlai records how Zhou Enlai stirred up the campaign and then examined, supervised, and pushed its progress in the various localities and work units.

The campaign had started in Beijing even before the One Strike document was formally issued. On January 9, 1970, the municipal military commission issued a notice about twenty people to be executed, including Yu Luoke. Nineteen of them, including the Cultural Revolution critics Ma Zhengxiu and Wang Peiying, were executed following a public trial before some one hundred thousand people at Beijing Workers' Stadium on January 27.

On February 11, the military commission issued a list of fifty-five "criminals," including Gu Wenxuan, Shen Yuan, Zhang Langlang, and Wen Jia, and eighteen of them were executed along with Yu Luoke after a public trial at the Beijing Workers' Stadium on March 5.[5]

With the nation's capital as a model, other localities rushed to implement the Central Committee document.

The day after Yu Luoke and the others were executed in Beijing, Nanjing held a mass public trial to execute several people, including Zha Jinhua, who had organized a dissenting Marxist-Leninist group. The official provincial newspaper *New China Daily* marked the occasion with a bloodthirsty editorial calling for a massive upsurge in reporting, exposing, denouncing, and purging class enemies. That night, Chen Zhuoran and Su Xiaobin cut out words from the newspaper and combined them into banners that they put up at Nanjing's major thoroughfares: "Immortality for the martyr Zha Jinhua!" "We want genuine Marxism-Leninism!" "Down with Lin Biao!" "Down with Jiang Qing!" The banners shocked the public, and the provincial public security apparatus launched a major investigation. Chen Zhuoran was exposed by an informant two months later and summarily executed after a public trial on April 28. Su Xiaobin was sentenced to fifteen years in prison.[6]

By then Nanjing had already sentenced another eleven "current counterrevolutionaries" to death and had imposed life sentences or other lengthy prison terms on dozens of others on March 6. Martial law was temporarily imposed on the city and all transportation was halted as the counterrevolutionaries were paraded through the streets in an impressive motorcade, the "criminals" gripped by their hair so the masses could view their "fearsome countenance." Once the motorcade reached the execution ground, the eleven were executed on the spot, and their remains were disposed of without their families being informed. After the "March 6 judgment," Nanjing's military control commission held three more public trials with great fanfare in 1970. Twenty-four dissidents were executed on July 30, and ten on December 10.[7]

The crimes of those fifty-seven executed "criminals" were virtually identical—venomously attacking the Great Leader Chairman Mao and his close comrade-in-arms, Vice-Chairman Lin Biao, the proletarian headquarters, the dictatorship of the proletariat, the Great Proletarian Cultural Revolution, and the socialist system, referred to in abbreviated form as "venomous attacks." After the Cultural Revolution, all fifty-seven executions were classified as unjust, and the victims posthumously rehabilitated.

During the OSTA campaign in Guangdong Province from January 1970 to June 1971, more than 26,000 "class enemies" were rooted out.[8] Zhejiang Province carried out investigations against 67,900 people and sentenced 2,200. Some people were labeled as counterrevolutionaries for sitting on sheets of newspaper printed with Mao's quotations while attending mass rallies.[9]

In May 1970, the Heilongjiang revolutionary committee's people's defense department reported that 5,927 people had been designated counterrevolutionaries, another 1,043 as historical counterrevolutionaries, 61 as traitors, 172 as secret agents, 1,805 as black elements, and 72,069 as having engaged in graft, embezzlement, or profiteering.[10]

In Hebei Province's Shijiazhuang Prefecture, 46,738 people were listed as "focal targets," including 3,942 categorized as a "contradiction between the enemy and us." One hundred people were executed, 2,372 imprisoned, and 1,078 "put under control."[11]

In Shaanxi Province, the core group of the Xi'an Municipal Revolutionary Committee began arranging its OSTA campaign on February 10, 1970, and by the end of March, reports had been filed against more than 42,000 people.[12]

The OSTA campaign in Hunan Province was managed by worker and PLA propaganda teams, who mainly targeted rebel faction leaders. Some were executed and many were imprisoned, while the rest were ejected from revolutionary committees, denounced, or put under isolation in "study classes" for months at a time. An editorial in *Changsha Evening News* proclaimed, "Unless they are killed, public outrage will not be appeased, and the laws of the state will not be upheld. Kill, kill, kill, kill, kill, kill, kill to create a glowing red new world of Mao Zedong Thought!"

THE EXECUTION OF CULTURAL REVOLUTION CRITICS

Zhang Langlang, who survived a death sentence during the OSTA campaign, compares it to Qin Shihuang's live burial of Confucian scholars because "most of those killed were intellectuals."[13] During that time, thousands of people who maintained and disseminated independent views regarding the Cultural Revolution and the auto-cratic system were executed. The atmosphere of bone-chilling terror created by the OSTA directive was heightened by the brutal torture and humiliation that dissidents were subject to before they were killed at public trials. Given the focus of the OSTA campaign on "thought crimes," the authorities went to outrageous lengths to prevent victims from expressing last words by wrapping their necks with ropes, stuff-ing objects in their mouths, or slitting their larynxes.

What follows are some of the more notable victims of the OSTA campaign.

ZHANG ZHIXIN

Zhang Zhixin, born in 1930 in Tianjin, began working in the Liaoning provincial party committee propaganda bureau in 1957. After being informed on by a fellow student at the provincial May 7 cadre school in Panjin in November 1968, Zhang was locked up in the school's "study class," and her verbal and written opinions resulted in her being de-nounced several times. In an essay titled "Viewpoints and Opinions Regarding the Cultural Revolution's Problems," she wrote: "Because of errors at the 1959 Lushan Conference, the experience and lessons that emerged during the Great Leap Forward could not be summarized and absorbed . . . I believe that the Cultural Revolution going on right now is a continuation, expansion, and development of the left-deviating po-litical line error of 1959." She criticized Mao for this leftist deviation from Marxism-Leninism, first in economics and then in the political realm. Zhang was arrested on September 24, 1969, and sentenced to death in May 1970, but at the recommendation of the top leader in Li-aoning Province, Chen Xilian, her death sentence was commuted to life imprisonment so she could "serve as a negative example." Deranged by her abusive treatment, Zhang wrote, "Down with Mao Zedong" and "Hack Mao Zedong to pieces." At a mass rally to criticize Lin Biao and Confucius on November 16, 1973, Zhang stood up and yelled, "The root of the CCP's ultra-rightist line is Mao Zedong," and other such slogans. She was tried again and executed on April 4, 1975, her larynx cut in advance so she couldn't yell any more slogans.

YU LUOKE

Yu Luoke was an outstanding student, but after his parents were both designated rightists in 1957, he was not allowed to enroll in college and could work only as an apprentice at the People's Machine Factory. He nevertheless persevered in studying classical Chinese and foreign philosophers and developed his own thoughts on the Cultural Revolution, which he recorded in a journal. During the terror of Red August, his journal was discovered and displayed at a Red Guard exhibition as a "secret account of a restorationist." After spending a month in a study class, he wrote in his journal, "The worst thing in my life would be to deceive myself or to surrender to anything but investigating the truth." He wrote his famous essay "On Family Background," which analyzed the absurdity of blood lineage theory and condemned the bias suffered by people in the political underclass. "If things go on this way, how different will it be from caste systems such as blacks in America, the Sudras in India, or the Burakumin in Japan?" The essay ended with the emphatic appeal: "All oppressed revolutionary youth, rise up and bravely fight!"

Yu sent his essay to the CCP Central Committee, but when he received no response, he mimeographed and distributed hundreds of copies, which were eagerly discussed by large numbers of victims of blood lineage theory. Students at the Beijing No. 4 Secondary School reprinted the essay in *Secondary School Cultural Revolution News*, and ninety thousand copies were eagerly snapped up. Inundated with letters of support from around the country, Yu Luoke wrote another essay in late 1967 in which he proposed pay based on seniority and then on contribution, as well as "Summing Up 1967," and a suggested reading list of 104 books. Five days later, Yu was arrested. Sentenced to death at the public trial at Beijing Workers' Stadium on March 5, 1970, Yu stood with his shaved head unbowed as a bullet ended his life at the age of twenty-seven.[14]

CAI TIEGEN

Cai Tiegen, born in 1911, joined the Red Army in 1936 and the Communist Party in 1939. As an army veteran at the rank of senior colonel, he was assigned a leading position at the Nanjing Military Academy in 1956.

After coming under attack as a "dogmatist" along with Marshal Liu Bocheng and General Xiao Ke in 1958, Cai was discharged from all his party and military positions, demoted, and sent to work in a company in Changzhou. The Great Famine led him into a period of deep reflection, and in his journal he recorded the tragic circumstances in which "mother and children are no longer close, father and son hate each other, and friends harm each other." His thinking touched on the leadership, the system of ownership, and the socialist system. He wrote: "Mao Zedong's brilliance and greatness truly deserves to be called 'singular from time immemorial.' He has been able to do what no other ruler has been able to, in the past or present, in China or in foreign lands: control people's mind." Regarding struggle within the party, he wrote:

> In order to seize power over the worldwide socialist camp and become the leader of the worldwide communist revolutionary movement, he demands that the entire party become his "docile tool," and he relegates all people with differing views and ideas to the titles of "rightist," "right-deviating opportunist," "anti-party element," "anti-party clique," and so on. He has trampled the party constitution until it is worthless bullshit, and has thoroughly eliminated any scrap of democracy within the party, intending to eliminate all differing views and dissent within or outside the party as well.
>
> In these years, so many people have "committed errors." Only one person is eternally correct, and that is Mr. Mao. He is in fact the ringleader of all error, but no one dares to say he is wrong, because his limitless authority is even greater than God's, because he is truth . . .
>
> . . . The experience of socialism in China proves that private assets are the economic basis of human freedom. Once personal assets disappear, personal freedom completely disappears with it; when the system of private ownership is completely abolished, personal freedom also completely disappears.[15]

Cai was eventually imprisoned as the "ringleader" of a number of people with independent political views. He went on a hunger strike three times and was finally placed in heavy manacles after trying to escape to petition Beijing.

Cai's case attracted renewed attention after the OSTA campaign was launched, and in early March 1970, Cai and his fellow dissidents were declared counterrevolutionaries. Cai and another defendant, Li Yefang were executed; another, Wu Yi, was given a suspended death sentence, while several others were imprisoned.[16]

ZHANG SHILIANG

Zhang Shiliang, a native of Hebei Province, graduated with a degree in economics from Beiping University in 1930 and then went to Japan for further studies, returning to China in 1936 and eventually becoming a college instructor. During an academic discussion at Gansu Normal University in autumn 1965, Zhang expressed disagreement with Mao's statement that "In class struggle, some classes triumph and some are eliminated; this is history, the history of thousands of years of civilization." Zhang felt that to speak only of class struggle without mentioning productive force, relations of production, the economic base, and superstructure was to lose a basic thread in studying history. This attracted criticism, and soon after the Cultural Revolution began, the university's work group organized a mass denunciation of Zhang. When Zhang defended his views, the work team accused him of opposing the work group, the party, and the Cultural Revolution. Zhang Shiliang was sentenced to death and summarily executed on March 17, 1970.[17]

MAO YINGXING

Mao Yingxing, born in 1921, graduated from Southwestern Agricultural College and then taught at the Lanzhou Agricultural Vocational School. Designated a rightist in 1957, she was banished to the Jiabiangou labor farm, and after returning to the agricultural school four years later, she and her husband were sent off to the Ningxia Hui

Autonomous Region. Observing the increasingly absurd deification of Mao during the Cultural Revolution, Mao Yingxing dismissed it as "bourgeois clamor and sycophantic flattery . . . The flatterers are taking advantage of revolution at the expense of the revolutionary undertaking and revolutionary people, including Chairman Mao himself." This led to her being denounced as a counterrevolutionary. Mao Yingxing's elder brother had left his stamp collection with Mao Yingxing when he went to study in the United States. When Mao Yingxing's home was ransacked, stamps printed with images of Chiang Kai-shek became evidence of her crime, and she was sentenced to five years in prison on July 1, 1969. While serving time in the Gansu Province No. 4 Prison, she engaged in deep reflection and kept a journal of more than three hundred thousand words in which she criticized the destruction of China's precious historical legacy during the "smashing of the four olds," among other things. Mao Yingxing's "crime" was upgraded during the OSTA campaign, and she was executed on April 14.[18]

XIN YUANHUA

Xin Yuanhua, born in Zhejiang Province in 1934, went to Xinjiang to build railroads in 1952. By 1962, he had schooled himself in university coursework and had read many volumes of political theory. While serving as an economic planner for the Xinjiang railway's Hami hydropower supply, he embarked on in-depth reflection on how the Three Red Banners had triggered the Great Famine, and observed in his journal that the famine "was clearly an error in the guiding ideology." He wrote a letter to Mao comparing Mao to the sun and hoping that Mao would "acknowledge that you are just one star in the Milky Way." After more letters and poems to Mao and other leaders and to newspapers and magazines, Xin was arrested on July 3, 1963, and sentenced to three years of reform under the supervision of the masses. On January 24, 1967, Xin wrote a letter to the security department of the Hami railway, saying, "The motherland is shrouded by a dark cloud of personality cult," and observing that after the 1957 anti-rightist movement and 1959 campaign against right-deviation, "Our industrious, courageous, and intelligent great nation has degenerated into a nation that routinely speaks political falsehoods . . .

Chairman Mao is living in a fog of eulogy and has become separated from the real world and from the worker and peasant masses. This is a thousand times more harmful than a sugarcoated bullet!" Predicting that the people would awaken in time to drive away this black cloud, Xin wrote, "A limitlessly beautiful motherland beckons to us with a smile."

On May 13, 1970, Xin Yuanhua's death sentence was approved. Interrogated one last time, he said calmly, "History will reach the correct conclusion on who was right and who was wrong." He was executed in Xinjiang on May 30, 1970.[19]

DING ZUXIAO

The Cultural Revolution stirred up a fanatical deification movement. Meetings were preceded by "loyalty dances," speeches were begun with expressions of loyalty to Mao, and people had to stand before a portrait of Mao every morning to "request instructions" and every evening to "report."[20] In Dayong County in the Tujia and Miao Autonomous Prefecture of Hunan Province, every home flew a "loyalty banner" and put up "loyalty plaques," and shrines that had once held images of deities or ancestral tablets now displayed Little Red Books. Objecting to this practice, a woman named Ding Zuxiao and her elder sister Ding Zuxia wrote and disseminated leaflets criticizing the loyalty campaign: "It resembles feudal society, making Chairman Mao into an emperor to whom respects must be paid every day . . . 700 million or 1.4 billion cries can go up every day for Chairman Mao to live for ten thousand years, but it still won't really happen . . . Chairman Mao isn't dead yet, but he's already being worshiped like the God of Death. That's just wrong." Ding called on "all true revolutionaries" to "clear your minds, don't be duped, don't resign yourself to being slaves. Make revolution against 'loyalty'!" Late at night on July 5, 1969, Ding Zuxiao was arrested, and her sister was imprisoned soon afterward. When Li Qishun, a young urban woman sent down to the countryside for reeducation, learned of Ding Zuxiao's being brutally tortured, she and her seventeen-year-old sister, Li Qicai, distributed leaflets describing Ding as "worthy of the name of revolutionary vanguard." The Li sisters were soon arrested. Ding Zuxiao was executed on May 8,

1970, and Li Qishun shortly thereafter. Ding Zuxia was sentenced to twenty years in prison, and Li Qicai to ten years.[21]

MA MIANZHEN

In January 1970, a technician at the Guiyang Construction Company, Ma Mianzhen, was arrested after putting up a big-character poster criticizing the chairman of the provincial revolutionary committee, Lan Yinong. She became a specimen of class struggle and was loaned out to various work units to be denounced at mass rallies. During a struggle rally at the Guiyang Pastry Factory, she shouted out, "Down with Lin Biao! Down with Jiang Qing!" She was immediately knocked down, a paint-soaked rag was stuffed into her mouth, and she was formally arrested. She went on a hunger strike, but the provincial revolutionary committee ordered her put on a feeding tube to keep her alive long enough to be executed. After her death sentence was pronounced on May 10 at a public trial attended by two hundred thousand people, springs were stuffed in her mouth to prevent her from shouting offensive slogans. Ma was paraded through the streets in a truck until four o'clock in the afternoon, after which she was executed in a wilderness area on the city's outskirts. She was only thirty years old.[22]

WU XIAOFEI

On February 17, 1970, a public trial was held in Jiangxi's provincial capital, Nanchang, for the execution of twenty-two-year-old Wu Xiaofei. His crime was writing two treatises saying that the Cultural Revolution was an "abnormal political incident" that "didn't bring people a shred of political or economic benefit." Wu criticized Lin Biao for "deifying Chairman Mao," and Jiang Qing as "the source of the flood of anarchism in the Cultural Revolution." He also said that Liu Shaoqi had been persecuted "by hook or by crook and without reason."[23]

SHI DAWEI

A technician at the Xi'an Eighth Institute of Design of the Ministry of the First Machinery Industry, Shi Dawei was executed in March 1970 as a counterrevolutionary because he had discussed his dissatisfaction with Lin Biao and Jiang Qing and his objections toward some policies from 1957 to the Cultural Revolution.

CHEN YAOTING AND XIE JUZHANG

Chen Yaoting, an instructor at Jiangxi's Gannan School of Medicine, and his wife, Xie Juzhang, wrote more than ten anonymous essays criticizing the Cultural Revolution in 1966 and 1967. Following an investigation, Chen was arrested in December 1967 and Xie in February 1968. Chen Yaoting was executed on March 16, 1970. Xie Juzhang was handed a suspended death sentence but died at the Jiangxi Labor Reform Farm on July 11, 1971.[24]

SHI RENXIANG

Shi Renxiang, born in 1942 in Anhui's He County, joined the army in 1964. While serving in Tibet in 1966, he criticized Lin Biao's fearmongering May 18 speech on coups. After he was demobilized and assigned work in his hometown in Anhui in 1968, Shi sent a letter to the Central Committee and to Mao, Zhou Enlai, and the Jinan and Nanjing Military Regions, as well as his former military unit, denouncing Lin Biao as a double-dealer "opposing the red flag by holding a red flag." After being arrested on January 8, 1969, he wrote "Down with Lin Biao" on the wall of his prison cell. Shi Renxiang was executed in a public trial on July 12, 1970, after his throat was cut so that he couldn't say any last words.[25]

OTHER VICTIMS OF THE CAMPAIGN

THE COMMUNIST SELF-STUDY UNIVERSITY

Just after the 1970 Spring Festival, the case of a "major current counterrevolutionary clique" in Ningxia's capital, Yinchuan, resulted in the arrest of thirteen young people. The clique was called the Communist Self-Study University.

These young people had enthusiastically taken part in the Cultural Revolution as secondary students in 1966 and 1967, but as the movement progressed, they became disillusioned and withdrew to immerse themselves in study. After they were sent to the countryside for "reeducation" like others their age in 1968, one of them, Wu Shuzhang, began organizing evening readings of the works of Marx and Lenin in his production team. In November 1969, the young people established the Communist Self-Study University with the objective of "understanding truth, persisting in truth, and fighting for achieving the truth." Over the next two years, they brought practical issues in the Cultural Revolution to their study of classical works by Marx and Engels, and published their findings in their school journal, including an essay titled "What Is Fascism?" When the Ninth Party Congress confirmed Lin Biao as Mao's successor, they said that Lin Biao was using the Cultural Revolution to usurp power and wrote the word "bullshit" in the margin of Lin Biao's preface to a new edition of *Quotations of Chairman Mao*. Among the members of the Communist Self-Study University, Wu Shuzhang, Wu Shusen, and Lu Zhili were executed as counterrevolutionaries. Chen Tongming was sentenced to life in prison, Xu Zhaoping to fifteen years, Zhang Weizhi to eight years, Zhang Shaochen to three years, and six others to detention, isolation, and denunciation in their work units. One of them, twenty-two-year-old Xiong Manyi, killed herself while in custody.[26]

FUJIAN'S CHINESE COMMUNIST PARTY HAPPINESS COMMITTEE

Xie Hongshui, born in 1938, was a peasant in Shizhong Commune in Fujian's Longyan County, where more than four hundred members of his commune starved to death during the Great Famine. With only a primary school education, Xie survived by leaving his village and working as a blacksmith, but he was detained as an unauthorized migrant and made to perform hard labor. Back at home, his child died of starvation and his wife deserted him. When the system of output assigned to households was adopted in Longyan County, things began to improve, and upon learning that Liu Shaoqi had advocated this policy, Xie Hongshui sympathized with Liu when he came under attack during the Cultural Revolution. In October 1966, Xie established the Chinese Communist Party Happiness Committee, which professed to be under the direct leadership of Liu Shaoqi; and established a secret network of like-minded people who produced two issues of a tabloid called *Voice of the Masses*, which formulated a name list for a Central Committee that included toppled leaders such as Liu Shaoqi and Peng Dehuai but not Mao, Lin Biao, or Jiang Qing. The group also compiled a document called "CMC Confidential" that emphasized the need to "follow Liu Shaoqi," "topple Mao Zedong," and "serve the interests of the people." In May 1967 they printed and distributed a slogan proclaiming, "Rise up and fight for freedom and happiness! Resolutely expunge all unjust systems, oppose the state monopoly for grain purchasing and marketing! . . . Long live the Chinese Communist Party! . . . Long live Chairman Liu!" In June, they drafted a party constitution that called for production assigned to households, freedom, and the elimination of classes and collectives. "Our ultimate objective is to thoroughly eliminate the Mao-Lin clique and fight for the people's greatest freedom and happiness." The Happiness Committee began operating semi-openly and gained three hundred members; peasants from the next county asked to join, while other counties established their own happiness committees. The authorities began targeting the organization in March 1970. Xie Hongshui and eighteen others were executed first, and two others were executed after they continued to defend Liu Shaoqi while serving time in a labor camp. Twelve others were driven to suicide, and eight died after being beaten. Wives and mothers of some of the victims also committed suicide.[27]

SHANXI'S CHINESE COMMUNIST LEAGUE

On March 28, 1970, the public security military control commission of Datong City, Shanxi Province, put up a notice announcing judgment against members of a "current counterrevolutionary rebel clique" called the Chinese Communist League, which had allegedly established two organizations inside a labor farm and had "openly acknowledged the Yugoslavian revisionist program and Soviet revisionist line." Its members had also written "sixty-five counterrevolutionary

essays," "more than 300 counterrevolutionary poems," and "179 counterrevolutionary letters" and had engaged in "venomous attacks."
Thirteen members of the group were summarily executed, and others
were sentenced to lengthy prison terms.[28]

Forcibly instilled official ideology poisoned many people's souls and
intensified the terror of the totalitarian system. Even family members
informed on the dissenting views of their loved ones during the OSTA
campaign. On February 13, 1970, in Anhui Province's Guzhen County,
Fang Zhongmao, her husband, Zhang Yuesheng, and their sixteen-
year-old son, Zhang Hongbing, were arguing about the Cultural Revolution when Fang said, "The leaders shouldn't create a personality
cult . . . I want the verdict against Liu Shaoqi overturned." Zhang
Yuesheng and Zhang Hongbing were horrified, and Zhang Yuesheng
said, "From now on, we're cutting off all relations with you. Write
down the toxic things you just said." Fang wrote what she'd said on a
piece of paper, and Zhang Yuesheng went out, saying he was going to
report her. Zhang Hongbing composed a written accusation that ended
with the words "Down with the current counterrevolutionary Fang
Zhongmao! Execute Fang Zhongmao!" He then stuffed his report with
a Red Guard badge into the doorway of the military representative.
After receiving the report, the military representative came to Fang
Zhongmao's home, kicked her to the ground, tied her up, and took her
away. Two months later, Fang Zhongmao was executed as a current
counterrevolutionary. Zhang Hongbing recalls, "At that time, I felt a
class struggle was going on in our home, and my father and I took a
firm standpoint. Our political performance passed the test." Guzhen
County's *Revolution in Education* exhibition included a display board
titled "Upholding Righteousness Above His Family: The Valiant and
Resolute Struggle of Secondary School Student Zhang Hongbing
against his counterrevolutionary mother." The father and son realized
their error after reading a newspaper report about the execution of
Zhang Zhixin in 1979. In a reexamination of the case on July 23, 1980,
the county court ruled that the original judgment was a travesty of
justice, exonerating Fang. Zhang Hongbing was left to regret this for
the rest of his life.[29]

TRAGIC ABSURDITIES

During the OSTA campaign, people who never ventured an opinion were also caught up in ways that were no less tragic for being absurd.

Mo Dingqin, a primary school teacher in Guizhou's Rongjiang County, strove to enhance his teaching credentials in his spare time by reading, copying, and cutting out photos and brief biographies of leading figures from China, America, England, the Soviet Union, and France that had been published in newspapers and magazines, along with famous quotes, aphorisms, and poems by great Chinese and foreign thinkers. He compiled this material into a scrapbook that he titled *More Precious Than Gold*, and kept this scrapbook on his desk at school, where students and other teachers fought for their turn to leaf through it. At the height of the OSTA campaign in April 1970, *More Precious Than Gold* became evidence of counterrevolutionary crime, and the school was plastered with posters denouncing the scrapbook while loudspeakers blasted imprecations against Mo Dingqin's heinous offense. In the months that followed, Mo was repeatedly denounced, his hair ripped out in patches, and his body covered with wounds and bruises. Unable to bear any more torment, he fled his village. Three months later he crept back home in the depths of night, only to be pounced upon by a group of watchmen. He was immediately declared under arrest, and on September 29, 1970, Mo was sentenced to twenty years in prison as a "current counterrevolutionary." While he was undergoing labor reform, a former female student of Mo's named Zhang Youzhen, who wrote to Mo on his wife's behalf, was repeatedly denounced for "colluding with a counterrevolutionary."[30]

In another inexplicable case, on June 10, 1968, a cadre at the Su County Oil Company in Anhui Province died after setting his bed alight while smoking in a drunken stupor. After the OSTA campaign began in 1970, the work group sent to that work unit decided that the Cleansing of the Class Ranks had not been thorough enough and that the cadre must have died in an arson attack by a "major corruption syndicate." Nearly three-fourths of the oil company's cadres and staff were interrogated under brutal torture, and twenty-two of the company's forty-three employees were detained for extended periods; three were beaten to death. A two-year witch-hunt produced not one scrap of evidence of corrupt dealings, but the special investigation team still didn't give up, and ordered the oil company to withdraw 2,965.58 yuan from its bank account, claiming that this money was proof of the corruption syndicate.[31]

In Hunan's Qianyang County, a production brigade deputy party secretary attempted to earn a promotion by killing his family dog and then reporting to the commune that someone had poisoned it. It so happened that the commune party secretary was feeling dejected over his inability to root out any counterrevolutionaries at that time, and he readily grasped this opportunity to order an investigation. The production brigade deputy party secretary set up a machine gun in his office and had all the commune members brought in for questioning, and then declared that he had uncovered a sixteen-member counterrevolutionary clique. One person was shot to death, two hanged themselves, two were permanently crippled, and 115 were implicated.[32]

18

MASS KILLINGS CARRIED OUT BY THOSE IN POWER

The mass killings referred to here were carried out against groups of ordinary citizens with no means of resistance. The people who organized, directed, and carried out these massacres were, for the most part, soldiers, police officers, People's Armed Forces militiamen, or core members of the CCP or Communist Youth League. They can therefore be considered killings of ordinary people by those in power at the local level.

Some of these mass killings targeted the rebel faction during the 1967 February Countercurrent, as in the case of the massacre that the Qinghai Military Region commander Zhao Yongfu carried out against the Xining August 18 Red Guard Battalion. Other mass killings were meant to ensure "purity" of lineage, to cleanse the class ranks, or to facilitate and safeguard the establishment of the revolutionary committees.

Su Yang, a professor at University of California, Irvine, analyzed county gazetteers for his research on mass killings, which he defined as involving at least ten victims at once. In 1966, China had around 2,250 counties. Su carried out in-depth research on a total of 235 counties in Guangdong, Guangxi, and Hubei, representing 71 to 90 percent of the counties in those provinces. Forty-three of the sixty-five county gazetteers he studied for Guangxi (66 percent) recorded mass killings, including fifteen counties in which the death toll exceeded 1,000; in Wuming County, 2,463 people died. The average number of killings per county in Guangxi was 526. Nearly half the fifty-seven counties that Su researched in Guangdong recorded mass killings, including six in which the death toll exceeded 1,000, and the overall average was 278 killings per county. In Hubei, thirty-eight county gazetteers (60 percent of the research sample) reported more than 1,000 beatings, many of which resulted in permanent disability, but none reported mass killings.[1]

County gazetteers are official publications that have undergone strict political vetting. Many gazetteers covered up massacres, and those recording mass killings would report only the lowest possible number. Yang Su's research conclusions regarding these county gazetteers must therefore be regarded as the bare minimum.

MASSACRES IN BEIJING'S SUBURBAN COUNTIES[2]

In August 1966, the red terror created by the Red Guards in Beijing rapidly spilled over into the suburbs, and shocking massacres occurred in Changping and Daxing Counties.

On August 27, 1966, the Changping County public security apparatus transmitted Xie Fuzhi's remarks from the day before at an enlarged meeting of the Beijing Municipal Public Security Bureau, which emphasized that "the People's Police have to take the side of the Red Guards" and must "give them information on five black category elements." Changping County immediately took action. In the space of around two weeks, killings occurred in fourteen of the county's twenty-four communes, with a total of 327 deaths. Two of the most shocking incidents occurred in the China-Vietnam Friendship Commune and Heishanzhai Commune.

On August 27, the head of the China-Vietnam Friendship Commune public security station called in the commune's vice-chairman, the deputy commander of the People's Armed Forces Department (PAFD), station personnel, and Red Guard leaders to arrange for "sweeping out the four olds." A pamphlet by Beijing's Xicheng Red Guard Pickets calling for "blood for blood and a life for a life" was read out and printed off, and it was decided that the commune would carry out a unified action. That night, a rumor circulated at the Yandan brickyard about plans for a counterrevolutionary rebellion, and four black elements were killed as a preventative measure. The public security station head expressed his support.

During telephone conferences carried out at the commune on August 28 and 30, each village reported the number of people killed, and the commune declared that "the 'smashing of the four olds' was proceeding smoothly and the killing of black elements had lifted everyone's hearts." Villages criticized for halfhearted efforts took further action, and by September 6, a total of 144 commune members were dead.

After hearing about the killing of black elements at China-Vietnam Friendship Commune, production brigades in the neighboring Heishanzhai Commune also began killing black elements. Under the slogan of "Destroying root and branch, and sparing females but not males," they did not even spare baby boys. By September 4, a total of sixty-seven people had been killed in the commune, including eighteen minors.

The death toll in Daxing County was close to that in Changping County: From August 29 to 31, a total of 324 people were killed (232 males and 92 females) in thirteen communes. Ranging in age from thirty-eight days to eighty years old, they included 175 black elements, 137 black element offspring, and 12 others. One hundred and seventy-one households were affected, and twenty-two were completely wiped out. The pretext for the killings was that "class enemies" in Ma Village had carried out an uprising and killed some poor and lower-middle peasants. It was sheer fiction.

The county public security bureau played a key role in accordance with Xie Fuzhi's speech and the Beijing Municipal Public Security Bureau's call to "support and protect the Red Guards." At Huangcun Commune, a county public security bureau leader surnamed Zhang briefed Red Guards and police personnel about twenty-seven black element families and organized combat units. Commune leaders took over from there. The political instructor of the Huangcun police station and cadres from the commune PAFD also urged production brigades to "kill and bury" all "misbehaving" black elements. The commune's Cultural Revolution committee organized Red Guards to carry out killings in one brigade, and the commune's management committee chairman went to another brigade to "light the fire."

At Tiantanghe Commune's Ma Village production brigade on August 30, the security head gathered up all the brigade's black elements and their children and divided them up in four jails for elderly men, adult men, women, or children. The brigade party secretary Li Enyuan led a dozen people to the production brigade headquarters to interrogate the prisoners, arbitrarily questioning, killing, and burying people in an "assembly line" process. By the time the Beijing municipal party committee sent the general secretary Ma Li and the garrison command political commissars Liu Shaowen and Zhang Yisan to the village to stop the killings, thirty-four people had died.

At Daxinzhuang Commune, the killings were directed by a "nine-man committee" led by the commune chairman Gao Fuxing and youth league secretary Hu Defu, and also including the commune deputy party secretaries Li Ziyong and Li Guanqing. Supported by Zhang from the county public security bureau, Gao Fuxing and Hu Defu called a secret meeting of the leading cadres of the commune's seventeen production brigades on the night of August 29 to devise a plan for killing black elements. This commune recorded the highest number of killings, with 110 people dispatched in one night, August 31. In the Liming production brigade alone, fifty-six people from eleven households were killed.

All kinds of methods were used to kill people, including clubbing, beheading with fodder choppers, and strangulation. The cruelest method was used on infants: The killer would step on one of the baby's legs and then yank on the other with both hands, tearing the baby in two. The chairman of the Poor Peasant Association (PPA) in Daxinzhuang Commune's Zhongxin brigade single-handedly chopped sixteen people to death with a fodder chopper until he finally collapsed with exhaustion. The dead were stuffed into a deep well, but when white froth and an appalling stench flowed from the well a few days later, the villagers dredged out some of the corpses and buried them in a reed pond, then filled in the well. At the Liming brigade, the dead were buried in a reed pond north of the village, and eventually people were killed by simply dragging them to the pond with a rope around their necks.

The cadres at Beizang Commune's Xibaituan production brigade opposed the killings. After the brigade party secretary Li Shuqing (a woman) attended the commune meeting requiring production brigades to kill all black elements and their families, she returned to the brigade quaking with fear and called in all the production team cadres to discuss what to do. One production team leader, Zhang Wanyi, adamantly opposed killing anyone, saying, "Our production brigade's black elements and their family members total more than 280 people! How are we to kill so many? None of us has ever killed anyone— killing even one would make us keel over with fear! What's more, if we're overly hasty in killing more than two hundred people, who can say who will end up killing who?" Zhang Wanyi was a poor peasant from generations back and had been a soldier in the Eighth Route Army, and therefore had courage to speak his mind. The other cadres were already reluctant to kill anyone, so once Zhang Wanyi poured cold water on the idea, everyone went along with him.

The random slaughter of innocent people in Changping and Daxing Counties shocked the Beijing municipal party committee and the Central Committee. On September 1, Beijing municipal party committee general secretary Ma Li broadcast a speech to the counties, and the municipal and county governments also sent work teams to the communes and brigades where people were being killed and brought the situation largely under control. On September 2, the municipal party committee handed down an "urgent notice" demanding "the greatest possible effort to patiently persuade and firmly halt all killing phenomena." On September 5, *People's Daily* published an editorial titled "Fight with Words, not Weapons." Although killings continued in Beijing after that, the tide of mass slaughter was effectively stemmed.

The killers were subsequently punished only minimally. For example, the chief culprits in Daxinzhuang Commune, Gao Fuxing and Hu Defu, were each sentenced to eight years in prison (another version is that they were sentenced to fourteen years, but six years were spent at a cadre school, and they were released early), and after release they enjoyed retirement benefits. The Liming production brigade party secretary Yang Wanjie was sentenced to eight years in prison, where he killed himself. The brigade's PPA chairman, Yang Jingyun, was also sentenced to eight years in prison, and he died of natural causes two or three years after his release.

HUNAN'S DAOXIAN MASSACRE

In 1986, the Hunanese journalist Tan Hecheng was assigned a story that gave him access to a large number of confidential documents relating to a Cultural Revolution massacre in Hunan's Dao County (Daoxian) and surrounding counties. His article was never published, but in the years that followed, he went to Daoxian several times to interview the people involved, verify facts, and correct and supplement his original text, collecting material totaling millions of words about nearly four hundred cases. Tan compiled his material into a book,[3] which I find a credible source, and most of the material in this section is derived from it.

Daoxian has a river called the Xiaoshui, which passes through the county seat, Daojiang, and flows into the Shuangpai Reservoir and on into the Xiangjiang River. At the height of the Daoxian massacre in August 1967, hundreds of bodies flowed through the county seat every day at a reported rate of 1.6 per minute. The stinking corpses flowed into the Shuangpai Reservoir and clogged the dam, tainting the water and forming a red scum on the surface and spreading an overpowering stench for miles in all directions.[4]

The Daoxian massacre lasted sixty-six days, from August 13 to October 17, 1967, and affected all the county's ten districts and thirty-three communes. The death toll of 4,519 (including 326 suicides) represented 2.7 percent of the county's population at the time, and 117 households were completely wiped out. In terms of class, 41.4 percent of the victims were black elements, and 49.9 percent were black elements' offspring. Influenced by Daoxian, killings also occurred in ten other counties in Hunan's Lingling Prefecture, bringing the total unnatural deaths to 9,093 (including 1,397 suicides). The killing methods included shooting, stabbing, drowning, blowing up with explosives, dropping into caves or mines, live burial, beating, strangulation, burning, and dashing to the ground (in particular for children). These methods don't encompass all the creativity and cruelty of the killers, who also eviscerated people, cut out their eyes or tongues, raped women and ran spears through their genitals, and nailed people to door planks to slice their flesh off piece by piece. In Qingxi District's Ganziyuan Commune, a rich peasant element was bound up and dropped into an abandoned lime pit, after which he was covered with quick lime and water to burn away his flesh. This method was called "lime-roasted egg."

During the Cultural Revolution, two opposing mass organizations emerged in Daoxian: the Red Alliance and the Revolutionary Alliance. Most members of the Red Alliance had inseparable ties with the local government, and therefore enjoyed the support of local officials and had conservative tendencies. The Revolutionary Alliance was mainly composed of young students and teachers, town residents, craftsmen, educated state or local employees, and a minority of cadres, and many of its members had suffered unfair treatment, so it was inclined toward the rebel faction. The Revolutionary Alliance was stronger in the county seat, where it had its headquarters in the No. 2 Secondary School. The Red Alliance enjoyed the support of the local PAFD and controlled most of the villages. The Red Alliance moved its headquarters to Yingjiang Commune and decided to "surround the city with the villages and then seize the city."

To demonstrate its revolutionary spirit, the Red Alliance aimed its spearhead at black elements, which was consistent with class-struggle theory and entailed little risk. A rumor circulated that the county's black elements were plotting to rebel by "killing party members, then cadres, then half of the poor and lower-middle peasants." Another rumor claimed that the No. 2 Secondary School was a den of black elements who hung a portrait of Chiang Kai-shek in the school and that it harbored air-dropped secret agents from Taiwan. As these rumors spread through proper and official communication channels, the people's militias adopted the guiding ideology of "The enemy is grinding his sword, and so must we," and "Taking the initiative gives the advantage, and lagging behind will bring disaster." Prior to the massacre, the county's leaders held three meetings and decided that all black elements should be killed off so that Chiang Kai-shek's troops wouldn't have anyone to show them the way when they attacked the mainland.

Although factional fighting was intense in Daoxian in 1967, the county, district, commune, and production brigade power structure was still largely functional. The county PAFD was the effective power-holder, handling the PLA's support-the-left work, and along with the county's leading cadres, it tacitly supported and encouraged the killings. Killings surged in the days after the Red Alliance held a "political and legal work conference" in Yingjiang from August 26 to 28; more than a hundred people were killed in Tangjia Commune from August 28 to September 1. The leaders in Yingjiang approved and encouraged "four chiefs' meetings"[5] for party secretaries, production brigade heads, militia commanders, and PPA chairmen in each production brigade, during which brigade leaders spoke of class struggle, planned killings, and arranged for the "double rush"[6] planting and harvesting to ensure that "neither revolution nor production was neglected."

Killings were always preceded by mobilization through customary administrative operational methods. The killings at Yingjiang Commune's Meihua production brigade were typical in that they carried out killings after each meeting in Yingjiang and held mass struggle rallies and delivered judgments by the Supreme People's Court of the Poor and Lower-Middle Peasants before each killing. At the meeting preceding the last batch of killings on August 29, the security chief He Guoqing, CRC chairman He Tao'an, and brigade cadre Wu Dexue proposed killing Wen Shangyi and his son, Wen Shoufu. Wen Shangyi had criticized Wu Dexue during the Four Cleanups campaign, and Wen Shoufu had to be killed in order to prevent him from avenging his father's death. Wen Shangyi was a poor peasant, however, which made it hard to justify killing him, so a rich peasant named Mo Desheng was added to the list. The commune leader, Liao Longguo, approved the killings, saying, "Not all poor peasants are guaranteed Reds. If they need to be killed, then kill them."[7]

There were killings at twelve of Xiaojia Commune's production brigades on August 29, and only the Xiaojia production brigade, where the commune headquarters was located, had no killings. The reason was that divergent views had emerged during the meeting to discuss the killings on August 24: One view was that even killing a pig required written permission, so it would be better to wait for written instructions from above before killing a human being. The second view was that killing off all the black elements would make future work arrangements difficult, especially for tasks that no one else wanted to do. The brigade continued to resist the commune's urging until the commune finally sent a group of core militiamen led by the PAFD commander Liao Longjiu to help the Xiaojia production brigade "carry out revolution" on August 28, blasting twelve class enemies and off-spring to death with dynamite. Ultimately Xiaojia Commune killed a total of 237 people, ordering activists applying for party membership and probationary party members to "redden their swords" on the front line of class struggle in order to "join the party on the battle front."[8]

Some grassroots cadres used suppression of class enemies as a pre-text for taking revenge for personal grudges. In the Hongxing produc-tion brigade of Qingxi District's Ganziyuan Commune, a poor peasant named Tang Congjiao, who had exposed the corruption of brigade lead-ers during the Four Cleanups campaign, was targeted during the massacre on the pretext that his son had joined the Revolutionary Alliance. All nine members of Tang's family were killed, including an infant less than a week old and a heavily pregnant daughter-in-law.[9]

The Daoxian massacre aroused the concern of the CCP Central Committee and the Hunan Revolutionary Committee Preparatory Committee and Forty-Seventh Army responsible for supporting the left in Hunan. The preparatory committee and Forty-Seventh Army headquarters telephoned the Lingling Military Sub-district and Dao-xian PAFD asking what was going on. However, after the Red Alli-ance's Yingjiang command post held its political and legal work conference from August 26 to 28 to discuss the killings, another 2,454 people were killed throughout the county, more than half of all the people killed during this incident. The meeting determined that the first stage of the revolutionary action of the poor and lower-middle peasants was "very well done" and that it was "a supplementary lesson in revolution," but that there should be "no random killing" and that only "one or two of the most heinous criminals could be killed." Some communes took these pronouncements as an indication that they should take this last opportunity to kill a few more class enemies.

On August 29, 1967, the Forty-Seventh Army's 6590 Unit (an ar-tillery regiment) entered Daoxian to halt the killings, and on Septem-ber 27, the Forty-Seventh Army and provincial preparatory committee issued an urgent notice stating, "So-called 'supreme people's courts of the poor and lower-middle peasants' are illegal and must be resolutely banned. The minority of bad leaders and their main co-conspirators must be harshly investigated and punished in accordance with law."

The notice was immediately air-dropped in leaflets over all counties in southern Hunan. The Forty-Seventh Army also sent work teams to each locality to end the killings. By late September, the killings had effectively ended.

THE GUANGXI MASSACRE[10]

Yan Lebin, a Public Security Ministry cadre who was a member of a Central Committee investigation team, wrote in January 1984 that his team was sent to the Guangxi Zhuang Autonomous Region's Office for Handling the Aftermath of the Cultural Revolution, and that a death toll of 89,700 named individuals had been reported, among whom 3,700 had died during factional fighting, 7,000 had been hounded to death, and more than 79,000 had been beaten or shot in organized operations. More than eight of the fourteen counties in Nanning Prefecture had death tolls exceeding 1,000, and 3,777 people had died in Binyang County alone. More than 20,000 other people had gone missing throughout the prefecture, and more than 30,000 unidentified people had also died.[11] In other words, out of 89,700 identified dead, more than 79,000, or 88 percent, were the victims of mass killings, without even taking account of the 50,000 who had gone missing or who were unidentified. Yang Zhiqing of the Guangxi Party committee's investigation and research office told the Central Committee investigation team that 130,000 fewer clothing coupons were issued by the commercial department in 1969 than in 1967. The Central Committee investigation group believed the death toll was at least 100,000.[12] Based on that smaller figure, the research group's statistical analysis determined that 80,000 people were victims of mass killings. A disproportionate number of victims belonged to the rebel April 22 faction, as opposed to the Alliance Command Post, which was the faction in power at the time. April 22 faction members were killed to ensure that revolutionary committees were controlled by one faction.

Apart from the factor of political rivalry, black elements were also targeted in the "Red tempest" that arose in Guangxi's villages from spring 1967 to spring 1968. On October 3, 1967, the Sanjiang production brigade of Quanzhou County's Dongshan Commune, led by the militia commander Huang Tianhui, killed seventy-six black elements and their offspring by burying them alive in a pit. Liu Xiangyuan, from a landlord family, was married to a poor peasant woman, and they had two children ages one and three. Before Liu was forced to jump into the pit, he begged the militia commander, "Tianhui, I have two sons. Can the government leave one of them for my wife? I'll jump into the pit with one, and my wife can have the other." Huang Tianhui said, "Not possible." Both children were buried alive with their father. From July to December, 859 black elements and their offspring were executed by shooting.[13] In Lingshan County's Tanli production brigade, the militia commander Huang Peili organized the militia in a unified operation that killed all the brigade's 130 landlord and rich-peasant elements and their offspring.[14]

The methods used to kill people in Guangxi were horrifying. In 1981, the Guangxi Autonomous Region Party Committee general office reported to a Central Committee investigation task force that thirty-eight people had been cut into pieces in Wuxuan County and that their flesh, hearts, and livers had been eaten. The *Yearbook of Major Events During the Cultural Revolution in Guangxi* recorded that from June 15 to the end of August 1968, seventy-five members of the Rebel Army and like-minded cadres and ordinary villagers in Wuxuan County were cannibalized. According to incomplete statistics, 113 state cadres and staff in Wuxuan County ate human flesh, hearts, and livers. In the Nashen production team of the Tigao production brigade in Shangsi County's Baibao Commune, with a population of just over one hundred, more than thirty people were killed, including all the men. The primary school teacher Liu Zhi and shop cashier Li Wenxing were bound back-to-back on a woodpile, and the killers cut out Liu's liver and showed it to Li before cutting out Li's liver. At the Wuming Overseas Chinese Farm, 560 people were denounced and 107 killed. Some of the victims were dismembered and decapitated, and some had their livers and flesh eaten by more than twenty people. At the Liuzhou Steelworks and Liuzhou No. 2 Chemical Plant, members of the April 22 faction had explosives tied to them and were blasted to smithereens.[15] One of the originators of this procedure at the Liuzhou Steelworks, Cen Guorong, was rewarded for his service by being promoted to chairman of the Guangxi Federation of Trade Unions, and he served as an alternate member of the Ninth CCP Central Committee, a full member of the Tenth Central Committee, and an alternate member of the Eleventh Central Committee. He wasn't expelled from the party until 1985.

On the night of July 1, the vice-principal of the Tongling Secondary School, Huang Jiaping, who sympathized with the Rebel Army, died during a struggle session led by the vice-chairman of the school's revolutionary committee preparatory committee, Xie Dong. The next morning, Huang Peinong, Zhang Jifeng, and others cut out his liver and sliced off his flesh, leaving only his bones behind. A group of people then roasted his flesh under the eaves of the school dormitory, the odor of it floating throughout the school grounds.

On July 17, the head of the Alliance Command Post in the Shangjiang production brigade organized a public denunciation of the Rebel Army members Liao Tianlong, Liao Jinfu, Zhong Zhenquan, and Zhong Shaoren, and after all four were killed, their bodies were dragged to the Pingzhao ferry wharf, where their flesh was cut off and their livers and sex organs removed and then taken back to the production brigade headquarters and fried up. Twenty-three people took part in the cannibal banquet.

Killers were rewarded rather than punished. Liu Muzhong, who killed forty-five people, was promoted to deputy party secretary of the Liuzhou Steelworks and then to vice-chairman of the Guangxi Federation of Trade Unions. According to the subsequent official investigation, nearly 50,000 party members took part in killings outside of factional battles. Among them, 20,875 were already party members at the time of the killings, and 9,956 were admitted to the party as a reward for the killings.

YUNNAN'S SHADIAN INCIDENT[16]

Shadian was a stockaded village inhabited by members of the Muslim Hui ethnic minority, with more than 1,500 households totaling more than 7,200 people. Several smaller Hui villages adjoined it, including Dazhuang, Maoke, and Xinzhai.

The forcible closure of Shadian's three mosques during the Four Cleanups campaign became the focus of two opposing viewpoints at the early stage of the Cultural Revolution. Yunnan's Cannon faction felt that China should have freedom of religion and that the mosques should be reopened, but the Eight faction felt that the mosques were part of the four olds and that reopening them would negate the great achievements of the Four Cleanups movement. Everyone in Shadian belonged to the Hui minority, and the vast majority belonged to the Cannon faction, so the mosques were reopened.

The Yunnan provincial military control commission and the provincial revolutionary committee supported the Eight faction, and leaders and core members of the Cannon faction were seized and struggled. In Shadian, however, there were not enough people in the Eight faction to go after the Cannon faction, so Cannon faction members from nearby cities and counties sought refuge in Shadian. They also put up big-character posters and sent people to Beijing to petition the Central Committee to end the suppression of one faction by the other. This led the provincial revolutionary committee to regard Shadian as a "hornet's nest."

The people in power decided to poke at that hornet's nest. In early December 1968, the provincial revolutionary committee sent a military propaganda team to Shadian under the pretext of "disseminating Mao Zedong Thought." Expecting the propaganda team to execute the government's policies on religious freedom for ethnic minorities, Shadian's Hui residents lined the streets to welcome the support-the-left troops and surrendered their militia's weapons. The propaganda team proceeded to search every home for fugitive stalwarts of the Cannon faction, who were hog-tied and led away for brutal public denunciations.

The military propaganda team was quartered in the mosques, which were once again closed to the Hui villagers. The soldiers ate pork and dumped the bones into the mosques' wells, and they danced and sang and caroused in the worship halls. The propaganda team proclaimed, "Believing in religion means opposing Marxism-Leninism and Mao Zedong Thought and opposing the party's leadership." Anyone caught worshipping or fasting was publicly denounced.

While carrying out its campaign against religion, the military propaganda team also cleansed the class ranks, and more than two hundred people were labeled "reactionary leaders opposing and disrupting the army," "daring vanguards of religious restoration," or "mischief-makers," and were subjected to utterly inhuman denunciation and beating. Eighty-four villagers were tortured, and fourteen died. At one struggle rally, a Hui villager was savagely beaten when he refused to lick a pig's head that was tied to his neck. At a mass struggle rally on January 30, 1969, sixty Hui villagers were marched through the streets and escorted to a public toilet, where they were forced to snuffle against the wall and scramble around and squeal like pigs. Later, more than fifty Hui villagers were forced to roll like pigs down a slope more than ten meters high. A pregnant woman among them suffered a miscarriage. A year of this kind of humiliation and torment had the Huis of Shadian burning with rage deep in their hearts.

In October 1973, representatives of the residents of Shadian asked the Shadian production brigade party branch to reopen the mosques for people to resume their normal worship activities. After the request was refused, Shadian's Jinjizhai Mosque was forcibly reopened that October, and the Great Mosque was reopened in February 1974. The authorities in Honghezhou and Mengzi Counties considered this "subverting the dictatorship of the proletariat" and "a religious restoration incited by counterrevolutionaries," and they immediately sent a new seventy-man work team to Shadian. When local residents thwarted the work team's attempt to close down the mosques, the work team released broadcasts during worship and used armed force to obstruct assemblies for the festival of Eid, which were treated as "counterrevolutionary gatherings." Members of the work team also ran into the worship hall to "disseminate Central Committee documents" during solemn religious rites. This profaning and disturbance of religious practice aroused intense resentment among the Hui.

During the Campaign to Criticize Lin Biao and Confucius in April 1974, the work team spread the word that "criticizing Lin Biao and Confucius had to be combined with criticizing the mosques," and specifically targeted the Shadian representatives Ma Bohua, Ma

Shaohua, and others. These men went to Beijing on May 10 and petitioned central leaders to withdraw the work team and implement the government's policies on the religious practices of ethnic minorities. On May 14, the Central Committee instructed the Yunnan provincial party committee to implement minority polices and submit a report on the situation.

In accordance with the Central Committee's demands, the provincial first secretary and revolutionary committee chairman, Zhou Xing, went to Shadian and convened all kinds of meetings to hear the views of local residents, who demanded the reopening of their mosques, an end to factional persecution and the rehabilitation of those who had been denounced, and improved living conditions through cash crop production, increases in grain rations, and the dismissal of officials who were taking more than their share.

Zhou Xing expressed no views on the first two points, and while he said the problems in living conditions could be resolved, he never followed through. Meanwhile, he reported to the Central Committee that the Shadian problem had been "solved." In September 1974, the Yunnan provincial party committee issued its Document No. 45 [1974], which stated that reopening the mosques would be a negation of the Cultural Revolution and that forcibly reopened mosques were to be closed. The document also restricted religious freedom through ten management regulations for Islam.

Hundreds of Shadian villagers went to Kunming to petition the provincial authorities in protest, and they were soon joined by more than a thousand Hui from Honghe, Wenshan, Yuxi, and other places. Some protesters climbed onto a Beijing-bound train to submit formal complaints to the central government. Zhou Xing and other provincial leaders labeled the Hui petitioning efforts as "stirring up trouble" and "opposing the party's leadership."

As the situation intensified, local authorities took measures that exacerbated the conflict. At the end of November 1974, a militia unified command post was established in Jijie District, just over a kilometer from Shadian, and the army sent armed militia to patrol the area around Jijie and Shadian. The Hui of Shadian responded by establishing their own Shadian militia unit, and from then on, the two militias faced each other with daggers drawn.

On January 1, 1975, the Central Committee summoned Ma Bohua and the other Hui representatives and leaders of the provincial party committee to Beijing to resolve the issue. In the meantime, the Central Committee issued its "Notice Prohibiting the Plundering of Weapons" (Central Committee Document No. 2 [1975]). The Yunnan provincial party committee confiscated weapons from the Hui in Shadian and other places, but guns held by the militia command post were not surrendered.

Acting under orders, the army surrounded the Hui villages of Najiaying and Yujidaying on March 5 and took some hundred Hui into custody in Yuji, Eshan, and Tonghai Counties. Hundreds of Hui were forced to attend study sessions, while dozens were sentenced to prison for "counterrevolutionary beating, smashing and looting." Extortion of confessions through torture became rampant, and numerous people were crippled for life.

The army and work team attempted to forcibly enter Shadian once again in May 1975, but with memories still fresh of the 1968 "poking of the hornet's nest," Shadian's residents refused them entry until the Hui representatives returned from Beijing. With a thousand people blocking the entrance to the village, the troops and work team were obliged to stay at the Jijie sugar refinery while waiting for a chance to enter Shadian at a moment's notice.

On July 29, 1975, several units of the PLA's Fourteenth Army encircled Shadian, cut off the supply of electricity to the village, and launched an assault with heavy artillery. On August 4, 157 villagers, men and women, old and young, emerged from the south end of Jinjizhai with their hands raised, pleading for their lives. When they reached the fields, machine guns opened fire, and in a flash, bodies tumbled into rivers of blood. Three people managed to survive the massacre. Around six o'clock that evening, artillery fire destroyed the remaining homes at the southern end of Jinjizhai, and Ma Bohua and the other Hui representatives were all killed.[17] This weeklong battle destroyed more than 4,400 homes and killed more than 900 villagers, with more than 600 others wounded. The army also suffered casualties.

Other nearby Hui villages were also subjected to armed suppression for participating in the "Shadian armed rebellion." More than 1,600 villagers were killed, and another 1,000 wounded. Casualties at Xinzhai were even higher than those at Shadian. Dozens of people were subsequently sentenced to death or lengthy prison terms because of the Shadian Incident, and hundreds were forced to attend study sessions.

In February 1979, the Central Committee approved a document by the Yunnan provincial party committee and Kunming Military Region party committee that revoked the original verdict of a "counter-revolutionary armed rebellion with Shadian as its hub" and rehabilitated the majority of Hui cadres and masses involved in this incident.

MASSACRES IN OTHER LOCALITIES

Available documents show that massacres were carried out against ordinary civilians in other localities as well.

In Guangdong Province, landlords and members of the China Youth Anti-Communist Salvation Corps in Yangjiang County were executed early in 1968. In May, 178 black elements in Haikang County were killed in a campaign against right-deviation, followed by 573 more deaths in June. By January 1969, 909 people had died. The killings employed guns, hoes, cudgels, stones, and kerosene, as well as drowning and live burial.[18]

Some localities in Jiangxi Province authorized civilian executions, in which commune and production brigade cadres could kill at their own discretion without opening a case file, collecting evidence, or requesting approval. According to reliable statistics, more than 270 people were killed in Xingguo County, more than 300 in Ruijin County, and more than 500 in Yudu County, through shooting, stoning, clubbing, stabbing, and other methods.[19]

THE GENERAL CIRCUMSTANCES AND BASIC REASONS FOR MASS KILLINGS

The situations described above indicate that mass killings during the Cultural Revolution shared several characteristics: First, the scale of killing was extensive, and the killing methods were appallingly brutal. Second, the victims were all innocent civilians, and the killings were completely unjustified. Third, the killings were carried out on the basis of the "class struggle" theory that had been instilled by the authorities over the long term, and accusations were fabricated and rumors circulated prior to the killings. And fourth, the killings were engineered by grassroots officials such as county PAFDs, revolutionary committees (or preparatory committees), and leading organs of communes and production brigades.

Mass killings surged during three stages of the Cultural Revolution. The first upsurge occurred during 1966's Red August under the banner of "sweeping away all ox demons and snake spirits" and "smashing the four olds," and against the backdrop of blood lineage theory, which required the vetting of family background going back three generations.[20] Beijing's Changping and Daxing counties are typical of massacres that occurred during this upsurge. The second upsurge occurred during the chaotic months of autumn 1967, when local officials who controlled rural communes, production brigades, and production teams mobilized militias and conservative mass organizations to kill members of the political underclass and opponents of the local bureaucratic machines in the name of eliminating class enemies. A larger number of localities experienced mass killings during this upsurge, with the massacres in Daoxian, Hunan Province, serving as a representative example. The third upsurge consisted of the military and government bureaucratic clique butchering members of mass organizations that opposed the revolutionary committees or military control committees. This upsurge, carried out under the banner of clearing away obstructions to the "great alliance" and "tripartite combination" and "defending the newborn red regime," occurred in many localities and had the largest number of victims, with the Guangxi massacre a representative example. In his audience with the "five great leaders" of the rebel faction Red Guards on July 28, 1968, Mao warned, "Those who steadfastly refuse to change are bandits and Kuomintang and must be surrounded, and if they continue to stubbornly resist, they must be annihilated." With this "highest directive," support-the-left units could feel justified in carrying out massacres against the rebel faction that they opposed to begin with. In each type of massacre, killings were also carried out by grassroots cadres in retaliation for personal grudges, or in order to seize women or property.

The victims of these massacres consisted of several types of people: The first type were the political underclass and their offspring. The second type consisted of members of mass organizations that opposed the support-the-left troops and revolutionary committees (or preparatory committees). The third type consisted of religious believers in ethnic minority areas such as Shadian, who were persecuted on the pretext of "smashing the four olds." Other victims included villagers who had exposed and criticized grassroots cadres during the earlier Four Cleanups movement or campaign to "rectify work styles and the communes." Combined estimates for these various incidents indicate that at least 300,000 people died in mass killings during the Cultural Revolution.

The people who directly encouraged and organized the mass killings were grassroots apparatchiks of the totalitarian system, specifically those in authority at the county level or below. The people who halted the killings were officials at the provincial level and above. Even so, the murderous actions of the grassroots authorities were a continuation and extremism of the policies of the higher-level authorities. The Central Committee and provincial-level officials constantly issued warnings about excessive violence, and upon receiving reliable information of mass killings, higher-level officials would issue criticisms and send out officials or troops to stop the violence. That doesn't absolve higher-level authorities of responsibility for the killings, however; the tendency toward power running amok and untrammeled killing was deeply rooted in the system and ideology of that time.

Under the line of "class struggle as the key link," the stratification of social classes prior to and during the Cultural Revolution continued to reference Mao Zedong's 1926 analysis of Chinese society that clearly demarcated the enemy from "us." The land reform movement in the countryside and the socialist transformation in the cities had already extinguished the economic basis of class, but this only enhanced the concept of "class" in the political sense (I use quotation marks here because Marx originally framed class as an economic construct). The standard for designating a political "class" was "revolutionary attitude." The revolution ended once the PRC was established, but the political identities of "enemy," "us," and "friend" became fixed, and treatment of groups of people was based on these labels. People with the political classifications of landlords, rich peasants, counterrevolutionaries, bad elements, rightists, or capitalists and their offspring were members of a political underclass. Prior to the Cultural Revolution, China's political underclass comprised an enormous mass of people; in October 1959, Public Security Minister Xie Fuzhi revealed in a document[21] that twenty million people were class enemies, and if each family was regarded as having an average of four members, by extension, eighty million people belonged to the political underclass. In the seventeen years prior to the Cultural Revolution, the government-controlled public-opinion tools constantly demonized the political underclass to the point where they were considered worthy of death. Without the slightest means of resistance at their disposal, members of the political underclass became meat on the chopping block of class struggle in every political campaign. In the early stage of the Cultural Revolution, mass organizations defending the bureaucracy could slaughter this underclass without the least resistance or legal penalty as a reflection of "enhanced class consciousness."

Under a harsh totalitarian system, the politically ignorant lived in terror of making a false step that would turn them into members of the political underclass, and their ignorance and terror made them abjectly obedient to the commands of those in power. A killer in the Daoxian massacre told an official questioner in the 1980s, "The higher-ups told me to kill, so I killed. If they told me to kill you now, I'd do it." Most of the mass killings in the first and second upsurges were carried out by the politically ignorant against the political underclass.

19

THE TWELFTH PLENUM OF THE EIGHTH CENTRAL COMMITTEE: ELIMINATING LIU SHAOQI

The party constitution passed by the Eighth National Party Congress in September 1956 stipulated that the party would hold a national congress once every five years. More than ten years later, on October 21, 1967, the CCP Central Committee and Central Cultural Revolution Small Group (CCRSG) issued a notice soliciting opinions regarding the Ninth Party Congress at Mao's request. In autumn 1968, with revolutionary committees now established in every province, the twelfth plenum of the Eighth Central Committee was tasked with preparing for the Ninth Party Congress. Zhou Enlai organized the plenum meticulously in accordance with Mao's intentions.

Mao presided over the twelfth plenum, which was held in Beijing from October 13 to 31, 1968. Ten of the ninety-seven members of the Eighth Central Committee had died, many had been stripped of their right to attend the plenum, and some of the forty who were able to attend had to be released from detention to do so. Lacking a quorum, Zhou Enlai announced that "the proletarian headquarters had decided after discussion" to select ten alternate members, including Huang Yongsheng, Xu Shiyou, and Chen Xilian, to become full Central Committee members. This brought attendance to fifty, producing a quorum. Extended to include people who took part in the CCRSG enlarged briefing meetings, members of the Central Military Commission Administrative Group, and leaders of provincial-level revolutionary committees and military regions, the plenum had 133 participants.[1] Zhou Enlai announced an agenda of four items: (1) the guiding ideology and methods for appointing delegates to the Ninth Party Congress; (2) the new draft party constitution; (3) the international and domestic situations; and (4) special investigations, in particular of Liu Shaoqi.

LIU SHAOQI PERMANENTLY EXPELLED FROM THE PARTY

The essential task of the twelfth plenum was to solve the Liu Shaoqi problem once and for all following a series of measures since August 1966.

The first measure involved thoroughly discrediting Liu Shaoqi. The eleventh plenum of the Eighth Central Committee had stripped Liu of his status as Mao's successor and had demoted him from second to eighth in power, but he was still a member of the Politburo Standing Committee and the president of the People's Republic of China. Mao said he still wanted Liu on the Central Committee, but that meant little; after all, hadn't Mao made his political rival Wang Ming a member of the Central Committee years ago? It first required a thorough political discrediting, and mass criticism was the main method used against Liu Shaoqi.

There was no mechanism for the CCP's highest officials to withdraw into peaceful obscurity. If the deposed person continued to exert any lingering influence over ideology or the party organization, it would be impossible for the victor to smoothly implement his own line. While in power, Liu had been fervently eulogized as the epitome of perfection, his every act held up as a model for others to emulate and every utterance proclaimed "important remarks," but the moment he was ousted, he became an arch-criminal devoid of any merit, and his past "important remarks" became "big poisonous weeds."

Mao himself had a hand in discrediting Liu Shaoqi.

The fifth issue of *Red Flag*, published on March 30, 1967, included an essay by Qi Benyu titled "Patriotism or Treason? On the Reactionary Film *Secret History of the Qing Palace*." Mao proclaimed this particular essay "very well written!" and also wrote one of its key paragraphs: "Was it the Chinese people who organized the Boxers and ran to imperialist countries such as Europe, America, or Japan to stage rebellions and commit murder and arson, or was it the various imperialist countries running over to invade this land of China and oppress and exploit the Chinese that caused the Chinese masses to rise with force and spirit to resist imperialism and its running dogs and corrupt officials in China? This is a major question of right and wrong that has to be argued clearly." Mao had expressed his support for the Red Guards by comparing them to the Red Lanterns among the Boxers, and he reiterated this comparison in his memo on the draft that Qi submitted for his approval: "With great discipline, they organized themselves and practiced martial arts to oppose the imperialists and their running dogs. It seems you could add a few sentences about them here."[2] Zhou Enlai convened several Politburo meetings to revise the essay sentence by sentence. The essay referred only elliptically to "the biggest capitalist roader holding power in the party,"[3] but anyone reading it knew it referred to Liu Shaoqi. The end of the essay raised eight questions regarding Liu and then said, "You're a bogus revolutionary, a counterrevolutionary; you're a Khrushchev sleeping beside us!"

When Liu Shaoqi read Qi's essay in the newspaper, he was infuriated. Ripping the newspaper to shreds, he stormed, "This essay is full of lies! When did I ever say that movie was patriotic? . . . I was the one who proposed Mao Zedong Thought during the Seventh Party Congress. No one has promoted Mao Zedong Thought more than I have!"[4]

The March 30 issue of *Red Flag* also had a commentary by Wang Li and Guan Feng titled "The Bourgeois Reactionary Line on the Cadre Issue Must Be Criticized." Mao had personally finalized this essay and added a paragraph referring to Liu Shaoqi's book *The Cultivation of a Good Communist* as a "fraud" that "advocated bourgeois individualism and slave mentality while opposing Marxism, Leninism, and Mao Zedong Thought . . . It is essential to thoroughly repudiate this book and eradicate its evil influence."[5]

On May 8, 1967, an essay describing *Cultivation* as "a betrayal of the dictatorship of the proletariat" was published under the bylines of the editorial departments of *Red Flag* and *People's Daily* after being discussed and approved by the Politburo Standing Committee, setting off a tide of criticism against "black cultivation."

In a speech while receiving representatives of the masses from Anhui Province on September 5, 1967, Jiang Qing said: "A mass campaign to criticize the leading capitalist roader is being carried out all over the country, and every battle line is opening fire on him. He must be thoroughly denounced and discredited . . . We needed to make him a household word as thoroughly discredited as Trotsky in the Soviet Union." The mass representatives believed she was expressing Mao's views.

From then on, mass criticism of Liu Shaoqi took off on a grand scale throughout the country, and every publication, from party magazines and newspapers to PLA and Red Guard newspapers, was filled with interminable screeds. The essay "Taking the Socialist Road or the Capitalist Road," attributed to the editorial departments of *Red Flag* and *People's Daily* on August 13, 1967, had been revised with additional evidence against Liu Shaoqi at Mao's request.[6]

The second measure to deal with Liu Shaoqi was to denounce his wife, Wang Guangmei. This was handled by Tsinghua University's Jinggang Mountain Corps. Wang had been a consultant for the Tsinghua work group that had labeled many students counterrevolutionaries, so now Tsinghua students demanded that Wang return to the university to undergo self-criticism. When Wang initially ignored their demand, she was lured there by trickery two weeks later. Detaining Liu Shaoqi's daughter Liu Pingping while she was carrying out self-criticism at a secondary school on January 6, members of Tsinghua's "demon-catching brigade" telephoned Wang Guangmei in the guise of being public security officers and said that Pingping had been sent to the hospital after being hit by a car. Wang didn't believe it and had Liu Shaoqi's bodyguards and another daughter, Liu Tingting, go to see if it was true. The "demon-catching brigade" made Liu Tingting telephone and confirm what they'd said, and when Liu Shaoqi and Wang Guangmei arrived at the hospital, the brigade made Liu Shaoqi leave and took Wang Guangmei to Tsinghua. Liu Shaoqi reported the matter to the Central Committee, and Zhou Enlai telephoned Kuai Dafu and instructed him that Wang Guangmei could be taken to Tsinghua for self-criticism, but she could not be beaten or humiliated and had to be allowed to go home afterward. That night, Wang Guangmei underwent self-criticism on the gymnasium balcony of the western sports ground, but she answered the students' questions without batting an eyelash or confessing to anything. Finally Zhou Enlai sent

Sun Yue from the Secretariat to bring Wang Guangmei home, and the members of the Tsinghua Jinggang Mountain Corps were left to argue over what some felt was a dishonorable as well as fruitless tactic.

On April 3, 1967, at the Great Hall of the People, Kuai Dafu wrote a note to Zhou Enlai asking permission to hold a mass rally denouncing Wang Guangmei. After getting the nod from Chen Boda, Kang Sheng, and Jiang Qing, Zhou told Kuai, "All right, give us time to prepare and communicate a little."[7] On April 10, more than three hundred thousand people gathered at Tsinghua to denounce Wang Guangmei. The Beijing municipal government sent more than a thousand police officers to maintain order. The speakers included Kuai Dafu; a student named Zhu Deyi, who was disabled from attempting suicide when the university work group persecuted him; the former work group head Ye Lin, exposing his former allies; a representative of the Taoyuan production brigade exposing Wang Guangmei's "evil acts during the Four Cleanups"; and the foreign anti-revisionist Sidney Rittenberg, who said that ferreting out Liu Shaoqi was "eliminating harm and performing meritorious service for the international communist movement." Peng Zhen, Lu Dingyi, Bo Yibo, Jiang Nanxiang, and more than two hundred Tsinghua cadres were brought in as secondary targets of criticism. Wang Guangmei was humiliated in every way possible, dressed in the *qipao* she'd worn on a state visit to India with Liu Shaoqi, and with her pearl necklace represented by a string of Ping-Pong balls.

Under increasing pressure, Liu Shaoqi on July 8 wrote a self-criticism to the 8-1 Combat Group at the Beijing Institute of Civil Engineering regarding remarks he'd made in August 1966 that were now being treated as "evidence of his crime." By then, however, the 8-1 Combat Group had split into new and old factions, and he'd unknowingly submitted his self-criticism to only the new one. The old 8-1 group immediately put up a tent and loudspeakers outside the west gate of Zhongnanhai and blasted the message "We will not rest until Liu Shaoqi is collared from Zhongnanhai and thoroughly discredited."

When it became clear that the CCRSG supported and encouraged the institute's campaign, other schools set up their own "collar Liu" strongholds around Zhongnanhai, and were soon joined by the rebel factions of government organs, factories, and enterprises. Within days, the surrounding streets were filled with banners, big-character posters, and the constant shouting of slogans. It is said that more than seven thousand sheds were built around Zhongnanhai, with more than five hundred loudspeakers and more than three thousand flags. This "Collar Liu Shaoqi Battlefront" became famous throughout the city, but it later became evidence of criminal activity when the May 16 clique was investigated.

The third measure to dispose of Liu Shaoqi involved designating him as a traitor. Mao planned this well in advance and developed his case against Liu Shaoqi in three steps.

STEP ONE: MOBILIZING THE PUBLIC TO FERRET OUT TRAITORS

Throughout the world and in Chinese history, surrender has been recognized as acceptable in order to preserve one's life. The CCP showed no such leniency, however. Back in 1963 and 1964, China's historians engaged in a debate over Li Xiucheng, a key leader of the Taiping Heavenly Kingdom. When Nanjing, the city that the Taiping Kingdom had proclaimed its capital, was stormed and captured by Qing troops on July 19, 1864, Li Xiucheng managed to break through the siege with the son of the Taiping leader Hong Xiuquan. Three days later, Li was taken prisoner, and before his death on August 7, he wrote a statement that the leader of the anti-Taiping forces, Zeng Guofan, shaped into "Li Xiucheng's Confession." The confession related Li's life experience and the history of the Taiping Heavenly Kingdom, while also summarizing the lessons of its failure. It included self-deprecating language and fawned on Zeng Guofan, but it didn't betray the Taiping revolution, and the mainstream viewpoint among Chinese historians had always been positive toward Li Xiucheng. In August 1963, the fourth issue of *Historical Research* published an essay by Qi Benyu that designated Li Xiucheng a traitor, creating a major controversy in academic and artistic circles. Prompted by Zhou Enlai, the Central Committee Propaganda Department brought together more than twenty historians to discuss the essay, and they criticized it as distorting history.[8] Jiang Qing provided Mao with that issue of *Historical Research*, along with related articles from *Beijing Evening News* and *Guangming Daily*, and

Mao wrote a memo saying that the evidence against Li Xiucheng was "ironclad." With tacit encouragement from Mao passed on through Jiang Qing,[9] Qi explicitly raised the issue of Li Xiucheng's traitorous behavior in another essay in *Historical Research* in 1964 that sent shock waves throughout the country.

The first victim of criticism of Li Xiucheng was the deceased Qu Qiubai.[10] Before being executed by the Kuomintang, Qu had written "Superfluous Remarks," which expressed weariness and resignation with the revolution. Now Mao said, "I can't finish 'Superfluous Remarks.' It's nothing but an apology to the enemy, surrender and defection."[11] In a speech at an enlarged Politburo meeting on May 21, 1966, Zhou Enlai cited Qi Benyu's essay while criticizing Qu Qiubai and Li Xiucheng in the context of "maintaining one's integrity in old age," observing, "Dying doesn't make someone a martyr. I suggest removing Qu Qiubai from Babaoshan and also destroying Li Qiucheng's former residence in Suzhou. These people are all shameless."[12] The Red Guards turned Zhou Enlai's words into action: Qu Qiubai was exhumed from the Babaoshan Revolutionary Cemetery, and Li Xiucheng's former residence in Suzhou was destroyed.

STEP TWO: DESIGNATING A "TURNCOAT CLIQUE"

The focus on turncoat behavior provided a rationale for dredging up Liu Shaoqi's relationship with the "sixty-one traitors" who formed his power base.[13]

Red Guards at Nankai University had alerted Zhou Enlai to the issue after discovering an "anti-Communist notice" by Liu Lantao in an old newspaper, but with Mao's approval, Zhou replied to the students on November 24, 1966, that the Central Committee was aware of the matter and that there was no need to pursue it at a mass rally.[14] After reading the material exposed by the Red Guards, however, Mao changed his mind. In a conversation with Albania's Beqir Balluku on February 3, 1967, Mao said, "I didn't know what kind of formalities they had to carry out. Now we learn that it involved endorsing the Kuomintang and opposing the Communist Party."

With the support of Kang Sheng and the CCRSG, the Nankai University Red Guards organized a further investigation and submitted a report on "Liu Shaoqi's Large Turncoat Clique" to Zhou Enlai, Xie Fuzhi, and the CCRSG in January 1967. After the Cultural Revolution, the matter of collaring the turncoats was laid entirely at the feet of Kang Sheng and the CCRSG, but in fact, Zhou Enlai also supported it. While receiving mass representatives from the finance and trade circles on March 21, 1967, Zhou praised the Red Guards for "tracking down a batch of traitors."[15] In her memoirs, Nie Yuanzi also mentions Zhou's consent to traitor-collaring activities at Peking University.[16]

On March 16, 1967, Central Document No. 96 [1967] explicitly stated: "The struggle to oppose the bourgeois reactionary line of Liu Shaoqi and Deng Xiaoping uncovered material regarding a turncoat clique of more than sixty people, including Bo Yibo, Liu Lantao, An Ziwen, and Yang Xianzhen. These traitors have been concealed within the party for a long time, and have occupied important positions in party and government leadership organs in the Central Committee and localities."[17]

The sixty-one former prisoners were formally designated a "turncoat clique," and since Liu Shaoqi had told them to "turn traitor" and had then appointed them to important positions, he was naturally designated the clique's leader.

STEP THREE: DESIGNATING LIU SHAOQI A "TURNCOAT, HIDDEN TRAITOR, AND SCAB"

Zhou Enlai headed up the Central Special Investigation Group (CSIG), which specifically investigated important personages under three subsidiary offices. Office One investigated Liu Shaoqi, Deng Xiaoping, Peng Zhen, Lu Dingyi, Yang Shangkun, Tao Zhu, and other high-level civilian officials. Office Two investigated Peng Dehuai, He Long, Huang Kecheng, Luo Ruiqing, Zhang Aiping, Chen Zaidao, and other high-ranking military officers. Office Three handled the investigations of officials at the level of party or state organ deputy director or above, leaders of the democratic parties, and other prominent individuals. (The May 16 clique was also handled by Office Three.)

On October 18, 1968, the CSIG submitted its "Investigation Report Regarding the Criminal Acts of the Turncoat, Hidden Traitor, and

Scab, Liu Shaoqi" to the second plenum of the Eighth CCP Central Committee. How would the report's accusations stand up today?

"(1) Liu Shaoqi's arrest and defection in Changsha in 1925"
The CSIG's report stated that in while serving as leader of the Shanghai Federation of Trade Unions in November 1925, Liu fled to Changsha but was arrested by the security apparatus of the governor of Hunan, warlord Zhao Hengti, on December 16. Following intervention by Liu Shaoqi's well-connected friends and relatives, Zhao agreed to spare Liu Shaoqi's life if Liu betrayed the revolution, and Liu left Hunan for Guangzhou on January 16, 1926. The CSIG's report stated that the extent of Zhao's betrayal was "leaving Hunan immediately" and accepting a set of the Four Books and Five Classics.[18] There were no specific allegations of betraying his comrades or giving up secrets.

"(2) In Wuhan in 1927, Liu Shaoqi acted as the running dog of the imperialist and Kuomintang reactionaries Wang Jingwei and Chen Gongbo,[19] engaging in a series of hidden traitor activities to betray the worker class and sabotage the revolution"
The CSIG report stated that Liu had provided the KMT with intelligence and colluded to sabotage the labor movement after being appointed head of the Kuomintang Central Committee's Labor Movement Committee in June 1927. After Liu Shaoqi was rehabilitated, the official version was that these allegations relied entirely on the false testimony of a former CCP member who was taken into custody during the Cultural Revolution.[20] In fact, similarly compromised testimony had also been drawn from three other former unionists. In any case, at the time of Liu Shaoqi's alleged "hidden traitor" activities, Wang Jingwei was still part of the KMT's leftist faction and regularly cooperated with members of the CCP.

"(3) Liu Shaoqi's major betrayal in 1929 while occupying the position of party secretary of Manchuria"
The CSIG report stated that around August 21, 1929, Liu Shaoqi (using the pseudonym Zhao Zhiqi) and Meng Yongqian (known then as

Meng Jian) were arrested by the warlord Zhang Xueliang[21] at the Fengtian Cotton Mill (in what is now Shenyang). Liu Shaoqi allegedly confessed to being the party secretary of Manchuria and gave up the name of other party committee members as well as exposed subsidiary party branches. Zhang Xueliang showed his appreciation by releasing Liu Shaoqi on the grounds of insufficient evidence, after which Liu wrote a letter saying, "Commander Zhang, you are the parent of my rebirth, and I will be beholden to you for the remainder of my days." The CSIG report claimed that Liu Shaoqi's betrayal resulted in serious damage to the party organization in Manchuria and the arrest and killing of many Communist Party members.

After Liu Shaoqi was rehabilitated, however, the official version of events was that Liu "stood firm without exposing his identity" following his arrest, and was therefore released on bail because of insufficient evidence. Meng Yongqiang's false testimony was blamed on the coercion of the "Jiang Qing Gang": "Although Meng Yongqian wrote more than twenty appeals while in custody requesting to retract his false testimony, he was not allowed to submit them to the upper levels, and the Investigation Report only selected the false testimony."[22] The CSIG report provided more than ten other collaborating testimonies from witnesses who, like Meng, had testified while deprived of their freedom. Mao had ordered Gao Gang to investigate this period of Liu's career back in 1953,[23] and was clearly predisposed to labeling Liu a traitor (there is no way to verify whether the report from that time was consistent with the CSIG report).

Although eventually officially debunked, this "criminal evidence" was enough to condemn Liu Shaoqi. After checking and approving the evidence on September 16, 1968, Jiang Qing wrote a memo stating, "How infuriating! Detestable! . . . Liu Shaoqi is a major turncoat, major inner traitor, major secret agent, and major counterrevolutionary. He incorporates all five vices and is the most insidious, most ferocious, most cunning, and most vicious class enemy."[24] Zhou Enlai wrote a letter to Jiang Qing agreeing with her views and denouncing Liu in equally strong language. Zhou Enlai personally read out dozens of pages of charges against Liu Shaoqi at the twelfth plenum, followed by a discussion and vote on a resolution to "permanently expel Liu Shaoqi from the party, dismiss him from all of his positions inside and outside of the party, and continue to expose and criticize the criminal acts of Liu Shaoqi and his cohort to betray the party and the country." Chen Shaomin, vice-chair of the All-China Federation of Trade Unions, resorted to silence to express her dissent and refused to raise her hand, but the vote against Liu was pronounced unanimous all the same.[25] After the plenum, the CSIG's "Investigation Report" and its accompanying evidence were issued to the grassroots level as Central Committee Document No. 155 [1968].

Liu Shaoqi was being treated in the hospital when he learned that the twelfth plenum had permanently expelled him from the party. He "immediately broke out in a sweat, he began gasping and vomiting, and his blood pressure and temperature shot up." From then on, he said nothing more and refused to answer any questions. In the final months before he died in November 1969,[26] Liu's face was haggard, his was body emaciated, and his hair and beard were long and dirty. No one changed or washed his clothes, no one took him to the toilet, and his clothing was covered with excrement. After long periods of his being confined to bed, his lower limbs became atrophied and as thin as kindling, and his body was covered with bedsores. To prevent him from killing himself, his legs were bound to his bed with bandages. On November 12, 1969, the ailing Liu Shaoqi died at the age of seventy-one in a makeshift prison in Kaifeng, Henan Province. When his body was sent to the crematorium, it was identified as that of a "highly contagious patient" named Liu Weihuang, unemployed, who had died of natural causes.[27]

Before the twelfth plenum, criticism of Liu Shaoqi had used the term "China's Khrushchev," but after this plenum Liu was denounced by name. Throughout the country, every work unit at every meeting had to shout "Down with Liu, Deng [Xiaoping], and Tao [Zhu]!" and every province and work unit had to add its own people to be struck down with Liu, Deng, and Tao.

RENEWED DENUNCIATION OF THE FEBRUARY COUNTERCURRENT

Criticizing the February Countercurrent was one of the main tasks of the twelfth plenum. On October 17, CCRSG members Kang Sheng,

Jiang Qing, Yao Wenyuan, and Xie Fuzhi joined in renewed exposure and denunciation of the February Countercurrent, each supporting the other in attacking people by name.[28] In a lengthy speech on October 26, Lin Biao described the February Countercurrent as an attempt to negate not only the Cultural Revolution and the verdicts on Liu, Deng, and Tao but also the Yan'an Rectification Movement and the verdict on Wang Ming more than twenty years earlier. Zhou Enlai made a point of criticizing several marshals. In particular, he blamed Nie Rongzhen and Ye Jianying for their roles in the February Countercurrent and for the more recent suppression of rebels in various parts of the country.[29]

The marshals acknowledged Zhou Enlai's criticism and ruthlessly berated themselves. Chen Yi stood up and said, "In past decades, I generally endorsed Chairman Mao and followed Chairman Mao in carrying out revolution, and from now on I'll never oppose him again. I'm afraid I won't meet the standards of a Ninth Party Congress delegate." Mao interrupted Chen Yi, saying, "You can represent the rightists!" Chen Yi stood there stunned with embarrassment, as if someone had hit him in the head with a club.[30] From then on, "rightist representatives" became a synonym for veteran cadres such as Chen Yi and Ye Jianying.

Mao had completely demoralized the veteran marshals with all his talk about the February Countercurrent before the twelfth plenum, but after they all admitted their errors, Mao said at the twelfth plenum, "This matter can't be considered minor; it's a major issue. At the same time, we can't say it's extremely important. They have their opinions and we have to talk about it, right? They're all Politburo members and vice-premiers, some are CMC vice-chairmen. I think it's permissible for them to talk. Weren't there two big arguments—one in the Huairentang and one in the Jingxi Hotel? The commotion they raised put their views out in the open. But some details aren't known to anyone, not even me. Only recently I've read about these things in the bulletin."

Mao understood the virtue of not pushing someone to the wall. He knew that if he took the matter too far and irreparably offended all the marshals and veteran cadres, it would be very difficult to continue the Cultural Revolution, so he looked for a face-saving opportunity.

After the second round of strident denunciations of the February Countercurrent at this plenum, he went back to presenting himself as kindhearted and lenient.

The objective of denouncing the February Countercurrent was to defend the Cultural Revolution. In his speech on the twenty-sixth, Lin Biao used high-sounding words to affirm the Cultural Revolution: "I've said in the past that its achievements are the greatest, greatest, greatest, and its losses are the smallest, smallest, smallest. Now these losses are getting smaller all the time, even smaller than when I spoke those words, while the achievements are becoming ever greater than at the time I spoke those words, and will be even greater in the future; this is irrefutable. So the losses versus the gains are in fact one to a hundred, one to a thousand, or one to ten thousand; it a massive profit from a small investment." The bulletin of the twelfth plenum of the Eighth Central Committee quoted Mao as saying, "This Great Proletarian Cultural Revolution is absolutely essential for strengthening the dictatorship of the proletariat, preventing the restoration of capitalism, and building socialism, and it's extremely timely." The bulletin also affirmed the important role of the CCRSG, which had been the main target of attack by the veteran marshals in the February Countercurrent. Once the bulletin was published, it gave even greater encouragement to the rebels and was welcomed with drums and gongs throughout the country.

Speaking at the plenum's closing ceremony on October 31, Mao put in a few good words for senior cadres such as Deng Xiaoping, observing, "It should be said that there is a difference between Deng Xiaoping and Liu Shaoqi." He also called for "February Countercurrent comrades" to be elected as delegates to the Ninth Party Congress and put a word in for some prominent intellectuals: "Jian Bozan, a professor and historian at Peking University, is a bourgeois historical authority, right? It's hard to expect him not to talk about emperors, generals, and ministers. We shouldn't engage in methods that humiliate such people. For instance, only giving them a salary of twenty-four yuan a month, or at most forty yuan—don't dock their pay too severely." At the same time, Mao presented the new political star Wang Hongwen, having Wang stand up before everyone and praising his involvement in the Anting Incident. The twelfth plenum passed the

"(Draft) Constitution of the Chinese Communist Party," produced by a committee led by Kang Sheng, Zhang Chunqiao, and Yao Wenyuan, which said: "Comrade Lin Biao has always held high the great red banner of Mao Zedong Thought, and has most loyally and most steadfastly executed and defended Comrade Mao Zedong's proletarian revolutionary line. Comrade Lin Biao is Comrade Mao Zedong's close comrade in arms and successor." Lin suggested removing the word "successor," but Kang Sheng refused, saying, "Comrade Lin Biao is Chairman Mao's successor—this was universally acknowledged at the plenum, and is fully deserved."[31] Before the Ninth Party Congress began, Lin again asked Mao to remove that word, but Mao said, "Excessive modesty could be untruthful. For example, if everyone wants to elect me chairman and I decline, it would not be convincing." During the drafting process, Zhang Chunqiao had included the words "Jiang Qing is the standard-bearer of the Cultural Revolution." But Kang Sheng said, "You can't raise issues this way. If we're not careful, we may end up losing everything we've already gained." That's why Jiang Qing's name didn't appear in the party constitution.[32]

The plenum bulletin stated, "The plenum held that after undergoing the tempest of the Great Proletarian Cultural Revolution, the ideological, political, and organizational conditions are in place to hold the party's Ninth National Party Congress. The plenum decided to convene the Ninth National Party Congress of the Chinese Communist Party at an appropriate time."

20

THE NINTH NATIONAL PARTY CONGRESS: FROM UNITY TO DIVISION

On the night of March 3, 1969, Mao called the members of the en-larged Central Cultural Revolution Small Group into room 19 of the Great Hall of the People for an informal session to discuss prepara-tions for the Ninth National Party Congress. Mao suggested that the CCRSG wouldn't need to be incorporated into the post-congress orga-nizational structure because the Cultural Revolution would soon be ending and the Politburo Standing Committee would suffice as the leading body.[1] On the afternoon of March 22, Mao called this group together again, along with Chen Yi, Li Fuchun, Li Xiannian, Xu Xiangqian, and Nie Rongzhen, who had just been called back from the factories they'd been sent to for "work experience." He comforted these party elders, saying: "You're old now, but I don't agree with not putting you to use. Old comrades can be delegates to the Ninth Party Con-gress. The political report will make no mention of the February Countercurrent. We'll follow the old rules and bring everyone into unity as much as possible; we'll allow people to make mistakes and to correct their mistakes. Most will be handled as a contradiction among the people and not as a contradiction between the enemy and us."[2] Mao intended the Ninth National Party Congress to be a conference that would create unity and a new central leadership structure, and then gradually bring the Cultural Revolution to a close. But was that how it actually turned out?

A HIGHLY CENTRALIZED AND SECRETIVE MEETING

The Ninth National Party Congress was held in Beijing from April 1 to 24, 1969. The delegates attending the congress weren't elected but were designated by the "core party groups" of revolutionary committees at various levels; at that time, the party organization had yet to be restored in the provinces, so military-dominated core party groups played a decisive role.

The congress was a secret meeting; its timing was not announced in advance, no outside guests were invited, and no journalists were allowed to cover it. All the delegates except for a tiny number of senior military and civilian cadres had spent the preceding two to three months assembled in local guesthouses and cut off from all outside contact while they underwent comprehensive study to prepare for attending the congress at a moment's notice.

Toward the end of March, the delegates began heading off to Beijing and checking into the Beijing Hotel, Qianmen Hotel, and Jingxi Guesthouse, where they continued to live under tight security and were not allowed to go outside for any reason. The telephones in their rooms were disconnected, windows that opened onto the street had to be kept closed, and they had to draw their curtains at night. The delegates were transported to the congress sessions in buses, which would stop with their doors open at the door of the hotel, at which point the delegates would race onto the bus and sit in assigned seats. Two buses arrived every three or four minutes, allowing all the delegates in a given hotel to be picked up within about half an hour. The bus routes were carefully arranged so that none of the delegates could be observed entering the Great Hall of the People through the main entrance, and the assembly hall's windows were covered with blackout curtains.[3]

By March 27, all 1,512 delegates had assembled in Beijing and had begun considering the name list for the presidium. Mao stated that the presidium would not have a standing committee but would be led by a chairman, vice-chairman, and secretary-general—predictably Mao, Lin Biao, and Zhou Enlai, respectively.[4]

Normally plenary sessions began at 9:00 a.m., but the congress held its opening ceremony at 5:00 p.m. to accommodate Mao's normal working and resting patterns. Everything revolved around Mao, and the meeting schedule also followed his biological clock.

The seating on the rostrum was meticulously arranged. Mao sat in the middle; at his right were seated Zhou Enlai, Dong Biwu, Liu Bocheng, Zhu De, Chen Yun, Li Fuchun, Chen Yi, Li Xiannian, Xu Xiangqian, Nie Rongzhen, and Ye Jianying; and on his left, Lin Biao, Chen Boda, Kang Sheng, Jiang Qing, Zhang Chunqiao, Yao Wenyuan, Xie Fuzhi, Huang Yongsheng, Wu Faxian, Ye Qun, Wang Dongxing, and Wen Yucheng. It was said that the rightists sat on the right and the leftists on the left. As the meeting was called to order, Mao announced the agenda: First, Comrade Lin Biao would represent the Central Committee in presenting the political report; second, the constitution of the Chinese Communist Party would be amended; and third, the members of the CCP Central Committee would be elected.

Mao then asked the assembly if everyone agreed to the 176-member presidium list that had been distributed to the delegates. The response was thunderous applause from the assembly and unanimous passage by a show of hands.

When it came time to elect the chairman, vice-chairman, and secretary-general of the presidium, a curious scene occurred. Mao said, "I nominated Comrade Lin Biao as chairman of the presidium. Do all of you agree?" Lin Biao rushed to the microphone and said loudly, "Our Great Leader Chairman Mao will be chairman of the presidium!" Mao said again, "Comrade Lin Biao will be chairman, and I will be vice-chairman, all right?" Lin Biao stood up, smiled at the crowd, and said, "Our Great Leader Chairman Mao will be chairman of the presidium—all who agree, please raise your hands!" The delegates smiled and raised their right arms high in the air, and Lin Biao shouted, "Passed!" The conference hall once again rang with thunderous applause and shouts of "Long live Chairman Mao!" Mao said, "If you insist, I can be chairman." He then nominated Lin Biao as vice-chairman and Zhou Enlai as secretary-general, and both were readily elected by a show of hands and applause.

The Ninth Party Congress raised Mao's personality cult to a new high. Mao's half-hour opening speech was interrupted dozens of times as someone would shout a slogan, sometimes in the middle of a sentence, and then everyone would repeat after him, the slogans taking up more time than Mao's speech, which as arranged for publication consisted of less than eight hundred characters, including punctuation.

Mao mainly spoke of the CCP's history from the First to the Eighth Party Congress, and each speech that followed further mythologized Mao's role in this history. The Ninth Party Congress gave legal standing to the "theory of continuing revolution under the dictatorship of the proletariat" as laid out in the political report delivered by Lin Biao.

Presiding over the assembly on April 14, Mao requested that no slogans be shouted and said that this meeting would have three orders of business: to pass the report Lin Biao had presented on behalf of the Central Committee, to pass the party constitution, and to hear speeches by several comrades.

Mao was seventy-six years old by then, so the question of succession was a matter of urgency. The party constitution passed by the congress explicitly stated that "Comrade Lin Biao is Comrade Mao Zedong's close comrade-in-arms and successor." Because at one point Mao had proposed stepping back to allow Liu Shaoqi to succeed him as chairman, the Eighth Party Congress had stipulated that "at the necessary time the Central Committee can establish an honorary chairman," but the Ninth Party Congress constitution eliminated this stipulation, indicating that Mao would have to die before Lin Biao could succeed him. This would not have escaped the notice of someone as shrewd as Lin Biao.

The first two items on the agenda were completed smoothly, and the order of business proceeded to speeches by Zhou Enlai and others extolling Mao and endorsing Lin Biao's political report.

CONTROVERSIES DURING THE DRAFTING OF THE POLITICAL REPORT

The political report was always a major part of every party congress, and delegates to the Ninth Party Congress found it regrettable that Lin Biao read from the script in a stumbling fashion. It was only after Lin's death that they learned that Mao and Lin had wrangled over the political report. Zhou Enlai disclosed this in his political report at the Tenth Party Congress on August 24, 1973:

> Before the Ninth Party Congress, Lin Biao colluded with Chen Boda to draft a political report. They opposed continuing revolution under the dictatorship of the proletariat, and felt that the main task after the Ninth Congress was to develop production. This was a new version of the revisionist fallacy that Liu Shaoqi and Chen Boda had crammed into the Eighth Party Congress resolution, which was that the main domestic contradiction was not that between the proletarian and capitalist class, but rather the "contradiction between an advanced socialist system and backward productive force." This political report by Lin Biao and Chen Boda was naturally rejected by the Central Committee. Regarding the political report that Chairman Mao took charge of drafting, Lin Biao secretly supported Chen Boda to oppose it, and only after being frustrated was he forced to accept the Central Committee's political line and read out the Central Committee's political report at the plenary session.

The incident began at an enlarged CCRSG briefing meeting on February 7, 1969, when Mao assigned Chen Boda with the task of drafting the political report for the Ninth Party Congress with the assistance of Zhang Chunqiao and Yao Wenyuan and overseen by Lin Biao. When Chen Boda reported this exciting news to his secretaries, Wang Wenyao and Wang Baochun, he told them what he was thinking of for the political report: There should be no more campaigns, and the main task now was to seize production.[5] By then, Chen Boda's relations with Jiang Qing, Zhang Chunqiao, and Yao Wenyuan were very strained, so Chen simply ignored Zhang and Yao and drafted the report on his own. He wasn't up to the task, however, and failed to deliver the draft on time. Impatient with Chen's delay, Mao told Kang Sheng, Zhang Chunqiao, and Yao Wenyuan to start working on a competing draft and dictated the theme for them as well: "You need to write about conflict, about the struggle between the proletarian and capitalist class, about why we need to carry out the Cultural Revolution, and about the additional serious problem of obstructing the mass movement."[6]

Meanwhile, Chen Boda discussed his report outline with Lin Biao, who had given Chen, Zhang, and Yao carte blanche to draft the report. Chen then wrote up the outline with ten subheadings under the title "The Struggle to Build Our Country into the Most Powerful Socialist Country," and wrote a report to Mao with the outline appended to it.[7] After reading the outline, Mao returned it to Chen without comment.

When Chen finally finished the first draft, he sent it to Mao, and on Zhou Enlai's instructions, he presented the draft at an enlarged CCRSG briefing meeting during which Zhang Chunqiao and Yao Wenyuan also presented their draft report. Argument ensued: Zhang and Yao said Chen's draft talked up the singular importance of productive forces, while Chen summarized Zhang and Yao's draft as "embracing Eduard Bernstein's idea that movement is everything and aim is nothing!"

Mao took Zhang's and Yao's side against Chen. As it turned out, Mao never read Chen's draft at all but edited Zhang and Yao's draft many times before finalizing it on the eve of the Ninth Congress. After Mao decided to use Zhang and Yao's report, the Politburo held a meeting to criticize Chen Boda for placing productive force above all else. Mao thundered, "The inherent quality of imperialism will not change, the inherent quality of Marxism-Leninism will not change, and your inherent quality, Chen Boda, will also not change!" Accusing Chen of "straddling two boats" from the Yan'an period to the present,[8] Mao seemed most infuriated by Chen's emphasis on economic construction over continuous revolution. The "other boat" could only have been Lin Biao, which indicated a major split between Mao and Lin on what should be the main task after the Ninth Party Congress.

Mao sent all his edits to Zhang Chunqiao and Yao Wenyuan's draft to Lin Biao,[9] but Lin's secretary Zhang Yunsheng recalls that Lin never read the drafts or made any changes; at most, he had his secretary tell him what parts Mao had changed.[10] Zhang Chunqiao wanted Lin Biao to sign the written report before it was delivered, but Lin refused, and rather than delivering an oral report, Lin Biao just haltingly read out the report that Mao had finalized[11] as a way of showing his dissatisfaction.

Li Zuopeng believes that the difference of opinion between Mao and Lin regarding the political report for the Ninth Party Congress was a major turning point that led Mao to sense that Lin Biao was unreliable.[12]

THE ELECTION AND BALLOTS

The main task of the third and last plenary session on the afternoon of April 24 was the election. The assembly hall was divided into seven sections, and each section and the rostrum had its own ballot box. The members of the presidium, as the smallest group, finished their balloting first and returned to their seats. Suddenly, a young delegate who had just cast his ballot turned back to the rostrum, leaped lightly onto the stage, and then walked quickly to the center of the front row, where he reached out and grasped the hands of Mao, Lin Biao, and Zhou Enlai in turn. Inspired by this delegate's success, many other young delegates dashed onto the rostrum, quite a few of them managing to reach Mao, Lin, and Zhou before the guards standing backstage could rush out and create a human wall to regain control of the situation. Anyone fortunate enough to have shaken hands with Chairman Mao refused to wash his hand for a long time afterward, and others tried to shake that same hand in order to share his blessing.[13]

There were 1,510 delegates present (only 2 having requested leave), and Mao was elected by the full 1,510 votes, while Lin Biao had 1,508 votes. An authoritative source said afterward that Lin Biao and his wife, Ye Qun, voted against Lin to ensure that Mao would have the largest number of votes. Zhou Enlai gained 1,509 votes, and Jiang Qing 1,502 votes. Resentful of missing 8 votes, Jiang alleged mischief and demanded an investigation.[14]

Her suspicions were not baseless. At that time the two most powerful organizations, the Central Military Commission Administrative Group (CMCAG) and Central Cultural Revolution Small Group (CCRSG), were constantly trying to undermine each other behind the scenes. Wu Faxian and Qiu Huizuo acknowledge in their memoirs that several members of the CMCAG were up to something during the election.

Before the election, Ye Qun said to Wu Faxian, "Marshal Lin says

Jiang Qing has become too fanatical. Zhang Chunqiao and Yao Wenyuan used to be mediocre pawns, but now they've gained so much prestige that it looks like they'll have no problem being elected to the Central Committee. At least we can make sure they lack a few votes and take some of the wind out of their sails." After that, Wu Faxian and others arranged for designated military delegates to decline to vote for Jiang Qing and her cohort.[15] Consequently, when the election results were stated, Jiang Qing was short eight votes, while Zhang Chunqiao and Yao Wenyuan lacked ten votes or more, and some ballots even had Jiang, Zhang, and Yao's names crossed out. Members of the CMCAG received more votes than members of the CCRSG did.[16] At an informal meeting of the Central Committee after the session closed, Yao Wenyuan and Zhang Chunqiao demanded an investigation, with Zhang observing, "Anyone who voted against Jiang Qing couldn't have been a minor delegate but must have been a major one. It's not a matter of lacking a few votes—it's an insidious political struggle." When Zhou Enlai informed Mao of their demands, Mao said, "If they want to investigate the election, let them. I'm not going to join any cantata that violates the party constitution."[17] On the afternoon of April 25, Zhou Enlai told Qiu Huizuo, "Go back and tell Wu and Huang that the Chairman has issued instructions on the election issue and it's been resolved, so there's no need to worry. You need to be true to yourselves on issues of principle, but not necessarily on petty matters like this that might backfire on you."[18]

In a speech on April 11, Mao said, "I recommend electing several old comrades, the ones you refer to as old opportunists . . . We should elect the veteran marshals, and also Li Xiannian and Li Fuchun."[19] He repeated this on April 23, the day before the election. However, the "opposition" wasn't to be elected to the Central Committee unconditionally. The presidium secretariat issued a stipulation that they had to receive a lower number of votes in order to ensure that they recognized the gravity of their error and felt compelled to change their ways. To this end, each delegation was tasked with voting for or against certain of the ten. The delegations took this very seriously, and some even went through practice drills. Even at that, the congress secretariat took the precaution of carrying out a pre-election on the night of April 23 among the large groups, with the results proving satisfactory.[20]

The formal election results on the twenty-fourth were just as Mao had intended: Zhu De, 809; Chen Yun, 815; Li Fuchun, 886; Chen Yi, 867; Xu Xiangqiang, 808; Nie Rongzhen, 838; Ye Jianying, 821; Deng Zihui, 827; Li Xiannian, 922; Zhang Dingcheng, 1,099.

The Ninth Party Congress elected 170 members to the Central Committee, along with 109 alternate members. They included 53 members and alternate members of the Eighth Central Committee, less than a third of the original 167 (apart from those who had died).

Why did the military cadres oppose Jiang Qing? The memoirs of several military leaders emphasize that they personally opposed the Cultural Revolution, but that was the politically correct position after the Cultural Revolution was negated, and the reality is not that simple. Military leaders had several reasons for opposing Jiang Qing and the CCRSG: (1) There was an ongoing power struggle between the CCRSG and CMCAG during the Cultural Revolution, and the CMCAG felt compelled to defend itself from Jiang Qing's attempts to gain control over the military. (2) Jiang Qing's outrageous behavior disgusted many, especially generals who had risked their lives in years of battle. (3) Wang Dongxing, as "imperial steward," vented his outrage over the eccentric behavior of the "lady of the manor" by spreading false rumors that Mao and Jiang didn't get along.

The first plenum of the Ninth Central Committee on April 28 included an election for the central leadership structure, with Mao elected chairman of the Central Committee and Lin Biao the sole vice-chairman. The members of the Politburo Standing Committee were Mao, Lin Biao, and (according to stroke order) Chen Boda, Zhou Enlai, and Kang Sheng. The Politburo members, apart from Mao and Lin, were (again, according to stroke order) Ye Qun, Ye Jianying, Liu Bocheng, Jiang Qing, Zhu De, Xu Shiyou, Chen Boda, Chen Xilian, Li Xiannian, Li Zuopeng, Wu Faxian, Zhang Chunqiao, Qiu Huizuo, Zhou Enlai, Yao Wenyuan, Kang Sheng, Huang Yongsheng, Dong Biwu, and Xie Fuzhi. The alternate Politburo members were Ji Dengkui, Li Xuefeng, Li Desheng, and Wang Dongxing. The way the names were listed gave the utmost prominence to Lin Biao's status as second-in-command, while Zhou Enlai dropped from third to fourth place, possibly through his own arrangement. After the results were announced, Zhou immediately stepped down to the first row below the stage, but Mao invited him back onto the stage.

It is worth noting that the people who didn't vote for Jiang Qing in the Central Committee election also didn't vote for her in the election for the Politburo. This bore out what Zhang Chunqiao said: "The people who didn't vote for Jiang Qing were not minor delegates but major delegates," in other words, members of the new Central Committee and naturally also members of the CMCAG. Chen Boda was one of them.

On the military side, Mao continued as chairman of the CMC, with Lin Biao, Liu Bocheng, Chen Yi, Xu Xiangqian, Nie Rongzhen, and Ye Jianying as vice-chairmen. Huang Yongsheng was made chairman of the CMCAG, with Wu Faxian as vice-chairman, and the eight other members included Ye Qun, Li Zuopeng, and Qiu Huizuo. Lin Biao effectively controlled the military through the CMCAG, and the other veteran marshals took no part in day-to-day operations. The CMCAG became more powerful as the CCRSG was phased out, and the number of documents co-issued by the CCRSG dwindled until it ceased all operations on September 12, 1969. The conflict between the Cultural Revolution faction and the CMCAG nevertheless persisted within the Politburo, developing into two utterly irreconcilable cliques. Zhou Enlai's power increased: Before the Ninth Party Congress, he was the convener of enlarged CCRSG briefing meetings, but now he virtually presided over Politburo meetings. Within the large framework set by Mao, Zhou was the decision-maker in the executive process, concentrating the power of State Council premier, general secretary of the Central Committee Secretariat, and half of a state president (Dong Biwu acted as president without being in charge of anything) in a single person. For years, Mao had placed himself above the Politburo, and once Zhou Enlai took charge, this was even more apparent; the Politburo's collective leadership had to request instructions from Mao and obey his directives. According to Qiu Huizuo, then a Politburo member, "Anything important that happened in the central government at that time was decided by Chairman Mao and carried out by Zhou Enlai."[21]

THE SUBTLETIES OF CENTRAL POLITICS

Prior to the first plenum of the Ninth Central Committee, Mao entrusted a committee consisting of Zhou Enlai, Kang Sheng, and Huang Yongsheng with drawing up a list of Politburo nominees. Members of the committee were not allowed to take telephone calls from anyone but Mao or Lin Biao, or to have any contact with others.

The first list that the committee submitted included twenty-three names: Mao, Lin Biao, Zhou Enlai, Dong Biwu, Zhu De, Liu Bocheng, Chen Boda, Kang Sheng, Jiang Qing, Zhang Chunqiao, Yao Wenyuan, Huang Yongsheng, Wu Faxian, Li Zuopeng, Qiu Huizuo, Xu Shiyou, Chen Xilian, Wang Dongxing, Ye Jianying, Xie Fuzhi, Li Xiannian, Li Xuefeng, and Wang Xiaoyu.

Huang Yongsheng subsequently said, "At first I didn't know what was really going on. I said Jiang Qing had contributed a lot to the Cultural Revolution and should be given due credit, but that it would be better for the overall situation and for the Chairman for her not to be a Politburo member. Kang Sheng immediately flew into a rage. After the meeting, Premier Zhou said to me, 'You just don't understand.' 'What don't I understand?' The Premier didn't reply."[22]

Mao looked at the list on the afternoon of April 26. He crossed out Jiang Qing's name and added Ye Qun's, and he underlined Wang Xiaoyu's and Ye Jianying's names. Later Mao said not to consider Wang Xiaoyu.

After Lin Biao looked at the list, he crossed out Ye Qun's name but didn't add Jiang Qing's name. Qiu Huizuo says, "This was really a stroke of genius. It helped to clarify the Chairman's attitude toward Jiang Qing."

At the meeting of the three-man committee, Zhou Enlai said, "The Chairman and Vice-Chairman Lin crossed names off the list, but we have to consider them. We should insist on keeping those two people on the list in consideration of the current situation." Jiang Qing and Ye Qun's names were then added back onto the list.[23]

On the new list, Mao once again crossed out Jiang Qing's name and added the names of Li Desheng and Ji Dengkui in the margin. Lin Biao once again crossed out Ye Qun's name.

Lin Biao was in poor health and was not always able to attend meetings, so Ye Qun attended in his place. As head of Lin's office, Ye Qun represented Lin to a certain extent, fielding all telephone calls and serving as "quality control" for Lin's views; when she suggested a better idea, Lin Biao would accept it. Likewise, Jiang Qing was not only Mao's wife but also a key player in the Cultural Revolution. Zhou Enlai knew that Mao and Lin were both being disingenuous and racked his brain to include both wives in the Politburo.

When the three-member group went back to work on the night of the twenty-sixth, Zhou Enlai said, "The whole problem with the name list is Jiang Qing and Ye Qun. Once that problem is solved, we can settle on the list. Based on the current situation, Jiang Qing and Ye Qun have to join the Politburo. We have to sincerely express our attitude to Chairman Mao and Vice-Chairman Lin from the political standpoint. The three of us will report to the Chairman tomorrow morning, and in the afternoon we'll report to Vice-Chairman Lin, and do our best to resolve this issue with each of them."

The group went to see Mao at ten o'clock the next morning. Zhou Enlai said, "We sincerely recommend that Comrade Jiang Qing be included among the candidates for the Politburo. Including her will have a definite political effect, but not including her will also have a political effect and possibly give rise to an even bigger political problem. After weighing the pros and cons, we recommend definitely including her in the list of candidates." Mao said, "If that's what you want, then go ahead. In any case, if she's included on the list, the responsibility is mine, so we'll leave it at that."

The committee then went to see Lin Biao with a similar message. Huang Yongsheng said they'd just seen Chairman Mao and he had basically accepted their view, and they hoped Vice-Chairman Lin would also agree. Kang Sheng made a similar request. Lin said, "Whether or not I agree with including Ye Qun among the Politburo nominees, I'll go along with Chairman Mao's decision."

At a meeting in Mao's quarters, they finally fixed the list of Politburo candidates, and Mao, Lin, Zhou, Kang, and Huang all signed their names to the list.[24]

After Huang, Wu, Li, and Qiu joined the Politburo, Zhou Enlai repeatedly spoke with them on the nature and scope of "central politics," which Zhou defined as "managing the relationships between

Chairman Mao, Vice-Chairman Lin, and Jiang Qing." Qiu Huizuo had expected "central politics" to be very profound and never guessed it would be so mundane. Only after he himself was struck down on September 13 did he realize just "how brilliant and profound" the Premier was. Qiu Huizuo eventually understood "central politics" to mean that (1) one's attitude toward Jiang Qing was not toward her as an individual but was also bound up with the Chairman; (2) the Chairman wasn't greatly opposed to Jiang Qing, in spite of what Wang Dongxing had said; and (3) one couldn't be swayed by emotion and lack shrewdness.[25] In fact, Mao wanted Jiang Qing on the Politburo, and by crossing off her name and adding Ye Qun's he had laid the groundwork for Jiang Qing to join. Jiang Qing was stronger than Ye Qun in terms of both experience and political influence, so if Ye Qun joined the Politburo, how could Jiang Qing not join?

Jiang Qing was very hard to deal with, and Zhou Enlai was always compromising with her for the sake of the overall situation. Huang Yongsheng told his son, Huang Zheng, that he'd personally witnessed Zhou Enlai acting like a bullied daughter-in-law in Politburo meetings, submitting to Jiang Qing's harangues without retort:

> One Politburo meeting had an important topic to discuss, but before the meeting began, Jiang Qing raised a fuss, saying, "Premier, you need to solve a serious problem for me, otherwise there will be real trouble!" Zhou Enlai asked, "Comrade Jiang Qing, what is this serious problem?" Jiang Qing said, "The toilet in my quarters is so cold that I can't use it in chilly weather—I'll catch the flu the moment I sit on it, and once I catch the flu, I can't go to see Chairman Mao for fear he'll catch it. Isn't this a serious matter?" Zhou Enlai said, "How shall we deal with this? Shall I send someone to have a look at it after the meeting?" Jiang Qing found this unacceptable, saying, "Premier, you lack class sentiment toward me; the class enemies are just waiting for me to die as soon as possible!" Zhou Enlai had no choice but to cancel the meeting and take us all over to Jiang Qing's quarters. Zhou Enlai looked at Jiang Qing's toilet and rubbed his chin thoughtfully without coming up with a solution. Finally he said, "Comrade Jiang Qing, how about this: We don't have the

technology to heat this toilet, but we could wrap the seat with insulating material, and also pad it with soft cloth, and that should solve the problem temporarily." Jiang Qing agreed to this, and Zhou Enlai immediately told the Central Committee Secretariat to send someone over to deal with it.[26]

After the eleventh plenum of the Eighth Central Committee, whenever Mao appeared at any event, Jiang Qing's status was equivalent to Lin Biao's. Under most circumstances, Jiang Qing entered shoulder-to-shoulder with Lin Biao, or at the very least followed directly behind him. Whenever Zhou Enlai appeared at a function, Jiang Qing entered along with him. Whenever the Central Cultural Revolution Small Group appeared solely at an event, Jiang Qing stood at the head of it, and those behind her had to maintain a certain distance. One time, Jiang Qing had to take medicine at an informal meeting of the Central Committee. A nurse brought a cup of boiled water, and Zhou Enlai felt the glass with his hand, then said to Jiang Qing, "The water isn't too hot. Please take your medicine."[27] Given Jiang Qing's special relationship with Chairman Mao, there was no one among the party's senior cadres who didn't show her respect and defer to her.[28]

THE RELATIONSHIP BETWEEN LIN BIAO AND JIANG QING AFTER THE NINTH PARTY CONGRESS

The relationship between Jiang Qing and Lin Biao was very delicate. Lin Biao was obliged to respect Jiang Qing as Mao's wife, but Jiang Qing often made herself disagreeable with her inappropriate behavior. Most crucially, Jiang Qing followed Mao by supporting the rebel faction in the armed forces, while Lin Biao wanted to stabilize the army. This brought their viewpoints into conflict.

Wu Faxian recalls attending a small-scale conference held by the Central Military Commission, Central Cultural Revolution Small Group, and All Forces Cultural Revolution Small Group at the Jingxi Guesthouse on February 19, 1967. At the meeting, Chen Boda blamed the CMC for many ongoing problems, calling General Xiao Hua "a bourgeois politician" who didn't allow the Cultural Revolution to gain traction in the military. The CMC cadres in attendance were highly offended by Chen Boda's remarks, especially since Xiao Hua's home had recently been ransacked by rebels from the song-and-dance troupe of the Beijing Military Region and some military academies. The next morning, Ye Jianying reported the situation to Lin Biao, who flew into a rage and had his secretary summon Jiang Qing. "You're treating the army and the CMC as the enemy, and I won't have it! I won't have it! Shall I resign? I'm reporting this to Chairman Mao. Without even discussing it with me you went off berating Xiao Hua and inciting people to ransack his home and steal his files—what's going on here? You don't go through the CMC but directly intervene in military matters. You want to get rid of the General Political Department—is that in line with Chairman Mao's instructions? I'm going to Chairman Mao and asking him to relieve me of all my positions."

Jiang Qing tried to interrupt him to explain, but Lin Biao wouldn't let her get a word in edgewise. In his anger, Lin Biao repeatedly shouted for his security officer to arrange for a car to take him and Jiang Qing to see Mao. Ye Qun stood between the two of them, weeping and pleading for them to stop fighting. She even knelt before Lin Biao and clutched his legs to keep him from leaving. Jiang Qing apologized to Lin Biao: "You're the vice-chairman of the Central Committee and of the CMC, and I was wrong. You can criticize and blame me, even curse me, and I'll accept it, but do we have to go to Chairman Mao?"

The day after he rebuked Jiang Qing, Lin Biao told Ye Jianying and Xu Xiangqian to preside over a meeting of the CMC, and asked CCRSG members Chen Boda, Jiang Qing, Kang Sheng, and others to attend for the transmission of Mao's views on how to handle the Xiao Hua issue: "Seizing Xiao Hua, ransacking Xiao Hua's home, and snatching his files was wrong. Allow Xiao Hua to cross the hurdle by writing a self-criticism." He also notified Xiao Hua himself to attend the meeting. As it turned out, the only CCRSG member who showed up was Guan Feng, who said, "Chen Boda made some thoughtless and erroneous comments last night because he'd been drinking. Jiang Qing criticized him at the CCRSG meeting, and he's carried out a self-criticism, admitting that he hadn't discussed it with Jiang Qing beforehand." Guan Feng's remarks aroused intense criticism from the military leaders.[29]

Soon after Huang Yongsheng became chief of staff, the CMCAG clashed with the CCRSG. In summer 1968, the CMCAG suggested to Mao that CMC documents concerning war preparedness, troop deployment, and other major issues be sent only to Mao, Lin Biao, and Zhou Enlai for approval. Mao agreed. Jiang Qing demanded that Huang Yongsheng carry out self-criticism for blocking the CCRSG's access to information on military matters, but he refused. In autumn 1968, the Central Committee decided that Huang would lead a delegation to Albania, but Jiang Qing tried to prevent Huang from leaving the country and accused him of running a military junta and rejecting the leadership of the party. Mao allowed the delegation to go, infuriating Jiang Qing even more.

After the first plenum of the Ninth Central Committee, on April 30, Jiang Qing gave notice that the enlarged CCRSG briefing meeting would be held as normal. Jiang was the first to arrive at the meeting, and she sat in Zhou Enlai's usual seat and presided over the meeting herself. She said, "I want to discuss a problem with all of you. Someone is engaged in a plot right now, refusing to tell me anything and not even telephoning me. This is a serious problem . . . You think the Cultural Revolution is over and that you're safe because you're the members of some committee or other? Your historical accounts are still locked in my safe. If anyone has the guts, let's have it out!" After these raving remarks, Jiang Qing left.[30]

At a full meeting of the Politburo held in the Great Hall of the People on May 4, Zhou Enlai transmitted instructions from Mao and Lin Biao: "From now on, the central leadership's work will be led collectively by the Politburo, and day-to-day work will be managed by its standing committee." The Politburo members Mao named to take part in the central leadership's day-to-day operations were Zhou Enlai, Chen Boda, Kang Sheng, Jiang Qing, Yao Wenyuan, Huang Yongsheng, Wu Faxian, Li Xiannian, Ye Qun, Li Zuopeng, Qiu Huizuo, Ji Dengkui, and Li Desheng.[31] This effectively eliminated the role of the CCRSG.

Once Huang, Wu, Li, and Qiu became members of the Politburo, they constantly discussed the relationship between Lin Biao and Jiang Qing. Huang Yongsheng told Li Zuopeng and Qiu Huizuo, "We're all in this together—if anything happens, none of us will get away. Are you afraid? If you are, you can withdraw."[32] The four of them spent more than ten hours during the Ninth Party Congress holed up in a room in the Jingxi Guesthouse discussing Lin and Jiang's relationship.[33]

On the morning of May 17, 1970, Jiang Qing summoned Huang Yongsheng, Wu Faxian, Qiu Huizuo, Li Zuopeng, Li Desheng, Xie Fuzhi, and Yao Wenyuan to her quarters at No. 11 Diaoyutai for a meeting. Jiang Qing talked for three hours straight about her revolutionary experience and her marriage with Mao in Yan'an, and then went on to critique the Standing Committee members Zhou Enlai, Kang Sheng, and Chen Boda one by one. She said Zhou Enlai had administrative ability and was conscientious and hardworking, but he wasn't strong on major political orientation and principles, didn't see things clearly, and was insufficiently resolute, so he was really suited only to concrete work in the Central Committee. She said this was "related to the opportunistic road he's taken in his personal history; historically, he's always gone along with the prevailing wind, and when he followed Wang Ming, the loss to the Soviet areas was immense." Of Kang Sheng, she said, "He has theoretical proficiency and performed meritorious service in his resolute struggle against revisionism, but he has very little practical work experience." She said Chen Boda was "just a bookworm who doesn't know how to run anything and who takes no stands, and we're always having to wipe his ass after he says the wrong thing. The whole burden of the CCRSG is on me."[34]

Offended, Huang Yongsheng withdrew from the meeting, with Wu, Li, and Qiu following close behind, and they went to Lin Biao's home to tell him about Jiang Qing's inappropriate remarks. Lin told Huang and Wu to report the situation to Mao, and he had Ye Qun personally contact Mao by telephone.[35] Since they had to immediately attend a Politburo meeting convened by Zhou Enlai, Huang and Wu made only a brief report. The first thing Mao said was, "It's all right for a member of the Politburo to call in Politburo members to discuss some issues." The second thing he said was, "You know that Jiang Qing is a force to be reckoned with." The third thing he said was, "Don't let Jiang Qing know that you told me about these problems, and I won't tell her, either. If she finds out, you'll be in trouble."[36] Wu Faxian recalls, "Huang Yongsheng and I were rather disappointed. We felt Chairman Mao wasn't interested in our report . . . It was as if nothing had happened, and as if Jiang Qing had done nothing wrong. Mao Zedong's attitude was not at all what we expected."[37]

Wang Dongxing had a close relationship with the CMCAG, and the members of the CMCAG were always sounding him out on Jiang Qing's relationship with Mao. Wang hated Jiang Qing as much as they did, but lacking the courage to oppose her himself, he merely fed the others negative information. Later Huang, Wu, Li, and Qiu discovered that Wang Dongxing had taken them in, especially after Mao commended Jiang Qing's participation in two-line struggle in remarks during his southern tour in August and September 1971.[38] Qiu observed, "In fact, the Chairman and Jiang Qing had a very profound relationship. Mao never really criticized Jiang Qing, nor did he ever even think of striking her down. People who pay attention to history will discover that whenever Mao said anything bad about Jiang Qing, he never took any real action against her."[39]

MAO'S ANXIETY REGARDING "MILITARY BUREAUCRATIC DICTATORSHIP"

The Ninth Party Congress and the first plenum of the Ninth Central Committee were a victory for the military and Lin Biao. Of the twenty-one Politburo members produced by the Ninth Party Congress, eleven, or just over half, were military cadres, with Lin Biao's associates occupying dominant positions. Military cadres composed nearly half of the 170 members and 109 alternate members of the Ninth Central Committee. The vast majority of leaders in the provinces, municipalities, and Central Committee ministries and commissions were "support-the-left" military cadres. In Tianjin, for example, among the 4,035 military cadres taking part in "Three Supports and Two Militaries" work, 3,172 joined the leading bodies of local governments, enterprises, and state-run institutions. Among sixty urban district and departmental party secretaries, forty-four (73.3 percent) were military cadres, as were ten of the eleven chairmen of municipal-level organs.[40] Tianjin was not exceptional in this regard. Xu Shiyou, who was the top man in Jiangsu's party, government, and military, concentrated all local administrative power in the hands of his trusted military cadres.

By 1970, military cadres were the top party and government leaders of all Jiangsu Province's fourteen prefectures and of sixty-one of its sixty-eight counties.[41] The prevailing trend at that time put the military in control of the entire country. At the first plenum of the Ninth Central Committee, Mao said, "The Soviet revisionists are attacking us with their TASS broadcasts, Wang Ming material, and tirades in *The Communist,* saying we now have a . . . military bureaucratic system. 'System' is a Japanese term. The Soviets call it 'military bureaucratic dictatorship.'" Although Mao expressed disagreement, that didn't mean he didn't have similar deep-seated anxieties.

After the Ninth Party Congress, the rift deepened between the Lin Biao clique (Huang, Wu, Li, Qiu, etc.) and the Jiang Qing clique (former members and supporters of the CCRSG), and Mao's suspicions toward Lin Biao also gradually increased. Lin Biao had always stayed out of the limelight and did all in his power to avoid offending Mao, but he was bound to slip up eventually. One matter that deepened Mao's suspicions was "Vice-Chairman Lin's first verbal order."

The Zhenbao (Damansky) Island incident occurred on March 2, 1969, during the most strained year in Sino-Soviet relations,[42] and the situation on the Sino-Soviet border deteriorated with the Tielieketi (Terekty) Incident in Xinjiang on August 13.[43] To mitigate tensions arising from these two incidents, Zhou Enlai met with the Soviet leader Alexei Kosygin, who was passing through Beijing on his way back from Vietnam, on September 11 in the VIP room of Beijing Capital Airport, and the two engaged in lengthy talks. However, Kosygin was cold-shouldered by key political figures after returning to the Soviet Union, and the Soviets refused a demand by the Chinese side for an exchange of diplomatic letters documenting the understanding reached by Zhou and Kosygin. China's leaders became convinced that the Soviet Union had a concrete plan to launch a surprise attack on China. On October 5, Lin Biao flew to Zhangjiakou with Huang Yongsheng, Wu Faxian, and others to inspect the terrain and battle preparations by military units there. After Lin Biao returned to Beijing, Mao had him convene a Politburo meeting to analyze the trend in Sino-Soviet relations and look into specific measures to guard against a surprise attack. Around the same time, Kosygin sent a letter to Zhou Enlai proposing talks in Beijing regarding Sino-Soviet border issues.

Kosygin sent another letter on October 14 notifying Zhou Enlai that a Soviet delegation would arrive in Beijing by October 20. Based on the lessons of the "Prague Incident,"[44] Chinese leaders believed that the day when the Soviet delegation arrived in Beijing was the very day on which the Soviet Union would launch its attack, and they decided to have all necessary preparations in place by October 19.

The Central Committee issued a notice for urgent dispersal in preparation for war, and large numbers of party, state, and military leaders in Beijing were sent to other locations after the National Day celebrations. On October 17, 1969, Lin Biao, who had been sent to Suzhou just two days before, issued an "urgent directive on strengthening defenses and guarding against an enemy surprise attack" to Huang Yongsheng. Huang had deputy chief of staff Yan Zhongchuan note it down and transmit it to the troops, which Yan did by having the staff officer of the battle operations security post compose a script to be read over the telephone. This was the first directive by a leading cadre after a frontline command post was established in preparation for a surprise attack by the Soviet Union, so it was referred to as the "first verbal order under Vice-Chairman Lin's direction." Handed down by telephone on the eighteenth, it consisted of six points: (1) to greatly enhance vigilance against being duped by the Soviet revisionists when their negotiating delegation was due to arrive in Beijing; (2) for all military regions, especially those in the north bordering the Soviet Union, to immediately disperse and conceal all heavy weapons such as tanks, aircraft, and large canons; (3) for military regions along the coast to enhance precautions against a possible attack by the American imperialists and Soviet revisionists; (4) to step up production of anti-tank weapons; (5) to immediately incorporate command teams of crack troops into wartime command positions; and (6) to strengthen on-duty leadership at all levels to promptly grasp the situation and rapidly report execution. Before the directive was passed to Huang Yongsheng, Ye Qun had the secretary add one sentence: "Comrade Dongxing has been asked to report the above six points to Chairman Mao. If Chairman Mao has other instructions, Chairman Mao's directives are to be considered the standard." Later Wang Dongxing telephoned Ye Qun and said that Mao had no problem with Lin's six points.[45] In accordance with the "first verbal order," 95 divisions totaling some 940,000 soldiers, 4,100 aircraft, large numbers of tanks and canons, and 600 naval vessels were dispersed and concealed.[46] Lin Biao was responding appropriately to the situation, but the massive effect of the "first verbal order" aroused Mao's suspicion and jealousy. Mao was in Wuchang on the nineteenth when he read the telephone record that Wang Dongxing gave him for his "urgent perusal," and with a scowl on his face he said, "Burn it!" and then struck a match and did so himself. Wang Dongxing saved the envelope in order to retain a serial number for the communication.[47] "The Fight to Smash the Lin-Chen Anti-party Clique's Counterrevolutionary Coup d'État," issued on December 11, 1971, explicitly referred to this incident as "a preview of usurping the party's power." After the September 13 Incident, Yan Zhongchuan was imprisoned for seven years for his part in the "first verbal order."

Mao's main objective in carrying out the Cultural Revolution was to put into practice his theory of continuous revolution under the dictatorship of the proletariat, but concrete implementation required taking one step and then observing the results before proceeding. It was called a "great strategic plan," but in fact it was issue-driven, proceeding as the opportunity arose. How could Mao have anticipated that by enlisting Lin Biao's support to eliminate Liu Shaoqi, he would find Lin an even more troublesome opponent? This cast into complete disarray Mao's strategic plan of holding the Ninth Party Congress to consolidate the structure arising from Cultural Revolution and gradually restore order. The day of the Ninth Party Congress's closing ceremony was when Mao and Lin parted company. Mao's vision of establishing a new order popped like a bubble.

While the entire country was celebrating the success of the Ninth Party Congress with gongs and drums, the conflict between Mao and Lin was rapidly fermenting. Fifteen months later, during the second plenum of the Ninth Central Committee in autumn 1970 (the Lushan Conference), the conflict between Mao and Lin burst into the open.

21

FOGGED IN ON LUSHAN: THE SECOND PLENUM OF THE NINTH CENTRAL COMMITTEE

Lushan (Mount Lu) is situated within Jiujiang City in northern Jiangxi Province, towering over the shores of Poyang Lake in the middle reaches of the Yangtze River. With its enchanting scenery and refreshing summer temperatures, it has always been a favorite vacation spot for China's elite. For the Chinese Communist Party, Lushan was already associated with a major event, namely the denunciation of Peng Dehuai and the adoption of policies that intensified the ongoing Great Famine during the 1959 Lushan Conference. The 1970 Lushan Conference was likewise the scene of intense political struggle, shrouded among the mountain's heavy mists.

This Lushan Conference, the second plenum of the Ninth Central Committee, held from August 23 to September 6, 1970, was attended by 155 members of the Central Committee and 100 alternate members. A power struggle had already become fierce before Central Committee members ascended the mountain, and Mao was aware of a turbulent undercurrent in the upper reaches of the party. At a meeting of the Politburo Standing Committee on August 22, he warned, "I want this to be a plenum of unity and victory, not of division and failure."

In this newest power struggle, one side consisted of members of the Central Military Commission Administrative Group[1] plus Chen Boda, who had all been elected members of the Politburo during the Ninth Party Congress and who were backed by Lin Biao, and were therefore known as the Lin Biao clique; and the other side consisted of members of the Central Cultural Revolution Small Group, including Jiang Qing, Kang Sheng, Zhang Chunqiao, and Yao Wenyuan, who had likewise been elected to the Politburo during the recent congress and who were backed by Mao. Chen Boda had originally been the head of the CCRSG, but he had become a whipping boy for Jiang Qing and the others during the Cultural Revolution. Lin Biao's wife, Ye Qun, had seized the political opportunity to reel Chen in when he was frozen out of Diaoyutai and began betting his political future on Lin succeeding Mao. Several core members of the Lin Biao clique had established a power base back during the war years as members of the First Red Army Group of the First Front Red Army. Their alliance had formed during the May 13 Incident in 1967, when all of them supported the conservative faction against the rebel faction within the armed forces,[2] and it became even tighter after Huang Yongsheng became chairman of the CMCAG. Lin Biao's secretary Zhang Yunsheng records that the guests received at Lin's residence in Maojiawan in summer 1970 were basically the same few people: Chen Boda, Huang Yongsheng, Wu Faxian, Li Zuopeng, and Qiu Huizuo. They usually gathered at night to escape the notice of the CCRSG; Chen Boda would arrive by a roundabout route from Diaoyutai, while Huang, Wu, Li, and Qiu would discreetly turn up to "watch movies." Any member of the clique who clashed with CCRSG members would immediately report it to the others, and they would discuss how to deal with it.

An environment lacking open debate and a free press easily gives rise to backstage battles between cliques. That is why "anti-party cliques" emerged one after another in both the Soviet Union and Communist China.

THE FIRST ROUND BEFORE ASCENDING THE MOUNTAIN: WHETHER OR NOT TO ELECT A PRESIDENT

The second plenum of the Ninth Central Committee was convened to prepare for the Fourth National People's Congress (NPC). It had been six years since the Third NPC in December 1964, surpassing the stipulated five years between congressional sessions. By 1970, mass organizations had been disbanded, and the "Monkey Kings" that Mao had loosed were imprisoned under Five Finger Mountain, bringing an end to the "great chaos under heaven." Revolutionary committees had been set up in the provinces and cities, and local party organizations were being restored, so this seemed the right time to rebuild the government structure.

This process raised an unavoidable question: After Liu Shaoqi was removed as president of China, Dong Biwu had occupied this largely ceremonial position in an acting capacity for several years. Now Dong was eighty-four years old, and a new president had to be chosen. Mao had always detested receiving visiting VIPs and had no interest in administrative affairs. He already held ultimate power and didn't need the position of president, but the only alternative was Lin Biao, and Mao didn't want Lin to be president, either. Under the "Three Supports and Two Militaries," Lin Biao was more powerful than ever. Mao feared losing control of the military, especially after losing trust in Lin during the Ninth National Party Congress.

Lin Biao considered his ascent to the presidency a matter of course, given that his status as Mao's successor was enshrined in the party constitution, he was deputy commander in chief, and he had held the rank of vice-premier of the State Council since 1954. During the Second and Third NPCs in 1959 and 1964, Mao's designated successor, Liu Shaoqi, had served as president, but now Mao wasn't allowing Lin Biao to assume this position. Given Lin Biao's health issues and personality, he didn't necessarily want the position, but his mulish Hubei character made him more determined to assume this office the more Mao seemed set against it. He knew that assuming the presidency was the litmus test of Mao's trust in him, and his back-and-forth with Mao from early March to mid-May forced Mao to come clean on the issue.

While in Wuhan on March 8, 1970, Mao proposed holding the Fourth NPC and amending the constitution, and at the same time changing the state organizational system to eliminate the position of president. Wang Dongxing returned to Beijing to communicate Mao's views to Zhou Enlai,[3] who, in turn, had Ye Qun communicate them to Lin Biao in Suzhou. On March 9, Lin Biao told Ye Qun to tell Huang Yongsheng and Wu Faxian that "Vice-Chairman Lin endorses having a state president."[4]

On March 16, the Politburo wrote a report requesting instructions from Mao on amending the constitution, and Mao explicitly stated that there should be no state president.[5] Huang Yongsheng, Wu Faxian, and others argued fiercely for the post of president during a Central Committee work conference from March 17 to 20, but Mao held his ground, and when Lin Biao had his secretary telephone Mao's secretary and say, "Vice-Chairman Lin recommends that Chairman Mao serve as president," Mao merely had his secretary make a courtesy phone call in response.[6]

Late at night on April 11, Lin Biao, still in Suzhou, had his secretary telephone the Politburo and communicate his proposal that Mao serve as president, along with his own lack of interest in the position of vice-president.[7] Zhou Enlai endorsed Lin Biao's proposal of Mao becoming state president at the Politburo meeting the next day, but Mao repeated his refusal in a memo on the Politburo's report.[8] This was the first major issue since the Cultural Revolution began in which both Mao and Lin adamantly persisted in their own views.[9] Mao repeated his opposition to the position of president at another Politburo meeting in the latter part of April following his return to Beijing.[10]

On the afternoon of May 17, Huang Yongsheng, Wu Faxian, Li Zuopeng, and Qiu Huizuo went to Lin Biao's home and told him that Mao had said, "If there's a state president, Lin Biao should serve." Lin Biao said, "For a major country of a billion people not to have a state president or head of state is utterly improper. Only Chairman Mao can serve as this state president and head of state; no one else is appropriate."[11]

Qiu Huizuo holds that Politburo Standing Committee members endorsed having a state president out of consideration for the state organizational structure, while Mao may have linked the issue to the question of succession.[12]

Mao's proposal to not have a state president was meant to test Lin Biao's ambition, while Lin's insistence on having a president was meant to test whether his position as Mao's successor was real or fake. The position of state president was therefore only an outward manifestation of the fact that Mao no longer trusted his chosen successor. Under an autocratic system, a change of successors would be disastrous for Lin Biao, as he could see from what had happened to Liu Shaoqi. Mao later said that "establishing the position of state president" was Lin Biao's "anti-party program" at the Lushan Conference. From the perspective of the fight over succession, Mao hit the nail on the head.

THE SECOND ROUND BEFORE ASCENDING THE MOUNTAIN: REGARDING POLITICAL WEAPONS

In this new round of political struggle, the Lin Biao clique assembled the political weapon of "Mao worship" as a show of strength.

This weapon had been tempered over a period of years. The deification of Mao began during the Yan'an Rectification Movement and became established practice during the Seventh National Party Congress. The energetic adulation of Liu Shaoqi, Zhou Enlai, Lin Biao, Tao Zhu, Ke Qingshi, and other party leaders, and twenty years of vigorous propaganda, had made one's attitude toward Mao and toward Mao Zedong Thought the highest standard for judging right from wrong and good from evil. Worshiping Mao was politically correct, and refusing to worship him was a disastrous political error. After decades of bloody suppression of those who opposed Mao, anti-Mao language aroused insecurity and even terror. In political struggles at the highest levels, seizing the initiative to worship Mao gave the advantage, and Lin Biao grasped this opportunity after taking charge of the military. Ostentatiously deifying Mao by every available means increased Lin's political capital and created a political atmosphere in which Mao worship was an even more formidable political weapon, and its wielder all but invincible.

Mao initially needed personality cult and used Lin Biao's adulation against Liu Shaoqi. Although too shrewd to become intoxicated by a billion people treating him like a god, Mao used the worship of others to achieve his political objectives. Once he discovered that Lin Biao had parted ways with him politically, he found Lin's bogus adulation disgusting. Perceiving that the Lin Biao clique had turned Mao worship into a political weapon for their own use, Mao stealthily deconstructed that weapon, and members of the Cultural Revolution faction quickly caught on. The military men, as yet unaware that their political weapon had become useless, continued to uphold it through opposition to the Cultural Revolution faction.

An intense dispute broke out while Kang Sheng was presiding over a meeting of the constitution revision group on the afternoon of August 13, 1970, with neither side backing down on whether or not to have a state president. Then Wu Faxian proposed that the constitution's chapter on the State Council should say, "Mao Zedong Thought is the guiding principle of all of the State Council's work." Kang Sheng and Zhang Chunqiao said, "That's redundant, and Chairman Mao won't agree to it." Zhang added, "Some people go on and on about ingeniously, comprehensively, and creatively developing Marxism-Leninism; even Khrushchev ingeniously and creatively developed Marxism-Leninism. It's a complete joke." Recognizing that Zhang was referring to a quote by Lin Biao, Wu Faxian immediately accused him of ridiculing Lin and added that Zhang was "using Chairman Mao's great modesty to belittle Mao Zedong Thought." Chen Boda, who had just returned to the meeting after a trip to the restroom, advised Wu, "The situation today is complicated. You should report it to Vice-Chairman Lin and to Premier Zhou and Chief of Staff Huang." Wu accordingly contacted Zhou and Ye Qun, and obtained an endorsement from both Zhou and Lin Biao for including his sentence in the constitution.[13]

On the morning of August 15, Huang Yongsheng telephoned Li Zuopeng in Xuzhou and told him, "There was a big argument in the constitution revision group, and Fatty Wu is very isolated. You need to hurry back." Li returned to Beijing that afternoon, and Huang briefed him on the dispute.[14]

Lin Biao was an astute and cunning man. To the outside observer, he had always followed Mao closely, but this was only a public performance. Ye Qun made sure that whenever Lin went to the Tiananmen gate tower, he would arrive a minute or two early so that he could greet Mao in front of the elevator. Everyone thought of Lin Biao as always having a Little Red Book in his hands, but in fact, Lin's chief of security, Li Wenpu, carried the book for him, and once they arrived at a mass rally, Li would hand the book to Lin, and Lin would raise the Little Red Book high and wave it in the air as the crowd shouted slogans. As soon as the shouting stopped, the book would return to Li Wenpu's hands.[15] Lin Biao extolled Mao as the "Great Teacher, Great

Leader, Great Commander in Chief, and Great Helmsman," but in private he said, "He worships himself and has blind faith in himself; everything he does is in his own interests." Having seen through Mao, Lin adopted a modus operandi: "Don't advise, don't criticize, don't report bad news . . . Respond as rapidly as possible to his every new proposal, because he urgently waits for others to reveal their attitudes . . . Don't take a different stand and you'll never get into trouble; follow orders . . . If you say east, he will insist on saying west, so let him talk first and go along with him."[16] Among all the party's leaders, Lin Biao's private criticism of Mao was the most intense and struck right to the heart of Mao's political character.

A totalitarian political system is a breeding ground for hypocrites and schemers. Lin Biao himself said that under this kind of system, "it's impossible to do anything important without lying," and he was the ultimate double-dealer. Mao tolerated and accepted Lin's hollow accolades when they were needed, but once they came to repulse him, Mao took the initiative to "oppose personality cult" while maintaining a state of high alert against the commanding power of the military.

First, he eradicated the "three adverbs." Lin Biao had first said that "Comrade Mao Zedong ingeniously, comprehensively, and creatively developed Marxism-Leninism" back on May 18, 1966. The phrase was later written into the bulletin of the eleventh plenum of the Eighth Central Committee, and Lin included the "three adverbs" in his preface to the reprint of *Quotations of Chairman Mao* on December 16, 1966. But Mao crossed out the "three adverbs" when the twelfth plenum of the Eighth Central Committee discussed the party constitution in October 1968,[17] as a result of which they were missing from the bulletin of the twelfth plenum and from the revised party constitution. Members of the Lin Biao clique apparently hadn't noticed this when they defended the sentence at the August 13 constitution revision group meeting, and it wasn't until August 27, after the clique suffered a crushing defeat at the Lushan Conference, that Lin Biao sent his copy of the revised party constitution for Wu Faxian to read, and Wu found that the "three adverbs" were already missing there. Later that day, Wu asked Zhou Enlai why the three adverbs had been removed, and inquiries by personnel from the general office determined that Mao himself had edited them out.[18]

Second, on July 27, 1970, Zhou Enlai presided over a Politburo meeting to discuss an editorial for the main party publications titled "Enhance Vigilance, Defend the Motherland," which added two words to the formulation that had been used for years: "the Chinese People's Liberation Army that the Great Leader Chairman Mao personally founded and led, and that *Chairman Mao* [italics added] and Vice-Chairman Lin directly command," so that the military was no longer directly commanded by Lin alone. Chen Boda argued that changing the standard formulation would give rise to debate, but Zhang Chunqiao refused to back down, and further inquiries established that Zhang Chunqiao and Yao Wenyuan had already added the words to the editorial marking National Day (October 1) the previous year,[19] clearly in accordance with Mao's intentions. During his southern tour one year later, Mao explicitly pointed out, "Why would the founder not be able to command?"

Third, while receiving the American journalist Edgar Snow on December 18, 1970, Mao said, "It's different now—the worship has become excessive and has led to a lot of formalism. For example, the 'four greats'—disgusting! One day I'll get rid of all of it and leave only 'teacher,' because I've always been a teacher and I'm still a teacher now. The rest can all go." Snow asked, "Was all that necessary in the past?" Mao replied, "In the past few years there was a need for personality cult, but now there's no need, and we have to lower the temperature." Following vetting by Mao, the Central Committee turned the summary of this conversation into a formal document and on May 31, 1971, distributed it to "party grassroots branches, to be orally transmitted to all party members."[20] Anyone aware of this document would automatically think of Lin Biao.

It was also at this time that Mao criticized the various manifestations of formalism while speaking with members of the Politburo. He said, "It would be best for you to take down all the quotes from the Great Hall of the People; until then, I won't enter the Great Hall of the People." Accordingly, the head of the PLA's General Political Department, Li Desheng, put in place pictures or paintings of all the Mao quotes in the Great Hall of the People and the Jingxi Guesthouse.[21] This was at a time when Mao's quotes were displayed in homes and offices and on walls throughout the country.

THE THIRD ROUND BEFORE ASCENDING THE MOUNTAIN: CHOOSING LIN BIAO'S SUCCESSOR

On April 25, 1970, Mao brought Zhang Chunqiao and others with him on a rare visit to Lin Biao in Suzhou.[22] In the course of conversation, Mao observed that the Premier was getting old and asked if Lin had any thoughts on who should succeed him. He then got to the real purpose of his visit by saying, "I'm old and your health is poor. Who do you have in mind to succeed you?" Lin Biao said nothing, so Mao went on, "What would you think of Xiao Zhang [Zhang Chunqiao]?" Lin Biao said nothing at first, but during a discussion of countering and preventing revisionism a few minutes later, he said, "We need to rely on Huang, Wu, Li, and Qiu, who've been carrying out revolution with the Chairman since their youth, to prevent the petty bourgeoisie from seizing power."[23] By "petty bourgeoisie" he meant Zhang Chunqiao. Given Lin's poor health, Zhang could replace him at any time once designated as successor, but Lin Biao disliked Zhang Chunqiao and had his own ideas about a successor.

In autocratic countries, the supreme leader often designates his son as his successor. Mao had taken pains to groom his eldest son, Mao Anying, who had been sent to the Soviet Union in 1936, at the age of fourteen, to study at the military and political school and at the military academy and then fought with the Red Army during the Second World War. Mao Anying returned to Yan'an in 1946 and joined the Chinese Communist Party that same year, after which Mao sent him to the villages to attend the "university of manual labor" and gain an understanding of the countryside. As soon as the Korean War began, Mao entrusted his son to Peng Dehuai so that he could gain some battle experience, but Mao Anying was killed during the war. It had become clear that if Lin Biao succeeded Mao, he was likely to hand over power to his son, Lin Liguo. This would foil Mao's plans to designate Zhang Chunqiao as Lin Biao's successor while also hitting Mao where it hurt the most.

Lin Liguo, born in 1945, began studying physics at Peking University in 1963 and was in the third year of a six-year program when the Cultural Revolution began. In 1967, Lin Biao and Ye Qun arranged through Wu Faxian for Lin Liguo to be assigned to the air force headquarters. Wu energetically groomed Lin Liguo in the air force party committee office, and half a year later, Lin Liguo joined the party. In October 1969, he was promoted to deputy director of the air force headquarters office and of the air force's war department. In front of other senior staff, Wu Faxian told Lin Liguo, "You can move troops and command operations within the air force as you please." Although mere flattery, the comments enhanced Li Liguo's status within the air force.

According to Chen Zhao, who worked with Lin Liguo, Lin was charismatic and eloquent, and helped upgrade the air force's radar antennas, which Mao described in a memo as a "technological innovation."[24] Lin Biao took advantage of the situation to push Lin Liguo into the limelight, bringing him along on an inspection of a large ordnance factory on July 23, 1970. Lin Liguo walked close behind Lin Biao along with Huang Yongsheng, Wu Faxian, Li Zuopeng, and Qiu Huizuo as they were welcomed by troops lining the street on the factory grounds. A seven-hour speech on learning and applying Chairman Mao's works that Lin Liguo gave at a conference of air force headquarters cadres on July 31 was recorded and replayed at a larger conference on August 4, with Wu Faxian and others praising him as "a great, versatile, and comprehensive talent."[25] Lin Biao encouraged this flattery, but Mao was clearly displeased, telling Jiang Qing, Kang Sheng, and Zhang Chunqiao in a private conversation, "I'm not dead yet, but Comrade Lin Biao's health is poor and he's impatient to prepare his own successor."[26]

Since Lin Biao didn't want Zhang Chunqiao as his successor, Zhang became a target of the Lin Biao clique in this new battle.

LIN BIAO'S SPEECH AT THE OPENING CEREMONY

Mao presided over the opening for the second plenum of the Ninth Central Committee at the Lushan Auditorium on the afternoon of August 23, after which Zhou Enlai announced the agenda, and Kang Sheng reported on amending the constitution. Then Lin Biao spoke for an hour and a half on the draft amendments enshrining Mao's status as "Great Leader," head of state of the dictatorship of the proletariat, and supreme commander and affirming Mao Zedong Thought as China's guiding ideology: "This point is extremely important—extremely important. Using the form of the Constitution to confirm this is extremely good—extremely good! It can be considered the soul of the Constitution." Emphasizing Mao's genius, Lin Biao reiterated the "three adverbs" and observed, "Now someone has raised this issue, as if the genius theory is wrong. It would be excusable if someone below said something like this, but if someone in the central leadership says it, it will affect the whole country and give rise to chaos." Unaware that Mao had already removed the "three adverbs," Lin was aiming his criticism at Zhang Chunqiao, but most of those present were completely clueless and applauded wildly. After Lin Biao finished speaking, Kang Sheng endorsed Lin's views on Mao's historical status and the constitution's amendments and said that "all views were unanimous" regarding Chairman Mao serving as state president and Lin Biao as vice-president. At this point Mao declared the meeting adjourned.

Wu Faxian recalls that Ye Qun told him twice that Lin Biao would not be speaking at the meeting,[27] but Chen Boda told Qiu Huizuo that he convinced Lin Biao to give a speech by blaming the nonstop campaigns on the influence of Jiang Qing, Kang Sheng, and Zhang Chunqiao: "You can't knock Jiang Qing, but you may be able to knock Zhang Chunqiao."[28] Wu Faxian later learned from Ye Qun that just before the plenum, Mao asked Lin if he was going to speak, and Lin said he wished to say "a few words" about the question of genius[29] and about the argument between Wu Faxian and Zhang Chunqiao regarding the draft amendments to the constitution: "Zhang Chunqiao disagreed with writing that state organs have to treat Mao Zedong Thought as their guiding principle, and said that Khrushchev ingeniously and creatively developed Marxism-Leninism. I want to talk about that problem." Mao said, "This isn't Zhang Chunqiao's view, it's Jiang Qing's view, and it's Jiang Qing causing trouble behind the scenes. You can talk about it, but don't mention Zhang Chunqiao."[30]

The official *Biography of Mao Zedong: 1949–1976* says that Lin Biao gave Mao only last-minute notice of his desire to "express some views."[31] Chen Boda, who was present, recalls that before the opening ceremony, Lin Biao had a lengthy private conversation with Mao while Chen, Zhou Enlai, and others waited in another room, and that after the meeting, Lin told him that "Chairman Mao knew what he was going to say."[32] What requires further study is whether Mao actually agreed to Lin's criticizing Zhang Chunqiao without naming him, and if so, whether it was Mao's attempt to "lure the snake from his den." If so, Lin Biao took the bait and Mao should have been happy. But the head of Mao's security detail, Chen Changjiang, says, "All of the delegates attending the conference applauded Lin Biao's speech; only the Chairman didn't applaud, and he had a depressed expression on his face."[33] Mao's attendant Zhang Yufeng says, "After the meeting, the Chairman was very unhappy. At dinner he kept pushing his food away, and it had to be reheated several times. When he was told to eat, he lost his temper."[34]

"A BLAST THAT COULD LEVEL LUSHAN"

Wu Faxian, Ye Qun, Qiu Huizuo, and the others were overjoyed by Lin Biao's speech. Back in Beijing, Huang Yongsheng learned the details from Wu Faxian and told Qiu Huizuo, "I'm delighted! I allowed myself an extra bowl of rice tonight."[35] That night, Chen Boda, Wu Faxian, Qiu Huizuo, and others gathered in Wu's quarters and talked until 3:00 a.m., mainly about Zhang Chunqiao.[36]

On the morning of August 24, Ye Qun, Wu Faxian, and the others decided that each of them would give a speech at meetings of the six regional subgroups that day, endorsing Lin Biao's speech, expounding on the "genius" quotes, calling for a state president, and demanding that opponents of Chairman Mao be "rooted out."[37] Wu and Qiu also recruited others to give supporting speeches.[38]

Before Qiu Huizuo attended the Northwest subgroup meeting that afternoon, Wu Faxian telephoned him and told him to bring along *Quotations of Engels, Lenin, and Chairman Mao on Genius*, compiled by Chen Boda, which Mao's head of security, Wang Dongxing, had given them to support their positions.[39]

A recording of Lin Biao's speech was played back twice for

discussion by the regional subgroups. Apart from a small minority, attendees didn't know who was being targeted in Lin Biao's speech, nor did they know about the split between Mao and Lin; they knew only that they couldn't go wrong by flattering Mao and endorsing Lin's speech.

In the North China subgroup meeting, Chen Boda and Wang Dongxing vigorously endorsed Lin Biao's speech and attacked those who denied the importance of genius. Wang in particular warned against reactionary careerists in the party who opposed Mao as president and rejected Mao Zedong Thought. Wu De, who attended the plenum, recalls, "When Chen Boda spoke, everyone was still suspicious, but as soon as Wang Dongxing spoke, that changed. He was someone at Chairman Mao's side, and people were more inclined to believe him."[40] Under the highly charged atmosphere, many other members of the North China group endorsed Lin Biao's speech. Chen Yi described the denier of Mao's genius as a "counterrevolutionary and an imperialist running dog who should be expelled from the party and subjected to mass criticism."[41] The chairman of the subgroup, Li Xuefeng, arranged for a bulletin of the meeting to be issued the next day to the other subgroups as Bulletin No. 6 of the second plenum:

> Listening to the speeches by Comrade Boda and Comrade Dongxing at the group meeting greatly deepened understanding of Vice-Chairman Lin's speech. In particular, intense indignation was expressed at the realization that someone in our party is making a vain attempt to deny that our Great Leader Chairman Mao is the greatest genius of modern times, and it was considered a very serious matter that the party still had someone with this kind of reactionary thinking after four years of the Cultural Revolution. This kind of person is a careerist, conspirator, an extreme reactionary, and a genuine counterrevolutionary revisionist, a proxy of the Liu Shaoqi reactionary line without Liu Shaoqi, a running dog of the imperialist revisionist reactionaries, a villain, and a counterrevolutionary who should be rooted out and publicly exposed, expelled from the party, and denounced until thoroughly discredited, subjected to death by a

thousand cuts, punished by the entire party, and despised by the entire country.

After his secretary read Bulletin No. 6 out to him, Lin Biao said, "Of all the bulletins I've heard, this is one of the few that have any weight and substance."[42] Other subgroups responded by demanding the uprooting of the villain who opposed Chairman Mao. Wu Faxian, Li Zuopeng, and Qiu Huizuo gave similar speeches to the Northwest and Southwest subgroups, and eventually some people learned that the person to be "punished by the entire party, and despised by the entire country," was Zhang Chunqiao. When the East China subgroup held a discussion on the afternoon of August 25, the political commissar of the Fifth Airborne Group, Chen Liyun, leaped to his feet and shouted at Zhang Chunqiao, "Come forward on your own!" Everyone present was shocked. Zhang's expression was ghastly as he evaded Chen's eyes and stared at the carpet, puffing hard on his cigarette as group members chanted thunderously, "Whoever opposes Chairman Mao must be struck down! Down with careerists! Down with conspirators! Defend Chairman Mao to the death! Defend Vice-Chairman Lin to the death!"[43]

Endorsing the "genius theory," extolling Mao Zedong Thought, and endorsing the presidency became the political equivalent of opposing those associated with the CCRSG, so even the marginalized Chen Yun and Chen Yi took the side of those extolling Mao Zedong Thought and supported Lin Biao.

Qiu Huizuo recalls that a "significant number of Central Committee members" joined with Chen Boda and the CMCAG members against Jiang Qing and other members of the CCRSG.[44] Several military region commanders wrote letters to Mao, Lin, and Zhou calling for the "person committing the error" to be sent down to the countryside for manual labor and to be educated by the workers, peasants, and soldiers.[45] By then the political wind had shifted, and Zhou Enlai gave the letters to Ye Qun and told her not to pass them further upward.[46] Li Zuopeng records in his memoirs, "As soon as the discussion began, all of the Central Committee members were vying to sign up to speak first, and every speech was loud and high-toned with fierce diction, using words like 'machine gun,' 'canon,' 'saber,' and 'hand grenade.'"[47] Mao finally realized the intense antipathy of Lin Biao's military clique toward the Cultural Revolution and its main proponents, especially Jiang Qing and Zhang Chunqiao, describing the meeting as "a blast that could level Lushan."

Mao regarded this fight at the Lushan Conference very seriously, and some people have compared it to the February Countercurrent by referring to it as the "August Countercurrent," but Mao called it the "August Con-current." Xie Xuegong recorded in his journal that on September 3, Zhou Enlai told the North China subgroup, "The Chairman says that the August 'Con-current' has converged with the 'February Countercurrent,' and the two Chens have formed a confluence";[48] the "two Chens" were Chen Boda and Chen Yi. At the April 1971 meeting to "criticize Chen and conduct rectification," Mao Yuanxin referred to the Lushan Conference as a "failed coup d'état."[49]

MAO TOSSES OUT CHEN BODA

The "Three Supports and Two Militaries" had put the military in control of the Politburo, Central Committee ministries and commissions, and provincial revolutionary committees, and the military was under the control of Lin Biao's close confederates in the CMCAG. This made military leaders impervious to any attack by Jiang Qing.[50] When Mao raised the issue of a "military bureaucratic dictatorship" during the first plenum of the Ninth Central Committee, Jiang Qing added, "Chiang Kai-shek ran a party state, and now we're running a military party and a military state."[51] How could Mao tolerate the "military bureaucrats" rooting out CCRSG member Zhang Chunqiao at Lushan? On August 25, Zhang Chunqiao and Jiang Qing informed Mao about what had happened during the subgroup discussions, and Mao was surprised and annoyed when he learned of Bulletin No. 6.[52] He felt compelled to frustrate the Lin Biao clique's attempts to root out a steadfast supporter of the Cultural Revolution, Zhang Chunqiao, and extend its influence in the process.

On the afternoon of the twenty-fifth, Mao called a meeting of the Politburo Standing Committee, enlarged to include the convener of each regional subgroup, and wrathfully repeated his refusal to serve as China's president: "Don't even mention the idea of a state president again. Anyone who insists on it can be president himself. In any case, I won't do it!" He threatened to leave Lushan and resign as chairman of the Central Committee if arguments over the issue continued. Calling an end to discussion of Lin Biao's report, Mao demanded a recall of Bulletin No. 6 and ordered Chen Boda and others to carry out self-criticism.[53] He declared a recess the next day.

During the recess, most Central Committee members went sightseeing in the daytime and watched movies at night, but Zhou Enlai was in a frenzy of activity. Pulling together the minutes of all the subgroup meetings, Zhou discovered a striking similarity between the speeches of Wu Faxian, Li Zuopeng, Qiu Huizuo, and others, suggesting that they'd been in contact beforehand. Zhou and Kang Sheng questioned Wu, Li, and Qiu and found out how *Quotations of Engels, Lenin, and Chairman Mao on Genius* had been compiled by Chen Boda and printed and distributed by Wang Dongxing.[54]

On August 27,[55] Zhou Enlai and Kang Sheng went to Lin Biao's quarters, and Kang Sheng said, "There are three major culprits at this Lushan Conference . . . Wu Faxian started rumors, Wang Dongxing lit the fire, and Chen Boda stirred up the trouble, and Chen Yi also jumped out." Lin Biao said, "I understand Wu Faxian very well. He's been with me for decades and has never started rumors. You were there during the argument on August 14—how is that starting rumors?" The next day, Zhou Enlai told Wu Faxian to make self-criticism to protect Lin Biao, but Lin told Wu, "Don't make self-criticism! You did nothing wrong. I'm the one who spoke, and I take responsibility for any error." He added, "People like us are born soldiers. We know how to fight, but we can't beat them in civilian matters. I shouldn't have given that speech."[56]

On the afternoon of August 27, Chen Boda arranged for Wu, Qiu, and Li Zuopeng to come to his quarters and told them, "Chairman Mao has criticized me for joining the Military Club! He says I've betrayed the CCRSG and he wants me to admit my error to Jiang Qing and Kang Sheng and obtain their forgiveness." Before they left, he said, "I committed errors. I won't be in contact with you anymore."[57]

On August 30, Huang Yongsheng arrived at Lushan on Mao's

orders, and Mao had Li Desheng return to Beijing to take Huang's place. As soon as Huang arrived, Mao called him in and asked why the military leaders were attacking the "completely unarmed" Zhang Chunqiao. He asked for Zhang to be given another three years to prove himself. Huang said, "I took part in the Autumn Uprising under the Chairman's leadership, and I've followed the Chairman through hails of bullets for decades, always supporting the Chairman." Mao urged Huang to unite with others in executing the Ninth Party Congress line and carrying the Cultural Revolution on to the end.[58] Wu Faxian recalls Lin Biao also telling him that Mao had asked for Zhang to be given more time to prove himself.[59]

When Huang Yongsheng returned to his quarters late that night, he, Wu, Li, and Qiu talked until 4:00 a.m., with Ye Qun joining them. They reached an agreement on several principles: They would make self-criticism without implicating each other, Lin Biao, or Huang Yongsheng, nor would they expose Chen Boda or Wang Dongxing, and they would deny any contact between Lushan and Beijing. Wu Faxian said, "Premier Zhou wants me to make self-criticism. I'm the deputy group leader, so I'll take responsibility in my self-criticism and protect Vice-Chairman Lin." All of them agreed with Wu's suggestion.[60] Huang Yongsheng urged everyone not to admit to a conspiracy.[61]

After talking with individual Politburo members from August 25 to 31, Mao decided to first take action against Chen Boda. On August 31, he wrote the following words in the margin of *Quotations of Engels, Lenin, and Chairman Mao on Genius*:

> Comrade Chen Boda produced this material and deceived quite a few comrades. First, there's nothing by Marx in here. Second, there's only one sentence by Engels, and *The Eighteenth Brumaire of Louis Bonaparte* is not one of Marx's major works. Third, there are five quotes by Lenin, of which the fifth says it is necessary to have a leader who has been tested, undergone special training and long-term education, and who can work well with others, four conditions. Very few comrades in the Central Committee, not to mention others, meet all these conditions. For example, I've worked for more than thirty years with this great theoretical genius, Chen Boda, and on many major

issues we haven't cooperated at all, not to mention cooperated
well. If we take the three Lushan Conferences as an example,
at the first, he went over to Peng Dehuai; at the second . . . he
left after a few days, and I don't know why or where he ran off
to. This time he has cooperated very well, adopting a surprise
attack and stirring up trouble . . . Finally, my words will certainly not help him much, because I say that social practice is
more important than genius. I've exchanged views with Comrade Lin Biao, and we both believe that on this question over
which historians and philosophers have argued nonstop . . . we
can only take the position of Marxism-Leninism, and absolutely
cannot go along with Chen Boda's rumors and sophistry . . . I
hope that comrades will take the same attitude and unite and
fight for even greater victories, and not claim to understand
Marx or be taken in by those who understand nothing about
Marx.[62]

Zhou Enlai said that Mao thought this over for three days before
writing it.[63] On September 1, Zhou passed the text to Lin Biao, who
said he agreed with it. Zhou made a few edits and then had it printed
and sent to Chen Boda.[64]

Chen Boda was one of the CCP's early revolutionaries, joining the
party at its most perilous moment, during Chiang Kai-shek's purge of
Communists from the Kuomintang in 1927. In that year, the CCP sent
Chen to the Soviet Union to study, and soon after he returned to China
in 1930, he became propaganda head for the CCP's North China Bureau. From 1934 onward, he joined Ai Siqi and others in launching the
New Enlightenment Movement, a Marxist take on the "science and
democracy" concept of the May Fourth Movement. Chen Boda arrived
in Yan'an in 1937 and began working as Mao's de facto political secretary in 1939, making an important contribution to establishing Mao's
theoretical system. In April 1948, Chen called Mao out of his quarters
just before they were destroyed by Kuomintang bombers, thereby saving
Mao's life. Yet Mao was willing to deny Chen any merit in the past or
present, while still claiming shared views with Lin Biao despite all
evidence to the contrary. Mao knew very well that Lin Biao had
teamed up with Chen Boda, but he dealt with them separately,

stabilizing Lin Biao and the military first while tossing out the "unarmed" Chen Boda for a harsh attack. Mao likewise shielded Wang Dongxing, believing that Wang was loyal to him and not to the Lin Biao clique. Mao would never have imagined that six years later, Wang Dongxing would be one of the main people responsible for arresting Jiang Qing.

Zhou Enlai knew very well that this whole controversy had been stirred up by Lin Biao's speech and that Chen Boda was just a scapegoat, but he still went along with Mao by advising Wu Faxian to make self-criticism and say that he had "misunderstood" Lin Biao's speech.[65] In return, Zhou protected Wu Faxian from criticism when the plenum turned toward denouncing Chen Boda.[66]

After several days of unusual silence from Ye Qun, Lin Biao's secretary, Zhang Yunsheng, received a phone call from Lin Liguo saying, "The director stirred up trouble and provoked a major disturbance. Chen Boda took the lead in jumping out, and the Chairman grabbed him, and he's been denounced. The director and Li, Wu, and Qiu have all made self-criticism at the conference. Damn! They're blaming the director for everything. Deep down I'm happy that the director got in a car wreck, but the price is too damned high."[67] Ye Qun's son Lin Liguo and daughter Lin Liheng both referred to her as the "director," and neither was on good terms with her.

At an enlarged Politburo Standing Committee meeting in his lodgings on September 4, Mao said that Chen Boda was a Trotskyite, a traitor,[68] and a Kuomintang agent who had always followed Wang Ming, but added, "We still have to look further at Chen Boda. If there are no political or historical problems, we can let him be a Central Committee member." At Ye Jianying's insistence, a special investigation group composed of Zhou Enlai, Kang Sheng, and Li Desheng entrusted Ye Jianying with going to Fujian to look into Chen Boda's historical problems.[69] After the Lushan Conference, Chen Boda became a political leper and his three requests for a meeting with Mao in Beijing were refused.[70] He was soon placed under house arrest, and after Lin Biao's death, he was sent to Qincheng Prison, finally completing his eighteen-year sentence at the age of eighty-five (the last few years spent on medical parole).

Chronology of Mao Zedong: 1949–1976[71] mentions that Mao spoke with Lin Biao on September 4 but doesn't divulge the content of a conversation that appears to have affected Mao and Lin's relationship.[72]

The second plenum of the Ninth Central Committee passed an amended constitution that did not include the position of state president. Chen Boda was not among the four Politburo Standing Committee members who sat on the rostrum for the closing ceremony on September 6, and Lin Biao, wearing a Sun Yat-sen suit instead of his usual military uniform, was silent and deathly pale.[72] In his closing speech, Mao observed, "Lushan wasn't leveled, and the world is still turning as before." He put an emphasis on "unity built on the foundation of Marxism-Leninism, and not unity without principle," and spoke of the "convergence of the two Chens."[73] The report on the conference published in *People's Daily* four days later made no mention of the controversy, noting only that "Chairman Mao and his close comrade-in-arms Vice-Chairman Lin spoke at the conference." It ended with the sentence: "Under the leadership of the party Central Committee led by Chairman Mao and with Vice-Chairman Lin as his deputy, unite and strive for even greater victory!"

On the afternoon of September 6, Ye Qun, Huang, Wu, Li, and Qiu went to see Jiang Qing. After keeping them waiting, Jiang Qing finally saw them for just half an hour. Jiang's secretary, Yang Yinlu, recalls Jiang and Ye Qun walking out of the office shoulder-to-shoulder, with their hands clasped and looking happy, and Ye Qun saying, "Comrade Jiang Qing, having a chance to see you today has really moved me. I'll never forget the help you've given me as long as I live."[74] Qiu Huizuo recalls, "Jiang Qing made us wait half an hour before coming down in her pajamas and saying, 'I've always opposed Chen Boda, and you know that. Now things are easier. In the past you didn't listen to me and made mistakes. From now on just listen to the Chairman. His and my attitude toward you is the same as before. You were just taken in by Chen Boda.'" When the five of them left Jiang Qing's quarters, they all said together, "What a prima donna! She has us twisted in knots, damn it!"[75]

Before Lin Biao left Lushan on September 7, Zhou Enlai went to see him. The two of them shook hands and faced each other without speaking. Huang, Wu, Li, and Qiu saw Lin Biao off at Jiujiang Airport and took a photo with him on the aircraft. Lin Biao said, "We didn't do anything against our conscience, so we don't need to worry about the devil knocking at the door. Eat and work as normal; at worst I'll be a second Peng Dehuai. If something comes up, report it to the Premier."[76]

Mao kept waiting for Lin Biao to make self-criticism, and it wasn't until his southern tour in August and September 1971 that he began to harshly criticize the actions of Chen Boda and the military leaders at the Lushan Conference:

> At the 1970 Lushan Conference, they mounted a surprise attack and carried out covert activities. Why didn't they dare to do it openly? That shows they had ill intentions . . . Peng Dehuai operated a Military Club and openly declared war, but they weren't even up to Peng Dehuai's standard.[77]

Lin Liguo had his own view. He told Jiang Tengjiao, Wang Weiguo, and Chen Liyun: "This was a preview and drill for a future fight—camp and field training. Both sides lined up and showed their faces, and Chen was the hero of the fight and Wu was a coward. Our side was good above and below but came apart in the middle, and lacked a good chief of staff . . . These old commanders have a low political proficiency and seldom study, so when the time came they didn't have a plan in place and didn't consider the matter from all possible angles. They can lead a military campaign but not a political campaign. The political struggle can't depend on their leadership from now on. The actual leadership power has to be in our hands."[78] This shows that the young radicals in the Lin Biao clique were ready to engage in an independent extremist movement.

22

CHEN BODA'S DENUNCIATION AND LIN BIAO'S ESCAPE ATTEMPT

The controversy at the Lushan Conference led Mao to perceive the power of the Lin Biao clique and the momentum it was building for collective action. To reverse a situation that threatened his control over the military, Mao struck out at the "unarmed" Chen Boda, launching a nationwide "criticize Chen and carry out rectification" campaign and forcing members of the Lin Biao clique to admit their error and express their complete submission. At the same time, he aimed to disband the Lin Biao clique by "mixing in sand, tossing rocks, and digging up cornerstones."

THE NORTH CHINA CONFERENCE AND REORGANIZATION OF THE BEIJING MILITARY REGION

The Lushan Conference's Bulletin No. 6 had come out of the North China subgroup, and since Mao considered the bulletin to be "counter-revolutionary," North China naturally became a focus of investigation. The rock Mao tossed was a report by the Thirty-Eighth Army, which led to the North China Conference.

The Thirty-Eighth Army's report grew out of a conflict that developed with the Hebei Provincial Military District when the Thirty-Eighth Army was transferred to Baoding Prefecture to carry out support-the-left work in early 1967. The provincial military district sided with the more stable and conservative local mass organizations, while the Thirty-Eighth Army aligned itself with the more radical faction. The Beijing Military Region took the side of the Hebei Provincial Military District in criticizing the Thirty-Eighth Army's support-the-left measures. With both of Baoding's factions enjoying military support, armed clashes proliferated.

With Mao's approval, Chen Boda went on an inspection visit in Hebei from December 1967 to January 1968 along with the Beijing Military Region's acting commander, Zheng Weishan, and political commissar, Li Xuefeng, to facilitate establishing the provincial revolutionary committee. Seeking to stabilize the situation, Chen Boda suppressed the more radical faction supported by the Thirty-Eighth Army, but after the provincial capital was moved from Baoding to Shijiazhuang in November 1968, the Beijing Military Region's new political commissar, Xie Fuzhi, put the Thirty-Eighth Army in charge of Baoding, where it suppressed all factional struggle and restored order under the grand alliance and three-in-one combination.

Chen Boda, Zheng Weishan, and Li Xuefeng were all implicated in the Bulletin No. 6 matter during the second plenum of the Ninth Central Committee at Lushan. Soon after that, on December 10, 1970, the party committee of the Thirty-Eighth Army submitted the "Report Exposing Chen Boda's Anti-Party Crimes" to the Central Military Commission Administrative Group and the Central Committee. This report accused Chen of "involving himself in the military and engaging in factional activities in a vain attempt to create chaos in the military and seize power."[1] On December 16, 1970, Mao wrote a memo on the report to Lin Biao, Zhou Enlai, and Kang Sheng, recommending that the Beijing Military Region party committee hold a meeting to discuss "why they listened to Chen Boda running around and spouting off," given that Chen had no official jurisdiction over the military region. "What reason was there for Chen Boda to become the backstage ruler of the Beijing Military Region and North China Region?" Mao demanded. No one in the Central Committee bothered to defend Chen by pointing out that his inspection visit to Hebei had been arranged by Zhou Enlai as part of the effort to establish the revolutionary committees (Zhang Chunqiao, Yao Wenyuan, and Kang Sheng had also been sent to various regions for the same purpose).[2]

On December 19, Zhou Enlai wrote a report to Mao stating that the Politburo had discussed Mao's memo and unanimously agreed to convene an enlarged meeting of the Beijing Military Region's party committee a few days later. This meeting, which at Mao's suggestion also included Li Desheng, Ji Dengkui, Huang Yongsheng, and Li Zuopeng, came to be known as the North China Conference.[3]

By this time, Mao had already expressed his intention to alter the power balance in the military. On November 13, 1970, Mao reproached Huang Yongsheng for helping to "lead the revolt at the Lushan Conference" and said that he was going to end the CMCAG's dominating power.[4] Mao was referring to Lin Biao, Huang, Wu, Li, and Qiu all coming from his former personal power base in the First Front Red Army and First Red Army Group, and becoming a power unto themselves during the Cultural Revolution when Mao needed their support. Increasingly uneasy over their influence, Mao had begun seeking out veteran cadres such as Xie Fuzhi, Xu Shiyou, Chen Xilian, Han Xianchu, and Li Desheng from the Fourth Front Red Army Group, which had been under the leadership of his old rival Zhang Guotao in the 1930s.[5] Li Desheng was commander of the Twelfth Army and chairman of the Anhui provincial revolutionary committee. After coming to Mao's attention through his handling of the Wuhu Incident,[6] Li had become an alternate Politburo member during the Ninth Party Congress and had been appointed director of the PLA's General Political Department on April 30, 1970. On December 20, Mao called Li back from an inspection tour in Anhui and appointed him commander of the Beijing Military Region[7] in a move he referred to as "digging up cornerstones." Combined with "tossing rocks" in the form of his opinions on Chen Boda's *Quotations of Engels, Lenin, and Chairman Mao on Genius* and his memo on the Thirty-Eighth Army's report, Mao also "mixed sand" into the CMCAG, telling its members, "Your CMCAG is like clay that's hardened into a sheet; it's become airtight and needs some sand mixed in. Mixing in Li Desheng alone doesn't seem to be enough. I'm also sending you a civilian official, my old friend Ji Dengkui. How about that? Will you welcome him?"[8]

The North China Conference, which began on December 22, was attended by leaders of the Beijing Military region, various provincial military districts, the Beijing Garrison Command, the Tianjin

Garrison Command, and various departments in northern China. It started with the transmission of Mao's memo and studying the Thirty-Eighth Army's report. Apart from exposure and denunciation of Chen Boda, Li Xuefeng and Zheng Weishan also carried out self-criticism. Mao felt this conference wasn't tough enough on Chen Boda, and the concurrent CMC symposium also drew his criticism for "going on for a month without actually criticizing Chen,"[9] so those attending the CMC symposium also began attending the North China Conference on January 9, 1971, with Zhou Enlai presiding.

In a speech before the closing ceremony of the North China Conference on January 24, 1971,[10] Zhou Enlai listed Chen Boda's "criminal acts," and accused Li Xuefeng and Zheng Weishan of colluding with Chen against the Ninth Party Congress's line and "amplifying his influence" to "form an independent kingdom." He announced a new lineup in the Beijing Military Region: Li Decheng would become commander and first party secretary, with Xie Fuzhi as first political commissar and second secretary, and Ji Dengkui as second political commissar and third secretary. By this time, Xie Fuzhi was gravely ill, and he died in March 1972. After Lin Biao's plane crash on September 13, 1971, Li Xuefeng was expelled from the party, and he and Zheng Weishan were sent to labor in the countryside in Anhui. Many others were implicated along with them.

DENOUNCING CHEN, MAO WAITS FOR LIN BIAO'S SELF-CRITICISM

After the Lushan Conference, Lin Biao went straight to Beidaihe and didn't return to Beijing until the end of September 1970 for National Day festivities. Mao and Lin Biao both attended the grand celebration marking the twenty-first anniversary of the People's Republic of China on October 1, and Lin Biao, to all appearances still Mao's successor and close comrade-in-arms, gave a speech.

After the celebration, the campaign to "criticize Chen and carry out rectification" was launched. On November 16, the CCP Central Committee issued "Instructions Regarding Transmitting Chen Boda's Anti-Party Problem," first to the prefectural and military company level, with distribution gradually expanding from there. The Central Committee's "Materials on the Criminal Acts of the Anti-Party Element Chen Boda," issued on January 26, 1971, was followed by a series of long and tedious denunciations in the newspapers. For ordinary party members and cadres, this campaign involved little more than study and meetings, but at the upper level, Mao and Lin Biao were engaged in a secret battle.

Wu Faxian recalls that after Lin Biao and Ye Qun returned to Beijing for the 1970 National Day celebrations, Mao had Lin Biao come to his quarters and told him of plans that included replacing Wu Faxian as air force commander. Lin made an unsuccessful attempt to protect Wu and then advised him to carry out self-criticism, but when Mao refused three requests by Wu to see him, Lin said, "There's nothing to be done."[11]

Wu Faxian's self-criticism was delivered to Mao on September 29, 1970. On October 14, Mao wrote comments about "the lack of spirit of being just and honorable" and observed, "One has to dare to go against the tide; that's a principle of Marxism-Leninism. At the Lushan Conference, my attitude was one of going against the tide."[12] He also noted a willingness to "read the views of the other orators," meaning that he wanted Huang, Ye, Li, and Qiu to also carry out self-criticism.

On October 13, Ye Qun wrote a letter to Mao criticizing her own errors at the Lushan Conference. Mao underlined many of her phrases and wrote harsh comments,[13] in particular observing, "Whether one's ideological and political line is correct or not decides everything," and accusing her of following Chen Boda's line in opposition to the line of the Ninth Party Congress. At the end of Ye Qun's letter, Mao wrote a memo stating, "Doesn't mention the Ninth Party Congress or the Party Constitution. And doesn't listen to me. As soon as Chen Boda boasts, she shows interest. Many comrades in the CMCAG are like that." As with Wu Faxian's self-criticism, Mao sent Ye Qun's self-criticism with his comments to Lin Biao, Zhou Enlai, Kang Sheng, and other leaders to read. Comparing the comments with those on Wu Faxian's self-criticism, Huang, Wu, Li, and Qiu felt that "Mao's criticism of Ye Qun was even harsher. Criticizing Ye Qun is directly related to Lin Biao, but he gave Lin Biao some face and didn't refer to him by name."[14]

After the Ninth Party Congress, the Central Cultural Revolution Small Group (CCRSG) ceased functioning, and although its key members joined the Politburo, they held no military or government positions. Mao engineered the establishment of a Central Organization and Propaganda Group (COPG) under the direct leadership of the Politburo on November 6, 1970. The work units under its oversight included the Central Committee Organization Department, Central Party School, *People's Daily*, the Xinhua News Agency, *Red Flag* magazine, the Central Broadcasting Enterprise Bureau, *Guangming Daily*, the Central Compilation and Translation Bureau, central-level organs relating to workers, youths, and women, and so on. The chairman of the group was Kang Sheng, and its other members were Jiang Qing, Zhang Chunqiao, Yao Wenyuan, Ji Dengkui, and Li Desheng.[15] Kang Sheng was ill, and Li Desheng was later transferred to the Shenyang Military Region, so the COPG was controlled by Jiang Qing and her close associates, but in fact it was under Mao's direct control and became a rival organization to the CMCAG.

Mao relentlessly pursued what he considered a line struggle while hoping that Lin Biao would voluntarily carry out self-criticism and resolve the matter peacefully. During the meeting to criticize Chen and carry out rectification in June 1971, Lin Biao asked Jiang Qing to take a photo of him. In the photo, a hatless Lin Biao is reading a copy of Mao's works. Jiang Qing gave this photo the title "Diligence," and using the pseudonym Junling (meaning "lofty range"), she had it published in the July–August 1971 combined issue of *PLA Pictorial* and *People's Pictorial*. This last close-up photo of Lin Biao was taken just three months before the September 13 Incident.

With the passing of the New Year in 1971, Lin Biao directed his office staffer Li Genqing to leave a note on Ye Qun's bedroom wall that said, "In the final analysis, not all that bad." It appears that he was still feeling secure and that he wanted to comfort Ye Qun, who was very anxious at the time.[16]

On February 19, 1971, Mao wrote a memo on the campaign against Chen Boda: "Please tell comrades in all places that . . . the emphasis is on denouncing Chen and only then carrying out rectification." This heightened the exposure and criticism of people and matters connected with Chen Boda.

On March 21, Huang Yongsheng, Li Zuopeng, and Qiu Huizuo wrote self-criticisms, and then on Mao's instructions carried out self-criticism along with Wu Faxian and Ye Qun at a reporting meeting on the campaign against Chen. Mao was satisfied, and in a March 24 memo wrote, "Now it's a question of putting these declarations into practice."[17] That afternoon, he had Zhou Enlai, Kang Sheng, Huang, Wu, Li, Qiu, Ji Dengkui, Li Desheng, and Wang Dongxing come in to discuss the issue of denouncing Chen and carrying out rectification. He approved the decision by Zhou and others to hold a reporting meeting, required Wu Faxian and Ye Qun to write self-criticisms again, and asked Zhou Enlai to send Huang's, Li's, and Qiu's written self-criticisms and Mao's memo to Lin Biao for his review. Mao told all but Kang Sheng to go to Beidaihe and report to Lin Biao after Lin had read the self-criticisms.[18]

Mao hoped that sending Zhou Enlai and the others to Beidaihe would compel Lin Biao to write a self-criticism, Mao's usual method for keeping his subordinates under control. Submitting self-criticism or confessions was a kind of surrender, and once put on record, the old offenses could be dredged up again if the offender erred in the future. It was even more important for the commander in chief of the Lin Biao clique to surrender in this way, because it would allow Mao to take the initiative to resolve the Lin Biao problem. If the self-criticism expressed sincere submission, Mao would not need to change his successor; otherwise, it would provide a basis for replacing Lin Biao.

On March 29, 1971, Zhao Enlai and the others took Zhou's chartered train to Beidaihe and met with Lin Biao on March 30 and 31. Lin had turned the heat on in his quarters, and his face was chalky and expressionless. Zhou reported that the Central Committee was preparing to hold a reporting meeting on the campaign to denounce Chen during the next month, which would also provide an opportunity to resolve the Lushan Conference issue. Zhou said tactfully that the Chairman recommended that Vice-Chairman Lin attend the reporting meeting and say a few words. Lin Biao said that he "completely endorsed" the instructions and arrangements Mao had issued since the Lushan Conference; was "very happy" with the self-criticisms of Huang, Li, and Qiu; and wanted Wu Faxian and Ye Qun to "carry out another written self-criticism." He had "absolutely never imagined" that the Chen Boda problem was so serious, and ferreting out Chen was a "very great victory." He "completely agreed" with the Central Committee holding the reporting meeting, but he didn't say he would attend and expressed no intention to carry out self-criticism.[19]

When Zhou Enlai and the others reported to Mao on their trip to Beidaihe on April 1, Mao harshly criticized Huang, Wu, Li, and Qiu to their faces, saying, "You're already at the edge of the precipice. It's just a question of whether you'll jump, be pushed in, or be pulled back. Whether or not you can be pulled back is completely up to you!"[20] Mao was actually referring to Lin Biao.

The CMCAG members consistently failed to have their self-criticisms accepted, and losing faith in Mao's promise that the problems at Lushan would go no further, they suggested to Ye Qun that Lin Biao should carry out a small amount of self-criticism. Three days later, Ye communicated Lin Biao's views, as recalled by Qiu Huizuo:

> (1) Self-criticism is part of daily life in our party, but I'm not to blame in any way for the Lushan problem. Chairman Mao agreed to the speech I gave at the opening ceremony and said, "Don't speak under orders; it's only good if you speak your own mind." I spoke in that spirit. (2) They vainly hope to get something out of our self-criticisms, but that's impossible. At Lushan a lot of people were dragged into quarrels for several days over the "genius theory" and the position of state president. The first of those two issues is old and toothless. I did put forward the view insisting on genius, but don't I have the right to a personal opinion? (3) The Lushan problem is not one that will end with self-criticism.[21]

Lin anticipated trouble from Mao over his refusal to make a self-criticism. One day, Ye Qun read out Mao's remarks on a document and then flapped it in front of Lin Biao's face, saying, "Look at this—isn't this aimed at you?" Lin Biao roared at Ye Qun, "Don't come here bothering me! Get out! I want to rest!" Lin Biao was no longer as calm as he'd been at the beginning of the year, and his nerves were on edge.[22]

The reporting meeting for the campaign to denounce Chen and carry out rectification began on April 15, 1971, with ninety-nine leading military and government cadres in attendance. Mao particularly ordered Chen Yi, Xu Xiangqian, and Nie Rongzhen to attend. Huang Yongsheng and Wu Faxian gave self-critical speeches that were then discussed during the first seven days. The last days were devoted to exposing and criticizing Chen Boda and exchanging experience on the campaign in the various localities.

On April 18, Mao ordered that the meeting be extended, continuing to wait for Lin Biao to make his attitude known. At first Lin Biao remained at Beidaihe, even as Zhou Enlai had Huang Yongsheng telephone Ye Qun daily, but when it came out that Qiu Huizuo had gone to the Northeast subgroup to share information and agitate during the Lushan Conference, Lin Biao became worried about the consequences of this information and rushed back to Beijing on April 19. While delivering the meeting papers and Mao's related instructions, Zhou Enlai asked Lin to speak at the meeting, but Lin said he would "absolutely not speak" and had no intention of attending the meeting.[23] Zhou still hoped to smooth things over, and on April 24, he stated, "The meeting hopes that the Chairman and Vice-Chairman Lin can see everyone once, and if they can say a few words, so much the better." With Lin refusing to attend the meeting, how could Mao condescend to do so? He said, "I'm staying in for the next few days."[24]

With both lead actors refusing to appear, Zhou Enlai had to put on a one-man show. On April 29, 1971, Zhou gave a summing-up speech on behalf of the Politburo and in line with Mao's tone. Still trying to smooth things over, he distinguished the "directional and line errors of the five comrades of the CMCAG" from "the heinous crimes of the Kuomintang anti-communist element, Trotskyite, traitor, and secret agent Chen Boda in attempting to usurp the power of the party," and said that if they were genuinely willing to mend their ways, they would be treated with welcome and assistance.[25]

Soon after that came the May 1 International Labor Day, celebrated with the usual fireworks at Tiananmen Square. Lin Biao was determined to stay home but finally gave in to Zhou Enlai's urging and the tearful entreaties of Ye Qun, who knelt at his feet and said, "Please go. If you don't, our whole family will die!"[26] The Xinhua photojournalist Du Xiuxian, who was present at the Tiananmen gate tower that night, recalls what happened:

Mao Zedong took the lead in going to the terrace of the gate tower. He sat on the eastern side of the round table in the middle, and sitting close by him was Prince Sihanouk, and Dong Biwu sat to the right of Sihanouk. Lin Biao sat there quietly. Mao Zedong lifted his chin slightly and cast a glance at Lin Biao across from him, then turned to speak to Sihanouk as if he'd seen nothing. In full view of others, Lin Biao wore a listless expression and didn't say a word. He didn't shake hands with Mao Zedong, who was so close by, and didn't even look at him. In the May weather Lin Biao was wearing an army overcoat; his brow was creased, his hands were in his sleeves, and he looked bored and lonely . . . Although Lin Biao didn't look straight at anyone, he studied everything around him. Whenever Mao moved slightly off to the side, his body would react with an almost imperceptible shudder. He was ready to respond to Mao Zedong at any moment, but Mao Zedong showed absolutely no intention of talking to him or greeting him, and didn't even seem willing to look straight at him. Lin Biao's bushy eyebrows trembled several times, and his gloomy eyes suddenly lit up with aggressive anger. Then Dong Biwu was drawn into a conversation with Mao, and he was left on his own. In that split second, he suddenly stood up, turned, and disregarding everyone he left the room.[27]

While steadfastly refusing to admit wrongdoing, Lin Biao wrote a letter to Mao proposing conditions. After the September 13 Incident, Beijing Garrison commander Wu Zhong discovered this unsent letter while searching Lin Biao's quarters in Maojiawan. The full text of the letter, dated May 23, 1971, reported Lin's suggestions regarding "unity within the party and the safety of personnel at the equivalent level of Politburo member or above," which he said he'd discussed with Zhou Enlai. Lin observed the need to consolidate the "great victory" of the Cultural Revolution and "implement the Ninth Party Congress's line of unity," and described the campaign to denounce Chen Boda as "necessary and correct, because Chen Boda is a counterrevolutionary and a great scoundrel; he used the opportunity of the Lushan Conference to create chaos, and for that reason it is necessary to purge his influence." He called for specific measures to "guard against ideologically muddled persons and adventurers adopting unimaginably risky behavior that sabotages the party's unity and leads to a breakdown in order resulting in undesirable repercussions domestically and abroad."

Lin Biao then went on to outline a policy under which top military leaders who were current or alternate Politburo members would not be arrested, imprisoned, killed, or dismissed for a period of ten years, but would be dealt with through internal criticism, and those with long-term illnesses would be allowed to retire. Violation of this policy should be harshly punished. Lin also recommended defending the capital with independent regiments from East China, North China, and Shandong, and to transfer the Thirty-Eighth Army from North China and replace it with troops from the Second, Third, or First Field Army. He concluded, "I would very much like to talk with the Chairman. If the Chairman has time at any time, please arrange to see me."

Wu Zhong says that after writing the letter, Lin Biao set it aside for three days and considered not sending it, and that he consulted Zhou Enlai, who asked him, "Is this necessary?"[28] Li Genqing recalls that Lin Biao dictated this letter to his secretary Yu Yunshen, who had Li make a clean copy and then gave it to Lin Biao to sign. The letter was never handed back to Li to send through confidential channels.[29]

How are we to interpret this letter that was never sent? Was it because Lin Biao's health was poor and he was exhausted and looking for a way to step down, given that the CCP line struggle provided no mechanism for senior leaders to retire or retreat? If Lin Biao wanted to step down, he still needed to protect his supporters, which was why he proposed exempting senior military cadres from punishment for ten years. Lin Biao's suggestion of transferring the Thirty-Eighth Army, a unit that he had commanded, away from Beijing was a way of expressing to Mao that he had "disarmed" himself and that Mao could relax.

Zhou probably objected to sending the letter to Mao because he anticipated a negative reaction and feared that Mao would suspect him of colluding with Lin.

On June 3, 1971, Mao told Lin Biao to accompany him in receiving the general secretary of the Communist Party of Romania, Nicolae

Ceaușescu. At first Lin said he was suffering from cold sweats and couldn't go, but he finally went after Ye Qun's entreaties. Even so, Lin withdrew right after the exchange of conventional greetings and sat alone in a corner of the main hall, waiting for the meeting to end.[30] This was the last encounter between the two "close comrades-in-arms," Mao and Lin.

On the night of July 9, 1971, Zhou Enlai, Xiong Xianghui, and others went to Mao's quarters to report on their talks with the U.S. national security adviser Henry Kissinger. Xiong had long been engaged in undercover intelligence work at the side of Hu Zongnan and at this point was deputy director of the Second Department of the PLA's General Staff Headquarters. Ignoring this major event in Sino-American relations, Mao asked Xiong whether Huang Yongsheng had talked about "how he and his CMCAG made mischief during the Lushan Conference" and whether Xiong had read the self-criticism of the "five senior generals." When Xiong pled ignorance (although the self-criticisms should have been issued to officers at his level), Mao slapped the tea table and roared, "Their self-criticisms were fake! The Lushan matter isn't finished and hasn't been resolved at all. Someone is up to something. They have a secret backer." Zhou Enlai tried to smooth things over by pointing out errors he himself had made in the past, but Mao said, "That was different. You made mistakes out in the open, but Huang Yongsheng and the others are plotting and causing division as a covert opposition faction. Engaging in conspiracy and causing division is engaging in revisionism."[31] Mao was trying to get Zhou Enlai to take his side in the Lin Biao matter.

In early July, Lin Biao and Ye Qun left Beijing for Beidaihe, but Ye Qun returned to Beijing on August 3 for a physical examination for possible breast cancer. After being given a clean bill of health, Ye Qun telephoned Mao's secretary on August 6 to report her presence in Beijing and her intention to return to Beidaihe very soon. She asked if Mao had any instructions for her, the usual way of requesting to see Mao. Two days passed with no word, and Ye Qun returned to Beidaihe on August 9.[32] While in Beijing she had been visited by Huang, Wu, Li, and Qiu at Maojiawan.

MAO TARGETS LIN BIAO WHILE TOURING THE SOUTH

In the campaign to denounce Chen and carry out rectification, Mao exempted Lin Biao and protected him in hopes that Lin Biao would carry out profound self-criticism and demonstrate thorough submission. The self-criticisms of the CMCAG members didn't touch on Lin Biao, and the campaign against Chen Boda didn't trace Chen's wrongdoings back to Lin Biao. To Mao's great disappointment, Lin had absolutely no intention of admitting wrongdoing, so Mao scheduled a party process to resolve the problem. A Politburo meeting on August 12 communicated Mao's suggestion to hold the third plenum of the Ninth Central Committee before National Day, and then the Fourth National People's Congress. A preparatory committee established for this purpose was headed by Lin Biao opponent Zhang Chunqiao and excluded members of the Lin Biao clique.

While Zhou Enlai prepared for the third plenum and the NPC, Mao took a chartered train out of Beijing on the afternoon of August 15, 1971, for a secret and spur-of-the-moment tour of the south. Mao was accompanied by a squadron of more than a hundred men from the Central Guard Regiment under Zhang Yaoci, all armed with handguns, rifles, and machine guns.[33] Wu Faxian later wrote, "He toured the south to prepare to thoroughly take us down in the eyes of the organization and public opinion."[34]

Mao's trip to the south was mainly to unite the thinking of leading cadres and prevent them from following Lin Biao during the third plenum. Mao stayed in Wuhan from August 16 to 27, in Changsha from August 27 to 31, in Nanchang from August 31 to September 2, and in Hangzhou from September 3 to 10, followed by a brief stop in Shanghai before his train headed north and reached Beijing's Fengtai Station early in the afternoon on September 12. Mao met with military and provincial government leaders at each stop,[35] admonishing them to engage in Marxism and not revisionism and reminding them, "Whether one's ideological and political line is correct or not decides everything." He urged them to stay united and to avoid schemes and intrigues.

Mao said, "There have been ten major line struggles in our party's fifty-year history. In these ten line struggles, some wanted to split our party but didn't succeed . . . Based on history, there's hope for our party." He counted the conflict during the 1970 Lushan Conference as one of these line struggles: "The program was to have a state president, to promote a 'genius' theory, and to oppose the line of the Ninth Party Congress . . . Someone was in a hurry to become state president, and wanted to split the party in their rush to seize power." Mao said that the 1970 Lushan Conference was "a fight between two headquarters" like previous fights with Peng Dehuai and Liu Shaoqi.

Mao put Lin Biao in the league of "leading persons" in history who had committed line errors and who were incapable of change, like Chen Duxiu, Li Lisan, Wang Ming, and Gao Gang. He said, "The Lushan matter isn't finished and hasn't been resolved . . . I don't believe our army will revolt; I don't believe that Huang Yongsheng can command the Army to revolt!" By referring to Huang Yongsheng, he actually meant Lin Biao. In Changsha, he told the leaders of the Guangzhou Military Region, Liu Xingyuan and Ding Sheng, "You have such a deep relationship with Huang Yongsheng, what are you going to do if he's overthrown?"

The more Mao talked with people, the harsher his comments became. He went from attacking Lin Biao by innuendo to openly naming him and increasingly elaborated on the seriousness of the problem. Over the course of his trip, Mao constantly sent records of his conversations with party and government leaders to Zhou Enlai so that Zhou could keep up with the direction he was taking. Zhou knew that a showdown between Mao and Lin was unavoidable, and that Lin was no match for Mao. After studying and weighing the situation, he shifted from trying to smooth things over to firmly taking Mao's side, even though he and Lin Biao had held the same views on China's direction after the Ninth Party Congress. Gao Wenqian, who has specifically studied Zhou Enlai, says that Zhou never took the side of the loser.[36]

From the end of August until early September, Wu Faxian telephoned Ye Qun several times to report on Mao's movements in Wuhan, Changsha, and Nanchang. Since he was in charge of air traffic, Wu could track Mao's location by the officials who flew to see him, but he didn't know what they discussed. Mao repeatedly told Liu Feng to keep the content of their conversations strictly confidential, especially from Beijing. Meanwhile, with Mao's permission, Liu Xingyuan briefed cadres at the division level and above in the Guangzhou Military Region on the main content of Mao's remarks during a cadre conference that Liu and Ding Sheng held on September 5. The air force chief of staff for the Guangzhou Military Region, Gu Tongzhou, stealthily took notes on the inside of a cigarette packet, and that night he discussed Liu's remarks over the telephone with Yu Xinye (who, like Zhou Yuchi, was a secretary in the general office of the air force party committee) but without mentioning comments directly related to Lin Biao. Around this time, Li Zuopeng accompanied a North Korean military delegation to Wuhan, where Liu Feng told him some of the things Mao had said, and Li discussed the matter with Huang Yongsheng after returning to Beijing on September 6. That night, Huang telephoned Ye Qun and told her what he'd heard. Early in the morning on September 6, Zhou Yuchi telephoned Lin Liguo, and that afternoon he flew by helicopter to Beidaihe with a fifteen-page telephone record.[37] On Lin Liguo's instructions, Gu Tongzhou put together a fifty-page document and had his wife take it to Beijing on a chartered flight on the afternoon of September 9.[38]

THE "FLOTILLA'S" ARMCHAIR STRATEGIST

As Mao pressed in on the Lin Biao clique, Lin himself hibernated at home, passive in all but his refusal to acknowledge error. Informed sources say that after Lin learned what Mao had been saying on his southern tour, his first thought was to sit tight and wait. Early in the afternoon on September 11, office staff heard Lin Biao tell Ye Qun, "In any case, I don't have long to live. If I'm going to die, I'll die here. I'll either go to prison or die like a hero."[39] Lin may have been making the best choice available to him at the time, given that he was no match for Mao. Banking on his meritorious service to the regime, he felt that if he remained passive, he'd simply be denounced and could retire on medical grounds without his family being dragged into it.

His wife, Ye Qun, and son, Li Liguo, were unwilling to admit defeat, however. Lin Liguo, young and brash, told his elder sister, Lin

Liheng, "Rather than sit and wait for death, it would be better to take the initiative to launch an attack—there could still be hope!"[40] Lin Liheng opposed his taking the risk.

Ye Qun had served as a section chief at Yan'an's Chinese Women's University and married Lin Biao after he'd returned from the Soviet Union in 1942. Outgoing, well read, and canny, Ye Qun increasingly gained Lin Biao's trust and reliance, and became as dominant in the CMCAG as Jiang Qing was in the CCRSG. Apart from representing Lin at Politburo meetings and controlling his personal communications, she was also Lin's conduit to his trusted followers.

Lin Liguo had come into his own in the air force. Attributing the defeat at the Lushan Conference to the impotence of the old soldiers, he wanted to push them aside and make a fresh start. In 1968, before becoming deputy director of the war department, Lin Liguo had formed an "investigation and research group" with Wang Fei and Zhou Yuchi. It was the embryo of what came to be jokingly referred to within the air force party committee as the "United Flotilla," and which eventually became the core of a "counterrevolutionary organization" (after the September 13 Incident, twenty-five air force personnel were sent to Qincheng Prison as alleged members of Lin Liguo's "flotilla"). As Lin Biao became increasingly imperiled, Lin Liguo resolved to go all-out.

In Shanghai on March 21, 1971, Lin Liguo, Zhou Yuchi, Yu Xinye, and Li Weixin discussed Lin Biao's succession issue and felt there were three possibilities: a peaceful transition, someone else seizing power, or Lin himself seizing power ahead of schedule. Their preference was for Lin to seize power, and there were two ways to bring this about: One was to do away with Zhang Chunqiao and his coterie while preserving Lin Biao's status and maintaining the peaceful transition; the other was to assassinate B-52 (their code name for Mao), but given the target's immense prestige, turmoil was sure to result, so that could be only a last resort. They decided to focus their efforts on a peaceful transition while preparing for an armed insurrection. They referred to their coup d'état as Project 571 (which in Mandarin sounded similar to "armed insurrection").[41]

From March 22 to 24, 1971, Lin Liguo and the others outlined Project 571, which, as recorded in Yu Xinye's notebook, was apparently still a work in progress. After the September 13 Incident, this notebook was found in one of their Beijing strongholds. Huang Yongsheng, Wu Faxian, Li Zuopeng, and Qiu Huizuo never read this outline, and it is not known if Lin Biao or Ye Qun ever did. The outline's designation of Huang, Wu, Li, and Qiu's CMCAG as a "borrowed force" and not an "essential force" shows that the CMCAG members were not participants in the armed insurrection. The Project 571 outline had nine parts: feasibility, necessity, basic conditions, the opportune moment, resources, slogans and guiding principles, main points of implementation, tactics and strategies, and confidentiality and discipline.

The outline noted the instability of the political situation following the Lushan Conference, as well as increasing social instability attributed to China's state apparatus becoming "a meat grinder of mutual slaughter and strife" under a "modern-day Qin Shihuang." It defined Chinese socialism as essentially "fascism."

The outline analyzed the conditions beneficial to an armed insurrection: "The dictators are increasingly losing popular support," and "there is increasing unspoken resentment among cadres who have been rejected and attacked in internal party struggle and during the Cultural Revolution." "The peasants lack food and clothing," and "sending educated youth up the mountains and down to the countryside is just reform through labor in disguised form." "Government cadres are being retrenched, and being sent to a May 7 cadre school is tantamount to losing one's job." "Workers (especially young workers) are seeing their wages frozen, which is just disguised exploitation." "Red Guards were first duped, used, and treated as cannon fodder, and then suppressed and treated as scapegoats." Of Mao, the outline noted, "He is paranoid, sadistic . . . Once he purges someone, he won't quit until the person is doomed; when you get on his wrong side, it's for keeps, and all blame for what goes wrong is shifted onto others . . . People around him fall from power like figures on a shadow lantern, but in fact they're all his scapegoats!"

Project 571 raised the slogans: "Down with the modern Qin Shihuang—B-52!" "Topple the feudal dynasty under a socialist signboard!" and "Establish a socialist state that genuinely belongs to the proletariat and the working people!" To achieve their goal, the conspirators were prepared to use all available tactics: "poison gas, bacterial warfare, explosions, 543 [the code name for a kind of weapon], traffic accidents, murder, kidnapping, and urban guerrilla warfare squads."

Some content of the Project 571 outline said what many people were thinking but didn't dare express. Demonstrating the drive of the young military men, as well as a rather horrifying fascist mentality, this document was a profound criticism of social reality and was the strongest voice assailing the modern Qin Shihuang dictatorship.

After learning the content of Mao's remarks during his southern tour, the members of the flotilla intensified their planning. According to official documents issued after his downfall, Lin Biao personally wrote an order on September 8: "Hoping that all will be done according to the orders communicated by comrades Liguo and Yuchi." At 9:48 p.m. on September 8, Lin Liguo, Liu Peifeng, and others returned to Beijing from Beidaihe with the intention of assassinating Mao.

From late at night on the eighth to the early hours of the ninth, Lin Liguo called meetings of the flotilla at the Air Force Academy and Xijiao Airport. Those who attended included Zhou Yuchi and Jiang Tengjiao. At the meeting they discussed murdering Mao by attacking his train with flamethrowers, rocket launchers, or an antiaircraft gun; ambushing his car on the way to a meeting; or carrying out a bombing or arson to distract troops while the assassination was carried out. Each of these methods was ruled out because of insurmountable difficulties in execution. As a last resort, they called in Guan Guanglie, who had worked in Lin Biao's office and was then political commissar of the Luoyang Infantry Division. After Guan arrived in Beijing by express train on the night of September 10, Zhou Yuchi let him read Lin Biao's "handwritten order" (different from the one discovered at the site where the helicopter was forced down) and proposed deploying two brigades to attack Diaoyutai and sending a flame-throwing company to Shanghai. Guan Guanglie said, "Even one platoon would be impossible, much less a company. No individual officer can transfer troops unless under orders from the CMC. Furthermore, a lot of paperwork is required, reporting it upward level by level, as well as applying for railway carriages from the military transport allocation to carry the troops."[42] Lin Liguo said, "Can we pass something off as a

CMC command?" "The call signal frequency is different, and there's a password that makes it even more difficult." It really did seem impossible, so Lin Liguo decided not to launch the operation for the time being.

At 7:30 p.m. on September 12, Lin Liguo took Trident aircraft 256 to Shanhaiguan, preparing to fly straight to Guangzhou the next day. Before leaving, he called Wang Fei, Jiang Tengjiao, Yu Xinye, and Li Weixin to the Air Force Academy. Zhou Yuchi told them to go to Guangzhou, where Lin Biao would create a separatist regime by force of arms after flying down from Beidaihe the next morning. Huang, Wu, Li, and Qiu would be ordered in Lin Biao's name to fly down from Beijing, and the Shanghai group would be flown to Guangzhou in an Ilyushin Il-18 aircraft. Zhou Yuchi and the others had no idea that Zhou Enlai had already taken control of air traffic and that fleeing to Guangzhou was out of the question.

The armed uprising that Lin Liguo and the others devised in secret was an impractical daydream, and the Project 571 outline just armchair strategizing that was never carried out. The detailed investigations after the September 13 Incident turned up no material evidence of the operation. If Lin Biao had taken part in the plot, his abilities and his influence in the military might have led to a different outcome, with Mao away from Beijing and only Zhou Enlai in charge. But if the powerful Lin Biao had wanted to carry out a coup d'état, why would Lin Liguo's totally impractical methods be necessary?

Some writers attempting to prove that the Lin Biao clique engaged in a counterrevolutionary coup d'état have sensationally described how Mao sharp-wittedly evaded Lin Liguo's assassination attempt. Some of the details originated with Wang Dongxing, highlighting his own role in Mao's escape. Having said that, given his intensely antagonistic relationship with Lin Biao's powerful military clique, the ever-vigilant Mao would certainly have taken precautions.

At 4:00 p.m. on September 10, Mao's chartered train left Hangzhou for Shanghai at high speed, arriving at the feeder line near the airport before 10:00 p.m. Mao had Shanghai's party and government leaders board the train to talk with him.

On the morning of September 11, Mao spoke with Xu Shiyou and Wang Hongwen on his train. Around noon, Mao said, "I'm not going to keep you here for lunch. Wang Hongwen, take this old general out for a few drinks. The two of you go, and I'll wait for you here." Before Xu and Wang could return, Mao's train left Shanghai at 12:30 p.m.

Mao's train reached Nanjing's Xiaguan train station at 6:35 that evening, but stopped for only fifteen minutes for refueling, water, and upkeep before setting off again, and Xu Shiyou, who had flown over from Shanghai, wasn't allowed to see Mao.

The train also made brief stops of only fifteen to twenty minutes at Jinan, Dezhou, and Tianjin on September 12. After arriving at Beijing's Fengtai station at 1:10 p.m., Mao spent about two hours talking with Ji Dengkui, Li Desheng, Wu De, Wu Zhong, Chen Xianrui, and others, but didn't proceed to downtown Beijing immediately afterward, uncertain of the security situation there. After their talk, Mao had Li Desheng remain behind and told him to transfer a division of the Thirty-Eighth Army to the Beijing suburb of Nankou.

Mao's train reached Beijing station at 4:05 p.m., and Mao took a car back to Zhongnanhai.

The actions of the flotilla during the crucial days of September 11 and 12 are described in the memoirs of Lu Min,[43] who had become a hero in the Korean War for shooting down an American F-86 Sabre aircraft on December 5, 1952. At the time of the September 13 Incident, he was director of the air force's war department, and he recalled several key moments during those two days:

> At 8:30 p.m. on September 11, 1971, Jiang Tengjiao drove me to a small building at Xijiao Airport. When Li Liguo saw me he said, "We have to attack now. The deputy commander in chief has issued an order. Take it out and show them." Zhou Yuchi took out a piece of stiff white paper, and Lin Liguo handed it to me. What I saw was a note written in red pencil stating, "Do as ordered by comrades Liguo and Yuchi. Lin Biao, September 8." Lin Liguo said, "The situation is very tense now. The third plenum will be held soon, and as soon as it starts, Vice-Chairman Lin will no longer enjoy the advantage. The deputy commander-in-chief has handed down the order to take the initiative to attack. Jiang Tengjiao will take the lead in Shanghai and try to take him down in Shanghai, and if he fails, we'll need Director

Lu to carry out a second attack using explosives on the railroad in a second Huanggutun Incident."[44]

Alarmed but reluctant to refuse the armed men, Lu Min said, "I've fought plenty of air battles but I've never handled ground forces, and I've never dealt with explosives or even seen them. Isn't there a better way?" The discussion went nowhere, and then Yu Xinye telephoned and said that Mao had left Shanghai. Lin Liguo announced in a panic, "The situation has changed. All our discussion today was wasted. We'll act as if nothing happened. Don't let any of this get out, or we're dead." Everyone then hurried off.

Lu Min wanted to shake off Lin Liguo and the others, and his wife, a doctor, thought of a way. At that time, pink eye was running rampant, so she used strong brine and out-of-date Aureomycin to turn Lu's eyes dark red so he would be admitted to the air force general hospital. That wasn't enough, however. After 8:00 p.m. on September 12, Wang Fei telephoned and told Lu Min to immediately report to the office for the transmission of an important document. (By that time, Lin Liguo had already taken the Trident 256 to Shanhaiguan.) Lu Min arrived at the office and found the atmosphere extremely strained. Wang Fei said, "There's no time to waste! Deputy Director Lin [Liguo] has already arrived at Beidaihe. He told us by telephone to immediately organize a group of dependable personnel and get ready to escort Huang, Wu, Li, and Qiu to Xijiao Airport tomorrow and fly to Guangzhou The task at present is to immediately draft a name list, organize groups, and make all operational preparations!" Yu Xinye was off to the side taking notes, checking the list, organizing groups, and recording more than twenty names. The first of six groups included Wang Fei and Lu Min.

A call came around 11:00 p.m. Answering it, Wang Fei blanched, and in a panic he told the others, "Disperse immediately! Everyone disperse! Nothing happened tonight! Everyone go home and go to sleep!" It turned out that the call was from Zhou Yuchi, who said, "It's been exposed! Drop it!" The aircraft they were to take to Guangzhou were under Zhou Enlai's control.

LIN BIAO'S DEATH IN ÖNDÖRKHAAN

Earlier that day, at a little after 4:00 p.m., air force deputy chief of staff Hu Ping had arranged for six aircraft to fly to Guangzhou on orders from Zhou Yuchi. At 7:00 p.m., Hu notified the deputy political commissar of the Thirty-Fourth Division, Pan Jingyin, to pilot Trident 256 taking Lin Liguo to Shanhaiguan that night. Fifteen tons of fuel were loaded onto the aircraft, three more than for a typical day's flight.[45]

At 7:40 p.m., Lin Liguo, Liu Peifeng, Cheng Hongzhen, and others took Trident 256 to Shanhaiguan Airport, arriving there at 8:15 p.m. and reaching Lin Biao's quarters at Beidaihe around 9:00.

The Hong Kong film *Sweet as Honey* was being shown at Beidaihe to celebrate Lin Liheng's engagement to Zhang Qinglin. Lin Liguo quickly congratulated his sister and then had a confidential talk with their mother, followed by a secret talk between Lin Biao, Ye Qun, and Lin Liguo around 10:00 p.m. What Lin Liguo said at that time is the key to understanding Lin Biao's subsequent actions: If Lin Liguo told Lin Biao about the failure of his assassination plan, Lin Biao was certain to know the problem was serious. No historical materials relate the content of this crucial conversation between Lin Biao and his son. (Lin Liheng said that she told an office staffer to listen in on the conversation, and he indistinctly heard Lin Biao say, "I'm a nationalist," but the claim is dubious.) If it can be said that Lin Liguo was previously able to keep his father in the dark, now that the plot had failed, he had to tell his father the truth and discuss how to deal with the extremely dangerous situation. Lin Liguo had come up with the idea of establishing a separate regime in Guangzhou, but now he was aware of Mao's remarks on his southern tour, and that the Guangzhou Military Region had communicated Mao's remarks to cadres at the division level and above. Even if the Guangzhou Military Region was willing to support the establishment of a second central government, it was unlikely to hold out for long against Mao's might. Always relying on certainty in battle, Lin Biao was unlikely to take a chance on heading south. Fleeing the country was the only real choice, and the sooner the better.

Lin Liguo's return to Beidaihe with news of his failed plot was a surprise, and Lin Biao, Ye Qun, and Lin Liguo's decision to flee was made in haste. It was inconceivable to the vast majority of people (including the officers and men in the Central Security Unit in Beidaihe) that Mao's successor would flee the country. The September 13 Incident was a sudden incident, even though it had been brewing for a long time.

Before talking to Lin Biao and Ye Qun that night, Lin Liguo had told Lin Liheng to go to Guangzhou right away. Instead, Lin Liheng went to the Central Security Unit's Second Brigade and reported, "Ye Qun and Lin Liguo are trying to take Vice-Chairman Lin away, and the aircraft is already at Shanhaiguan Airport." At 10:20 p.m., the deputy commander of the Second Brigade, Zhang Hong, telephoned the deputy director of the Central Security Unit, who was also deputy director of the Central Committee General Office, Zhang Yaoci,[46] and Zhang reported it to Wang Dongxing. Wang Dongxing immediately telephoned Zhou Enlai, who was holding a meeting at the Great Hall of the People. Zhou's secretary, Ji Dong, recalls receiving a phone call from the leader of Lin Biao's security detail at Beidaihe saying that Lin Liheng had reported Lin Biao's intention to leave the country. Soon after that he received another phone call reporting that Lin Liguo had arrived at Shanhaiguan Airport.[47] A little after 11:00, Zhang Hong telephoned Zhang Yaoci and said, "Lin Liguo and Ye Qun are discussing abducting Lin Biao and fleeing the country tonight, and have arranged for an aircraft to bomb Zhongnanhai in a murder plot against Chairman Mao. Lin Liheng wants me to immediately report this . . . and protect Chairman Mao."[48] (Zhang Yaoci may have added the bombing plot as his own surmise.) Aware of the strained relations between Lin Liheng and her mother, Zhou Enlai suspected that this report arose from a domestic dispute, but he took the precaution of asking Wu Faxian and Li Zuopeng to check into whether an aircraft had flown to Beidaihe or Shanhaiguan. Li Zuopeng soon reported an air force Trident aircraft at the naval aviation airport at Shanhaiguan. Ji Dong relayed the message to Zhou, who said simply, "Got it." Ji Dong sensed that Zhou hadn't returned to his meeting and had been waiting by the phone.[49]

Wu Faxian telephoned Hu Ping to verify the report, and Hu Ping said that a newly refitted Trident had made a test flight to Shanhaiguan.

Zhou Enlai ordered the aircraft to be immediately flown back to Beijing without passengers. Hu Ping informed Zhou Yuchi that Zhou Enlai was asking about the aircraft, and told him to tell Lin Liguo. He then telephoned Pan Jingyin, and they came up with the story that a malfunctioning oil pump was being repaired, so the aircraft couldn't return yet. Zhou Enlai told them to send the aircraft back as soon as it was repaired and repeated that it should carry no passengers.

In a telephone conversation around 11:30, Zhou Enlai asked Ye Qun[50] about Lin Biao's health, and Ye said that he was feeling well. Zhou asked if Ye knew about an aircraft at Beidaihe, and after hesitating, Ye said, "There is an airplane. My son took it here. His father said that if the weather is good tomorrow, they can take it up and fly around." Zhou asked, "Do they plan to take it somewhere else?" Ye answered, "They were thinking of going to Dalian. It's getting a bit cold here." Zhou said, "It's not safe to fly at night." Ye said, "They won't fly at night. They'll wait until tomorrow when the weather is good." Zhou said, "They shouldn't fly. It's unsafe. They need to be clear about the weather situation." Zhou Enlai tested Ye Qun further by saying, "If necessary, I can come to Beidaihe to visit Comrade Lin Biao." Ye Qun quickly said, "If you come to Beidaihe, it will just make Lin Biao more anxious and uneasy . . . It's better for the Premier not to come."[51]

Zhou could tell from Ye's stammering and hesitation that something was up, and he immediately telephoned Li Zuopeng, who wrote down four points: (1) There might be movement at Beidaihe (referring to Lin Biao), possibly a night flight, which wouldn't be safe and was undesirable; (2) If Lin wanted to make a night fight, Shanhaiguan Airport should telephone Zhou after Lin arrived at the airport; (3) the air force should obey the instructions of Zhou, Huang Yongsheng, Wu Faxian, and Li Zuopeng regarding the movements of that aircraft; and (4) Zhou had told Wu Faxian to go to Xijiao Airport to make necessary preparations.[52] At 11:35 p.m., Li Zuopeng communicated the Premier's orders to Shanhaiguan Airport: "This aircraft must obey the Premier's directives, Chief of Staff Huang's directives, Deputy Chief of Staff Wu's directives, and my directives before it can take off." At 12:06 a.m. on the thirteenth, Li Zuopeng once again telephoned Shanhaiguan Airport and repeated that authorization from one of the four of them was required in order for the aircraft to take off. Zhou Enlai later said that the authorization of all four were needed, and Li Zuopeng claimed that he had misunderstood Zhou's instructions.

Zhou Enlai's inquiries regarding the Trident and his offer to visit Lin Biao at Beidaihe sent Lin Liguo and Ye Qun into a panic. At 11:40 p.m., Ye Qun told the chief of Lin Biao's security detail, Li Wenpu, to arrange for a car as soon as possible. She added, "Hurry up! We're not taking anything! Someone wants to seize the Commander—we can't wait any longer!" Lin Liguo told Li Wenpu the same thing and said, "I'll telephone Zhou Yuchi and you keep an eye on things here." Lin notified Zhou Yuchi that he'd abandoned the plan to flee south and had decided to go north instead.

When the car arrived at Lin Biao's residence at 11:50 p.m., the scene was complete chaos. Ye Qun's hair was disheveled, Lin Liguo was scrambling, and Liu Peifeng was dashing around with four travel bags. Li Wenpu carried out the two briefcases that Lin Biao always used. As soon as Yang Zhen drove up, Lin Biao, Ye Qun, Lin Liguo, Liu Peifeng, and Li Wenpu leaped inside the car. About two hundred meters down the road, Li Wenpu shouted for the car to stop and leaped out. Two shots rang out, leaving Li with a wound on his left upper arm, and the car sped off for Shanhaiguan.

At 12:22 a.m., Lin Biao's car reached the airport and roared up behind the Trident aircraft. The first to leave the car, Ye Qun shouted, "Someone wants to hurt Vice-Chairman Lin! Take the fuel tanker away fast, we need to leave!" Lin Biao was next out of the car, and all of them ran to the aircraft's hatch and began climbing the utility ladder into the pilot's cabin. At this time, Tong Yuchun had just rushed over from the field dispatcher's office to pass on the order to Pan Jingyin that the aircraft was not allowed to take off, but he didn't see Pan, so he told the machinist, Tai Qiliang, who was on the telephone with the head dispatcher. As Tai Qiliang hesitated in confusion, Lin Liguo forced him onto the aircraft at gunpoint. The aircraft immediately moved forward, its right wing clipping the top of the fuel truck, which had not yet pulled away, and damaging the red navigation light on the tip of the wing. Personnel from the Central Security Unit 8341 rushed over in a jeep but didn't have time to stop the aircraft, and it rose rapidly into the air at 12:32 a.m.[53] The copilot, navigator, radio operator, and other members of the flight crew had not been able to board.

Shanhaiguan Airport telephoned Li Zuopeng and reported that Trident 256 had taken off. Li immediately telephoned Zhou Enlai, who told Li to chart the aircraft's course. After making inquiries, Li told Zhou that the aircraft was heading northwest.[54] By then it was 12:55 a.m. on the thirteenth. Zhou Enlai ordered radar surveillance to monitor the flight and told aircraft controllers to send out calls to the aircraft telling Lin Biao and the others to return: "Wherever this aircraft lands, I, Zhou Enlai, will be there to meet you." There was no response.[55]

At 12:32 a.m., Wang Dongxing received phone calls from Zhang Hong at Shanhaiguan Airport and Lin Liheng at Beidaihe saying that the aircraft had taken off. Wang immediately telephoned Zhou Enlai and said, "Chairman Mao doesn't know about this yet. You should leave the Great Hall of the People and go to the Chairman, and I'll go to him from Zhongnanhai, and we'll meet up there." The two of them arrived at the Zhongnanhai swimming pool at almost the same time.[56]

While Zhou and Wang were reporting to Mao, Wu Faxian telephoned requesting instructions. The aircraft had been flying for thirty minutes and was about to enter Inner Mongolia;[57] should he send a fighter plane to intercept it? Mao said, "Lin Biao is still vice-chairman of our party. The rain must fall, a widow must get married—don't stop him, just let him keep flying!"[58] At 1:55 a.m., Lin Biao's aircraft crossed the Chinese-Mongolian border at the No. 414 boundary marker and entered Mongolian airspace, gradually disappearing from the radar screen. Afraid that Zhongnanhai might come under air attack, Zhou Enlai arranged for Mao to take up temporary residence in room 118 in the Great Hall of the People.

A directive preventing any further flights without an order jointly signed by Chairman Mao, Vice-Chairman Lin, Premier Zhou, Chief-of-Staff Huang, and Commander Wu was transmitted at 2:00 a.m. Zhou Enlai sent Li Desheng to air force headquarters to follow up, while sending Yang Dezhong with Wu Faxian to Xijiao Airport, and Ji Dengkui to the Beijing Military Region air force headquarters. From the early hours of September 13 until the afternoon, Zhou Enlai personally telephoned eleven military regions and the main provincial-level leaders, saying, "The person who gave the first speech at the first plenum of the Lushan Conference has fled in an aircraft with his wife and son to the People's Republic of Mongolia! You must follow the directives of the Central Committee and Chairman Mao. Effective immediately, we are in a state of urgent war preparation!" In the afternoon, Zhou called in deputy chief of staff Zhang Caiqian, Yan Zhongchuan, Wang Xinting, Peng Shaohui, and Chen Jide to Xinjiang Hall in the Great Hall of the People for a Politburo battle conference. He said solemnly, "My first consideration now is war, the second is war, and the third is also war!"[59] Zhou Enlai was worried that once Lin Biao reached the Soviet Union, the Soviets would launch an air attack on China.

At the same time that flight ban was issued, the entire military was ordered into first-degree combat readiness. Zhou Enlai told the navy fleet and all regional air forces to directly answer to their respective military regions and had the army occupy all major airports. This relieved the command of the navy and air force headquarters because of a lack of trust of Wu Faxian and Li Zuopeng.

After Zhou Yuchi received Lin Liguo's telephone call telling him that the southern exodus had been shifted north, he and the deputy commander of the Thirty-Fourth Division's helicopter brigade, Chen Shiyin, went to Beijing's Shahe Airport and used Lin Biao's "September 8 handwritten order" to commandeer a helicopter from the pilot Chen Xiuwen. At 3:15 a.m., Shahe Airport sent an urgent report that a helicopter had taken off with five people on board, including Zhou Yuchi, Yu Xinye, Li Weixin, and the copilot. Zhou Enlai issued an order for the helicopter to be intercepted and forced to land or shot down. When the helicopter entered the airspace of Zhangjiakou, Chen Xiuwen realized that they were about to leave the country and tried to turn around, but Zhou Yuchi forced him at gunpoint to continue flying north. Chen Xiuwen took the helicopter into Beijing's suburbs, and at 6:47 a.m. the helicopter made a forced landing in Shayu, Huairou County, where Zhou Yuchi shot and killed Chen Xiuwen.[60] The Beijing Garrison commander Wu Zhong ordered the garrison's Third Division to send a motorized unit to surround the landing site, dispatching militia at the same time. Having heard the helicopter land and shots fired, nearby residents and militia ran over from all directions as Zhou

Yuchi, Yu Xinye, and Li Weixin jumped out of the helicopter and fled into the hills, only to be surrounded by militia. After a brief discussion, they shot themselves. Zhou and Yu died on the spot, but Li shifted his aim and saved himself, and was taken prisoner along with Chen Shiyin.

At 12:20 p.m. on September 14, the Foreign Ministry received an urgent telegram from the Chinese embassy in Mongolia stating that at 8:00 a.m., the Mongolian deputy foreign minister had notified the Chinese ambassador Xu Wenyi that a Chinese aircraft had crashed inside the Mongolian border around 2:30 a.m. on September 13, and that all nine people on board were dead. Since the deceased were armed and on a military aircraft, the Mongolian government issued a protest to China. It was later learned that the Trident crashed at a place called Öndörkhaan. Shortly after 2:00 p.m., the deputy foreign minister Wang Hairong arrived at the Great Hall of the People with an urgent telegram from the Chinese embassy in Mongolia. Zhou Enlai's secretary, Ji Dong, observed that after Zhou opened the brown paper envelope, "at first, the Premier's brows were knitted, but as his eyes passed over the document, the expression on his face gradually relaxed. His hands trembled slightly as he held the report. Suddenly he said excitedly, half to himself and half to me, 'Good! Good! Look here, they crashed and died! Crashed and died!'" Zhou told Ji Dong, "I have to go to Room No. 118 to report this to the Chairman. Come with me." Zhou then changed clothes and brought Ji Dong and Gao Zhenpu with him to Mao's quarters in room 118. Ji Dong and Gao Zhenpu waited in the hallway until Zhou came back twenty minutes later, his step much lighter.[61]

The nine people who died on the Trident aircraft were Lin Biao, Ye Qun, Lin Liguo, Liu Peifeng, Lin Biao's chauffer's Yang Zhengang, the pilot Pan Jingyin, and the mechanics Li Ping, Tai Qiliang, and Zhang Yankui. Based on the grass beneath them, their clothing, and the state of their bodies, it appears that they burned to death after the plane crashed.

On the night of September 14, Zhou Enlai presided over a Politburo meeting where he announced the death of Lin Biao and the others in the plane crash and issued the report from the Chinese embassy in Mongolia. Zhang Chunqiao went to the outside reception desk and grabbed a bottle of Maotai liquor and several glasses and laughingly told everyone, "Today the drinks are on me!" Pouring out glasses of liquor, he said, "From now on, we'll work well under Chairman Mao's leadership."[62]

Over the course of three days and nights, seventy-three-year-old Zhou Enlai had slept only three hours. Shortly after the crisis was over, Ji Dengkui and Li Xiannian went to see Zhou in his provisional office at the Great Hall of the People and found him sitting at his desk in a trance, pensive and gloomy. Attempting to comfort him, Ji said, "Since Lin Biao has self-combusted, we should be happy, because now we can focus on the country's economic construction." Apparently, those words triggered something in Zhou Enlai: He began to weep, "first silently, with tears running down his face, and then gradually with weeping sounds, and after that with great howls." After a long while, the Premier calmed down and said, "You don't understand. The situation isn't so simple, and it's not over yet." Ji Dengkui understood this to mean that Zhou and Mao had different thinking about governing the country and about economic construction.[63] With Lin Biao dead, Zhou became second-in-command, so now it was his turn to experience friction with Mao. That's why he said, "It's not over yet."

At the Xishan battlefront command post on September 17, Huang Yongsheng faced an enormous wall map of the North China, Northeast, and Northwest Military Regions and shouted angrily, "Why run off?! You've killed us all!"[64] Huang believed that many others would be dragged under by Lin Biao's stupid move. In the subsequent exposure and criticism campaign, many military cadres were purged, and Huang Yongsheng, Wu Faxian, Li Zuopeng, Qiu Huizuo, and other members of the Lin Biao counterrevolutionary clique were handed lengthy prison sentences.

On September 18, the Central Committee issued an official notice: "On September 13, 1971, Lin Biao fled the country in a panic in a despicable defection to the enemy, betraying party and country and inviting his own destruction. All available material and testimonial evidence amply proves that the evil intention of Lin Biao leaving the country was to surrender to the Soviet revisionist social imperialists. According to confirmed information, the Trident aircraft crossed the border and crashed in Mongolia near Öndörkhaan. Lin Biao, Ye Qun,

Lin Liguo, and the others all burned to death, and became turncoats and traitors whose crimes cannot be expiated by death."[65] To reduce the social reverberations of Lin Biao's flight, this document was first transmitted to provincial-level cadres before being handed down to the prefectural and divisional levels on September 28, and then to the county and regimental levels on October 6.

MULTIPLE MYSTERIES SURROUNDING THE SEPTEMBER 13 INCIDENT

Although the Central Committee drew its conclusion about the September 13 Incident, major questions continue to be disputed.

1. WAS LIN BIAO A PARTICIPANT IN THE MILITARY COUP D'ÉTAT AND PLAN TO ASSASSINATE MAO?

The official version is that Lin Biao was a participant, based on his handwritten order to follow the orders of Lin Liguo and Zhou Yuchi. Some researchers believe that the September 8 order was a forgery, since Lin Liguo, Zhou Yuchi, and others had practiced imitating Lin Biao's handwriting. Three copies of the "September 8 handwritten order" were found after the event, which supports the possibility of forgery. If Lin Biao wanted to mount a military coup, why not make use of the CMC supreme command or his confidants Huang, Wu, Li, and Qiu? Lin Biao was a great military leader, and the childish plot devised by Lin Liguo and the others was totally out of character for him.

2. DID LIN BIAO LEAVE CHINA VOLUNTARILY?

The mainstream opinion is that Lin Biao fled voluntarily, with no better options available after the failed assassination plot. Although Lin Biao knew this move would instantly destroy the heroic image he had taken a lifetime to build, he considered the welfare of his family members and went along with Ye Qun and Lin Liguo. The alternative view is that he was deceived and abducted by Ye Qun and Lin Liguo.

3. DID LIN BIAO ET AL. PLAN TO ESTABLISH ANOTHER CENTRAL COMMITTEE IN GUANGZHOU AND SECEDE SOUTHERN CHINA (PER THE OFFICIAL VIEW)?

Ding Sheng, who was commander of the Guangzhou Military Region at the time, said that none of the top-level officers at the military command had any idea that Lin Biao might flee south. When Ding Sheng's successor, Xu Shiyou, investigated Lin Biao's die-hard followers, he found no evidence that the Guangzhou Military Region aided and abetted Lin Biao.[66]

4. AFTER LIN LIHENG REPORTED THAT YE QUN AND LI LIGUO WANTED TO FLEE THE COUNTRY, WHY DID THE TOP CENTRAL LEADERS DO NOTHING TO STOP THEM?

On March 20, 1980, Lin Liheng and her husband, Zhang Qinglin, wrote a report to the Central Commission for Discipline Inspection stating that on the night of September 12, they on five occasions begged the 8341 Unit and Zhang Yaoci in Beijing to use troops to prevent Lin Biao and the others from fleeing from Beidaihe, but nothing was done, and Lin Liheng and Zheng Qinglin were told to get on the aircraft as well.[67] For this reason, some researchers believe that Mao and Zhou intended to let Lin Biao escape as part of a major political plot.

More researchers negate this theory, because the escape attempt by Lin Biao and the others came as a complete surprise to Mao and Zhou. Unaware of the power struggle, military personnel would hardly dare to obstruct Lin Biao without an explicit directive from the central leadership after years of being told that Lin Biao was Chairman Mao's close comrade-in-arms and successor.

5. DID LIN BIAO PLAN TO DEFECT TO THE SOVIET UNION?

The official version is that Lin Biao was a defector and traitor. Another view is that Lin Biao had no intention of defecting to the Soviet Union. In the many years since the September 13 Incident, no evidence has come to light that Lin Biao and the others had been in contact with the Soviet or Mongolian governments before their attempt to flee China, but it cannot be denied that Lin Biao attempted to flee to the Soviet Union. After Lin Liguo's assassination attempt failed, the family could save themselves only by fleeing, their only real choice being the Soviet Union or Hong Kong. Of course, it could be argued that fleeing to the Soviet Union would not be treason but rather "political exile."

6. WHAT HAPPENED ON BOARD THE AIRCRAFT FROM THE TIME IT TOOK OFF UNTIL IT CRASHED?

There were reports that the aircraft changed course a number of times. Was there a struggle on board? Did Lin Biao hear the call from Zhou Enlai telling him to come back? A black box might answer these questions, but one has never been found, and some aviation experts believe there was no black box on Lin Biao's aircraft.[68]

In spite of all the mysteries and disagreements surrounding the September 13 Incident, no one disputes that Lin Biao died in a plane crash while fleeing China. This was a world-class scandal that dealt a harsh blow to Mao and symbolized the failure of the Cultural Revolution. Every day, propaganda organs had talked of Chairman Mao's close comrade-in-arms and successor, and China's people had been told to wish him "eternal good health," but now he'd been killed while trying to flee the country. This was deeply shocking to the Chinese people and shattered the lies that the government had created since the beginning of the Cultural Revolution.

23

CRITICIZING LIN BIAO — AS A LEFTIST OR RIGHTIST?

As the reverberations of the Lin Biao incident began to subside, a guarded search for a way forward gave rise to contention between two forces.

The first, led by Mao, staunchly defended the Cultural Revolution and refused to acknowledge its failures. It consisted of members of the former Central Cultural Revolution Small Group occupying the highest positions in the Politburo, mass representatives who had been pushed out of the power structure during the campaigns against factionalism and the May 16 clique, radical rebels relentlessly purged by the bureaucratic clique, and those who believed that "continuous revolution" would provide China with a new way forward. This group favored carrying out the Cultural Revolution to the end and opposed restoration of the pre–Cultural Revolution bureaucratic structure.

The second force consisted of ousted officials restored or waiting to be restored to their positions, along with some military leaders and ordinary people who had lost patience with "continuous revolution" and who were exhausted by factional struggle. They called for redressing the errors of the preceding years, restoring order, and liberating purged officials to resume their postings as soon as possible.

Backed by Mao, the first group controlled the party organization and propaganda apparatus and dominated the power core. The second group took advantage of Mao's willingness to acknowledge some of the problems resulting from errors during the previous few years, and made the most of policy adjustments premised on continued endorsement of the Cultural Revolution. As the problems of the Cultural Revolution became increasingly apparent, and purged officials were gradually reinstated, the second force grew increasingly powerful.

Mao had kept the revolutionary veterans in check through his ability to maintain a political power balance. When the Lin Biao incident destroyed the political balance established during the Ninth Party Congress, Mao was compelled to make concessions to bureaucrats who had come under attack at the outset of the Cultural Revolution. While receiving military leaders for a symposium in Chengdu on the night of November 14, 1971, Mao called for putting the February Countercurrent behind them: "Wang [Li], Guan [Feng], and Qi [Benyu] wanted to overthrow everyone, including the Premier and the marshals. The marshals were angry and vented their irritation. They did it at a party meeting and in the open, raising a commotion at Huairen Hall! There were problems, and it was all right for you to complain a little."[1] He attended Chen Yi's memorial service and called for an end to "fascist investigation methods" exposed in the treatment of Liu Jianzhang, vice-minister of railways.[2] When receiving the prime minister of Sri Lanka, Sirimavo Bandaranaike, on June 28, 1972, Mao criticized China's leftists as "the people who set fire to the British mission in Beijing. Today they want to unseat the Premier, and tomorrow they want to unseat Chen Yi, and the next day they want to unseat Ye Jianying. These so-called 'leftists' are now all in jail."[3] When receiving the members of the Central Military Commission on December 21, 1973, Mao hailed Zhu De as a "red commander" and blamed Lin Biao for the attacks on Luo Ruiqing and other military leaders.[4]

Mao made these concessions in order to defend but also to end the Cultural Revolution and restore the country to normalcy. He supported Zhou Enlai in allowing veteran cadres to resume leadership positions, while at the same time keeping Cultural Revolution stalwarts such as Zhang Chunqiao and Wang Hongwen in key positions. By criticizing Zhou, Mao prevented negation of the Cultural Revolution; and by criticizing the Cultural Revolution faction, Mao steered them toward more strategic action to rally support for continuous revolution under the dictatorship of the proletariat. Political struggle over the next five years therefore focused on the question of whether to defend the Cultural Revolution and maintain continuous revolution or to negate the Cultural Revolution and restore order.

MAO CRITICIZES THE RIGHT, ZHOU CRITICIZES THE LEFT

After the Lin Biao incident, the campaign against Chen Boda transitioned into a campaign against Lin Biao. The first force described above called for criticizing Lin's rightism, defined as advocating a restoration of order and therefore opposing the Cultural Revolution, while the second force called for criticizing Lin's leftism, defined as endorsing the Cultural Revolution.

Under the social conditions at that time, most people hoped for production to be restored, the economy to be developed, and social order to be reinforced, while opposing anarchy and criticizing ultra-leftist thinking. Zhou Enlai made the restoration of social order a priority after Lin Biao died, and his speeches over the following year frequently included criticism of ultra-leftist thinking and anarchism and advocated a return to professional quality.[5] While listening to reports before the commencement of the 1972 national planning conference, Zhou called for rectification of China's businesses,[6] the first mention of "rectification" since the Cultural Revolution began. While attending a military cultural performance, he emphasized the need to eliminate ultra-leftist thinking in cultural work.[7] On August 1 and 2, Zhou again strongly criticized ultra-leftism during a long talk to returning ambassadors and foreign affairs section leaders.[8] Well aware that Zhou Enlai's criticism could negate the Cultural Revolution, Mao unleashed the Cultural Revolution faction.

Mao didn't appear in public for a long time after the Lin Biao incident, and at the end of November 1971, he became seriously ill; although saved by the all-out efforts of his doctors, his health remained poor from then on. On January 6, 1972, one of the main instigators of the February Countercurrent, Chen Yi, passed away. Although Mao crossed out a sentence in Chen's eulogy stating that Chen's "merits outweighed his demerits,"[9] he turned up without notice at Chen's memorial ceremony at the Babaoshan Revolutionary Cemetery on

January 10, wearing a bathrobe covered with an army overcoat, and told Chen Yi's widow, Zhang Qian, "Chen Yi was a good comrade." Mao also said that Deng Xiaoping's problem qualified as a contradiction among the people. Zhou Enlai told Chen Yi's family members to disseminate Mao's words.[10]

Mao was trying to placate veteran cadres for political objectives, but Zhou spun Mao's action in a way that effectively liberated the cadres politically. An April 24, 1972, *People's Daily* editorial vetted by Zhou called for "learning from past mistakes" and referred to veteran cadres as "the party's treasures" who should be returned to public service as soon as possible.[11] A large number of ousted officials returned to their old positions, and few were ever again disparaged as capitalist roaders.

Zhou Enlai's actions drew retaliation from the Cultural Revolution faction. In July 1972, Zhou Enlai told the physicist and former Peking University vice-president Zhou Peiyuan that it was necessary to eliminate leftist interference in the educational and scientific fields and to attach importance to basic theoretical research.[12] Recognizing Zhou Enlai's influence in an essay that Zhou Peiyuan published in *Guangming Daily* in early October, Zhang Chunqiao said, "Zhou Peiyuan has a backstage supporter, but no matter how great and how firm that supporter is, he has to be criticized!"[13] Shanghai's *Wenhui Bao* soon afterward launched criticism of Zhou Peiyuan's essay.

The 1972 National Day editorial was yet another test of strength. When Yao Wenyuan crossed out the words "It is necessary to criticize ultra-leftist thinking" in the draft editorial, Zhou Enlai compromised by emphasizing the need to "continue implementing Chairman Mao's proletarian policies, including those on cadres, intellectuals, and the economy," and to "encourage people to be both red and expert."[14]

On November 28, 1972, Zhou Enlai approved a report by the Central Committee's International Liaison Department and the Foreign Ministry that stated the need to "thoroughly denounce the ultra-leftist ideological trend and anarchy stirred up by the Lin Biao anti-party clique." Zhang Chunqiao wrote a memo on the report stating, "I'm wondering if criticizing Lin is the same as criticizing ultra-leftist thought and anarchy." Jiang Qing said straight out that "criticizing Lin means criticizing ultra-rightism" and "should emphasize the success of the Great Proletarian Cultural Revolution." Zhou Enlai compromised by agreeing to strike out the offending phrase.[15]

A March 1972 situation report by the leaders of the State Council's routine work group, Hua Guofeng, Li Xiannian, and Yu Qiuli, stated that anarchy was a serious problem in Heilongjiang Province and that discipline had broken down in key factories and mines. The Heilongjiang revolutionary committee's writing group responded with a pseudonymous essay opposing anarchy, which, along with a similar essay by the Hebei provincial revolutionary committee's writing group, was published in a full-page spread in *People's Daily* on October 14.

The essays attracted notice from all quarters, including the foreign news agency AFP, which issued a dispatch describing the essays as speaking up for veteran cadres and criticizing the Red Guards. Nine provincial and city newspapers reprinted the essays in full, and eight newspapers published their own essays criticizing anarchism. However, Shanghai's *Wenhui Bao* explicitly opposed these articles, and the November 4 issue (number 312) of its internal reference bulletin, *Wenhui Situation* (*Wenhui Qingkuang*), quoted speakers at a Shanghai workers' symposium who criticized the essays for "negating the Cultural Revolution" and "criticizing the masses."

Yao Wenyuan demanded that *People's Daily* discuss the workers' views as well as Central Committee documents, but in the process, a manager of the newspaper's theory department, Wang Ruoshui, discovered that documents approved by Mao to criticize Lin Biao repeatedly referred to anarchism. Believing that Zhang Chunqiao and Yao Wenyuan were the originators of leftism and that they were opposing Zhou Enlai, Wang Ruoshui wrote a letter to Mao on December 5 asking him to weigh in.[16] The day after Wang Ruoshui submitted his letter, Mao had Jiang Qing circulate the letter to Zhou Enlai, Zhang Chunqiao, Yao Wenyuan, and others. After the Politburo spent two days discussing Wang's letter, Mao told Zhou, Zhang, and Yao on December 17, "I think Wang Ruoshui's letter is wrong; we should criticize ultra-leftism a little less." Mao declared that the Lin Biao line was "ultra-rightist. It is revisionist, splittist, scheming and intriguing, and betraying the party and the country."

On the night of December 19, Wang Ruoshui and other leading cadres at *People's Daily* were summoned to the Great Hall of the

People for an audience with central leaders and to hear Mao's views on the Lin Biao line. Zhou Enlai said, "Comrade Wang Ruoshui heard my August 1 speech. When I said that ultra-leftist thinking had to be thoroughly criticized, I was referring to foreign affairs policies and certain operational problems, not the entire Lin Biao line. Lin Biao was a traitor to the party and our country, and that's ultra-rightism . . . Saying Lin Biao is leftist is wrong in principle." Jiang Qing reproached Wang for using the Premier's words to "sow dissension among central leaders." The meeting lasted more than five hours, until 2:00 a.m. When everyone shook hands as usual at the end, Wang Ruoshui gripped Zhou Enlai's hand, trying hard to discern his actual feelings, but Zhou's face was completely expressionless.

After the meeting with the central leaders, *People's Daily* launched a mass exposure and criticism. The head of the newspaper's theory department, Hu Jiwei, was transferred out of *People's Daily*, and Wang Ruoshui was sent down to a May 7 cadre school.[17]

Mao's standpoint was now clear, and from 1972 to 1973 all China's newspapers and radio stations were caught up in a wave of anti-rightism. In practice, however, the leftist deviations of the Cultural Revolution's first five years were being corrected. The different directions resulted from the Cultural Revolution faction controlling the propaganda work while the pragmatic faction headed by Zhou Enlai controlled the operations of the government and the economy. Restoring order was consistent with the wishes of the majority of people at that time, and Zhou Enlai was in complete control of the situation in 1972.[18] Reconstitution of the government apparatus proceeded apace, with thirty-one ministries and commissions operating by the end of 1973, compared with only eighteen in 1969, and the State Planning Commission resumed work in July 1972. The proportion of military representatives in the government declined from 57 to 40 percent with the reinstatement of ousted cadres. Orderly industrial production resumed, and colleges and research institutes revived classes and research.

THE REPORTING MEETING ON THE CAMPAIGN TO CRITICIZE LIN BIAO

After the Lin Biao incident, Mao and Zhou were all that remained of the five Politburo Standing Committee members confirmed during the Ninth Party Congress, and the number of Politburo members attending the informal enlarged meetings of the PSC had also declined by half. Zhou Enlai was now second only to Mao, and as State Council Premier, he was keenly aware of the difficulties anarchy created. After supporting Mao in the Cultural Revolution and helping him get rid of Liu Shaoqi, Zhou became the patron of ousted bureaucrats and the hope of those longing for the restoration of order. Mao couldn't run the country without Zhou, but he didn't trust him, and his grip on Zhou tightened as he faced the possible negation of the Cultural Revolution.

After attending Chen Yi's memorial service, Mao came down with pneumonia, which developed into pulmonary heart disease. He suddenly fell into a coma on February 12, 1972, and revived only after emergency measures were taken.[19] Zhou rushed to Mao's bedside, and Mao told him, "I don't think I'll make it. Everything depends on you." Zhou immediately replied, "There is no great problem with the Chairman's health, and everyone still depends on the Chairman." Mao shook his head and said, "No, I'm finished. After I die, you'll have to take care of everything." Then he said, "Let's leave it at that. You all can go."[20] Believing he had little time left, Mao felt compelled to hand everything over to Zhou, but once his health took a turn for the better, he became even more suspicious and jealous of Zhou.

On May 3, 1972, Mao told Zhou to convene a reporting meeting on the campaign to criticize Lin Biao. The meeting, held in Beijing from May 21 to June 23 with 312 attendees, focused on interpreting the Lin Biao incident in a way that would dispel its negative influence. To prove that Mao had perceived what Lin was up to early on, a letter that Mao wrote to Jiang Qing on July 8, 1966, was distributed during the meeting:

> . . . The Central Committee is in a hurry to issue my friend's speech,[21] and I'm prepared to agree to issuing it. He focuses on the problem of coups d'état. No one has talked about this problem the way he does. Some of his wording makes me uneasy. I've

never believed that my little books have such magical power. Now that he's promoting them, the whole party and the whole country have joined in. It's really a case of blowing one's own trumpet. They've forced me to go their way, and it seems I can't disagree with him . . .

. . . At the Hangzhou conference in April this year, I expressed disagreement with the wording my friend was using, but what use was it? He repeated what he had said at the May conference in Beijing, and the flattering words in the newspapers were blown out of proportion, so I could only give in . . .

. . . Of more than one hundred [communist] parties in the world, the majority no longer believe in Marxism-Leninism; Marx and Lenin have been broken to pieces, so why not us? I advise you to also take note of this problem and not let success go to your head. Regularly consider your weaknesses, flaws, and errors. I've spoken to you about this problem many times—you must remember, we spoke of it in Shanghai in April.

What I've written above sounds rather ominous. Don't some anti-party elements say similar things? But they want to completely strike down our party and myself; I'm simply saying that certain comments on my influence are not entirely appropriate. That's the difference between me and the reactionary gangs. This matter cannot be made public at present; all of the leftists and the broad masses talk this way, so saying it openly will only pour cold water on them and help the rightists. The current task is to strike down the rightists throughout the party and the country (it's impossible to get all of them), and after seven or eight years we will need another campaign to sweep away the ox demons and snake spirits, and we'll need several more such sweeps thereafter . . .

. . . If China experiences an anti-Communist rightist coup d'état, I can guarantee it will be unstable and of brief duration, because the revolutionaries who represent the interests of more than 90 percent of the people will not tolerate it. The rightists may be able to use my words to their advantage for a time, but the leftists will use other words of mine to organize and strike down the rightists . . . Wherever the rightists have been most aggressive, they will fail most miserably, and the leftists will be more vigorous. This [Cultural Revolution] is a drill for the entire country; the leftists, rightists, and vacillating centrists will each learn their own lesson.

In conclusion, as the saying goes, the future is bright, but the path is crooked . . .

In a speech at the reporting meeting on May 21, 1972, Zhou Enlai said that when he arrived in Wuhan, Mao had him read a "corrected" copy of the letter, and that everyone should note how "prophetic" it was.[22] Jiang Qing also spoke of Mao's "sagacious foresight" regarding Lin Biao. The historian Chen Xiaoya has nevertheless expressed the belief that the letter was made public in 1972 as a "conspiracy between husband and wife" to create an impression of foresight.[23] The Australian Chinese historian Warren Sun postulates that Mao altered a letter he had written six years earlier in an effort to cover up his mistaken judgment and promotion of Lin Biao and to pass off his belated realization as prophetic vision.[24]

At the reporting meeting, Mao called in Zhou Enlai and told him to deliver a speech on the six line struggles that the party experienced before the founding of the PRC. This was to make Zhou take responsibility for his own errors during these line struggles.

From 1927 onward, Zhou Enlai had been a key member of the CCP's Comintern faction, which was blamed for the CCP's failure to take root in Shanghai and other cities. Mao, who advocated focusing on the countryside, was forced out of the military leadership in 1932. This period of conflict in the party's upper echelons was subsequently summed up as six line struggles. During the Yan'an Rectification Movement, the Comintern faction was purged, and Zhou Enlai submitted himself completely to Mao's authority. At subsequent key junctures, Mao used these six line struggles to put pressure on Zhou Enlai and keep him under control, and now he was doing it again. Did Mao want Zhou to release his historical baggage so he could become a suitable successor, or did he want to destroy Zhou's image so he could never be the successor? Whoever lived longest was likely to determine China's political future, and the largely bedridden Mao was unlikely to outlive the younger and healthier Zhou.

Then, in a bolt from the blue, Zhou Enlai was diagnosed with bladder cancer on May 18, 1972. The medical team wrote a report to the Central Committee urging early treatment, which promised an 80 to 90 percent chance of recovery.[25]

Why didn't Zhou receive timely treatment? Zhou's personal physician, Zhang Zuoliang, said that Zhou's busy work schedule was "also an important reason." He didn't say what the other reasons were. The Central Committee's health system required the treatment plan for any leader at the Politburo level or above to be approved by Mao. Mao transmitted a four-point directive to Zhou Enlai's medical team: (1) Maintain secrecy, and don't tell the Premier or his wife, Deng Yingchao; (2) don't carry out further examinations; (3) don't operate; and (4) step up medical attention and nutrition.[26] The prime treatment stage was missed, the cancer spread rapidly, and now the ailing Zhou Enlai was expected to criticize his previous errors.

Zhou spent the period from May 29 to June 7 drafting the outline of "My Reflections on the Six Line Struggles During Our Party's New Democratic Revolution Phase." He wrote until his face was puffy and his legs were so swollen with edema that he couldn't wear shoes.[27] On June 7, Zhou submitted his outline to Mao, who marked it as read, and he produced a second draft on June 9.

Zhou delivered his report during a Politburo meeting held from June 10 to 12. At the end of his speech, Zhou declared, "I have always and will always believe that I cannot be the helmsman but only the assistant . . . After you understand my historical errors, it will rid you of any blind faith . . . You have the right to require me to reform, and if I don't reform well enough and the errors I committed are great, you have the right to make the Central Committee discuss it and issue a warning to me, if lenient, or relieve me of my duties, if severe."[28]

On June 23, 1972, the last day of the Central Committee reporting meeting on the campaign to criticize Lin Biao, Zhou Enlai delivered the report "Regarding the Truth of the Kuomintang's Rumor-Mongering and Slanderous Publication of the So-Called 'Wu Hao [Anti-Communist] Notice,'" Wu Hao being an alias of Zhou Enlai's. An audio recording, transcripts, and documents relating to this 1972 case were compiled on Mao's orders and deposited in the Central Archives and all provincial-level archives.[29]

THE DENUNCIATION OF ZHOU ENLAI

The Korean War had put China at odds with the United States, but after that, China's relations with the Soviet Union had also soured. Now Mao wanted to remove China from its isolation. On April 7, 1971, Mao authorized inviting an American table tennis team to China, and this "Ping-Pong diplomacy" led to a breakthrough in Sino-U.S. relations. President Richard Nixon's national security adviser Henry Kissinger made a secret visit to Beijing in July 1971. On October 25, 1971, the twenty-sixth session of the United Nations General Assembly passed a resolution recognizing the People's Republic of China as "the only legitimate representative of China to the United Nations." Nixon's official visit to China on February 21, 1972, restored diplomatic relations that had been cut off for twenty-five years. By the end of 1972, the PRC had diplomatic relations with eighty-eight countries, compared with forty-seven in 1965.

Implementing the policies set by Mao, Zhou Enlai played his diplomatic role to perfection, but that didn't save him from being harshly denounced. Gao Wenqian believes that Mao was jealous of Zhou because major Western newspapers were lauding "Zhou Enlai diplomacy" after Nixon visited China.[30] With the Tenth Party Congress imminent, resistance was building within the party against Wang Hongwen as Mao's successor, while Zhou's succession was enthusiastically applauded. Worried that if Zhou succeeded him the Cultural Revolution might be negated, Mao put pressure on Zhou to undermine his impetus as potential successor.

In June 1973, Soviet leader Leonid Brezhnev visited the United States, and he and Nixon signed the Agreement on the Prevention of Nuclear War as well as other agreements on the use of nuclear power and weapons. At Mao's suggestion, Zhou Enlai met with the head of the U.S. liaison office in China, David Bruce, on June 25, and Zhou gave his revised version of the Foreign Ministry's summary of the conversation to Mao for his examination and approval. Mao crossed out all Zhou's revisions, feeling the tone was too soft and lacked backbone, and he passed a message to the Foreign Ministry saying, "In alliances with the capitalists, struggle is often forgotten."[31]

While the U.S.-Soviet talks were still ongoing, Zhou Enlai

prompted Foreign Minister Ji Pengfei to provide an analysis of U.S.-Soviet relations. A research article by the ministry's Americas and Oceania Department on the Nixon-Brezhnev talks published in issue number 153 of the ministry's journal *New Situation* (*Xin Qingkuang*) on June 25 held that the talks were "largely deceptive" and that the "atmosphere of U.S.-Soviet hegemony is even stronger."[32] Mao was displeased with the article, however, so Zhou Enlai ordered the recall of that issue of *New Situation* and confessed, "The main responsibility for that error falls on me."[33]

That wasn't enough for Mao. On July 4, he summoned Zhang Chunqiao and Wang Hongwen and criticized the Foreign Ministry for superficially identifying hegemony without seeing the turbulence and division beneath it, and for focusing on minor matters at the expense of major issues. "If this doesn't change, it's bound to end in revisionism. Don't say I didn't warn you!"[34] He told Zhang and Wang, "You're not too old yet. Learn some foreign languages so you won't be taken in by those old codgers and be deceived into boarding their pirate ship."[35]

Zhang Chunqiao communicated the content of Mao's conversation at a Politburo meeting that night. Ignorant of the background, Politburo members were alarmed by Mao's harsh criticism and wondered what had happened.[36] Zhou Enlai, who had just undergone treatment for his bladder cancer, spent all that night writing a self-criticism for Mao. On July 12, Zhou arranged a meeting with relevant personnel from the Foreign Ministry to research and draft an article criticizing issue number 153 of *New Situation*, and he revised the Foreign Ministry's draft on July 14. In a letter appended to the article submitted to Mao and Politburo members for vetting, Zhou took responsibility for the errors described. Mao wrote a memo saying no self-criticism was necessary. The article was distributed to all of China's overseas embassies, as well as to provincial-level civilian and military departments.[37] With that, the matter finally came to an end.

But before that wave subsided, another rose. Henry Kissinger made his sixth official visit to China from November 10 to 14, 1973, his first as secretary of state, and he came offering a "nuclear umbrella." On the night of the tenth, Zhou Enlai and Ye Jianying met with Kissinger and his attaché, Winston Lord. Kissinger disclosed the circumstances of his visit to the Soviet Union in May and June, saying that Brezhnev had told him it was the joint responsibility of the United States and the Soviet Union to prevent China from becoming a nuclear power. Kissinger revealed that the Soviet Union was preparing to destroy China's nuclear capability, but that the United States was willing to help China by giving advanced warning of a Soviet attack in order to minimize fatalities.[38] Zhou didn't believe that the Soviet Union would immediately attack China, but he said, "Thank you anyway for your information and for your notification."[39] On the afternoon of the eleventh, Zhou received Kissinger for the first formal talks in the Great Hall of the People. Unaware of what was going on within China's top leadership, Kissinger praised Zhou: "There is no other state leader in the world who can ponder matters as comprehensively as the Prime Minister." Zhou immediately replied, "This can be said about Chairman Mao. I have merely learned from him as his comrade-in-arms, and my learning has been insufficient."[40]

In a meeting with Mao on November 12, Kissinger reiterated the Soviet Union's intention to destroy China's nuclear capability and observed that for the sake of its own self-interests, the United States was "determined to oppose" a Soviet attack on China. Mao said, "Their ambitions are contradictory to their capacity."[41] Mao was displeased to realize that Kissinger was offering to help China rather than requesting China's help to deal with pressure from the Soviet Union.[42]

During another talk that Zhou Enlai and Ye Jianying had with Kissinger on the night of November 13, Kissinger went a step further by suggesting that in case of a prolonged attack on China by the Soviet Union, the United States could supply equipment and other services. He suggested establishing a hotline through which U.S. satellites could relay early warnings of a Soviet missile launch to Beijing. "Another way is to sign between ourselves an agreement on accidental nuclear war." Zhou agreed to study the matter and see Kissinger before he left the next day.[43] Zhou told Qiao Guanhua that they needed to go immediately to Zhongnanhai to report to the Chairman,[44] but by then it was well past midnight, and Mao was asleep, so Zhou decided to continue talking with Kissinger along the lines Mao had set.[45]

Zhou Enlai and Kissinger held their last face-to-face talk at 7:35 a.m. on November 14. Zhou was accompanied by his interpreter, Tang Wensheng, and Kissinger by Commander Jonathan T. Howe and their interpreter. Regarding the suggestion that the United States could help China, Zhou merely said, "Under those circumstances, if as you envisaged it would be possible for you to cooperate with warnings, that would be intelligence of great assistance. And, of course, there are also communications networks. But this must be done in a manner so that no one feels we are allies . . . And therefore, indeed that would require very good consultations." Kissinger said that the hotline could not be established secretly, but that once established, "we can give it the purpose you described yesterday and that can be kept secret." Kissinger left with an agreement to establish a hotline, and another to jointly prevent a Soviet attack, with Huang Zhen assigned to continue communicating with Kissinger on intelligence cooperation between China and the United States.[46]

On the night after Kissinger left, Mao had his contacts in the Foreign Ministry, Wang Hairong and Tang Wensheng, immediately produce a record of the conversations. On November 17, Mao told Zhou and relevant Foreign Ministry personnel, "Someone wants to lend us an umbrella that we don't want, and it's a nuclear umbrella . . . We have to take note that in dealing with the U.S., there's a tendency to go 'left' during struggle and to go 'right' during alliance. I say we shouldn't engage in any military alliance with them." He also said, "I'm telling you to your faces, you can go to the Politburo meeting and sit in the back row. Whoever attempts revisionism will be criticized!"[47]

In accordance with Mao's decision, the Politburo convened a meeting that night to "criticize Zhou and Ye's revisionist line." Jiang Qing accused Zhou of "right-deviating capitulationism," "humiliating the nation and forfeiting its sovereignty," and "kneeling down before the Americans." Zhou pounded the table and said, "I, Zhou Enlai, have made many mistakes in my life, but I refuse to be labeled a 'right-deviating capitulationist'!"[48] While reporting to Mao on the meeting the next day, Zhou acknowledged that he "hadn't done well enough" during this round of Sino-U.S. talks.[49]

Seeing no in-depth self-criticism from Zhou, Mao ordered further criticism of Zhou and Ye at an enlarged Politburo meeting in the Great Hall of the People, with Wang Hongwen presiding. An "assistance committee" for denouncing Zhou was composed of Wang Hongwen, Zhang Chunqiao, Jiang Qing, Yao Wenyuan, Wang Dongxing, and

Hua Guofeng. Mao designated the following additional people to attend the meeting: Deng Xiaoping, who had been restored to his position just half a year before; Foreign Minister Ji Pengfei and Vice-Ministers Qiao Guanghua and Zhong Xidong; the head of the PRC liaison office in the United States, Huang Zhen; and interpreters Luo Xu and Zhang Hanzhi. Mao's Foreign Ministry contacts Wang Hairong and Tang Wensheng spent eight hours communicating Mao's instructions for the denunciation, which was carried out every night from November 21 to early December.[50] Much of the language was identical to that used by Mao against Liu Shaoqi and Lin Biao, for example, stating that the Foreign Ministry was Zhou's independent kingdom and impervious to outside input, and that the ministry wasn't implementing Mao's foreign affairs policies. Describing the current discord as the eleventh line struggle,[51] Jiang Qing accused Zhou of being "impatient to replace Chairman Mao."[52] Xu Shiyou leaped onto his chair and accused Zhou of wanting to engage in revisionism and become a puppet emperor.[53] After every meeting, Zhou emerged from the conference room with his face ashen and lips drawn, a desolate look in his eyes as he staggered away.[54]

It was notable that Mao had Deng Xiaoping attend the denunciation meeting, because although Deng had resumed his work as vice-premier, he was not yet a Politburo member. Mao planned to replace Zhou with Deng but wanted to test him first. Deng was the last to speak at the meeting, and he warned Zhou against inordinate ambition: "You're just one step away from the Chairman's position, and no one else can do more than hope for it. I hope you'll watch out."[55] When learning of Deng's remarks from Wang and Tang, Mao said happily, "I knew he would speak, even though I didn't tell him to." Mao became determined to appoint Deng to a key position.[56]

While presiding over a Politburo meeting on December 12, 1973, Mao criticized the Politburo for not discussing politics and the Central Military Commission (CMC) for not discussing military matters, clearly targeting Zhou Enlai and Ye Jianying. At an enlarged Politburo meeting on December 15, Mao introduced Deng Xiaoping, saying: "I've engaged a chief of staff. Some people are afraid of him, but he handles things decisively. His lifetime record is about seventy percent achievements to thirty percent errors. I've invited your old superior back. The Politburo invited him back, not me alone." Mao then turned and said to Deng, "As for you, people are scared of you, so here are some words of advice: Be firm but gentle, an iron hand in a velvet glove. You can correct your previous flaws little by little."[57] At the same time, Mao endorsed Wang Hongwen and others from the rebel faction: "Nowadays a lot of people look down on the Children's Corps, but I also came over from the Children's Corps and so did all of you. I don't believe that any of you were all that smart back when you were young people in your twenties."[58]

It appeared that Mao had made some preliminary arrangements for his succession in hopes that once he and Zhou were gone, rebels such as Wang Hongwen and veteran cadres such as Deng Xiaoping would work together on major affairs of state.

Throughout the denunciation process, Zhou Enlai waited at home for notice to attend the meetings rather than arriving ahead of time as normal. When the meeting was adjourned, he immediately left the Great Hall of the People while the others remained behind to discuss how to deal with him next time. People who had once greeted him warmly now gave him the cold shoulder, and even his support staff were snubbed.[59]

On December 4, Zhou Enlai tearfully carried out self-criticism "on the highest plane of principle" at the enlarged Politburo meeting after Mao refused his request for a face-to-face meeting. In the name of the "assistance committee," Jiang Qing ordered Zhou to write his self-criticism himself without assistance from others,[60] and Zhou was rebuked for asking Wang Hairong and Tang Wensheng to help him because of his advanced age, poor eyesight, and hand tremors. At the end of this self-criticism, Zhou emphasized that he could only assist, and that someone else should take charge of the Politburo's work.[61] Mao declared Zhou's self-criticism acceptable and ordered that the content of the enlarged Politburo meeting be communicated to the Foreign Ministry and the CMC.[62]

Once Zhou was unmanned, Mao relented. After meeting with the king of Nepal on December 9, Mao told Zhou Enlai, Wang Hongwen, Wang Hairong, and Tang Wensheng: "This [Politburo] meeting went very well, except that someone [Jiang Qing] misspoke twice. Once was by saying that this is the eleventh line struggle—she shouldn't have said that, because it's not true . . . The other was by saying the Premier was impatient [to replace Mao]. He's not impatient, it's she herself who's impatient."[63] He told Zhou, "Premier, you've been made a political victim. I hear they treated you terribly, saying you like to interrupt me, so now you don't dare say anything and have given me the sole say-so." Pointing to Wang Hairong and Tang Wensheng, he said, "They persecuted me and persecuted the Premier, shitting and pissing on my head, and in the future it will be said that they persecuted the Premier." He also said, "Poor Premier, a few women have caused you such suffering!" Knowing full well that Mao was the actual tormentor, Wang Hairong and Tang Wensheng could only grumble behind Mao's back, "He's the face and we're the ass!"[64]

MAO REINSTATES DENG XIAOPING

Mao had spent a lifetime working with Zhou Enlai, but they'd clashed repeatedly, and Mao had never trusted Zhou. However, Mao had historical and practical reasons for trusting Deng Xiaoping.

Mao never forgot that Deng had been disciplined along with Mao's younger brother, Mao Zetan, and Xie Weijun and Gu Bai for taking Mao's side when he was forced out by the Comintern faction in 1932. Deng's daughter Mao Mao (Deng Rong) writes, "Forty years later, this incident that occurred in the 1930s was an important and active factor deciding Father's political life."[65]

Deng steadfastly upheld Mao's policies from 1949 onward. He took a leading role in the 1957 Anti-Rightist Campaign, and headed the secretariat that took over the functions of the State Council when Mao reprimanded Zhou Enlai for opposing the "rash advance" ahead of the 1958 Great Leap Forward. Deng remained on the front line of struggle against the Soviet Union and revisionism from 1963 onward. In autumn 1965, Zhou Enlai told Wang Jiaxiang that Mao had authorized him to speak of impending "significant personnel changes": "The main successor in the party Central Committee could be Lin Biao or Deng Xiaoping."[66]

Although Mao disapproved of Deng and Liu Shaoqi sending in

work teams at the outset of the Cultural Revolution, he always differentiated between them. In 1967, Mao sent Wang Dongxing with a message to Deng: Hold tight and don't be anxious; Liu and Deng could be treated differently; if anything came up, Deng could send a letter to Mao. Not long after that, Mao met with Deng.[67]

Aware of Mao's hopes in him, Deng repeatedly carried out in-depth self-criticism and promised never to engage in verdict reversal.

During a self-criticism at a Central Committee work meeting on October 23, 1966, Deng denounced himself and Liu Shaoqi as the two representatives of a "bourgeois reactionary line." In a confessional narrative that he wrote on July 5, 1968, Deng said: "I sincerely and without reservation accept the criticism and censure of the party and the revolutionary masses toward me . . . The Cultural Revolution has rescued me and kept me from falling into an even deeper abyss of evil . . . I am willing to spend my remaining years repenting and making a fresh start and striving to reform my bourgeois worldview with Mao Zedong Thought. For someone like me, no treatment is excessive. I promise never to demand verdict reversal, and I am absolutely unwilling to be an incorrigible capitalist roader. My greatest hope is to be able to remain in the party, and I pray that when it is possible the party will allot me some small task and allow me an opportunity for expiation and renewal. I ardently hail the great victory of the Great Proletarian Cultural Revolution!"

On November 6, 1971, Deng Xiaoping and his wife, Zhuo Lin, came home from a factory meeting during which the September 13 Incident had been revealed. Zhuo Lin pulled their daughter into the kitchen and excitedly wrote on her palm: "Lin Biao is dead." Then the entire family played poker deep into the night.

Deng Xiaoping perceived that China's political situation was going to take a turn for the better. On November 8, 1971, he wrote a letter to Mao expressing his loyalty and asking to be assigned work, but he received no reply. He wrote a long letter to Mao on August 3, 1972, in which he hailed the great victory of the Cultural Revolution and of Mao Zedong Thought and reiterated his acknowledgment of his errors and his promise to never demand verdict reversal. "I have no way of knowing whether someone who has committed such great errors and crimes as I have, and who has been completely discredited in society, can obtain the trust of the masses or be given important work anymore. However, I feel my health is still good, and although I'm sixty-eight years old, I can still carry out some work of a technical nature (for instance, investigative and research work), and I can still work for the party and the people for another seven or eight years in order to make some small expiation."

On August 14, Mao wrote a memo on Deng's letter stating that he should be treated differently from Liu Shaoqi, especially in view of his historical integrity and his steadfast resistance to Soviet revisionism. "I've mentioned these things many times in the past and mention them once again."[68] Mao's memo removed the ban on reinstating Deng.

In early 1973, Deng took his entire family on a pilgrimage to Jinggang Mountain and southern Jiangxi, where the course of his life had been set, and on March 10, the Central Committee issued the "Decision to Restore Comrade Deng Xiaoping's Organizational Life and Posting as State Council Vice-Premier" to the entire party. On April 12, Deng Xiaoping made his first public appearance at a grand banquet that Zhou Enlai held at the Great Hall of the People for Cambodia's Norodom Sihanouk and his wife. Deng enjoyed a rapid ascent, and Zhou also found him the most acceptable candidate for succeeding Mao, but the Cultural Revolution faction tried to obstruct him.

On January 18, 1974, Deng joined the Central Military Commission Group of Five, led by Ye Jianying, to discuss major issues in the CMC.[69] In March that year, Mao designated Deng as China's delegate to the upcoming special session of the United Nations, although Zhou Enlai was the natural choice to attend as State Council premier and had expressed his desire to go.[70] Jiang Qing objected, but Mao wrote a memo to Jiang saying, "Comrade Deng Xiaoping's trip abroad is my idea, and it's best if you don't oppose it. Be prudent, and don't oppose my suggestions."[71] Jiang also tried to intervene when Mao recommended that Deng be appointed first vice-premier of the State Council as preparations were being made for the Fourth National People's Congress.[72]

Deciding on the successor to the supreme leader is always a thorny issue in an autocratic system. To prevent the chaos caused by constant competition for succession in ancient times, imperial China adopted the method of succession by primogeniture, but even this method failed to prevent repeated tragedies. Lacking a democratic mechanism for determining selection, the Mao era fell back on the time-tested method of giving the supreme leader absolute power to decide on this matter. That meant constant ingratiation and scheming while Mao was alive, and endless antagonism and conflict after his death. As Mao's health gradually worsened and he drew closer to "meeting Marx," the question of succession became increasingly urgent, and Mao needed to consider whether his chosen successor could actually hold the fort after his death. Zhang Chunqiao had the best understanding of Mao's thinking and was the most steadfast proponent of the Cultural Revolution, but he was deeply unpopular with veteran leaders. Jiang Qing played an important role in the struggles against Liu Shaoqi and Lin Biao, but she was impulsive and radical and tended toward self-sabotage. Mao therefore began actively grooming thirty-eight-year-old Wang Hongwen, who had been a peasant, a soldier, and a worker and was a steadfast supporter of the Cultural Revolution. Starting with the visit by the French president Georges Pompidou on September 12, 1973, Mao had Zhou Enlai and Wang Hongwen sit on each side of him when he received foreign guests; newspapers had published photos of the three of them receiving foreign dignitaries sixteen times by May 1974, and foreign journalists believed that Wang was Mao's chosen successor.[73] But two years of observation made Mao disappointed in Wang's performance, and even more critically, top-level military and civilian officials considered him an utter lightweight. Mao's appointment of Deng as first vice-premier satisfied the demands of his most able cadres, as well as provided a successor to Zhou Enlai, who by then had been suffering from cancer for more than two years.

After the Tenth Party Congress (August 1973), Mao agreed to consider Ye Jianying's suggestion that Deng take on responsibility for military work as well as joining the Politburo.[74] On January 5, 1975, the Central Committee announced Deng's appointment as vice-chairman of the CMC and general chief of staff of the PLA, and Zhang Chunqiao's appointment as director of the PLA's General Political Department.

The plan was for a collective succession by Wang Hongwen, Deng Xiaoping, and Zhang Chunqiao. After Zhou Enlai was hospitalized, Mao arranged for Wang Hongwen to take charge of the party's work

and preside over Politburo meetings, while Deng Xiaoping was responsible for the State Council and foreign affairs, and Zhang Chunqiao
handled ideological work as well as serving as chairman of the PLA's
General Political Department. Mao probably intended for Wang and
Zhang to maintain the political line of the Cultural Revolution while
Deng took charge of practical matters, but in fact Wang and Zhang
were no match for Deng. Wang was soon sent to Shanghai for "work
experience," and Deng took over the Central Committee's work. Deng
and Zhang Chunqiao were incapable of cooperating, so Mao felt compelled to choose Hua Guofeng in hopes that Zhang would be willing to
assist him.[75] Ultimately it was Deng, with his deep-seated base in the
bureaucratic clique, who emerged the victor, but the old-timer Chen
Yun opposed Deng, and given his advanced age, Deng was obliged to
be satisfied with the power of first in command while relinquishing
the formal title. But that came later.

THE TENTH PARTY CONGRESS AND TRANSFERS AMONG THE MILITARY REGIONS

The CCP's Tenth Party Congress, moved up because of the Lin Biao
incident, was held in Beijing from August 24 to 28, 1973, and was
attended by 1,249 delegates representing 28 million party members.
The proportion of military delegates dropped to 16 percent, compared
with 28 percent during the Ninth Party Congress, while the proportion of cadre delegates rose from 12 to 19 percent, reflecting changes
in the political situation following the Lin Biao incident. The agenda
included a political report drafted under the oversight of Zhang Chunqiao and delivered by Zhou Enlai and a report on revisions to the
party constitution delivered by Wang Hongwen.

In preparation for the congress, the Central Committee's special
investigation group had submitted its "Investigation Report Regarding the Counterrevolutionary Crimes of the Lin Biao Anti-Party
Clique" to the Central Committee on July 10. On August 20, the Central Committee passed a resolution approving the recommendation of
the special investigation group to permanently revoke Lin Biao's

474 | THE WORLD TURNED UPSIDE DOWN

membership in the party and to expel Chen Boda, Huang Yongsheng, Wu Faxian, Ye Qun, Li Zuopeng, Qiu Huizuo, and Li Xuefeng from the party and from all their official positions.

Like the Ninth Party Congress, the Tenth Party Congress was held in secret. Mao directed that the meetings, documents, and speeches be kept short. A presidium composed of Wang Hongwen as chairman and Zhou Enlai, Kang Sheng, Ye Jianying, Jiang Qing, Zhang Chunqiao, Ji Dengkui, and Li Desheng as vice-chairmen, was tasked with drawing a list for the congress's chairman, vice-chairman, secretary-general, and other members. Doing this through discussion rather than election allowed Mao to control the situation.

While the Ninth Party Congress had strengthened the power of the Lin Biao clique, the political report delivered by Zhou Enlai affirmed both "the political and organizational line of the Ninth Congress" and the campaign against the Lin clique after the Ninth Congress. This ongoing campaign, the report said, was "not the end of the struggle between two lines," but an integral part of "continuous revolution under the dictatorship of the proletariat." Internationally, the report attributed worldwide chaos to the contention for supremacy between the two nuclear superpowers, the United States and the Soviet Union.

The draft amendments to the party constitution removed all reference to Lin Biao and emphasized the "absolute necessity and timeliness" of the Cultural Revolution to prevent a capitalist restoration, explicitly stating, "This kind of revolution must be carried out many more times henceforth."

On August 28, 195 Central Committee members and 124 alternate members were elected. The members of the Tenth Central Committee included Deng Xiaoping, Wang Jiaxiang, Ulanhu, Li Jingquan, Li Baohua, Liao Chengzhi, and other leading cadres who had previously been struck down. On August 30, the first plenum of the Tenth Central Committee selected the new central leadership structure, with Mao as chairman and Zhou Enlai, Wang Hongwen, Kang Sheng, Ye Jianying, and Li Desheng as vice-chairmen. These leaders, along with Zhu De, Zhang Chunqiao, and Dong Biwu, became members of the Politburo Standing Committee. Among the rest of the twenty-one Politburo members were Jiang Qing, Xu Shiyou, Ji Dengkui, Wu De, Wang Dongxing, Chen Xilian, Li Xiannian, and Yao Wenyuan.

Wu De recalls: "Chairman Mao truly placed his hopes in Wang Hongwen, Zhang Chunqiao, Jiang Qing, and Yao Wenyuan. After the Tenth Party Congress in August 1973, Chairman Mao called me to the swimming pool at Zhongnanhai for a talk, and asked me to support Wang Hongwen, Zhang Chunqiao, Jiang Qing, and Yao Wenyuan. He pointed at some vegetables growing in a garden nearby and said, 'It's like cultivating those.'"[76]

Official histories of the Cultural Revolution hold that after the Tenth Party Congress, Jiang Qing, Zhang Chunqiao, Yao Wenyuan, and Wang Hongwen formed a "Gang of Four" within the Politburo.[77] That would mean there was no Gang of Four during the first eight years of the Cultural Revolution, and the Lin Biao clique likewise existed only from April 1969 to September 1971. Yet the Cultural Revolution lasted for ten years, so the official claim that "the Cultural Revolution was a period of domestic strife wrongfully launched by the leader and made use of by counterrevolutionary cliques [referring to the Gang of Four and the Lin Biao clique] to the severe detriment of the party, the country, and people of all ethnicities"[78] is inconsistent with fact.

After the Lin Biao incident, a search of Lin's home yielded materials including letters from some military leaders. Lin had held on to letters that the military region commanders Xu Shiyou, Yang Dezhi, Han Xianchu, and others had sent to Mao, Lin, and Zhou Enlai during the second plenum of the Ninth Central Committee. Later, letters that the newly appointed Central Committee vice-chairman Li Desheng had sent to Lin were also discovered. There were also letters from some military leaders venting their anger at the Central Cultural Revolution Small Group when the military had come under attack in 1967. Mao was deeply worried about the loyalty of these powerful military leaders and felt it would be safest to loosen their control over local forces. Deeply familiar with the ancient practice of frequently changing commanders to prevent the formation of separatist regimes, Mao decided to transfer the leaders of China's various military regions.

Mao announced his decision at a Politburo meeting on December 12, 1973: "It's not good for someone to stay too long in one place. He becomes an old hand. There are several military regions where the political commissar has no influence and where whatever the commander says goes."[79] Mao announced the following transfers among the eight military region commanders:

Li Desheng, commander of the Beijing Military Region, switched places with Chen Xilian, commander of the Shenyang Military Region. (Not long afterward, Li Desheng was removed from his posts as vice-chairman of the Central Committee and head of the General Political Department, while Chen Xilian became vice-premier and a member of the Central Military Commission standing committee.) The commander of the Jinan Military Region, Yang Dezhi, switched places with the commander of the Wuhan Military Region, Zeng Siyu. The commander of the Nanjing Military Region, Xu Shiyou, switched places with the commander of the Guangzhou Military Region, Ding Sheng. The commander of the Fuzhou Military Region, Han Xianchu, switched places with the commander of the Lanzhou Military Region, Pi Dingjun. Three other military region commanders remained in place: Qin Jiwei in the Chengdu Military Region, Wang Bicheng in the Kunming Military Region, and Yang Yong in the Xinjiang Military Region.

24

—

INTERNAL STRUGGLE DURING THE CAMPAIGN TO CRITICIZE LIN BIAO AND CONFUCIUS

The Cultural Revolution was doomed to fail, but Mao couldn't admit defeat, and as he neared the end of his life, he did all in his power to instill in the people the theory of continuous revolution under the dictatorship of the proletariat, hoping that subsequent generations would continue to carry out revolutions every seven or eight years. Most cadres and the general public nevertheless supported Zhou Enlai's stand of denouncing the ultra-left and anarchy. Ever adept at carrying out political struggle through misdirection and innuendo, Mao came up with "the campaign to Criticize Lin [Biao] and Criticize Confucius" (hereafter, the CLCC campaign), which was ostensibly a dispute over history and culture, but in fact was a fight over the Cultural Revolution.

THE BACKGROUND TO THE CAMPAIGN

After the Lin Biao incident, people became increasingly disenchanted with political struggle and longed for the restoration of order. However, because the Cultural Revolution involved only destruction and not systemic innovation, this meant reverting to the order and system that had existed before the Cultural Revolution. The marginalized rebels referred to this phenomenon as "restoration," as reflected in the following circumstances:

1. Although the May 16 Circular and Sixteen Articles had made

"purging capitalist roader power-holders" the focus of the Cultural
Revolution, the vast majority of purged cadres returned to office, and
not one leading cadre was designated a capitalist roader. This was inevitable, given that the term was never explicitly defined, and any errors cadres may have committed and any privileges they may have
enjoyed were products of the system. Not all were blameless, but all
were exonerated in the course of implementing rehabilitation policies.
Inevitably, officials bore grudges toward their tormentors, and once
restored to office, they avenged themselves on the rebels. Some even
dared to express opposition to the Cultural Revolution in private conversation. Gao Yangwen, former vice-minister of metallurgy, was detained as a "current revolutionary" for such remarks, but they resonated
among many veteran cadres. Wang Zhen said, "I've said the same
things as Gao Yangwen." Zhou Enlai added, "Yes, in fact, you've said
even more." Ultimately Mao was obliged to write a memo downgrading
the Gao Yangwen controversy to a "contradiction among the people."

2. Since the implementation of the grand alliance and three-in-one
combination, rebels had been repeatedly purged and suppressed
throughout the country. Even in Shanghai, where the Cultural Revolution faction had played such an important role, nearly half the mass
representatives in the leadership ranks of industrial and financial organs had been driven out,[1] not to mention in less radical localities. As
Mao's instrument in creating "great chaos under heaven," the rebels
inevitably resented this persecution.

3. Distribution of benefit clearly favored officials over citizens, especially in arrangements for their children. After Mao handed down
the directive that it was "very necessary for educated youth to go to
the countryside and receive reeducation from the poor and lower-
middle peasants" in December 1968, more than sixteen million urban
youths were sent up into the mountains and down to the villages to
engage in physical labor. Largely incapable of earning their keep, urban young people were subjected to shocking incidents of beating and
rape.[2] A Central Committee work conference on the issue of sent-down
youths held from June 22 to August 7, 1973, reported at least twenty
thousand cases of sexual abuse of young urban women, mostly by
party cadres. An influential minority of parents managed to have
their children recruited into the military, which exempted them from

the hardships of rural life and brought them the economic, political, and career advantages of military status. From the 1970s onward, rusticated urban youths were gradually allowed to return to the cities for jobs, for the treatment of illnesses, real or alleged, or to take over the jobs of their retiring parents. If an official had yet to be reinstated, it was difficult for his son or daughter to return, but as soon as cadres were restored to their positions, they did all in their power to rescue their offspring, while the children of ordinary citizens continued to languish in the countryside.

On June 27, 1970, the Central Committee approved the "Report Requesting Instructions from Peking University and Tsinghua University Regarding College Admissions (Pilot Project)," which stated that colleges were scrapping the examination system in favor of a combination of "recommendations from the masses, approval by work unit leaders, and review by the schools." Students recruited in this way were referred to as "worker-peasant-soldier students." Apart from a minority whose performance was genuinely outstanding, a large share of these students were admitted through the influence of their elders. The offspring of ranking officials could be admitted to famous universities, while the children of ordinary officials could only gain admission to run-of-the-mill schools, and the offspring of people with no power or influence had basically no chance of obtaining a referral. The report submitted by the 1973 conference on sent-down youths stated: "The problem of going through the back door has become quite serious and widespread . . . Each job or college space becomes a contest among various political forces." According to a popular doggerel, "A major official relies on his bureaucratic influence, a minor official relies on his personal relationships, and a non-official relies on his effort." A young man named Zhong Zhimin gained admission to Nanjing University through the influence of his father, the deputy political commissar of the Fuzhou Military Region, Zhong Xuelin, in April 1972. When he discovered that some 70 to 80 percent of the thirty students in his class came from the military, and that a third of these were the offspring of cadres, he was so ashamed that he requested to be sent back to the countryside. This incident had major reverberations in society at that time, prompting a special report in the January 18, 1974, issue of *People's Daily*.

Mao couldn't afford to offend military leaders such as Ye Jianying, but the Tsinghua University party secretary Chi Qun and the deputy party secretary Xie Jingyi, who were protégés of Mao's, criticized the practice of going through the back door as "a complete betrayal of Marxism-Leninism" at a CLCC rally on January 25, 1974, and Jiang Qing and others relentlessly forced Ye Jianying to undergo self-criticism. The self-criticism that Ye eventually submitted to Mao was actually a complaint against Jiang Qing. On February 6, Zhou Enlai advised Mao, "Studying the issue of going through the back door alone is too narrow; the unhealthy tendencies are much broader than this. Furthermore, cases of going through the back door vary and should be treated accordingly for the best results."[3] On February 25, Mao wrote to Ye Jianying, "Some people who use the back door are also good people, and some people who use the front door are bad people; the anti-dialectic mentality is running rampant and becoming one-sided. Mixing in criticism of using the back door might dilute the criticism of Lin and Confucius. The remarks by young Xie and Chi Qun are flawed and should not be circulated to the lower levels."[4]

Of the two powers engaged in a contest of strength in 1974, the veteran cadre faction represented by Zhou Enlai, which advocated the restoration of order, enjoyed greater public support than the Cultural Revolution faction, represented by Jiang Qing, which advocated "continuous revolution." Zhou Enlai now enjoyed more power than either Liu Shaoqi or Lin Biao, and was second only to Mao in his control of the party, civil administration, and military. Mao adopted the policy of both using and pressuring Zhou in hopes that as Mao's successor, Zhou would continue supporting the Cultural Revolution and also be less powerful than the Cultural Revolution faction. Increasingly fearful of chaos as his health declined, Mao suppressed the Cultural Revolution faction whenever its extremism derailed the state machinery, but then supported the Cultural Revolution faction whenever the bureaucrats tried to negate the Cultural Revolution.[5] This seesawing between the contending forces became even more apparent after the Lin Biao incident. Understanding that it would be impossible to realize his Cultural Revolution objectives during his lifetime, Mao took the long-term view of leaving behind "seeds of fire" that would reignite revolution in the future. Among the masses, the CLCC campaign was a propaganda campaign for Mao's last wishes, but among the party's upper reaches, it was a fight to the death.

THE LAUNCH OF THE CAMPAIGN

The CLCC campaign began in 1974 and never officially ended. Some scholars say that it lasted around half a year, but in fact the government work report for the Fourth National People's Congress on January 13, 1975, still emphasized, "Our chief task is to sustain the spread, penetration, and continued development of the campaign to Criticize Lin and Criticize Confucius."

Zhou Enlai had the image of a modest, self-restrained Confucian scholar, but Mao's philosophy of struggle was incompatible with Confucianist thinking. It so happened that a search of Lin Biao's residence in Maojiawan turned up quotations from Confucius and Mencius, note cards reflecting what Lin had learned from history, and calligraphic scrolls including the Confucian saying "Subdue the self and return to propriety." Some propagandists claimed this was evidence of Lin Biao's desire to restore capitalism. Mao was always comparing himself to China's first emperor, Qin Shihuang, while Lin Biao had repeatedly criticized Qin Shihuang, and the Project 571 outline also attacked the "modern Qin Shihuang." This could be why Mao tied criticism of Lin Biao to criticism of Confucius.

In a conversation with Zhang Chunqiao and Wang Hongwen on July 4, 1973, Mao brought Confucius into his criticism of Zhou Enlai's diplomatic philosophy: "I officially advise comrades to read some books so they won't be deceived by intellectuals . . . Mr. Guo[6] not only venerates Confucius, but also opposes Legalists . . . It was the same with the Kuomintang! And Lin Biao! . . . It's wrong to berate Qin Shihuang. He's too mixed-up."[7]

On August 5, 1973, Mao spoke with Jiang Qing regarding the historical dispute between Confucians and Legalists,[8] and pointed out that the most outstanding historical political figures were all

Legalists and advocated stressing the present and ignoring the past, while Confucians were always talking about virtue and morality and advocating stressing the past at the expense of the present.

While receiving Vice-President Husayn ash-Shafi'i of Egypt on September 23, 1973, Mao said, "Qin Shihuang is famous as China's first emperor. I am also Qin Shihuang. Lin Biao berated me as Qin Shihuang. China has always had two schools of thought, one that says Qin Shihuang was good, and the other that says he was evil. I endorse Qin Shihuang and I don't agree with Confucius, because Qin Shihuang was the first to unite China and unify the Chinese language and construct vast roadways."[9]

Jiang Qing had Peking University and Tsinghua University's mass criticism groups compile material on "Lin Biao and the doctrines of Confucius and Mencius." With Mao's permission, the Central Committee issued the resulting report on January 18, 1974, along with a notice describing Lin Biao as "an out-and-out disciple of Confucius and Mencius. He was like the dying-out reactionary faction, venerating Confucius and opposing the Legalists, vilifying Qin Shihuang, and making Confucian and Mencian doctrines into a reactionary ideological weapon for plotting to usurp the party's power and restore capitalism." A conference of cadres from Central Military Commission organs and Beijing-based military units was held on January 24, 1974, to mobilize the CLCC campaign, followed by a rally for Central Committee and State Council organs and their subsidiary work units the next day. Jiang Qing was a key speaker at both conferences.

One of the key elements of the CLCC campaign was expounding on the "history of dispute between Confucianism and Legalism." Some scholars simplified China's intellectual history by generalizing the dispute between Confucianism and Legalism as one "between reform and conservatism, and between advancement and reversal." Mao wanted to "make the past serve the present" by using an academic historical issue to support the "new things" of the Cultural Revolution against the "restorationist" negation of the Cultural Revolution, and by opposing a "sham benevolent government" to defend his own governing through violence.

A Sun Yet-sen University professor, Yang Rongguo, who had long venerated Legalism, became the man of the hour after *People's Daily* published his essay "Confucius—a Thinker Who Stubbornly Defended the Slave System" on Mao's recommendation on August 7. Jiang Qing spoke on the historical dispute between Confucianism and Legalism at the Tianjin Cadres' Club on June 19, 1974. The famous philosopher Feng Youlan wrote twenty-five poems praising Legalism and criticizing Confucianism.[10] Scholars of the history of philosophy suddenly became very busy as publishers engaged them to translate and annotate large quantities of ancient Legalist works to serve as material for political study in the CLCC campaign, and local governments all over China asked them to write reports on the history of struggle between the Confucianists and Legalists. Jiang Qing, Zhang Chunqiao, and Yao Wenyuan organized several writing groups that used historical events to reflect critically on the present.

For quite some time, China's periodicals were filled with lengthy pseudonymous essays by the mass criticism groups at Peking University and Tsinghua University and the writing groups of the Shanghai municipal party committee, the Central Party School, and the Ministry of Culture. The universities in particular enlisted famous scholars such as Feng Youlan and Zhou Yiliang, whose essays had the greatest influence on public opinion. As of October 1976, some 181 essays were published under the Liang Xiao ("two schools") byline, some of them targeting Zhou Enlai by innuendo.[11]

While public opinion was being shaped through reading about the historical conflict between Confucianism and Legalism and writing big-character posters, Central Committee vice-chairman Wang Hongwen mobilized the marginalized rebel faction to defend the Cultural Revolution.

At a "central book-reading class" for representatives of provincial revolutionary committees on January 14, Wang Hongwen delivered a speech emphasizing "the necessity and great significance of the Cultural Revolution," denouncing those who "depicted the Cultural Revolution as wholly negative, like some kind of great scourge," and criticizing cadres who "took attacks by the masses to heart, and punished the masses as soon as they were liberated and back in power." He complained: "Why are old cadres educated on their errors, but new cadres aren't educated and are only suppressed? It's not fair! . . . Some criticize us as rising to power from rebellion, but what's wrong with rebelling against the bourgeoisie?! The myriad principles of Marxism can ultimately be summed up in one sentence: To rebel is justified. Our old forefather Marx leads us to rebel."

The CLCC campaign gave hope to the rebel leaders who had been labeled as counterrevolutionaries and "May 16 elements," and to mass representatives who had been ejected from the three-in-one combination of the revolutionary committees. Regarding this campaign as a second Cultural Revolution, they surged in political waves all over China, never guessing that Mao would once again regard them as a stumbling block and that their actions during this campaign would only be added to their crimes.

FARCICAL INCIDENTS DURING THE CAMPAIGN

During the CLCC campaign, the manipulation of public opinion by Jiang Qing and others often descended into farce.

THE MA ZHENFU INCIDENT

Performing abysmally on the English exam at Ma Zhenfu Secondary School in Tanghe County, Henan Province, in July 1973, the student Zhang Yuqin wrote on her exam paper: "I'm Chinese, why should I learn a foreign language? Someone who didn't learn his ABCs could become successor, take over the revolution, and bury imperialists, revisionists, and counterrevolutionaries." Subjected to ridicule at her school, Zhang committed suicide. In January 1974, Jiang Qing published an article in an internal publication saying that Zhang Yuqin had been persecuted to death by the resurgent "revisionist education line," and the head teacher and principal were sentenced to two years in prison.

ANTONIONI'S FILM *CHUNG KUO, CINA*

With Zhou Enlai's permission, the leftist Italian filmmaker Michelangelo Antonioni came to China in 1972 and that December released his documentary *Chung Kuo, Cina,* which objectively reflected China's situation, including its backwardness. A year later, someone wrote a letter to Jiang Qing and Yao Wenyuan calling the film an "extremely venomous reactionary film attacking China." While launching a mass criticism campaign, Jiang Qing said, "There are traitors in China, otherwise a foreigner wouldn't be able to shoot this kind of film!"—implicitly attacking Zhou Enlai and Foreign Ministry officials.

DENOUNCING THE SHANXI OPERA *THREE TRIPS TO TAOFENG*

In January 1947, the Shanxi opera *Three Trips to Taofeng* was performed in a theater festival in northern China. Previously known as *Three Trips to Taoyuan,* it related how two production teams sold and then bought back a sick horse, an incident previously reported and praised in *People's Daily.* Since Liu Shaoqi's wife, Wang Guangmei, had taken part in the Four Cleanups movement in the Taoyuan production brigade, Jiang Qing and others launched a mass criticism of this opera as an attempt to reverse the verdicts against Liu and Wang. The deputy director of the Shanxi Province Cultural Bureau, who was one of the authors of the play, was dismissed.

ZHANG TIESHENG'S BLANK EXAM PAPER

Zhang Tiesheng, who had been sent to a production brigade in Xing-cheng County, Liaoning Province, was recommended for the university entrance exam in 1973. Stymied by the physics and chemistry portions, he wrote a letter on the back of his blank exam paper describing how his arduous labor in agricultural production had deprived him of the opportunity to prepare. "I'm extremely disgusted with those bookworms who have spent years not engaged in honest work but just loafing about. The exam allows them to monopolize the universities." After *Liaoning Daily* published and commended Zhang's letter on July 19, *People's Daily* reprinted it on August 20 with an editorial note stating, "This letter points out a serious problem in the struggle between the two roads and two ideologies on the educational battlefront." In short order, Zhang became a national hero of "going against the tide," and with the encouragement of Jiang Qing, Mao Yuanxin, and others, he went around giving speeches for the CLCC campaign. After the Gang of Four was put on trial, Zhang Tiesheng was imprisoned for fifteen years.

JIANG QING'S "TEN NEW THINGS"

Jiang Qing took three trips to Xiaojinzhuang in Tianjin to support "ten new things" there, most of which involved writing doggerel and songs in accordance with the political needs of the times. *Tianjin Daily* published 466 propaganda articles regarding Xiaojinzhuang from June 25, 1974, to the end of 1976, and more than 18,000 people from 512 work units in 27 provinces, cities, and autonomous regions went on tours of Xiaojinzhuang in less than three months in 1974.[12] Other incidents during the CLCC campaign included the criticism of a Hunan opera called *The Teacher's Song* as "channeling the spirit of the revisionist education line," and an attack on "black pictures" that Zhou Enlai commissioned from well-known artists such as Li Keran, Huang Zhou, and Li Kuchan to decorate Beijing's guesthouses.

THE LI QINGLIN INCIDENT

If the incidents above come off as farcical, the Li Qinglin incident leaves the bitter taste of a genuine tragedy.

Li Qinglin was a language teacher at the Xialin Primary School of the Chengjiao Commune in Putian County, Fujian Province. With one son enduring the appalling hardship of "reeducation" in the mountains, and another facing the same grim prospect, Li wrote a letter to Mao on December 21, 1972, describing his elder son's deprivation, and observing that other young people had leveraged the influence of friends and relatives to return to the urban areas for work or schooling, or to become cadres, "completing a bona fide gilded rustification process." The letter was sincere, plain, and moving.

On May 6, 1973, the postman delivered a letter to Li Qinglin in a large brown envelope stamped with the words "CCP Central Committee General Office." With trembling hands he pulled out a printed copy of Mao's reply letter (the original manuscript preserved in the archives of the Central Committee General Office): "Comrade Li Qinglin: I'm sending three hundred yuan to supplement hunger. There are many such instances throughout the country that must be resolved through planning as a whole. Mao Zedong, April 25, 1973." Li Qinglin read Mao's letter over and over again with tears streaming down his face.

Meanwhile, the Central Committee held meetings in April and May to discuss policies relating to sent-down youths, and on June 10, the Central Committee printed and distributed Li Qinglin's letter and Mao's reply. A three-month State Council work conference over the summer resulted in draft trial regulations relating to the problems of sent-down youths, and their situation began to improve.

At an enlarged Politburo meeting on December 15, 1973, Mao said, "Some say that that letter from Li Qinglin in Fujian has hidden barbs, but I think it's quite good even if it does have barbs! I held on to it here for months and read it often; I read it through several times before I decided to write a reply."[13] Mao's handling of Li Qinglin's letter balanced out his criticism of those who opposed using the back door and enhanced his image of caring about people in the lower strata.

Regarded as a "hero going against the tide," Li Qinglin gradually rose from vice-chairman of his school's revolutionary leading group to member of the State Council's Educated Youth Office and of the standing committee of the Fourth National People's Congress. Invited to make speeches all over China during the CLCC campaign and the counterattack against the right-deviating verdict-reversal wind that followed it, Li took the side of the rebel faction and boldly criticized the bureaucratic system. But soon after the Gang of Four was arrested in October 1976, Li was put under isolation and investigation, and eventually he was handed a sentence of life imprisonment as a "current counterrevolutionary" and permanently stripped of his political rights.

In the early 1980s, some former sent-down educated youths from Beijing and Shanghai who were touring the scenic area of Mount Wuyi heard that Li Qinglin was imprisoned nearby. Bearing fruit and pastries, they hiked more than five kilometers to the labor reform farm, where they crowded around Li and told him how his letter to Mao had changed their lives.

In December 1990, Li Qinglin's sentence was commuted, and he was released in March 1994. He constantly received letters and remittances from former sent-down youths from around the country. One man in Shantou, Guangdong Province, sent him six hundred renminbi for medical treatment, referring to Li as "the guardian angel of Chinese educated youth."

THE CAMPAIGN IN VARIOUS PROVINCES

In some places, rebels who had come under attack after the establishment of the revolutionary committees saw the CLCC campaign as an opportunity to launch new struggles. Following are episodes in several provinces.

HUBEI PROVINCE

A mobilization rally for the CLCC campaign held by the provincial party committee and Wuhan armed forces party committee on January 28, 1974, was followed in March by the release of the jailed rebel leaders Hu Houmin and Li Xiangyu, among others, who were restored to their positions in the provincial and municipal revolutionary committees. Hu Houmin oversaw the drafting of a five-word policy toward rebel leaders of "release, rehabilitate, reappoint, promote, and recruit." Following implementation of this policy, Hu Houmin, Zhu Hongxia, Deng Jinfu, Pan Hongbin, and Ping Yi were added as vice-chairmen of the newly resurrected Hubei Province Federation of Trade Unions.

Rebel leaders used every opportunity to mold public opinion. A writing group in Wuhan wrote weekly critical essays about administrative and military leaders in Hubei and Wuhan that were pasted on a massive "democracy wall" at the Hankou water tower, and big-character posters plastered Wuhan's major thoroughfares. The rebel re-empowerment was short-lived, however. After forming a temporary alliance, members of the New and Steel factions took possession of black dossiers compiled by the military region until Zhou Enlai ordered the files returned. After the Cultural Revolution was negated, this was designated an incident of "snatching confidential files," and the instigators were sentenced to four years in prison.[14] Similarly, rebel leaders who had been reincorporated into the power structure were all sent down to "eat, live, and work with the peasants" in the counties and communes under a directive by Deng Xiaoping in 1975.

HUNAN PROVINCE

Although many of Hunan's rebel leaders were purged during the One Strike and Three Antis campaign and the investigation of the May 16 clique, others remained in power in revolutionary committees at various levels, and one of them, Tang Zhongfu, was even promoted to both the Ninth and the Tenth CCP Central Committees as well as the standing committee of the CCP Hunan provincial party committee. After the CLCC campaign was launched, the rebel leaders who remained in power pushed for the rehabilitation and reinstatement of purged rebel leaders and the destruction of investigative files.

In February 1974, Tang Zhongfu and the former Changsha Workers' Alliance leaders Hu Yong and Lei Zhizhong composed and distributed a pseudonymous leaflet demanding that power be seized back from the capitalist roaders and bourgeois rightists, and they united with their former antagonists in Xiang River Storm to orchestrate a resurgence of the rebel faction. As a result, many marginalized rebel leaders resumed their positions in the provincial and municipal revolutionary committees, and some long-imprisoned rebel leaders were released.

ZHEJIANG PROVINCE

The Central Committee put Tan Qilong and Tie Ying in charge of the provincial party committee in April 1972 to replace military leaders purged after the Lin Biao incident. During the campaign to criticize Lin Biao and carry out rectification, deposed cadres rejoined the leadership ranks, and some leaders with rebel backgrounds were sent off to the grassroots level. After Wang Hongwen publicly criticized the unjust treatment of rebels while in Zhejiang in January 1973, rebel leaders wrote to Wang complaining of persecution, and Wang passed the letters to Tan Qilong, putting him under pressure.[15] The pressure increased in October and November 1973, as workers and students, some of whom were members of the provincial revolutionary committee, began posting open letters and sending reports to the Central Committee accusing Tan Qilong and Tie Ying of negating the Cultural Revolution and suppressing new cadres.

Wang Hongwen directed the provincial party committee to carry out self-criticism and organize study sessions, and on January 13, 1974, Jiang Qing sent Chi Qun and Xie Jingyi to Zhejiang to "set the prairie ablaze" with letters and reports naming Tan Qilong as Zhejiang's biggest capitalist roader.

On February 7, 1974, more than thirty thousand workers staged a rally and march denouncing the provincial leadership for negating the Cultural Revolution. A rebel-led Hangzhou militia command post led by He Xianchun was established a few days later with the blessings of the municipal party committee, and similar command posts were soon established in 81 percent of the province's cities and counties.[16]

On March 2, the Hangzhou Municipal Workers' Representative Assembly joined a petitioning group in holding a mass rally to criticize Lin Biao and Confucius and launch a "frontal assault on the right-deviating ideological trend of negating the Cultural Revolution." A leading group for the campaign was established a few days later, with Tan Qilong as a figurehead chairman and Chai Qikun, Zhang Yongsheng, Hua Yinfeng, and Weng Senhe as the vice-chairmen and actual leaders. During the CLCC campaign, 174 detained rebel leaders were released, and some leading cadres came under attack.

Denunciations of Tie Ying, Xia Qi, Chen Weidong, and Nanjing Military Region commander Xu Shiyou continued over the next few months, while ousted rebels forced themselves onto party committees. Led by Weng Senhe, He Xianchun, and others, they revived earlier Cultural Revolution practices such as unauthorized detention, torture, and factional violence. On January 29, 1975, rebels burst in on a provincial party committee work conference and abducted Tan Qilong, who had to be rescued through an all-out effort by security guards and soldiers. When Deng Xiaoping learned of this matter, he had the Central Committee Secretariat telephone Hangzhou and say, "Tan Qilong cannot be struck down!"

The utter chaos unleashed by the CLCC campaign produced a backlash, resulting in the disbanding of the militia command posts. In July 1975, the Central Committee reorganized the provincial party leadership, and more than two hundred rebel leaders were brought in for collective study classes that included manual labor. Weng Senhe was put under investigation, and Zhang Yongsheng and He Xianchun were sent to the countryside for labor reform.

JIANGSU PROVINCE

Unlike those in Zhejiang Province, Jiangsu's rebel leaders were suppressed during the period of military control and were therefore unable to play a role in the CLCC campaign when it was launched in January 1974. Nevertheless, reinstated veteran cadres, in particular Peng Chong and Xu Jiatun,[17] did all in their power to speak up for persecuted rebels. Peng Chong called for the CLCC campaign to focus on the crimes of Lin Biao's die-hard followers and the injustices perpetrated during the investigations of the May 16 clique, as a result of which the campaign targeted the provincial leaders Xu Shiyou, Wu Dasheng, and Jiang Ke. The actions of Peng and Xu led the local rebel faction to welcome the resurgence of Jiangsu's veteran cadres instead of protesting "restoration of the old order." Urban residents who had been expelled to the countryside during the horror of Red August and the Cleansing of the Class Ranks[18] likewise hoped that the CLCC campaign would give them an opportunity to return to the cities. They repeatedly petitioned and protested in Nanjing, and at one point even obstructed the Nanjing-Shanghai Railway.[19]

At a provincial party committee meeting in mid-April 1974, Wu Dasheng admitted that the provincial party committee should bear responsibility for the many errors in Jiangsu's investigation of the May 16 clique, and he agreed to release Zeng Bangyuan and other jailed rebel leaders. From mid-May to the end of June, the provincial party committee held CLCC mass rallies during which Peng Chong and Xu Jiatun led former rebels and May 16 victims in denouncing their persecution at the hands of the military.[20]

On August 15, Wu Dasheng admitted to supporting the Lin Biao clique during the 1970 Lushan Conference and to having covered up Xu Shiyou's ties with the clique, and later that month the provincial party committee proposed measures to rehabilitate victims of the May 16 investigations.[21]

The Central Committee demonstrated its support on November 13 by inviting Peng Chong, Xu Jiatun, Ding Sheng, and other leaders of the Nanjing Military Region and Jiangsu provincial party committee to Beijing, where they were received by Politburo Standing Committee members. The central leaders announced the appointment of Peng Chong as provincial first secretary and chairman of the provincial revolutionary committee, as well as second political commissar of the Nanjing Military Region. On December 30, the Jiangsu provincial party committee and military district jointly issued a notice ordering all military personnel in local party and government organs to return to their ranks,[22] and veteran civilian cadres replaced military personnel in the party and government leadership.

Wu Dasheng and Jiang Ke were suspended and continued to be denounced and investigated, while rebel leaders were released from prison and had their "counterrevolutionary" labels removed. However, once the veteran civilian cadres replaced the military cadres, they no longer supported the rebel faction and explicitly stated that rebel leaders could not return to the leadership positions they had held in 1968.[23]

JIANGXI PROVINCE

Jiangxi's rebel faction was active for a time during the CLCC campaign. At the end of 1973, rebel leaders informed Jiang Qing, Wang Hongwen, and Zhang Chunqiao of the "score settling" actions of some provincial party leaders, and in early February 1974, rebel leaders mobilized the CLCC campaign in various cities to expose the "right-deviating restorationist" behavior of certain provincial party leaders. Negotiations with provincial leaders resulted in the release of 224 people who had been locked up during the One Strike and Three Antis campaign. Many counties experienced waves of protest against "restorationist reversion" in the early months of 1974.[24]

Given Mao's desire for the entire country to head toward "great order," however, these rebel actions were short-lived, and the CLCC campaign in Jiangxi focused on Li Jiulian.

Li Jiulian had been the propaganda head for the Youth League committee of Ganzhou's No. 3 Secondary School, as well as head of the student union study department. During the Cultural Revolution, she became a leader of a Red Guard organization and then was assigned a job as a worker at the Ganzhou Metallurgical Machinery Factory. However, in May 1969, Li was arrested as a counterrevolutionary after her soldier boyfriend handed over a letter in which Li expressed her disenchantment with the Cultural Revolution as a top-level power struggle, her sympathy with the views of Liu Shaoqi, and her suspicion of Lin Biao's motives. Her journal was also found to contain criticism of Lin Biao.

The chairman of the provincial revolutionary committee, Cheng Shiqing, declared Li Jiulin's case to be a contradiction between the enemy and us, and Li was sentenced to five years in prison. Following Cheng Shiqin's ouster as a diehard follower of Lin Biao, Li was released and her case downgraded to that of a "current counterrevolutionary handled as a contradiction among the people," but she was still expelled from the Communist Youth League and assigned a job at the tungsten mill in Xingguo County.

On April 4, 1974, Li Jiulian put up a big-character poster in her own defense titled "It Is Not a Crime to Oppose Lin Biao," garnering significant public support and spurring criticism of the Ganzhou provincial leadership. In a panic over the intense public outcry, the Ganzhou prefectural party committee had Li Jiulian secretly arrested on the night of April 20, 1974. Massive protests demanded Li's release, including more than forty trucks full of protesters accused of attacking the Xingguo County prison where Li was being held. Some local party leaders were sympathetic to the public's demands and hoped that the higher-ups would handle the matter discreetly. However, Cheng Shiqing's replacement as chairman of the provincial revolutionary committee, a former Mao bodyguard named Chen Changfeng, declared Li Jiulian a bona fide current counterrevolutionary and the attack on the Xingguo County prison a serious political incident. In spite of even more organized public protests on her behalf, Li Jiulian was sentenced to fifteen years in prison as a current counterrevolutionary in May 1975, and more than forty of her defenders were imprisoned, while more than six hundred others were punished in various ways. Paying a heavy price on behalf of a woman who was a complete stranger to them, some of these people committed suicide, some went to prison, some became homeless, divorced, or insane, and some were crippled by beatings.

Imprisoned for a second time, Li Jiulian protested her torture by going on a hunger strike until she was tied down and given glucose injections. After Li began criticizing what she considered a new personality cult for Mao's successor Hua Guofeng, her prison sentence was changed to capital punishment, and she was executed on December 14, 1977, after a public trial before thirty thousand people at the Ganzhou sports stadium. When Li refused to kneel, the executioner shot her in the leg so she could no longer stand. She was only thirty-one years old on the day of her execution. Under the terrifying political atmosphere, Li's family didn't dare claim her corpse, which was defiled by a local deviant.

Among the people protesting the injustice against Li Jiulian was a primary school teacher named Zhong Haiyuan, who often brought her two-year-old daughter with her. After producing leaflets protesting the arrest of some of Li's other defenders, Zhong was sentenced to twelve years in prison. Continuing her protests in prison in spite of brutal physical abuse, Zhong was sentenced to death on April 30, 1978, and summarily executed for "venomous attacks on Chairman Hua." She was kept alive long enough to have her kidneys harvested in a truck on the execution ground for transplant to an airman at Nanchang's Ninety-Second Field Hospital.[25]

The officials involved in persecuting Li Jiulian and her supporters resisted all calls to redress the case until Hu Yaobang intervened in January 1980. The Jiangxi provincial court finally pronounced Li's verdict unjust in April 1981.

CENTRAL COMMITTEE DOCUMENTS REIN IN THE REBEL FACTION

The actions of rebels during the CLCC campaign threatened newly reinstated officials and went against Mao's strategy to achieve stability and unity, as well as the public's desire for a return to normalcy. On April 10, 1974, the Central Committee issued its "Notice Regarding Several Problems in the Campaign to Criticize Lin and Confucius" (Document No. 12 [1974]), which required the campaign to be carried out under the leadership of the party committees and prohibited the establishment of battle groups as well as trans-sectoral and transregional networking. Activist groups were to return to their work units to take part in the campaign and to seize revolution and push production, operations, and war preparedness. The document also prohibited "plucking out" support-the-left personnel, whose errors would be dealt with by their military units.

To stabilize the military ranks, the Central Committee issued another notice on May 18 limiting investigation of the Lin Biao incident to the activities of the Lin Biao anti-party clique. Any errors committed prior to Mao's inspection tour in August and September 1971 would not be called into account if confessed to the party with a disavowal of the Lin Biao clique, and military personnel were to be dealt with through positive education.

A June 18, 1974, the State Planning Commission report to the Politburo on current problems in industrial and agricultural production stated that the chaos caused by the CLCC campaign had led to a decline in the national economy: "In the first half of 1974, industrial production in many localities and departments failed to fulfill the state's plan . . . In terms of railway transport, due to upheavals, many lines were blocked, so transport by train was reduced by around 1/3."[26] These worrying figures allowed the State Council under Zhou Enlai to keep the CLCC campaign from becoming a "second Cultural Revolution."

On July 1, 1974, the Central Committee reframed this grim situation in its "Notice Regarding Seizing Revolution and Pushing Production" (Document No. 21 [1974]). It demanded that the rebel masses "properly treat cadres who had committed errors," and prohibited seizing and beating people. Cadres and masses were to join together against their common enemies.

As soon as the CLCC campaign began, Zhou Enlai endorsed Mao's "strategic plan" while ignoring the large quantities of reports and essays that Jiang Qing and others were producing to attack him by innuendo through the "struggle between the two lines of Confucianism and Legalism." Although terminally ill and admitted to the hospital, Zhou held fast to his authority and continued to inquire into the daily work of the party, government, and army.

On September 30, 1974, the ailing Zhou presided over a grand celebration of the twenty-fifth anniversary of the establishment of the People's Republic of China. Only a small number of the more than two thousand people attending the celebration belonged to the rebel faction; the majority were cadres who had been reinstated after being "roasted," including some whom Zhou Enlai had personally protected. People stood up and constantly called out, "Premier Zhou! Premier Zhou!" The assembly seethed with excitement, and Zhou Enlai's brief toast was interrupted more than ten times by thunderous applause. Mao was obliged to consider the possibility that openly denouncing Zhou might have serious ramifications and cause the situation to spin out of control. With a public denunciation of Zhou no longer an option, the CLCC campaign lost its purpose. Coupled with concerns over the chaos caused by the rebel faction, the campaign was allowed to ebb after a little more than half a year.

CONFLICT OVER FORMING THE CABINET IN THE FOURTH NATIONAL PEOPLE'S CONGRESS

The Central Committee finally issued its "Notice Regarding Preparations for Holding the Fourth National People's Congress in the Near Future" (Document No. 26 [1974]) on October 11, 1974. That was nearly ten years after the Third NPC was held at the end of 1964. Although Zhou Enlai had been admitted to the No. 305 Hospital on June 1, 1974, and his work had been handed over to Wang Hongwen, Deng Xiaoping, and Zhang Chunqiao, he frequently called people in to talk with him about preparations for the Fourth NPC.

In the run-up to the NPC, the "pragmatist faction" of reinstated veteran cadres, led by Zhou Enlai, began locking horns with the Cultural Revolution faction led by Jiang Qing, each hoping to gain the advantage in the distribution of power at the congress.

The Cultural Revolution faction created the "SS *Fengqing* Incident" in an attempted show of strength. The SS *Fengqing* was an oceangoing freighter built in Shanghai's Jiangnan Shipyard in 1973 that had been handed over to the Shanghai branch of the Transportation Ministry's High Seas (Yuanyang) Company. During the SS

Fengqing's trial voyage, the receiving company discovered that the ship's main engine cylinder coupling was worn down by 0.15 millimeter and was of substandard quality, and its radar had also developed problems. Shanghai officials felt that the Transportation Ministry was nitpicking and unwilling to use Chinese-made ships, and when the Transportation Ministry refused to authorize this vessel for the high seas, the Shanghai Revolutionary Committee supported the Jiangnan Shipyard in organizing big-character posters accusing the Transportation Ministry of favoritism toward foreign products. The Transportation Ministry finally permitted the ship to travel the high seas, and the SS *Fengqing* set off for Europe on May 9, 1974. During the voyage, arguments between Transportation Ministry and Shanghai personnel over the ship's quality issues developed into political arguments. The background of these arguments was a State Planning Commission plan, endorsed by Zhou Enlai, to meet shipping needs on the high seas by purchasing foreign-made vessels rather than making ships in China at a much higher cost. After the SS *Fengqing* returned to Shanghai on September 30, a report by Shanghai personnel published in the Xinhua News Agency's October 13 issue of *Galleys of Domestic Trends* carried the dispute into the upper levels of government. Jiang Qing wrote a memo on the magazine saying, "The Transportation Ministry truly has a small number of West-worshippers and people with comprador-class mentality imposing dictatorship on us . . . The Politburo should take a stand on this issue and adopt the necessary measures." Zhang Chunqiao wrote a memo describing the incident as a continuation of "the struggle between the two roads in the shipbuilding industry." At a Politburo meeting on October 17, Jiang Qing insisted that Deng Xiaoping take a stand on the SS *Fengqing* controversy until Deng sternly replied, "When the Politburo holds meetings to discuss issues, everyone should be equal, and no one's views should be forced on others. Is it absolutely necessary for me to say I agree with your view?" The arrogant Jiang Qing was unused to being treated with such impertinence, and a raucous argument ensued. Deng Xiaoping said, "The issue is not yet clear. How can we have a meeting if you're going to act so high and mighty?" With that, he stormed out.[27]

After the quarrel at the Politburo meeting, Jiang Qing, Wang Hongwen, Zhang Chunqiao, and Yao Wenyuan decided to send Wang

Hongwen to Changsha to tell Mao what Zhou Enlai and Deng Xiaoping were up to. Just before he left on October 18, Wang wrote a letter to Mao saying that conflict over personnel arrangements had risen to the surface in preparations for the Fourth NPC and appended three reports by Jiang Qing. After arriving in Changsha later that day, Wang told Mao that the atmosphere in Beijing was like that at the 1970 Lushan Conference and that Zhou Enlai was having constant meetings in his hospital room with Deng Xiaoping, Ye Jianying, and Li Xiannian, apparently over personnel arrangements for the Fourth NPC.[28] Wang also praised Jiang Qing, Zhang Chunqiao, and Yao Wenyuan, implying that they should be included in the leadership of the Fourth NPC. Mao just told Wang to go back to patch things up with Deng Xiaoping and to exchange views with Zhou Enlai and Ye Jianying, and not to get embroiled in Jiang Qing's activities.

During the last two years of his life, Mao was nearly blind, and those around him were his only source of information, in particular his interpreters Wang Hairong and Tang Wensheng. After Wang Yongwen set off for Changsha, Jiang Qing expressed her views to the two young women in hopes that they could bring influence to bear on Mao; instead, they reported the matter to Zhou Enlai. Soon after that, on October 20, Wang and Tang went to Changsha and passed on reports to Mao that were detrimental to Jiang Qing. Mao told them to tell the Central Committee: "The Premier is still the Premier. If his health allows, let him have a discussion with Comrade Hongwen and propose a list . . . Deng Xiaoping is First Vice-Premier and Chief of General Staff." He also said, "The SS *Fengqing* problem was originally a small matter that Li Xiannian had already resolved, but Jiang Qing has still raised such a fuss over it." He told the interpreters to tell Wang Hongwen, Zhang Chunqiao, and Yao Wenyuan not to go along with Jiang Qing in issuing unauthorized documents to stir up trouble.[29]

Hoping to bring the country back to normalcy while he was still alive, Mao squelched antics by Jiang Qing that threatened to derail the Fourth NPC once again. His stance was highly advantageous to the pragmatic faction.

On December 23, Zhou Enlai and Wang Hongwen took separate flights to Changsha to report to Mao on the NPC preparations. In conversations with both over the next few days, Mao continued to disparage the Gang of Four and said that Deng Xiaoping had "strong political thinking and is a rare talent," reiterating that Deng should be first vice-premier, vice-chairman of the Central Military Commission, and chief of General Staff. Mao recommended holding the second plenum of the Tenth Central Committee before the Fourth NPC and making Deng Xiaoping vice-chairman of the Central Committee and a member of the Politburo Standing Committee. Mao had decided to make Deng Xiaoping his successor instead of Wang Hongwen.

Accordingly, Deng Xiaoping attained the highest position of his career during the second plenum of the Tenth Central Committee from January 8 to 10, 1975. Even so, Mao ensured that the Cultural Revolution faction would keep Deng in line by having Wang Hongwen and Zhang Chunqiao become members of the Central Military Commission standing committee and additionally making Zhang the director of the General Political Department, empowered to appoint or dismiss military personnel.

The Fourth NPC was held from January 13 to 17, 1975, preceded by a weeklong preparatory meeting. As with the Ninth and Tenth Party Congresses, the NPC was held in complete secrecy, with delegates entering and exiting the Great Hall of the People through underground tunnels. The Xinhua News Agency didn't report on the Congress until after it had ended.

Zhang Chunqiao delivered the "Report on Amending the Constitution," the drafting of which he had overseen, and which enshrined "the theory of continuous revolution under the dictatorship of the proletariat." The constitution stated that "the Chinese Communist Party is the leadership core of all of China's people," "the People's Republic of China is a socialist state under the dictatorship of the proletariat, led by the worker class and with the worker-peasant alliance as its foundation," and "Marxism, Leninism, and Mao Zedong Thought are the theoretical foundation of our country's guiding ideology." This became the basic content of the "Four Cardinal Principles" that Deng Xiaoping proposed four years later.

Deng Xiaoping had overseen the drafting of the government work report, which in view of Zhou Enlai's poor health was limited to 5,200 words. Zhou read only the beginning and the end of the report on January 13. The highlight of the report was its proposal of "Four Modernizations," which rehashed the Third NPC's objectives of establishing an independent and relatively complete industrial system and national economic apparatus by 1980 and of bringing about a comprehensive modernization of agriculture, industry, national defense, and science and technology that would advance China's national economy to the world's front ranks. It stated that the next ten years would be the key decade for realizing this two-step plan and that the State Council would map out a ten-year long-range plan, five-year plans, and annual plans toward achieving this objective.

This was the first time since the Cultural Revolution began that economic construction was made a national objective, and it was received with enthusiastic applause. At the same time, the report called for the campaign to criticize Lin and Confucius to continue and go deeper.

The Cultural Revolution faction was obliged to take a back seat to the pragmatic faction in the distribution of power during the Fourth NPC. Zhou Enlai remained Premier, with twelve vice-premiers: Deng Xiaoping, Zhang Chunqiao, Li Xiannian, Chen Xilian, Ji Dengkui, Hua Guofeng, Chen Yonggui, Wu Guixian (the only woman), Wang Zhen, Yu Qiuli, Gu Mu, and Sun Jian. Deng Xiaoping was first vice-premier, and a few days after the NPC ended, he took over from Zhou Enlai in overseeing the work of the State Council. The pragmatic faction completely controlled the economy and foreign relations. Chen Yonggui, Wu Guixian, and Sun Jian had come up from the grassroots and had limited political influence. Zhang Chunqiao's sphere of authority, in the cultural and education sector, was far smaller than Deng Xiaoping's. Wang Hongwen, Jiang Qing, and Yao Wenyuan had no formal government positions. The heads of the twenty-nine State Council ministries and commissions were almost all veteran cadres and reinstated military officials; the only ones who had come up through the Cultural Revolution were Minister of Culture Yu Huiyong, Minister of Health Liu Xiangbing, Minister of Metallurgy Chen Shaokun, and the State Sports Committee chairman Zhuang Zedong.

REPROACHING JIANG QING

Mao's desire to protect the Cultural Revolution while also stabilizing social order during the last year of his life were mutually incompatible goals, and the best he could do was to seek a delicate balance between the "restorationists" Zhou and Deng and the Cultural Revolution faction. Protecting the Cultural Revolution no longer entailed supporting the rebel faction's rebellions, but rather imbuing the masses with the theory of opposing and preventing revisionism. In December 1974, the Central Committee handed down Mao's "Summary of Comments on Theoretical Issues," which called for fighting revisionism by expounding on Lenin's demand for dictatorship to be imposed on the bourgeois class. Mao felt that the dictatorship of the proletariat was the only way to restrain the development of a commodity system in China "That's why we need to read more Marxist-Leninist books."

On orders from Mao, Zhang Chunqiao and Yao Wenyuan took charge of selecting thirty-three quotes from Marx, Engels, and Lenin regarding the dictatorship of the proletariat as the basis for Mao's theory of continuous revolution. *People's Daily* published all the quotes on February 22, 1975, followed by Yao Wenyuan's essay "On the Social Foundation of the Lin Biao Anti-Party Clique," published on March 1, 1975, and Zhang Chunqiao's "On Comprehensive Dictatorship over the Bourgeoisie," published on April 1, both on Mao's instructions. Mao ordered all work units throughout the country to run study classes aimed at bolstering the Cultural Revolution through Marxist orthodoxy in hopes that understanding of the theory of continuous revolution under the dictatorship of the proletariat would help the masses complete what Mao had left unfinished.

Mao was fading fast, largely immobilized and with his speech indistinct, as he tried to strike a balance between opposing political forces and prevent major turmoil while he was still alive. This forced him to once again compromise with the bureaucratic clique. The CLCC campaign and the subsequent campaign to beat back the right-deviating verdict-reversal trend represented the last gasp of the Cultural Revolution, and of Mao himself.

At this juncture Jiang Qing was nothing but trouble. Jiang suffered from severe neuroses that made her dependent on sleeping pills.

She saw enemies behind every bush and was prone to hysteria, and she used her status as Mao's wife to lord over everyone. There was discord between Mao and Jiang in their domestic life during Mao's last years, but Jiang was Mao's faithful follower and reliable partner in the political sphere. Even so, Jiang's propensity toward inappropriate remarks and actions caused Mao considerable grief, and Mao felt obliged to reproach Jiang from 1974 onward to prevent the Cultural Revolution faction from sabotaging the political balance and triggering renewed turmoil. On March 20, 1974, Mao wrote a letter to Jiang saying: "It's better if you stay out of sight . . . There are books by Marx and Lenin and myself, but you don't study them. I'm seriously ill and eighty-one years old, and you still don't take that into consideration. You have special privileges, but after I die, how will you manage? You're the kind of person who ignores major matters but obsesses over small things." Mao sent a number of letters admonishing Jiang, but they were the complaints of a husband to a wife and didn't treat Jiang as a political dissident; the letters made no mention of the Gang of Four.

During a Politburo meeting at his swimming pool on July 17, 1974, Mao said, "Comrade Jiang Qing, you need to pay attention! Others resent you, but they don't say it to your face, so you don't know." Mao also said, "She can be considered part of the Shanghai Gang! You all need to be careful not to form a four-member mini-faction!" He added, "She doesn't represent me, she represents herself."[30] This was the first time that Mao criticized Jiang Qing by name in a Politburo meeting, and the first time that he referred to the Gang of Four in the party's highest reaches. Even so, Mao was merely referring to relations among members of the Politburo and wasn't designating them a counterrevolutionary gang. Factions had always existed within the Politburo, and Mao warned Jiang Qing to guard against it rather than saying that the "mini-faction" already existed. The pragmatic faction nevertheless used Mao's criticism of Jiang Qing as a political weapon against the Cultural Revolution faction. Conversely, the Cultural Revolution only shot themselves in the foot when they tried to make use of the political weapon Mao prepared for them against the pragmatic faction: Zhou Enlai's history of empiricism.

When Zhou Enlai attempted to use criticism of the ultra-left to negate the Cultural Revolution in spring 1973, Mao dug out nine essays he had written in 1941 during the Yan'an Rectification Movement to denounce dogmatism and empiricism.[31] The essays vented the sense of grievance Mao had built up while being suppressed in the Central Soviet Area in the early 1930s. Two of the essays named Zhou Enlai as a "representative of empiricism" and "errand runner and sedan-bearer" of dogmatism, the latter term referring to the Comintern faction that had spent time in the Soviet Union, represented by Wang Ming. Thirty years later, Mao had these nine essays reproduced in a large-print edition for circulation among the top leaders, and he told his nephew Mao Yuanxin to make a voice recording of the two essays relating to Zhou Enlai and take it back to Liaoning.[32] When Jiang Qing and the others went all out to denounce Zhou Enlai by innuendo as the "major Confucianist within the party" in June 1974, Mao brought out the nine essays again and revised them for future use. Shortly after that, on July 17, Mao told Politburo members that he had "burned" the essays and "didn't want them anymore,"[33] but in fact, even after Zhou Enlai's death, Mao was still revising the essays and telling people to read them.[34] Jiang Qing probably knew that Mao hadn't burned the essays and believed that Mao would support her and her cohort if they criticized empiricism as a pretext for criticizing Zhou Enlai.

On March 1, the newly appointed head of the PLA General Political Department, Zhang Chunqiao, expounded on "opposing empiricism" at a seminar of military political department heads. The essays published by Yao Wenyuan on March 1 and Zhang Chunqiao on April 1, suggested and vetted by Mao, also mentioned opposing empiricism. In two speeches on March 4 and 5, Jiang Qing referred to empiricism as the "accomplice of revisionism" (a phrase out of Mao's nine essays criticizing Zhou Enlai) and said that it was a greater danger to the party than dogmatism. She also demanded a discussion on opposing empiricism at a Politburo meeting in mid-April.

The Cultural Revolution faction hoped to use Mao's criticism of empiricism to block Deng Xiaoping's rectification of the system when he took charge as first vice-premier in early 1975, but Deng leveraged

Mao's trust in him to neutralize their effort. After accompanying Mao in receiving North Korea's Kim Il-sung on April 18, Deng told Mao how Jiang Qing and Zhang Chunqiao had been actively opposing empiricism since March and expressed his own disagreement with the claim that "empiricism is the greatest danger at present." Mao indicated that he agreed with Deng.[35]

The influence of Deng's remark soon became apparent. On April 23, Mao wrote a memo stating that opposition to revisionism should include both empiricism and dogmatism: "Both of them revise Marxism-Leninism, so one should not be mentioned while ignoring the other." Mao also castigated party officials who scolded people on theoretical issues despite their own ignorance of Marxisim-Leninism, and suggested that the Politburo discuss this issue.[36]

After Yao Wenyuan read out Mao's memo at a Politburo meeting on April 27, everyone but Jiang Qing, Wang Yongwen, Zhang Chunqiao, and Yao Wenyuan demanded that it be issued. Wu De took the opportunity to criticize reports being circulated without the approval of Mao or the Politburo, and said that opposition to empiricism was targeting veteran cadres: "You're engaging in factionalism!"[37] Ye Jianying and Deng Xiaoping added their own harsh criticism, with Ye saying, "The Chairman has called you a 'Gang of Four' and told you to halt your activities. Did you stop or keep on going?" Jiang Qing was forced to carry out self-criticism. In a subsequent letter to Mao, Wang Hongwen said that Zhou Enlai, Ye Jianying, and Deng Xiaoping had presented a bleak picture at the Politburo meeting and were supporting and tolerating the worst rumors that were going around: "During this dispute, Ye and Deng said what the Premier wanted to say but wouldn't, and their objective was to reverse the verdict of last December's meeting."[38] Jiang Qing said Deng and the others had engaged in a "surprise attack" and that she'd been "besieged from all sides."

The critical moment for a confrontation between the pragmatic faction and Cultural Revolution faction had arrived.

On April 29 and 30, Zhou Enlai had separate discussions with Deng Xiaoping, Hua Guofeng, Wu De, Chen Xilian, and Wang Hongwen to gain an understanding of what had occurred at the Politburo meeting. On May 2, Zhou had his secretary pull out the editorial note to Yao Wenyuan's March 1 essay as well as a March 21 *People's Daily* editorial titled "Leading Cadres Must Take the Lead in Learning Well," both of which criticized empiricism.

On the night of May 3, Mao called a Politburo meeting at his Zhongnanhai swimming pool. It was the last Politburo meeting over which Mao presided, and Zhou Enlai left the hospital to attend. Mao shielded the Cultural Revolution faction by taking responsibility for the attack on empiricism, but he also gently rapped them on the knuckles: "Don't form a Gang of Four. Why do you keep doing this? Why don't you engage in unity with the more than two hundred Central Committee members?" He admonished Jiang Qing: "Don't be so willful. You need to be disciplined and circumspect. Don't go off on your own. If you have an opinion, discuss it in the Politburo and issue it as a document in the name of the Central Committee, not in any individual's name, including mine."[39]

On the afternoon of May 4, Deng Xiaoping went to the hospital to talk with Zhou Enlai about criticizing the Gang of Four, and then Zhou had a long talk with Wang Hairong and Tang Wensheng. That night, Zhou Enlai presided over a meeting of the Politburo Standing Committee in the Great Hall of the People to discuss how to implement Mao's remarks at the May 3 Politburo meeting. Mao wasn't allowing publication of his April 23 memo since the gist of it had been reflected in an article in *Red Flag*.

On May 4 and 5, Zhou drafted an opinion paper on theoretical studies and on the Politburo's work. The opinion paper identified recent attacks on empiricism in the media and internal publications as mistaken because they discouraged "those with long-term qualifications and who know how to fight battles . . . and agitated millions of people."[40] After discussions with Li Xiannian, Ji Dengkui, Su Zhenhua, Wu De, Ye Jianying, and Deng Xiaoping, Zhou on May 21 sent a letter to the entire Politburo saying that Yao Wenyuan's essay had been the first to state that "at present, empiricism is the greatest danger," and that Zhang Chunqiao had one-sidedly emphasized the "danger of empiricism" at a meeting of the PLA General Political Department. Zhou suggested sending this letter to Mao. When Zhang Chunqiao wrote a memo suggesting that Zhou's letter contained "some inaccuracies," Zhou Enlai backed up his claims with cables from the political departments of the various military regions, apparently wanting to nail down Zhang Chunqiao's errors in preparation for the Politburo meeting to criticize Jiang Qing. Zhou's failing health gave him a sense of urgency. He told Tan Zhenlin and Wang Dongxing, "I estimate I have half a year left," and he asked hospital staff to tell him the truth about his condition so that he could make the necessary arrangements.[41]

Opposing empiricism became a major issue because it meant opposing the reinstated veteran cadres as well as Zhou Enlai. Given Mao's need for Zhou Enlai and the other veteran cadres to achieve "stability and unity," this issue highlighted his dilemma over the contradiction between defending the Cultural Revolution and restoring order.

While presiding over a Politburo meeting in the East Hall of the Great Hall of the People on May 27, Deng Xiaoping used Mao's words to denounce Jiang Qing and the others, saying that Mao's May 3 criticism of the Gang of Four was related to the stability and unity of the Politburo and the issue of the "three wants and three don't wants."[42] Regarding the claim that the criticism of Jiang on April 27 had been "excessive," Deng said, "Not even 40 percent was spoken of—perhaps not even 20 percent, much less was it 'excessive' or a 'surprise attack.'" Speaking sternly and pounding the table, Deng emphasized the need to clarify three things about Jiang Qing: her description of the December 1973 criticism of Zhou Enlai and Ye Jianying as the "eleventh line struggle"; the 1974 CLCC campaign opposing use of the back door as a betrayal of Marxism-Leninism; and the criticism of empiricism in 1975. Li Xiannian, Wu De, and Chen Xilian also gave speeches along the same lines. The next day, Zhou Enlai asked Deng Xiaoping and others to brief him on the Politburo's denunciation of the Gang of Four.[43]

The Politburo held another meeting to denounce Jiang Qing on June 3. There was an awkward silence at first, because no one was certain about Mao's attitude. Ye Jianying broke the ice by defending the April 27 Politburo meeting and saying that Jiang Qing hadn't requested instructions from Mao before speaking of an eleventh line struggle and opposing the back door and empiricism. Closely questioned by the majority of Politburo members, Wang Hongwen was obliged to engage in self-criticism.[44] Criticism of Jiang Qing carefully followed Mao's tone and did not extend the focus beyond the "three matters," while the Politburo members also cautiously endorsed the criticism of Zhou Enlai and Ye Jianying at the December 1973 Politburo meeting.

In early June, Mao told Jiang Qing to have a talk with Deng Xiaoping. Deng subsequently said that the conversation didn't go well, with a lot of useless spouting off by Jiang.[45] This suggests that Jiang admitted no wrongdoing and was only patching things up at Mao's request. After the first denunciation meeting, Jiang complained to Mao that Deng had engaged in a "surprise attack" and "score settling," but Mao didn't relent and told her to write a self-criticism. On June 28, Jiang Qing submitted a self-criticism, which Zhou Enlai distributed to Politburo members on June 30 with a memo saying that he welcomed it and suggesting that it be sent to Mao. Mao drew a circle on the document to show he had read it.

After carrying out self-criticism, the usually overbearing Jiang reportedly became unusually subdued and didn't appear in public for a long time. At Mao's suggestion, Wang Hongwen was sent to Zhejiang and Shanghai to "assist operations" in the latter half of June 1975, and soon after that Deng Xiaoping took over management of the Politburo's daily operations.

Jiang Qing made her displeasure known at a banquet for more than a hundred journalists and cultural workers during the conference "Learn from Dazhai in Agriculture" in Xiyang County, Shanxi Province, in September 1975. She said, "They persecuted this old lady for more than a month in Beijing."

Although Mao himself criticized Jiang and the others for opposing empiricism, he also said, "I don't think it's a major issue and it shouldn't be blown out of proportion." Had Deng Xiaoping blown it out of proportion? As usual, it was Zhou Enlai who truly understood Mao. On April 28, 1975, the day after Jiang Qing was denounced for the first time, Zhou had Wu De come to see him at the No. 305 Hospital and said solemnly, "You know, the Chairman is taking a wait-and-see attitude toward both sides; they're going to fight back, and when they do, you won't be able to stand it."[46] Ji Dengkui also recalls Zhou expressing worries at this time. He repeatedly reminded Ji to take note of Mao's attitude and said that Mao was still watching and had not yet made a final determination, so it was possible that the situation would still change.[47]

25
—

FROM GENERAL OVERHAUL TO THE CAMPAIGN AGAINST DENG AND RIGHT-DEVIATING VERDICT-REVERSAL

DENG XIAOPING'S GENERAL OVERHAUL

Veteran cadres gained the advantage in the formation of the cabinet at the Fourth National People's Congress, and Jiang Qing drew back for a while after being reprimanded. Once Mao put Deng Xiaoping in charge of the government's overall operations, Deng was in the position to accomplish great things, and he chose to undertake a general overhaul[1] to mend the chaos caused by the Cultural Revolution. The people wanted social order restored, the economy to develop, and living conditions to improve. Political fervor is always difficult to sustain in the population at large, and with even the most enthusiastic activists exhausted by the constant upheaval of the Cultural Revolution, Deng's efforts to end the turmoil gained widespread support. Even so, Mao was still alive, and years of propaganda work ensured that the theory of continuous revolution continued to influence the public mindset, and that the marginalized rebel faction remained a force to be reckoned with. Knowing that he was at loggerheads with long-imbued theory and the situation created by the Cultural Revolution, Deng cowed his opponents into submission by playing the Mao card and making the "Three-Point Directive" the guiding principle for his general overhaul.

Mao's "Three-Point Directive" called for (1) stability and unity, (2) improving the national economy, and (3) studying the theory of dictatorship of the proletariat. Mao had repeatedly called for stability and unity since the Lin Biao incident, and had also spoken of the need to improve the national economy on several occasions since Li Xiannian reported to him on the national economy on October 20, 1974. Studying the theory of dictatorship of the proletariat was what mattered most to Mao, and the Central Committee had issued Mao's comments on theoretical issues in December 1974 and a directive to study them in February 1975 (Central Committee Document No. 5 [1975]).

The first two items were urgent issues, while the third was Mao's long-term strategy of continuous revolution. Mao regarded distribution according to work done, currency transactions, and small production to be hotbeds of capitalist restoration, and since improving the national economy required developing the commodity economy, Mao's first two directives came into conflict with the third. Deng Xiaoping bound all three together as "general principles for the work of the entire country and party," but he actually implemented only the first two and paid mere lip service to "studying theory." Essentially, the "Three-Point Directive" hoisted Mao by his own petard.

This conflict carried into the ongoing contest of strength between the Cultural Revolution faction, which stressed studying theory, and the bureaucratic faction, which emphasized stability and unity and improving the national economy. Since the bureaucratic faction's position answered China's most urgent needs at that time, it was regarded as the "pragmatic faction." The pragmatists saw the rebel faction's lack of submission to the power structure as a source of disorder, so rebels were the main targets of suppression in the name of "establishing orderly production." In some places, "suppressing factionalism" became a pretext for veteran cadres to avenge themselves on rebels.

For the purpose of the general overhaul, Deng had the State Council's Political Research Department (effectively Deng's think tank, established on July 5, 1975) draft three documents.

The first document was "On a General Program for the Work of the Entire Party and Entire Country," drafted by Hu Qiaomu, Deng Liqun, and Hu Jiwei. It accused those who "rebelled under the red banner" of "engaging in revisionism under the banner of opposing revisionism, and in restoration under the banner of opposing restoration," and warned them to "correct their errors and be good party members" or face the risk of "stumbling into the pit of counterrevolution."

The document was completed in October 1975, but due to changes in the political wind, it was never issued.

The second document, "Regarding Certain Issues in Accelerating Industrial Development" (known as "Twenty Articles on Industry"), was drafted by Hu Qiaomu, Yu Guangyuan, Deng Liqun, and others and completed in November 1975. This programmatic document for reorganizing the management of enterprises stipulated the need to "especially be on guard against sabotage carried out by evildoers in the name of 'rebelling' and 'going against the tide.'" Although the political wind shifted before it could be issued, its spirit was communicated to the grassroots level.

The third document, "Several Issues Regarding Scientific and Technological Work" (also known as "Report Outline on the Work of the Academy of Sciences"), was drafted under the direction of Hu Yaobang, Li Chang, and others. This document emphasized allowing intellectuals to truly fulfill their purpose by engaging in scientific and technological work and quoted Mao as saying, "Science and technology is productive force" (Mao subsequently denied ever saying that). The shifting political wind also prevented this document from being officially issued, but it circulated among intellectuals, who warmly welcomed it.

Even without being officially issued, the three documents served as the guiding ideology for Deng Xiaoping's general overhaul.

The railways served as a classic case. These arteries of the national economy were constantly blocked, impeding the conveyance of goods and routinely transporting passengers to their destinations hours behind schedule. Some lines were completely paralyzed. Improving the national economy required first making the railways operational again. With a mighty push from Deng Xiaoping, the "CCP Central Committee Resolution Regarding Enhancing Railway Work" (Document No. 9 [1975]) was issued on March 5, 1975, putting railway transport under the centralized management of the Railways Ministry. It emphasized the need to transfer and discipline "leading cadres and supervisors with serious bourgeois factionalism" and to "overhaul railway transport, battle all kinds of sabotage, and enhance dictatorship of the proletariat."

Once Mao marked the document with a circle, it became an

imperial sword that Railway Minister Wan Li wielded at a mass rally on March 9 to resolutely reorganize the leadership ranks of the Xuzhou Railway Bureau. Rebel leaders such as Gu Binghua were arrested, and the seriously disrupted Xuzhou railway was quickly restored to order. In April, Wan Li led a work group that extended the Xuzhou experience to Taiyuan, Zhengzhou, and Nanchang. Nearly ten thousand factionalists were denounced, more than two thousand lawbreakers arrested, and more than one hundred executed.[2] On June 2, 1975, the Central Committee endorsed and transmitted the Jiangsu provincial party committee's report on the implementation of Central Committee Document No. 9 in Xuzhou Prefecture, which required all localities to reference the experience in Jiangsu and denounce excessively factional leading cadres. With orderly railway service restored and blockages removed, the vast majority of railway bureaus were able to exceed their planned objectives. Given the scale of the campaign, however, it was inevitable that some people were wrongfully victimized, and these injustices planted the seeds for the "counterattack against right-deviating verdict reversal" that followed several months later.

Deng Xiaoping used the railways as a model for readjustments in the industrial sector, even having Wan Li describe his reorganization of the railways at a seminar on the iron and steel industry from May 8 to 29. In his concluding speech on the twenty-ninth, Deng called for ridding the iron and steel industry of persistent factionalists "without giving an inch, and with great fanfare," and for establishing leadership that would strengthen enterprises.[3] In this speech, Deng for the first time referred to Mao's issuing the "Three-Point Directive": "This will be the guiding principle for every item of our work in the period going forward." The 1983 edition of *Selected Works of Deng Xiaoping* edited out this sentence.

Deng Xiaoping's ambition was all-encompassing. His general overhaul included not only the railways but also the military, the cultural and scientific communities, education, and agriculture.

In a speech at a conference for military cadres on January 25, 1975, Deng communicated Mao's directive to reorganize the military. The "Three Supports and Two Militaries" policy had resulted in several rounds of military cadres being sent to the localities and promoted, and now that military cadres had been recalled to the ranks, the establishment had become badly bloated, with seven to eight deputies under commanders and political commissars at every level. The expansion of the military's power had also resulted in rampant corruption. Deng Xiaoping diagnosed the military's main problems as "bloat, slackness, arrogance, extravagance, and indolence." At an enlarged Central Military Commission meeting from June 24 to July 15, Ye Jianying and Deng Xiaoping reduced every level of leadership to one principal and one or two deputies,[4] and on August 30, 1975, the Central Committee and Mao approved a CMC notice that completely restructured the PLA's headquarters, branches, and military regions. Although Zhang Chunqiao was in charge of appointing and dismissing cadres as head of the Political Department, Deng Xiaoping was an insider, and as chief of General Staff he stacked all levels of the military leadership with people he trusted. Zhang Chunqiao grumbled to Wang Hongwen, "I'm just a rubber stamp; someone else has arranged a leadership structure for the General Political Department to submit for approval under the name of Zhang Chunqiao, but my views were never solicited."[5]

Deng's general overhaul also focused on the provincial leadership, and in the course of a little more than half a year, attacks on a large number of factionalist cadres were accompanied by a positive turnaround in production. Deng Xiaoping then ventured onto Jiang Qing's turf: the cultural sector. Under Deng's repeated advice, Mao acknowledged that artistic production had become limited to a handful of model operas as creativity was stifled by political criticism. "The party's cultural policies need to be adjusted, and there should be gradual expansion of cultural programs."[6] All this was consistent with public demand.

Deng's attempts to rally support among senior cadres occasionally backfired, however.

Before the Central Committee sent Jia Qiyun to Yunnan as provincial party secretary and chairman of the provincial revolutionary committee in autumn 1975, Deng repeatedly warned Jia to resolutely oppose factionalism and to take reorganization of the leadership ranks firmly in hand, in particular relying on veteran cadres: "If people accuse you of being a restorationist, that means you're doing it right."

Deng said the same things when Zhao Ziyang was sent to Sichuan. Later, when Deng was denounced in March 1976, Jia revealed what Deng had told him, and it became "heavy-duty artillery" in the attacks on Deng. Zhao Ziyang, however, said nothing. When the Gang of Four was arrested and Deng was once more restored to power, Jia Qiyun was discharged, and Zhao Ziyang was appointed to a key post in the central government.

Betrayal also came from another senior cadre whom Deng took into his confidence. After seeing off foreign guests he'd accompanied to Shanghai on June 12, 1975, Deng invited Ma Tianshui to his guesthouse for a confidential chat. Born in 1912 and joining the party in 1931, Ma Tianshui was a ranking official who served as Shanghai's party secretary and vice-chairman of its revolutionary committee and was a member of the Central Committee. Under his leadership, Shanghai's industry was showing signs of improvement. Taking Ma aside to "keep him in the loop," Deng complained about the attack on empiricism and advised him, "From now on when you come to Beijing, go straight to Li Xiannian and Yu Qiuli. You can also come straight to my home and talk with me." After Deng left, Ma Tianshui told Xu Jingxian, Wang Qiuzhen, and other members of the Shanghai municipal party committee what Deng had said, and he also submitted a report to Wang Hongwen titled "Deng Xiaoping's Incitement of Me to Defect." With Zhang Chunqiao's encouragement, Ma Tianshui gave a speech at a Central Committee meeting in February 1976 that became another "heavy artillery shell" lobbed at Deng.[7]

MAO'S ATTITUDE CHANGES

Deng Xiaoping's negation of the Cultural Revolution crossed Mao's bottom line and cost Deng his support. Mao's nephew, Mao Yuanxin, played a key role in keeping Mao informed of the consequences of Deng's general overhaul.

Mao Yuanxin, born in Xinjiang in 1941, was the son of Mao's younger brother, Mao Zemin. Mao Zemin was killed along with Chen Tanqiu when the warlord who controlled Xinjiang, Sheng Shicai, arrested more than a hundred Communist Party members in September 1942. Mao Yuanxin's mother eventually remarried Fang Zhichun, the vice-governor of Jiangxi, and after attending top schools in Beijing, Mao Yuanxin was admitted to Tsinghua University's radio department and then to Harbin's Military Engineering Institute, where he joined the Red Rebel Regiment when the Cultural Revolution began. In 1974, Mao Yuanxin was appointed to a key position in the Shenyang military, and eventually became party secretary of Liaoning Province and vice-chairman of its revolutionary committee.

Since his father had been a martyr to the cause in Xinjiang, Mao Yuanxin accompanied a Central Committee delegation to celebrate the twentieth anniversary of the establishment of the Xinjiang Uighur Autonomous Region in late September 1975. While passing through Beijing on September 27, Mao Yuanxin reported to his uncle on the progress of the Cultural Revolution in the northeast. When Mao Yuanxin passed through Beijing again on his way back from Xinjiang on October 10, Mao had him stay behind to serve as his liaison man with the Politburo. By then, Mao could move only with great difficulty. His hands shook so much that others had to help him eat and drink, and his speech was reduced to an unintelligible croak. The fate of China rested on this ailing man.

Mao Yuanxin told Mao that there were mixed feelings in Liaoning regarding the Cultural Revolution and that the mood "seemed to be worse than when ultra-leftism was criticized in 1972." He observed that Deng Xiaoping "very seldom talks of the accomplishments of the Cultural Revolution, and very seldom criticizes Liu Shaoqi's revisionist line," and he felt there were "problems in the speeches of several vice-premiers" at a State Council meeting discussing ideological guidelines earlier that year.[8]

It wasn't only Mao Yuanxin who changed Mao's attitude toward Deng Xiaoping. Mao made his comments on the classical novel *The Water Margin* before Mao Yuanxin began accompanying him.

Nearly blind, Mao had a female Peking University instructor, Lu Di, read classical works to him. In the early hours of August 14, 1975, Lu Di asked Mao's appraisal of classics such as *The Water Margin* and *The Romance of the Three Kingdoms*. Mao said: "*The Water Margin* serves as negative teaching material so people will recognize the capitulationist faction. *The Water Margin* only opposes corrupt officials and not the emperor . . . Song Jiang capitulates and engages in revisionism. He changes Chao Gai's hall of rebellion into a hall of loyalty and righteousness, and later accepts amnesty and pledges loyalty to the emperor. The struggle between Song Jiang and Gao Qiu is a struggle between different factions within the landlord class."[9] Mao agreed with Lu Xun's critique that by turning against their fellow bandits on behalf of the empire, Song Jiang and the others become slaves. Mao said that the shorter version of *The Water Margin* was less authentic, and he called for all three versions—with 100 chapters, 120 chapters, and 70 chapters—to be published with Lu Xun's commentary at the beginning.[10]

Upon learning of Mao's instructions, Yao Wenyuan, who was in charge of publishing, wrote to Mao on August 18 with a plan to discuss *The Water Margin* in *People's Daily* and *Guangming Daily* and to draft essays from the perspectives of criticizing capitulationism, revisionism, and class-struggle concessionism. Mao responded with a memo stating, "I agree."[11] From then on, a large number of articles were published criticizing *The Water Margin*, and some work units organized "theory groups" to criticize the novel.

The Cultural Revolution faction immediately made use of Mao's directive to critique *The Water Margin*. Toward the end of August, Jiang Qing told Minister of Culture Yu Huiyong and Vice-Minister Liu Qingtang, "The crucial point in *The Water Margin* is making a figurehead of Chao Gai,[12] as some in the party are now making a figurehead of Chairman Mao."[13] She was clearly referring to Zhou Enlai's and Deng Xiaoping's influence, but since Zhou Enlai was gravely ill, she mainly meant Deng Xiaoping. Jiang and Deng presented their rival viewpoints at the national conference "Learn from Dazhai in Agriculture" in mid-September. Deng Xiaoping quoted Mao on the need for an overhaul in everything from the military and local governments to industry, agriculture, commerce, culture, education, and the ranks of science and technology, while Jiang Qing focused on *The Water Margin* and the "struggle between the two roads."

Zhou Enlai, still hospitalized, had someone bring him the various editions of *The Water Margin* to study and said, "It's very clear who's being targeted in the criticism of the 'capitulationist faction' in critiquing *The Water Margin*. If there really were a capitulationist faction, of course it should be criticized, but that is not the reality. Although I've made mistakes in the past, I've spent decades devoting my efforts to the best interests of the party and the people!"[14] After receiving guests from Thailand in the company of Li Xiannian and Qiao Guanhua on July 1, Zhou agreed to have his photo taken with hospital staff, but he told them, "This is the last time I'll have a photo taken with you, and I hope you won't cross my face off afterward."[15] Before going into surgery on September 20, Zhou Enlai requested the transcript of his speech on the "Wu Hao issue," which he gave at the reporting meeting for the campaign to criticize Lin and Confucius in June 1972. He signed his name to the transcript and noted clearly, "Before going into surgery, September 20, 1975." As he was wheeled into the operating room, Zhou called out, "I'm loyal to the party and the people! I'm not a capitulator!"[16]

Deng Xiaoping did all he could to downplay Mao's remarks about *The Water Margin*, telling Hu Qiaomu on August 21 that they were purely literary criticism and in no way referred to struggle within the party.[17] When a group of journalists from New Zealand asked him for "actual examples of capitulationism" on September 5, Deng replied, "It's Liu Shaoqi and Lin Biao."

Deng was present when Mao received the first secretary of the Vietnam Labor Party, Le Duan, on September 24 and told him, "We have a leadership crisis at present," describing his own advanced age and the poor health of Zhou Enlai, Kang Sheng, and Ye Jianying. Pointing at Deng, Mao said, "He's the only able-bodied man." Afterward, Deng reported to Mao on recent work, and upon hearing of Jiang Qing's speech at the "Learn from Dazhai" conference, Mao said, "Bullshit! It's totally irrelevant! They were supposed to be learning about agriculture and she's off criticizing *The Water Margin*. That woman just doesn't understand. Few people trust her up there." (Mao was referring to the Politburo.) Hua Guofeng told Mao that Jiang Qing wanted the recording of her speech at the conference broadcast, but Mao directed, "The transcript is not to be circulated, the recording is not to be broadcast, and the speech is not to be printed."[18]

Facing a leadership crisis, Mao needed the "able-bodied man" Deng Xiaoping to hold the fort, but two letters from Tsinghua University's

Liu Bing finally made Mao shift his remaining energy toward defending what he considered the second greatest accomplishment of his life, the Cultural Revolution.

Liu Bing, the deputy party secretary of Tsinghua University before the Cultural Revolution, had been struck down by the work group sent in by Liu Shaoqi, but was eventually reinstated as the university's deputy party secretary in January 1970 because he "genuinely came to stand with Chairman Mao's revolutionary line." In January 1972, Chi Qun, propaganda chief of the Central Security Unit 8341 and leader of Tsinghua's Mao Zedong Thought Propaganda Team, was named university party secretary and chairman of the university's revolutionary committee. Mao's confidential assistant, Xie Jingyi, became deputy party secretary along with Liu Bing, who was in charge of day-to-day operations. Known as "Chairman Mao's two soldiers," Chi and Xie completely controlled the university. Some Cultural Revolution histories describe them as members of the rebel faction, but that's incorrect; Mao sent them to Tsinghua after he abandoned the rebel faction. Chi and Xie followed Mao ideologically, and they endorsed the Cultural Revolution.

Inclined toward Deng Xiaoping, Liu Bing was at odds with Chi Qun and Xie Jingyi. When Liu transmitted a speech that Deng had given on August 3 at a conference of key defense industry enterprises, Xie yelled, "Chi Qun and I have told you, transmitting the speeches of any central leaders has to be cleared by us first. Why did you transmit that without telling us?" Liu Bing later recalled her "enraged face, and the veins popping out of her neck." Liu replied, "Deng Xiaoping is vice-chairman of the party Central Committee, so why can't his speech be transmitted? I'm the deputy secretary in charge of the party committee's day-to-day operations, so don't I have the authority and the responsibility to transmit it?" Xie Jingyi just tossed her head and stomped off huffing and puffing.[19]

Once the conflict between Chi Qun, Xie Jingyi, and Liu Bing erupted, the university party committee could not operate effectively. On August 13, 1975, Liu Bing and the other university party leaders Hui Xianjun, Liu Yi'an, and Lü Fangzheng wrote a letter of complaint to Mao about Chi Qun. Hui, Liu, and Lü had come to Tsinghua as leaders of the propaganda team in July 1968.

The letter started by affirming that the situation of Tsinghua University's "education revolution" was "excellent" and that "the numerous cadres and teachers and staff are elated about it." The letter said that Chi Qun's head had been turned by success, making him arrogant and domineering and entrenched in a bourgeois lifestyle. It described in vivid detail Chi's rage when he wasn't made a minister or Central Committee member after the Tenth Party Congress and Fourth NPC, and how he had descended into binges of alcohol and sleeping tablets, neglected his hygiene and responsibilities, and went running around the streets at night: "He cursed people unceasingly, jumping up and down and breaking his glasses and bruising his ribs. He smashed several sets of state-owned tea services . . ." The letter of complaint had written on it, "To Comrade Xiaoping to forward to the Chairman."

A month passed with no response, so on October 13, Liu and the others sent a second letter saying that it was becoming increasingly obvious that Xie Jingyi was "covering up Chi Qun's errors . . . When Chi Qun was venting his wrath, she knelt before Chi Qun and grasped his hand and said some unprincipled things . . . We hope the Central Committee will solve this problem in our leadership ranks."

Mao had directed his secretary to put the first letter aside, but the second letter touched on one of Mao's most trusted confidants. After reading it, Mao told his secretary to bring him the first letter to read again. Mao asked Mao Yuanxin about Chi Qun and Xie Jingyi's situation, and Mao Yuanxin reported that they had been "quite energetic in executing the Chairman's education revolutionary line, and can be rated seven out of ten." After hearing this, Mao said, "If Chi Qun leaves, won't we need a second Cultural Revolution?" He raged, "When they revile Chi Qun, in fact they're opposing me; perhaps because they don't dare, they put all their anger on Chi Qun."[20] Mao was already displeased with Deng Xiaoping's undermining of the Cultural Revolution, and Liu Bing's letters served as the fuse for him to take action.

On October 19, Mao had a conversation with Li Xiannian and Wang Dongxing, saying: "Rumor has it that I criticized Jiang Qing. I did criticize her, but Jiang Qing didn't get it. Tsinghua University's Liu Bing and others sent me a letter complaining about Chi Qun and Little Xie. Their letter actually targets me. Is Chi Qun a counterrevolutionary? He's made mistakes and should be criticized, but does that mean he has to be struck down and beaten to death? Little Xie led 30,000 people into Tsinghua University."[21] The fact that Mao shifted the topic from Jiang Qing to Chi Qun and Xie Jingyi shows that he was still feeling wounded by the denunciation of Jiang Qing several months earlier. Mao also said, "I'm in Beijing, so why not write directly to me? But they passed it through Xiaoping. You should tell Xiaoping to be careful not to be taken in. Xiaoping is partial toward Liu Bing."[22]

Back when Jiang Qing was being denounced on April 28, Zhou Enlai had predicted, "They're going to fight back, and when they do, you won't be able to stand it."[23] In Zhou's view, this was a crucial juncture in the Politburo's development; with Mao at the brink of death and Deng Xiaoping firmly ensconced in power, it was enough to move ahead steadily and strike sure blows. Zhou had shared these views within a small circle, and Ye Jianying agreed, but Deng Xiaoping ignored him. When things took a turn for the worse, Ye said, "He's always been that way, so opinionated and unwilling to listen to others' views, preferring to do everything single-handedly and never turning back until he hits a brick wall."[24]

Mao finally struck back, but he didn't start out intending to strike down Deng Xiaoping; he merely wanted to make Deng affirm the Cultural Revolution.

MAO TRIES TO MAKE DENG AFFIRM THE CULTURAL REVOLUTION

After hearing a report from Mao Yuanxin on November 2 regarding the attitude of Deng Xiaoping and others toward the Cultural Revolution, Mao said, "The problems relating to Tsinghua aren't isolated; they reflect the current struggle between the two roads. You should have a talk with Xiaoping, Dongxing, Xilian, and the others and express your views to them; put all your cards on the table and don't waffle. You need to help them improve."[25]

Accordingly, Mao Yuanxin had a talk that night with Wang

Dongxing, Chen Xilian, and Deng Xiaoping, and didn't hold back in his criticism. Deng said, "Comrade Yuanxin, to hear you talk, I'm executing a revisionist line! You're saying that the party Central Committee led by Chairman Mao has been engaging in a revisionist line. Put bluntly, we have to consider whether the situation of the entire country has gotten better or worse since Document No. 9."[26] Young and brash, Mao Yuanxin rudely replied, "That's right, you've been engaging in revisionism!"[27] Deng didn't agree with Mao Yuanxin, but he acknowledged the need for self-criticism.

On November 3, Mao Yuanxin went to Mao's swimming pool and told him about the conversation. Mao said, "You weren't mentally prepared and he also didn't expect it, so you butted heads. You had your reasons but things got a little rough and you butted up against him. That's called helping." When Mao Yuanxin said that Deng had taken back what he'd said, Mao was pleased: "He needs to turn around and he's begun to turn. Comrade Xiaoping has a good attitude." Mao directed Mao Yuanxin to bring in four more people—Li Xiannian, Ji Dengkui, Hua Guofeng, and Zhang Chunqiao—and discuss the merits and achievements of the Cultural Revolution. "The Cultural Revolution has two flaws: first, striking down everything, and second, full-scale civil war. Some things were struck down correctly, such as the Liu and Lin cliques, but some were attacked wrongly, including many old comrades. Those people also made mistakes, and it was fine to criticize them a little. The eight of you discuss it first, and if the first meeting doesn't go well enough, meet a second or third time. Don't rush things."[28]

On the night of November 4, Mao Yuanxin reported that participants in the discussion took great exception to what had happened since Deng Xiaoping took over. Wang Dongxing had said he preferred how Mao would criticize various people in order to maintain a unanimous line and not to strike them down. Mao nodded and said, "That's right. It wasn't to strike people down but to correct errors and bring about unity so work would go better. That was why I criticized Jiang Qing, for stability and unity. It's not that we don't want class struggle—class struggle is the guiding principle, and everything else is just a detail." He added that Lenin was right in saying that small production always gives rise to capitalism and in calling for building a capitalist state without the bourgeois class in order to guarantee the bourgeois prerogative.

Mao didn't want commodity production or commodity exchange, or distribution according to work done. He wanted to use executive power to implement his ideal of "Great Harmony," in which everyone was equal. For the sake of this ideal, he had caused the Great Famine that led to the deaths of more than thirty million people. The Cultural Revolution was meant to "smash the old state apparatus" and establish his ideal paradise. He had resigned himself to this being his last National Day celebration, but he hoped to pass down this ideal for others to bring to fruition.

Mao told Mao Yuanxin to keep adding people to the meetings and achieve unity so work could be done better, but told him not to tell Jiang Qing anything about the meetings,[29] fearing that she would do something rash that would upset his political balance.

After the eight-man criticism sessions began, Deng Xiaoping concluded that Mao no longer trusted him and offered to resign as chief of general staff. Mao accepted his resignation but told Deng to remain in charge of foreign affairs.[30] Deng had learned from Lin Biao's example that retaining a tight grip on the military after losing Mao's trust was very dangerous.

To provide ideological encouragement for more cadres to criticize Deng, Mao wrote a memo on November 13 directing the "cautioning" of "old comrades like Zhou Rongxin, Li Chang, Hu Yaobang, Hu Qiaomu, and Li Jingquan."[31] Also vulnerable because of their support for Deng Xiaoping's general overhaul were Zhou Rongxin, in charge of education; Li Chang and Hu Yaobang, in charge of science and technology; and Hu Qiaomu, who had helped draft the "Three-Point Directive."

The general overhaul ground to a halt after nearly nine months.

In accordance with Mao's instructions, a Politburo meeting was held on November 15 and 16, with Deng Xiaoping presiding and Zhou Rongxin, Li Chang, Hu Yaobang, Hu Qiaomu, Liu Bing, and others attending as nonvoting members. Mao Yuanxin communicated Mao's memo regarding Liu Bing's letters, and the nonvoting attendees were obliged to carry out self-criticism regarding their part in writing and transmitting letters. By then, more than ten "debate sessions" had been held at Tsinghua University to denounce Liu Bing, and another mass rally was held to denounce him after this Politburo meeting.

Deng Xiaoping made a strategic retreat and sounded out Mao's attitude toward him with a letter on November 15 suggesting that Wang Hongwen resume his responsibilities for the Central Committee's daily work now that he had returned from Shanghai. Mao wrote a memo: "Comrade Xiaoping should remain in charge for the time being. We'll discuss it again later."[32] Mao's memo didn't clarify his attitude toward Deng, mainly because he had encountered problems over the matter of his successor.

Although Wang Hongwen had a well-rounded background and was more amiable and level-headed than the typical rebel, his rapid promotion had prevented him from accumulating experience at each level, and he was not the kind of person who devoted great effort to study. One time, receiving a foreign head of state without bothering to read the material the Foreign Ministry had sent him, he could think of nothing more meaningful to say than to repeatedly ask, "How do you like the food in China? Are you living comfortably?" Mao was infuriated when Foreign Ministry personnel reported this to him. On another occasion, when Mao was talking to Wang about the restoration of Zhang Xun,[33] Wang didn't know who Zhang Xun was, and all Mao could say was, "Go look it up." He told Zhou Enlai and Deng Xiaoping that Wang was not strong in politics and lacked prestige. That's why Wang was sent back to Shanghai and Zhejiang in the latter half of 1975, and Mao agreed to Ye Jianying's recommendation to have Deng Xiaoping take charge of the Central Committee's work.[34]

The politically thwarted Wang Hongwen had no plans to return to Beijing after being sent to Shanghai. He told the vice-chairman of the Shanghai revolutionary committee, Wang Xiuzhen: "Some people don't acknowledge me as vice-chairman, don't acknowledge the Cultural Revolution, and don't acknowledge the new cadres, and in many places the new cadres have been struck down. We're still struggling over the Cultural Revolution. Look at Deng Xiaoping's speech—isn't it obvious?" With nothing much to do in Shanghai apart from inspecting local work, Wang spent much of his time eating, drinking, hunting, fishing, and watching movies. Ma Tianshui says that he, Xu Jingxian, and Wang Xiuzhen repeatedly urged Wang to return to Beijing: "Hongwen had nothing to do in Shanghai, and Deng Xiaoping was very good at grasping power, so we urged him to hurry back to Beijing. If he kept putting it off, he would gradually lose power and would also lose influence among the masses."

Wang Hongwen returned to Beijing on November 15, but continued his life of leisure, with Ye Jianying inviting him to dinner most often. After one feast, Wang's study adviser, Xiao Mu, spent three hours urging Wang to use his time more constructively. Wang said, "It's hard for me. I can't get anywhere in my work. A lot of people basically refuse to acknowledge the political line of the Tenth Party Congress, or my status as vice-chairman of the Central Committee. Only Marshall Ye supports me. He told me to come back, and I didn't like to refuse."[35]

Having abandoned Wang Hongwen as his designated successor, Mao could only place his hopes on Deng Xiaoping's voicing support for the Cultural Revolution. He put Deng in charge of a resolution stating that the Cultural Revolution had a record of 70 percent achievements and only 30 percent errors, hoping that the bureaucratic clique and the Cultural Revolution faction could reach a consensus and form a joint succession. At a Politburo meeting on November 20 to discuss assessing the Cultural Revolution, Deng Xiaoping stated that it would be inappropriate for him to take charge of writing this resolution because he had been out of circulation for too many years.[36]

Subsequent books and articles claim that Deng locked horns with Mao over assessing the Cultural Revolution, but I believe this requires further study.

After the establishment of the People's Republic of China, Deng always followed Mao closely and stood steadfastly at the front line of the anti-rightist movement, Great Leap Forward, and struggle against Soviet revisionism. Although at the outset of the Cultural Revolution he took Liu Shaoqi's side on sending in work groups and seizing "rightists" among students and the masses, the self-criticisms he sent to Mao made it clear that he endorsed and embraced the Cultural Revolution and would never demand a verdict reversal. Two months before Mao had him preside over the meeting to assess the Cultural Revolution, on September 5, 1975, Deng made remarks to the journalists from New Zealand that were consistent with Mao's attitude toward the Cultural Revolution. The Xinhua News Agency passed along Deng's comments to editors and journalists, and I still have the notes I took at the time.[37] Regarding Mao's comments on *The Water Margin* relating to capitulationism, Deng said:

> This novel is a classical literary work that is very influential in China, but for a long time incorrect viewpoints have existed in assessments of it. This work in fact promotes capitulationism, so it's necessary to clarify its assessment among the people. Second, carrying out assessment of *The Water Margin* has practical significance . . . in denouncing revisionism. Revisionism is capitulationism. Since Khrushchev came to power in the Soviet Union, over the past twenty years, Lenin's socialist state has become a social imperialist state, and engaging in a restoration of capitalism is capitulating to the bourgeoisie. Based on the experience of the Soviet Union, the conclusion we've reached is that if a socialist country completely restores capitalism domestically, it is capitulating to the bourgeoisie and will inevitably become a social imperialist country . . . The Great Proletarian Cultural Revolution, the campaign to criticize Lin and Confucius, and Chairman Mao's recent call to study the theory of the dictatorship of the proletariat are all aimed at opposing revisionism, restorationism, and capitulationism, and are all aimed at strengthening the dictatorship of the proletariat and the socialist system . . . Criticism of *The Water Margin* is part of the content for theoretical study.

Mao put Deng in charge of drafting a resolution in hopes of reaching a consensus that would allow the Cultural Revolution to be brought to a close during his lifetime. Deng considered Mao's request seriously enough to ask Ji Dengkui to draft the resolution for him, but Ji eventually declined, at which Deng stomped off in a rage.[38] Based on Deng's conversation with the delegation of New Zealand journalists, he could have taken on the task if he'd wanted to. Deng's failure to satisfy Mao on this point enabled the Cultural Revolution faction to gradually escalate criticism against Deng.

THE COUNTERATTACK AGAINST THE RIGHT-DEVIATING
VERDICT-REVERSAL TREND

The counterattack against the right-deviating verdict-reversal trend can be said to have begun when Mao took an explicit stand on Liu Bing's letters: that is, on October 19, 1975. Gradually expanding discussions, culminating in the November 20 Politburo meeting, were aimed at forcing Deng Xiaoping to formally affirm the Cultural Revolution and at cautioning other leading cadres to adopt a proper attitude toward the Cultural Revolution.

On November 21, Deng sent Mao a report requesting instructions regarding the "cautioning" meeting slated for 136 cadres. The report said that in accordance with Mao's instructions, "Main Points of Cautioning" had been drafted, which referred to Liu Bing's letters of complaint as "calumny, slander, and rumor that confused black with white," and said that the problem at Tsinghua reflected the existing struggle between the two classes, two roads, and two political lines, "which is a right-deviating verdict-reversal wind" aimed at "squaring accounts over the Cultural Revolution." The cautioning meeting was meant to "use debate to clean up ideology and bring comrades into unity."[39] Time and time again, Mao emphasized that the bourgeois class still existed under socialism and that repeated campaigns were needed to battle against the capitalist roaders who continued to influence the party itself. That's why he couldn't let go of the Cultural Revolution and wanted posterity to continue it on his behalf.

Deng read out the main points approved by Mao at the cautioning meeting that the Central Committee held on November 24. Two days later, the Central Committee issued "Main Points" to the provincial level as Document No. 23 [1975], with Liu Bing's letters appended. This document was further distributed down to the grassroots level on December 10. From then on, the campaign to beat back the right-deviating verdict-reversal trend spread throughout the country. At a Politburo meeting on December 20, Deng Xiaoping carried out self-criticism regarding some methods used in the general overhaul and placed the main blame on his attitude toward the Cultural Revolution, in particular ideological issues.[40]

Deng seemed less than receptive to the Cultural Revolution

faction's exposure and criticism at Politburo meetings, however. Zhang Chunqiao told Ma Tianshui, "We've criticized Deng Xiaoping so much, but he's never said anything, just sitting in his chair smoking one cigarette after another and taking it in calmly . . . He says he's deaf and can't hear what people are saying, but when it was time for the Politburo meeting to end and Hua Guofeng, sitting on the other side of the table, said softly that the meeting was adjourned, Deng heard it right away and jumped up and left."[41]

In another self-criticism at a Politburo meeting on January 3, 1976, Deng faulted himself for not consulting Mao, the Politburo, or the State Council on such a major issue as the "Three-Point Directive as Guiding Principle." Afterward, Deng sent the record of his self-criticism to Mao and asked for a face-to-face meeting to "obtain the Chairman's admonition." Mao wrote a memo, saying, "Print off and distribute Comrade Deng Xiaoping's second self-criticism for discussion by the Politburo."[42] He didn't grant Deng's request for an audience.

By then, Mao was no longer having Deng accompany him in receiving foreign guests. After carrying out self-criticism at another Politburo meeting on January 20, Deng sent a letter to Mao enclosing the text of his self-criticism and again asked for a meeting to seek Mao's approval for relieving him of his responsibilities in the Central Committee.[43] After hearing Mao Yuanxin's report on the Politburo meeting the next day, Mao said that Deng's issue should be treated as a contradiction among the people. "I think his workload can be reduced, but he should not leave his position, that is, don't beat him to death." Mao Yuanxin reminded him, "Hua Guofeng, Ji Dengkui, and Chen Xilian proposed that the State Council request that the Chairman designate someone to take the lead, while the three of them do the concrete work." Mao said, "Ask Hua Guofeng to take the lead; he sees himself as a person of limited political abilities, so Xiaoping can focus on foreign affairs."[44] In this way Mao designated his fourth successor, Hua Guofeng. Mao still hoped that Zhang Chunqiao could be an "adviser," and he had Mao Yuanxin pass on these words to Zhang: "Didn't I serve as an assistant for ten years after the Zunyi Conference?"[45]

Prodded by the Cultural Revolution faction, Tsinghua and Peking Universities began publicly denouncing Deng Xiaoping on January 21,

1976. A week later, Mao had Hua Guofeng take over the Central Committee's day-to-day operations, and Deng Xiaoping surrendered all his authority.

On February 2, 1976, the Central Committee issued Document No. 1 [1976], which was distributed down to the county and brigade level. The notice consisted of two sentences announcing Hua Guofeng's appointment as acting premier of the State Council and Chen Xilian's being put in charge of the Central Military Commission "during the illness of Comrade Ye Jianying." Chen Xilian had become part of Mao's reliable force in the military since the Lin Biao incident. Chen had risen to fame as a twenty-two-year-old regimental commander in the Eighth Route Army during the War of Resistance against Japan when he destroyed twenty-four enemy aircraft in a surprise attack on Shanxi's Yangmingbu Airport on October 19, 1937. In 1955 he was conferred with the rank of general. During the Cultural Revolution, Chen put his full support behind Mao Yuanxin as commander and political commissar of the Shenyang Military Region and chairman of the Liaoning provincial revolutionary committee. Ye Jianying, for his part, had repeatedly sided with Zhou Enlai and Deng Xiaoping in conflict with the Cultural Revolution faction since the February Countercurrent.

In a speech at a meeting that the Central Committee convened for provincial, municipal, autonomous region, and military region leaders on February 25, 1976, Hua Guofeng said that Deng Xiaoping could now be criticized by name. Soon after that, Hua Guofeng's speech was issued as Central Committee Document No. 5 [1976], and the campaign against the right-deviating verdict-reversal trend became a nationwide campaign to "criticize Deng and carry out a counterattack against the right-deviating verdict-reversal trend," with Deng Xiaoping labeled a "still incorrigible capitalist roader."

Despite the fanfare, the campaign against Deng consisted largely of lip service, as opposed to the criticism of work unit leaders at the outset of the Cultural Revolution. Battle groups were not allowed, and the campaign was led by party organizations at the various levels. Industry, agriculture, commerce, and the military were not to be attacked. For this reason, this campaign didn't create major chaos. Much of the criticism was a formality, and big-character posters, criticism rallies, and critical essays largely pandered to the upper levels and news organizations, their numbers often greatly exaggerated.

Some cadres involved in political and ideological work or propaganda followed the political tide and published articles to shape public opinion, which gave the campaign a superficial momentum, but it attracted little genuine enthusiasm, and many among the cadres and masses were suspicious or antagonistic toward it.

On February 8, 1976, a technician at the Chongqing Iron and Steel Company's machine repair shop, Bai Zhiqing, put up a big-character poster at Chongqing's liberation memorial titled "I Love My Motherland," signed with his own name. The poster stated that "heartless beasts" had caused massive economic devastation over the years, and he praised Deng's leadership as leading to "the greatest and fastest increase in the steel industry's annual yield in the past ten years and a comprehensive recovery of the national economy and people's living standards." He was arrested in late March after putting up another big-character poster in Chengdu attacking Zhang Chunqiao at great length. Bai was eventually released on July 3, 1978, and after retiring from the Chongqing Steel Group as an engineer in February 2005, he published *A Detached Look at China, a Tearful Look at China* and other works.

Tsinghua University was a test site for Mao's campaign to criticize Deng and beat back the right-deviating verdict-reversal wind, and people flocked there to read the many big-character posters, which were eventually collected and published in multiple volumes and distributed throughout the country. Some work units were also intensely engaged in the campaign. When the head of the State Commission of Science for National Defense, General Zhang Aiping, was labeled a key Deng follower, the commission's deputy director, the famous guided-missile expert Qian Xuesen, publicly distanced himself from Zhang and put up a big-character poster exposing him as a "chauvinist." At a denunciation rally, Qian said, "Zhang Aiping is a demon! He wants to pull me down with him, beckoning to me like a demon!" Zhang Aiping suffered a heart attack on the spot and had to be hospitalized.[46]

THE CAMPAIGN ON THE GROUND

Once Mao's attitude changed, the Cultural Revolution faction's deep resentment of the general overhaul immediately became a force against Deng Xiaoping. The railway apparatus is one example.

In the new political climate, people who had come under attack in the railway reorganization began filing complaints with the Railways Ministry. The ministry's walls were plastered with banners proclaiming, "Wan Li's suppression of the rebel faction is a crime deserving death," "Ferret out the daring vanguard of Deng Xiaoping's negation of the Cultural Revolution, Wan Li," and "The trains won't run until Wan Li is struck down." At one point, four hundred people besieged the ministry with petitions.[47] The leader of the Zhengzhou Railway Bureau, Tang Qishan,[48] threw his support behind a protest march involving a hundred vehicles and organized a large-scale demonstration.

On February 8, 1976, the Henan provincial party committee leaders Liu Jianxun and Tang Qishan submitted a report to the Central Committee accusing the Zhengzhou Railway Bureau's first party secretary, Su Hua, of "stirring up a right-deviating verdict-reversal wind to reverse the verdict on the Great Proletarian Cultural Revolution." The report placed the main blame on the Railways Ministry and criticized Deng's general overhaul for failing to "distinguish between the two types of contradictions" and "negating the new things and new forces that emerged during the Cultural Revolution." A leader in the Gansu provincial party committee, Xian Henghan, blamed the Railways Ministry and called for beating back the right-deviating verdict-reversal trend under the centralized leadership of the provincial party committee. The Politburo supported Liu Jianxun and Xian Henghan's views, and Wan Li was compelled to carry out self-criticism.

People who had been attacked at various times before 1975 wanted to use the new campaign as an opportunity for rehabilitation. In particular, some former rebel faction leaders hoped to reclaim the status they'd held at the early stage of the Cultural Revolution. This led to turmoil in some localities.

Yunnan Province: In January 1976, leaders of the Eight faction[49] including Huang Zhaoqi (vice-chairman of the provincial revolutionary committee and standing committee member of the provincial party committee), Liu Yinnong (standing committee member of the Kunming municipal party committee and vice-chairman of the municipal revolutionary committee), and Tu Xiaolei put up a number of pseudonymous big-character posters on the streets of Kunming. The posters described the Yunnan provincial party committee's measures against factionalism as a "hacking massacre of the newly emerging force" and Deng Xiaoping as a "fanatical restorationist of capitalism," and called for seizing back power from the capitalist roaders in all sectors.

The trio won the support of Zhu Kejia, who, along with Jia Qiyun and Qilin Wangdan, attended the meeting that Hua Guofeng convened on February 25 to denounce Deng Xiaoping. Zhu was a secondary student from Shanghai who had been sent to Yunnan's Xishuangbanna production brigade in 1969. Reports on his achievements were published in Shanghai's *Wenhui Bao* and other publications in March 1973, and nominated by Zhang Chunqiao, Yao Wenyuan, and others, he became an alternate Central Committee member and a delegate to the Fourth National People's Congress. Approached by the Cultural Revolution faction during the February 25 meeting, Zhu agreed to help turn around the provincial party committee leadership. After returning to Yunnan, he joined Huang Zhaoqi and Liu Yinnong as an energetic leader of the campaign against Deng and the right-deviating verdict-reversal trend.

From March 6 to 28, 1976, the provincial party committee held an enlarged conference for prefectural and municipal party secretaries to transmit the Central Committee's "Notice Regarding Studying Chairman Mao's Important Directives" and Hua Guofeng's speech at the February 25 meeting. Zhu, Huang, Liu, and others denounced Deng and the provincial party committee while at the same time organizing the masses to storm the meeting and seize and struggle some of the attending party committee leaders. On March 13, provincial party secretary Jia Qiyun gave a speech in which he revealed what Deng Xiaoping had said to him in autumn 1975, and criticized himself for "executing a revisionist line" after arriving in Yunnan.

Under pressure from Huang Zhaoqi and others, in late March and early April 1976, the provincial party committee released more than

120 people, largely Eight faction members who had been arrested for their brutal violence against members of the rival rebel faction in late 1968. In some places, those released were greeted with floral wreaths and motorcades, grand processions of drums and gongs, and the setting off of firecrackers. Zhu, Huang, and Liu saw to it that Jia Qiyun, the provincial party committee, and newly reinstated veteran cadres were denounced, and in June and July carried out "crash recruitment and promotion" to "reorganize and replenish the leadership ranks" and bolster the influence of like-minded rebels at all levels of the power structure.[50]

Hubei Province: During Deng Xiaoping's general overhaul, the provincial party committee sent rebel faction leaders such as Hu Houmin, Zhang Liguo, Zhu Hongxia, and Xia Bangyin to rural areas for "tempering during suspension." In February 1976, the provincial party committee notified sent-down individuals that they were to return to Wuhan to take part in the campaign to criticize Deng and beat back the right-deviating verdict-reversal wind. Rebel leaders took this opportunity to begin networking to launch a new struggle. They pasted open letters to the provincial and municipal revolutionary committee leaders all over the city center and strung an enormous banner proclaiming "Closely Follow Chairman Mao, Reascend Jinggang Mountain, Strike Down Deng Xiaoping, Exterminate the Landlord Restitution Corps!" across the Yangtze River Bridge. They organized reporting groups that went around to different work units, and they demanded that provincial party committee leaders "come around" ideologically and allow rebels into the leadership ranks.[51] During this time, some people also tried to reverse the verdict on the imprisoned leader of the Steel faction's Second Command Post, Yang Daoyuan.[52]

Hunan Province: In spring 1976, formal rebel leaders in the provincial and municipal revolutionary committees, led by Tang Zhongfu and Hu Yong, launched a new assault on the Hunan provincial party committee under Zhang Pinghua with the intention of reallocating positions and regaining the power they held in 1968.

Zhejiang Province: As soon as the campaign began, previously disciplined rebels began networking. Five people attending the Central Committee's cautioning meeting in February 1976 drafted an opinion paper criticizing the right-deviating verdict-reversal trend in Zhejiang in 1975, and Wang Hongwen had Tan Qilong remain in Beijing to carry out self-criticism. The provincial party committee's work was taken over by Lai Keke, former secretary of the party committee secretariat and a member of the provincial revolutionary committee.

Sichuan Province: The original Chengdu rebel organizations had dissolved long ago, but during the new campaign, some of their core members joined forces to challenge party committees at various levels. They demanded that wrongfully arrested and sentenced individuals be rehabilitated, people expelled from the revolutionary committees be reinstated and allotted actual power, and people with appropriate family backgrounds be allowed to join the party. Deng's general overhaul in 1975 had led to many rebels being purged, so Mao's launch of the campaign against Deng and right-deviating verdict reversal, especially the directive to "be lenient with rebels," gave them hope of resolving their personal difficulties.

At a rally convened by the provincial party committee on April 2, 1976, to denounce Deng and the right-deviating trend, rebel representatives criticized the provincial party committee under Zhao Ziyang and Zhou Cangbi for executing Deng's political line in 1975 and for promoting capitalist roaders to leadership positions while retaliating against rebels. They pasted their statement of protest on the city's main streets to increase pressure on the provincial revolutionary committee.

Long out of power, rebel leaders now felt able to gather in public, and even members of antagonistic factions began banding together to amplify their influence. Zhao Ziyang made a genuine effort to pacify the rebels and carefully mended various relationships in hopes of resolving the conflict through dialogue. Although the issue of adding mass representatives to the revolutionary committee continued to drag on, rebels with "red" family backgrounds were able to join the party from March to July 1976, and rebels in the party and in revolutionary committees were in many cases allowed to enjoy actual authority.[53]

26

THE APRIL FIFTH MOVEMENT

Deng Xiaoping's comprehensive readjustment in 1975 reflected the public's desire for social stability and economic development, and although arousing the displeasure of steadfast supporters of the Cultural Revolution, it was embraced by the majority of Chinese citizens. For this reason, the campaign to criticize Deng and beat back the right-deviating verdict-reversal trend not only failed to realize Mao's desire to protect the Cultural Revolution but actually exacerbated public discontent and increased people's resentment of Mao and the Cultural Revolution faction. This resentment brewed into political turmoil that was touched off by the death of Zhou Enlai and public mourning for the beloved Premier.

CONFLICT SURROUNDING COMMEMORATIVE ACTIVITIES FOR ZHOU ENLAI

In January 1976, as the Cultural Revolution faction pressed forward and Deng Xiaoping was repeatedly forced to carry out self-criticism, Zhou Enlai was on the brink of death.

On January 1, *Poetry*, *People's Daily*, and *Red Flag* magazine published two poems by Mao titled "Reascending Chingkang Mountain—to the Tune of Shui Tiao Keh Tou" and "Two Birds: A Dialogue—to the Tune of Nien Nu Chiao."[1] Mao had written both poems in 1965, and now they were published for the first time, apparently in coordination with the ongoing campaign against the right-deviating verdict-reversal trend. *People's Daily, Liberation Army Daily*, and *Red Flag* also published a joint editorial in their first editions of the New Year titled "Nothing in the World Cannot Be Overcome, as Long as We Dare to Climb," which included Mao's directive of two months before: "Stability and unity does not mean rejecting class struggle. Class struggle is the guiding principle, and all the rest is detail," meant as a criticism of Deng Xiaoping's "Three-Point Directive as Guiding Principle." That sentence had previously been published only in Central Committee documents circulated at a certain level, but now it was being made public to show that the campaign to criticize Deng and beat back the right-deviating verdict-reversal trend would be ramped up in the new year.

On that day, the comatose Zhou Enlai regained a measure of consciousness. Hearing the broadcast of Mao's poems, he ordered his staff to buy the book and read the poems to him and then place the book beside his pillow.

Just before 10:00 a.m. on January 8, Zhou Enlai died at the No. 305 Hospital at the age of seventy-eight.

Zhou Enlai had faithfully executed Mao directives throughout the first six years of the Cultural Revolution, but his popularity hadn't suffered, because people had not yet become hostile toward the Cultural Revolution. After the Lin Biao incident, an increasing number of people became disenchanted with the Cultural Revolution or even opposed it outright, and they sided with Zhou Enlai in his disagreement with Mao over what Lin Biao represented. The average Chinese knew nothing about the leadership's denunciation of Zhou in 1973, but most knew that Zhou had become a target of the campaigns to criticize Lin Biao and Confucius and to beat back the right-deviating verdict-reversal trend; and his death, while he was under criticism, won him widespread public sympathy. Throughout the country, people who were unhappy with the Cultural Revolution launched commemorations for Zhou Enlai.

Zhou's death before Mao's was advantageous to the Cultural Revolution faction at this key juncture and certainly was a source of private glee. Yet they countered public sentiment by discouraging commemorative activities, knowing full well that these spontaneous actions were an expression of discontent. They didn't realize that their suppression would only intensify public rancor.

On January 9, the Xinhua News Agency requested instructions on how to report on Zhou Enlai's death. Yao Wenyuan replied, "A eulogy has not yet been issued, so there are no plans at this time. Once the eulogy is issued, request instructions on whether or not to issue organized responses." Under Yao's prohibition order, in the six days following Zhou's death, Xinhua published only two news items regarding commemorative activities by the leadership.

A farewell ceremony was carried out in the mortuary of Beijing Hospital. In the past, such ceremonies for state leaders had been held in spacious and dignified venues such as the Hall of Supreme Harmony or in the Workers' Cultural Palace, and ordinary citizens were indignant that Zhou Enlai's ceremony was held in this cramped and depressing place. Everyone attending the ceremony looked sorrowful except Jiang Qing, who glanced around disrespectfully while standing in front of Zhou's remains. Her behavior exacerbated the mounting public antipathy toward her.

In accordance with instructions from above, many work units restricted memorial activities on the basis that they were not to interfere with the campaign to beat back right-deviating verdict reversal. In many places, people were forbidden to wear black armbands, deliver floral wreaths, put up memorial shrines, hold memorial meetings, or display portraits of Zhou. These prohibitions only inflamed public indignation.

On the afternoon of January 11, Wang Hongwen, Wang Dongxing, Deng Yingchao, the funeral committee, and Zhou's closest friends delivered Zhou Enlai's remains to the Babaoshan Revolutionary Cemetery for cremation. A million people lined the route in the freezing weather to pay their last respects, and wails of sorrow accompanied the hearse's slow progress, with some people kneeling down before the hearse and weeping. Zhou's public reputation had been burnished by his unstinting efforts for China's revolution, as well as his restrained personal habits and unusually scandal-free and childless marriage to Deng Yingchao, and his degraded posthumous treatment aroused widespread sympathy. But there was more to the public mourning than that. Thirty years later, Bao Tong[2] astutely observed, "It wasn't because they understood Zhou Enlai so well, but rather because they understood Mao Zedong all too well. The entire significance of the mourning for Zhou was in the loss of faith in Mao." Knowing very well that beneath the sorrow roiled deep-seated hostility toward Mao, the authorities did all they could to suppress the grieving and protect Mao. Xinhua journalists wrote a lengthy article describing how the masses saw off Zhou Enlai's hearse, only to have it edited down to nothing and then finally spiked under Yao Wenyuan's orders.

From January 12 to 14, more than forty thousand people from all sectors of Beijing society attended a ceremony for Zhou Enlai at the Workers' Cultural Palace, after which Zhou's ashes were laid to rest in the Great Hall of the People.

As the official media, acting under Yao Wenyuan's instructions, continued to deflect attention from the memorial activities and play up reports on the campaign to criticize Deng and beat back the right-deviating verdict-reversal trend, public resentment seethed.

On January 15, flags were flown half-staff throughout the country, and at the official memorial ceremony held that afternoon in the Great Hall of the People, Deng Xiaoping represented the Central Committee in delivering the eulogy. Then, in accordance with Zhou Enlai's last wishes, his ashes were scattered from an airplane over Beijing, Tianjin, and the Yellow River estuary in northeastern Shandong. Since Mao had attended Chen Yi's memorial meeting, people expected him to attend Zhou Enlai's as well, but Mao said, "I can't move." People did not fail to notice, however, that Mao continued to receive foreign guests after Zhou's death.[3] Meanwhile, Yao Wenyuan spiked a Xinhua roundup of memorial activities on January 16, and on January 28, Jiang Qing suppressed a documentary film titled *In Immortal Memory of Our Esteemed and Beloved Premier Zhou Enlai*, while the increasingly strident denunciations of Deng Xiaoping were accompanied by aspersions against Zhou.

Public commemorations of Zhou Enlai continued to proliferate from January to April, and displaying photographs of Zhou became a way to resist the Cultural Revolution faction. Some ninety million copies were printed of a 1973 photo by the Italian photographer Georgio Lotti showing Zhou Enlai reclining on a sofa, titled "Zhou Enlai Lost in Thought."[4]

Public discontent came to a head in the Nanjing Incident, which had nationwide repercussions. In the first week after Zhou Enlai's death, more than 320,000 people from more than 2,500 Nanjing work units went to a memorial hall in the Meiyuan Residential Quarter to mourn Zhou Enlai, only to find the memorial hall closed to the public. Then, on the March 5th Lei Feng commemoration day,[5] Shanghai's *Wenhui Bao*, controlled by the Cultural Revolution faction, omitted Zhou Enlai's tribute to Lei Feng while publishing those by Mao and Zhu De. On March 12, students from Nanjing University signed a joint letter calling *Wenhui Bao* to account: "What is your standpoint? . . . Whose interests do you represent?" On March 24, more than two hundred students and staff from the traditional Chinese medicine department of the Jiangsu New Medical School went to the Yuhuatai Revolutionary Martyrs' Park to commemorate Zhou Enlai, after which students from several major Nanjing universities began planning a large-scale commemoration.

On March 25, *Wenhui Bao* published a report that included the sentence "That capitalist roader within the party wanted to put in power a capitalist roader who was struck down and remains unrepentant to this day." The unrepentant capitalist roader was Deng Xiaoping, and his supporter was Zhou Enlai. This "flogging of Zhou's corpse" drew 421 letters and telegrams of protest and more than 1,000 telephone calls demanding an explanation from the newspaper. Big-character posters and banners went up at Nanjing University and then throughout the city in memory of Zhou Enlai and opposing the Gang of Four. People gathered to exchange information, read out poems and essays, or give speeches. Banners proclaimed, "Dearly cherish the memory of the martyr Yang Kaihui!,"[6] "Denouncing Zhou will bring chaos, opposing Zhou will destroy our country!," "Down with *Wenhui Bao*'s backstage supporter, Zhang Chunqiao!," and "Down with the major careerist and conspirator Zhang Chunqiao!"

To expand the influence, more than eight hundred students from Nanjing University split into groups and gave speeches in the streets and put up banners on the streets, at bus stations, and on buses. On the evening of March 29, Nanjing University students went to the Nanjing Train Station, and on trains bound for Chengdu and Shanghai they painted the words "*Wenhui Bao* deserves ten thousand deaths for targeting Premier Zhou!" and "Beware of Khrushchev-type careerists and schemers plotting to usurp leadership of the party and state!" Students from other schools soon arrived, and in a little more than ten hours, nearly two hundred slogans painted on trains were carrying their messages across the country.

After a late-night meeting presided over by Hua Guofeng on April 1 to discuss the Nanjing Incident, the Politburo issued a notice stating: "In recent days, big-character posters and banners have appeared in Nanjing targeting comrades in the central leadership. This is a political incident to split the party Central Committee led by Chairman Mao and to shift the general orientation of criticism of Deng. You must immediately take effective measures to cover up all of these posters and banners . . . Beware of people with ulterior motives who take the opportunity to enlarge the situation and create disturbances and carry out sabotage . . . We must thoroughly investigate the backstage instigator of this political incident." The notice was communicated to the general public on April 3, but over the next three days, some 600,000 Nanjing residents took part in protests and other activities to commemorate Zhou Enlai.[7]

During the last two years of the Cultural Revolution, the political force calling for the restoration of social order and a swift end to the Cultural Revolution had been growing, and the rival force calling for maintaining continuous revolution and safeguarding the achievements of the Cultural Revolution was waning but had not yet admitted defeat. Representatives of these two forces clashed in Zhengzhou over commemoration of Zhou Enlai.

In early April 1976, wreaths, elegies, and anonymous posters appeared beneath the February 7 Monument in Zhengzhou's city center, some attacking the Cultural Revolution faction or Mao. Some workers at the Zhengzhou Meat Processing Plant discussed the incident and felt a need to take a stand against what they regarded as a counterrevolutionary countercurrent. Early in the morning of April 5, the meat plant employees wrote a "stern statement" on a big-character poster signed by dozens of people and placed it at the Zhengzhou Telecommunications Bureau office near the February 7 Monument. The poster, which took a diametrically opposite stand to the posters at the monument, soon attracted other posters endorsing its views.

That night, the Henan branch of the Xinhua News Agency informed the people who had signed the stern statement that their poster and their names had been reported to the Politburo. Encouraged by this news, the poster's signers drove a truck to the February 7 Monument and began taking away "reactionary" wreaths and depositing them at the provincial party committee office across the way. Truckloads of soldiers arrived to help them clean up the monument area. These workers and "revolutionary masses" from other factories and work units then went through the streets painting banners and posters expressing their views until well into the night, clashing with residents who had commemorated Zhou Enlai. An employee of the Zhengzhou Telecommunications Bureau, Jiao Chunliang, was beaten to death near the February 7 Monument. (The municipal revolutionary committee eventually proclaimed Jiao a martyr, and a man scapegoated for killing him, Liu Jing, was sentenced to death. But typical of the reversals of that time, after the Cultural Revolution ended, Liu Jing was released and became a hero of the April Fifth Movement, while Jiao Chunliang's martyr designation was revoked, along with the monthly twenty-yuan bereavement allowance his young child received, and the people involved in the stern statement were investigated and punished.)[8]

Counterprotests of the Zhengzhou variety were rare, however, in the atmosphere of seething discontent during the last stage of the Cultural Revolution. Salaries had been frozen since 1963, and workers lived in poverty. People who had been pulled into the various political campaigns were fed up with being kneaded and pummeled like dough. Intellectuals were unhappy because their political and economic status had plummeted. Educated youths who had been sent to the countryside and their parents were unhappy, and cadres sent to the May 7 cadre schools were unhappy. These long-suppressed grievances poured out whenever the opportunity arose. With the Cultural Revolution in tatters, the various opposition factions and malcontents converged in commemorations for Zhou Enlai, giving rise to an unprecedented surge of protest.

Beijing's Tiananmen Square has always been a hub for popular protest. The commemoration of Zhou Enlai was initially limited to the Monument to the People's Heroes. On March 19, police confiscated a wreath laid down by Chaoyang District's Niufang Primary School. On March 25, the number of people laying wreaths multiplied. On March 30, a troop of PLA soldiers laid a wreath at the monument, and this bolstered the courage of others to defy the ban. By the thirty-first, more than a hundred wreaths had been laid at the square, along with poems and eulogies boldly criticizing Jiang Qing and other members of the Cultural Revolution faction. On April 2, employees of the Chinese Academy of Sciences organized a protest march led by four trucks bearing wreaths dedicated to Zhou Enlai, Chen Yi, and Yang Kaihui along with huge signs praising the loyal heroes of revolution and vowing destruction against "monsters and demons." On the south side of Chang'an Avenue, wreaths covered the square all the way from the monument to the flagpole. On the north side of the avenue, the reviewing stand beneath Tiananmen was filled with wreathes, the largest more than seven meters in diameter. White paper flowers brought in by millions of people covered the cypress trees along the roads south of the Monument to the People's Heroes and the bushes surrounding the Great Hall of the People and Chinese National Museum. Elegiac couplets, poems, and leaflets covered the square, most of them targeting the Cultural Revolution faction. One poem displayed on the Monument to the People's Heroes used veiled language anticipating the fall of Jiang Qing, Zhang Chunqiao, and Yao Wenyuan.

This protest by the general public against officialdom and against Mao was the largest peaceful revolt the party had faced since the founding of the PRC.

THE DEEPER LEVEL: IDEOLOGICAL REBELLION

The massive and intense movement at Tiananmen Square reflected the social mood. Beneath public sentiment lay trends of thought.

While the Cultural Revolution kept most people on a mad dash to follow the larger trend, a few people always kept reading, thinking, and probing. As the movement developed, people started dashing in different directions, and the content of contemplation also changed, but the main common thread was criticism of bureaucratic privilege and of the social system. Almost everyone was feeling battered after nearly ten years of constant reversals, and as even the most fervent began to cool down, the number of people engaged in thinking and probing increased. Beneath the mass fervor of the April Fifth Movement roiled nonconformance to the mainstream ideology.

Long closed off from the rest of the world, China's young thinkers had access to only Marxist materials. For years, the social model envisaged by Marxism had been depicted as perfect and sacred, but seventeen years of reality presented a starkly different picture, and it was this disparity that led many people to enthusiastically embrace the Cultural Revolution. The ideology of the radical wing of the rebel faction was rooted in negating the PRC's first seventeen years. At the outset of the Cultural Revolution, young thinkers used Marx's theory of state to analyze the Cultural Revolution and Mao's theory of continuous revolution under the dictatorship of the proletariat.

On October 17, 1966, a physics student at Beijing Normal University, Li Wenbo, put up a big-character poster titled "A Commune Is No Longer a State in the Original Sense." Li proposed "thoroughly reforming the socialist system and thoroughly improving the dictatorship of the proletariat." His poster said, "Our current system is an organizational form originating with the bourgeoisie; it is a capitalist state without a capitalist class. It remains a hotbed for a capitalist class, revisionism, and bureaucracy." Li called for adhering to the principles of the Paris Commune, in particular keeping official salaries at the same level as those of the workers and allowing the people to remove government officials at will. The title of the poster came from Engels's comments on the Paris Commune; Li felt that China was a state in its "original sense"—one dominated by class, employing violent suppression, and allowing bureaucrats to enjoy special privileges.[9] A revamp of the socialist system and dictatorship of the proletariat was likewise espoused by *New Thought Trend*, a magazine published by students at Beijing Normal University.

Li Wenbo's poster soon came under criticism from Kang Sheng, a "theoretical authority" who had never published a theoretical essay but who had a keen political nose for theoretical issues. Then, on February 24, 1967, the deputy head of the Central Cultural Revolution Small Group, Zhang Chunqiao, transmitted Mao's directive stating,

"'Thoroughly improve the dictatorship of the proletariat' is a reaction-ary slogan; it repudiates the dictatorship of the proletariat and estab-lishes bourgeois dictatorship. The proper expression is to partially improve the dictatorship of the proletariat."[10] Mao felt that China had become a capitalist state without a capitalist class, and the Cultural Revolution was meant to correct this, so Li Wenbo's thinking was in sync with Mao's on this point. But Mao disliked the word "thoroughly," because being "thorough" would touch on the foundation of the Commu-nist regime. How much "partial" improvement would be allowed—80 percent, 20 percent? There was no clear boundary, given Mao's own swings between radicalism and compromise.

Around the same time as Li Wenbo's poster, the Red Cannon Team at the Chinese University of Science and Technology, Peking Univer-sity student Qiao Jianwu, and Liu Wozhong and Zhang Licai at the Beijing Agricultural University Affiliated Secondary School (using the pen name Yilin Dixi) also demanded changing an obsolete system in which the bureaucratic class exploited the people.[11] A poster in the form of an open letter by Qiao Jianwu (born Qiao Junli) and Du Wenge (born Du Wenzhong) said that the inability of non-party members to elect the members of party organs gave rise to revisionism and bureaucratism.

On June 11, 1967, the Beijing secondary school student journal *4-3 Battle Communiqué* published "On the New Thought Trend—the Dec-laration of the 4-3 Faction," which stated: "Socialist society emerges from capitalist society, so the distribution system and prerogatives of capitalist society cannot be eliminated in one fell swoop . . . It still leads assets and power to be concentrated for the time being in the hands of a minority—those in power." These assets and power would eventually become privatized and serve the sole interests of the "coun-terrevolutionary restorationist clique" and their families and descen-dants. "Privileged individuals strenuously avoid redistribution and renewed transformation, and this is the 'conservative' essence of the bourgeois reactionary line . . . The Cultural Revolution is the eruption of this main class contradiction, the contradiction between 'revolution' and 'conservatism.'"[12]

When the Central Committee reined in the rebel faction in late 1967, the Cultural Revolution lost direction, and many people withdrew from the movement. Disenchanted young people such as the Bei-Jue-Yang group described earlier in this book began exploring other options. Bei-Jue-Yang in particular endorsed replacing the revolutionary committees with a "Wuhan People's Commune." They enthusiastically praised Wang Renzhou, the leader of the Ba River First Command Post in Hubei's Xishui County,[13] for creating a "new village" even more radical than the 1958 people's communes. If Wang Renzhou had succeeded, he might have become like Pol Pot in Cambodia.

Yang Xiguang (a.k.a. Yang Xiaokai), a student at the Changsha No. 1 Secondary School whose cadre father had been attacked as a right-deviating opportunist and "counterrevolutionary revisionist," was among the rebels who opposed the blood lineage theory and had been locked up for opposing his school's work group. After being released, he concentrated on reading and contemplation. In January 1968, Yang wrote a pseudonymous big-character poster titled "Whither China," which he also distributed in leaflet form. The essay stated, "The contradiction between the new bureaucratic bourgeois class and the broad masses remains fundamentally unresolved." It was therefore necessary to "topple the product of the bourgeoisie's reformism— the rule of the revolutionary committees—and reestablish a Paris Commune–type regime." The Central Committee leaders Kang Sheng, Zhou Enlai, Chen Boda, and others criticized this essay while receiving representatives of Hunan's various mass organizations and the preparatory committee for the Hunan provincial revolutionary committee on January 24, 1968. Kang Sheng said this essay couldn't have been written by a secondary school student or even a university student, and must have a hidden instigator behind it. From then on, Yang Xiguang and his parents were persecuted, and Yang spent ten years behind bars.[14]

Likewise employing Marxist discourse, Wang Shenyou surpassed the thinking of his era in 1976. Born in 1944, Wang was a physics student at East China Normal University when he was imprisoned for fifteen months during the 1968 Cleansing of the Class Ranks because of his "reactionary journal," and then sent to labor in a May 7 cadre school. Wang Shenyou saw Mao's May Seventh Directive as a blueprint for "an Asian autocratic system that inevitably creates a situation in which peasants are eternally uncivilized and backward, and has not

THE APRIL FIFTH MOVEMENT | 545

the slightest element of socialism." Wang Shenyou held that the alternative road represented by Liu Shaoqi, Zhou Enlai, and Deng Xiaoping "allows the law of value to play the most beneficial historical role and promotes the rapid enhancement of social productive force." He criticized Mao as having a "grossly insufficient understanding of the historical role and historical necessity of the capitalist mode of production, and of the historical conditions for its transition to socialist modes of production," and advocated "giving full rein to the function of profit."[15] Wang Shenyou was arrested again soon after the fall of the Gang of Four, and he was executed under the Hua Guofeng regime on April 3, 1977.

In November 1974, a controversial big-character poster was put up in the bustling downtown of Guangzhou. Titled "On a Socialist Democracy and Legal System," it was a collective work using the pen name Li Yizhe, which represented the names of its contributors, Wang Xizhe (a factory furnace-stoker who had been sent to the countryside as a high school student), Li Zhengtian (an unemployed former art student who had spent several years in prison for criticizing Lin Biao), and Chen Yiyang (who had been sent to the countryside as a high school student and had only recently returned to Guangzhou), with the additional participation of Guo Hongzhi, a middle-age cadre at Guangdong People's Broadcasting, and some other supporters. The four core members had been members of Guangzhou's rebel Red Flag faction during the first three years of the Cultural Revolution until the faction was forcibly disbanded by the military and the revolutionary committees.

The essay sharply criticized privilege as incubating "the social foundation for capitalist roaders and careerists within the party," and indirectly criticized Mao for tolerating the practice of "going through the back door": "Why must we avoid criticizing privilege? Why must we use the problem of so-called 'good people' and 'bad people' as a substitute for the cardinal line principles of right and wrong reflected in 'going through the back door'?" The essay pointed out an "enormous contradiction" that existed within the Cultural Revolution's guiding ideology in its focus on rectifying the capitalist roaders within the party while insisting on maintaining the stability of the central leadership. The only solution was to "demand democracy, demand a socialist legal system, demand safeguarding the revolutionary rights and personal rights of the broad masses . . . In the current world trend, the reactionary faction opposing democracy is a mere countercurrent."[16]

Similar thinking often emerges under similar social conditions.

In the mid-1970s, a young former rebel named Xu Shuiliang put up a big-character poster in Nanjing's downtown area opposing privilege and demanding democracy.[17] Around the same time, a dozen disaffected former rebels in Sichuan's Wan County, including Zhang Chuang, Mou Qizhong, and Liu Zhongzhi, organized a Marxist Research Association that published several essays with titles such as "Whither China," "Challenging Labor Value Theory," "From Cultural Revolution to Armed Revolution," and "Socialism's Retreat from Science to Utopia," warning that China's backward productivity was the economic foundation for the "restoration of feudal fascism." They also complained of having been cynically used during the Cultural Revolution. Mou Qizhong said, "I worshiped Chairman Mao infinitely. When I discovered that he violated Marxism-Leninism and stubbornly maintained these errors, Chairman Mao's divine nimbus dimmed in my heart."[18]

In spring 1976, during the campaign to beat back the right-deviating verdict-reversal trend, a young man in Yunnan Province named Chen Erjin wrote a long essay titled "On Privilege,"[19] which held that China's privilege system "doesn't take the form of blatant private ownership, but rather is cloaked in the sacred surplice of public ownership . . . Through political and economic unification, the bureaucratic privileged class combines political leadership and economic distribution power in one body, turning all of society's human and material resources into a highly organized, highly centralized, highly monopolistic capital accumulation system with enormous competitive power." Under this system, "the working people and the bureaucratic privileged class are routinely in a situation of white-hot antagonism." Chen called for a "proletarian democratic revolution" that "insists on Marxism while also drawing on the experience of Western political systems' principles of separating the legislative, executive, and judicial powers, a two-party system, and safeguarding human rights."

By spring 1976, the Cultural Revolution was already a lost cause.

At that time the various thought trends formed a political spectrum that ranged from the ultra-leftist theory of thorough revolution to the theory of continued revolution under the dictatorship of the proletariat, to the restoration of the social order existing before the Cultural Revolution,[20] to calls for democracy. The furthest-left thinking on the political spectrum was suppressed by the authorities and also rejected by ordinary citizens who longed for social order. The theory of continuous revolution under the dictatorship of the proletariat was the mainstream at the time, but it had come under suspicion. Restoration of the pre–Cultural Revolution social order had a growing number of supporters and eventually replaced the theory of continuous revolution as the mainstream. Although pro-democracy thinking remained relegated to illegal terrain, it flashed like lightning in the night. Apart from the theory of continuous revolution under the dictatorship of the proletariat, all this thinking combined into an enormous force that opposed the Cultural Revolution and propelled the April Fifth Movement forward. The greatest number of people demanded restoration of the social order that existed before the Cultural Revolution.

Chen Ziming[21] believed that the April Fifth Movement was actually the confluence of two trends of thought in society. One part, by far the majority, consisted of veteran cadres and old intellectuals and workers who were intensely critical of the Cultural Revolution and wanted to return to the conditions before 1957. The other part, perhaps 10 to 20 percent, consisted of the vanguards of the movement, young workers and intellectuals who espoused the new social thought trend of democracy and modernization.[22] The young vanguards were just "small granules" in the mighty torrent of the movement but "agglomerated" the many people who were unhappy with the reality created by the Cultural Revolution. The people who gathered on the square, whether inclined toward the left or the right, were all attacking the Cultural Revolution and its representative figures, Jiang Qing and Zhang Chunqiao, and in some cases even Mao and the system that his generation had established. At that time, the most shocking cry was a line from a free-verse poem written under the pen name Huang Sun: "The feudalist society of the Qin Emperor, once gone, can never return!"

SUPPRESSION OF PUBLIC SENTIMENT ESCALATES PROTESTS

Long accustomed to docile citizenry, China's totalitarian officials responded to the people's rebellion with suppression. That further outraged the masses and escalated their revolt.

In 1976, the traditional Qing Ming festival, when Chinese remember their dead, fell on April 4. At least two million black-clad people marked the day by flooding Tiananmen Square with white floral wreaths and jostling among one another to copy down the poems and elegies displayed or orated there.

One of those present was Chen Ziming, who recalls that most people there were only following a few who took the initiative; but under the circumstances of those times, even following was taking the initiative. Chen Ziming had just been expelled from the Beijing Institute of Chemical Engineering for "reactionary speech" and was about to set off for a stint of labor in the countryside. Concerned as he was with politics, he took advantage of his brief interval of freedom to observe what was going on at Tiananmen Square. He was standing on the southwest corner of the Monument to the People's Heroes reading an essay denouncing Jiang Qing, "The Eleventh Line Struggle," when someone behind him yelled, "Will the comrade in front please read it out loud?" and a hand tapped him on the shoulder. After a moment's hesitation, Chen and a young man beside him began reading the essay in unison, and the people around them repeated each sentence in turn, this "human megaphone" transmitting the essay in relay fashion across the square. Some people cheered and others yelled, "Well written!" "Read it again!" "Jiang Qing is shameless!" "The people believe in Deng Xiaoping!" Chen read out the essay until he was hoarse, at which point another took over from him.[23]

Wu Zhong recalls seeing people at the monument who were "giving a speech and openly condemning Jiang Qing. The crowd around them kept growing and was packed together. They reviled Jiang Qing until they were hoarse."[24] That was probably Chen Ziming and the other youth reading "The Eleventh Line Struggle." Around that same time, a young worker from Shanxi, Wang Lishan, drew a similar crowd with a poem he posted at the monument: "Grieving, I hear demons howl /

Weeping while jackals laugh / Tearfully mourning a hero / I raise my head with sword unsheathed."

That night, Hua Guofeng presided over a Politburo meeting that determined the Tiananmen Incident to be "counterrevolutionaries inciting the masses to oppose the Chairman and the Central Committee and to interfere with and sabotage the general orientation of struggle."[25] When the *People's Daily* editor in chief, Lu Ying, reported the berating of Jiang Qing, Jiang furiously pointed at Chen Xilian, saying, "You're the commander," and then at Ji Dengkui, saying, "You're the political commissar," and adding, "Plus there are Beijing's two Wus [referring to Wu De and Wu Zhong], but is anyone looking after the safety of the Central Committee?" Jiang Qing and others demanded "immediately clearing away the wreaths and arresting the counterrevolutionaries."[26]

In the early hours of April 5, the municipal authorities deployed 150 trucks to remove the floral wreaths from the square. Some people who were still at the square were interrogated, and a small number were taken away. People arriving at the square on the morning of April 5 found it empty and surrounded by guards. An enraged crowd of more than one hundred thousand people gathered around the square shouting, "Give back our wreaths! Give back our comrades-in-arms!" Around eight o'clock that morning, two vehicles equipped with loudspeakers drove slowly along the west side of the square repeatedly broadcasting the message "The Qing Ming festival has ended. Memorial activities are finished. Revolutionary comrades are requested to leave the square. Beware of the destructive activities of a smattering of class enemies!" A crowd surrounded one of the vehicles and flipped it over. Chen Ziming recalls:

> When I arrived at Tiananmen Square on the morning of April 5th, at least a thousand people had gathered on the steps in front of the monument. Soon after that, a company of soldiers encircled the monument and drove away the crowd, shouting, "In accordance with the Central Committee's order, the monument is being repaired today. Qing Ming is over; no more wreaths can be laid." At that time, a youth pulled a small

wreath wrapped in a plastic bag out of his backpack and asked to be allowed to place it on the relief sculpture of the monument. Soldiers shoved the youth and blocked his way. I was standing next to the youth, and while criticizing the soldiers' unreasonable obstruction, I led the crowd in breaking through the human wall the soldiers had formed by linking their arms. People rushed forward and knocked the soldiers all over the place, and clustered around the young man as he placed his wreath on the monument . . . Suddenly, someone jumped out of the crowd and began scolding the youth and demanding to know his work unit, and the crowd became indignant. Someone in a blue uniform said, "No one wants to be provoked by counterrevolutionaries. Don't cause any more trouble. Don't risk your life for capitalist roaders. The newspapers are about to name the capitalist roaders." The crowd immediately surrounded that man and questioned him, and some wanted to beat him. At that time, two people stepped forward to help him out, and members of the public recognized them as plainclothes policemen and yelled, "Beat up the plainclothes cops!" With the people turning on them, the plainclothes policemen ran toward the Great Hall of the People with the crowd close at their heels, and the people on the square charged at the Great Hall of the People.[27]

Someone yelled, "There are wreaths inside the Great Hall of the People!" and someone tried to run into the Great Hall and grab a wreath. Enraged people surrounded the hall's eastern entrance and clashed with policemen and militiamen. Someone was injured. The situation spun out of control.

THE FORCED CLEARANCE OF THE SQUARE

To deal with the events at Tiananmen Square, a "joint command post" was established for the Beijing Garrison Command, Beijing Municipal Public Security Bureau, and Capital Militia Headquarters in a small gray building at the southeast corner of the square. Upon learning of the situation outside the Great Hall of the People, the joint command post decided to send militia and police to coordinate with the army in sealing off the square from south to north.

Someone who served in the militia recalls that each work unit located near the square had to select several people, each of whom was issued with several buns and a wooden pole, to lie in ambush at Zhongshan Park and the Imperial Ancestral Temple and block anyone who attempted to lay down a wreath.[28] But that didn't solve the problem in front of the Great Hall of the People. Wu Zhong recalls:

> The person in charge of the Great Hall made an urgent telephone call telling me that the situation was very strained and that a staff officer had been injured, and asking what he should do. Wang Dongxing also telephoned and said that the masses were storming the eastern entrance of the Great Hall. A moment later, Zhang Yaoci telephoned and said, "Commander Wu, the situation at the Great Hall is very tense; you need to protect the safety of the Great Hall." Zhang Yaoci's phone call made me pay attention. He was close to Chairman Mao [in charge of the Chairman's security details]. So Chairman Mao probably already knows about it. So I found Ma Xiaoliu and mobilized the militia to maintain order, and had the masses step back and not make the conflict worse. The militia went out, but they had no effect whatsoever. The militiamen's feelings were the same as the masses charging at the eastern entrance of the Great Hall, and telling them to mobilize the masses who were crowding around the Great Hall had not the slightest effect . . . The crowd was growing, and the square was becoming more chaotic. I went back to the Garrison Command auditorium and called in the leaders of the First and Second divisions of the security force . . .
>
> The situation continued to develop, and the security force's First and Second divisions were unable to maintain order . . . Comrade Chen Xilian agreed that it was acceptable to bring the Third and Fourth divisions into the city, and that we and [Beijing mayor] Comrade Wu De could discuss how many to bring in. After completing the plan, 5,000 to 6,000 troops were transferred in three groups. But the problem of the crowd storming

552 | THE WORLD TURNED UPSIDE DOWN

the eastern entrance wasn't resolved, and you couldn't just drag them away! Wang Dongxing telephoned and asked when the problem at the Great Hall would be solved, and I said two o'clock in the afternoon . . . In fact, it was resolved before noon. A Japanese was discovered taking photos, and the masses snatched his camera from him and pulled the unexposed film out of it and beat him up. The Japanese ran toward the History Museum, and the crowd all rushed toward the History Museum, and no one was left at the eastern entrance of the Great Hall.

Chen Ziming recalls that people didn't leave the Great Hall of the People to chase down the Japanese man, but rather that they went to the joint command post. Singing "The Internationale," they cut across Tiananmen Square and rushed toward the small gray building, where worker militiamen had already formed a human wall. The crowd yelled, "Give back our wreaths! Return our comrades-in-arms! Down with the scabs!" and at the same time stormed the building. The crowd sent Chen Ziming, Zhao Shijian, Sun Qingzhu, and Hou Yuliang into the building to negotiate as their representatives. The four of them scrambled over the shoulders of the people guarding the building, but once they were inside, the negotiations went nowhere.

When the four of them came out without any resolution, the crowd was enraged and began a protest march, during which a vehicle in front of the small gray building was burned and two fire trucks sent to the scene were blocked by the crowd. When a van arrived to deliver food to the building just before 3:00 p.m., someone among the protesters said, "We haven't eaten all day, and we're not letting them be fed so they can suppress us!" The crowd seized the food inside the van and then tipped it over and set it on fire. Two jeeps parked in front of the building were also set on fire, and dozens of bicycles were thrown into the flames. Around 5:00 p.m., the guards in front of the building dispersed and the crowd burst in, setting rice straw ablaze so that the flames spread to the second floor. Tables, chairs, books, radios, and other items were thrown out the windows into the bonfire in front of the building as the people inside fled out the back door.

Some veteran cadres who had been persecuted during the Cultural Revolution were secretly delighted. Describing Deng Xiaoping's situation during those few days, Deng Rong (Mao Mao), wrote, "Every day, every item of news that arrived, every stirring poem, made us feel very excited. The hearts of Deng Xiaoping's family were beating in the same rhythm with those of the masses at Tiananmen Square."[29] Wang Dongxing says, "Some old comrades who had come under attack were gloating over the Tiananmen Incident, and Yang Shangkun bought bottles of wine to celebrate."[30] On the afternoon of April 5, some Politburo members observed what was happening on the square from Jiangxi Hall in the Great Hall of the People, and Deng Xiaoping was called to the Great Hall and denounced. Zhang Chunqiao wrote in a letter to his son, "On April 5th, I went to the Great Hall, and it was like watching the Hungarian Incident.[31] I could see everything clearly through the binoculars. I cursed Deng Xiaoping to his face as a Nagy."[32]

After an emergency Politburo meeting at 2:00 p.m., a speech by Wu De was broadcast at 6:30 p.m. to make people leave the square. The speech had been drafted by the director of the Beijing Municipal Public Security Bureau, Liu Chuanxin, and then revised by Wu De and approved by the Central Committee, and reportedly also by Mao. The speech accused "a tiny minority of evildoers with ulterior motives" of using the Qing Ming festival to create a political incident targeting Mao and the Central Committee, and warned the public not to be taken in by this attempt to derail the struggle against "that unrepentant capitalist roader's revisionist line" and the right-deviating verdict-reversal trend.

The number of people on the square only increased, however, as people finished work and joined the protesters. The focus of the protest shifted from the small gray building to the monument. In the meantime, Wu De and Wu Zhong prepared to deploy personnel to clear the square at 8:30 p.m. Because of the size of the crowd, Wu Zhong waited until 11:00 p.m. to order the army, public security police, and militiamen to begin forcibly clearing the square. Many people were injured by clubs, fists, and kicks, but no one was killed. Wu Zhong recalls arresting around 150 people, but in fact as many as 388 were seized.[33]

After hearing a report on the incident in the early hours of April 6, some Politburo members designated it a "bona fide counterrevolutionary incident." Mao Yuanxin gave Mao a report on the Politburo meeting at 3:00 a.m., after which Mao wrote a memo: "Morale is up. Good, good, good!"[34]

Mao Yuanxin again reported to Mao on the situation at the square on the morning of April 7, and Mao said, "Dismiss Deng from all his positions but preserve his party membership and see how he behaves." He told Mao Yuanxin to call an urgent top leadership meeting to appoint Hua Guofeng as premier. That day at noon, Mao Yuanxin reported to Mao on the views expressed during the Politburo's discussion, and when it came to the decision for Hua Guofeng to become premier, Mao proposed that he become first vice-chairman of the party as well.[35] All Mao's proposals were formalized as the Politburo's unanimous decisions and made public by radio broadcast on the evening of April 7.

Someone at the April 7 Politburo meeting suggested that Deng Xiaoping had personally gone to the square and directed the masses to create chaos, but Hua Guofeng said that Deng himself had to be asked about this, and Jiang Qing suggested sending Wang Dongxing. On his way to Deng's quarters, Wang stopped to see Mao and said that Deng might be coming under attack. Mao explicitly directed Wang to make sure that Deng was not further attacked or taken away, so Wang put Deng under protection at the Legation Quarters. Wang asked Deng if he had gone to the square, and Deng replied that he had only gone to the Beijing Hotel (about half a mile away from the square) for a haircut. The next day, Deng wrote a letter asking Wang to tell the Central Committee and Chairman Mao that he endorsed the appointment of Hua Guofeng as first vice-chairman and premier, and that he was grateful to be allowed to retain his party membership.[36] Over the next few days, mass rallies and parades were organized by the authorities in Beijing and other major cities to celebrate Deng's downfall. On April 10, *People's Daily* published an editorial celebrating the quashing of the rebellion on Tiananmen Square as a great victory of Mao's revolutionary line. Eventually, with Mao's permission, Deng Xiaoping and his family were allowed to return to their original living quarters in mid-July.

The various provincial party committees and military regions vied to be the first to declare their political allegiances, and for days the newspapers were filled with telegrams stating unity with the Central

Committee led by Mao and determination to fully mobilize the masses to denounce the criminal acts of Deng Xiaoping and carry out the great struggle against right-deviating verdict reversal to the very end.

Public sentiment is easily manipulated in a totalitarian system, and organized declarations of political standpoints do not necessarily reflect people's actual feelings. Many of the people who had been most active in the square also took part in street demonstrations celebrating the "great victory."

Hua Guofeng, born Su Zhu in 1921, was a native of Shanxi's Jiaocheng County. He joined the CCP in 1938, and in 1948 was appointed party secretary of Yangqu County and political commissar of the local Communist forces. He was soon reposted as the PLA advanced southward during the civil war. In 1954, he was named party secretary of Xiangtan Prefecture, Hunan Province. Mao invited him to describe his experience there when the sixth plenum of the Seventh Central Committee discussed issues concerning the agricultural cooperative movement in October 1955, and found Hua's report very interesting. Every time Mao went to Hunan, Hua warmly received him and requested his advice, and Mao often told people, "Hua Guofeng is an honest man." During the Cultural Revolution, Hua Guofeng was vicechairman of the Hunan provincial revolutionary committee, and he maintained an impartial attitude during the intense political conflicts. He was elected to the Central Committee during the Ninth National Party Congress in April 1969, and then promoted to first party secretary of Hunan Province in November 1970 and to political commissar of the Guangzhou Military Region in October 1971.

After the Lin Biao incident, Mao brought Wang Hongwen from Shanghai and Hua Guofeng from Hunan. Mao considered Wang Hongwen successor material because of his steadfast attitude toward the Cultural Revolution, but the bureaucratic clique's loathing of Wang gave Hua Guofeng his opportunity to rise to the pinnacle of power. Hua was elected to the Politburo in 1973, and in January 1975, he became vice-premier and minister of public security. On January 28, 1976, at Mao's recommendation, Hua replaced Deng Xiaoping in managing the Central Committee's work, and the 1976 April Fifth Movement elevated Hua to the status of Mao's successor.

After the quelling of the April Fifth Movement, peace returned to

Tiananmen Square, but people remained agitated and uneasy, and a critical mood pervaded society. This movement liberated people's thinking, serving as a harbinger of the Democracy Wall movement and "great debate over the standard of truth" that occurred two years later. It not only breached the forbidden zone of Reform and Opening but also cracked the eggshell of liberalism that prepared the way for China's democratization. As Chen Ziming said, "The April 5th Movement was a turning point in the process of China's modernization."

Bao Zunxin[37] observed, "The April 5th Movement's criticism targeted Mao Zedong and the single-party dictatorship that he represented." If the temporal-spacial conditions of that time limited the movement's demands to indirect expression through commemorating and eulogizing Zhou Enlai, then the period of Democracy Wall and underground journals that followed two years later more explicitly expressed the wishes of the April Fifth generation: an end to single-party autocracy, the need for human rights, freedom, democracy, and rule of law, and for China to incorporate these basic conditions of modern human civilization into reform of its political and social systems.

27

THE CURTAIN FALLS ON THE CULTURAL REVOLUTION

THE DEATH OF MAO

Shortly after midnight on September 9, 1976, Mao abandoned his one billion subjects and abruptly passed away.

Mao had been suffering from the torments of various age-related infirmities since 1971, and the attempt that year by his handpicked successor, Lin Biao, to flee the country, with its attendant international political scandal, had dealt him a severe mental blow. In his last years, he became obsessed with the war years and the first years of the People's Republic, constantly watching movies related to these events. He broke down in sobs one time when the movie screen showed the ecstatic public welcoming PLA troops entering a city. In May 1976, Mao's condition began steadily deteriorating, and emergency measures were required to save him from a stroke in early June. The ailing Mao asked to return to his native Shaoshan, Hunan Province, so his "leaves would return to their roots," but the Politburo denied his request in view of his serious health issues. The last document to which he affixed his approving circle was the Central Committee's "Notice Regarding Earthquake Relief for the Tangshan and Fengnan Region."[1]

Mao's personal life was unhappy. One son had died in the Korean War, and another suffered from mental problems. He spent much of his last years living apart from his wife and lacked a loving home environment. During his illness, he ordered large-print annotated editions of the prose poems "Withered Tree," "Moon," "Snow," and

"Parting," their sorrowful tone reflecting Mao's desolate state of mind. Spending his last Spring Festival in his quarters at Zhongnanhai accompanied only by the staff who attended to the needs of his declining body, Mao had them set off a few firecrackers to break up the monotony of the whistling cold night wind. In the new year, his health declined to the point where his attendants had to feed him his food and medicine, and he found it increasingly difficult to move. Although retaining sight in only one eye, he maintained his lifelong reading habits until his dying day, assisted by staff who held books and documents for him. On the afternoon of September 7, he tremblingly wrote the number "3" and then knocked on the headboard of his bed, which his attendant interpreted as a wish to read a book by the Japanese author Takeo Miki (Miki was written with the Chinese characters for "three" and "wood"), and when the book was brought to Mao, he nodded his head with satisfaction. Miki was head of Japan's Liberal Democratic Party and was running for reelection as prime minister at that time, an event in which Mao took great interest,[2] but after reading for a few minutes, he lost consciousness. On September 8, Mao spent nearly three hours reading documents and books. He even read while being given emergency treatment.[3]

Mao died worrying that the Cultural Revolution would be negated and that China would fall into chaos. Others shared his concern. In the early hours of September 9, the Central Committee and Central Military Commission sent an urgent cable telling the main leaders of all provinces, cities, autonomous regions, and military regions to keep the situation stable, and the military rapidly went into battle preparation mode. The Central Committee's arrangements were based on the common knowledge that in a totalitarian country, the death of the supreme political strongman often results in social reverberations and even upheaval.

At 4:00 p.m., the Central People's Broadcasting Station in mournful tones broadcast an announcement of this sad news issued jointly by the Central Committee, the standing committee of the National People's Congress, the State Council, and the Central Military Commission. Xinhua journalists reported on displays of grief all over China, with people gathering in public places to weep together, vehicles stopping in the middle of streets, and people waiting in long lines to buy Mao portraits or collapsing in sorrow along roadways.

These reports weren't fabricated. I personally witnessed these kinds of scenes. Why the collective anguish at the death of a leader? This had much to do with the two-thousand-year tradition of imperial politics as well as Mao's long-standing personality cult.

After lunch on September 9, the leader of Xinhua's Tianjin branch office told me to go to the Tianjin No. 1 Machine Tool Factory to listen along with workers to an important announcement at 4:00 p.m. and then report on the response. He didn't tell me the content of the announcement, but I had a pretty good idea what it was. When I reached the factory, hundreds of people had already gathered in the outdoor plaza (because of the recent earthquakes, all activities were carried out in the open air). At 3:00 p.m., the factory leader came back from a meeting in the city. Covering his face with his hands as he climbed weeping from his vehicle, he said with a choked voice, "Chairman Mao is dead!" As soon as he finished speaking, several people began weeping loudly, and as the workers listened to the announcement over the loudspeaker, sobs filled the plaza.

Weeping can be contagious; I seldom cry and maintain a detached attitude toward life and death, but I found my face covered with tears. A few days later, I went to Tiananmen Square and strolled there deep in thought, recalling the many National Day activities and other political gatherings I had attended there as a student, and the many times I'd seen Chairman Mao waving at us from the gate tower. Looking at the empty gate tower now, I profoundly felt the loneliness and emptiness behind a political strongman and experienced the intensely painful feeling of the end of an era. This may have been one reason why China's people wept. Another important reason may have been that it could be politically risky not to cry along with everyone else; in private the situation may have been quite different. Years later, I read in the memoirs of some political victims that they were secretly joyful at the news of Mao's death, and some even had a celebratory drink on the sly.

At 3:00 p.m. on September 18, one million people took part in a memorial gathering at Tiananmen Square as a billion people mourned for Mao in innumerable similar gatherings all over China. Reporting on these activities in Tianjin, I rode my bicycle through the usually bustling commercial district from Munan Road to the city square without seeing any vehicles or pedestrians in the streets or a single customer in any shop.

The passing of a great political leader brings more shock than sorrow. When the famous philosopher and Peking University professor Feng Youlan learned of Mao's death, the first thing he said was, "This is earthshaking news."[4] It was indeed as if the great pillar of the national government had crumbled, and the effect on the people working within that government can only be imagined. Was the feeling behind the wracking sobs one of sorrow, dread, anxiety, hesitation, or liberation? All those feelings existed, but among different people.

For people who during the Cultural Revolution had joined the Great Leader in attacking capitalist roader power-holders, the feelings of sorrow were undoubtedly accompanied by dread, for some of their victims had already been restored to power and constituted the "pragmatist faction" that now dominated the regime. In China, whenever an emperor died, his hatchet men met with disaster. These people increased their private contact while acting with greater circumspection.

Among the intellectuals, anxiety prevailed. They knew that Mao died in the midst of fierce infighting over his succession, which in a totalitarian system is typically accompanied by bloodshed. The intellectuals believed that anything could happen now, and constant rumors fueled their apprehension.

Black elements, the "landlords, rich peasants, counterrevolutionaries, bad elements, and rightists" who had been attacked and suppressed for years, hoped to cast off their status as a political underclass. For people exhausted by endless class struggle and poverty, hope of change glimmered vaguely on the horizon.

Some people fastened their expectant gaze on a small, elderly man, Deng Xiaoping. And what was Deng doing at that time?

Deng was still in his Kuan Street home, labeled the "chief bourgeois representative, the biggest unrepentant capitalist roader within the party, and China's Imre Nagy." He was reading when his daughter told him of Mao's death. Laying down his book, he became lost in thought amid the funereal music.

DAGGERS DRAWN

As mentioned before, by the time Mao died, China's various political powers had formed a spectrum ranging from an ultra-leftist faction promoting thorough revolution, to the Cultural Revolution faction promoting continuous revolution, to the bureaucratic faction calling for a restoration of the pre–Cultural Revolution order, and then to the liberal democratic faction, but the ultra-leftist faction had been suppressed, and the liberal democratic faction was just a spark. The only factions that had any influence were the Cultural Revolution faction and the bureaucratic faction. Since the bureaucratic faction emphasized "building the four modernizations" and paid little attention to the "theoretical problems" Mao raised, it was referred to as the "pragmatic faction." Mao's death removed the supreme authority that had maintained a balance between these two completely irreconcilable factions, and the only possible outcome was that one would obliterate the other. The Cultural Revolution faction had disintegrated over the course of the Cultural Revolution, and all that remained of it in the Central Committee were Jiang Qing, Wang Hongwen, Zhang Chunqiao, and Yao Wenyuan; their grassroots support was very fragile, while an increasing number of ordinary people supported the pragmatic faction, which held power at all levels of the government. The campaign to criticize Deng and beat back the right-deviating verdict-reversal trend went against public sentiment and caused little harm to the pragmatic faction in terms of the political balance.

After Mao died, the two factions pulled out their daggers for a fight to the death.

From September 11 to 17, a condolence ceremony was held in the Great Hall of the People. Among the endless stream of three hundred thousand people in black armbands who came to pay their respects, party and government leaders representing both political forces stood with mournful faces before Mao's remains while busily calculating how to defeat the opposition.

The Cultural Revolution faction enjoyed the advantage of controlling the tools of public opinion and pursuing the mainstream policy of continuous revolution under the dictatorship of the proletariat. After Mao's death, the Politburo Standing Committee had just four members: Hua Guofeng, Wang Hongwen, Ye Jianying, and Zhang Chunqiao, but Mao had put Ye Jianying on "sick leave" in early February, giving the Cultural Revolution faction the majority.

The rival pragmatic faction, although powerful, had no dominant personality. Deng Xiaoping had been struck down, and Ye Jianying, on "sick leave," was not allowed to intervene in military affairs. Hua Guofeng was a key person. He had been personally promoted by Mao, and as minister of public security, he had been an active participant in the campaign to criticize Deng and beat back the right-deviating verdict-reversal wind.[5] If the Cultural Revolution faction had vigorously supported Hua Guofeng, with Zhang Chunqiao content to serve as Hua's facilitator, the outcome might have been much different. Instead, they cast Hua Guofeng as their opponent.

On September 11, Wang Hongwen set up a security post independent of the Central Committee Secretariat security post and notified all provincial-level party committees that they should request instructions from his cohort on all major matters. Feeling muzzled in the Politburo Standing Committee by Wang and Zhang, Hua Guofeng began holding enlarged Standing Committee meetings in order to bring in Ye Jianying and Li Xiannian.

What was Jiang Qing up to at this time?

In early September, Jiang Qing had gone to Dazhai to "carry out work at the lower levels and create public opinion." Chen Yonggui says that when Jiang Qing received the secret cable about Mao's deteriorating condition, her hands trembled, but as soon as someone else entered the room, she pulled herself together and yelled, "Let's play cards!" She played poker while waiting for her train but kept making wrong plays and glancing at her watch.[6]

After returning from Dazhai, Jiang Qing moved from Diaoyutai to quarters next to Mao's in Zhongnanhai. The documents that Mao kept in his quarters included self-criticisms and written accusations relating to many Politburo members, and controlling those documents could serve as a "weapon" for subduing others. The documents might also contain "highest directives" left by Mao, which could be put to advantageous use in political struggle and gaining legitimacy as successor. Mao's documents therefore became the primary focus of struggle after Mao's death. On September 12, Jiang Qing telephoned Hua Guofeng and demanded that he call an emergency meeting of the Politburo Standing Committee but refused to tell him why. When Hua asked who should be included in the meeting, Jiang specified that Ye Jianying should not take part but that Mao Yuanxin, a nonmember, should. As soon as the meeting began, Jiang Qing demanded that she and Mao Yuanxin be entrusted with sorting through Mao's papers and books. She said that as the Chairman's wife and secretary, she was the natural person to deal with this, and noted that Lenin's manuscripts had been mainly handled by his widow, Nadezhda Krupskaya.

Wang Dongxing said it had been decided that Mao's documents would be sealed up for safekeeping, and he and Hua Guofeng also rejected Jiang Qing's alternative suggestion that Mao's personal secretary, Zhang Yufeng, take care of the documents. Hua Guofeng likewise quashed Zhang Chunqiao's suggestion that Mao Yuanxin help Zhang Yufeng sort through the papers. The wrangling continued for four or five hours until Hua Guofeng finally insisted that Wang Dongxing be put in charge of all Mao's papers and books and that they be sealed up for safekeeping for the time being.

On September 17, Wang Dongxing and his trusted subordinate, Wu Jianhua, pasted paper seals on Mao's bedroom and study. Prevented from entering that night, Jiang Qing telephoned Hua Guofeng at two o'clock in the morning, weeping and wailing and claiming that the seal was affecting her personal quarters: "The Chairman's remains are not yet cold, and you're already forcing me out?"

When Central Committee General Office staff examined the documents on September 21, they discovered that Zhang Yufeng had allowed Jiang Qing and Mao Yuanxin to "have a look" at two documents, which had not been returned. One was a copy of a record of a foreign journalist's interview with Jiang Qing, and the other was the record of the conversation between Mao, Yang Dezhi, and Wang Liusheng in Wuhan in 1974. Wang Dongxing and the others demanded the return of what they felt were important top-secret documents. After much arguing, Jiang Qing finally returned the documents on the condition that Hua Guofeng circulate them to Wang Hongwen and Zhang Chunqiao after he read them. Hua Guofeng ignored her.

Late at night on September 29, Hua Guofeng presided over a Politburo meeting to discuss how National Day should be celebrated following Mao's demise. Jiang Qing proposed first sorting out the leadership of the Central Committee, and she criticized Hua Guofeng for indecisiveness on such pressing issues as the prolonged factional violence in Baoding, Hebei Province. Wang Hongwen and Zhang Chunqiao proposed strengthening the collective leadership and providing Jiang Qing with a formal role, but Ye Jianying and Li Xiannian preferred to discuss whether Mao Yuanxin should return to Liaoning. Mao Yuanxin had written to Hua Guofeng to sound him out on the subject now that he wasn't needed as Mao's liaison. Much to the vexation of the Gang of Four, Hua Guofeng clearly stated that Mao Yuanxin should return to Liaoning.

Jiang Qing angrily insisted that Mao Yuanxin should remain in Beijing to help sort out Mao's affairs, and the argument dragged on into the early hours of the next morning. Everyone was thoroughly exhausted. Hua Guofeng suggested that Ye Jianying and Li Xiannian leave first, given their age, and only six or seven people were left to continue the meeting. Jiang Qing and her allies then pushed for holding a third plenum of the Central Committee, and Jiang Qing wanted to discuss drafting the report for the plenum. Hua Guofeng said the Politburo couldn't discuss the third plenum without a quorum: "Even if a political report is required for the third plenum, I should be the one to prepare it. As for personnel matters relating to the Central Committee, that should be decided through discussion by the Politburo." Having said this, he rose to his feet and declared the meeting adjourned.[7]

In this battle, the Gang of Four had nothing on their side but control of the media. Hoping to consolidate their power in the Central Committee through a third plenum of the Tenth Central Committee, they were expending all their effort on soliciting votes. Zhang Chunqiao had told Wang Hongwen's secretary, Xiao Mu, on September 18, "Now that the Chairman is gone, it looks like the Central Committee may rely on collective leadership from now on . . . We need to keep the emphasis on criticizing Deng and talking about unity."[8] Their main emotion was one of fear for their future, partially fueled by information passed on to them from military and civilian bureaucrats. Yao Wenyuan and his wife, Jin Ying, both had ominous presentiments and started thinking about how to deal with their children. Yao told his youngest daughter, "If Papa dies, you mustn't be sad."

Xu Shiyou's son, a regimental commander in the Beijing Military Region, wrote in a letter to his girlfriend, a nurse in the No. 301 Hospital:

> By no means say anything to anyone about Luo and Fu concealing handguns; I think they're preparing to make a move. When I saw Papa a few days ago, he said, Now that the Chairman is dead, there may be some internal upheaval in China, mainly aimed at vying for supreme leadership. If someone makes trouble in Beijing, he'll lead his troops north and occupy Beijing and take control of Zhongnanhai and Diaoyutai, round up those people and kill them all off. Papa said that the Shanghai Gang is rotten through and through, and used the Chairman's backing to go around tyrannizing people and carrying out all kinds of wicked deeds. Now that the Chairman is gone, they're finished. Papa also said it doesn't matter that Wang Hongwen is vicechairman of the CMC or that Zhang Chunqiao is director of the General Political Department; the troops don't listen to them, and the military is in our hands. All they can do is mobilize a few militia divisions, and that doesn't amount to anything. Papa says he would only need one army to wipe out Shanghai's entire militia. He's positioned the Sixtieth Army at Wuxi to keep an eye on Shanghai.[9]

"Luo and Fu" referred to the generals Luo Ruiqing and Fu Chongbi. This letter fell into Wang Hongwen's hands, and he gave it to Mao Yuanxin, saying anxiously, "It looks like they're really going to make a move. Without any troops, how will we manage?" They discussed having the deputy commander of the Shenyang Military Region, Sun Yuguo,[10] send two divisions from Shenyang, but deploying even one battalion required the approval of the Central Military Commission. Although Wang Hongwen was vice-chairman of the CMC, he had no authority to deploy troops, and although Zhang Chunqiao was director of the General Political Department, his deputy directors ignored him.

In summer 1976, Ji Dengkui's son had gone to visit the head of the organization department of the Henan provincial party committee, who was in Beijing recovering from an illness. They'd talked about the conflict between the old and new factions in the Politburo, and how the old faction wasn't saying anything at the time because Chairman Mao was still alive, but it was already establishing secret contacts and preparing, and that after Mao died, it would take the first opportunity to declare Zhang Chunqiao a traitor[11] and establish military control over the entire country, with massive bloodshed to follow. This news rapidly spread. In July, a journalist in the Xinhua News Agency's Henan branch sent a letter reporting this conversation to the head office and asked that it be passed to Mao through Yao Wenyuan. After reading the letter, Yao thought about it several times but didn't pass it on. The letter was later discovered during a search of Yao's home, and Xie Lifu, who worked at Xinhua's head office, and the director of the Henan branch office, Zhou Mingying, became targets of investigation. Yao Wenyuan later said, "That letter was like a huge stone pressing down on my heart."[12]

The Gang of Four had for some time felt imperiled by their lack of military backing. When in Shanghai for a seminar on militia work a year earlier, in September 1975, Wang Hongwen had told leaders of the Shanghai municipal party committee and militia headquarters to establish a militia headquarters that combined the people's armed defense forces: "You need to be mentally prepared to hold up in case the others launch an attack."[13] He also told Ma Tianshui not to store arms in the military arsenal. "Instead, place them in the hands of the people so the militia will be armed if a war starts."[14] The Shanghai militia began distributing arms in June 1976, and by September 10 more than seventy thousand weapons had reached the grassroots level.[15] However, some researchers believe that Shanghai gave arms to the militia in case of another mass incident like the Tiananmen Incident. After Mao's death, the militia took on an even greater value for defensive purposes but never commanded a scale that would permit sending it to Beijing for a coup.

The Cultural Revolution faction made full use of the media to prolong the campaign to criticize Deng and beat back the right-deviating verdict-reversal trend. On September 16, *People's Daily*, *PLA Daily*, and *Red Flag* published a joint editorial titled "Chairman Mao Lives Forever in Our Hearts," which publicized Mao's "parting exhortation": "Handle things according to the fixed policy." The "fixed policy" was of course continuing revolution under the dictatorship of the proletariat, which meant ramping up the campaign against Deng and the right-deviating verdict-reversal trend. Under Yao Wenyuan's repeated urging, Beijing's and Shanghai's main publications published hundreds of long-winded articles publicizing the need to "handle things according to the fixed policy." *People's Daily* and *Guangming Daily* both turned the phrase into banner headlines, and *Guangming Daily* incorporated it into columns, essays, and news reports for more than two weeks. The message being communicated was that even though Mao was dead, the Cultural Revolution and criticism of Deng had to continue. This naturally put enormous political pressure on the pragmatic faction.

But the Gang of Four made the error of misquoting Mao's actual words, which were "Handle things according to past policy." There was in fact no great difference in the meanings of the two sentences, but the pragmatic faction seized on this error to accuse the Gang of Four of "falsifying" and "counterfeiting" Mao's "parting exhortation."

"Handle things according to past policy" was one of three sentences that Mao wrote in Hua Guofeng's notebook after receiving a delegation from New Zealand on April 30, 1976. The other two sentences were "Take things slowly, don't be in a hurry," and "With you in charge, I'm at ease." The error occurred when Hua made these sentences public for the first time at the State Planning Conference in July, and the person taking the minutes, Chen Feizhang, incorrectly wrote "Handle things according to the fixed policy." When vetting a speech by Foreign Minister Qiao Guanhua on October 2, Hua Guofeng crossed out the sentence "Handle according to the fixed policy" and wrote on the document, "This speech contains an error. It quotes Chairman Mao, and I looked at the original document and found that the wording is different from what Chairman Mao himself wrote. What Chairman Mao wrote and what I passed along at the Politburo meeting was 'Handle things according to past policy.' In order to prevent the error from being passed along, I have crossed it out." Afraid of "giving rise to unnecessary dispute," Zhang Chunqiao decided not to pass along Hua Guofeng's memo but to have the newspapers reduce references to the sentence in order to gradually correct the error. The next day, Yao Wenyuan told the *People's Daily* editor in chief, Lu Ying, to implement Zhang Chunqiao's views, but it was too late: A lengthy article titled "Forever Handle Things According to Chairman Mao's Fixed Policy" under the byline Liang Xiao[16] was published by *Guangming Daily* on October 4. The pragmatic faction was alarmed by this article and later referred to it as a "counterrevolutionary mobilization order," "counter-revolutionary declaration," and "counterrevolutionary signal flare" by the Gang of Four for its coup d'état. As it happened, on the same day that *Guangming Daily* published its article, Jiang Qing proposed going to Shijiazhuang, but her train made a stop at Baoding, where she got out and picked wildflowers for a while before heading back to Beijing. She didn't seek out the local rebel faction or Thirty-Eighth Army to take action, and she didn't go on to Shijiazhuang. If this essay had been a mobilization order for a coup d'état, why would Jiang Qing, a lead player in such a coup, be so leisurely?

Even so, given that the two opposing sides were always putting the worst possible construction on what the other did, the *Guangming Daily* essay provided a rationale for the pragmatic faction to push ahead with its coup d'état.

THE OCTOBER COUP

The pragmatic faction decided to "dispose of" the Cultural Revolution faction once and for all, and private discussions resulted in two possible scenarios: struggle within the party or "extraordinary measures." The first option meant holding a meeting, specifically the third plenum of the Tenth Central Committee, while the second meant taking sudden and harsh action involving a limited amount of armed force to subdue the political opponents, or what is typically referred to in Chinese as a "palace coup."

Yao Yilin recalls that when he delivered a report depicting Jiang Qing as a traitor[17] to Chen Yun's home, he found Chen pondering whether the third plenum could be used to solve the Gang of Four problem. After studying the list of names for the Central Committee over and over again, he felt that the Gang of Four had too many supporters and that it would be difficult to strike them down during the third plenum.[18] Chen Yun was an expert strategist, and his judgment was correct; Li Xiannian and others agreed that their only option was to take harsh measures.

Even so, taking harsh measures required an ironclad rationale. The pragmatic faction recalled a sentence that Mao used on May 3, 1974, to criticize the Cultural Revolution faction: "Don't form a Gang of Four. Why do you have to do that? Why not engage in unity with the 200-plus Central Committee members? It's never been good to band just a few together." Mao's remark was a warning to the Cultural Revolution faction not to form a small clique and to unite with as many people as possible to "continue the revolution." Mao repeatedly criticized Jiang Qing and the others, but mainly because they had failed to meet his expectations.[19] Even so, the pragmatic faction coopted the term "Gang of Four" in order to claim that seizing their political opponents was executing Mao's "unfulfilled will."

The first person in Hua Guofeng's circle to propose taking harsh measures was Li Xin, Kang Sheng's former secretary and then deputy director of the Central Committee General Office and deputy commander of the Central Security Unit. While accepting this recommendation, Hua knew he would need military support, and he thought of Ye Jianying.

In the period before Mao's death, Ye Jianying was networking and secretly plotting in the Western Hills. Although ostensibly on sick leave, Ye was still a member of the Politburo Standing Committee and vice-chairman of both the Central Committee and the Central Military Commission, so he had legitimate status. Because Chen Xilian, who was in charge of the CMC's operations, greatly respected him, Ye still had immense influence within the military, and people he secretly talked to included Tan Zhenlin, Kang Keqing, Geng Biao, Li Qiang,

Luo Qingchang, Xiong Xianghui, Wang Zheng, Yang Chengwu, Liang Biye, Su Yu, Song Shilun, Hua Nan, Liu Zhijian, and Li Desheng. Most of these powerful men had been attacked and marginalized during the Cultural Revolution, and they loathed the Cultural Revolution faction to the depths of their souls.

When Mao was on the brink of death, Major General Xiao Jinguang went to see Ye Jianying and said they had to think of a way to get rid of Jiang Qing and Zhang Chunqiao to avert the disaster of their taking power after Mao's death. Xiao suggested deploying troops to seize Jiang, Zhang, and the others separately. Ye Jianying thought about it for a while, then waved his hand and said, "The Chairman is seriously ill. This isn't the time."[20] The most active of the plotting veterans was Wang Zhen, who constantly circulated among the various homes spreading news and discussing tactics. While Mao was near death, Wang repeatedly went to Ye Jianying's home to talk. Once while they were discussing Wang, Zhang, Jiang, and Yao, Wang Zhen asked Ye, "Why are we letting them run amok like this? Wouldn't rounding them up solve all our problems?" Ye Jianying remained expressionless and merely motioned with his hand, which Wang Zhen understood to mean: "Chairman Mao is still alive. Let's not act rashly. Wait until the time is ripe."[21]

After Mao's death, Ye Jianying stepped up his contacts and preparation. On September 21, Nie Rongzhen passed a message to Ye through Yang Chengwu expressing the worry that the Gang of Four might assassinate Deng Xiaoping and place Ye under house arrest. "The Gang of Four relies on Jiang Qing's special status to act shamelessly at meetings and overbearingly refuses to talk reason, so the usual channel of inner-party struggle won't solve the problem. It's up to us to make the first move and take drastic measures to prevent a mishap.[22]

Ye Jianying naturally agreed with Nie Rongzhen's view to "make the first move."

Hua Guofeng didn't know what to expect from Ye Jianying and urgently needed to get in touch with him, so he went to Li Xiannian. Using the pretext of a medical appointment at Beijing Hospital, Hua dropped in at Li Xiannian's home in West Huangchenggen Street on September 11 and told him, "We're not going to be able to avoid a fight with the Gang of Four. Please go see Marshal Ye on my behalf and ask him to think of when and how to solve the Gang of Four problem. I also ask you to consider this question."

On September 14, Li Xiannian arranged a drive to the Xiangshan Botanical Garden in the Western Hills, saying he was out of sorts and needed a walk. When his car had nearly reached the garden, Li suddenly told his driver and bodyguard to drive to Ye's home nearby. Ye took Li inside and turned on the radio in case the house was bugged. This caused problems for Ye, who was hard of hearing, so the two wrote notes to each other and then burned them. Li wrote, "This fight is unavoidable," and Ye wrote, "This is a fight to the death." Li wrote, "Please consider when and how," and Ye nodded his head in agreement. Ye then wrote Chen Xilian's name with a question mark after it. Li wrote, "Completely reliable, please don't worry."

Why did Li Xiannian have such confidence in Chen Xilian? Li and Chen had kept a deathwatch over Mao together, and when Li went to the restroom, Chen followed him out. While they were in the restroom, Chen said to Li, "Those people might make a move, so be careful."

Hua Guofeng's conversation with Li Xiannian lasted less than ten minutes. Li Xiannian's talk with Ye Jianying lasted less than half an hour.[23]

Apart from having Li Xiannian contact Ye Jianying, Hua Guofeng also contacted Wang Dongxing, a Politburo member and head of the Central Committee General Office. Wang had no great political differences with the Gang of Four, but he dreaded the idea of Jiang Qing taking power. Before the Lin Biao incident, Wang had spread exaggerated rumors about Mao's discord with Jiang in hopes of using the military's power to quash Jiang. When Mao issued instructions from 1975 onward that he didn't want to see Jiang Qing, it was Wang who warded her off, and Jiang hated him for it. Wang Dongxing knew that once Mao was dead, Jiang Qing might wield even greater power, and that decisive measures were needed to "dispose of" Jiang Qing to ensure Wang's personal safety and the welfare of his family. When his subordinate Li Xin advised Hua Guofeng to use harsh measures to dispose of the Gang of Four, it was probably Wang's idea. Wang was head of the Central Committee General Office and controlled the Central Security Unit, which gave him the best opportunity to mount a palace coup. The fact that the Gang of Four was disposed of using only the Central Security Unit without the military's participation also indicates Wang Dongxing's initiative and key role.

Hua Guofeng also gained the support of the Beijing Party secretary and Beijing Military Region political commissar Wu De. Ye Jianying contacted Chen Yun, Deng Yingchao, and other veteran leaders, and they were also completely supportive.

The greatest concern in arresting the Gang of Four was Jiang Qing. Ye Jianying repeatedly used an old saying about fearing to swat a rat on a valuable vase. In this case, the rat was Jiang Qing, and the vase was Mao.

Although Mao criticized Jiang Qing toward the end of his life, and his marriage had been disharmonious for some time, Jiang Qing always stood firmly on Mao's side on political issues, and Mao trusted her in spite of his criticism. Mao's deification lent Jiang Qing an aura that gave her considerable influence, which had intensified under the public fawning of central leaders from 1966 onward.

Even though Jiang Qing sometimes behaved inappropriately, Mao still considered her family. When Mao Yuanxin balked at Jiang Qing's request to summarize the content of some documents they were putting in order in 1975, Jiang Qing wrote a letter to Mao asking him to intercede. Mao drew a circle on Jiang Qing's letter and sent it on to Mao Yuanxin. Mao Yuanxin didn't know what the circle meant, so he went to Mao and asked. Mao told him, "Help her out. We don't have much family left now."[24] Ordinary people were even more inclined to regard Jiang as the person closest to Mao.

In spite of fears of "breaking the vase while swatting the rat," the decision was made to arrest the Gang of Four; preparations were made, and bows were drawn.

In accordance with the plan drawn up by Hua Guofeng, Ye Jianying, and Wang Dongxing, Wang would be responsible for arresting the Gang of Four; Wu De and Wu Zhong would be responsible for putting Chi Qun, Xie Jingyi, Jin Zumin,[25] and others under isolation and investigation; if anything unexpected occurred within Zhongnanhai, Wu De would organize troops from the garrison command as backup; and the Beijing Garrison Command would be responsible for *People's*

Daily, the Xinhua News Agency, the broadcasting stations, central organs, and Tsinghua and Peking Universities.

Wang Dongxing directed Zhang Yaoci, the deputy director of the Central Committee General Office, and Wu Jianhua, deputy director of the Central Security Unit, to select fifty-odd officers and soldiers to participate in the operation. To obtain authority to command troops from the Beijing Garrison, Wu De communicated with Wu Zhong, the Beijing Garrison commander, and liaised with Chen Xilian, who was in charge of the CMC's day-to-day operations. Li Xin was responsible for preparing all the documents needed for the coup. While mobilizing the security guards and soldiers who would carry out the operation, Wang Dongxing said, "Jiang Qing and the others are taking advantage of Chairman Mao's death to plot a restoration of capitalism in China." This was the most irredeemably heinous crime at that time, and anyone involved in political struggle would impose that label on the opposition.

In the afternoon of October 6, Ye Jianying received a phone call in his home in the Western Hills notifying him of a meeting at Huairen Hall at eight o'clock that night and requesting that he arrive one hour in advance. Accordingly, Ye arrived at Zhongnanhai at seven o'clock and went to a side room to rest before proceeding to Huairen Hall.

Bright lights lent Huairen Hall a congenial atmosphere, and some of the men assigned to the special mission posed as guards. When Ye entered the hall, he saw that Hua Guofeng and Wang Dongxing had already arrived. They communicated with each other through their eyes and said nothing. All the tables and chairs had been removed, making the hall look very spacious. A screen in the middle divided the room into two sections. In front of the screen were two high-backed sofas. Behind the screen, Wang Dongxing and guards were hiding on either side, watching the door.

That afternoon, Wang Hongwen, Zhang Chunqiao, and Yao Wenyuan had been notified of a Politburo Standing Committee meeting in Huairen Hall for the purpose of vetting the final proof of volume 5 of Mao's *Selected Works* and a plan for the construction of a memorial hall for Mao. Yao Wenyuan wasn't a standing committee member, but he was responsible for publications, so it was natural to invite him to the meeting. It was also natural that Jiang Qing, who was not a standing committee member, was not notified to attend the meeting. Jiang Qing required special handling on her own.

At 7:55 p.m., Zhang Chunqiao swaggered into the hall with his briefcase, but his bodyguards were told to wait outside. Sensing something amiss, he asked, "What's going on? What's going on?" at which point the leader of the operations group, Ji Hefu, came over with several others and "protectively" ushered him into the main hall. Zhang looked around for his usual seat, but saw only a stern-faced Ye Jianying and a wrathful Hua Guofeng. Before Zhang could say anything, Hua Guofeng said sternly, "Zhang Chunqiao, you listen here. You colluded with Jiang Qing, Wang Hongwen, and others to oppose the party, oppose socialism, and commit unforgivable crimes!" He then read out a prepared decision to place Zhang under "isolation and investigation" with immediate effect. Zhang was led away without putting up any resistance.

The next to come in was Wang Hongwen. As soon as he entered the doorway, another leader of the operations group rushed over with several guards and apprehended him. Wang yelled, "I'm here for the meeting. What are you doing?" He struck out frantically at them with his hands and feet but was quickly subdued. The guards twisted his arms around his back and took him into the main hall, where Hua Guofeng once again read out the decision. Before he reached the end, Wang suddenly yelled, broke free from the guards, and charged like a raging beast at Ye Jianying, who was about five meters away. Quarters were too close for gunfire, so the guards raced over and hurled him to the ground. He was then half dragged outside in handcuffs and pushed into a car, which drove off.

Yao Wenyuan was late, occasioning some tension. When being notified of the meeting by phone, he had said, "This meeting is long overdue," but for whatever reason he was late getting around, and without summoning his guard or putting on his hat, he grabbed his briefcase and jumped into his car. After arriving at Huairen Hall, he was taken to the large vestibule in the East Hall, where a deputy director of the Central Security Unit, rather than Hua Guofeng, read out the decision to place him under isolation and investigation. Yao didn't try to defend himself or resist, but simply said, "Let's go," and followed the guards out the door.

While Wang, Zhang, and Yao were being dealt with at Huairen Hall, Zhang Yaoci, Wu Jianhua, Li Lianqing, and a dozen others arrived at Mao Yuanxin's quarters at Zhongnanhai. Zhang Yaoci informed Mao Yuanxin that Hua Guofeng had relayed instructions from the Central Committee to place him under protection and investigation, and he was to hand over the keys to his filing cabinet and his gun: "Instructor Li Lianqing will be responsible for your living arrangements and your safety. You are not allowed to make outside phone calls, and must observe the rules. Anything you write will be passed to the Central Committee through Comrade Li Lianqing." Mao Yuanxin said, "The Chairman's remains aren't yet cold, and you're already . . ." But then he said no more. When he refused to hand over his keys and gun, a cadre took them from him.[26]

Zhang Yaoci and the others then proceeded to Jiang Qing's quarters nearby, arriving at 8:20 p.m. Zhang Yaoci informed Jiang Qing that under instructions from Hua Guofeng, she was being placed under isolation and investigation for engaging in activities to split the party Central Committee: "You will go to another place, where you must frankly confess your crimes to the party and observe the rules. Hand over your documents and your keys." Jiang Qing glared at him from her sofa and didn't say a word. With a pencil, she wrote a brief note on red-lined high-quality letter paper: "Comrade Guofeng, people came here and claimed that they are acting under your orders to declare me under isolation and investigation. Is this the Central Committee's decision? I'm sending you the key to my filing cabinet along with this letter. Jiang Qing, October 6." She then wrote, "To be personally opened by Comrade Hua Guofeng" on a large envelope, and at the bottom wrote, "Entrusted by Jiang Qing." She wrapped her key in a piece of paper and placed it with her letter inside the envelope, then put two seals on each end of the envelope, pressed down hard on the seals, and handed the envelope to Zhang Yaoci. At that point, Wu Jianhua came over and led Jiang Qing out of the room. A Red Flag sedan was waiting for her outside, and Jiang Qing entered it with her customary hauteur.[27]

At the same time, the Beijing Garrison Command was placing Chi Qun, Xie Jingyi, and Jin Zumin under isolation and investigation, while other allies of the Cultural Revolution faction were also taken into custody.

Hua Guofeng also sent people to take control of the broadcast stations, the Xinhua News Agency, and other important media units, starting that night. He first called Geng Biao[28] to Zhongnanhai and had him read two duplicated documents of Mao's notes stating, "With you in charge, I'm at ease," and "Take things slowly, don't be in a hurry," and then told Geng Biao to take troops to the Central and Beijing broadcast stations. Geng Biao, Deputy Commander Qiu Weigao of the Beijing Garrison Command, and others hurried straight to Central People's Broadcasting Station. Geng Biao showed Hua Guofeng's personal order to the head of the broadcasting department, Deng Gang, and told him to notify all his assistants to come with bedrolls to the office, as they would not be allowed to return home. He told them to go through the recordings that were to be broadcast the next day and edit out all mentions of the phrase "Handle things according to the fixed policy." When Deng Gang hesitated to hand over the keys to the live broadcast room, Geng Biao said, "If you don't, we can telephone Yao Wenyuan." Deng Gang quickly said, "That's not necessary, I suspect his number is out of order now." For safety's sake, Geng Biao and the others ate and drank only items brought from outside. Geng Biao also called in the party secretary of the Beijing People's Broadcasting Station, Zhao Zhengjing, and repeated the process there.[29]

A five-member group took control of the Xinhua News Agency the next day. One member of the group was the head of Xinhua's Beijing branch, Li Pu, and the others were Zheng Bingnian (head of a military political department), Xu Guinian (Li Xiannian's secretary), Yang Jiaxiang (a Signal Corps officer), and Huang Zonghan (Kang Sheng's secretary). Li Pu and the others had been called over to Zhongnanhai's Ziguang Pavilion, where Ji Dengkui had everyone read the copies of Mao's two notes and revealed that the Gang of Four had been placed under isolation and investigation. The group was then tasked with taking over management of the Xinhua News Agency.[30] The Central Committee also sent a work group led by Chi Haotian[31] to take control of *People's Daily*.

As soon as the Gang of Four was "disposed of" on the night of October 6, all Politburo members who were in Beijing at the time received an urgent notification to report immediately to Building No. 9 at Jade Spring Hill for a meeting. By ten o'clock, everyone had arrived: Hua Guofeng, Ye Jianying, Li Xiannian, Wang Dongxing, Chen Xilian, Su Zhenhua, Ji Dengkui, Wu De, Ni Zhifu, Chen Yonggui, and Wu Guixian. The meeting lasted until four o'clock the next morning.

Hua Guofeng presided over the meeting and gave a speech. Ye Jianying reported on the process and significance of arresting the Gang of Four. The Politburo unanimously passed a motion by Ye Jianying making Hua Guofeng chairman of the Central Committee and of the Central Military Commission. Wang Dongxing notified Politburo members who were outside Beijing, including Wei Guoqing, Xu Shiyou, Li Desheng, and Sai Fuding, and solicited their views.

The reaction of Deng Xiaoping and his family is vividly described by his daughter Mao Mao:

> On October 7, after He Ping [Mao Mao's husband] learned the news, he rode his bicycle at full speed to Kuan Street to share it with our family. As soon as he entered our house, he said, "Come here! Hurry!" The whole family looked at his excited face, dripping with sweat, and knew that a major event had occurred. At this time, we were afraid there were listening devices in the house, so whenever there was something important, we would use anti-bugging methods and speak quietly. Our entire family—Father, Mother, Deng Lin and Deng Nan, who were at home at the time, and myself—all went into the bathroom and turned on the water taps full blast. Amidst the sound of pouring water, we surrounded He Ping and heard him describe the smashing of the Gang of Four. Father's hearing was not good, and the sound of flowing water was too loud, so he didn't hear clearly and asked for it to be repeated. The Gang of Four had been smashed! Could it be true? We didn't dare believe it. When we heard about the interesting spectacle, we three girls jumped up and down with excitement! Our hearts thumped so violently that the sound rang in our ears. Amazement, doubt, tension, joy, for a time all feelings of joy, anger, sorrow, and happiness

flooded our hearts at once. Father was very agitated, and the cigarette he was holding trembled in his hand. Locked in the bathroom amidst the sound of rushing water, our entire family asked, talked, discussed, and softly rejoiced, venting our emotions through furious cursing. It seemed that no method could fully express the excitement and joy in our hearts.[32]

On October 10, the overjoyed Deng Xiaoping wrote a letter to Hua Guofeng:

> Dear Chairman Hua, Party Central Committee:
> This recent struggle against careerists and schemers usurping the party's power happened at the crucial moment immediately after the death of our Great Leader Chairman Mao. The party Central Committee led by Comrade Guofeng conquered that bunch of rotten eggs and won a great victory. This is the victory of the great undertaking to consolidate the party, and the victory of Mao Zedong Thought and Chairman Mao's revolutionary line. Like the people of the entire country, I feel extreme and heartfelt joy at the victory in this great struggle, and cannot keep myself from yelling, "Long live! Long live!" With this letter I express the sincere emotions in my heart.
> Long live the party Central Committee led by Chairman Hua!
> Long live the great victory of the party and the socialist undertaking!

It was natural for Deng Xiaoping to rejoice at the downfall of the Gang of Four, and he wrote his letter in hopes of being given an opportunity to go back to work. Marshal Ye Jianying did in fact immediately recommend allowing Deng Xiaoping to come back to work, but his recommendation was rejected under the prevailing circumstances. Not long afterward, Ye brought Deng's family to live in the Western Hills and secretly sent over periodic batches of documents using someone else's name in order to keep Deng apprised of the situation.

Over the next week, the Politburo notified central, provincial-level, and military region leaders of what official documents referred to as the "smashing of the Gang of Four." This expression continued to be used for many years, but historically speaking, it is more appropriate to refer to it as the "October Coup," because it was a classic palace coup.

The Central Committee officially notified the entire party of this major event on October 18 through Document No. 16 [1976]. By the time this document was circulated among the general population on October 20, its content was common knowledge. The reception was positive; Jiang Qing's imperious antics had made her highly unpopular, and few sympathized with her. A grand celebratory parade of some 1.5 million people in Beijing on October 21 was replicated in cities all over China in the days that followed. It is likely that the participants were largely the same as those who just half a year earlier had celebrated the fall of Deng Xiaoping.

Shanghai was an important base area for Mao's launch of the Cultural Revolution; the Cultural Revolution faction was still in power there, and three of the members of the Gang of Four were from Shanghai. So how did Shanghai react to the October Coup?

At three o'clock in the morning on October 7, the Central Committee General Office telephoned the Shanghai party secretary in charge of operations, Ma Tianshui, and summoned him to Beijing for a meeting, but declined to state the purpose. Ma immediately telephoned Zhang Chunqiao and Yao Wenyuan in Beijing to ask what was going on, but he couldn't get through to them. The Central Committee sent a chartered plane to bring Ma and the commander of the Shanghai Garrison, Zhou Chunlin, to Beijing, where they were then taken to the Jingxi Guesthouse and told not to make any outside telephone calls, go out, write letters, or receive visitors.[33]

Xu Jingxian and Wang Xiuzhen had told the secretary who was accompanying Ma, Fang Zuoting, to telephone to report their safe arrival, and when no phone call came from Fang, Xu Jingxian and the others tried to contact Beijing through various channels, but without success. On October 8 they learned that all contact channels with Beijing had been cut off. To find out what was really going on, Wang Xiuzhen sent Jin Zumin's secretary, Miao Wenjin, to Beijing and told him to call back with the message of "heart failure" if the situation was serious.[34]

On the afternoon of the eighth, Xu Jingxian, Wang Shaoyong, Wang Xiuzhen, and Feng Guozhu held a meeting with leaders of the people's militia headquarters and the public security bureau, during which Xu reported that a coup seemed to have occurred and that Ma Tianshui was under house arrest in Beijing. Xu then called in the heads of the city's newspapers and radio station, followed by an enlarged meeting of the municipal party committee's standing committee, to expand the number of people informed. At seven o'clock in the evening, Miao Wenjin telephoned Kang Ningyi at the party committee's security unit and said, "My mother has died of a heart attack," and three hours later, a phone call came from Liu Qingtang at the Ministry of Culture saying, "Old Ma isn't taking phone calls. We're all ill." That put an end to two days of guessing. Zhu Yongjia, the leader of the municipal party committee writing group, called for bringing out the militia. "If we can't fight for a week, we'll fight for five days or even three days, as long as the whole world knows, just like the Paris Commune." Wang Xiuzhen told the militia leaders of the apparent coup and that Ma Tianshui and others from Shanghai had been apprehended. "We have to fight. Shanghai was where the January revolution started; we're bound to the Great Proletarian Cultural Revolution like flesh and blood." But they prepared without a decent military map, and the security troops could produce only a single battalion.

After several more attempts, Xu Jingxian finally reached Ma Tianshui at seven o'clock on the night of October 9. Wang Xiuzhen asked if Ma had seen Zhang Chunqiao, Wang Hongwen, and Yao Wenyuan, and Ma said, "They are unwell and rather busy with work, so they haven't had time to talk with me." This made the others feel they'd been worried for nothing, and they told the militia to stand down. Later that night, Ma Tianshui telephoned and told Xu Jingxian and Wang Xiuzhen to come to Beijing for a meeting the next day.

With all three of Shanghai's party secretaries called to Beijing, just four veteran cadres from the party committee standing committee—Feng Guozhu, Wang Shaoyong, Zhang Jingbiao, and Huang Tao—were left behind. After Xu Jingxian and Wang Xiuzhen arrived in Beijing on the tenth, the Politburo clearly spelled out the situation to them and advised them to be prudent. Ye Jianying said, "The Central Committee trusts you and will give you a free hand;

we'll count on you to handle things in Shanghai." They were told to telephone Shanghai every day to keep the situation stable.[35] Ma Tianshui and Zhou Chunlin had already been brought in line by then, and they convinced Xu and Wang. Xu Jingxian telephoned Feng Guozhu in Shanghai and told him, "Wait for us to get back before deciding on anything."

On the twelfth, Feng and the other standing committee members held a meeting with unionists, militia, and core members of the municipal party committee writing group. Zhu Yongjia called for "taking immediate action" and "putting the will of the people to use," saying they'd already missed the chance to act on the eighth, and if they didn't act now, by tomorrow they would have no further opportunity. Ye Changming, Chen Ada, and Ma Zhenlong from the municipal federation of trade unions were also in favor of immediate action. The four standing committee members agreed that something should be done but advocated waiting for the three secretaries to come back first.

The three party secretaries returned to Shanghai the next day and called an enlarged standing committee meeting on the afternoon of the thirteenth to communicate the Central Committee's message. Weeping broke out at the meeting and lasted for five or six minutes.[36] That night, Ma Tianshui called in core members of the federation of trade unions, the militia, and the public security bureau and passed along the Central Committee's message to them as well. One of the activists, who still wanted to rebel, later went to Ma Tianshui's home and urged him to mobilize the militia and carry out a revolt like the Paris Commune. "You lead us, Old Ma, and we will follow you!" Ma Tianshui replied, "We don't have control of the military, and the militia is no match for the army." The two of them wept in each other's arms, knowing that the situation was hopeless and there was no going back. At that time, the Sixtieth Army, which was loyal to the Central Committee, was stationed near Shanghai.

Although Shanghai was an important base area for the Cultural Revolution faction, many of its residents resented the Cultural Revolution. On the night of the thirteenth, banners calling for the downfall of Wang Hongwen, Jiang Qing, Zhang Chunqiao, and Yao Wenyuan appeared all around the streets of Shanghai. From the fifteenth onward, Shanghai residents held celebratory rallies during which upward of ten thousand people poured into the Shanghai municipal party committee offices demanding to know why news of the smashing of the Gang of Four wasn't being passed on. When *People's Daily* published a report on the smashing of the Gang of Four on October 22, the city roiled with excitement, and celebrations with drums, gongs, and firecrackers filled the streets.

A Central Committee work group sent by Hua Guofeng and led by Su Zhenhua, Ni Zhifu, and Peng Chong arrived in Shanghai on October 26. On November 1, one hundred thousand armed militiamen in helmets and uniforms paraded in the streets, holding aloft portraits of Mao and Hua Guofeng and celebrating the victorious smashing of the Gang of Four. It was the largest parade since the formation of the Shanghai militia.[37]

Mao was dead and the Cultural Revolution faction was "smashed." The ten-year-long Cultural Revolution had effectively ended. However, the official end of the Cultural Revolution was not declared until ten months later, at the Eleventh National Party Congress.

Hua Guofeng's political report to the Eleventh Party Congress on August 12, 1977, stated that "the smashing of the Gang of Four was yet another great victory of the Great Proletarian Cultural Revolution." After emphasizing the necessity of the Cultural Revolution, Hua said that seizing back the power stolen by Liu Shaoqi, Lin Biao, and the Gang of Four had consolidated the dictatorship of the proletariat and cleared the road for comprehensive, correct, and thorough implementation of Chairman Mao's revolutionary line: "Now that the Gang of Four has been struck down, we can bring about stability and unity in accordance with Chairman Mao's instructions, and achieve great order under heaven. I hereby declare that our country's first Great Proletarian Cultural Revolution, lasting eleven years, has ended in victory, marked by the smashing of the Gang of Four."

Please note, Hua Guofeng said that the Cultural Revolution lasted eleven years, not ten years, as subsequently stated.

In order to legitimize the October Coup, a public trial was held from November 1980 to January 1981, binding together two mutually antagonistic groups of people: the Lin Biao clique and the Gang of Four under the name of the "Lin Biao, Jiang Qing counterrevolutionary clique." Jiang Qing and Zhang Chunqiao were both sentenced to death, suspended for two years, and permanently stripped of their political rights; Wang Hongwen was sentenced to life in prison and permanent deprivation of political rights; Yao Wenhuan was sentenced to twenty years in prison and five years' deprivation of political rights. Qi Benyu was sentenced to eighteen years in prison (he had been jailed in 1967), Chi Qun to eighteen years, and Liu Qingtang to seventeen years. Among the members of the Lin Biao clique, who had been imprisoned five years earlier, Huang Yongsheng, Chen Boda, and Jiang Tengjiao were sentenced to eighteen years in prison; Wu Faxian and Li Zuopeng to seventeen years; and Qiu Huizuo to sixteen years.

When Jiang Qing took her place in the defendant's dock, Judge Zeng Hanzhou slapped the table and said sternly, "Jiang Qing, you are a criminal, you are a defendant, you have to be afraid of us!" Jiang Qing was taken aback at first, but then shot back, "Afraid of you? You're afraid of me!" The two of them went back and forth arguing who was afraid of whom. Finally Jiang Qing laughed and said, "Ask Jiang Hua, who's sitting beside you, whom I've ever been afraid of!" The pronouncement of Jiang Qing's verdict was another farce. Head judge Jiang Hua tried to intimidate Jiang Qing by declaring, "Jiang Qing is sentenced to death!" and pausing there. Jiang Qing shouted, "Revolution is not a crime, to rebel is justified! Down with the Ye and Deng counterrevolutionary clique!" Jiang Hua then went on to say that the death sentence was suspended for two years.[38]

When Zhang Chunqiao was interrogated before his public trial, the judges first asked him if there was anything he wanted to say. Zhang said he would not say anything unless it was truthfully reported. After being repeatedly questioned by the judges, Zhang Chunqiao finally said, "Although the Cultural Revolution launched and led by Chairman Mao failed, its spirit and principles are eternal, and if the governing Communist Party doesn't sincerely resolve the problem of degeneration and becomes a privileged class separated from the vast masses, remote and high above and acting like mighty and paternalistic officials, sooner or later the masses will launch another revolution according to Chairman Mao's instructions, and will strike down the capitalist class within the party."[39] At the actual public trial, Zhang Chunqiao maintained a stony silence.

Wang Hongwen seemed like a completely different person while on trial; he was thoroughly submissive. Qiu Huizuo, who was in prison with him, says, "After Wang Hongwen was arrested, the suffering he experienced was appalling! When we were in prison together, an injury to his brain prevented Wang Hongwen from talking intelligibly. He just rambled on and on nonsensically."[40] Wang Hongwen, Wu Faxian, Jiang Tengjiao, and Qiu Huizuo were sent to prison together on July 15, 1981, almost five years after Wang Hongwen was arrested. His speech problems suggest how badly he'd been treated in the intervening years.

For China to stage a public trial after years of lawlessness was a kind of progress. It showed that the bureaucrats who had come under attack during the Cultural Revolution had learned the importance of the law after their bitter taste of anarchy. It would be difficult to say that the trial process was carried out in accordance with law, however. Zhang Sizhi, who was head of the legal team during the trial of the Lin-Jiang clique, said the judges were temporarily transferred officials, and many had no knowledge of law, leading to some farcical episodes. The defense lawyers, appointed by the authorities, were not allowed to challenge the facts of the case or the charges against the defendants. Since carrying out a defense involved these two very things, once they were ruled out completely, what could a lawyer do? The witnesses who appeared in court had been coached in advance and were required to cooperate with the prosecution and prove that the charges were factual. Once all that was settled, it was a matter of going through several "dress rehearsals" before the public trial. The people attending the hearings had been selected in advance from among the politically reliable.[41]

28

CHINA'S FOREIGN RELATIONS DURING THE CULTURAL REVOLUTION

During its first ten years, the diplomatic policy of the People's Republic of China was heavily weighted toward the Soviet Union. The USSR was China's best friend, and the United States its archenemy. After the twentieth party congress of the Communist Party of the Soviet Union, Sino-Soviet relations went into steady decline, and China's best friend became its most malevolent foe. Countries that sided with either "American imperialism" or the Soviet Union's "social imperialism" were likewise regarded as hostile and reactionary, and China's full-scale attack on "imperialists, revisionists, and reactionaries" made a shambles of its foreign relations. After the Lin Biao incident, Mao's adjustments to the strategy of the Cultural Revolution were reflected in a shift in China's diplomatic policies from all-out attack to allying with the United States against the Soviet Union.

He Fang[1] says, "Mao Zedong insisted on continuous revolution, so domestic affairs continued to be handled according to the approach of a revolutionary party rather than a governing party, while foreign affairs were carried out according the rules of world revolution rather than modern international relations."[2] Mao's adjustment of diplomatic policies, although somewhat easing the tensions in China's international relations, never abandoned the particular approach of world revolution.

TAKING PRIDE IN BEING THE "HUB OF WORLD REVOLUTION"

Communism calls for world revolution, and the Soviet Union had long been the leader of world revolution. After deciding that the Soviet Union had turned "revisionist," the Chinese Communist Party hoped to take its place. Mao's theory of world revolution, shaped before the Cultural Revolution, held that Asia, Africa, and Latin America were the world's "countryside," while Western Europe and North America were the world's "cities," and that victory in world revolution could be achieved by following China's revolutionary path of using the villages to besiege the cities. By the time the Cultural Revolution began, it was claimed that "the world had entered the new era of Mao Zedong Thought," that China was the "base area of world revolution," and that Beijing was the "hub of world revolution."

The Chinese who lived in the hub of world revolution were nevertheless unable to set foot outside China. At that time, only high-level leaders and diplomats had the opportunity to visit foreign countries; even ordinary cadres and intellectuals were forbidden to do so, much less workers and peasants. Foreigners were a rare sight, and any who turned up on China's streets became targets of intense interest as the Chinese surrounded and trailed them, marveling over blue eyes and blond hair. Foreign goods could not be purchased in the Chinese marketplace, and foreign publications were not available in libraries (apart from some scientific journals). Scientific and cultural exchanges with the outside world basically ended.

Since China was the hub of world revolution, one of its chief tasks was to export Mao Zedong Thought. According to incomplete statistics, from October 1966 to May 1967, the China International Bookstore distributed more than eight hundred thousand copies of *Quotations from Chairman Mao* in English, French, Spanish, Japanese, Russian, German, Italian, Nepalese, Vietnamese, Hindi, Arabic, Burmese, Swahili, Persian, and other languages to 117 countries and regions.[3] On November 24, 1967, the Xinhua News Agency reported that 25 foreign-language editions of Mao's works totaling more than 4.6 million copies had been distributed to 148 countries and regions. Mao badges were also exported in mass quantities as symbols of revolution.

The mass export of Mao's works gave rise to many diplomatic disputes. Chinese embassy staff drew protests from one host country when they went around the main thoroughfares distributing leaflets proclaiming that "to rebel is justified" and putting up posters stating, "Long Live the Victorious Great Proletarian Cultural Revolution" on walls near the embassy. Engineers sent to assist a construction project in another country clashed with local police when the host government prohibited them from erecting a gigantic poster stating, "Socialism will definitely replace capitalism" at the worksite. Embassy staff in a certain African country created considerable ill feeling by reading Mao's quotes out loud on public buses and forcing Little Red Books and Mao badges on pedestrians in the streets, punching and cursing at people who rejected their gifts. Embassy staff in another country waylaid veiled Muslim women to promote "liberated thinking" and were hurled from tents while trying to propagate atheism among the devout.[4]

Ever since Mao resurrected class struggle at the tenth plenum of the Eighth Central Committee in 1962, the domestic policy of "three freedoms and one contract"[5] and diplomatic policy of "three appeasements and one reduction"[6] had been dismissed as "a general program for the restoration of capitalism." Criticism turned the "three freedoms and one contract" into the "three capitulations and one extinguishing"[7] during the Cultural Revolution and called for implementing the "three fights and one increase": fighting imperialists, revisionists, and reactionaries, and increasing support to national liberation movements. These fights were endless, and the amount of aid steadily increased; in 1972, 1973, and 1975, foreign aid composed 6.7 percent, 7.2 percent, and 6.3 percent, respectively, of the national budget. From 1954 to 1970, aid to Albania reached more than 9 billion yuan, or an average of 4,000 yuan per Albanian citizen.[8] By way of comparison, in 1972, 1973, and 1975, China's national average-per-capita consumption was 147 yuan, 155 yuan, and 158 yuan, respectively.[9] After the United States and Vietnam went to war, Mao announced in a December 19, 1967, cable to the Vietnamese Southern National Liberation Front: "The seven hundred million people of China are the staunch backup force of the Vietnamese people, and the vast Chinese national territory is the reliable rear area of the Vietnamese people." Mao was as good as his word, providing Vietnam with enough light and heavy weapons to arm more than two million soldiers in its naval, land, and air forces. China also provided Vietnam with equipment for 450 industrial factories, hospitals, and research institutes, and built hundreds of kilometers of railways and thousands of kilometers of petroleum pipelines in Vietnam. China also provided large quantities of various kinds of raw materials, nonstaple foods, and other material goods. Over the course of the war, China sent more than twenty thousand specialist advisers to Vietnam and more than three hundred thousand troops for ground-to-air missiles, antiaircraft guns, and minesweeping. More than five thousand Chinese died while aiding the Vietnamese war effort.[10] From 1950 to 1978, the total value of China's aid to Vietnam reached US$20 billion, according to the international market value at that time. The vast majority was voluntary aid requiring no repayment, while a small portion consisted of interest-free loans.[11]

In the dense atmosphere of struggle, everyone vied for the front ranks of opposition to imperialists, revisionists, and reactionaries. Massive protests against the United States, the Soviet Union, India, and Indonesia filled the streets of Beijing on a regular basis. The most notable diplomatic incidents in 1967 were the "three smashings and one burning." The Indian embassy was damaged by protesters on June 18, the Burmese embassy on July 3, and the Indonesian embassy on August 6, while protesters set fire to the British mission on August 22. It wasn't only Red Guards who engaged in these extremist actions—workers, cadres, and foreign affairs officials also took part.

The series of violent protests was set off after two secretaries from the Indian embassy were arrested on June 4 on allegations that they had secretly photographed a restricted area. On June 13, the Beijing Higher People's Court found one of the secretaries guilty of espionage and expelled him with immediate effect, while the other was declared persona non grata and ordered to leave the country within three days. India retaliated on June 14 by expelling a secretary of the Chinese embassy in Delhi, Chen Luzhi, and declaring another secretary, Xie Chenghao, persona non grata. This provoked a strong protest from China on June 15. After more than one thousand Indians attacked the Chinese embassy in Delhi on June 16 and beat up embassy staff, Red

Guards and mass organizations in Beijing staged a protest in front of the Indian embassy on June 18, breaking several of its windows and removing the embassy sign bearing the national emblem of India.[12]

The Burma incident was set off around the same time when Chinese embassy staff ignored the dissuasion of the Burmese government and forced copies of *Quotations from Chairman Mao* and Mao badges on overseas Chinese and Burmese citizens. Students in Burma were forbidden to wear the insignia of a foreign country, and conflicts erupted when administrators of Burmese schools for overseas Chinese required students to remove their Mao badges. On June 27 and 28, Burmese people surrounded and attacked the Chinese embassy, killing a Chinese aid specialist named Liu Yi and injuring five others. From June 29 onward, protesters surrounded the Burmese embassy in Beijing, shouting "Down with Ne Win!" and "Hang Ne Win!"[13] Some people pelted the embassy with bricks, and the outside walls and road in front of the embassy gate were plastered with posters and banners.

China had supported the Indonesian Communist Party (ICP) all along. After a failed coup in September 1965 allegedly involving the ICP, the new Suharto regime killed off ICP members, expelled Indonesia's overseas Chinese, and took diplomatic action against China. Window displays promoting Mao Zedong Thought at the Chinese Embassy in Jakarta in the early stage of the Cultural Revolution brought constant attacks on the embassy and on Chinese organs in Indonesia, which in turn drew protests from the Chinese government. After Indonesia declared the interim chargé d'affaires in the Chinese embassy, Yao Dengshan, and Consul General Xu Ren persona non grata on April 4, 1967,[14] more than half a million Chinese protested outside the Indonesian embassy in Beijing from April 24 to 28, breaking down its gate. An attack on the Chinese embassy in Jakarta by the Indonesian armed forces on August 5 injured four embassy staff. China's Foreign Ministry issued a diplomatic notice of protest on August 6, and ten thousand people besieged the Indonesian embassy, smashing up furnishings and vehicles, setting fire to the offices, and assaulting embassy staff.

The burning of the British mission was sparked by the "1967 Incident" in Hong Kong, when leftist workers went on strike following a labor dispute at the Hong Kong Artificial Flower Factory in May, and

590 | THE WORLD TURNED UPSIDE DOWN

mainland workers voiced support. On June 3, *People's Daily* published an editorial titled "Resolutely Beat Back the Provocation of British Imperialism," and Chinese militia crossed the Hong Kong border for a punitive attack on the Hong Kong British authorities in July, with two people killed on the Chinese side and five on the Hong Kong side. Tensions eased until August, when the Hong Kong authorities ordered three left-wing newspapers to cease publication and arrested some reporters and staff. A million people began protesting in front of the British mission in Beijing on August 15 and then set it on fire after the Hong Kong authorities ignored China's diplomatic notice demanding retraction of the publication ban and the unconditional release of the reporters and staff. Enraged students and workers forced the mission's British staff to admit their error and request punishment in front of a portrait of Mao, and the acting chargé d'affaires, Donald Hopson, was beaten. Zhou Enlai later took responsibility for the incident,[15] and a leader of Tsinghua University's 4-14 faction, Jiang Nanfeng, was subjected to years of investigation for his part in the arson attack.

This chaos in China's diplomatic affairs resulted from the prevailing guiding ideology on foreign affairs, and from the Cultural Revolution movement within the Foreign Ministry, described earlier in this book.[16] Responding to a call to take part in the Cultural Revolution, around two thousand personnel of China's overseas embassies returned to China in early 1967. They organized battle groups based on their embassy units, and they publicly denounced the ambassadors and attachés, as well as their wives, as power-holders.

Within a year of the launch of the Cultural Revolution, more than thirty of the fifty-odd countries with which China had established relations or was negotiating or preparing to establish relations became involved in diplomatic disputes with China, and China's overseas consulates decreased from fourteen to five, while the number of foreign consulates in China decreased from more than thirty to just six.[17] Of course, China was not solely responsible for these diplomatic disputes, but the "three fights and one increase" policy was a key factor.

THE DIPLOMATIC SITUATION IMPROVES AS THE
REBEL FACTION IS CONTAINED

The year 1967 was marked by the launch of "all-out class struggle." Encouraged by Wang Li's August 7 remarks, the Foreign Ministry's Revolutionary Rebel Liaison Station took control of the political department, denounced Foreign Minister Chen Yi in a mass rally, rebuffed Premier Zhou Enlai, and sent unauthorized cables to foreign embassies, further developing the ultra-leftist diplomatic thinking that had formed before the Cultural Revolution.[18]

As this chaos was emerging in foreign affairs, the entire country was becoming enveloped in "great chaos under heaven" as rebels who had been suppressed by support-the-left military units seized the momentum of Wuhan Military Region commander Chen Zaidao's downfall and began launching attacks on military units. After making his escape from Wuhan's July 20 Incident, Mao had considered arming the rebel faction as a check and balance against military leaders who didn't support the Cultural Revolution, but ultimately he chose to protect the army and contain the rebel faction as his strategy shifted from "great chaos under heaven" to a gradual push toward "great order under heaven." Zhou Enlai seized on this opportunity by using Wang Li's August 7 speech against him, and once Mao pronounced the speech a "big, big, big poisonous weed," Wang Li, Guan Feng, and Qi Benyu were removed from the political stage.[19] This cleared the way for Zhou Enlai to call in the core group of the Foreign Ministry's rebels and criticize the major political errors they'd committed in August. Zhou reiterated, "Power over foreign relations remains with the Central Committee, and the Central Committee has delegated this power to me, and no one else has any say in the matter. I'm in charge." He further stated that ultra-leftist thinking and actions had affected China's diplomatic work and damaged China's international reputation:[20] "My support for the [Revolutionary Rebel] 'Liaison Station' ends on August 31." Having lost Zhou Enlai's support, the ministry's rebel faction quickly collapsed.

In spite of Mao's and Zhou's efforts to turn the situation around, ultra-leftist thinking continued to influence China's diplomatic policies.

China closed its embassy in Tunisia in September 1967 after

protesting that Tunisia's president had "slandered our Great Leader Chairman Mao" with "extreme savagery," and then severed relations with Indonesia on October 27. On October 31, the Chinese government accused Burma's Ne Win government of "selling out the interests of the Burmese people to seek refuge with American imperialism and Soviet revisionism," and Mao soon afterward received the leader of the opposition Burmese Communist Party, Thakin Ba Thein Tin, for a "cordial and friendly dialogue." In November, the president of Zambia, Kenneth Kaunda, expressed opposition to African countries being pulled into the vortex of the Sino-Soviet squabble.[21]

Although the arrest of Wang Li and the denunciation of the Foreign Ministry's rebel faction cooled the fanaticism over the hub of world revolution, previous campaigns had left Foreign Ministry personnel afraid of their own shadows. Mao had to personally come forward if the situation was to be effectively corrected.

In late November 1967, Mao issued a memo stating agreement with the views of Anzai Kuraji, a member of the Japanese Communist Party Secretariat, who felt that "excessively emphasizing the universal significance of China's road of surrounding the cities with the villages in fact negates the road of the October Revolution, which went from the cities to the countryside."[22] On May 1, 1968, Mao underlined the phrase "world hub—Beijing" in a conference notice and commented, "This expression should not be used by Chinese; it is the erroneous thinking of 'putting oneself at the center.'" On May 18, the Central Committee and the Central Cultural Revolution Small Group issued an "important notice" authorized by Mao that prohibited using the expression "hub of world revolution" in publications, internal documents, and speeches and when receiving foreign guests. "We must always be on guard against and criticize the erroneous thinking of 'putting oneself at the center.'"[23] On March 22, 1969, Mao called in Chen Yi, Li Fuchun, Li Xiannian, Xu Xiangqian, Nie Rongzhen, Ye Jianying, and others for a meeting and said, "It's better to be more moderate [in foreign relations]; we're isolated now, and no one is paying attention to us."[24] On May 1 (Labor Day) in 1969, Mao communicated China's wish to improve its relations with various countries by meeting with several diplomatic envoys in the Tiananmen gate tower.

With Mao taking a clear stand, Zhou Enlai actively set about putting it into practice. In a conversation with the Foreign Ministry's core party group on September 18, 1970, Zhou said, "Don't think that China is the only country doing things right and that China can take on the entire job of world revolution. How is that possible? Foreign affairs departments must continue to criticize ultra-leftist thinking." In another such conversation on September 24, Zhou stated that "personnel in foreign embassies who are still committed ultra-leftists must be transferred back to China to undergo study."[25]

From then on, China's diplomatic situation began to improve. China resumed and developed diplomatic relations with Kenya, Tunisia, Burundi, Ceylon, Ghana, and other countries. There were official visits, the development of trade and new routine contacts, and cables expressing the desire for mutual cooperation and understanding. Existing diplomatic relationships improved or developed to varying degrees, with the exception of the Soviet Union, India, and Indonesia. Eleven countries in Asia, Africa, Latin America, Europe, and North America established diplomatic relations with China from 1968 to July 1971.[26]

FROM TWO FRONTS TO ONE LARGE STRIP

Regarding both the Soviet Union and the Unites States as enemies, China fell into the disadvantageous position of fighting on two fronts, and Mao began seeking a way out of this precarious international situation. He fastened his eyes on "intermediate zones" between the United States and the Soviet Union.

Mao described these intermediate zones during a meeting with a member of the Japanese Communist Party Politburo, Katsumi Kaori, on January 5, 1964: "One part consists of the vast economically backward countries in Asia, Africa, and Latin America; the other part consists of imperialist and advanced capitalist countries, represented by Europe." Both parts opposed American control, and various Eastern European countries were opposing Soviet control.[27] The diplomatic strategy in the years immediately preceding the Cultural Revolution was to focus on diplomacy with countries in the first intermediate zone and try to win over countries in the second intermediate zone, including Japan. Chinese leaders made many visits to Asian and African countries during this period while also developing relations with European countries (for instance, establishing diplomatic relations with France in January 1964). Forty-seven countries had established diplomatic relations with China by 1965, but these overtures ended in the first two years of the Cultural Revolution.

After China clashed with the Soviet Union over Zhenbao Island in 1969, Mao called for the country's entire armed forces to prepare for a surprise attack from the Soviet Union, but at the same time sought an international united front against American and Soviet hegemony. At Mao's suggestion, around the time of the Ninth Party Congress in 1969, Zhou Enlai asked the four marshals Chen Yi, Ye Jianying, Xu Xiangqian, and Nie Rongzhen to study the international situation and advise the Central Committee on appropriate policies. The marshals held a series of meetings with the foreign affairs specialists Xiong Xianghui and Yao Guang, among others, from June to mid-September and submitted two reports. The marshals' "preliminary appraisal" in July held that the United States would not rashly attack China, and that America's strategic emphasis was the West. The Soviet Union was the greatest threat, but would have many misgivings and difficulties in launching a major attack on China. Their "Views on the Current Situation," submitted on September 17, held that the conflict between China and the Soviet Union was greater than that between China and the United States, and that the conflict between the Soviet Union and the United States was greater than that between China and the Soviet Union. They also felt that a war targeting China was unlikely, and that China held the advantage at a time when both the Soviet Union and the United States were eager to play the "China card."

There are no documents indicating whether Mao accepted the views of the four marshals, but he said, "We must win over one of the two hegemons; we can't fight on two fronts."[28] He cast his gaze on the United States.

China and the United States had been antagonists since 1949, and relations had been severed between the two countries for more than twenty years, but by the mid-1960s, they needed each other. China needed to break out of "fighting two hegemons at the same time," and the United States wanted to extricate itself from the quagmire of the Vietnam War. After Richard Nixon was elected president in 1969, he directed National Security Adviser Henry Kissinger to fully explore the possibility of improving relations with China in order to gain an advantage in talks with the Soviet Union. The United States took more initiative on improving Sino-American relations than China did.

At a fashion show in Warsaw on December 2, 1969, the U.S. ambassador to Poland, Walter Stoessel, tried to engage a Chinese diplomat in conversation. Embassy secretary Li Juqing and interpreter Jing Zhicheng evaded him, but Stoessel caught up with Jing and hastily told him that Nixon wanted to carry out "major and specific talks" with Chinese leaders. After requesting instructions from Beijing, on December 11 the Chinese temporary chargé d'affaires to Poland, Lei Yang, invited Stoessel to the embassy for a conversation, during which he formally received Nixon's proposal. After reading a telegram from the Warsaw embassy that night, Zhou Enlai immediately reported the situation to Mao and told him happily, "We've found a brick to knock on the door."[29] While receiving the Pakistani ambassador the next day, Zhou Enlai asked him to inform President Yahya Khan that Nixon could use official channels to contact China. After that, the Sino-U.S. Warsaw ambassadorial talks that had been suspended for three years were resumed, but they were suspended again when the United States supported the military coup in Cambodia in March 1970. On May 20, Mao issued the statement: "People of the World Unite and Defeat the American Aggressors and All of Their Running Dogs."

Sino-U.S. relations were already on their own trajectory, however. In mid-March 1970, President Yahya Khan told the Chinese ambassador to Pakistan, Zhang Tong, that during his recent visit to the United States, President Nixon had asked him to relay a message to China that he was prepared to open a direct communication channel between the White House and Beijing. The existence of this channel would be kept secret from anyone outside the White House. Zhang Tong passed this message to Zhou Enlai on March 21,[30] and frequent verbal messages were passed between the leaders of the United States and China in late spring and early summer 1971, almost always through the "Pakistan channel."[31]

In early October 1970, Nixon told *Time* magazine, "If there is anything I want to do before I die, it is to go to China." In a face-to-face discussion later that month, Nixon asked Yahya Khan to be the middleman to assist in normalizing Sino-U.S. relations. Nixon later had the Romanian leader Nicolae Ceaușescu carry a verbal request for high-level contact with China.[32] After receiving Nixon's messages, Zhou Enlai reiterated China's position through both the Pakistan and Romanian channels: Taiwan was Chinese territory, solving the Taiwan problem was China's domestic affair, and outsiders were not allowed to interfere. The crux of tensions in Sino-U.S. relations was the U.S. military presence in Taiwan and the Taiwan Strait. While receiving his old friend the American journalist Edgar Snow on December 18, Mao said, "If Nixon is willing to come, I'm willing to talk with him. It's all right regardless of whether the talks succeed, or whether or not we argue; he can come as a tourist or as President. In short, it's all right regardless."

A direct dialogue between the top leaders of two hostile countries without diplomatic relations required an innocuous pretext. The thirty-first World Table Tennis Championship in Nagoya, Japan, in April 1971, was the first time that China took part in an international sporting event since the launch of the Cultural Revolution. Mao approved a set of stipulations that if there was an encounter with American officials, Chinese officials should not take the initiative to talk, and that if there was a contest with the American team, team pennants could not be exchanged, but the teams could shake hands in greeting. The leader of the U.S. delegation did in fact contact the Chinese delegation six times expressing the wish for a friendly visit to China. On April 3, the Foreign Ministry and State Sports Commission jointly submitted a report requesting instructions: "The U.S. team can be told that the time is not yet ripe for a visit to China, but that it is believed that an opportunity will arise in the future." Zhou Enlai wrote a memo on the report, "Tentatively agree." He added, "They can be given an address for communications. But in direct contact with the delegation head, it should be made clear that the Chinese people resolutely oppose 'two Chinas' or 'one China, one Taiwan' conspiratorial activities." The report was sent to Mao, who did not reply. On the afternoon of April 6, as the competition was about to end, the Foreign

Ministry informed the Chinese table tennis team of Zhou Enlai's memo. That night, Mao decided on his response to the report: "Immediately invite the American table tennis team to visit China." On April 10, the American table tennis team entered China through Shenzhen, Guangdong Province, and a contest between the Chinese and American teams was held in Beijing on April 13. The next day, Zhou Enlai met with the delegations from the United States and other countries in the Great Hall of the People. Also present was the American journalist John Roderick, who had interviewed Zhou in Yan'an years before. Zhou told Roderick, "The door is open now."[33]

The American table tennis team's visit to China whipped up a "Ping-Pong diplomacy" whirlwind. On May 29, Zhou Enlai sent a verbal message welcoming Henry Kissinger to Beijing for a secret preparatory meeting. Briefed by Kissinger on June 2, President Nixon said, "This is the most important communication that has come to an American President since the end of World War II." Kissinger made secret visits to China in July and October, during which both sides agreed to a simultaneous announcement that Nixon would visit China in February 1972. As Kissinger reached the end of his second visit to Beijing, the twenty-sixth session of the United Nations General Assembly on October 25 passed a motion to restore the People's Republic of China's UN seat, and to eliminate the UN seat of the Republic of China on Taiwan. Some Western scholars say that the United States played a key role in securing this vote.[34] The next day, the United States and China reached agreement on a preliminary draft for what came to be known as the "Shanghai Communiqué."

Throughout these negotiations, China rebuffed U.S. offers of protection from the Soviet Union. During a visit to Beijing in early January 1972, the deputy assistant to the president for national security affairs, Alexander Haig, passed a verbal message to Zhou that the Soviet Union planned to organize China's enemies or their agents to encircle China, and the United States was willing to safeguard China's independence and viability. He also noted that the enhancement of Nixon's international image resulting from his visit to China would be advantageous to both sides. Zhou reported all this to Mao, and the two of them shared the belief that the United States was using the Soviet Union's threat to China as a means of intimidating China into yielding ground in the Sino-U.S. talks. On the night of January 6, Zhou told Haig, "No country should ever rely on external forces to maintain its independence and viability. If it does so, it can only become a protectorate or a colony."[35]

The Taiwan problem was the greatest roadblock to improving Sino-U.S. relations. Before Nixon's visit, Kissinger and Zhou Enlai repeatedly discussed, argued, compromised, and reached a preliminary solution on this difficult problem.

In the early hours of February 21, 1972, President Nixon and his entourage arrived in Beijing for a weeklong visit. As Nixon walked down the ramp from his aircraft, he immediately reached out for a warm handshake with Zhou Enlai, who had come to meet him. Zhou said, "Your hand has stretched across the world's largest ocean to shake mine—after twenty-five years without contact!"

On that day, Mao constantly asked about Nixon's movements. It was the ninth day after Mao had emerged from his coma, and his legs were so swollen with edema that he had to wear extra-large shoes. When Mao met with Nixon in his library at 2:50 p.m., emergency medical equipment and medical staff were standing by behind a screen. After a conversation regarding the international situation, bilateral relations, philosophy, and history, Nixon and his entourage were taken on a tour of Beijing's cultural, industrial, and agricultural sights. They then visited Hangzhou and Shanghai, but the talks continued as they traveled; Zhou Enlai and Nixon met six times, and Zhou met with Kissinger even more often. On February 28, the Sino-U.S. Shanghai Communiqué was issued.[36]

The communiqué started with each side laying out its position. China stated, "The Chinese side stated that it firmly supports the struggles of all the oppressed people and nations for freedom and liberation." The U.S. side stated, "The United States supports individual freedom and social progress for all the people of the world, free of outside pressure or intervention."

The communiqué said, "The United States believes that the effort to reduce tensions is served by improving communication between countries that have different ideologies so as to lessen the risks of confrontation through accident, miscalculation or misunderstanding . . . Countries should treat each other with mutual respect and be willing to compete peacefully, letting performance be the ultimate judge. No country should claim infallibility and each country should be prepared to re-examine its own attitudes for the common good." The statement went on to note:

> The two sides agreed that countries, regardless of their social systems, should conduct their relations on the principles of respect for the sovereignty and territorial integrity of all states, nonaggression against other states, noninterference in the internal affairs of other states, equality and mutual benefit, and peaceful coexistence. International disputes should be settled on this basis, without resorting to the use or threat of force. The United States and the People's Republic of China are prepared to apply these principles to their mutual relations.

On the Taiwan issue, China reiterated its position in the communiqué:

> The Government of the People's Republic of China is the sole legal government of China; Taiwan is a province of China which has long been returned to the motherland; the liberation of Taiwan is China's internal affair in which no other country has the right to interfere; and all U.S. forces and military installations must be withdrawn from Taiwan. The Chinese Government firmly opposes any activities which aim at the creation of "one China, one Taiwan," "one China, two governments," "two Chinas," an "independent Taiwan," or advocate that "the status of Taiwan remains to be determined."

The United States stated:

> The United States acknowledges that all Chinese on either side of the Taiwan Strait maintain there is but one China and that Taiwan is a part of China. The United States Government does not challenge that position. It reaffirms its interest in a peaceful settlement of the Taiwan question by the Chinese themselves. With this prospect in mind, it affirms the ultimate objective of

the withdrawal of all U.S. forces and military installations from
Taiwan. In the meantime, it will progressively reduce its forces
and military installations on Taiwan as the tension in the area
diminishes.

The Shanghai Communiqué turned a new page in Sino-U.S. relations. One year later, the two countries agreed to establish liaison
offices in each other's capitals. In the meantime, on September 29,
1972, Japan became the thirty-third country to establish diplomatic
relations with China during that period, bringing the number of countries with which China had diplomatic relations to eighty-eight, up
from forty-seven in 1965. On January 1, 1979, the United States became the 117th country to establish formal diplomatic relations with
the PRC. Even Deng Xiaoping, who completely negated the Cultural
Revolution, said that foreign affairs made great strides during the
Cultural Revolution, and that even while the country was in chaos,
China's international status was enhanced by international acknowledgment that it was a great nation.[37]

On February 17, 1973, during Secretary of State Henry Kissinger's
fourth visit to China, Mao put forward his strategic thinking of establishing "a horizontal line" from China and Japan through Pakistan,
Iran, Turkey, and Europe to the United States, with all the countries
on this line uniting to oppose Soviet hegemony.[38] Improving relations
with the United States, Japan, and other capitalist countries allowed
China to take this idea of Mao's a step further. Even so, Mao's basic
objective of world revolution hadn't changed; only the strategy had
changed. After the United States and China established relations,
Mao developed his idea of "two intermediate zones" into a concept of
"three worlds."

Mao explicitly raised the concept of "three worlds" in a meeting
with President Kenneth Kaunda of Zambia at his Zhongnanhai swimming pool on February 22, 1974. He said, "I see the U.S. and the Soviet Union as the First World. The centrists, Japan, Europe, and
Canada, are the Second World. We're the Third World . . . Apart from
Japan, Asia is the Third World. All of Africa is the Third World, and
Latin America is the Third World."[39] Mao elaborated on the idea in a
conversation with guests from Algeria on the twenty-fifth: "China

belongs to the Third World. Because China cannot compare with the rich and great nations politically and economically, it can only be grouped with relatively poor nations."

The concepts of "two intermediate zones" and "three worlds" didn't cast off the guiding ideology of "world revolution," but rather formed a united front for world revolution.

Mao to a certain extent perceived the significant change that had taken place in the world situation from the Second World War to the 1960s and adjusted his foreign affairs strategy accordingly. However, he didn't perceive the enormous transformation of that era. The Shanghai Communiqué reflected that Mao still maintained Lenin's definition of the current era as "the era of imperialism and proletarian revolution," and hence an "era of war and revolution."[40] This epochal outlook was the foundation of domestic and foreign affairs policies. An "era of war and revolution" required "class struggle as the key link" in domestic policies, and "three fights and one increase" in foreign affairs policies.

It wasn't until the 1980s that Chinese with greater strategic vision saw that the times had changed. While meeting with a delegation from the Japanese Chamber of Commerce and Industry in 1985, Deng Xiaoping said, "The significant issues confronting the world today, issues of global strategic significance, are: first, peace, and second, economic development."[41] After in-depth study, He Fang in 1986 concluded that after the Second World War, the world began to change from an era of war and revolution to an era of peace and development, and that this transition ended in the late 1950s and early 1960s. "Social and economic construction and scientific and technological development were delayed for thirty years after our country was founded, mainly because of this erroneous judgment of the era."[42]

It was the fundamental appraisal that the world had transitioned from the "age of war and revolution" to the "age of peace and development" that allowed China to make a fresh start on its domestic and foreign policies: Domestically, it replaced "class struggle as the key link" with "economic construction as the focus," and externally, it abandoned the "three fights and one increase" in favor of openness to the outside world, joining the World Trade Organization and merging itself into the international mainstream.

29

REFORM AND OPENING UNDER THE BUREAUCRATIC SYSTEM

THE POLITICAL SPECTRUM AFTER THE CULTURAL REVOLUTION

After the Cultural Revolution ended, four main political forces tried to control China's future path.

The first political force maintained the path of Mao's last years both politically and economically, insisting on continuous revolution under the dictatorship of the proletariat and a planned economic system. The smashing of the Gang of Four crippled this force, but those who crushed the Gang of Four did not necessarily oppose the theory of continuous revolution under the dictatorship of the proletariat, and this concept of Mao's latter years still enjoyed considerable mass support because of the long-term effect of ideological propaganda.

The second force wanted to maintain the political aspects of the socialist system, the existing ideology, and the Chinese Communist Party–led dictatorship of the proletariat but revert to the economic policies of the 1950s. People espousing this approach nevertheless felt that the economy of the 1950s was too centralized and concentrated, and advocated allowing some market adjustment within the scope of a planned economic system—what was termed "a mainly planned economy supplemented by market adjustment." Chen Yun represented this political force.

The third force maintained the existing ideology and the CCP-led dictatorship of the proletariat on the political level, but in the economic sphere was willing to abandon planned economy and undertake market-oriented reforms. People taking this stand were more aware of the abuses inherent in a planned economy, but at the outset of the reforms, no one dared to talk of abandoning the planned economic system or to explicitly propose a market economy. They emphasized only developing a commodity economy and corresponding economic system. It wasn't until the mid-1980s that a "market orientation" was proposed for the reforms, and not until the early 1990s that a "socialist market economy" was proposed. Deng Xiaoping represented this political force.

The fourth political force wanted to cast aside the planned economy in favor of a market economy and the dictatorship of the proletariat in favor of democratization. This was the liberal democratic faction, which existed mainly outside the government. No one within the system maintained this stand at the time, but it was the mainstream thinking in the West and in the Soviet Union and Eastern European countries undergoing transition, and therefore it continued to exert influence on China.

These four forces formed a political spectrum from left to right, with the remnant forces of the Gang of Four and those who insisted on the road of Mao's last years positioned furthest left, and the liberal democrats positioned furthest right. The strongest of the forces were the third, represented by Deng Xiaoping, and the second, represented by Chen Yun. The contest between the four forces continued throughout the thirty years of China's Reform and Opening, and their combined force decided China's direction.

Although there were divisions between the first three forces in terms of economic reform, they all maintained the political system left behind by Mao—that is, the Chinese Communist Party's single-party autocracy. When the fourth force was relatively weak, the first three battled among themselves over China's economic reforms, but as soon as the fourth force posed a threat to the CCP's leadership status, the first three forces united to suppress the liberal democrats.

Confronting these various political forces, China's top leader faced the choice of controlling and maintaining a balance among the various political forces or relying on the strongest political force and becoming its representative. Lacking the ability to control the various political forces, Hua Guofeng instead became a representative of the first one, which had no political future. This was his downfall.

How to deal with Mao's legacy was a thorny issue at that time. As Mao's successor, Hua Guofeng contributed little to solving this problem. When speaking to propaganda heads about exposing and denouncing the Gang of Four on October 26, 1976, Hua said that whatever the Chairman approved should not be opposed. At a Central Committee Work Meeting on March 14, 1977, he said, "Whatever policy decision Chairman Mao made must be upheld; whatever speech or actions damage Chairman Mao must be prevented." An editorial titled "Study Documents and Grasp the Guiding Principles," published by the party's main mouthpieces on February 7, 1977, stated, "We must resolutely uphold whatever policy decisions Chairman Mao made, and we must unswervingly follow whatever instructions Chairman Mao issued." This became known as the "Two Whatevers." Drafted by the Central Theoretical Study Group, the editorial clearly represented the thinking of the highest levels of the central leadership. Hua Guofeng also published an essay calling for "carrying out continuous revolution under the dictatorship of the proletariat to the end."[1]

Although the "offenses" Hua Guofeng was accused of when he was unseated in 1978 were clearly far-fetched, and although Reform and Opening was put on the agenda during his two years in power, the negative effects of Hua's Two Whatevers cannot be denied.

Hua Guofeng's Two Whatevers resulted from a virtually inescapable historical inertia. After years of Mao's personality cult, who dared to say that Chairman Mao's words weren't the truth? Who dared hesitate to implement his "highest directives"?

Restrained by the Two Whatevers, Hua Guofeng proposed a guiding principle of "grasping the key link and stabilizing the country." The key link was class struggle, and the specific content of class struggle was to expose, denounce, and investigate the Gang of Four and to continue the "in-depth attack on the right-deviating verdict-reversal trend." Stabilizing the country meant "learning from Daqing in industry and learning from Dazhai in agriculture," just as during Mao's lifetime.

Exposing and denouncing the Gang of Four was carried out

according to the past methods of class struggle through mass movements, mass investigations, and mass vetting throughout the country.

Exposing and denouncing the Gang of Four focused on their "conspiracy to seize power," but this didn't hold up under careful analysis. Hadn't the bureaucratic faction seized power? And had their power seizure been carried out in an open and aboveboard manner? The essence of the problem was the direction in which the Gang of Four was leading China, and required exposing and denouncing the Gang of Four's ideological line. This was a problem that Hua Guofeng found impossible to solve, because the ideological line of the Gang of Four was Mao's theory of continuous revolution under the dictatorship of the proletariat. Hua Guofeng needed to demonstrate that he was a faithful successor to Mao, which meant that he had to uphold that ideological line for the time being. This resulted in the bizarre distortion of claiming that the Gang of Four had betrayed the ideological line that they had, in fact, so fervently maintained—the line of Mao's last years.

The confused and far-fetched propaganda logic at that time claimed that "smashing the 'Gang of Four' was the great victory of Chairman Mao's theory of continuous revolution under the dictatorship of the proletariat, and the great victory of the Great Proletarian Cultural Revolution."[2] It said that "exposing the 'Gang of Four' anti-party clique once again proved the incomparable wisdom and correctness of Chairman Mao's judgment regarding the 'capitalist class within the party' . . . Their rise to power was the rise to power of the capitalist class, of revisionism, and of fascism, and the restoration of capitalism . . . The fruits of victory of the Great Proletarian Cultural Revolution would be lost."[3] It called for a renewed and deeper focus on the campaign to criticize Deng and beat back the right-deviating verdict-reversal wind, which had allegedly been derailed by the Gang of Four.

Cases of injustice abounded after the Gang of Four was smashed. In January 1977, Li Dongmin and several other Beijing youths were arrested as a "counterrevolutionary clique" for putting up banners on Chang'an Avenue calling for Deng Xiaoping to be given work in the government, and for the April Fifth Tiananmen Incident to be rehabilitated. In Lüda, Liaoning Province,[4] big-character posters calling for the rehabilitation of the Tiananmen Incident were designated "counterrevolutionary incidents." On December 9, 1976, Shi Yunfeng, a youth in Changchun, Jilin Province, was executed two years after being arrested for "counterrevolutionary crimes." On April 16, 1977, a Shanghai youth named Wang Shenyou was executed for his penetrating insights and critiques of Mao's views. A young Jiangxi woman, Li Jiulian, was executed on April 16, 1977, after years of imprisonment for criticizing Lin Biao and sympathizing with Liu Shaoqi. During the time Hua Guofeng was in power, around fifty people were executed as counterrevolutionaries, most of them young vanguards of liberal thought.

Most people's political attention at that time focused on two issues: rehabilitating the Tiananmen Incident and allowing Deng Xiaoping to resume working in government. Since both issues had been decided by Mao, they could not be resolved as long as the Two Whatevers were maintained. Deng Xiaoping therefore needed to challenge the Two Whatevers while avoiding the risk that would entail. He did this by using language that promoted Mao Zedong Thought to undermine the influence of Mao Zedong Thought. Deng said, "We must use accurate and complete Mao Zedong Thought to guide our entire party generation after generation."[5] Employing the flexible terms "accurate" and "complete" to replace the completely inflexible Two Whatevers, he explained, "What I mean is that we should have an accurate and complete understanding of Mao Zedong Thought and that we must effectively study, grasp, and utilize Mao Zedong Thought to guide all our work. Only in this way can we avoid damaging Mao Zedong Thought by gutting or distorting it."[6]

But how to distinguish what was accurate and complete? And who was to make this distinction? Without an objective criterion, only a new super-authority could serve as the ultimate arbiter, and that would require creating a new Mao, which was clearly impossible. Mass discussion of the criterion of truth resolved this problem.

For decades, Mao's words had served as the highest standard of truth, and judging right and wrong in any matter depended on what was consistent with Mao Zedong Thought. Mass discussion of the criterion of truth meant making practice the sole authority for deciding what truth was. Hu Yaobang, at that time the deputy director of the Central Party School, played an important role in pushing forward this mass discussion through publication of Sun Changjiang and Hu Fuming's essay titled "Practice Is the Sole Criterion for Testing Truth" in *Guangming Daily* on May 11, 1978.

Unlike the natural sciences, social practice does not allow a conclusion to be drawn within a short time in a laboratory; it requires a relatively long historical process to clearly distinguish what works and what does not. The thesis of "social practice as the criterion for testing truth" therefore contained the important task of objectively summarizing historical experience. But this would require subverting historical textbooks compiled for decades in accordance with ideological requirements. Those in power could not allow that to happen.

Even so, mass discussion of the criterion of truth began to break down the blind faith in Mao that had imprisoned the minds of Chinese for more than twenty years.

A TURBULENT DEMOCRATIC TIDE

Once reality smashed the spiritual shackles of the Chinese people, an irresistible tide arose and pounded against the ideological dikes built over the course of decades. Its symbols were the Xidan Democracy Wall among the general populace and the Theoretical Conference within the government.

Xidan Wall, about 250 meters long and 3 meters high, stretched along the street from the Telegraph Building to Xidan Road, enclosing a floodlit playing field, a tram depot, and other public facilities. Its central location near Tiananmen Square made it an ideal place for public expression of views.

Unjust cases had piled up during the Mao era, and after the Cultural Revolution ended, people from all over China came to Beijing to petition the authorities. Xidan Wall became a place for petitioners to post their appeals for justice, and for others to post essays on political or social issues. As posters proliferated and blanketed the wall, crowds began gathering day and night to read the posters, with those standing closest reading them out loud for those standing farther away to hear and copy down. People began calling this area Democracy Wall, and for a period of time it became a focus of discussion all over China and a plentiful source of news for foreign journalists. Eventually, other places such as Wangfujing Street and the Monument of the People's Heroes also became plastered with posters, and the Democracy Wall phenomenon spread to other major Chinese cities.

The posters at the Xidan Democracy Wall covered a vast range of topics, but tended to focus on several main themes:

1. Complaints over cases of injustice, both individual and social: A large number of posters called for rehabilitation of the Tiananmen Incident.
2. Appraisals of the Cultural Revolution: People began to take a critical stance against the Cultural Revolution, and some posters called for Liu Shaoqi to be rehabilitated.
3. Calls for democracy: Wei Jingsheng's essay added the establishment of a modern democratic system to the existing Four Modernizations. Ren Wanding's "Declaration of Human Rights in China" demanded "the implementation of freedom of thought and speech, and the release of all those imprisoned for their thinking or speech."
4. Appraisals of Mao: Posters put up by Guizhou's Enlightenment Society around the Monument for the People's Heroes used parables to hint that Mao was a feudal despot. In his "Fire God Symphony Poems," Huang Xiang wrote, "Send violence and force to perdition," and "Confound and destroy the idolatrous shrines in your hearts."[7]
5. Criticism of the "Two Whatevers faction."

The Xidan Democracy Wall developed into underground journals,[8] and from there to political organizations such as the Enlightenment Society and China Human Rights Alliance. The publications that went furthest were Wei Jingsheng's *Exploration* and Ren Wanding's *Human Rights in China*. An essay by Wei Jingsheng in *Exploration* referred to the dictatorship of the proletariat as "a feudal lord system cloaked with socialism," and to Marxism-Leninism and Mao Zedong Thought as "just a higher form of snake oil."

As the Democracy Wall phenomenon spread, the written word

could no longer meet the needs of all the people with views to express. When I went to the Xidan Democracy Wall to read posters on the night of December 28, 1978, a symposium was being held, and someone was regaling thousands of listeners with a vehement speech about how fighting for democracy and freedom was not enough, and that the most fundamental thing was to change the country's political system. The audience swelled to the point where it obstructed traffic, so someone suggested moving the gathering over to the Monument of the People's Heroes. Thousands of people filed toward Tiananmen Square, chanting, "We want democracy, not autocracy!," "The Chinese people are not idiots!," "Let thinking break out of its cage!," and other slogans. They sang "March of the Volunteers," "The Internationale," and "Unity Is Power." By the time they reached the monument, they numbered in the tens of thousands, and people took turns climbing the steps of the monument to speak. The stirring speeches gave me the sense of a democratic tide.

Theoreticians also began issuing demands for democracy through the Theoretical Conference. The conference was sparked by debate in the *Red Flag* editorial department and in the Chinese Academy of Social Sciences over an essay rebutting "Practice Is the Sole Criterion for Testing Truth." Ye Jianying suggested that the Central Committee hold the Theoretical Conference to put the various viewpoints on the table and arrive at a consensus.

The Theoretical Conference had two stages. The first stage, from January 18 to February 22, 1979 (with a five-day recess for the Spring Festival in late January), emphasized the theme of correcting the wrongs caused by the Cultural Revolution and restoring normalcy. Convened by the Central Committee Propaganda Department and the Chinese Academy of Social Sciences, it involved more than 160 theoretical and propaganda workers from the central government and Beijing, as well as liaisons from each province. The second phase was planned for March and April.

In his "Introduction to the Theoretical Conference" on January 18, the head of the Propaganda Department, Hu Yaobang, called on participants "to be liberated from ideological ossification or semi-ossification, from the influence of a small-producer mentality, and from various bureaucratic 'management, checks, and pressure,' to breach all restricted areas, smash all spiritual fetters, and give full rein to democracy in theoretical discussions."[9] Deng Xiaoping also directed that this conference should have "no restricted areas and no prohibitions."

The main discussion occurred during the first stage of the conference, which focused on criticizing the Two Whatevers. Remarks touched on the theoretical and practical problems of the Cultural Revolution; problems with continuing revolution under the dictatorship of the proletariat; the problem of class struggle during the socialist stage; the problem of line struggle within the party; the problem of socialist democracy and democracy within the party; the problem of personality cult; appraisal of Mao and Mao Zedong Thought; and the suggestion about eliminating lifelong tenure for cadres. Some participants virulently criticized feudal fascism and expounded on the continued need to fight feudalism in China today. Issues that no one had dared to raise before were now open for discussion.

In the context of those times, some of the speeches were extraordinary. The deputy head of the Central Committee's Third Group, Wang Huide, said, "It's been nearly thirty years since the People's Republic was founded, and there are still two hundred million people who don't get enough to eat. Facing this situation, the party and the people have to consider: we must have gone wrong somewhere." The head of this same group, Zhou Yang, said, "Was the Cultural Revolution really created by careerists and schemers like Lin Biao and the Gang of Four, or were there problems with the line and theory? Do problems exist in the theory of continuous revolution under the dictatorship of the proletariat? Until we clarify this point, we cannot get to the bottom of the problem with the Two Whatevers. The theory of continuous revolution under the dictatorship of the proletariat is a basic problem, and this problem involves Comrade Mao Zedong." The historian Li Shu criticized Mao for prematurely abandoning the new democracy that he had proposed and for unconditionally transitioning into socialism, creating an "impoverished socialism." Economist Xu Dixin tied together the Great Leap Forward, the campaign against right deviation, the Four Cleanups, and the Cultural Revolution, saying, "Were these the result of the development of our venerable Chairman Mao's volitionism? . . . The Chairman didn't consider objective laws . . . Chairman Mao didn't understand economics." An expert in foreign relations, Huan Xiang, directly criticized the "Nine Commentaries,"[10] saying that the viewpoints they raised "were as left as it was possible to go . . . Some of the essays are fundamentally wrong, and the writing style is execrable." The theoretician Li Honglin bluntly criticized Mao's personality cult and the personality cult that was forming around Hua Guofeng: "It should not be the people who are loyal to the leader, but rather the leader who should be loyal to the people." Others such as Bao Tong and Ruan Ming also gave thought-provoking speeches.

In squaring the accounts on the CCP's work since the founding of the People's Republic, the Theoretical Conference to some extent imperiled the image of the CCP and its leader, Mao, and blasted a great hole in the value system that the CCP had established.

The shock wave sent out by the Theoretical Conference among the liberal elite and the Xidan Democracy Wall at the beleaguered lower strata combined to create a tidal wave that surged through the China of the late 1970s.

At first, Deng Xiaoping supported the Xidan Democracy Wall. On November 26, 1978, he told the visiting chairman of the Japanese Socialist Party, Ryosaku Sasaki: "Wall posters are guaranteed by the Constitution. We have no right to deny or criticize the masses for promoting democracy or putting up posters. If the masses are angry, let them vent. Not all of the views of the masses have been carefully considered and it's not possible that all of them are completely correct, but there's nothing terrible about that."[11] Ye Jianying said in a speech on December 13 that "the third plenum of the Eleventh Central Committee is an example of democracy within the party, and the Xidan Democracy Wall is an example of democracy among the people." Deng made similar remarks to a French journalist after attending a ceremony for the signing of a Sino-French trade agreement in early December. In his battle against the Whatevers faction, Deng Xiaoping drew on the power of public opinion as well as on the democratic tide within and outside the party.

Even so, his support had its limits.

"SOVIET LEARNING AS THE BASE, WESTERN LEARNING FOR APPLICATION"

Faced with the intense commentary at the first stage of the Theoretical Conference, the public sentiment aroused by the Xidan Democracy Wall, and massive demonstrations in Shanghai demanding the return of sent-down youth, the CCP's top officials felt that their leadership status was under threat. Some were extremely displeased with the Theoretical Conference. Deng Liqun said, "The longer the conference goes on, and the more people speak, the more outrageous things are said. The worst of them is Wang Ruoshui, who negates Mao Zedong Thought and Mao himself on the basis of Mao Zedong's personal qualities." Hu Qiaomu observed, "Altogether there have been five negations: of socialism, of the dictatorship of the proletariat, of the party's leadership, of Marxism-Leninism, and of Mao Zedong." Deng Xiaoping said, "The more I read the Theoretical Conference bulletin, the less I want to read it."[12] Deng felt that the party's leadership was coming under pressure from various quarters within the party.

The first stage of the Theoretical Conference ended on February 22. When Deng Xiaoping gave his speech on March 30, the audience included many prominent Beijing residents along with the conference participants, and the Great Hall of the People was filled to capacity, giving the impression of an anti-rightist political mobilization rally. Deng's speech marked the end of the Theoretical Conference and of the Democracy Wall:

> The Central Committee feels that while implementing the Four Modernizations in China, we must maintain the Four Cardinal Principles in ideology and politics. This is the fundamental prerequisite for implementing the Four Modernizations. These four items are:
>
> > First, we must maintain the socialist road;
> > Second, we must maintain the dictatorship of the proletariat;
> > Third, we must maintain leadership by the Communist Party;
> > Fourth, we must maintain Marxism-Leninism and Mao Zedong Thought.

> Everyone knows that these four cardinal principles are nothing
> new, and that they have been consistently maintained by our
> party for a long time. From the smashing of the "Gang of Four"
> to the third plenum, the party Central Committee has imple-
> mented a series of general and specific policies and has main-
> tained these four cardinal principles.[13]

The view at the time was that the Four Cardinal Principles were
essential to maintaining social stability. Although there were differences between the Two Whatevers and the Four Cardinal Principles,
both were meant to carry on Mao's system. Even so, a wholesale per-
petuation of Mao's legacy would make Reform and Opening impossible. Deng Xiaoping therefore created a new interpretation of
socialism,[14] which, in terms of the economic system, negated Stalinist
socialism and also moved away from Maoist socialism.

To stem the tide stirred up by the Xidan Democracy Wall, the authorities arrested Wei Jingsheng on March 29 and Ren Wanding on
April 4. At the same time, they arrested a worker, Fu Yuehua, who
had led a group of petitioners to cause a commotion in the capital.[15]
Others were arrested elsewhere in China. On October 16, the Beijing
Intermediate People's Court sentenced Wei Jingsheng to fifteen years
in prison, with an additional three years' deprivation of political
rights.

On December 6, 1979, the Beijing Municipal Revolutionary Committee issued a notice stating that as of December 8, apart from posters put up in work units, all posters of any size were restricted to a
designated area of Yuetan Park, and those putting up the posters
must register their actual names, pen names, addresses, and work
units. This aroused a public uproar over the suppression of big-
character posters, one of the "four bigs" enshrined in the PRC constitution. The government responded by amending Article 45 of the
constitution to eliminate the four bigs during the third session of the
Fifth NPC in August that year. From then on, the big-character posters that had been all the vogue in China for thirty years were no
longer legal.

Carrying on Mao's political system and ideology required endorsing Mao's historical status. When the Italian journalist Oriana Fallaci

asked Deng Xiaoping in August 1980 whether Mao's portrait would always hang on Tiananmen, Deng answered, "It will remain there forever." He then added, "We will forever commemorate him as the founder of our party and our country . . . We must carry out an objective appraisal of Chairman Mao's lifetime achievements and errors. We will affirm Chairman Mao's achievements as primary, and his errors as secondary."[16]

By that time, Deng had in fact begun overseeing the drafting of an official verdict on Mao and his era: "Resolution Regarding Certain Historical Issues of the Party Since the Founding of the People's Republic of China." During the drafting process, which began in November 1979, Deng delivered ten speeches that thoroughly expressed his views. The draft went through seven revisions, which included consulting the views of four thousand high-level cadres and key individuals in various spheres before the final version was approved by the sixth plenum of the Eleventh Central Committee in June 1981. The discussion among so many high-level cadres was a process of compromise to reach a consensus on the political problems faced at that time. This consensus allowed the drama of Reform and Opening to be played out, but as a product of compromise, it could not be the final historical summary.

The resolution divided Mao into two stages: the Mao of his last years, when he directed the Cultural Revolution and committed serious errors, and the Mao who came before, who was "glorious." The resolution stated, "It is completely wrong to negate the scientific value of Mao Zedong Thought and the guiding role of Mao Zedong Thought on our country's revolution and construction just because Comrade Mao Zedong committed errors in his later years." It emphasized, "Mao Zedong Thought is our party's precious spiritual wealth, and will continue to guide our actions in the long term."

Mao Zedong left behind two major problems: economic hardship and political autocracy. Solving these two problems required economic and political reform. Deng Xiaoping decided to perpetuate Mao's political and ideological legacy through the Four Cardinal Principles while carrying out reforms on the economic system by introducing market economics.

In 1987, Zhao Zhiyang summarized Deng's thinking into "one

center, two basic points," and he raised this summary to the status of "the party's basic line" in his political report to the Thirteenth National Party Congress. The "one center" was "economic construction as the center," and the "two basic points" were "reform and opening" and the Four Cardinal Principles, alternatively expressed as maintaining China's existing political system and learning from the West in developing the economy. It was a modern version of the late Qing reformers' promotion of "Chinese learning for the essence, and Western learning for practical use."

It was Zhang Zhidong who suggested this guiding ideology during the reforms of the late Qing. "Chinese learning as the base" meant preserving the political system of the late Qing, and "Western learning for application" meant introducing and utilizing Western experience to strengthen the political system, consolidate rule, and prolong the life of the declining Qing dynasty. In Deng Xiaoping's era, "Chinese learning as the base" preserved the road, theory, and political system left behind by Mao, and "Western learning for application" was aimed at developing the economy and thereby bolstering and prolonging the political system that Mao left behind. However, since the political system of the Mao era was mainly imported from the Soviet Union, it would be more accurate to say "Soviet learning as the base."

Once "economic construction as the center" became the supreme consensus, it replaced "class struggle as the key link," resulting in the elimination of political categories such as landlord, rich peasant, counterrevolutionary, bad element, and rightist, and granting equal status to the vast political underclass and their families. Economic construction as the center required opening up to the outside world and changing the assessment of the world situation from "the age of war and revolution" to "the age of peaceful development." It meant ending opposition to imperialism and revisionism and joining the World Trade Organization.

Economic reforms drew China into a new era, but the reforms were led by the bureaucratic clique that was the ultimate victor in the Cultural Revolution. They controlled all the country's resources and the direction of reform, and in objective terms decided who would pay the cost of reforms and how the benefits of reform would be distributed.

Reform and Opening allowed China's long-suppressed social vitality to burst forth, and over the course of thirty-odd years, China became the world's second-largest economy in terms of GDP and was on track to overtake the United States as the number one economy. Living standards at all levels of Chinese society improved to varying degrees, and both cities and the countryside underwent radical change, presenting a flourishing appearance compared with those in the developed countries of Europe and North America. This was a universally acknowledged miracle created by turning a planned economic system into a market economic system, and by freeing the long-confined potential of China's workers.

Even so, a profound crisis lurked behind the superficial prosperity of a market economy dominated by a bureaucratic autocracy.

THE POWER MARKET ECONOMIC SYSTEM

Mao's use of the term "power-holders" explicitly pointed out the antagonistic relationship between officials and the people. The bureaucrats in power in China controlled all the country's resources and oppressed and exploited ordinary people, resulting in bureaucratic privilege and turning the state-owned economy into an "official-owned economy." Mao mobilized the masses to expose and criticize this problem and surmount it through continuous revolution, but without acknowledging that the bureaucratic class of capitalist roader power-holders was the inevitable product of the Communist Party's political and economic monopoly that combined Marx with Qin Shihuang. Mao himself was the originator and ultimate controller of the system that doomed his Cultural Revolution.

In a state that provides society with public goods and in which the bureaucracy takes on the task of managing society, only constant improvement of the system and laws, and strengthening of checks and balances, can prevent a public servant from becoming a master. At the outset of the Cultural Revolution, Mao called on the masses to use the principles of the Paris Commune to "smash the old state apparatus," but eventually the bureaucrats had to be brought back to manage society and provide communal products, with the result that the bureaucratic clique was the ultimate victor in the Cultural Revolution.

The thirty-odd years from the last stage of the Cultural Revolution through Reform and Opening saw a process of rebuilding the bureaucratic system, resulting in the most immense, strongest, and most tightly woven bureaucratic system since the founding of the PRC. The comprehensive bolstering of the bureaucratic system is clearly indicated in the swelling of the bureaucratic ranks, which began with the reconstruction of the political structure in the 1970s and accelerated during Reform and Opening.

An excessive number of officials creates too great a burden on the state budget and causes the structure to become bloated, overstaffed, and inefficient. Over the years, the authorities have been obliged to repeatedly streamline the structure and reduce manpower, but the number of officials has continued to grow in a spiral of swelling, shrinking, and then swelling again.

PERSONS EMPLOYED IN STATE ORGANS, PARTY ORGANS, AND SOCIAL ORGANIZATIONS[17] (END OF YEAR)

Year	1965	1975	1979	1980	1981	1985	1986	1987	1988	1989	1995
Personnel (millions)	2.87	3.576	4.51	4.771	5.067	7.99	8.72	9.25	9.71	10.22	12.48

In this table, "social organizations" refers to democratic parties, trade unions, women's organizations, the Communist Youth League, and other political organizations under the Communist Party, not NGOs. During the early stage of the Cultural Revolution, party and administrative organs came under attack, and the number of people in nonstate institutions supported by government funding dropped below 2.4 million. After the restoration of social order, the number of officials ballooned to 3.576 million in 1975. After that, the number was alternately trimmed and expanded several times. In 1996, an effort to downsize the government structure designated some work units under the Central Committee and State Council as state-run institutions (for example, *People's Daily*, the Xinhua News Agency, the Central People's

Broadcasting Station), the expenses of which were not paid out of the state administrative management expenses, which led to a reduction in the number of government employees. Even so, there were still 10.96 million government employees in 1996.[18]

As the number of government employees spiraled, each expansion was greater and more abrupt than the one before, while each shrinkage was more strained and less effective than the one before. I was unable to obtain figures from 1996 onward, but the inflation of administrative management expenses in the state budget provides a good indication of the expansion of the bureaucracy:

STATE ADMINISTRATIVE MANAGEMENT EXPENSES[19]

Year	1978	1985	1990	1993	1994	1995	1996	2000	2005	2006
Expenditure (billion RMB)	4.91	14.36	30.31	53.58	72.94	87.27	104.08	178.76	288.35	335.58

From 2007 onward, the National Bureau of Statistics figures no longer include an item for "state administrative management expenses" but instead have an item called "general public services," which should be the equivalent of "state administrative management expenditure"—that is, the administrative costs of the bureaucratic system. The figures for "general public services" are as follows:

GENERAL PUBLIC SERVICES EXPENDITURE[20]

Year	2007	2008	2009	2010	2011	2012
Expenditure (billion RMB)	851.42	979.59	916.42	933.72	1098.78	1298.08

It is worth noting that in the expansion of the cadre ranks,[21] the growth rate for leading cadres has exceeded that for ordinary cadres. For example, in 1987, cadres at the division (*chu*) level and above composed 29.2 percent of the State Council apparatus, but by 1989 they composed 33.6 percent.[22] Because the number of leading cadres increased faster than the number of ordinary cadres, some work units became excessively top-heavy. In organs directly subsidiary to a certain prefecture in Jiangxi Province, cadres at the rank of deputy section (*ke*) head and above composed 41.9 percent of the total personnel. In a certain prefecture in Hunan Province, cadres at the county (division, *chu*) level composed 54.2 percent of the total, while cadres at the section (*ke*) level made up 37.5 percent and ordinary cadres only 8.3 percent.[23]

At the same time that the bureaucratic ranks have swelled, the police ranks have also ballooned. During the political unrest in 1989, it was decided that "police strength was inadequate," so hundreds of thousands of PLA troops were deployed to crack down on student protests in Beijing. The expansion of the police ranks accelerated from then on. In 1992, there were 1.3 million police officers, and the number reached 2 million in the new millennium. The National Bureau of Statistics' *China Statistical Summary* included armed police force expenditure for a number of years, tabulated in the table below:

ARMED POLICE FORCE EXPENDITURE (ALL REGIONS COMBINED)[24]

Year	1997	1998	2002	2003	2004	2005	2006
Expenditure (billion RMB)	0.56111	1.04632	2.08522	2.42441	3.09307	4.10708	6.26459

The figures in the above table for police expenditure (nationwide total) do not include expenses for police at the central government level. With the emphasis on stability preservation from 2006 onward, expenditure on the police force will have increased even more rapidly, but the National Bureau of Statistics did not publish figures for those years.

The expansion and strengthening of the bureaucratic clique corresponds with the course of Reform and Opening: Reform and Opening provided the material conditions for expanding and strengthening the bureaucratic system, and the expansion and strengthening of the bureaucratic system distorted the progress of reform.

Reforms that employed "Soviet learning as the base and Western learning for application" created a freak: the power market economic system. After Deng Xiaoping used a military force of hundreds of thousands to suppress protesting masses in 1989, the bureaucratic system became even more unyielding. In 1992, China announced the establishment of a "socialist market economy," which was in fact a power market economy.

A power market economy is directed and controlled by state administrative power. The power refers to the structure left over from the planned economy era without undergoing major reform (i.e., a power structure without checks and balances). Some people refer to the power market economy as the China Model. The China Model is a market economy dominated by the government unconstrained by the constitution. The dominance of the government is effectively dominance by the bureaucratic clique, and the power market economy is the bureaucratic clique dominating the market economy and distorting its patterns through administrative power.

In China under the power market economic system, the ability to succeed in anything depends on relationships with key power-holders. The process of selling official positions and titles has formed a shadow network of personal bondage and gangs as power wielders at various levels serve one another's needs and utilize one another in a hotbed of corruption and protection removed from social justice. The ordinary people covered by this huge shadow network are powerless to defend justice or appeal against unjust treatment.

The party Central Committee had always criticized corruption, and its power to combat corruption has become ever greater. But in a power market economy system, this kind of anti-corruption effort is sometimes described as "swatting flies in a latrine." The elite stratum bred on the soil of systemic corruption perpetuates its benefits from the power market economy by obstructing political systemic reform in every way possible.

The power market economic system has given rise to a vicious combination of abuse of rights and greed for capital that has become the root cause of social injustice in China today.

Deng Xiaoping's eldest son, Deng Pufang, once had a conversation with Chen Yizi, director of the China Economic Reform Research Institute:

> Deng: Yizi, tell me, what is reform?
> Chen: Any reform involves a reallocation of benefit and

power. If destitute people are to become well-to-do, the government needs to give everyone the opportunity and environment for fair competition.

Deng: (laughing) You're talking about principles. Practically speaking, I feel that reform is this: Whoever has the capabilities can grab something from the state . . . In the past, the state managed everything, but now the state has to unleash power and share benefit, and whoever is able to grab a piece can do so.

Chen: The way you put it, those closest to power can grab more, so don't ordinary people lose out?

Deng: Look at past dynasties—it's always those with ability who have benefited first!

Chen: In fact, achieving a modern society means creating opportunities for fair competition for every person.

Deng: What you say is true, but this is a process, and it can't be done right from the outset. There will always be a portion of capable people who get rich first before a shared prosperity is achieved.[25]

This is why most of China's wealthy are close to those in power, as opposed to the vast impoverished community. After more than thirty years of Reform and Opening, China's income disparity has reached an intolerable level.[26] Social injustice and lack of upward mobility are causing people in the lower rungs of society to lose hope, intensifying conflict between the classes as manifested in mass protests and disturbances, which have burgeoned from 8,700 instances in 1993 to more than 100,000 in 2008. Upward of 75 percent of these mass incidents have been of a rights' defense nature involving mainly workers and peasants.

The response of the government at all levels has been an overriding emphasis on stability maintenance, not by fundamentally resolving the social conflicts involved, but rather by coercive or even violent suppression of the people attempting to defend their rights. The government's expenditure on stability maintenance is now higher than its expenditure on the military. In the long term, the government's oppressive tactics will fail, because citizens far outnumber officials, and their natural sense of justice will only increase under pressure until the power of their rights' defense surpasses the tipping point and gives rise to an unprecedented social explosion.

Most fundamental to social harmony is harmony between the classes, and the key to harmony between the classes is social justice. That's why a society with a power market economy will never be harmonious. Fairness requires a new system that provides checks and balances on power and controls capital. Power must be caged by a constitution and operate within the confines of law. Capital needs to be controlled through a system that gives free rein to its positive aspects while controlling the danger its rapaciousness poses to society.

The experience of humanity over the past two centuries has shown us that constitutional democracy is an effective system for applying checks and balances on power and controlling capital. That requires breaking through the modern version of "Soviet learning as the base, Western learning for application" that serves as the guiding ideology of reform, carrying out political systemic reform, and enacting fundamental change to the bureaucratic system. Of course, this will take time and cannot happen overnight. Sudden change is dangerous, and peaceful evolution is more appropriate.

NOTES

AUTHOR'S NOTE

1. Wang Meng, *Inexplicable China*, Anhui wenyi chubanshe, 2012.
2. General histories of the Cultural Revolution published in Chinese include Gao Gao and Yan Jiaqi, *Turbulent Decade: A History of the Cultural Revolution*, Tianjin renmin chubanshe, 1986; Wang Nianyi, *Era of Upheaval*, Henan renmin chubanshe, 1988; Xi Xuan and Jin Chunming, *A Concise History of the Cultural Revolution*, Zhonggong dangshi chubanshe, 1996; Bu Weihua, *Smashing the Old World: Havoc of the Chinese Cultural Revolution (1966–1968)*, Chinese University of Hong Kong Press, 2008; Shi Yun and Li Danhui, *The Difficulty of Continuing the Continuous Revolution*, Chinese University of Hong Kong Press, 2008; Roderick MacFarquhar and Michael Schoenhals, *Mao's Last Revolution* (Chinese edition), Xinke'er chuban (Xianggang) youxian gongsi, 2009 (English edition, Belknap Press of Harvard University Press, 2006).
3. "Resolution Regarding Certain Historical Issues Since the Founding of Our Country," *A Selection of Important Texts Since the Third Central Committee*, Renmin chubanshe, 1982, p. 757.
4. CCP Central Committee Party History Research Room, *History of the Chinese Communist Party*, vol. 2 (1959–1978), Zhonggong dangshi chubanshe, 2011, p. 752.
5. Wang Nianyi, "An Informal Chat About the Cultural Revolution," *Ershiyi Shiji* (Twenty-First Century; Hong Kong), October 2006.
6. Fu Sinian (1896–1950) was a famous Chinese educator and linguist and a leader of the May Fourth Movement.
7. The URLs of these online journals are as follows: *Remembrance*, http://prchistory.org/remembrance; *Yesterday*, http://prchistory.org/yesterday/; Virtual Museum of the Cultural Revolution, http://www.cnd.org/CR/halls.html.

PREFACE: THE ROAD, THE THEORY, AND THE SYSTEM

1. A line in Mao's poem "Two Birds: A Dialogue—to the Tune of Nien Nu Chiao": "The roc wings fanwise, / Soaring ninety thousand li / And rousing

a raging cyclone. / The blue sky on his back, he looks down / To survey Man's world with its towns and cities. / Gunfire licks the heavens, / Shells pit the earth. / A sparrow in his bush is scared stiff. / "This is one hell of a mess! / O I want to flit and fly away." / "Where, may I ask?" / The sparrow replies, / "To a jewelled palace in elfland's hills. / Don't you know a triple pact was signed / Under the bright autumn moon two years ago? / There'll be plenty to eat, / Potatoes piping hot, / Beef-filled goulash." / "Stop your windy nonsense! / Look, the world is being turned upside down." (Translators' note [hereafter *TN*]: English translation from Mao Zedong, *Poems*, Open Source Socialist Publishing, 2008, p. 45.) This poem was written in autumn 1965 and originally expressed opposition to Soviet revisionism, but when *Poetry* (*Shikan*) magazine published it on January 1, 1976, Chinese associated it with the turmoil of the Cultural Revolution.

2. See my earlier book *Tombstone: An Account of Chinese Famine in the 1960s*, Hong Kong: Cosmos Books (Tiandi tushu chubanshe), 2008 (English edition: *Tombstone: The Great Chinese Famine 1958–1962*, trans. Stacy Mosher and Guo Jian, New York: Farrar, Straus and Giroux, 2012).

3. What is referred to here as the "political underclass" are the groups targeted in repeated political campaigns, including landlords, rich peasants, counter-revolutionaries, bad elements, rightists, capitalists, and officials left behind from the nationalist regime. They were subjected to constant persecution under an ideology that treated them as threats to society.

4. F. A. Hayek, *The Road to Serfdom*, vol. 2 of *The Collected Works of F. A. Hayek*, University of Chicago Press, 2007, p. 168; Chinese edition, trans. Wang Mingyi and Feng Xingyuan, Beijing: Zhongguo shehui kexue chubanshe, 1997, p. 143.

5. Wang Ya'nan, *Research into China's Bureaucratic Politics*, Zhongguo shehui kexue chubanshe, 1981, p. 190. A famous economist, Wang Ya'nan (1901–1969) was the first person to translate *Das Kapital* into Chinese.

6. Milovan Djilas, one of Yugoslavia's first revolutionaries, became president of the Federal Assembly of the Socialist Federal Republic of Yugoslavia in 1953 and was slated to become successor to Tito as president of Yugoslavia. However, a series of articles he wrote on Yugoslavia's new privileged class in late 1953 and early 1954 led to him being stripped of his position and expelled from the Central Committee of the Communist Party of Yugoslavia in January 1954, and he resigned from Yugoslavia's League of Communists soon afterward.

7. Milovan Djilas, *The New Class*, trans. Chen Yi, CCP Central Committee Politics and Law Committee Theory Office, large-type edition for internal circulation, pp. 47, 78, 93. TN: English translation: Milovan Djilas, *The New Class: An Analysis of the Communist System*, London: Thames and Hudson, 1957, pp. 36, 60, 72.

8. Milovan Djilas, *New Class*, p. 90; English edition, p. 69.

9. TN: A term used by Marx and Lenin, as in V. I. Lenin, *The State and Revolution: The Marxist Theory of the State and the Tasks of the Proletariat in the Revolution*, Lenin Internet Archive (Marxists.org), 1993, 1999, pp. 31, 33, marxists.org/ebooks/lenin/state-and-revolution.pdf.

10. Wang Lixiong shares this view: Wang Lixiong, "What Did China Gain from the Cultural Revolution," April 2006 (accessible through the Boxun website: blog.boxun.com/hero/2006/wanglx/5_1.shtml).

11. According to statistics from the CCP Central Committee Organization

Department, a total of 2.3 million cadres were placed under investigation during the Cultural Revolution, constituting 19.2 percent of the 12 million cadres at that time. An even larger number of cadres who weren't formally investigated were subjected to wrongful criticism and detention, and many other individuals were implicated. About 75 percent of all cadres at or above the level of state vice-minister or provincial vice-governor were formally investigated, and more than sixty thousand cadres were persecuted to death. Nearly twenty thousand wrongful cases were brought against "cliques," involving hundreds of thousands of cadres, and many good officials were ruthlessly persecuted. See *History of the Chinese Communist Party*, vol. 2, *1949–1978*, Zhonggong dangshi chubanshe, 2011, p. 967.

12. See chapter 9.
13. Xi Xuan and Jin Chunming, *A Concise History of the Cultural Revolution*, 2nd ed., Zhonggong dangshi chubanshe, 2006, p. 196.
14. *Complete Works of Marks and Engels*, vol. 39, Renmin chubanshe, 1977, p. 149. TN: English translation: "Engels to Nikolai Danielson in St. Petersburg (Abstract)," 1983, trans. Donna Torr, International Publishers, 1968, Marxists.org, marxists.org/archive/marx/works/1893/letters/93_10_17 .htm.
15. Deng Xiaoping, "Reform of the Party and State Leadership System," *Selected Works of Deng Xiaoping*, vol. 2, Renmin chubanshe, 1993, p. 323.
16. "Opinions Regarding Opening Files on the Main Leaders of Rebel Faction Organizations at Tertiary Educational Institutions During the Cultural Revolution," CCP Central Committee Document No. 6 [1983], April 23, 1983.
17. Hayek, *Road to Serfdom*, p. 102; English edition, p. 136.
18. The economist Wu Jinglian refers to "power market economy" as "crony capitalism." See, for example, David Barboza, "China's Mr. Wu Keeps Talking," *New York Times*, September 27, 2009, BU1, nytimes.com/2009/09/27 /business/global/27spy.html.

I. MAJOR EVENTS PRECEDING THE CULTURAL REVOLUTION

1. For more on the military discipline inspection system, see Yang Jisheng, *Political Struggle in China's Reform Era*, Hong Kong: Cosmos Books (Tiandi tushu chubanshe), 2010, pp. 36–39.
2. For detailed analysis of this point, see Yang Jisheng, *The Deng Xiaoping Era*, Zhongyang bianyi chubanshe, 1998, pp. 25–27, 309–312.
3. Under the "(Draft) Central Level Administrative Personnel Wage Standards" tabled in April 1950. See Yang Kuisong, *The History of the Founding of the People's Republic of China*, vol. 1, Jiangxi renmin chubanshe, 2010, from figures in the table on p. 445.
4. Yang Kuisong, *The History of the Founding of the People's Republic of China*, p. 450.
5. During the rectification of work styles in 1956, the domestic editor for the Xinhua News Agency, Feng Dong, was nearly labeled a rightist for writing a big-character poster about "posterior rankings."
6. Li Fu, *Thoughts and Recollections of Seventy Years*, Xiliu chubanshe, 2012, p. 192.
7. Yang Kuisong, *History of the Founding of the People's Republic of China*, contains abundant material on the killing of landlords. See pp. 137–154.

8. Yang Kuisong, *History of the Founding of the People's Republic of China*, pp. 216–217.

9. TN: The German social democratic theorist Eduard Bernstein is regarded as the father of revisionism. Karl Johann Kautsky was a Czech-Austrian theoretician who adhered to orthodox Marxism and opposed Bolshevism. Nikita Khrushchev's revisionism was so objectionable to Mao that it became a major factor in the launch of the Cultural Revolution.

10. CCP Central Committee Documentary Research Room (ed.), *Chronology of Mao Zedong: 1949–1976*, vol. 5, Beijing: Zhongyang wenxian chubanshe, 2013, p. 592.

11. "Speech at the Chengdu Conference," March 1958, in CCP Central Committee Documentary Research Room, ed., *Collected Works of Mao Zedong*, vol. 7, Beijing: Renmin chubanshe, 1999, p. 369.

12. Li Rui, *A Personal History of the Great Leap Forward: The Handwritten Notes of Mao Zedong's Secretary*, vol. 1, Haikou: Nanfang chubanshe, 1999, p. 252.

13. Lin Biao, Speech to the enlarged meeting of the Central Committee Politburo, May 18, 1966.

14. Xi Xuan and Jin Chunming, *A Concise History of the Cultural Revolution*, Beijing: Zhonggong dangshi chubanshe, 1996, p. 357.

15. For a detailed account of the Great Famine, see Yang Jisheng, *Mubei*, Hong Kong: Cosmos Books (Tiandi tushu chubanshe), 2008; English edition: *Tombstone: The Great Chinese Famine, 1958–1962*, trans. Stacy Mosher and Guo Jian, New York: Farrar, Straus and Giroux, 2012. The book has also been translated into French, German, and Japanese.

16. Quoted in the Beijing municipal party organ's Mao Zedong Thought Red Flag Regiment, ed., *The Criminal History of the Great Careerist and Conspirator Peng Zhen*. This view is also expressed in Roderick MacFarquhar and John King Fairbank, *The Cambridge History of the People's Republic of China (1949–1965)*, Chinese edition, Zhongguo shehui kexue chubanshe, 1992, p. 344. Other scholars hold that an examination of documents at Changguanlou was proposed by Mao before the Seven Thousand Cadres Conference and that Mao and Liu Shaoqi did not oppose it. See Liu Zheng and Zhang Chunsheng, "Looking at the Relationship Between Peng Zhen and Mao Zedong Through Several Major Historical Junctures," *Lingdaozhe*, no. 4 (2013), p. 149.

17. Wang Nianyi shares this view. See Wang Nianyi, "On the Launch of the 'Cultural Revolution,'" *Zhonggong dangshi yanjiu*, September 30, 1983.

18. Zhang Yizhe, "The Great Famine and the Cultural Revolution," *Zuotian (Yesterday)*, no. 23 (supplementary issue), 2013.

19. Yang Xiaokai, "The Chinese Cultural Revolution's Breakthrough in the Socialist System," *Zhishi fenzi*, Spring 1986.

20. Hu Sheng, ed., *Seventy Years of the Chinese Communist Party*, Beijing: Zhonggong dangshi chubanshe, 1991, p. 367. For some notable examples, see "Central Committee Transmission of the Zhejiang Provincial Party Committee's 'Report on Policy Violations That Occurred During the Socialist Education Movement in a Minority of Localities in Wenzhou and Jinhua Prefectures,'" December 21, 1958, Central Committee Document No. 1010 [1959], *hai*; "Gansu Provincial Party Committee Inspection Report Regarding Certain Problems in Implementing and Executing the Spirit of the Northwest Bureau's Lanzhou Conference over the Past Two Years," adopted

by the fourth plenum of the third provincial party committee on December 3, 1962, Gansu Provincial Party Committee Document No. 6 [1963]; "Central Committee's Approval of the Qinghai Provincial Party Committee's Resolution Regarding the Errors of the Anti-Party Clique Led by Comrade Zhang Guosheng," October 14, 1959, Central Committee Document (sent to provincial level) No. 822 [1959], *you.*

21. Deng Xiaoping, "Remarks to the Central Committee Work Conference," in *Selected Works of Deng Xiaoping* under the title "Ways of Surmounting the Present Difficulties," but with the figures edited out. See *Selected Works of Deng Xiaoping*, vol. 1, Beijing: Renmin chubanshe, 1989, p. 319.

22. Wu Lengxi, "Working with Tian Jiaying," *Dang de wenxian* (Party Documents), no. 5 (1996).

23. Zhang Suhua, *Critical Juncture: The Beginning and End of the Seven Thousand Cadres Conference*, Zhongguo qingnian chubanshe, 2006, p. 75.

24. Bo Yibo, *Looking Back on a Number of Significant Policy Decisions and Events*, vol. 2, Beijing: Zhonggong zhongyang dangxiao chubanshe, 1993, pp. 1026–1027.

25. Zhang Suhua, *Critical Juncture*, p. 110.

26. Bo Yibo, *Looking Back*, pp. 1026–1027.

27. *Selected Works of Liu Shaoqi*, Beijing: Renmin chubanshe, 1985, pp. 418–443.

28. Record of an interview with Deng Liqun on July 1, 1994, in Zhang Suhua, *Critical Juncture*, p. 285.

29. Mao Zedong, "My Conversation with Comrades Kapo and Balluku," February 3, 1967, in *Long Live Mao Zedong Thought, 1961–1968* (further publication information unavailable), p. 88.

30. Zhang Suhua, *Critical Juncture*, pp. 143–145.

31. CCP Central Committee Documentary Research Room (ed.), *Chronology of Mao Zedong: 1949–1979*, vol. 5, Zhongyang wenxian chubanshe, 2013, p. 92.

32. Xi Xuan and Jin Chunming, *A Concise History of the Cultural Revolution*, p. 15.

33. Mao Zedong, "Speech at the Enlarged Central Committee Work Conference (January 30, 1962)," in *Long Live Mao Zedong Thought*, p. 17.

34. "Opinions Put Forward to the Central Committee and Its Leaders and Related Departments During a Meeting in Gansu Province of Party Cadres of Provincial Units of Grade 19 or Above to Study and Discuss Documents from the Meeting of the Enlarged Central Committee Working Group," February 28, 1962, compiled by the provincial party secretariat, Gansu Provincial Archives.

35. Bo Yibo, *Looking Back*, pp. 1051–1052.

36. Liu Shaoqi, "What Is the Actual Current Economic Situation?" (May 11, 1962), in *Selected Works of Liu Shaoqi*, Beijing: Renmin chubanshe, 1985, pp. 444–446.

37. Liu Shaoqi, *Selected Works of Liu Shaoqi*, p. 1058.

38. Huang Zheng, ed., *President of the Republic, Liu Shaoqi*, vol. 2, Beijing: Zhonggong dangshi chubanshe, 1998, p. 1274.

39. Bo Yibo, *Looking Back*, pp. 1084–1085.

40. Wang Guangmei, Liu Yuan, et al., *The Unknown Liu Shaoqi*, Henan renmin chubanshe, 2000, p. 90.

41. Zhu Liang, "Selfless and Fearless Seeker of Truth, Wang Jiaxiang: The Truth Behind the 1962 Accusation of 'Three Appeasements and One Reduction' Revisionism," *Yanhuang Chunqiu*, no. 8, 2006.

42. CCP Central Committee Documents Research Room, *Chronology of Liu Shaoqi*, vol. 2, Zhongyang wenxian chubanshe, 1996, p. 551.

43. Mao Zedong, *Long Live Mao Zedong Thought*, pp. 29–30.

44. Bo Yibo, *Looking Back*, pp. 1074–1077.

45. Bo Yibo, *Looking Back*, pp. 1074–1088.

46. Bo Yibo, *Looking Back*, p. 1093; Huang Kecheng, *The Autobiography of Huang Kecheng*, Beijing: Renmin chubanshe, 1994, p. 270.

47. Kang Sheng was an alternate Politburo member, a secretary of the Central Committee Secretariat, and the chairman of the Central Committee Theoretical Group.

48. Bo Yibo, *Looking Back*, p. 1096.

49. Bo Yibo, *Looking Back*, p. 1096.

50. Huang Kecheng, *Autobiography of Huang Kecheng*, p. 270.

51. Mao Zedong's first speech at the Wuchang Conference, the morning of November 21, 1958, at Hongshan.

52. Mimeographed copies of Ai Siqi's speech were widely circulated at the outset of the Cultural Revolution, and I personally read it. It is not included in *The Collected Works of Ai Siqi*.

53. Central Party School Party History Research Room, ed., *Collected Documents from Several Important CCP Meetings*, vol. 2, Shanghai: Shanghai renmin chubanshe, 1983, pp. 196–197.

54. "Remarks on the (Draft) 'Three Great Disciplines and Eight Matters for Attention' for Party and Government Cadres," January 9, 1961, in CCP Central Committee Party Literature Research Center, ed., *Manuscripts of Mao Zedong Since the Founding of the Country* (hereafter *Manuscripts of Mao Zedong*), vol. 9, Beijing: Zhongyang wenxian chubanshe, 1996, p. 417; Cong Jin, *An Era of Twists and Turns*, Zhengzhou: Henan renmin chubanshe, 1989, pp. 533–534.

55. "Written comments on a situation report on central organs transferring 10,000 cadres down to grassroots units," November 15, 1960, *Manuscripts of Mao Zedong*, p. 349.

56. TN: The Communist Wind, Exaggeration Wind, Coercive Commandism Wind, Cadre Privilege Wind, and Chaotic Directives Wind. See Yang Jisheng, *Tombstone*, chapter 7.

57. TN: That is, landlords, rich peasants, counterrevolutionaries, and bad elements.

58. "Summary by the CCP Hebei Provincial Party Committee Rectification of Work Styles and Cooperatives Office and Commission for Discipline Inspection Regarding Organizational Handling of the Rectification of Work Styles and Cooperatives Campaign in the Villages from Winter 1960 to Spring 1961," April 28, 1962, Hebei Provincial Archive, Collection no. 856, catalog 1, file 221.

59. Wang Guangmei, "Summary of One Production Brigade's Experience with the Socialist Education Movement" (also known as "The Taoyuan Experience"), July 5, 1964. See *Material for Criticism: A Collection of the Counterrevolutionary Revisionist Discourse of China's Khrushchev, Liu Shaoqi, June 1958 to July 1967*, ed. People's Publishing Reference Room, Beijing: internal distribution edition, 1967, pp. 471–570.

60. Guo Dehong and Lin Xiaobo, *A True Record of the Socialist Education Movement*, Zhejiang renmin chubanshe, 2005, p. 171.

61. Wang Li, *Wang Li's Record of Introspection*, vol. 1, Hong Kong: Beixing chubanshe, February 2008, p. 573.

62. Gao Hua, "Behind the Four Cleanups Campaign in Guizhou: An Analysis of a Contemporary Memoir," rev. version, *Lingdaozhe* 12, no. 1 (January 2006).

63. Luo Bing, "Deciphering Mao Zedong's Launch of the Socialist Education Movement," quoted in Song Yongyi, "Liu Shaoqi's Contribution to the Cultural Revolution," in *The Cultural Revolution: Historical Truth and Collective Memory*, vol. 1, ed. Song Yongyi, Hong Kong: Tianyuan shuwu, 2007, p. 264. Bu Weihua casts doubts on these figures.

64. Wang Guangmei, Liu Yuan, et al., *Unknown Liu Shaoqi*, p. 110.

65. Huang Zheng, *President of the Republic, Liu Shaoqi*, p. 1285; "Central Committee Transmission of the Memo 'Regarding the Summary of a Production Brigade's Experience During the Socialist Education Movement,'" September 1, 1964, Central Committee Document No. 527 [1964].

66. Yin Shusheng, "Viewing the 'Four Cleanups' Campaign Through the Farce of Denouncing a Corpse," *Yanhuang Chunqiu*, no. 7, 2010.

67. Wang Guangmei, Liu Yuan, et al., *Unknown Liu Shaoqi*, pp. 115-118. CCP Central Committee Documentary Research Room (ed.), *Chronology of Mao Zedong: 1949-1976*, vol. 5, pp. 451-453, states that this argument occurred on the afternoon of December 20.

68. Bo Yibo, *Looking Back*, p. 1131.

69. CCP Central Committee Documentary Research Room (ed.), *Chronology of Mao Zedong: 1949-1976*, vol. 5, p. 456.

70. CCP Central Committee Documentary Research Room (ed.), *Chronology of Mao Zedong: 1949-1976*, vol. 5, p. 475.

71. CCP Central Committee Documentary Research Room (ed.), *Chronology of Mao Zedong: 1949-1976*, vol. 5, p. 458.

72. *A Survivor of the Revolution: The Memoirs of Zeng Zhi*, Guangdong renmin chubanshe, 1998, pp. 432-432. Quoted in Guo Dehong, Lin Xiaobo, *A True Record of the Four Clean-Ups Movement*, Zhejiang renmin chubanshe, 2005, p. 268.

73. Wang Guangmei and Liu Yuan, *Unknown Liu Shaoqi*, p. 118.

74. Mao Zedong's conversation with Edgar Snow, *Chinese Cultural Revolution Database*, ed. Song Yongyi et al., 3rd ed., Universities Service Centre for China Studies, Chinese University of Hong Kong Press, 2013.

75. CCP Central Committee Party Literature Research Center, ed., *Biography of Mao Zedong: 1949-1976*, vol. 2, Beijing: Zhongyang wenxian chubanshe, December 2003, p. 1461.

76. CCP Central Committee Party Literature Research Center, *Biography of Mao Zedong: 1949-1976*, p. 1462.

77. CCP Central Committee Party Literature Research Center, *Biography of Mao Zedong: 1949-1976*, p. 1384.

78. Yin Xuyi, ed., *Selected Essays of Eduard Bernstein*, Renmin chubanshe, 2008, pp. 410-411.

79. *Concise Course in the History of the Communist (Bolshevik) Party of the Soviet Union*, Renmin chubanshe, 1975, p. 377.

80. CCP Central Committee Party History Research Room, *History of the Chinese Communist Party*, vol. 2, *1949-1978*, Zhonggong dangshi chubanshe, p. 377.

81. "Advancing Along the Road Forged by the October Socialist Revolution: Commemorating the Fiftieth Anniversary of the Great October Socialist Revolution," *People's Daily*, November 6, 1967.

82. Zhou Yang was deputy director of the Central Committee Propaganda Department, as well as vice-chairman of the Chinese Federation of Literary and Arts Circles and of the Chinese Writers' Association.

83. Peng Zhen was a Politburo member and secretary of the Central Committee Secretariat, as well as first secretary of the Beijing municipal party committee and mayor of Beijing.

84. Lu Dingyi was an alternate Politburo member, secretary of the Central Committee Secretariat, and director of the Central Committee Propaganda Department.

85. Wu Lengxi was director of the Xinhua News Agency and editor in chief of *People's Daily.*

86. Luo Pinghan, *China on the Eve of the Cultural Revolution*, Renmin chubanshe, 2007, p. 257.

87. Luo Pinghan, *China on the Eve of the Cultural Revolution*, p. 260.

88. Cong Jin, *Era of Twists and Turns*, p. 570.

89. Jian Bozan, "On Peasant Wars in Ancient China," *Xuexi* magazine, February 1951.

90. *Manuscripts of Mao Zedong*, vol. 10, 1996, p. 436.

91. *Manuscripts of Mao Zedong*, vol. 11, 1996, p. 91.

92. Qi Yanming was vice-minister and party secretary of the Ministry of Culture. Xia Yan was a writer and deputy party secretary of the Ministry of Culture. Tian Han was a playwright and chairman of the Ministry of Culture's Drama Improvement Bureau and Fine Arts Bureau. Yang Hansheng was a playwright and former vice-chairman and party secretary of the Chinese Federation of Literary and Arts Circles. Shao Quanlin was a writer and vice-chairman and party secretary of the Chinese Writers' Association.

93. Luo Pinghan, *China on the Eve of the Cultural Revolution*, p. 244.

94. Cong Jin, *Era of Twists and Turns*, pp. 556–557.

2. LIGHTING THE FUSE

1. Wu Han, "I'm Indignant, I Accuse! Speech During the Fourth Session of the First National People's Congress," *People's Daily*, July 7, 1957.

2. Xi Xuan and Jin Chunming, *A Concise History of the Cultural Revolution*, new edition, Zhonggong dangshi chubanshe, 2011, p. 34.

3. Mao Zedong's speech at the seventh plenum of the Eighth Central Committee, April 5, 1959, in Li Rui, *A Personal History of the Great Leap Forward: The Handwritten Notes of Mao Zedong's Secretary*, vol. 1, Haikou: Nanfang chubanshe, 1999, p. 469; CCP Central Committee Documentary Research Room (ed.), *Chronology of Mao Zedong: 1949–1976*, vol. 4, pp. 11–12.

4. CCP Central Committee Party History Research Office, *History of the Chinese Communist Party*, vol. 2, *1949–1976*, p. 754.

5. Li Rui, *Personal History of the Great Leap Forward*, vol. 1, Haikou: Nanfang chubanshe, 1999, p. 473.

6. Xu Jingxian, *The Ten-Year Dream*, Hong Kong: Shidai guoji chuban gongsi, 2003, p. 5.

7. Xi Xuan and Jin Chunming, *A Concise History of the Cultural Revolution*, p. 69.

8. Zhu Yongjia, as told to Jin Guangyao, "Before and After the Publication of 'A Critique of the New Historical Play *Hai Rui Dismissed from Office*,'" *Yanhuang Chunqiu*, no. 6, 2011.

9. Wang Chuncai, *The Marshal's Last Years: Peng Dehuai on the Third Line of Defense*, Sichuan renmin chubanshe, 1991, p. 33.

10. Wang Ming (1904–1974), born Chen Shaoyu, joined the CCP in 1926. With the support of the Communist International, he became a CCP leader during the fourth plenum of the Sixth Central Committee in January 1931. He became a political opponent of Mao's by promoting what was termed a "left-deviating opportunistic road" characterized by dogmatism and idealization of the Soviet Union.

11. Yang Chengwu quoted Lin Biao in referring to this matter in a speech on June 20, 1967. See Wang Lin, "Big-Character Poster News and Street Rumors Recorded in My Journal Entries," *Zuotian* (*Yesterday*), no. 1, 2012.

12. Author's conversation with Gao Gang's secretary, Zhao Jialiang. See Yang Jisheng, *Collected Interviews with Modern Chinese Notables and Commentaries*, Hong Kong: Cosmos Books (Tiandi tushu chubanshe), 2013, p. 87.

13. While inspecting operations in Tianjin in April 1949, Liu Shaoqi held several discussions with capitalists, encouraging them to play a part in the resumption of economic construction, using the phrase "meritorious exploitation."

14. Author's conversation with Gao Gang's secretary, Zhao Jialiang, in Yang Jisheng, *Collected Interviews*, pp. 93–94.

15. Hengshan County, Shaanxi Province, Gao Gang and Revolution Research Association, *Remembering Comrade Gao Gang*, Dazhong wenyi chubanshe, 2010, p. 88.

16. Author's conversation with Gao Gang's secretary, Zhao Jialiang, in Yang Jisheng, *Collected Interviews*, pp. 98–99.

17. Zhang Daoyi, "Why Did Mao Zedong Worry That Peng Dehuai Would Oppose Him?," Xinhua online, May 10, 2011. Zhang Daoyi was Peng Zhen's secretary.

18. "The Crimes of Counterrevolutionary Revisionist Fan Jin: Supplementary Material No. 1," Beijing: Ribao wenhua geming yundong bangongshi, 1967, p. 18. This source is quoted in the Chinese edition of Roderick MacFarquhar and Michael Shoenhals, *Mao's Last Revolution*, Hong Kong: Xinke'er chubanshe, 2009, p. 19; TN: English edition, Belknap Press of Harvard University Press, 2006, p. 11.

19. "Chronicle of the Struggle Between the Two Roads on the Cultural Front from September 1965 to May 1966," appendix to the May 16 Circular.

20. *History of the Chinese Communist Party*, vol. 2, *1949–1978*, p. 754.

21. Hao Huaiming, "The Central Propaganda Department at the Outset of the Cultural Revolution," *Yanhuang Chunqiu*, no. 12, 2010.

22. Zhu Yongjia, as told to Jin Guangyao, "Before and After the Publication of 'A Critique of the New Historical Play Hai Rui Dismissed from Office,'" *Yanhuang Chunqiu*, no. 6, 2011.

23. "Chronicle of the Struggle Between the Two Roads on the Cultural Front from September 1965 to May 1966," appendix to the May 16 Circular.

24. "Chronicle of the Struggle Between the Two Roads on the Cultural Front from September 1965 to May 1966," appendix to the May 16 Circular.

25. *Chronology of Mao Zedong, 1949–1976*, vol. 5, pp. 547–548.

26. *Chronology of Mao Zedong, 1949–1976*, vol. 5, p. 548.

27. "Chronicle of the Struggle Between the Two Roads on the Cultural Front from September 1965 to May 1966," appendix to the May 16 Circular.

28. "Outline of the Report by the Cultural Revolution Five-Member Small Group Regarding the Current Academic Discussion," *Chinese Cultural Revolution*

Database, ed. Song Yongyi et al., 3rd ed., Universities Service Centre for China Studies, Chinese University of Hong Kong Press, 2013.

29. Wang Li, *Wang Li's Record of Introspection*, vol. 1, Hong Kong: Beixing chubanshe, February 2008, p. 12.

30. Gong Yuzhi, "The February Outline and the Trip to East Lake," in *Recollecting the Cultural Revolution*, ed. Zhang Hua et al., Zhonggong dangshi chubanshe, 2007, pp. 286–287.

31. "Chronology of the Struggle Between the Two Roads on the Cultural Front from September 1965 to May 1966," appendix to the May 16 Circular. Wang Li says that in Zhou Enlai's experience, if Mao put only a circle on a document, it was not considered a matter of priority. If Mao supported something, he would state clearly whether he agreed with it or not. On this document, Mao didn't even bother to draw a circle, which indicated his attitude. Wang Li, *Wang's Li's Record of Introspection*, vol. 2, Hong Kong: Beixing chubanshe, January 2008, p. 13.

32. "Chronicle of the Struggle Between the Two Roads," appendix to the May 16 Circular. Mao's conversations on March 17–20, 28, 29, and 30 are recorded in *Chronology of Mao Zedong: 1949–1976*, vol. 5, pp. 568 and 572.

33. "Chronicle of the Struggle Between the Two Roads," appendix to the May 16 Circular.

34. "Chronicle of the Struggle Between the Two Roads," appendix to the May 16 Circular.

35. "Chronicle of the Struggle Between the Two Roads," appendix to the May 16 Circular.

36. Bu Weihua, *Smashing the Old World: Havoc of the Chinese Cultural Revolution (1966–1968)*, Chinese University of Hong Kong Press, 2008, p. 68.

37. "Chronicle of the Struggle Between the Two Roads."

38. CCP Central Committee Documentary Research Room (ed.), *Chronology of Mao Zedong: 1949–1976*, vol. 5, p. 580.

39. Wang Li, *Wang Li's Record of Introspection*, vol. 2, 2nd ed., Hong Kong: Beixing chubanshe, May 2011, p. 17.

40. Li Xuefeng, "My Inside Knowledge of How the Cultural Revolution Was Launched," in *Recollecting the Cultural Revolution*, ed. Zhang Hua et al., Zhonggong dangshi chubanshe, 2007.

41. Qiu Huizuo, *The Memoirs of Qiu Huizuo*, Hong Kong: Xinshiji chubanshe (New Century Press), 2011, p. 432.

42. CCP Central Committee Documentary Research Room (ed.), *Chronology of Mao Zedong: 1949–1976*, vol. 5, p. 581.

43. Li Xuefeng, "My Inside Knowledge of How the Cultural Revolution Was Launched," p. 597.

44. Bu Weihua, *Smashing the Old World*, pp. 48–49.

3. REMOVING OBSTRUCTIONS

1. After the Cultural Revolution, the government claimed that Yang Shangkun tape-recorded Mao's conversations because his work required it. Qi Benyu's memoir provided new information: Yang Shangkun's practice of setting up listening devices in Mao's bedroom and bathroom was carried out through Wu Zhenying and Kang Yimin of the Confidential Office, Wu being Liu Shaoqi's confidential secretary. Eventually the Ministry of Public Security sent professionals to remove all the listening devices. Mao had the devices

and the self-criticism of Yang and Kang sealed up in a secret pouch and handed over to Jiang Qing for safekeeping. The listening devices were shaped like rice grains and had been imported from abroad. Yang Shangkun headed up the department at that time. See Qi Benyu, *The Memoirs of Qi Benyu*, Hong Kong: Zhongguo wenge lishi chubanshe, 2016, pp. 387–388.

2. "Zhou Enlai's Speech at the Enlarged Meeting of the Central Committee Political Bureau," May 21, 1966.

3. The ten senior generals were Su Yu, Xu Haidong, Huang Kecheng, Chen Geng, Tan Zheng, Xiao Jinguang, Zhang Yunyi, Luo Ruiqing, Wang Shusheng, and Xu Guangda.

4. Wu Faxian, *The Memoirs of Wu Faxian*, Hong Kong: Beixing chubanshe, 3rd ed., February 2008, p. 566.

5. Wu Faxian, *The Difficult Years: The Memoirs of Wu Faxian*, vol. 2, Hong Kong: Beixing chubanshe, September 2006, pp. 539–540.

6. Qiu Huizuo, *The Memoirs of Qiu Huizuo*, Xinshiji chubanshe (New Century Press), 2011, p. 404.

7. Qiu Huizuo, *Memoirs of Qiu Huizuo*, p. 370.

8. Qiu Huizuo, *Memoirs of Qiu Huizuo*, pp. 378–379.

9. Luo Ruiqing's involvement in the Guo Xingfu training methods and the competition were both criticized in the Central Committee Work Group's "Report on the Question of Luo Ruiqing's Errors."

10. Central Committee Work Group, "Report on the Question of Luo Ruiqing's Errors."

11. Luo Diandian, *Red Clan Dossier*, Hainan chuban gongsi, 1999, p. 140.

12. Shu Yun, *Pictorial Biography of Lin Biao*, Mingjing chubanshe, 2007, pp. 550–551; Song Dejin, *The Real Lin Biao: The Last Recollections of Lin Biao's Secretary*, Huangfu tushu, 2008, p. 225. Quoted in Kaiwen Ding et al., *The Luo Ruiqing Incident in the Cultural Revolution* and checked against *Chronology of Ye Jianying*.

13. Cheng Guang, *Dialogue of the Soul: Qiu Huizuo Discusses the Cultural Revolution with His Son*, Hong Kong: Beixing chubanshe, 2011, p. 11. Wu Faxian may not have been among those given notice. When the Shanghai Conference began, he didn't know what Luo Ruiqing's problems were; see *Memoirs of Wu Faxian*, p. 557.

14. Wu Faxian said that Mao and Lin Biao did not put in an appearance, but that every day after the meeting ended, Mao called in Standing Committee members to hear their reports and make decisions. See *Memoirs of Wu Faxian*, pp. 558–559.

15. The Central Work Group's "Report Regarding Comrade Luo Ruiqing's Errors and Problems," from April 30, 1966, largely supports Ye Qun's accusations of Luo's machinations, but after the Lin Biao incident, the official story was that Ye Qun framed Luo Ruiqing. Huang Yao's article "On Some of the Things Said About Luo Ruiqing in *The Memoirs of Qiu Huizuo*" contradicts Ye Qun's contentions, but Ding Kaiwen feels that they actually reflected Luo's views on the tendencies of the CMC's leadership and his attitude toward Lin Biao. See Yu Ruxin, ed., *The Luo Ruiqing Case*, Hong Kong: Xinshiji chubanshe (New Century Press), 2014, p. 47.

16. Wu Faxian, *Memoirs of Wu Faxian*, p. 560.

17. Shi Niantang, as told to Sun Huanying, "Recollections of General Luo Ruiqing Being Secretly Escorted Away," *Military History*, no. 11 (2004).

18. Chen Hong, "Yang Chengwu Talks About the Actual Situation of Denouncing Luo Ruiqing," *Yanhuang Chunqiu*, no. 10, 2005.

19. Chen Hong, "Yang Chengwu Talks About the Actual Situation of Denouncing Luo Ruiqing."

20. Qiu Huizuo, *Memoirs of Qiu Huizuo*, p. 395.

21. Luo Diandian, *Red Clan Dossier*, p. 212.

22. Qiu Huizuo, *Memoirs of Qiu Huizuo*, pp. 400, 407.

23. Luo Diandian, *Red Clan Dossier*, p. 214.

24. Chen Qingquan and Song Guangwei, *Biography of Lu Dingyi*, Beijing: Zhonggong dangzhi chubanshe, 1999, p. 501.

25. Zhang Yunsheng, *Record of Actual Events at Maojiawan*, Chunqiu chubanshe, 1988, p. 47.

26. Chen Qingquan and Song Guangwei, *Biography of Lu Dingyi*, pp. 485–486.

27. Chen Qingquan and Song Guangwei, *Biography of Lu Dingyi*, p. 488.

28. Chen Qingquan and Song Guangwei, *Biography of Lu Dingyi*, pp. 491, 495.

29. Wang Nianyi, *Era of Upheaval*, Henan renmin chubanshe, 1988, pp. 18–19. Wang Li explicitly denies this version in his memoirs.

30. Wang Li, *Wang Li's Record of Introspection*, vol. 2, 2nd ed., Hong Kong: Beixing chubanshe, May 2011, p. 24.

31. Qiu Huizuo, *Memoirs of Qiu Huizuo*, pp. 438–440.

32. Li Xuefeng, "My Inside Knowledge of How the Cultural Revolution Was Launched," in *Recollecting the Cultural Revolution*, ed. Zhang Hua et al., Zhonggong dangshi chubanshe, 2007, p. 599.

33. Zhou Enlai, "Speech at the Enlarged Central Committee Politburo Meeting," May 21, 1966.

34. Han Zongping, "A True Record of the Thirteen-Year Injustice Against Lu Dingyi," *Yanhuang Chunqiu*, no. 8, 2006.

35. Chen Qingquan, *Fifty Years in the High Echelon of the Central Committee: The Amazing Life of Lu Dingyi*, PDF, p. 291.

36. Han Zongping, "True Record of the Thirteen-Year Injustice Against Lu Dingyi."

37. TN: That is, the families of Chiang Kai-shek, Charlie Soong, Kung Hsiang-hsi, and Chen Qi-mei.

38. Liu Shaoqi's remarks to a symposium of democratic personages convened by the CCP Central Committee on the afternoon of June 27, 1966, in the Anhui Hall of the Great Hall of the People, with Deng Xiaoping presiding.

39. Wang Wenyao and Wang Baochun, *Chen Boda Before and After the Cultural Revolution: A Secretary's Testimony*, Hong Kong: Cosmos Books (Tiandi tushu chubanshe), 2014, pp. 49–50.

40. Ye Xiangzhen, "My Father and I in the Cultural Revolution," in *Light and Shadow in Home and Country: Descendants of the Founding Fathers Talk About the Past and Present*, ed. Zhou Haibin, Renmin chubanshe, 2011. Zhou Enlai recounted this incident in detail on January 24, 1970, when he, Kang Sheng, and Jiang Qing received representatives of the PLA Mao Zedong Thought Propaganda Teams from the Ministry of Culture, Ministry of Education, and other units under the direct jurisdiction of the central apparatus. He remarked, "This wasn't a rebellious action of the Great Proletarian Cultural Revolution; it surpassed resorting to violence and became kidnapping. After that, many other places followed their example." *The Memoirs of Wang Dabin*, p. 100, also describes this incident.

4. THE MAY CONFERENCE

1. Many writers say Jiang Qing attended the May Conference, but based on Yan Changgui's detailed verification, Jiang Qing was in Shanghai at the time and didn't return to Beijing until July 20. See Yan Changgui and Wang Guangyu, *Inquiring of History and Seeking Truth*, Hongqi chubanshe, 2009, p. 239.

2. Qi Benyu told Yu Ruxin that this conference was ostensibly run by Liu Shaoqi, but in fact the core role was played by Zhou Enlai, who better comprehended Mao's intentions. See Yu Ruxin, "A Face-to-Face Talk with Qi Benyu," in the electronic magazine *Fenghuayuan*, no. 432 (January 9, 2004).

3. Lin Biao's speech to the enlarged meeting of the Central Committee Political Bureau, May 18, 1966, *Chinese Cultural Revolution Database*, ed. Song Yongyi et al., 3rd ed., Universities Service Centre for China Studies, Chinese University of Hong Kong Press, 2013.

4. Zhou Enlai's speech to the enlarged meeting of the Central Committee Political Bureau, May 21, 1966, in Song Yongyi et al., *Chinese Cultural Revolution Database*.

5. Wang Li, *Wang Li's Record of Introspection*, vol. 2, Hong Kong: Beixing chubanshe, May 2005, p. 214.

6. Li Xuefeng, "My Inside Knowledge of How the Cultural Revolution Was Launched," in *Recollecting the Cultural Revolution*, ed. Zhang Hua et al., Zhonggong dangshi chubanshe, 2007, p. 595; Chen Xiaonong, *Chen Boda's Final Oral Recollections*, Beijing: Dongfang chubanshe, 2010, pp. 286–287. Both books provide the same account.

7. Wang Li, *Wang Li's Record of Introspection*, vol. 2, pp. 213–214.

8. Qi Benyu told Yu Ruxin that Lin Biao gave his "May 18 speech" on Zhou Enlai's instructions. See Yu Ruxin, "Face-to-Face Talk with Qi Benyu."

9. Wang Li, *Wang Li's Record of Introspection*, vol. 1, Hong Kong: Beixing chubanshe, January 2008, p. 23.

10. Wang Nianyi, "An Informal Chat About the Cultural Revolution," *Ershiyi Shiji (Twenty-First Century;* Hong Kong), October 2006.

11. Quoted in Bu Weihua, *Smashing the Old World: Havoc of the Chinese Cultural Revolution (1966–1968)*, Chinese University of Hong Kong Press, 2008, p. 83.

12. Xi Xuan and Jin Chunming, *A Concise History of the Cultural Revolution*, new edition, Zhonggong dangshi chubanshe, 2011, p. 46.

13. *Down with the Three-Oppositionist Element He Long*, vol. 1, compiled by the Beijing Denounce Three-Oppositionist Element He Long Liaison Station, reproduced by the Red Guard Congress National Sports Committee Athletics Department Mao Zedong Thought Red Guard Unit, pp. 2–3.

14. Stated in a report given to Kang Sheng at the end of 1967 by the First Office of the Central Special Investigation Committee; see *History's Trials (Continued)*, Beijing: Qunzhong chubanshe, 1986, p. 91.

15. Cheng Guang, *Dialogue of the Soul: Qiu Huizuo Discusses the Cultural Revolution with His Son*, Hong Kong: Beixing chubanshe, 2011, pp. 70–71; Qiu Huizuo, *The Memoirs of Qiu Huizuo*, Hong Kong: Xinshiji chubanshe (New Century Press), 2011, p. 524, says that Lin Biao spoke of He Long's problems at the enlarged CMC Standing Committee meeting on September 6, 1966, in the Sichuan Hall of the Great Hall of the People, with Zheng Hantao and others from Xiao Hua's office taking notes. Page 884 of Qiu's

memoirs also mentions this speech by Lin Biao in early September but doesn't specify its content. It's possible that when editing the book, Cheng Guang spoke with Lin Biao and then added this in.

16. Li Zuopeng, *The Memoirs of Li Zuopeng*, Hong Kong: Beixing chubanshe, 2011, pp. 568–569; Xian Henghan, *Eighty Years of Trials and Hardships*, electronic edition; Huang Zhengzhao, *Soldier Yongsheng*, vol. 2, Hong Kong: Xinshiji chubanshe (New Century Press), 2011, p. 266.

17. Li Youhua, "The Whole Story of Li Zhonggong's Framing of He Long," *History World*, no. 11 (2009).

18. CCP Central Committee Documentary Research Room (ed.), *Chronology of Mao Zedong: 1949–1976*, vol. 6, p. 514.

19. CCP Central Committee Documentary Research Room, *Biography of Mao Zedong: 1949–1976*, Zhongyang wenxian chubanshe, 2003, p. 1689.

20. Speeches by Kang Sheng, Jiang Qing, and Chen Boda at Beijing Normal University, July 27, 1966, in Song Yongyi et al., *Chinese Cultural Revolution Database*.

21. Qian Gang, "The Truth About the 'February Coup d'Etat,'" *PLA Daily*, December 7, 1980.

22. Qian Gang, "Truth About the 'February Coup d'Etat.'"

23. CCP Central Committee Documentary Research Room (ed.), *Chronology of Zhou Enlai*, vol. 2, Zhongyang wenxian chubanshe, 1997, pp. 31–32.

24. Zhang Min, *Zhou Enlai and the Capital Work Group*, Zhongyang wenxian chubanshe, 2009, pp. 74–75.

25. Zhang Min, *Zhou Enlai and the Capital Work Group*, pp. 74–76.

26. Zhang Min, *Zhou Enlai and the Capital Work Group*, p. 77.

27. TN: The February Countercurrent will be described in detail in chapter 11.

28. Chen Boda joined the CCP in 1927. At the Eighth National Party Congress, he was made an alternate member of the Politburo, deputy director of the Central Committee Propaganda Department, deputy director of the Chinese Academy of Sciences, and editor in chief of the Central Party's official magazine *Red Flag*, among other postings.

29. Kang Sheng joined the CCP in 1925. During the Yan'an Rectification Movement, he served as vice-chairman of the Central General Study Committee, among other postings, and assisted Mao in labeling many revolutionaries as "secret agents." In September 1956, at the first plenum of the Eighth Central Committee, Kang was made an alternate Politburo member, and in 1958 he served as vice-chairman of the Central Committee's Cultural and Education Group and took charge of editing volume 4 of *The Selected Works of Mao Zedong* as well as other cultural and educational work. In September 1962, during the tenth plenum of the Eighth Central Committee, he was made a secretary of the Central Committee Secretariat.

30. Liu Zhijian was conferred with the rank of lieutenant general in 1955. He served as deputy director of the PLA General Political Department before the Cultural Revolution.

31. Wang Li, *Wang Li's Record of Introspection*, vol. 2, p. 33. According to Yan Changgui's recollections, Jiang Qing returned to Beijing on the July 20.

32. Wang Wenyao and Wang Baochun, *Chen Boda Before and After the Cultural Revolution: A Secretary's Testimony*, Hong Kong: Cosmos Books (Tiandi tushu chubanshe), 2014, pp. 45–46.

33. Song Yongyi et al., *Chinese Cultural Revolution Database*.

34. TN: Between urban and rural areas, industry and agriculture, and physical and mental labor.

35. In 1871, France's crushing defeat in the Franco-Prussian War led to an uprising by the people of Paris. The uprising established a political regime on March 18, 1871, called the Paris Commune, which was eliminated on May 28. There are enormous discrepancies in descriptions and commentaries regarding the Paris Commune. Marx gave it a very high appraisal as the first attempt in world history to overturn bourgeois rule and establish dictatorship of the proletariat.

36. Karl Marx, *The Civil War in France*, in *Selected Works of Marx and Engels*, vol. 2, Renmin chubanshe, 1972, pp. 375–378. TN: The English translation is taken from Karl Marx, *The Civil War in France*, English edition of 1871, as provided in the Marxists Internet Archive, marxists.org/archive/marx/works/1871/civil-war-france/ch05.htm.

37. Frederick Engels, "Introduction to Marx's *The Civil War in France*," in *Selected Works of Marx and Engels*, pp. 334, 336. TN: The English translation is drawn from the Marxists Internet Archive, marxists.org/archive/marx/works/1871/civil-war-france/postscript.htm.

38. Wang Li, *Wang Li's Record of Introspection*, vol. 2, p. 109.

39. In remarks at an enlarged Politburo meeting on December 6, 1966, Zhou Enlai said, "Now that we want to implement a rationing system, we must ensure a good ideological foundation." In a speech at the meeting on December 4, Kang Sheng said, "The old economic patterns haven't changed in our factories, and in terms of trading, the pattern of commodity equal value exchange hasn't changed. Wages are still paid based on labor, and the remnants of bourgeois prerogative still exist." While receiving representatives of the rebel faction in Beijing's tertiary institutions on December 18, Jiang Qing said, "Recently we've done away with rank." Wang Li recalls that Mao clearly stated in December 1966 that he wanted to implement a rationing system and do away with the salary system.

40. Specifically, Song Shuo, director of the Universities Department of the Beijing municipal party committee; Lu Ping, party secretary of Peking University; and Peng Peiyun, the university's deputy party secretary.

41. Song Yongyi et al., *Chinese Cultural Revolution Database*.

42. Guo Dehong and Lin Xiaobo, *A True Record of the Four Cleanups Campaign*, Zhejiang renmin chubanshe, 2005, pp. 187–203.

43. Nie Yuanzi, *The Memoirs of Nie Yuanzi*, Hong Kong: Shidai guoji youxian gongsi, 2005, pp. 115–116.

44. In the 1990s, Zhang Enci and Yang Keming both denied that they accompanied Nie Yuanzi to see Cao Yi'ou. It's possible that Nie went alone.

45. *Biography of Mao Zedong*, p. 1407.

46. CCP Central Committee Documentary Research Room (ed.), *Chronology of Mao Zedong: 1949–1976*, vol. 5, p. 593.

5. LIU SHAOQI'S ANTI-RIGHTIST MOVEMENT

1. There are different versions of the measures Liu Shaoqi and Deng Xiaoping took in opposition to Mao. Wang Nianyi believes that Mao "put his cards on the table to Jiang Qing, then Kang Sheng and Lin Biao," but that Liu and Deng didn't know Mao's true intentions, and that's why divisions arose

between them (Wang Nianyi, *Era of Upheaval*, Henan renmin chubanshe, 1988, pp. 26–27). I endorse an alternative view, which holds that Liu's and Deng's political insight should not be underestimated and that there was an intentionality in their resistance to Mao.

2. Chen Boda took the work group to *People's Daily* with Mao's agreement.
3. Zhou Enlai, Speech at Tsinghua University, August 5, 1966, in *Chinese Cultural Revolution Database*, ed. Song Yongyi et al., 3rd ed., Universities Service Centre for China Studies, Chinese University of Hong Kong Press, 2013.
4. TN: It is also the case that the author is most familiar with, as he was a student at Tsinghua at the time.
5. Chen Jifang and Ma Xiaozhuang, *Rising and Falling Tide*, [publisher not identified] 2001, p. 22.
6. Liu Tao, "Rebel Against Liu Shaoqi, Spend Your Life Making Revolution with Chairman Mao: My Preliminary Self-Criticism" (composed December 28, 1966), *Jinggang Mountain Daily* (Tsinghua University), December 31, 1966. Subsequently Liu Shaoqi denied saying this, but Liu Tao said, "It's for him to deny and me to expose."
7. Kuai Dafu, "Statement Regarding the June 27 Rally," June 28, 1966, *Fifty Days of the Cultural Revolution at Tsinghua*, Hong Kong: Zhongguo wenhua chuanbo chubanshe, 2014, p. 127.
8. Li Xuefeng, "Remembering the 'Fifty-Day Line Errors' of the Early Stage of the 'Cultural Revolution': From the 'June 18' Incident to the 'July 29' Rally," *CCP Party History Research*, no. 4, 1998.
9. CCP Central Committee Documentary Research Room (ed.), *Chronology of Mao Zedong: 1949–1976*, p. 593.
10. Mao Mao, *My Father, Deng Xiaoping: The Cultural Revolution Years*, Zhongyang wenxian chubanshe, 2000, p. 20.
11. Mao Mao, *My Father, Deng Xiaoping*, p. 20.
12. "Indignantly Denouncing the Bourgeois Reactionary Line's Persecution of Us," Red Guards Representative Meeting Central Finance Institute Beijing Commune 8-8 Battle Corps Beijing Commune, April 20, 1967.
13. TN: Referring to the Hungarian Uprising, a nationwide popular revolt against the government of the Hungarian People's Republic from October 23 to November 10, 1956.
14. Wang Dabin, *The Memoirs of Wang Dabin*, Hong Kong: Zhongguo wenge lishi chubanshe, 2015, p. 15; Red Guards Capital Third Department, ed., *Earthshakingly Vehement and Fervent: A Chronicle of the Great Proletarian Cultural Revolution (December 1963–October 1, 1967)*, Beijing, 1967; Song Yongyi et al., *Chinese Cultural Revolution Database*.
15. Li Xuefeng, "Remembering the 'Fifty-Day Line Errors' of the Early Stage of the 'Cultural Revolution.'"
16. Zhou Liangxiao and Gu Juying, *Chronicle of the Ten-Year Cultural Revolution*, Xindalu chubanshe youxian gongsi, 2008, p. 80.
17. Zhou Liangxiao and Gu Juying, *Chronicle of the Ten-Year Cultural Revolution*, p. 165.
18. Xu Hailiang, *Storm on the East Lake: Wuhan's Masses Recall the Cultural Revolution*, Yinhe chubanshe, 2005, pp. 7, 14, 16.
19. Liu Guokai, *A Brief Analysis of the Cultural Revolution*, Hong Kong: Boda chubanshe, 2006, p. 10.
20. Xu Hailiang, *Storm on the East Lake*, p. 27.

21. Zhou Liangxiao and Gu Juying, *Chronicle of the Ten-Year Cultural Revolution*, p. 94.

22. Ma Shitu, *Ten Years of Great Changes*, Beijing: Zhonggong Zhongyang dangshi chubanshe, 1999, p. 72. Ma Shitu (b. 1915) joined the revolution early on. After 1949, he served as director of the Sichuan provincial party committee's organization department and other positions, and he was a famous writer.

23. Xiao Xidong, "Fifty Days in 1966: Recalled and Forgotten Politics." The quotes from the material compiled by the New Peking University Commune 01621 Detachment are drawn from Xiao Xidong's article.

24. Liu Shaoqi, "Speech When Receiving a Report from the Work Team of the Beijing Normal University No. 1 Secondary School," June 20, 1966, in *Material for Criticism: Collected Counterrevolutionary Revisionist Discourse of the Chinese Khrushchev, Liu Shaoqi, June 1958 to July 1967*, ed. People's Publishing Reference Room, internal distribution edition, Renmin chubanshe ziliaoshi, September 10, 1967, pp. 669–670.

25. "'Attack a Large Part, Protect a Small Pinch,' How Venomous!," Capital Secondary School Red Guard Congress Army Battlefield Report, April 10, 1967; "Bombard Liu Shaoqi: Denouncing the Monstrous Crimes of Liu Shaoqi at the Beijing Normal University No. 1 Affiliated Secondary School," *Revolutionary Link-Up Daily* (Peking University), January 9, 1967.

26. Liu Shaoqi, "Instructions When Discussing the 'Preliminary Plan for the Cultural Revolution in Beijing Secondary Schools,'" July 13, 1967, in *Material for Criticism*, p. 689.

27. Deng Rong, "Exposure of Deng Xiaoping," in *Thorough Exposure and Criticism of Deng Xiaoping's Monstrous Crimes in the Great Proletarian Cultural Revolution*, ed. New Peking University Commune 02621 Detachment, 1967, p. 4.

28. CCP Jiangsu Provincial Party Committee Party History Office, *The Story of Chen Guang*, Jiangsu renmin chubanshe, 2005, p. 225.

29. Nanjing Municipal Archives, *Chronicle of the Cultural Revolution in Nanjing*, mimeographed first draft, 1985, p. 5.

30. "Thoroughly Denounce the Bourgeois Reactionary line of Wang Renzhong's Work Team on the Problem of Wuhan University Cadres," Wuhan Red Guards Third Department, *The East Is Red*, May 11, 1967.

31. "The Workers Have Spoken" was the title of the first essay that *People's Daily* published signifying the turn from rectification of the party's work styles to the Anti-Rightist Campaign in 1957.

32. Zhang Jiancheng, *The Scars Left by Time: A Personal Record of the Cultural Revolution at the Wuhan Institute of Hydraulic and Electric Engineering*, Hong Kong: Zhongguo wenhua chuanbo chubanshe, 2014, pp. 97–104.

33. Xu Hailiang, "Wuhan in Spring and Summer 1966," *Wangshi*, no. 21 (August 29, 2005).

34. Mao spoke of the incident at Xi'an Jiaotong University twice, on July 21 and 22, and he also said, "Xi'an Jiaotong University is restricting people from making telephone calls, sending cables, or petitioning Beijing. "See *Long Live Mao Zedong Thought (1961–1968)* (further publication information unavailable), p. 262.

35. Women involved in "inappropriate" relationships with men were referred to as "worn-out shoes" (similar to "round-heels" in English), and parading female students through the streets was extremely humiliating.

36. Deng Zhenxin, *Storm in Guizhou*, Hong Kong: Zhongguo guoji wenyi chuban-she, 2014, pp. 41–44.
37. Mao Mao, *My Father, Deng Xiaoping*, p. 21.
38. Li Xuefeng, "Remembering the 'Fifty-Day Line Errors' of the Early Stage of the 'Cultural Revolution,'" pp. 650–651.
39. Chen Xiaonong, *Chen Boda's Final Oral Recollections*, Beijing: Dongfang chubanshe, 2010, p. 312.
40. Wang Li, *Wang Li's Record of Introspection*, vol. 2, 2nd ed., Hong Kong: Beixing chubanshe, May 2011, p. 31.
41. Li Xuefeng, "Remembering the 'Fifty-Day Line Errors' of the Early Stage of the 'Cultural Revolution,'" pp. 650–651.
42. CCP Central Committee Documentary Research Room (ed.), *Chronology of Mao Zedong: 1949–1976*, vol. 5, Zhongyang wenxian chubanshe, p. 600.
43. Wu De, as told to Zhu Shiyuan et al., *Wu De's Oral Account: A Chronicle of Ten Years of Trials and Hardships—Some of My Experiences Working in Beijing*, Dangdai Zhongguo chubanshe, 2004, p. 10.
44. Wu De, *Wu De's Oral Account*, p. 10.
45. The first group was ten students who criticized the work teams, including Lei Rong, Wang Xiaoping, Zhang Dai'er, and Yang Jisheng (the author); the second group was ten students who protected the work team, including He Pengfei and Liu Tao.
46. Kuai Dafu, "Statement Regarding the June 27 Rally," pp. 87–91.
47. Wang Li, *Wang Li's Record of Introspection*, pp. 32–33.
48. Xu Aijing, *Tsinghua's Kuai Dafu*, Hong Kong: Zhongguo wenhua lishi chu-banshe, 2001, p. 93.
49. Mao Mao, *My Father, Deng Xiaoping*, p. 23.

6. MAJOR INCIDENTS DURING THE ELEVENTH PLENUM

1. Qiu Huizuo, *The Memoirs of Qiu Huizuo*, Hong Kong: Xinshiji chubanshe (New Century Press), 2011, p. 434.
2. Qiu Huizuo, *Memoirs of Qiu Huizuo*, p. 443.
3. Wang Li, *Wang Li's Record of Introspection*, vol. 2, 2nd ed., Hong Kong: Beixing chubanshe, May 2011, p. 35.
4. Zhou Liangxiao and Gu Juying, *Chronicle of the Ten-Year Cultural Revolution*, Xindalu chubanshe youxian gongsi, 2008, p. 109.
5. Xi Xuan and Jin Chunming, *A Concise History of the Cultural Revolution*, new edition, Zhonggong dangshi chubanshe, 2011.
6. Central Committee Documentary Research Office, *Anthology of Material from Ten Years of the Cultural Revolution*, quoted in Gao Wenqian, *Zhou Enlai's Later Years*, Mingjing chubanshe, 2004, 26th printing, p. 125.
7. TN: That is, he wasn't afraid of being dismissed, demoted, or expelled from the party, having his marriage broken up, or being imprisoned or executed.
8. Central Committee Documentary Research Office, *Anthology of Material from Ten Years of the Cultural Revolution*.
9. Bu Weihua, *Smashing the Old World: Havoc of the Chinese Cultural Revolution (1966–1968)*, Chinese University of Hong Kong Press, 2008, pp. 191–192.
10. CCP Central Committee Documentary Research Room (ed.), *Chronology of Zhou Enlai*, vol. 2, Zhongyang wenxian chubanshe, 1997, p. 46.

11. Bu Weihua, *Smashing the Old World*, p. 194.
12. Wu Faxian, *The Memoirs of Wu Faxian*, Hong Kong: Beixing chubanshe, 3rd ed., February 2008, pp. 506, 597.
13. Qiu Huizuo, *Memoirs of Qiu Huizuo*, p. 444.
14. Guan Weixun, *The Ye Qun I Knew*, Zhongguo wenxue chubanshe, May 1993, p. 218.
15. CCP Central Committee Documentary Research Room (ed.), *Chronology of Zhou Enlai*, vol. 2, p. 46.
16. Ma Encheng, "Tao Zhu in 1966," *Bainianchao*, no. 11 (1999). Ma was Tao Zhu's secretary.
17. Wang Nianyi, "An Informal Chat About the Cultural Revolution, *Ershiyi Shiji* (*Twenty-First Century*; Hong Kong), October 2006.
18. "Ye Jianying's Remarks When Receiving Representatives of Teachers and Students from 13 Beijing Art Institutes," September 25, 1996.
19. "Ye Jianying's Remarks at a Mass Rally of 100,000 People at the Beijing Workers' Stadium," October 5, 1966.
20. Cheng Guang, *Dialogue of the Soul: Qiu Huizuo Discusses the Cultural Revolution with His Son*, vol. 1, Hong Kong: Beixing chubanshe, 2011, p. 43.
21. Ibid., p. 43.
22. Ibid., p. 63.
23. Wang Li, *Wang Li's Record of Introspection*, pp. 36–37.
24. Zhou Liangxiao and Gu Juying, *Chronicle of the Ten-Year Cultural Revolution*, p. 114.
25. TN· The "four bigs," or *sida*, refer to the slogan from the anti-rightist movement to speak out freely, air views fully, write big-character posters, and hold great debates (*daming, dafang, dazibao, dabianlun*).
26. CCP Central Committee Party History Research Room, *History of the Chinese Communist Party*, vol. 2, *1949–1973*, Zhonggong dangshi chubanshe, 2011, p. 967.
27. Qin Xiao, as told to Tang Xin and Mi Hedu, "Leaving Utopia," in *Oral Histories of Notable People of the Red Guard Era*, vol. 1, Zhongguo shuju, 2001, pp. 98–99.
28. Sun Yancheng, "Blood Lineage Theory and the August 31 Daxing Massacre," *Yanhuang Chunqiu*, no. 2, 2012.
29. Mi Hedu, *Initiation of the Generation Growing Up with the PRC*, Zhongyang wenxian chubanshe, 2011, p. 82.
30. Xiao Ling, "Tsinghua Affiliated Secondary School and the Red Guard Movement," *Yanhuang Chunqiu*, no. 10, 2011.
31. Mi Hedu, *Initiation of the Generation Growing Up with the PRC*, p. 75.
32. Core Group of the 65-5 Class, Tsinghua University Affiliated Secondary School, "Stand tall," quoted in Mi Hedu, *Initiation of the Generation Growing Up with the PRC*, p. 137.
33. Luo Xiaohai, preface, in Song Bolin, *The Rise and Fall of the Red Guards*, Hong Kong: Desai chuban gongsi, 2006, p. 17.
34. Luo Xiaohai, *Rise and Fall of the Red Guards*, pp. 17–21.
35. Liu Shaoqi, "Directive While Discussing the 'Preliminary Plan for the Cultural Revolution in Beijing Secondary Schools,'" July 13, 1967, in *Material for Criticism: Collected Counterrevolutionary Revisionist Speech by China's Khrushchev, Liu Shaoqi*, Renmin chubanshe ziliaoshi, internally circulated in September 1967, p. 691.

36. Song Yongyi et al., eds., *Chinese Cultural Revolution Database*, 3rd ed., Universities Service Centre for China Studies, Chinese University of Hong Kong Press, 2013.

37. Song Yongyi et al., *Chinese Cultural Revolution Database*.

38. Song Yongyi et al., *Chinese Cultural Revolution Database*.

39. Luo Xiaohai, *Rise and Fall of the Red Guards*, p. 22.

40. Mao Zedong, "Letter to Tsinghua Secondary School Red Guards," August 1, 1966, Song Yongyi et al., *Chinese Cultural Revolution Database*.

7. THE RED GUARDS AND RED AUGUST

1. Zhang Min, *Zhou Enlai and the Capital Work Group*, Zhongyang wenxian chubanshe, 2009, pp. 118, 120.

2. Bu Weihua, *Smashing the Old World: Havoc of the Chinese Cultural Revolution (1966–1968)*, Chinese University of Hong Kong Press, 2008, p. 206. There are other versions of the Red Guards going into the Tiananmen gate tower: Qin Xiaoying and Ma Li's *Illusory Red August* says that this was arranged in advance and that Red Guards went there with paper invitations.

3. Zhang Min, *Zhou Enlai and the Capital Work Group*, p. 145.

4. Zhang Huican and Mu An, "The Inside Story of Mao Zedong Receiving the Red Guards Eight Times," *Yanhuang Chunqiu*, no. 4, 2006.

5. Yin Hongbiao, *Footprints of the Lost*, Chinese University of Hong Kong Press, 2010, pp. 32–33.

6. Song Bolin, *The Rise and Fall of the Red Guards*, Hong Kong: Desai chuban gongsi, 2006, p. 92.

7. After the Cultural Revolution, Tan Lifu changed his name to Tan Bin and published articles in *People's Daily* criticizing blood lineage theory as a prominent Old Red Guard, blaming Jiang Qing for the notion. In 1987, Tan Lifu, by then a senior colonel, changed professions and became general manager of the personnel department of Kanghua, the company run by Deng Xiaoping's son Deng Pufang. He subsequently served as party secretary and assistant director of the National Library, as party secretary of the Palace Museum, and as director of the Ministry of Culture's general office.

8. These incidents at various schools are drawn from Wang Youqin, "Horrifying Red August," *Yanhuang Chunqiu*, no. 10, 2010.

9. This group was organized by the university's work group, and its leading members included offspring of senior cadres such as Liu Tao (Liu Shaoqi's daughter), He Pengfei (He Long's son), Li Lifeng (Li Jingquan's son), and Qiao Zongzhun (Qiao Guanhua's son).

10. TN: A pejorative label for cadres and intellectuals allegedly associated with the old Beijing municipal party committee.

11. Liu Bing, *Years of Trials: Tsinghua 1964–1967*, Dangdai Zhongguo chubanshe, 2008, pp. 83–85.

12. Luo Zhengqi, "The Forgotten 'Red Terror': Remembering the 'Cultural Revolution' at Tsinghua University in 1966," revised August 20, 2008.

13. The "yin-yang" haircut, in which a person's hair was cut off on only one side, was a common way of humiliating people during the Cultural Revolution.

14. Wang Hui, *A Personal History of the Cultural Revolution in Tianjin*, self-published, 2011, p. 89.

15. Zhang Min, *Zhou Enlai and the Capital Work Group*, pp. 272–273.
16. *Beijing Evening News*, February 23, 1987.
17. A speech by Ma Yongjiang, a member of the Chinese People's Political Consultative Conference, published in *People's Daily* on April 9, 1985.
18. Beijing Municipal Party Committee Party History Research Office, *Concise History of the Chinese Communist Party in Beijing*, Beijing chubanshe, 2011, p. 113.
19. Wang Nianyi, *Era of Upheaval*, Henan renmin chubanshe, 1988, p. 71.
20. Mi Hedu, *Motivations: A Perspective on Contemporaries in the Republic*, Zhongyang wenxian chubanshe, 2011.
21. Editing Group of Historical Materials of the Cultural Revolution in Shanghai, *Historical Narrative of Shanghai's Cultural Revolution*, 1994, p. 105.
22. Xu Hailiang, *Storm on the East Lake: Wuhan's Masses Recall the Cultural Revolution*, Yinhe chubanshe, 2005.
23. Bu Weihua, *Smashing the Old World*, p. 233.
24. Bu Weihua, *Smashing the Old World*, p. 234.
25. TN: China's oldest Buddhist temple, built in the first century c.e.
26. The Capital Work Group's other responsibilities included the deployment and transfer of the security forces of the People's Armed Police; investigating private organizations and private radio transmission and confiscating privately owned radios; strengthening the ranks of prison and labor camp guards; and dealing with diplomatic security and overseas Chinese.
27. Wang Youqin, "Horrifying Red August."
28. Xi Xuan and Jin Chunming, *A Concise History of the Cultural Revolution*, new edition, Zhonggong dangshi chubanshe, 2011, p. 316.
29. Wang Hui, *Personal History of the Cultural Revolution in Tianjin*, p. 158.
30. Shandong Provincial Party Committee Party History Research Office, Shandong Provincial Archives, eds., *Chronicle of Shandong During the "Cultural Revolution" Period (May 1966–October 1976)*, March 2001.
31. Zhong Jieying, "A Rightist Seeing Off a Puppet Township Head," in *We in That Time*, vol. 1, ed. Zhe Yongping, Yuanfang chubanshe, 1998.
32. "Comrade Ye Jianying's Remarks When Receiving Some Teacher and Student Representatives of 13 Arts Academies," September 25, 1966, in United Compilation Group, *Anthology of Speeches by Leading Cadres*, March 1967, p. 169.
33. Wu De, as told to Zhu Yuanshi et al., *Wu De's Oral Account: A Chronicle of Ten Years of Trials and Hardships—Some of My Experiences Working in Beijing*, Dangdai Zhongguo chubanshe, August 2004, p. 27.
34. Wang Li, *Wang Li's Record of Introspection*, vol. 2, 2nd ed., Hong Kong: Beixing chubanshe, 2008, pp. 52–53.
35. Except where otherwise noted, the material in this section is drawn from Wang Youqin, "Horrifying Red August."
36. Red Guards of the Tsinghua University Affiliated Secondary School, Renmin University Affiliated Secondary School, and Beijing Institute of Aeronautics Affiliated Secondary School, "Red Guards Urgent Letter of Appeal," published in *I Ask, on this Boundless Land, Who Rules over Man's Destiny*, an anthology of Red Guard big-character posters compiled and printed by the Red Guards of the Tsinghua University Affiliated Secondary School in September 1966.
37. Zhang Min, *Zhou Enlai and the Capital Work Group*, p. 167.
38. The couple was posthumously rehabilitated on March 26, 1981.

39. See Zhou Enlai's speech to the Second Assembly of Capital University and Secondary School Red Guard Representatives on September 10, 1966.

40. Li Xiang, "The Murders at No. 20 Dahongluocang, Beijing," originally published in *Southern Weekend*, quoted in Song Yongyi, ed., *Cultural Revolution Massacres*, Hong Kong: Kaifang zazhishe, 2002, pp. 3–11.

41. Wang Nianyi, *Era of Upheaval*, p. 77.

42. Zhang Min, *Zhou Enlai and the Capital Work Group*, p. 172.

43. Zhang Min, *Zhou Enlai and the Capital Work Group*, p. 170.

44. Wang Youqin, "Horrifying Red August."

45. Du Junfu, "The Truth Behind the Xicheng Pickets Must Be Clarified," *Remembrance*, no. 58.

46. Wang Youqin, "Student Attacks on Teachers: The 1966 Revolution," Yannan Community, 2003.

47. Beijing No. 6 Secondary School Beijing Commune, "The Heinous Crimes of the Liu-Deng Line at the No. 6 Secondary School," *Chinese Cultural Revolution Database*, ed. Song Yongyi et al., 3rd ed., Universities Service Centre for China Studies, Chinese University of Hong Kong Press, 2013.

48. Speeches by Jiang Qing, Chen Boda, Zhou Enlai, etc., in "Speeches by Central Leading Cadres at the National Mass Rally for Rebel Factions in Beijing to Criticize the Reactionary Line," December 17, 1966, in Song Yongyi et al., *Chinese Cultural Revolution Database*.

49. Zhang Guangyu, *Farewell, Senior Statesman*, Hong Kong: Beixing chubanshe, 2007, pp. 60–64.

50. Mi Hedu, *Motivations*, p. 239.

51. TN: See chapter 22.

52. Quoted in Zhou Liangxiao and Gu Juying, *Chronicle of the Ten-Year Cultural Revolution*, Xindalu chubanshe youxian gongsi, 2008, pp. 217–218.

53. Wang Li, *Wang Li's Record of Introspection*, p. 175.

54. Wang Li, *Wang Li's Record of Introspection*, p. 179.

55. TN: The February Countercurrent will be described in detail in chapter 11.

56. Mao Zedong's remarks when receiving five major Red Guard leaders on July 28, 1968.

57. Wang Li, *Wang Li's Record of Introspection*, p. 180.

8. DENOUNCING THE BOURGEOIS REACTIONARY LINE

1. "The Bogus Self-Criticisms Recently Submitted by the Number One Capitalist Roaders Within the Shanghai Party, Chen Pixian and Cao Huoqiu" (provided for mass criticism purposes), July 1967, distributed by the Shanghai Municipal Periodicals Distribution Office, p. 20.

2. TN: "Five-good workers" had been assessed to perform well in executing tasks, observing discipline, undertaking regular political study, and displaying unity and mutual aid.

3. "The Bogus Self-Criticisms Recently Submitted," p. 21.

4. Zhang Wenbao, "Four Visits with Chen Pixian in 1966," *Yanhuang Chunqiu*, no. 7, 2011.

5. "Wei Guoqing's Faithful Execution of Liu Shaoqi's Counterrevolutionary Revisionist Line During the Struggle Between the Two Lines," Guilin Secondary and Tertiary School Red Guard Headquarters *Red Guard Daily*, May 10, 1967.

6. Deng Zhenxin, *Collected Writings on Major Events in the Guizhou Cultural Revolution*, 5th revised ed. and expanded draft.

7. Unless otherwise noted, the contents of this section are drawn from Yang Daqing, "Zhang Pinghua's September 24 Report and the Campaign to Attack 'Black Devils.'"

8. Yang Xiaokai, "Political Persecution in the Cultural Revolution and the Citizens' Movement Against Political Persecution," *China Spring*, May 1993.

9. TN: At that time, Hua Guofeng was a member of the provincial committee secretariat and party secretary of Xiangtan Prefecture. He later became provincial first secretary.

10. Wang Bifeng, *A Concise History of the CCP in Hunan (1921–2000)*, Hunan renmin chubanshe, 2001.

11. Zhang Jiancheng, *The Scars Left by Time: A Personal Record of the Cultural Revolution at the Wuhan Institute of Hydraulic and Electric Engineering*, Hong Kong: Zhongguo wenhua chuanbo chubanshe, 2014, pp. 114–117.

12. Drawn from "We Should Apply Remaining Courage to Pursuing the Hard-Pressed Foe, Do Not Stoop to Fame Like the Overlord Xiang Yu: Thoroughly Expose and Criticize the Heinous Crimes of the Counterrevolutionary Revisionist Li Jingquan and His Pinch of Confederates in the Great Proletarian Cultural Revolution," Chengdu Anti-Li Main Station Education Apparatus Liaison Station *Education Revolution*, no. 6, 1968.

13. Xiao Xidong, "Leaders and Masses in the Cultural Revolution: Discourse, Conflict, and Collective Action."

14. "A Record of the Restoration of the Underground Provincial Party Committee," *Worker Rebel Daily*, January 21, 1968.

15. "Record of Criminal Acts by Jiang Weiqing Hired Instrument the (Workers') Red Guards," combined issue of *Jiangsu Red Headquarters* and *Serf Trident*, January 3, 1968.

16. *Manuscripts of Mao Zedong*, vol. 12, Zhongyang wenxian chubanshe, 1998, p. 124.

17. Zhou Liangxiao and Gu Juying, *Chronicle of the Ten-Year Cultural Revolution*, Xindalu chubanshe youxian gongsi, 2008, p. 150.

18. Wang Li, *Wang Li's Record of Introspection*, vol. 2, 2nd ed., Hong Kong: Beixing chubanshe, May 2011, pp. 42–43.

19. Wang Li, *Wang Li's Record of Introspection*, p. 44.

20. Wang Dabin, *The Memoirs of Wang Dabin*, Hong Kong: Zhongguo wenge lishi chubanshe, 2015, pp. 20–23.

21. Zhou Enlai, "Speech at the Mass Pledge Rally to Fiercely Opening Fire on the Bourgeois Reactionary Line," October 6, 1966, in Song Yongyi et al., *Chinese Cultural Revolution Database*.

22. Zhang Jiancheng, *Scars Left by Time*, p. 124.

23. Wang Li, *Wang Li's Record of Introspection*, pp. 42, 44.

24. Wang Li, *Wang Li's Record of Introspection*, pp. 50–51.

25. Subsequently handed down under the title "A Summary of Two Months of the Movement."

26. *Manuscripts of Mao Zedong*, p. 141.

27. Ma Encheng, "Tao Zhu in 1966," *Bainianchao*, no. 11, 1999.

28. Wang Li, *Wang Li's Record of Introspection*, p. 47.

29. *Manuscripts of Mao Zedong*, p. 134.

30. Wang Li, *Wang Li's Record of Introspection*, p. 47.

31. Wang Li, *Wang Li's Record of Introspection*, p. 48.
32. "Liu Shaoqi's Self-Criticism at the Central Committee Work Conference, October 23, 1966," in *Written Self-Criticisms in the Cultural Revolution*, ed. Shi Shi, Taipei: Shiying chubanshe, 2011, pp. 16–25.
33. "Deng Xiaoping's Self-Criticism at the Central Committee Work Conference, October 23, 1966," *Written Self-Criticisms in the Cultural Revolution*, pp. 116–123.
34. Mao Zedong's speech during the Central Committee Work Conference, October 25, 1966, *Chinese Cultural Revolution Database*.
35. Gu Mu, *Gu Mu's Memoirs*, Zhongyang wenxian chubanshe, 2009, p. 222.

9. THE RISE, ACTIONS, AND DEMISE OF MASS ORGANIZATIONS

1. Wang Rui, "Regarding Several Topics in Cultural Revolution Tabloids," *Zuotian* (Yesterday), no. 10, 2012.
2. Yan Huai recalls that Wang Renzhong directed the provisional preparatory committee and that he proposed the "August 7 Proposal" according to the spirit of the Premier's speech. See Sun Nutao, ed., *History Refuses to Forget*, Hong Kong: Zhongguo wenhua chuanbo chubanshe, 2015, p. 149.
3. Liu Jufen, a student in Tsinghua's automatic control department, was the daughter of Liu Ningyi, the secretary of the Central Committee Secretariat.
4. Guo Jian and Wang Youqin hold that during the Cleansing of the Class Ranks, the rebel faction controlled some work units, such as Beijing Agricultural University, and should be held responsible for the persecution there.
5. Zhou Enlai's speech during the Central Committee Work Conference, October 28, 1966.
6. Tao Zhu's speech at the Ministry of Health, July 27, 1966.
7. Zhang Jiancheng, *The Scars Left by Time: A Personal Record of the Cultural Revolution at the Wuhan Institute of Hydraulic and Electric Engineering*, Hong Kong: Zhongguo wenhua chuanbo chubanshe, 2014, pp. 95, 97–100.
8. He Shu, ed., "The Memoirs of Li Musen," *Wangshi*, no. 32.
9. Bai Hua came under criticism in the 1980s for writing the screenplay *Unrequited Love* (*Kulian*), which was renamed *The Sun and the People* when made into a movie.
10. Dong Guoqiang, "The Origins and Factional Identification of Nanjing's Cultural Revolution Mass Movement," *Jiyi* (*Remembrance*), no. 73, August 2011.
11. "Advance on the Crest of Victory," editorial in *People's Daily*, *Red Flag* magazine, and *PLA Daily*, May 1, 1968.
12. TN: The "grand alliance" of all rebel forces, and the presence of cadres, military, and the masses in revolutionary committees.
13. National Defense University Party History and Party Building Research Department, *Cultural Revolution Research Material*, vol. 2, no. 1, p. 366.

10. THE "WORKERS COMMAND POST" AND SHANGHAI'S "JANUARY STORM"

1. CCP Central Committee Documentary Research Room (ed.), *Chronology of Mao Zedong: 1949–1976*, vol. 6, Zhongyang wenxian chubanshe, 2013, pp. 24–25.
2. TN: That is less than 108 square feet. An average American bedroom measures 120 to 150 square feet.

3. Wang Li, *Wang Li's Record of Introspection*, vol. 2, 2nd ed., Hong Kong: Beixing chubanshe, May 2011, p. 60.
4. Wang Li, *Wang Li's Record of Introspection*, p. 82.
5. Xi Xuan and Jin Chunming, *A Concise History of the Cultural Revolution*, new edition, Zhonggong dangshi chubanshe, 2011, p. 113.
6. Gu Mu, *Gu Mu's Memoirs*, Zhongyang wenxian chubanshe, 2009, p. 220.
7. Wang Li, *Wang Li's Record of Introspection*, p. 61.
8. Mao Zedong's remarks on Tao Zhu's errors, January 8, 1967, in *Chinese Cultural Revolution Database*, ed. Song Yongyi et al., 3rd ed., Universities Service Centre for China Studies, Chinese University of Hong Kong Press, 2013.
9. Chen Xiaonong, *Chen Boda's Final Oral Recollections*, Beijing: Dongfang chubanshe, 2010, p. 358.
10. CCP Central Committee Documentary Research Room (ed.), *Chronology of Mao Zedong: 1949–1976*, vol. 6, p. 22.
11. Wang Li, *Wang Li's Record of Introspection*, p. 82. CCP Central Committee Documentary Research Room (ed.), *Chronology of Mao Zedong: 1949–1976*, vol. 6, does not include this paragraph.
12. Chen Ganfeng, a student in the Urban Construction department of Shanghai Tongji University, was leader of the Tongji East Is Red rebel organization. During the Cultural Revolution he was chairman of the university's revolutionary committee and vice chairman of the Shanghai revolutionary committee, and during the Ninth Party Congress he became an alternate member of the CCP Central Committee. He was placed under investigation in 1971 and sent to a steel mill as a worker. After the Cultural Revolution he was sentenced to eight years in prison.
13. Li Xun, *The Revolutionary Rebel Era: A History of Shanghai's Cultural Revolution Movement*, Hong Kong: Oxford University Press, 2015, p. 275; Xu Jingxian, *The Ten-Year Dream*, Hong Kong: Shidai guoji chuban gongsi, 2003, p. 29, says that after the Anting Incident, when the Workers Command Post ranked its members, Wang Hongwen required everyone to report their family background, and he ranked first on the basis of his superior background.
14. Li Xun, *Revolutionary Rebel Era*, pp. 297–298.
15. Xu Jingxian, *Xu Jingxian's Final Memoir*, Hong Kong: Xingke'er chuban youxian gongsi, 2013, pp. 54–55.
16. Chen Xiaonong, *Chen Boda's Final Oral Recollections*, p. 341.
17. Xu Jingxian, *Xu Jingxian's Final Memoir*, p. 58.
18. Li Xun, *Revolutionary Rebel Era*, p. 331.
19. Xu Jingxian, *Xu Jingxian's Final Memoir*, pp. 62–63.
20. Wang Li, *Wang Li's Record of Introspection*, pp. 57–58.
21. Zhou Liangxiao and Gu Juying, *Chronicle of the Ten-Year Cultural Revolution*, Xindalu chubanshe youxian gongsi, 2008, p. 199; Xu Jingxian, *Xu Jingxian's Final Memoir*, p. 64.
22. Xu Jingxian eventually ranked third in Shanghai's leadership, and after the Gang of Four fell from power, he was sentenced to eighteen years in prison. He died of a heart attack in 2004.
23. Xu Jingxian, *Ten-Year Dream*, p. 15.
24. Xu Jingxian, *Xu Jingxian's Final Memoir*, p. 104.
25. Xu Jingxian, *Ten-Year Dream*, p. 21.

26. Xu Jingxian, *Ten-Year Dream*, p. 22.
27. Xu Jingxian, *Ten-Year Dream*, pp. 22–23.
28. CCP Central Committee Documentary Research Room (ed.), *Chronology of Mao Zedong: 1949–1976*, vol. 6, pp. 29–30.
29. Yan Changgui and Wang Guangyu, *Inquiring of History and Seeking Truth*, Hongqi chubanshe, 2009, p. 95.
30. Mao Zedong's remarks to the Central Cultural Revolution Small Group on the power seizure incidents at *Wenhui Bao* and *Liberation Daily*, January 8, 1967, in Song Yongyi et al., *Chinese Cultural Revolution Database*.
31. The main conference venue was at the Great Hall of the People, with a total of eight hundred thousand people gathering at various branch meeting places. The CCP Central Committee General Office Secretariat printed and distributed the text on January 24, 1967.
32. Xu Jingxian, *Ten-Year Dream*, p. 30.
33. Xu Jingxian, *Ten-Year Dream*, p. 45.
34. Xu Jingxian, *Ten-Year Dream*, p. 42.
35. Xu Jingxian, *Ten-Year Dream*, p. 48.
36. Jin Chunming, *An Exploration of the Era of Great Change*, Zhongguo shehui kexue chubanshe, 2009, pp. 117–118.
37. Record of Mao Zedong's remarks during the enlarged meeting of the CCP Central Committee Politburo Standing Committee, January 16, 1967, quoted in *Biography of Mao Zedong: 1949–1976*, Zhongyang wenxian chubanshe, 2003, p. 1461.
38. Xu Jingxian, *Xu Jingxian's Final Memoir*, p. 421.
39. Wang Li, *Wang Li's Record of Introspection*, p. 109.
40. Wang Li, *Wang Li's Record of Introspection*, p. 236.
41. The director of the Tianjin Academy of Social Sciences, Wang Hui, provided me with this information.
42. Xi Xuan and Jin Chunming, *A Concise History of the Cultural Revolution*, p. 199.
43. TN: The campaign against the May 16 clique will be described in Chapter 15.

11. THE "FEBRUARY COUNTERCURRENT" AND THE "FEBRUARY SUPPRESSION OF COUNTERREVOLUTIONARIES"

1. Cheng Guang, *Dialogue of the Soul: Qiu Huizuo Discusses the Cultural Revolution with His Son*, Hong Kong: Beixing chubanshe, 2011, p. 51.
2. Cheng Guang, *Dialogue of the Soul*, p. 110.
3. CCP Central Committee Documentary Research Room (ed.), *Chronology of Mao Zedong: 1949–1976*, vol. 6, p. 50.
4. According to an informed source (Yiwei Zhiqingzhe), Ye Jianying was pounding the table at Xu Xiangqian, who disagreed with him on the four bigs. In fact, throughout the Cultural Revolution, especially in its early stage, no one lost their temper with Jiang Qing face-to-face, and even the old marshals didn't dare offend Mao's wife. During the middle stage of the Cultural Revolution, Huang Yongsheng argued with Jiang Qing to her face, and in this case Lin Biao supported him, but they had been misled by Wang Dongxing, who said that Mao and Jiang were not on the same page. See Yiwei Zhiqingzhe, "On Reading Li Xiaohang," *Jiyi* (*Remembrance*), no. 21, April 30, 2009.
5. CCP Central Committee Party History Research Office, *History of the Chinese*

Communist Party, vol. 2, *1949–1973*, Zhonggong dangshi chubanshe, 2011, p. 788.

6. TN: The ousted Shanghai leader who was under attack.

7. Wang Li, *Wang Li's Record of Introspection*, vol. 2, 2nd ed., Hong Kong: Beixing chubanshe, May 2011, p. 238. The quote from Chen Yi was cited in Gao Wenqian's *Zhou Enlai's Later Years*, p. 201, quoting Central Committee Documentary Research Room, ed., *A Selection of Materials from the Ten Years of the Cultural Revolution*.

8. The "February 16 Huairen Hall Minutes" are quoted in Gao Wenqian, *Zhou Enlai's Later Years*, Mingjing chubanshe, 2004, 26th printing, pp. 202, 210.

9. TN: A *shenghuo hui* was a small group meeting at which attendees criticized themselves and others.

10. Gao Wenqian, *Zhou Enlai's Later Years*, p. 206.

11. Wang Li, *Wang Li's Record of Introspection*, pp. 240–241.

12. Ma Jisen, *A True Record of the Foreign Affairs Ministry During the Cultural Revolution*, Chinese University of Hong Kong Press, 2003, p. 98.

13. Wu Faxian, *The Memoirs of Wu Faxian*, Hong Kong: Beixing chubanshe, 3rd ed., February 2008, pp. 658–659.

14. Quoted in Gao Wenqian, *Zhou Enlai's Later Years*, p. 216.

15. Gao Wenqian, *Zhou Enlai's Later Years*, p. 216.

16. Central Committee Document No. 117 [1967].

17. Zhang Yunsheng, *The True Account of Maojiawan: The Memoirs of Lin Biao's Secretary*, Chunqiu chubanshe, 1988, pp. 86–89.

18. An Shaojie, ed., *General Liu Xianquan*, Zhongguo wenlian chubanshe, 1999, p. 331.

19. Xian Henghan, *Eighty Tempest-Filled Years*, electronic version.

20. TN: This refers to the long-standing practice of extorting false confessions through torture and then giving credence to such confessions.

21. From a speech given by Liu Xianquan at a conference of heads of military control commissions and cadres in Qinghai on the afternoon of April 10, 1967, "Speeches by Leading Cadres," quoted in *Chinese Cultural Revolution Database*, ed. Song Yongyi et al., 3rd ed., Universities Service Centre for China Studies, Chinese University of Hong Kong Press, 2013.

22. CCP Central Committee, State Council, Central Military Commission and Central Cultural Revolution Small Group Resolution Regarding the Qinghai Issue, March 24, 1967, Central Committee Document 110 (1967).

23. Xian Henghan, *Eighty Tempest-Filled Years*.

24. Fan Shuo, "The Origin of the Three Branches and Two Armies and the Eruption of the July 2 Incident," *China's Children*, no. 2, 2001, quoted in *Smashing the Old World: Havoc of the Chinese Cultural Revolution (1966–1968)*, ed. Bu Weihua, Chinese University of Hong Kong Press, 2008, pp. 459–460.

25. Wang Keli and Yuan Xunhui, "Understanding the Cultural Revolution, Rethinking the Cultural Revolution (Part 1): Gongshiwang Interview with Xu Youyu," September 24, 2012.

26. Mao Zedong, "Remarks at the Enlarged Twelfth Plenum of the Eighth Central Committee," October 13, 1968.

27. Rebel to the End Faction Chongqing Public Security First Front Red Army, *Public Security Rebel to the End*, no. 7 (February 26, 1968), quoted in He Shu, "An Overview of the Development and Evolution of Chongqing's Mass Organizations During the Cultural Revolution."

28. Liu Guoping, "Wanzhou's 'February Suppression of Counterrevolutionaries' and June 13 Incident,'" *Yanhuang Chunqiu*, no. 1, 2013; see also the record in *Wan County Gazetteer: Chronicle of Main Events*. This incident resulted in thirty-three deaths.

29. "Chen Zaidao's Oral Self-Criticism," December 1, 1967, in *Written Self-Criticisms in the Cultural Revolution*, ed. Shi Shi, Taipei: Shiying chubanshe, 2011, p. 322. See also Zhang Jiancheng, *The Scars Left by Time: Personal Experience of the Cultural Revolution at the Wuhan Institute of Hydroelectric Power*, Zhongguo wenhua chuanbo chubanshe, 2014, p. 153.

30. Bu Weihua, *Smashing the Old World*, p. 460.

31. Deng Zhenxin, *Guizhou's Storm*, Hong Kong: Zhongguo guoji wenyi chubanshe, 2014, p. 145.

32. Wu Caixia, *Frosted Leaves: Reviews and Reflections on the Cultural Revolution*, Hong Kong: Zhongguo wenhua chuanbo chubanshe, 2009, pp. 47–48.

33. Li Wenqing, *Xu Shiyou Close Up (1967–1985)*, Jiefang wenyi chubanshe, 2002, pp. 29–30, quoted in Bu Weihua, *Smashing the Old World*, p. 456.

34. Bu Weihua, *Smashing the Old World*, p. 458.

35. The State Council's various ministries and commissions were divided up into several divisions (*kou*), such as the agriculture and forestry division, the industry and communications division, the finance and trade division, and so on, which were handled by different vice-premiers. Tan Zhenlin was in charge of the agriculture and forestry division, which included the Ministry of Agriculture, the Ministry of Forestry, etc., and their related schools and universities.

36. Central Committee Document No. 117 [1967].

37. Hu Ping, "My Personal Experience of the Cultural Revolution in the Chengdu Area."

38. Quoted in Zhou Enlai's speech at a seminar for representatives of mass organization and military units stationed in Guangdong on April 18–19, 1967.

39. Hu Ping, "My Personal Experience of the Cultural Revolution in the Chengdu Region."

12. THE ARMED FORCES AND THE "THREE SUPPORTS AND TWO MILITARIES"

1. Wu Faxian, *The Memoirs of Wu Faxian*, Hong Kong: Beixing chubanshe, 3rd ed., February 2008, p. 615.

2. Qiu Huizuo, *The Memoirs of Qiu Huizuo*, Hong Kong: Xinshiji chubanshe (New Century Press), 2011, p. 457.

3. Qiu Huizuo, *Memoirs of Qiu Huizuo*, p. 453.

4. Qiu Huizuo, *Memoirs of Qiu Huizuo*, p. 455.

5. Yu Ruxin, "The Origin of the CMC's 1966 'Urgent Directive,'" *Extensive Collection of the Party History* (Dangshi bolan), no. 12 (2015).

6. Qiu Huizuo, *Memoirs of Qiu Huizuo*, p. 458.

7. Wu Faxian, *Memoirs of Wu Faxian*, pp. 622–624.

8. In accordance with Mao's directive to "make a self-criticism and get it over with," Ye Jianying was obliged to make public self-criticisms in speeches at two mass rallies of representatives of military academies from across the country and of "revolutionary teachers and students" from military academies in Beijing.

9. Wu Faxian, *Memoirs of Wu Faxian*, pp. 625–627. In addition, Yu Ruxin states that on that same day, the academies committee of the PLA Cultural

Revolution Small Group became aware of the rally to denounce Chen Yi, Ye Jianying, and others. That night, Zhou Enlai, Kang Sheng, Jiang Qing, Xiao Hua, Yang Chengwu, and others once again received the members of the mass rally preparatory office and did all they could to dissuade them from holding the rally, diverting their attention toward the PLA Cultural Revolution Small Group and Liu Zhijian, and protecting Chen Yi and Ye Jianying.

10. Wu Faxian, *Memoirs of Wu Faxian*, p. 647.

11. Zhang Jinchang, *Recounting Past Events*, Beijing shidai wenhua fazhan gongsi, 2012, pp. 63–64. Why purge Li Jukui and the others? Qiu Huizuo, *Memoirs of Qiu Huizuo*, p. 524, explains: "On September 6, 1966, at an enlarged CMC meeting, when Lin Biao was talking about He Long's problems, he mentioned Li Jukui and Rao Zhengxi as being members of the Peng-Huang clique who had slipped through the net."

12. Tang Guangxue, *Youth Like Fire, the Setting Sun Even Redder*, self-printed memoir, 2012, pp. 172–175; Zhang Jinchang, *Recounting Past Events*, p. 64. Qiu Huizuo's son, Qiu Luguang, dismissed the sex-slave story as slander in his conversation with me on January 13, 2016.

13. Tang Guangxue, *Youth Like Fire*, pp. 208, 209.

14. Zhou Liangxiao and Gu Juying, *Chronicle of the Ten-Year Cultural Revolution*, Xindalu chubanshe youxian gongsi, 2008, p. 535.

15. Tang Guangxue, *Youth Like Fire*, pp. 225, 235, 247. Qiu Huizuo, in his memoirs, denies that he purged so many people. He says, "There was a total of 1,000 or so people in the three rebel organizations put together . . . The number who were dealt with and received demerits, including those wrongly handled, were few. The indictments during the subsequent public trials contained countless falsehoods." Qiu Huizuo, *Memoirs of Qiu Huizuo*, p. 519.

16. Wu Faxian, *Memoirs of Wu Faxian*, p. 648.

17. Qiu Huizuo, *Memoirs of Qiu Huizuo*, p. 456.

18. "Chen Zaidao's Oral Self-Criticism," December 1, 1967.

19. TN: Referring to the army, navy, and air force.

20. Wu Faxian, *Memoirs of Wu Faxian*, pp. 641–642.

21. Qiu Huizuo, *Memoirs of Qiu Huizuo*, pp. 527–528.

22. Li Zuopeng, *The Memoirs of Li Zuopeng*, Hong Kong: Beixing chubanshe, 2011, p. 583. Bu Weihua, *Smashing the Old World: Havoc of the Chinese Cultural Revolution (1966–1968)*, Chinese University of Hong Kong Press, 2008, p. 501, says that more than two hundred were injured, dozens of them seriously.

23. Bai Erqiang, "I Planned the Incident of Attacking the Three Armies Performance," *Yanhuang Chunqiu*, no. 2, 2011.

24. Qiu Huizuo, *Memoirs of Qiu Huizuo*, p. 528.

25. Qiu Huizuo, *Memoirs of Qiu Huizuo*, p. 529.

26. Li Zuopeng, *Memoirs of Li Zuopeng*, p. 585.

27. Cheng Guang, *Dialogue of the Soul*, Hong Kong: Beixing chubanshe, 2011, p. 403.

28. Wang Nianyi, *Era of Upheaval*, Henan renmin chubanshe, 1988, pp. 286–287.

29. Bai Erqiang, "I Planned the Incident."

30. Cheng Guang, *Dialogue of the Soul*, p. 380; Qiu Huizuo, *Memoirs of Qiu Huizuo*, p. 540, says that nearly three million people were sent out for the "three supports and two militaries." Other material states that up to the end of 1971, more than 220,000 military cadres carried out the "three supports

and two militaries." See Liu Zhiqing, "The Military's Exposure and Criticism Campaign after the '9-13' Incident," *Extensive Collection of the Party History*, no. 7 (2005).

31. TN: The "grand alliance" of all rebel forces, and the presence of cadres, military, and the masses in revolutionary committees.

32. CCP Central Committee Documentary Research Room (ed.), *Chronology of Mao Zedong: 1949–1976*, vol. 6, p. 75.

33. The Four-Member Small Group, also called the Guardian Small Group, established on July 17, 1967, included Wu Faxian, Ye Qun, Qiu Huizuo, and Zhang Xiuchuan, with Wu serving as chairman. It had overseen the Cultural Revolution in the General Political Department and among military organs in Beijing.

34. Qiu Huizuo, *Memoirs of Qiu Huizuo*, pp. 539–540.

35. CCP Central Committee Documentary Research Room (ed.), *Chronology of Mao Zedong: 1949–1976*, vol. 6, p. 146.

36. Qiu Huizuo, *Memoirs of Qiu Huizuo*, p. 546. Wu Faxian, *Memoirs of Wu Faxian*, pp. 713–714, refers to the *Outline of Struggle Between the Two Lines*, but says that only Mao, Lin Biao, and Jiang Qing were included, and that Jiang refused to have the document mention Zhou Enlai.

37. Qiu Huizuo, *Memoirs of Qiu Huizuo*, p. 549.

38. Qiu Huizuo, *Memoirs of Qiu Huizuo*, p. 549.

39. Another version is that Yang Chengwu's secretary received an anonymous letter from someone in an air force organ exposing various outrages and misconduct committed by close associates of Lin Biao's son Lin Liguo and others in the air force party committee office. This letter ultimately reached the hands of Zhou Yuchi and the others, who identified the handwriting as that of Shan Shichong, who was then framed with accusations of an improper relationship with Yang Chengwu's daughter. See Dong Baocun, *The True Story of the Yang-Yu-Fu Incident*, Jiefangjun chubanshe, 1987, pp. 117–124. Dong Baocun interviewed Yang Chengwu after the Lin Biao clique fell from power, so this might be Yang's version of events.

40. Wu Faxian, *Memoirs of Wu Faxian*, pp. 717–721.

41. Qiu Huizuo, *Memoirs of Qiu Huizuo*, p. 554.

42. Yu Nan, "A Preliminary Exploration of the Rise and Fall of the Lin Biao Clique," *Commentary Ten Years Later*, Zhonggong dangshi ziliao chubanshe, 1987, p. 82.

43. Chen Hong, "My Experiences in the Rao Shushi Special Investigation Team," *Yanhuang Chunqiu*, no. 10, 2015.

44. Wu Faxian, *Memoirs of Wu Faxian*, pp. 722–723.

45. Wu Faxian, *Memoirs of Wu Faxian*, p. 727.

46. Lin Biao, "Speech at the Military Cadre Mass Rally," March 24, 1968, in *Chinese Cultural Revolution Database*, ed. Song Yongyi et al., 3rd ed., Universities Service Centre for China Studies, Chinese University of Hong Kong Press, 2013, p. 2006.

47. "Central Committee Leading Cadres' Remarks When Receiving Military Cadres," Zhou Enlai, Jiang Qing, Chen Boda, March 24, 1967, in Song Yongyi et al., *Chinese Cultural Revolution Database*.

48. Qiu Huizuo, *Memoirs of Qiu Huizuo*, pp. 556–557.

49. Wu Faxian, *Memoirs of Wu Faxian*, p. 725.

50. Huang Zheng (son of Huang Yongsheng), *Soldier Yongsheng*, vol. 2, Hong Kong: Xinshiji chubanshe (New Century Press), 2011, p. 235.

51. Cheng Guang, *Dialogue of the Soul*, p. 174.
52. Li Zuopeng, *Memoirs of Li Zuopeng*, p. 614. TN: According to *Chronology of Zhou Enlai*, vol. 3, p. 222, the original request to find the manuscript came from Zhou Enlai at the behest of Lu Xun's widow, Xu Guangping, through her son, Zhou Haiying.
53. CCP Central Committee Documentary Research Room (ed.), *Chronology of Mao Zedong: 1949–1976*, p. 157.

13. "RED THROUGH EVERY HILL AND VALE"

1. Wang Li, *Wang Li's Record of Introspection*, vol. 2, 2nd ed., Hong Kong: Beixing chubanshe, May 2011, p. 256.
2. Deng Lifeng, "On the Three Supports and Two Militaries," *Modern China Historical Research*, no. 6, 2001, quoted in Bu Weihua, *Smashing the Old World: Havoc of the Chinese Cultural Revolution (1966–1968)*, Chinese University of Hong Kong Press, 2008, p. 591.
3. *Heilongjiang Province Gazetteer, Vol. 70: Communist Party Gazetteer*, Heilongjiang renmin chubanshe, 1996, pp. 247–249, 262. These figures were calculated by opponents of Pan after he fell from power, so they may be exaggerated.
4. Kang Sheng communicated this in the December 27, 1969, "Important Remarks by Central Leaders Receiving All Comrades from the Sichuan Province Revolutionary Committee and Chengdu Military Region Attending Study Classes in Beijing."
5. Zhou Enlai's remarks on the fourth occasion of receiving leaders of the Wuhan rebel faction, May 27, 1969.
6. Xu Zhengquan, "Footprints in the Snow," *Zuotian* (*Yesterday*), no. 7, 2012. Cao Chengyi, first draft, "Speaking of the Cultural Revolution with Mixed Feelings," ed. Chuan Yi, pp. 5–6.
7. CCP Wuhan Municipal Party Committee Party History Office, *Chronicle of Wuhan During the Cultural Revolution Period (May 1966–October 1976)*.
8. CCP Wuhan Municipal Party Committee Party History Office, *Chronicle of Wuhan*.
9. Xu Zhengquan, "Footprints in the Snow."
10. Shang Xinren, a researcher who personally experienced the Cultural Revolution in Wuhan, feels that the "Staff Federation," although "royalist," was relatively disciplined and moderate, unlike the royalist Million Heroes subsequently established with the support of the Wuhan Military Region's Chen Zaidao.
11. The top leader of the Red Militia (the Red Armed Core Militia), Yu Wenbin, was deputy director of the people's armed forces department of the Wuhan Municipal Machine Industry Bureau. Support from the provincial military district and municipal people's armed forces led to the group growing to 270,000 members in a few days, and all of them were armed. The Million Heroes, initiated by the Red Militia, was also led by Yu Wenbin, who had two guards from the municipal armed forces department protecting him around the clock.
12. Tan Zhenlin was considered representative of the leaders who suppressed the rebel faction, and in spring and summer 1967, rebels throughout the country protested against local "Tan Zhenlin–type persons," or "Old Tan."

13. Rong Gen, *The 40th Anniversary of Wuhan's "July 20 Incident": A Record of Interviews with Million Heroes Leaders Yu Wenbin, Zhang Dijie, and Others*.

14. Cao Chengyi, "Speaking of the Cultural Revolution," p. 34; Rong Gen, *The 40th Anniversary*; Wu Yanjin, as told to Zhong Yi, *Forty-three Years: A Memoir of Hope* (electronic edition. Print edition published in 2009).

15. Wang Haiguang, "A Popular History of Wuhan's Cultural Revolution," preface to *A True Record of Wuhan's July 20 Incident*.

16. Wu Yanjin et al., *Forty-three Years: A Memoir of Hope*.

17. Wu Yanjin et al., *Forty-three Years: A Memoir of Hope*.

18. Wu Yanjin et al., *Forty-three Years: A Memoir of Hope*.

19. "The CCP Central Committee's Approval of the 'Hubei Provincial Revolutionary Committee's Report on Solving Wuhan's "Anti-reversion" Problem,'" Central Committee Document No. 28 [69].

20. Mao Zedong on the May 16 clique, September 1967, in *Chinese Cultural Revolution Database*, ed. Song Yongyi et al., 3rd ed., Universities Service Centre for China Studies, Chinese University of Hong Kong Press, 2013. These words moved me deeply at the time, so I copied them down in my journal.

21. Preface by Fang Fang for Lu Li'an's *Crying Out to Heaven*, Hong Kong: Chinese University Press, 2005.

22. Central Committee Document No. 67 [1969].

23. The details of the crackdown on the May 16 clique will be related in chapter 15.

24. Wu Yanjin et al., *Forty-three Years: A Memoir of Hope*.

25. Zeng Siyu and Zhang Tixue both say the number exceeded 600,000.

26. This content is drawn from Deng Zhenxin, *Storm in Guizhou*, Hong Kong: Zhongguo guoji wenyi chubanshe, 2014. Further page citations will not be made except for figures.

27. Deng Zhenxin, *Storm in Guizhou*, p. 44.

28. CCP Central Committee Documentary Research Room (ed.), *Chronology of Mao Zedong: 1949–1976*, vol. 6, p. 36.

29. Unless otherwise stated, the material in this section is drawn from He Shu, *Chronicle of the Violence in Chongqing*; and He Shu, *Fighting for Chairman Mao: A True Record of the Great Battles in Chongqing in the Cultural Revolution*, Hong Kong: Sanlian shudian (Xianggang) youxian gongsi (Joint Publishing), 2010 edition.

30. The article was titled "'National Defense Literature' Was the Slogan of Wang Ming's Right-Deviating Opportunist Line" and referred to the great slogan dispute between the famous writer Lu Xun and literary theorist Zhou Yang in the 1930s. Ren Baige supposedly supported Zhou Yang.

31. CCP Central Committee, State Council, Central Military Commission, Central Cultural Revolution Small Group Order Forbidding the Plundering of People's Liberation Army Weapons, Equipment, and Various Military Supplies, September 5, 1967, Central Committee Document No. 288 [1967]. This document was publicly posted throughout the country.

32. Quoted in He Shu, *Fighting for Chairman Mao*, p. 303.

33. Yu Dian, "Why Was the Fighting in Chongqing During the Cultural Revolution so Violent?" (on the forty-fourth anniversary of the Cultural Revolution battles).

14. THE WUHAN INCIDENT AND MAO'S STRATEGIC SHIFT

1. Li Zuopeng, *The Memoirs of Li Zuopeng*, Hong Kong: Beixing chubanshe, 2011, p. 592; Wang Li, *Wang Li's Record of Introspection*, vol. 2, 2nd ed., Hong Kong: Beixing chubanshe, May 2011, p. 252.

2. Chen Zaidao believed that the CCRSG and Wu Faxian conspired to have Liu Feng meet Zhou at the airport rather than the military region political commissar Zhong Hanhua, against Zhou Enlai's wishes. See Chen Zaidao, *The Whole Story of Wuhan's July 20 Incident*, quoted in National Defense University Party History and Party Building Research Department, *Cultural Revolution Research Material*, 1988, p. 514.

3. Wang Li, *Wang Li's Record of Introspection*, vol. 2, 2nd ed., p. 252.

4. Li Zuopeng, *Memoirs of Li Zuopeng*, pp. 592–593.

5. CCP Central Committee Documentary Research Room (ed.), *Chronology of Mao Zedong: 1949–1976*, vol. 6, pp. 100–101.

6. Xu Hailiang, *A True Record of the July 20 Incident*, Zhongguo wenhua chuanbo chubanshe, 2010; Li Zuopeng, *Memoirs of Li Zuopeng*, p. 592.

7. Li Zuopeng, *Memoirs of Li Zuopeng*, p. 593.

8. Zhou Enlai's remarks at a conference of cadres at the division level and above in the Wuhan Military Region and Hubei Military District, July 18, 1967, in *Chinese Cultural Revolution Database*, ed. Song Yongyi et al., 3rd ed., Universities Service Centre for China Studies, Chinese University of Hong Kong Press, 2013. Wang Li, *Wang Li's Record of Introspection*, pp. 252–253, contains similar content.

9. In Yang Chengwu's memoir, *Traveling Incognito: Yang Chengwu in 1967*, he writes, "Late at night on July 17, [Yang] had just come over from being with Zhou Enlai . . . Handed several sheets of paper to Mao Zedong," and also: "The Premier made a summing-up speech, which was a speech outline drafted by the Premier, and which he asked the Chairman to vet . . . Mao Zedong broke with convention by not staying behind to manage it, immediately looking it over and then giving it to Yang Chengwu and saying, 'I agree, let him say it.'"

10. Zhang Jiancheng, *The Scars Left by Time: Personal Experience of the Cultural Revolution at the Wuhan Institute of Hydroelectric Power*, Zhongguo wenhua chuanbo chubanshe, 2014, p. 183.

11. CCP Central Committee Documentary Research Room (ed.), *Chronology of Mao Zedong: 1949–1976*, vol. 6, p. 102.

12. Li Zuopeng, *Memoirs of Li Zuopeng*, p. 594; Wang Li, *Wang Li's Record of Introspection*, p. 253.

13. "Chen Zaidao's Oral Self-Criticism" (December 1, 1967), in *Written Self-Criticisms in the Cultural Revolution*, ed. Shi Shi, Taipei: Shiying chubanshe, 2011, p. 322; Qiu Huizuo, *The Memoirs of Qiu Huizuo*, Hong Kong: Xinshiji chubanshe (New Century Press), 2011, p. 533, also records this unified approach taken by the Wuhan Military Region.

14. Zhong Hanhua's self-criticism: "Premier Zhou's directive repeatedly told us not to transmit it to the lower levels, but I approved Cai Bingchen transmitting it. This was the first blaze I lit in the '7-20' counterrevolutionary rebellion." This is according to the synthesized record of two self-criticisms carried out before the full assembly of the Hubei Province Study Class on November 30 and December 1, 1967, the edited draft of which was approved by Zhong himself.

15. Xu Hailiang, "The Wuhan 'July 20 Incident': Historical Facts and Viewpoints That Remain Controversial to the Present Day," in *The Cultural Revolution: Historical Truth and Collective Memory*, ed. Song Yongyi, Hong Kong: Tianyuan shuwu chubanshe, 2010, p. 466.

16. Xu Hailiang, who was present at the Hydraulic and Electrical Engineering Institute at the time, holds that Wang Li did not speak of the Four-Point Directive. The Million Heroes leaders Yu Wenbin and Zhang Dijie say the same thing, and Wang Li told the central leaders that he did not speak of the Four-Point Directive.

17. CCP Wuhan Municipal Party Committee Party History Office, *Chronicle of Wuhan in the Cultural Revolution Period (May 1966–October 1976)*. Chen Zaidao states, "Xie Fuzhi and Wang's Li's activities that night were the direct cause of the outbreak of the '7-20' Incident." See Chen Zaidao, *Whole Story of Wuhan's July 20 Incident*, p. 515. Bu Weihua, *Smashing the Old World: Havoc of the Chinese Cultural Revolution (1966–1968)*, Chinese University of Hong Kong Press, 2008, p. 533, states that the record of Wang Li's speech shows that Wang Li supported the rebel faction but did not specifically mention the central leadership's Four-Point Directive to resolve the Wuhan problem.

18. Xu Hailiang, "Wuhan 'July 20 Incident,'" pp. 466–467.

19. Rong Gen, *The 40th Anniversary of Wuhan's "July 20 Incident": A Record of Interviews with Million Heroes Leaders Yu Wenbin, Zhang Dijie, and Others*.

20. Years later, one of the leaders of the Million Heroes, Yu Wenbin, said of the night of July 17, "The leader of the Provincial Government Agencies Allied Headquarters, Yang Yicai, picked me up and drove to the East Lake, where he told me in a mysterious tone of voice that Mao Zedong was in Wuhan. 'You should go see him.' He also said, 'Chairman Mao also wants to see you.'" See Rong Gen, *The 40th Anniversary*.

21. Zhang Gencheng was a regimental-level army cadre and an enthusiastic student of Mao's works. During the Cultural Revolution he was sent to work with the CCRSG. He spent seven years in Qincheng Prison after the Cultural Revolution.

22. Xu Hailiang, *True Record of the July 20 Incident*, electronic edition. The following material also comes from this source.

23. Yu Yan, "More on the '8201' in the 'July 20 Incident': To Mr. Yu Ruxin," Fenghuahuan, February 25, 2005, Cultural Revolution Museum (Bwg535).

24. Xie Jingyi, *Trivial Memories of Working Alongside Mao Zedong*, Zhongyang wenxian chubanshe, January 2015, p. 58.

25. Xu Hailiang, "Wuhan 'July 20 Incident,'" p. 473.

26. Wang Li, *Wang Li's Record of Introspection*, pp. 253–254.

27. Yu Yan, "More on the '8201' in the 'July 20 Incident.'"

28. Xu Hailiang, *True Record of the July 20 Incident*.

29. Xu Hailiang, *True Record of the July 20 Incident*.

30. Zhang Chunting, "My Unforgettable Past as a Reporter at the 'Central Cultural Revolution Reporters' Station," in *Flying Arrow: A Record of What I Saw and Heard as a Reporter at the Central Cultural Revolution Reporters' Station*, Zhongguo wenhua chuanbo chubanshe, 2011.

31. Wu Faxian, *The Memoirs of Wu Faxian*, Hong Kong: Beixing chubanshe, 3rd ed., February 2008, pp. 684–685. Wu Faxian recalls that Zhou Enlai called a CCRSG briefing meeting the night he returned to Beijing, but the timing seems inaccurate, because Zhou flew out of Wuhan at 11:30 p.m. and would

have reached Beijing in the early hours of the next morning. The record in *Chronology of Zhou Enlai*, stating that the meeting was held on July 20 is reliable.

32. Qiu Huizuo, *Memoirs of Qiu Huizuo*, p. 533; Qian Sijie and Gu Baozi, *Mao Zedong During China's Eventful Years: 1964–1968*, Renmin wenxue chubanshe, 2013, p. 259.

33. Qiu Huizuo, *Memoirs of Qiu Huizuo*, p. 533.

34. Xu Hailiang, *True Record of the July 20 Incident*; Wu Faxian, *Memoirs of Wu Faxian*, p. 687.

35. Qiu Huizuo, *Memoirs of Qiu Huizuo*, p. 534.

36. Qian Sijie and Gu Baozi, *Mao Zedong During China's Eventful Years*, pp. 259–261.

37. Qiu Huizuo, *Memoirs of Qiu Huizuo*, pp. 534–535.

38. Li Zuopeng, *Memoirs of Li Zuopeng*, p. 595.

39. Rong Gen, *The 40th Anniversary*.

40. Li Zuopeng, *Memoirs of Li Zuopeng*, p. 596.

41. Chen Zaidao says that Lin Biao and Jiang Qing ordered the aircraft to circle overhead in order to create a bigger impression. See Chen Zaidao, *Whole Story of Wuhan's July 20 Incident*.

42. Li Zuopeng, *Memoirs of Li Zuopeng*, p. 596; Wang Li, *Wang Li's Record of Introspection*, p. 255. Wang Guangyu recalls that there were a few thousand people in the welcoming party. See Wang Guangyu, "Several Matters Regarding the Central Cultural Revolution Small Group after the '7-20' Incident," *Jiyi (Remembrance)*, no. 16.

43. Wang Guangyu, "Several Matters Regarding the Central Cultural Revolution Small Group."

44. Wang Li, *Wang Li's Record of Introspection*, p. 255.

45. Qiu Huizuo, *Memoirs of Qiu Huizuo*, pp. 532–535; Bu Weihua, *Smashing the Old World*, p. 540.

46. Shang Xinren and Peng Zulong, "Resentment Scattered Throughout Mankind: A Summary of the History of the Great Proletarian Cultural Revolution in Wuhan," electronic edition.

47. Xu Jingxian, *Xu Jingxian's Final Memoir*, pp. 223–224.

48. Wang Li, *Wang Li's Record of Introspection*, p. 256.

49. "Comrade Zhang Guohua's Speech at the Sichuan Province Agricultural Production Planning, Finance and Trade, and Metal Materials Production and Supply Conference," August 28, 1967, *Zuotian (Yesterday)*, no. 3, 2012.

50. Yan Changgui, "The Guan Feng I Knew," *Tonggongjin*, no. 4, 2013.

51. While Wang Li was speaking, the Foreign Ministry stenographer Ye Jiwen took notes, which are quoted in Yang Rongjia, *Secrets of the Republic's Foreign Ministry*, Hong Kong: Dashan wenhua chubanshe, 2011, pp. 119–121.

52. Wang Nianyi, *Era of Upheaval*, Henan renmin chubanshe, 1988, p. 267.

53. Wang Li, *Wang Li's Record of Introspection*, p. 257.

54. Bu Weihua, *Smashing the Old World*, p. 558.

55. Gao Wenqian, *Zhao Enlai's Later Years*, Mingjing chubanshe, 2004, 26th printing, p. 241.

56. CCP Central Archives Research Office, Jin Chongji, ed., *Biography of Zhou Enlai*, Zhongyang wenxian chubanshe, 1998, p. 1926.

57. CCP Central Committee Documentary Research Room (ed.), *Chronology of Zhou Enlai*, vol. 2, p. 183.

58. *Biography of Zhou Enlai*, p. 1928.

59. Yan Changgui, "Qi Benyu and Yan Changgui Talk of the Cultural Revolution," *Wangshi*, no. 119, March 29, 2013. Yan Changgui was Jiang Qing's secretary at the time.

60. Han Suyin, *Zhou Enlai and His Century*, Zhongyang wenxian chubanshe, 1992, p. 472.

61. Wu De, as told to Zhu Shiyuan et al., *Wu De's Oral Account: A Chronicle of Ten Years of Trials and Hardships—Some of My Experiences Working in Beijing*, Dangdai Zhongguo chubanshe, 2004, p. 66.

62. Wang Hairong, a grandniece of Mao's, was a Foreign Ministry official and one of the few people who could see Mao at that time.

63. Zong Daoyi, "The 'son-of-a-bitch's speech' and the Foreign Ministry's 'power seizure' farce," quoted in Gao Wenqian, *Zhao Enlai's Later Years*, p. 242.

64. CCP Central Committee, State Council, Central Military Commission, and Central Cultural Revolution Small Group General Order, June 6, 1967, Central Committee Document No. 178 [1967]. This general order called for "defending the order of the Great Proletarian Cultural Revolution, defending the authority of the proletarian dictatorship, protecting the Great Democracy under the dictatorship of the proletariat, protecting the normal carrying out of speaking out freely, airing views fully, big-character posters, and mass debate [the four bigs], and correcting the recently emerging unhealthy trend of beating, smashing, robbing, ransacking, and grabbing."

65. CCP Central Committee Documentary Research Room (ed.), *Chronology of Mao Zedong: 1949–1976*, vol. 6, pp. 115–111.

66. *Manuscripts of Mao Zedong Since the Founding of the Country*, vol. 12, Zhongyang wenxian chubanshe, 1998, pp. 385–390.

67. Cheng Guang, *Dialogue of the Soul*, Hong Kong: Beixing chubanshe, 2011, p. 158.

68. Chen Zaidao says that during the 1974 campaign to criticize Lin Biao and Confucius, Jiang Qing received Zhong Hanhua in Guangzhou and said, "I wronged you. I was also taken in by Lin Biao. He was Vice-Chairman, and when he went to Tiananmen, I followed him to Tiananmen. Lin Biao killed two birds with one stone back then. Through the 'July 20 Incident' he struck down Comrade Chen Zaidao and also plotted against Chairman Mao." Chen Zaidao, *Whole Story of Wuhan's July 20 Incident*, p. 524. Chen Zaidao and Ding Sheng (see below) may have been talking about the same thing.

69. Ding Sheng, *Hero in Hardship: The Memoirs of General Ding Sheng*, ed. Jin Guang and Yu Ruxin, Hong Kong: Xingke'er chuban gongsi, 2008, p. 236.

15. THE BAFFLING "MAY 16" INVESTIGATION

1. Wang Li says that 10 million people were investigated in the campaign against the May 16 clique, and 3.5 million were detained, giving rise to the most massive injustice in the Cultural Revolution. Wang Li, *Wang Li's Record of Introspection*, vol. 2, 2nd ed., Hong Kong: Beixing chubanshe, May 2011, p. 261.

2. Wu De, as told to Zhu Shiyuan et al., *Wu De's Oral Account: A Chronicle of Ten Years of Trials and Hardships—Some of My Experiences Working in Beijing*, p. 69.

3. Quoted in Song Yongyi et al., eds., *Chinese Cultural Revolution Database*, 3rd ed., Universities Service Centre for China Studies, Chinese University of Hong Kong Press, 2013.

4. Capital Red Guard Congress Beijing Iron and Steel Institute Yan'an Commune, ed., *Chronicle of the Criminal Activities of the Counterrevolutionary Conspiratorial Organization "May 16 Corps,"* December 1967.

5. Capital Red Guard Congress Beijing Iron and Steel Institute Yan'an Commune, *Chronicle of the Criminal Activities.*

6. Zhou Liangxiao and Gu Juying, *Chronicle of the Ten-Year Cultural Revolution*, Xindalu chubanshe youxian gongsi, 2008, pp. 486–487.

7. Record of Mao Zedong's remarks to Yang Chengwu, Zhang Chunqiao, Wang Dongxing, and Yu Lijin, September 19, 1967, quoted in CCP Central Committee Party History Research Office, *History of the Chinese Communist Party*, vol. 2, *1949–1973*, Zhonggong dangshi chubanshe, 2011, p. 795.

8. Wu De, *Wu De's Oral Account*, p. 68.

9. Zhou Enlai, Chen Boda, Kang Sheng, Jiang Qing, et al., "Remarks to the College Red Guard Congress, Workers' Red Guard Congress, and Three Armies Proletarian Revolutionary Faction," August 11, 1967.

10. Jiang Qing, Chen Boda, Zhou Enlai, Kang Sheng, et al., "Remarks at the Enlarged Meeting of the Beijing Municipal Revolutionary Committee Standing Committee, Reprinted by the Cultural Ministry Organs Revolutionary Combat Organization Liaison Station," September 1, 1967.

11. Liu Shaoqi's essay "On the Self-Cultivation of Communist Party Members" was a target of criticism at that time, and was called "reactionary 'Self-cultivation.'" TN: The title is sometimes also translated as "How to Be a Good Communist."

12. *Manuscripts of Mao Zedong Since the Founding of the Country*, vol. 12, Zhongyang wenxian chubanshe, 1998, pp. 401–405.

13. At the outset of the movement, the Foreign Ministry's leading party group labeled Vice-Ministers Chen Jiakang, Wang Bingnan, and others as anti-party elements. During the criticism of the bourgeois reactionary line, Chen and the others were released. After that, Chen Jiakang took the side of the rebel faction and revealed that Chen Yi had said at a study session at the outset of the Cultural Revolution that Mao's launch of the Cultural Revolution was "an arbitrary dictatorial act of sovereign power." Zhou Enlai berated Chen Jiakang's action as that of a "petty scoundrel" and said he was a "bad person."

14. TN: See chapter 12.

15. TN: See chapter 13.

16. Song Yongyi et al., *Chinese Cultural Revolution Database.*

17. Zhou Enlai, Kang Sheng, and Jiang Qing, "Remarks While Receiving Representatives of PLA Propaganda Teams of Cultural, Education, Academic Departments, and Other Work Units Directly Under the Central Committee, from 8:30 p.m. on January 24, 1970, to 12:40 a.m. on January 25," in Song Yongyi et al., *Chinese Cultural Revolution Database.*

18. "Zhou Enlai's Instructions Regarding Investigating the May 16 Clique While Receiving Leaders of PLA and Worker Propaganda Teams and Core Groups of the Foreign Affairs Apparatus," November 1, 1970. In Song Yongyi et al. *Chinese Cultural Revolution Database.*

19. "Zhou Enlai's Remarks Regarding Investigating the May 16 Clique," November 20, 1970, in Song Yongyi et al., *Chinese Cultural Revolution Database.*

20. Wu De, *Wu De's Oral Account*, pp. 67–68.

21. Wu De, *Wu De's Oral Account*, p. 72.

22. Song Yimin, preface to Yang Rongjia, *Secrets of the Republic's Foreign Ministry*, Hong Kong: Dashan wenhua chubanshe, 2011, p. 11.

23. He Fang, *The Autobiography of He Fang: Reflections on the Road from Yan'an*, Hong Kong: Ming bao chubanshe, 2007, simplified character edition self-printed in 2011, p. 355.

24. He Fang, *Autobiography of He Fang*, p. 355.

25. He Fang, *Autobiography of He Fang*, p. 355.

26. He Fang, *Autobiography of He Fang*, p. 355.

27. Yang Rongjia, *Secrets of the Republic's Foreign Ministry*, pp. 219–223.

28. Yang Rongjia, *Secrets of the Republic's Foreign Ministry*, pp. 219–223.

29. Ma Jisen, *A True Record of the Foreign Ministry During the Cultural Revolution*, Chinese University of Hong Kong Press, 2003, p. 258. Yang Rongjia, *Secrets of the Republic's Foreign Ministry*, p. 224, states, "A total of 1,500–1,700 May 16 elements were seized; He Fang, *Autobiography of He Fang*, pp. 312, 361–362.

30. The agriculture and forestry division included the Ministry of Agriculture, Ministry of Forestry, Ministry of Aquatic Products, Ministry of Agricultural Reclamation, the State Council's Agriculture Office, etc., and their related colleges, universities, and research institutes. Vice-Premier Tan Zhenlin was in charge of all of them.

31. "Zhou Enlai's Remarks to Representatives of Beijing Agricultural University East Is Red," September 16, 1967, in Song Yongyi et al., *Chinese Cultural Revolution Database*.

32. Xu Renjun, "My Experience of the Investigation of the May 16 Clique from Beginning to End," Chinese Communist Party News Online, August 17, 2010, 08:32.

33. Xu Renjun, "My Experience of the Investigation."

34. Unless otherwise noted, the content of this section is drawn from Chen Qizhen, "Painful Memories of the Investigation of the May 16 Clique in the Food Ministry," *Yanhuang Chunqiu*, no. 10, 2011.

35. Liao Zhunan, "Plugging the Gaps in the Article 'My Experience of the Investigation of the May 16 Clique in the Food Ministry,'" letter sent by Liao to *Yanhuang Chunqiu*, unpublished.

36. Before the Cultural Revolution, Wu Chuanqi and Lin Yushi were departmental-level cadres in the Philosophy Research Institute. On May 23, 1966, they took the lead in putting up a big-character poster criticizing Yang Shu's *Youthful Ramblings*, becoming part of the rebel faction in the Academic Department.

37. Pan Zinian (1893–1971), a native of Yixing, Jiangsu Province, joined the CCP in Shanghai in March 1927. Before the Cultural Revolution, he was a member of the party leading group of the Chinese Academy of Sciences and party secretary and deputy director of the academy's Philosophy and Social Sciences Department, as well as head of the Philosophy Research Institute.

38. Meng Xiangcai, "I Became Political Commissar of the Academic Departments' May 16 Clique," *Yanhuang Chunqiu*, no. 9, 2008.

39. Du Junfu, "How I Came to Be Labeled a 'May 16' Element," *Jiyi (Remembrance)*, no. 20, August 13, 2009.

40. "Zhou Enlai's remarks regarding investigating the May 16 Clique," November 4, 1970, in Song Yongyi et al., *Chinese Cultural Revolution Database*.

41. "Zhou Enlai and Li Xiannian's Remarks While Receiving Representatives of the Health and Sanitation Apparatus," December 10, 1967.

42. Zhou Guangzhen, *History of the Central Philharmonic Orchestra (1956–1996)*, Hong Kong: Sanlian shudian (Xianggang) youxian gongsi, December 2009.

43. "Decision Regarding Rehabilitation of the Guangxi 'May 16' Counterrevolutionary Conspiratorial Clique Case," [Guilin] Document No. 37 [1983], June 22, 1983; Leading Group of the [Prefectural] Party Committee to Handle the Aftermath of the Cultural Revolution, June 15, 1983.

44. Wang Chunnan, "An Incident I'll Never Regret: Criticizing Jiangsu's Campaign to Investigate the 'May 16' Clique During the Cultural Revolution," *Zuotian (Yesterday)*, no. 47.

45. Liu Dinghan, ed., *A Concise History of Contemporary Jiangsu*, Beijing: Dangdai Zhongguo chubanshe, 1999, p. 235; *Jiangsu Province Gazetteer: CCP Gazetteer*, 2002, p. 320; Pan Zhuping, "The Injustice of Jiangsu's Investigation of the 'May 16' Clique," *Yanhuang Chunqiu*, no. 11, 2007.

46. Ding Qun, "A Mountain of Unjust Cases, All Fabricated: Jiangsu Province's Campaign to Investigate and Excavate the 'May 16' Clique," quoted in Wang Chunnan, "Incident I'll Never Regret."

47. Liu Dinghan, *Concise History of Contemporary Jiangsu*, p. 235.

48. Compilation of exposure and criticism materials from the enlarged CCP Nanjing municipal committee standing committee meeting, November 20, 1974, p. 44.

49. Pan Zhuping, "Injustice of Jiangsu's Investigation." In Du Wenzhen's *Memoirs*, Dong Guoqiang saw around 1,100 people on the school's investigation list, with 359 designated May 16 elements, 248 named at a mass rally at the school, 158 locked up and investigated, and more than 20 persecuted to death. See Dong Guoqiang et al., "Interview with Professor Jiang Guangxue," *Jiyi (Remembrance)*, no. 30.

50. Dong Guoqiang, ed., *The Cultural Revolution as Personally Experienced: An Oral History by 14 Teachers and Students of Nanjing University*, Kejie chubanshe, 2000, p. 347.

51. Pan Zhuping, "Injustice of Jiangsu's Investigation."

52. There is material indicating that the person who exposed Wu Dasheng was suffering a mental disorder after being tortured. See Dong Guoqiang et al., "Interview with Professor Jiang Guangxue."

53. Dong Guoqiang et al., "Interview with Professor Jiang Guangxue."

54. Dong Guoqiang et al., "Interview with Professor Jiang Guangxue."

55. Dong Guoqiang et al., "Interview with Professor Jiang Guangxue."

56. Dong Guoqiang et al., "Interview with Professor Jiang Guangxue."

57. Dong Guoqiang et al., "Interview with Professor Jiang Guangxue."

58. Descendants of Yu Yao, "Xu Shiyou and Jiangsu's 'Two Excavations.'"

59. Pan Zhuping, "Injustice of Jiangsu's Investigation."

60. On May 29, 1975, Deng Xiaoping said, "During the investigation of 'May 16,' Xuzhou investigated more than 6,000 people. That's a horrifying number." *See Selected Works of Deng Xiaoping*, vol. 2, Renmin chubanshe, 1994, p. 10.

16. THE CLEANSING OF THE CLASS RANKS

1. Mao Zedong's speech to the Ninth Party Congress, April 11, 1969.

2. *Manuscripts of Mao Zedong Since the Founding of the Country*, vol. 12, Zhongyang wenxian chubanshe, 1998, p. 209.

3. "Advance on the Crest of Victory," editorial, published in *People's Daily*, *Red Flag* Magazine, and *PLA Daily*, May 1, 1968.

4. Mao Zedong's conversation with Beqir Balluku, the evening of October 5, 1968, in the Great Hall of the People, in *Chinese Cultural Revolution*

Database, ed. Song Yongyi et al., 3rd ed., Universities Service Centre for China Studies, Chinese University of Hong Kong Press, 2013.

5. The "six factories" were the Beijing Xinhua Printing Factory, the February Seventh Locomotive Factory, the Nankou Locomotive Machine Factory, the Beijing Knitting Industrial Complex, the Beijing Northern Suburbs Sawmill, and the Beijing Third Chemical Engineering Factory, and the "two schools" were Tsinghua University and Peking University.

6. Xia Junsheng, "The Cultural Revolution Prototype: The Cleansing of the Class Ranks in the Beijing February Seventh Factory," *Yanhuang Chunqiu*, no. 8, 2008.

7. Compilation Committee of the Chronicle of the Cultural Revolution in Beijing (November 1965–October 1976) draft soliciting opinions, 1987, in Song Yongyi et al., *Chinese Cultural Revolution Database*.

8. *Chronicle of Contemporary Beijing (1949–1989)*, Dangdai Zhongguo chubanshe, 1992, p. 265.

9. Mao Zedong's remarks while inspecting northern, south-central, and eastern China, July–September 1967.

10. Yin Shusheng, "Uncovering the Secret Files of the 'CCR' During Anhui's Cultural Revolution," *Yanhuang Chunqiu*, no. 1, 2011.

11. *Jiangsu Province Gazetteer: CCP Gazetteer*, Jiangsu renmin chubanshe, 2003, p. 318.

12. Li Bingduo, "Investigating Enemy and Puppet Regime Files." Li Bingduo took part in sorting through files on the enemy and puppet regimes in Sichuan. He submitted this article to *Yanhuang Chunqiu*, but it was never published. I thank him for allowing me to use his figures here.

13. Ding Shu, "The 'Cleansing of the Class Ranks' Campaign That Persecuted People on a Massive Scale," in *The Cultural Revolution: Historical Truth and Collective Memory*, ed. Song Yongyi, Hong Kong: Tianyuan shuwu chubanshe, 2010, p. 605.

14. Ding Shu, "The 'Cleansing of the Class Ranks' Campaign," p. 607.

15. Quoted in Roderick MacFarquhar and Michael Schoenhals, *Mao's Last Revolution* (Chinese edition, trans. Guan Xin, proofreader Tang Shaojie), Hong Kong: Xinke'er chuban (Xianggang) youxian gongsi, 2009, p. 265. TN: English edition, Belknap Press of Harvard University Press, 2006, p. 262, quoting from Andrew Walder and Yang Su, "The Cultural Revolution in the Countryside: Scope, Timing and Human Impact," *China Quarterly*, no. 173, March 2003, p. 77.

16. Xi Xuan and Jin Chunming, *A Concise History of the Cultural Revolution*, new edition, Zhonggong dangshi chubanshe, 2011, p. 196.

17. Yin Shusheng, "Uncovering the Secret Files of the 'CCR.'"

18. CCP Shanghai Party Committee Party History Research Room, *The Chinese Communist Party's 80 Years in Shanghai*, Shanghai renmin chubanshe, 2001, pp. 657–658.

19. Li Xun, *The Revolutionary Rebel Era: A History of Shanghai's Cultural Revolution Movement*, Hong Kong: Oxford University Press, 2015, p. 1194.

20. *Jiangsu Province Gazetteer: CCP Gazetteer*, p. 318.

21. *Gaoyou County Gazetteer*, Jiangsu renmin chubanshe, 1990, p. 69.

22. *Wujin County Gazetteer*, Shanghai renmin chubanshe, 1988, p. 46.

23. *Chronicle of the History of the Chinese Communist Party in Zhejiang*, Zhongguo dangshi chubanshe, 1996, p. 164.

24. *Guangzhou City Gazetteer, Vol. 1: Chronicle of Major Events*, Guangzhou chubanshe, 1999, p. 479.

25. *Guangdong Province Gazetteer: Political Summary*, Guangdong renmin chubanshe, pp. 228–229.

26. CCP Nanning Prefectural Party Committee Consolidated Party Office, "Nanning Prefecture Cultural Revolution Chronicle of Events (1966–1976)" (top secret), May 11, 1987.

27. *Shaanxi Province Gazetteer: Government Gazetteer*, Shaanxi renmin chubanshe, 1997, p. 680.

28. *Gansu Province Gazetteer, Vol. 1: Chronicle of Major Events*, Gansu renmin chubanshe, 1989, p. 441.

29. *Dingbian County Gazetteer*, Fangzhi chubanshe, 2003, p. 20.

30. CCP Shandong Party Committee Party History Research Room, Shandong Provincial Archives, eds., *Chronicle of Major Events in the Cultural Revolution in Shandong (May 1966–October 1976)*, March 2001, quoted in Song Yongyi et al., *Chinese Cultural Revolution Database*.

31. *Heilongjiang Province Gazetteer, Vol. 70: Communist Party Gazetteer*, Heilongjiang renmin chubanshe, 1996, pp. 250–251.

32. Jilin Province Public Security Organs Military Control Commission, "Some Circumstances of the Cleansing of the Class Ranks at Present," in *The Situation of Safeguarding Operations*, no. 15, October 21, 1968.

33. *Changchun City Gazetteer: Public Security Gazetteer*, Jilin renmin chubanshe, 2000, p. 267.

34. Bu Weihua, *Smashing the Old World: Havoc of the Chinese Cultural Revolution (1966–1968)*, Chinese University of Hong Kong Press, 2008, p. 678.

35. *A Brief History of Contemporary Jiangxi*, Dangdai Zhongguo chubanshe, 2002, quoted in Yao Shuping, "The Untold Story of the 1968 Civilian Executions: Killing at Will Without Evidence."

36. Ru Qi, "Support-the-Left Diary (1967–1968)," originally published in *Tianya*, no. 1, 1999.

37. *Jiangxi Province Gazetteer: Jiangxi Public Security Gazetteer*, Fangzhi chubanshe, 1996, pp. 351, 353.

38. *Yunnan in the 1950s: A Chronicle of the CCP in Yunnan Province During the Socialist Period*, Renmin ribao chubanshe, 1999, p. 149.

39. Ding Longjia and Ting Yu, *Kang Sheng and the Unjust Case Against Zhao Jianmin*, Beijing: Renmin chubanshe, 1999, pp. 176–177.

40. Ding Longjia and Ting Yu, *Kang Sheng and the Unjust Case*, p. 179.

41. Ding Longjia and Ting Yu, *Kang Sheng and the Unjust Case*, pp. 201–205.

42. Zhou Liangxiao and Gu Juying, *Chronicle of the Ten-Year Cultural Revolution*, Xindalu chubanshe youxian gongsi, 2008, p. 591.

43. *Contemporary China's Beijing*, Zhongguo shehui kexue chubanshe, 1989, p. 169.

44. Du Junfu, "A Narrative of the Cultural Revolution Movement in the Chinese Academy of Sciences," *Zuotian* (*Yesterday*), no. 59, October 30, 2015.

45. Petition Bulletin Editorial Office, ed., *Spring Wind and Rain Collection*, vol. 1, Qunzhong chubanshe, 1981, p. 441.

46. Hu Yaobang's memo regarding Dan Kuizhang's persecution of intellectuals in Jilin Province, April 8, 1978.

47. Bai Jiefu, "My Painful Friendship with Xiao Guangyan," *Yanhuang Chunqiu*, no. 7, 2005.

48. Mao Zedong once said that he wanted to bring 95 percent of the cadres and 95 percent of the masses into unity, known as "unifying two 95 percents."

49. Yu Fenghua, "My Experience of the Cleansing of the Class Ranks," *Yanhuang Chunqiu*, no. 2, 2008.

50. *Chongyi County Gazetteer*, p. 26.

51. *Heping County Gazetteer*, Guangdong renmin chubanshe, 1999, "Chronicle of Events, 1986," p. 25.

52. *Heping County Gazetteer: Government Gazetteer*, 1986, p. 33.

53. Yin Shusheng, "Uncovering the Secret Files of the 'CCR.'"

54. Song Keli, "The Petroleum River Is Weeping," in *Cultural Revolution Record of Vindication*, ed. Han Shangyu, Tuanjie chubanshe, 1993, pp. 291–298.

55. *Timetable of Major Events in Guangxi's Cultural Revolution*, Nanning, Guangxi renmin chubanshe, July 1990.

56. Xu Yong, "Wei Guoqing's Massacre of the Guangxi April 22 Faction."

57. Yan Lebin, "Guangxi's 'Cultural Revolution' Movement," unpublished manuscript.

58. Teng Haiqing, "Report Outline Regarding the 'IMPRP' Problem," December 22, 1968, in Song Yongyi et al., *Chinese Cultural Revolution Database*.

59. Altandelhei (Alateng Delihai), ed., *A True Record of the "Root Out and Eradicate" Disaster in Inner Mongolia*, self-printed, September 2008.

60. Bu Weihua, *Smashing the Old World*, p. 103, provides an alternative version: During the 1964 Four Cleanups campaign, a "Declaration to the People of Inner Mongolia" was printed and distributed within the autonomous region. It was a declaration that was issued in Mao's name on December 20, 1935, while the KMT was still in power, and that proposed national autonomy for the people of Inner Mongolia. On the basis of this declaration, the North China Bureau meeting said that Ulanhu was engaged in national separatism.

61. Altandelhei, *True Record*, pp. 7, 10.

62. A letter from the Second Party Secretary of Inner Mongolia, Ting Mao, to Huang Kecheng, August 1, 1981, quoted in Altandelhei, *True Record*, p. 236.

63. Altandelhei, *True Record*, pp. 85–95.

64. Bu Weihua, *Smashing the Old World*, p. 649.

65. Inner Mongolia *Bulletin of the Autonomous Region Pastoral Area Grassland Construction Work Conference*, no. 11, June 8, 1978.

66. *Bulletin of the CCP Yikezhao League Party Committee Policy Implementation Office*, no. 3, August 5, 1978.

67. Altandelhei, *True Record*, p. 119.

68. Indictment of the People's Republic of China Supreme People's Procuratorate Special Prosecutor's Office (concerning the case of the "Lin Biao and Jiang Qing Counterrevolutionary Clique"), November 2, 1980.

69. Cheng Tijie, "Looking Back Around Forty Years, Another Look at the Cultural Revolution in Inner Mongolia," *Cultural Revolution: Historical Truth and Collective Memory*, Hong Kong: Tianyuan shuwu chubanshe, 2010, p. 746.

70. CCP Central Committee's transmission of the report submitted by the core group of the Inner Mongolian Revolutionary Committee, "Several Opinions on Resolutely Implementing and Executing the Central Committee's Directives Regarding the Present Work in Inner Mongolia," May 22, 1969, Central Committee Document No. 24 [1969].

71. Altandelhei, *True Record*, p. 316.
72. Altandelhei, *True Record*, p. 249.
73. *Bulletin of Speeches at the Enlarged Plenum of the Chinese Federation of Cultural Circles*, speech by Sun Futian, p. 4; Petition Bulletin Editorial Office, ed., *Spring Wind and Rain Collection*, pp. 196–204.
74. Ma Zhigang, ed., *Cases of Gross Injustice and Great Redress*, Beijing: Tuanjie chubanshe, 1993, p. 261.
75. *Lingyuan County Gazetteer*, 1995, pp. 24, 416.
76. *Miyun County Gazetteer*, Beijing chubanshe, 1998, p. 30.
77. *Chronicle of Forty Years in Shandong*, 1989, p. 138.
78. Yin Shusheng, "Uncovering the Secret Files of the 'CCR.'"

17. THE ONE STRIKE AND THREE ANTIS CAMPAIGN

1. Wang Nianyi, *Era of Upheaval*, Henan renmin chubanshe, 1988, p. 337.
2. Wang Rui, "Who Signed Yu Luoke's Execution Order," Hongshiwang, January 20, 2010, 20:04.
3. Ding Shu, "Grim Times: The 1970 'One Strike and Three Antis' Movement," *Huaxia Wenzhai*, no. 343, 2003 supplement, pp. 1–14.
4. CCP Central Committee Documentary Research Room (ed.), *Chronology of Zhou Enlai*, vol. 2, Zhongyang wenxian chubanshe, 1997, p. 346.
5. Beijing Municipal Public Security and Judicial Military Commission Criminal Judgment No. [70] 30.
6. Yang Jian, *Underground Literature During the Cultural Revolution*, Chaohua chubanshe, 1993, p. 126.
7. Fang Zifen, "The Fortieth Anniversary of Nanjing's '3-6' Public Trial," Gongshiwang, January 20, 2010. Fang Zifen says that the March 6 public trial was the first, but in fact, Zha Jinhua was killed on February 12.
8. *Guangdong Province Gazetteer: Political Summary*, Guangdong renmin chubanshe, p. 229.
9. Cheng Chao and Wei Haoben, eds., *Chronicle of the Cultural Revolution in Zhejiang*, Zhejiang fangzhi bianjibu, 1989.
10. *Heilongjiang Province Gazetteer, Vol. 70: Communist Party Gazetteer*, Heilongjiang renmin chubanshe, 1996, p. 251.
11. CCP Shijiazhuang Municipal Party Committee Party History Research Room, *Chronicle of the Cultural Revolution in Shijiazhuang (May 1966–December 1978)*, March 1997, quoted in *Chinese Cultural Revolution Database*, ed. Song Yongyi et al., 2nd ed., Universities Service Centre for China Studies, Chinese University of Hong Kong Press, 2006.
12. Xi'an shi difangzhi bianzuan weiyuanhui, ed., *Xi'an City Gazetteer: Political and Military Volume*, Xi'an chubanshe, September 2000, p. 73.
13. Zhang Langlang, "Regarding the 'One Strike and Three Antis' Campaign in the Cultural Revolution."
14. Wang Chen and Zhang Tianlai, "Meteorite Ripping the Curtain of Night," in *History Pondered Here: A Record of 1966–1976*, vol. 3, Beijing: Huaxia chubanshe, 1986, pp. 253–282.
15. Cai Jingang, "The Rightist Senior Colonel Cai Tiegen," *Yanhuang Chunqiu*, no. 9, 2012.
16. "Wang Rui, Zhou Enlai, and the 'One Strike and Three Antis' Campaign," *Jiyi (Remembrance)* 57, no. 16 (September 13, 2010).

17. Yan Shugui, "The Old Professor Who Died for His Words," in *Cultural Revolution Record of Vindication*, ed. Han Shangyu, Tuanjie chubanshe, 1993, pp. 17–24.

18. Liu Yu, "Sentenced to Death for a Letter," in Han Shangyu, *Cultural Revolution Record of Vindication*, pp. 43–52.

19. Wu Tiexuan, "Record of the Xin Yuanhua 'Counterrevolutionary Case' That Shook Xinjiang," in Han Shangyu, *Cultural Revolution Record of Vindication*, pp. 53–64.

20. On November 13, 1967, the PLA 8341 Unit's "Report Regarding the Circumstances of Aiding Production at the Beijing Municipal Knitting Complex," submitted to Mao, quoted workers as saying, "Before going to work, we request instructions from Chairman Mao so we can see and think clearly and with direction; after finishing our shifts, we report to Chairman Mao and examine our work and thinking." At the same time that this report was given to Mao, the Beijing Knitting Complex revolutionary committee on November 11, 1967, sent a letter to Mao reporting happy news. On November 15, Mao wrote a memo on these two reports: "Read, very good, thank you, comrades!" The Central Committee issued these two reports and Mao's memo to the entire party. From then on, the ludicrous activities of "requesting instructions in the morning and reporting in the evening" spread like wildfire throughout the country. On June 12, 1969, the Central Committee handed down a document forbidding such "formalistic activities."

21. Tian Daye and Wu Zhaolin, "The Whole Story of the Western Hunan 'No. 1 Secret Agent,'" in Han Shangyu, *Cultural Revolution Record of Vindication*, pp. 25–32.

22. Deng Zhengxin, *Major Events in the Cultural Revolution in Guizhou*, 5th supplemented draft, electronic edition.

23. Petition Bulletin Editorial Office, ed., *Spring Wind and Rain Collection*, vol. 1, Qunzhong chubanshe, 1981, p. 406.

24. Wang Youqin, *Victims of the Cultural Revolution*, Hong Kong: Kaifang zazhi chubanshe, 2004, p. 46.

25. Ji Xichen, *An Era Unprecedented in History: The Notebook of a Veteran "People's Daily" Reporter*, Renmin ribao chubanshe, 2006, pp. 253–255.

26. Chen Chuan, "The Communist University Murder Case," in Han Shangyu, *Cultural Revolution Record of Vindication*, pp. 33–42.

27. Dai Huang, *Directly Facing Life*, Beijing: Zhongyang bianyi chubanshe, 1998, p. 315.

28. Chinese People's Liberation Army Datong City Public Security Apparatus Military Control Commission, "Criminal Judgment Regarding the Chinese Communist League," March 28, 1970, Criminal Judgment No. [70] 29.

29. Zhu Liudi, "A Red Guard's Regret: Never Forgiving Himself for 'Matricide,'" *New Beijing Daily*, August 7, 2013.

30. Qian Rong, "Sentenced to Twenty Years for Compiling a Book," in Han Shangyu, *Cultural Revolution Record of Vindication*, pp. 178–183.

31. Yin Shusheng, "Uncovering the Secret of the Anhui Cultural Revolution 'CCR' Files," *Yanhuang Chunqiu*, no. 1, 2001.

32. Ding Shu, "Grim Times."

18. MASS KILLINGS CARRIED OUT BY THOSE IN POWER

1. Su Yang, "Collective Killings During the Cultural Revolution: Research on Three Provinces," Modern China Studies 94, no. 3, 2006. TN: See also Yang Su, *Collective Killings in Rural China During the Cultural Revolution*, Cambridge University Press, 2011.
2. Unless otherwise noted, the material in this section is drawn from the following sources: Sun Yancheng, "'Bloodline Theory' and Daxing's 'August 13' Incident," *Yanhuang Chunqiu*, no. 2, 2012; Yu Luowen, "Investigation of the Cultural Revolution Massacre in Daxing, Beijing," online document posted May 4, 2010.
3. Tan Hecheng, *Blood Myth: A True Record of the 1967 Daoxian Massacre*, Hong Kong: Tinhangkin Publications, 2010, pp. 16–17. TN: The book was translated into English by Stacy Mosher and Guo Jian and published by Oxford University Press in 2017 under the title *The Killing Wind: A Chinese County's Descent into Madness During the Cultural Revolution*.
4. Tan Hecheng, *Blood Myth*, pp. 16–17.
5. Some production brigades also had public security deputies and Communist Youth League secretaries taking part, in which case these were referred to as "six chiefs' meetings."
6. "Double rush" refers to the rapid harvesting of summer crops and sowing of autumn crops within a few days' time to take maximum advantage of the growing season.
7. Tan Hecheng, *Blood Myth*, pp. 117–118.
8. Tan Hecheng, *Blood Myth*, p. 169.
9. Tan Hecheng, *Blood Myth*, p. 125.
10. Unless otherwise noted, the material for this section is drawn from *Chronology of Major Events in Guangxi's Cultural Revolution*, Editorial Committee, ed., *Chronology of Major Events in Guangxi's Cultural Revolution*, July 1990.
11. Yan Libin, "Guangxi's Cultural Revolution: Participating in Handling the Aftermath of Guangxi's 'Cultural Revolution.'" This article was published in edited form in *Yanhuang Chunqiu*, no. 11, 2012, but what is quoted here comes from the unedited version of Yan Libin's article.
12. CCP Central Committee Commission for Discipline Inspection, Central Committee Organization Department Policy Implementation Guangxi Investigation Group, Appendix I to "Guangxi Policy Implementation and Investigation Report: Situation Report on the Problem of Numerous Killings in Guangxi During the Cultural Revolution," July 15, 1981.
13. *Quanzhou County Gazetteer*, Guangxi renmin chubanshe, 1998, p. 17.
14. CCP Central Committee Commission for Discipline Inspection, Appendix I to "Guangxi Policy Implementation and Investigation Report: Situation Report on the Problem of Numerous Killings in Guangxi During the Cultural Revolution."
15. CCP Central Committee Commission for Discipline Inspection, Appendix I to "Guangxi Policy Implementation and Investigation Report."
16. Unless otherwise noted, the material in this section is drawn from Zhou Kang, "The Shocking Yunnan Shadian Tragedy," *Yanhuang Chunqiu*, no. 7, 2007.
17. *Renmin Luntan*, "A Narrative of Yunnan's 'Shadian Incident.'"

18. Chen Baode and Li Xuechao, "The Whole Story of Yangjiang's Random Killing Incident," *Yanhuang Chunqiu*, no. 11, 2014.

19. Ru Qi, "Support-the-Left Diary," quoted in Yao Shuping, "The Untold Story of the 1968 Civilian Executions: Killing at Will WITHOUT Evidence."

20. Zhao Enlai called for this vetting while receiving ten students from Tsinghua University at the Great Hall of the People on July 30, 1966. This writer was one of those students.

21. Xie Fuzhi summarized the findings of the Zhijiang Provincial Public Security Bureau regarding the "black elements" of Zhuji County's Fengqiao District in a report titled "Regarding Ten Good People Wrapping and Reforming One Bad Person, the Experience of Social Transformation Without Turning Over Contradiction to Authorities," which was submitted to Mao. After being praised and approved by Mao, the report spread throughout the country, resulting in the launch of a "socialist transformation of black elements campaign."

19. THE TWELFTH PLENUM OF THE EIGHTH CENTRAL COMMITTEE

1. Zhou Enlai's speech at the opening ceremony for the twelfth plenum of the Eighth Central Committee, October 13, 1968.

2. *Manuscripts of Mao Zedong Since the Founding of the Country*, vol. 12, Zhongyang wenxian chubanshe, 1998, pp. 292–293.

3. Yan Changgui, "Qi Benyu and Yan Changgui Talk of the Cultural Revolution," *Wangshi*, no. 119, March 29, 2013.

4. Liu Pingping, Liu Yuan, and Liu Tingting, "The Flowers of Victory Presented to You: In Cherished Memory of Our father, Liu Shaoqi," in *History Pondered Here: A Record of 1966–1976*, vol. 1, Beijing: Huaxia chubanshe, 1986, pp. 16–17.

5. Yang Changgui, "The Mass Criticism That Mao Zedong Launched and Led Against Liu Shaoqi," a speech delivered at National Association of Major Party History Writings; Wang Li, *Wang Li's Record of Introspection*, vol. 2, 2nd ed., Hong Kong: Beixing chubanshe, May 2001, p. 993.

6. *Manuscripts of Mao Zedong*, vol. 12, p. 397.

7. *Manuscripts of Mao Zedong*, vol. 12, p. 224.

8. Lei Yi, "Mao Zedong's Discussion and Appraisal of Superfluous Remarks: Apologizing to the Enemy, Surrender and Defection."

9. Qi Benyu, "Remembering Comrade Jiang Qing," *Red Reference*, July 29, 2015.

10. TN: Qu Qiubai (1899–1935) was an early CCP leader and theoretician.

11. Zhou Yang's conversation with the Central Commission for Discipline Inspection at his Wanshou Road residence on August 28, 1979, quoted in Lei Yi, "Mao Zedong's Discussion and Appraisal of Superfluous Remarks."

12. Song Yongyi et al., eds., *Chinese Cultural Revolution Database*, 3rd ed., Universities Service Centre for China Studies, Chinese University of Hong Kong Press, 2013.

13. TN: See chapter 2.

14. CCP Central Committee Documentary Research Room (ed.), *Chronology of Zhou Enlai*, vol. 2, Zhongyang wenxian chubanshe, 1997, pp. 93–94.

15. Song Yongyi et al., *Chinese Cultural Revolution Database*.

16. Nie Yuanzi, *The Memoirs of Nie Yuanzi*, Hong Kong: Shidai guoji youxian gongsi, 2005, p. 232.

17. CCP Central Committee memo regarding the printing and distribution of materials regarding the issue of Bo Yibo, Liu Lantao, An Ziwen, Yang Xianzhen, and others being released from prison.

18. Central Special Investigation Group, "Eighth Item of Evidence Against Liu Shaoqi Turning Traitor After Being Arrested in Changsha in 1925: The Handwritten Statement of the Counterrevolutionary Element Yang Jianxiong in 1952 Regarding Liu Shaoqi Being Arrested and Turning Traitor."

19. TN: Wang Jingwei and Chen Gongbo were leading members of the Kuomintang's leftist faction at this time. Later, during the Japanese occupation in the 1940s, Wang and Chen broke ranks with the KMT and led the collaborationist Nanjing Nationalist Government.

20. Xi Xuan and Jin Chunming, *A Concise History of the Cultural Revolution*, new edition, Zhonggong dangshi chubanshe, 2011, p. 175.

21. Zhang Xueliang effectively ruled all northeastern China and was an ally of the Kuomintang at this time.

22. Xi Xuan and Jin Chunming, *A Concise History of the Cultural Revolution*, p. 176.

23. Zhang Xiushan, *My Eighty-Five Years: From the Northwest to the Northeast*, Zhonggong dangshi chubanshe, 2007, p. 321. I learned further details from Gao Gang's daughter, Li Jie, on July 19, 2012, in the editorial office of *Yanhuang Chunqiu*. On October 4, 2001, Gao Gang's former secretary, Zhao Jialiang, also spoke of this matter with me. See Yang Jisheng, *Collected Interviews with Modern Chinese Notables and Commentaries*, Hong Kong: Tiandi tushu chubanshe (Cosmos Books), 2013, p. 98.

24. Gao Wenqian, *Zhao Enlai's Later Years*, Mingjing chubanshe, 2004, 26th printing, pp. 247–248.

25. Cheng Guang, *Dialogue of the Soul*, Hong Kong: Beixing chubanshe, 2011, pp. 191–192.

26. Huang Zheng, "Liu Shaoqi and the Cultural Revolution," *Party Documents*, no. 5, 1998.

27. Gao Gao and Yan Jiaqi, *Ten-Year History of the Cultural Revolution*, Tianjin renmin chubanshe, 1986, p. 178; English edition, *Turbulent Decade: A History of the Cultural Revolution*, trans. and ed. D. W. Y. Kwok, Honolulu: University of Hawai'i Press, 1996, pp. 162–164.

28. Kang Sheng, Jiang Qing, Yao Wenyuan, and Xie Fuzhi's speeches at the First Small Group Meeting of the twelfth plenum of the Eighth Central Committee, October 17, 1968, in Song Yongyi et al., *Chinese Cultural Revolution Database*.

29. "Zhou Enlai's remarks on the problems of several marshals at the twelfth plenum of the Eighth Central Committee," October 1968, in Song Yongyi et al., *Chinese Cultural Revolution Database*.

30. Cheng Guang, *Dialogue of the Soul*, p. 203.

31. Kang Sheng's speech to the Fourth Small Group at the Twelfth Plenum of the Eighth Central Committee.

32. Qiu Huizuo, *The Memoirs of Qiu Huizuo*, Hong Kong: Xinshiji chubanshe (New Century Press), 2011, p. 614.

20. THE NINTH NATIONAL PARTY CONGRESS

1. CCP Central Committee Documentary Research Room (ed.), *Chronology of Mao Zedong: 1949–1976*, vol. 6, Beijing: Zhongyang wenxian chubanshe, 2013, p. 231.

2. CCP Central Committee Documentary Research Room (ed.), *Chronology of Mao Zedong: 1949–1976*, vol. 6, p. 237.
3. Chi Zehou, "Trivial Memories Behind the Scenes of the CCP's Ninth Congress," *Yanhuang Chunqiu*, no. 3, 2003.
4. CCP Central Committee Documentary Research Room (ed.), *Chronology of Mao Zedong: 1949–1976*, vol. 6, p. 238.
5. Wang Wenyao and Wang Baochun, *Chen Boda Before and After the Cultural Revolution: A Secretary's Testimony*, Hong Kong: Tiandi tushu chubanshe (Cosmos Books), 2014, p. 137.
6. Mao Zedong's remarks at the enlarged CCRSG routine meeting, March 12 and 15, 1969, quoted in CCP Central Committee Document Research Office, *Biography of Mao Zedong: 1949–1976*, vol. 2, Zhongyang wenxian chubanshe, 2003, pp. 1538–1539.
7. Wang Wenyao and Wang Baochun, *Chen Boda Before and After the Cultural Revolution*, p. 137.
8. Mao Zedong's remarks at an informal meeting of the CCRSG, quoted in Gao Wenqian, *Zhou Enlai's Later Years*, Mingjing chubanshe, 2004, 26th printing, pp. 270–271. Gao's book says Mao made these remarks on March 7, but it's possible that it was sometime between mid-March and the Ninth Party Congress.
9. See *Manuscripts of Mao Zedong Since the Founding of the Country*, vol. 12, Zhongyang wenxian chubanshe, 1998, pp. 11–18.
10. Zhang Yunsheng, *The True Account of Maojiawan: The Memoirs of Lin Biao's Secretary*, Chunqiu chubanshe, 1988, pp. 213–215.
11. Wu Faxian, *The Memoirs of Wu Faxian*, Hong Kong: Beixing chubanshe, 3rd ed., February 2008, pp. 741, 742.
12. Li Zuopeng, *The Memoirs of Li Zuopeng*, Hong Kong: Beixing chubanshe, 2011, p. 674.
13. Chi Zehou, "Trivial Memories Behind the Scenes."
14. Chen Boda's secretary recalls that in the practice election before the formal one, Jiang Qing received full votes and was very pleased with herself. During the actual election, Chen Boda didn't vote for Jiang. See Wang Wenyao et al., op. cit., pp. 143–144.
15. Wu Faxian, *Memoirs of Wu Faxian*, p. 744.
16. Qiu Huizuo, *The Memoirs of Qiu Huizuo*, Hong Kong, Xinshiji chubanshe (New Century Press), 2011, p. 645.
17. Qiu Huizuo, *Memoirs of Qiu Huizuo*, p. 647. Wu Faxian, *Memoirs of Wu Faxian*, p. 745, says that Mao didn't respond when Zhou Enlai told him of the demand for an investigation.
18. Qiu Huizuo, *Memoirs of Qiu Huizuo*, p. 647.
19. Transcript of a recording of Mao Zedong's speech at the Ninth National Party Congress, April 11, 1969, in Song Yongyi et al., *Chinese Cultural Revolution Database*, 2nd ed., Universities Service Centre for China Studies, Chinese University of Hong Kong Press, 2006.
20. Chi Zehou, "Trivial Memories Behind the Scenes."
21. Cheng Guang, *Dialogue of the Soul*, Hong Kong: Beixing chubanshe, 2011, p. 280.
22. Qiu Huizuo, *Memoirs of Qiu Huizuo*, p. 650.
23. Qiu Huizuo, *Memoirs of Qiu Huizuo*, pp. 650–651.
24. Qiu Huizuo, *Memoirs of Qiu Huizuo*, pp. 651–652.
25. Qiu Huizuo, *Memoirs of Qiu Huizuo*, pp. 680–681.

26. Huang Zheng, *Soldier Yongsheng*, vol. 2, Hong Kong: Xinshiji chubanshe (New Century Press), 2011, pp. 257–258.
27. Qiu Huizuo, *Memoirs of Qiu Huizuo*, pp. 578–579.
28. Qiu Huizuo, *Memoirs of Qiu Huizuo*, p. 611.
29. Qiu Huizuo, *Memoirs of Qiu Huizuo*, pp. 651–656.
30. Qiu Huizuo, *Memoirs of Qiu Huizuo*, pp. 656–657.
31. Qiu Huizuo, *Memoirs of Qiu Huizuo*, pp. 657–658. Qiu Huizuo may have forgotten Xie Fuzhi.
32. Qiu Huizuo, *Memoirs of Qiu Huizuo*, p. 581.
33. Qiu Huizuo, *Memoirs of Qiu Huizuo*, p. 582.
34. Li Zuopeng, *Memoirs of Li Zuopeng*, p. 645. *The Memoirs of Wu Faxian* also quotes Jiang Qing on p. 745, and the two accounts are largely consistent.
35. Li Zuopeng, *Memoirs of Li Zuopeng*, pp. 644–646.
36. Qiu Huizuo, *Memoirs of Qiu Huizuo*, p. 683. *The Memoirs of Wu Faxian* also describes this incident on pp. 753–756, and the accounts are basically identical.
37. Wu Faxian, *Memoirs of Wu Faxian*, p. 756.
38. Li Zuopeng, *Memoirs of Li Zuopeng*, p. 687.
39. Qiu Huizuo, *Memoirs of Qiu Huizuo*, p. 727.
40. Information from the author's reporting notes when visiting the Tianjin municipal revolutionary committee in 1972.
41. Zhou Zhihua, "Criticizing the Splittist Cadre Line of Comrade Wu Dasheng and Others," speech at the Rally for Provincial-Level Organs to Criticize Lin Biao and Confucius, quoted in Dong Guoqiang and Andrew G. Walder, "Nanjing's 'Second Cultural Revolution' of 1974," *China Quarterly*, no. 212, December 2012, pp. 893–918.
42. In March 1969, China and the Soviet Union engaged in an armed conflict over a sovereignty dispute concerning Zhenbao (Damansky) Island in the Ussuri River shipping channel in Heilongjiang. Reportedly, Soviet troops carried out an armed invasion of the island several times and fired shells deep into Chinese territory on the opposite shore. Chinese forces carried out a counterattack.
43. On August 13, 1969, in the disputed Tielieketi (Terekty) area in Xinjiang's Yumin County on the western segment of the Sino-Soviet border, the Soviet Union deployed helicopters, tanks, and armored cars against a thirty-eight-member Chinese frontier defense patrol unit carrying only light weapons, resulting in the deaths of all members of the Chinese unit.
44. The Soviet Union's invasion of Prague in 1968 occurred without warning while the Soviet Union and Czechoslovakia were engaged in bilateral talks.
45. Wu Faxian, *Memoirs of Wu Faxian*, p. 767.
46. Li Ke and Hao Shengzhang, *The PLA During the Great Cultural Revolution*, Beijing: Zhonggong dangshi ziliao chubanshe, 1989, p. 125, quoted in Roderick MacFarquhar and Michael Schoenhals, *Mao's Last Revolution* (Chinese edition, trans. Guan Xin, proofreader Tang Shaojie), Hong Kong: Xinke'er chuban (Xianggang) youxian gongsi, 2009, p. 322; TN: English edition, Belknap Press of Harvard University Press, 2006, p. 318.
47. Wang Dongxing, *Memoirs of Wang Dongxing: Mao Zedong's Fight with the Lin Biao Counterrevolutionary Clique*, Dangdai Zhongguo chubanshe, 1997, pp. 14–15.

21. FOGGED IN ON LUSHAN

1. Namely, Huang Yongsheng, PLA chief of staff and chairman of the Central Military Commission Administrative Group; Wu Faxian, vice-chairman of the CMCAG, deputy chief of staff of the PLA, and Air Force commander; Ye Qun, Lin Biao's wife and a member of the CMCAG; Li Zuopeng, a member of the CMCAG, deputy chief of staff of the PLA, and first political commissar of the navy; and Qiu Huizuo, a member of the CMCAG, deputy chief of staff of the PLA, and director of the general logistics department.
2. See chapter 12.
3. CCP Central Committee Documentary Research Room (ed.), *Chronology of Zhou Enlai*, vol. 2, Zhongyang wenxian chubanshe, 1997, p. 356.
4. Wang Dongxing, *Memoirs of Wang Dongxing: Mao Zedong's Fight with the Lin Biao Counterrevolutionary Clique*, Dangdai Zhongguo chubanshe, 1997, p. 20.
5. Wang Dongxing, *Memoirs of Wang Dongxing*, p. 20.
6. CCP Central Committee Documentary Research Room (ed.), *Chronology of Zhou Enlai*, p. 285.
7. Wang Dongxing, *Memoirs of Wang Dongxing*, p. 21.
8. CCP Central Committee Documentary Research Room, *Biography of Mao Zedong: 1949–1976*, Zhongyang wenxian chubanshe, 2003, p. 1560.
9. CCP Central Archives Research Room, Jin Chongji, ed., *Biography of Zhou Enlai*, Zhongyang wenxian chubanshe, 1998, p. 1970.
10. Wang Dongxing, *Memoirs of Wang Dongxing*, p. 21.
11. Wu Faxian, *The Memoirs of Wu Faxian*, Hong Kong: Beixing chubanshe, 3rd ed., February 2008, p. 778.
12. Qiu Huizuo, *The Memoirs of Qiu Huizuo*, Hong Kong: Xinshiji chubanshe (New Century Press), 2011, p. 681.
13. Wu Faxian, *Memoirs of Wu Faxian*, pp. 780–783. Wu Faxian is mistaken when he says the quarrel occurred on August 14.
14. Li Zuopeng, *The Memoirs of Li Zuopeng*, Hong Kong: Beixing chubanshe, 2011, p. 657.
15. Zhang Yunsheng, *Record of Actual Events at Maojiawan*, Chunqiu chubanshe, 1988, pp. 230–232.
16. Li Genqing, "Lin Biao's Reflections on Mao Zedong in His 'Random Notes,'" *Yanhuang Chunqiu*, no. 11, 2014.
17. CCP Central Committee Documentary Research Room (ed.), *Chronology of Mao Zedong: 1949–1976*, vol. 6, Beijing: Zhongyang wenxian chubanshe, 2013, p. 207, states that on October 13, 1968, Mao crossed out these three adverbs while vetting the "(Draft) Constitution of the Chinese Communist Party" that Kang Sheng, Zhang Chunqiao, and Yao Wenyuan had submitted to him on October 12.
18. Wu Faxian, *Memoirs of Wu Faxian*, p. 805.
19. Gao Wenqian, *Zhao Enlai's Later Years*, Mingjing chubanshe, 2004, 26th printing, p. 284.
20. "CCP Central Committee Notice Regarding Summary of Conversation in the Meeting of Chairman Mao with the Good American Snow," Central Committee Document No. 39 [1971], May 31, 1971, quoted in *Chinese Cultural Revolution Database*, ed. Song Yongyi et al., 3rd ed., Universities Service Centre for China Studies, Chinese University of Hong Kong Press, 2013.

21. Zhu Tingxun, *The Tumultuous Life of Li Desheng*, Zhongyang wenxian chubanshe, 2010, p. 170.

22. CCP Central Committee Documentary Research Room (ed.), *Chronology of Mao Zedong: 1949–1976*, p. 294, states that Mao left Shanghai and arrived in Suzhou on April 25. Official histories do not reveal that Mao visited Lin Biao or what they discussed, but in fact this was an important historical incident.

23. Gao Wenqian, *Zhao Enlai's Later Years*, p. 276; Wang Nianyi, *Era of Upheaval*, Henan renmin chubanshe, 1988, p. 388.

24. Chen Zhao, "Mao Zedong Didn't Fear Lin Biao, but Feared Lin Liguo," Duowei News reporter Li Jie's interview with Chen Zhao, *Cultural Revolution Museum*, no. 918.

25. "CCP Central Committee Notice and Documents Regarding Organizing the Transmission and Discussion of 'The Fight to Smash the Lin-Chen Anti-Party Clique's Counterrevolutionary Coup d'État'" (Document No. 1), December 11, 1971, Central Committee Document No. 77 [1971].

26. Gao Hua, "A Reinvestigation of the 'Lin Biao Incident,'" collection of Netease commentaries, August 1, 2008, 16:32:18.

27. Wu Faxian, *Memoirs of Wu Faxian*, p. 791.

28. Qiu Huizuo, *Memoirs of Qiu Huizuo*, p. 691. Chen Boda's memoirs do not mention him advising Lin Biao to give a speech.

29. Wu Faxian, *Memoirs of Wu Faxian*, p. 793. This incident is also described in Qiu Huizuo, *Memoirs of Qiu Huizuo*, p. 687; and Li Zuopeng, *Memoirs of Li Zuopeng*, p. 660. All three drew their information from Ye Qun.

30. Record of Gao Wenqian's interview with Wu Faxian on November 18–25, 1993, quoted in Gao Wenqian, *Zhao Enlai's Later Years*, p. 291. Qiu Huizuo, *Memoirs of Qiu Huizuo*, p. 697, has similar content.

31. *Biography of Mao Zedong: 1949–1976*, p. 1565.

32. Chen Xiaonong, *Chen Boda's Final Oral Recollections*, Beijing: Dongfang chubanshe, 2010, p. 406.

33. Chen Changjiang and Zhao Guilai, *Mao Zedong's Last Ten Years: Recollections of the Chief of Security*, Zhonggong zhongyang dangxiao chubanshe, 1998, p. 134.

34. Record of interview with Zhang Yufeng, November 1, 2000, quoted in *Biography of Mao Zedong: 1949–1976*, p. 1566.

35. Qiu Huizuo, *Memoirs of Qiu Huizuo*, p. 696.

36. Qiu Huizuo, *Memoirs of Qiu Huizuo*, p. 697.

37. *Biography of Mao Zedong: 1949–1976*, p. 1567.

38. Xie Jiaxiang, "My Self-Criticism and Confession," June 20, 1972, in Song Yongyi et al., *Chinese Cultural Revolution Database*.

39. Qiu Huizuo, *Memoirs of Qiu Huizuo*, p. 699.

40. Wu De, as told to Zhu Shiyuan et al., *Wu De's Oral Account: A Chronicle of Ten Years of Trials and Hardships—Some of My Experiences Working in Beijing*, Dangdai Zhongguo chubanshe, 2004, p. 117.

41. Biography of Chen Yi Compilation Group, *Biography of Chen Yi*, Dangdai Zhongguo chubanshe, 1991, p. 617.

42. Wang Haiguang, *Crushing at Öndörkhaan*, Jiuzhou chubanshe, 2013, p. 114.

43. Xu Jingxian, *The Ten-Year Dream*, Hong Kong: Shidai guoji chuban gongsi, 2003, pp. 213–214.

44. Qiu Huizuo, *Memoirs of Qiu Huizuo*, p. 705.

45. The Central Committee Secretariat's deputy director, Wang Liang'en, handed these three letters over to Zhou, who sent them to Lin Biao, and they never reached Mao. The letters were confiscated from Lin's quarters after the Lin Biao Incident. During the campaign to denounce Lin Biao, Wang Liang'en was implicated in this matter and subsequently committed suicide.

46. Qiu Huizuo, *Memoirs of Qiu Huizuo*, p. 717.

47. Li Zuopeng, *Memoirs of Li Zuopeng*, p. 663.

48. "Xie Xuegong's Journal During the Second Plenum of the Ninth Central Committee," *Yanhuang Chunqiu*, no. 6, 2015.

49. Li Zuopeng, *Memoirs of Li Zuopeng*, p. 681.

50. Qiu Huizuo, *Memoirs of Qiu Huizuo*, p. 610.

51. Qiu Huizuo, *Memoirs of Qiu Huizuo*, p. 810.

52. Xiao Mu, "The Petrel and the Sun: A Preliminary Exploration of Zhang Chunqiao's Mental Trajectory," afterword to Zheng Zhong, *Zheng Chunqiao from 1949 Onward*, Chinese University of Hong Kong Press, 2017, PDF, p. 64; Yang Yinlu, "Jiang Qing During the Second Plenum of the Ninth Central Committee," *Dangshi Bolan*, no. 1, 2006; Xu Jingxian, *Ten-Year Dream*, pp. 218–219. Yang Yinlu says that Jiang Qing went on her own, while Xu Jingxian says she was accompanied by Zhang and Yao. Wang Haiguang, professor at the Central Party School, believes Xu's version is more reliable.

53. CCP Central Committee Documentary Research Room (ed.), *Chronology of Mao Zedong: 1949–1976*, vol. 6, p. 327.

54. Xu Jingxian, *Ten-Year Dream*, p. 216.

55. Wu Faxian, *Memoirs of Wu Faxian*, pp. 805–806.

56. Wu Faxian, *Memoirs of Wu Faxian*, p. 802, says it was on August 26. Qiu Huizuo says it was August 27.

57. Qiu Huizuo, *Memoirs of Qiu Huizuo*, pp. 710–712.

58. Qiu Huizuo, *Memoirs of Qiu Huizuo*, pp. 717–178.

59. Wu Faxian, *Memoirs of Wu Faxian*, p. 807.

60. Wu Faxian, *Memoirs of Wu Faxian*, pp. 808–809.

61. Qiu Huizuo, *Memoirs of Qiu Huizuo*, p. 719.

62. *Manuscripts of Mao Zedong Since the Founding of the Country*, vol. 13, Zhongyang wenxian chubanshe, 1998, pp. 114–115. The CCP Central Committee issued these comments along with instructions regarding the transmission of Chen Boda's anti-party problems on November 16, 1970.

63. CCP Central Committee Documentary Research Room (ed.), *Chronology of Zhou Enlai*, p. 392.

64. CCP Central Committee Documentary Research Room (ed.), *Chronology of Zhou Enlai*, p. 391.

65. Record of Gao Wenqian's interview with Wu Faxian on November 18–25, 1993, quoted in Gao Wenqian, *Zhao Enlai's Later Years*, pp. 298–299.

66. Gao Wenqian, *Zhao Enlai's Later Years*, p. 299.

67. Zhang Yunsheng, *Record of Actual Events at Maojiawan*, p. 397.

68. In fact, Chen Boda didn't sign an anti-communist notice when the Kuomintang released him from Beijing's Caolanzi Prison, because he was critically ill and near death; a townsman (a Shanxi warlord) bailed him out to receive medical treatment. Wang Li, *Wang Li's Record of Introspection*, vol. 2, 2nd ed., Hong Kong: Beixing chubanshe, May 2011, p. 113.

69. Qiu Huizuo, *Memoirs of Qiu Huizuo*, p. 722; Zhu Tingxun, *Tumultuous Life of Li Desheng*, pp. 155, 156.

70. Chen Xiaonong, *Chen Boda's Final Oral Recollections*, p. 396; Wang Wenyao and Wang Baochun, *Chen Boda Before and After the Cultural Revolution: A Secretary's Testimony*, Hong Kong: Cosmos Books (Tiandi tushu chubanshe), 2014, p. 146.
71. CCP Central Committee Documentary Research Room (ed.), *Chronology of Mao Zedong: 1949–1976*, vol. 6, p. 332.
72. Xu Jingxian, *Ten-Year Dream*, p. 227.
73. Xu Jingxian, *Ten-Year Dream*, p. 227.
74. Yang Yinlu, "Jiang Qing During the Second Plenum of the Ninth Central Committee."
75. Qiu Huizuo, *Memoirs of Qiu Huizuo*, p. 723.
76. Qiu Huizuo, *Memoirs of Qiu Huizuo*, p. 723.
77. Summary of Mao Zedong's remarks to leading cadres during his tour of the provinces, August–September 1971, in Song Yongyi et al., *Database of the Chinese Cultural Revolution*.
78. "CCP Central Committee Notice and Documents Regarding Organizing the Transmission and Discussion of 'The Fight to Smash the Lin-Chen Anti-Party Clique's Counterrevolutionary Coup d'État'" (Document No. 3), July 2, 1972, Central Committee Document No. 24 [1972].

22. CHEN BODA'S DENUNCIATION AND LIN BIAO'S ESCAPE ATTEMPT

1. CCP Central Committee transmission of the Thirty-Eighth Army party committee's "Report Exposing Chen Boda's Anti-Party Crimes," December 16, 1970, Central Party Document No. 76 [1970].
2. Chen Xiaonong, *Chen Boda's Final Oral Recollections*, Beijing: Dongfang chubanshe, 2010, p. 360.
3. *Manuscripts of Mao Zedong Since the Founding of the Country*, vol. 12, Zhongyang wenxian chubanshe, 1998, p. 188.
4. Wu Faxian, *The Memoirs of Wu Faxian*, Hong Kong: Beixing chubanshe, 3rd ed., February 2008, p. 830.
5. Zhang Guotao was one of the founders of the Chinese Communist Party and worked in Central Committee organs before becoming the leader of the E-Yu-Wan (Hubei-Henan-Anhui) Soviet Area in 1932. During the Long March, his Fourth Front Red Army had more than eighty thousand men, compared with fewer than ten thousand commanded by Mao. Zhang and Mao developed differences of opinion, and after arriving in Yan'an, Zhang's subordinates Li Te and Huang Chao were falsely accused of being Trotskyites by Wang Ming and were killed in early 1938. Feeling increasingly unsafe, Zhang Guotao left the CCP and joined the Kuomintang in April 1938. From then on, he was considered a representative of the erroneous line that split the party.
6. As hostilities intensified in Wuhu in summer 1968, Li Desheng convinced the participants to lay down their arms before a shot could be fired. The Anhui provincial revolutionary committee and Twelfth Army party committee submitted the "Summing-Up Report on Handling the Wuhu Problem" to the Central Committee, and it was issued to the entire country as Central Committee Document No. 120 [1968].
7. Zhu Tingxun, *The Tumultuous Life of Li Desheng*, Zhongyang wenxian chubanshe, 2010, pp. 160, 161.
8. Ji Pomin, "In Power and Out of Power, in Office and Out of Office: Listening to My Father Talk of the Past," *Gongshiwang*, October 1, 2013.

9. *Manuscripts of Mao Zedong Since the Founding of the Country*, vol. 13, p. 206.

10. Zhou Enlai's remarks were first written up in outline form and sent to Mao for vetting on January 22. Mao had Zhou come in to discuss the outline the next day, and Zhou amended it in accordance with Mao's views, then submitted it again for his approval. See *Manuscripts of Mao Zedong Since the Founding of the Country*, vol. 13, pp. 203–204. Zhou's speech was subsequently issued to the county and regimental levels as Central Committee Document No. 6 [1971].

11. Wu Faxian, *Memoirs of Wu Faxian*, pp. 827–828.

12. *Manuscripts of Mao Zedong Since the Founding of the Country*, vol. 13, pp. 137–142.

13. The following quotes come from *Manuscripts of Mao Zedong Since the Founding of the Country*, vol. 13, pp. 143–146.

14. Wu Faxian, *Memoirs of Wu Faxian*, p. 830.

15. CCP Central Committee Documentary Research Room (ed.), *Chronology of Zhou Enlai*, vol. 2, Zhongyang wenxian chubanshe, 1997, p. 403.

16. Li Genqing, "Lin Biao's Reflections on Mao Zedong in His 'Random Notes,'" *Yanhuang Chunqiu*, no. 11, 2014.

17. CCP Central Committee Documentary Research Room (ed.), *Chronology of Mao Zedong: 1949–1976*, vol. 6, Beijing: Zhongyang wenxian chubanshe, 2013, p. 374.

18. CCP Central Committee Documentary Research Room (ed.), *Chronology of Mao Zedong: 1949–1976*, vol. 6, pp. 374–375.

19. Zhu Tingxun, *Tumultuous Life of Li Desheng*, pp. 172–172; CCP Central Committee Documentary Research Room (ed.), *Chronology of Zhou Enlai*, vol. 2, p. 447.

20. Zhu Tingxun, *Tumultuous Life of Li Desheng*, p. 173.

21. Qiu Huizuo, *The Memoirs of Qiu Huizuo*, Hong Kong: Xinshiji chubanshe (New Century Press), 2011, pp. 779–780.

22. Li Genqing, "Lin Biao's Reflections on Mao Zedong."

23. Zhu Tingxun, *Tumultuous Life of Li Desheng*, p. 174.

24. CCP Central Committee Documentary Research Room (ed.), *Chronology of Mao Zedong: 1949–1976*, vol. 6, p. 380.

25. CCP Central Committee Documentary Research Room (ed.), *Chronology of Zhou Enlai*, vol. 2, p. 454.

26. Li Genqing, "Lin Biao's Reflections on Mao Zedong."

27. Gu Baozi and Du Xiuxian, *Mao Zedong's Tumultuous Last Ten Years*, Renmin wenxue chubanshe, 2010, pp. 63–64. Wang Haiguang believes that Du Xiuxian's recollection is inaccurate and that Lin Biao let Mao know that he was leaving.

28. Wu Zhong, as told to Chen Chusan and Li Dazhen, "Wu Zhong Talks About the September 13 Incident," *Yanhuang Chunqiu*, no. 1, 2012. According to Wu Zhong, Lin Biao's letter contained some errors because "some parts of the tape recording were inaudible." This book has made some corrections according to the version provided in Yu Ruxin, "The True Features of Lin Biao's Draft Letter."

29. Li Genqing, "Lin Biao's Reflections on Mao Zedong."

30. Gao Wenqian, *Zhao Enlai's Later Years*, Mingjing chubanshe, 2004, 26th printing, p. 322.

31. Xiong Xianghui, *History's Footnotes: Recalling Mao Zedong, Zhou Enlai, and Four Veteran Marshals*, Zhongyang dangxiao chubanshe, 1995, pp. 30–33.
32. Cheng Guang, *Dialogue of the Soul*, Hong Kong: Beixing chubanshe, 2011, pp. 577–583.
33. Zhang Yaoci, *The Memoirs of Zhang Yaoci: The Days with Mao*, Zhonggong dangshi chubanshe, 2008, p. 178.
34. Wu Faxian, *Memoirs of Wu Faxian*, p. 860.
35. The timing of Mao's travels on his southern tour and his meetings with officials are recorded in *Chronology of Mao Zedong*, vol. 6. The remarks by Mao cited below, unless otherwise indicated, come from National Defense University Party History and Party-Building Research Department, *Cultural Revolution Research Material* 1, vol. 2, "Summary of Remarks by Chairman Mao to Leading Comrades of Various Places During His Inspection Tour to the Outer Provinces" (Mid-August to September 12, 1971).
36. Gao Wenqian, *Zhao Enlai's Later Years*, p. 339.
37. Supreme People's Court Research Office, ed., *Record of the Trial of Prime Culprits of the Lin Biao-Jiang Qing Counterrevolutionary Clique by the Special Court of the Supreme People's Court of the People's Republic of China*, Lalü chubanshe, 1982, 1st ed., pp. 122–123.
38. "Prosecution of Gu Tongzhou for Aiding the Enemy by the Chinese People's Liberation Army Procuratorate," February 25, 1982, quoted in Shu Yun, *A Complete Investigation of the Lin Biao Incident*.
39. Jin Chunming, ed., *A Critique of the Cambridge History of the People's Republic of China*, p. 632, quoted in *Retrying the Lin Biao Case*, vol. 2, ed. Ding Kaiwen, Mingjing chubanshe, 2004, p. 997.
40. Zhang Ning, *Misfortune of Life*, Mingjing chubanshe, 1997, p. 193.
41. Li Weixin's written confession, "The Struggle to Smash the Lin-Chen Anti-Party Clique's Counterrevolutionary Coup d'État" (Document No. 2), January 13, 1972, Central Committee Document No. 4 [1972].
42. Record of interview with Lin Biao's secretary Guan Guanglie, September 9, 2000, quoted in Shu Yun, *Complete Investigation of the Lin Biao Incident*.
43. "Lu Min cannot bear to recall the past," in Song Qun, *The Back View Remains in the Heart*, Beijing shidai mingyu wenhua fazhan youxian gongsi chuban, 2013, pp. 158–165.
44. TN: This was an assassination committed with explosives on June 4, 1928, by the Japanese Kwantung Army against the Fengtian warlord Zhang Zuolin.
45. Shi Niantang, *History Will Expose the Deeper Layer of the Lin Biao Case: Recollections of an Air Force Chartered Plane Division Commander*, says that the amount of fuel loaded onto the plane indicates that the intention was to fly directly to Guangzhou. Flying to the Soviet Union would have required more than twenty tons of fuel.
46. Zhang Yaoci, *Memoirs of Zhang Yaoci*, p. 193.
47. Ji Dong, *Unusual Times: Recalling the Last Eight Years of Premier Zhou Enlai*, Zhongyang wenxian chubanshe, 2012, p. 121. CCP Central Committee Documentary Research Room (ed.), *Chronology of Zhou Enlai*, vol. 2, p. 480, states that it was around 11:00 p.m., while Zhang Yaoci says it was at 11:20.
48. Zhang Yaoci, *Memoirs of Zhang Yaoci*, p. 194.
49. Ji Dong, *Unusual Times*, p. 122.

50. Wang Dongxing, Li Zuopeng, and Guo Yufeng recall that it was Zhou Enlai who telephoned Ye Qun (Wang Dongxing, *Memoirs of Wang Dongxing: Mao Zedong's Fight with the Lin Biao Counterrevolutionary Clique*, Dangdai Zhongguo chubanshe, 1997, p. 205; Li Zuopeng, *The Memoirs of Li Zuopeng*, Hong Kong: Beixing chubanshe, 2011, p. 698; Yan Jingming, *My Husband, Guo Yufeng*, Hong Kong: Zhongguo wenhua chuanbo chubanshe, 2010, p. 55). Zhang Yaoci, Wu Faxian, and Qiu Huizuo recall that Ye Qun telephoned Zhou Enlai (Zhang Yaoci, *Memoirs of Zhang Yaoci*, p. 195; Wu Faxian, *Memoirs of Wu Faxian*, p. 862; Qiu Huizuo, *The Memoirs of Qiu Huizuo*, Hong Kong: Xinshiji chubanshe [New Century Press], 2011, p. 793). Lin Liheng also said that Ye Qun telephoned Zhou Enlai. On August 26, 1972, Zhou told Lin Liheng that Ye Qun telephoned to request leave to go to Guangzhou ("Material Written by Lin Liheng for the Central Commission on Discipline Inspection Regarding the Events of September 13," in Yu Ruxin, ed., *Looking Back at "9-13": Historical Fact and Analysis of the Lin Biao Incident*, Hong Kong: Xinshiji chubanshe [New Century Press], 2013, p. 45). At that time, the edited record by staff from the Central Security Bureau recorded that Ye Qun telephoned Zhou at 11:22.

51. Wang Dongxing, *Memoirs of Wang Dongxing*, pp. 205–206.

52. Li Zuopeng, *Memoirs of Li Zuopeng*, vol. 2, p. 481.

53. Kang Tingzi, "A Chartered Flight Copilot's Personal Experience of '9-13,'" Zhongqing chubanshe, 2013, pp. 60, 68, 69, quoted in Wang Haiguang, *Analyzing the Enigma of the "9-13 Incident": A Critique of Ms. Shu Yun's Ten Great Enigmas of "9-13."*

54. Li Zuopeng, *Memoirs of Li Zuopeng*, vol. 2, p. 697.

55. CCP Central Archives Research Office, Jin Chongji, ed., *Biography of Zhou Enlai*, Zhongyang wenxian chubanshe, 1998, p. 1998.

56. Wang Dongxing, *Memoirs of Wang Dongxing*, pp. 207–208.

57. Wu Faxian, *Memoirs of Wu Faxian*, p. 864, states, "When the aircraft reached the vicinity of Chifeng, we had a fighter plane unit there, and I asked Zhou Enlai if we should intercept the Trident. Zhou said he would request instructions from the Chairman."

58. Wang Dongxing, *Memoirs of Wang Dongxing*, p. 208.

59. Ji Dong, *Unusual Times*, pp. 125, 126–127.

60. Zhu Tingxun, *Tumultuous Life of Li Desheng*, p. 211. Li Desheng saying that he had the helicopter intercepted and attacked is inconsistent with fact. One explanation is that the helicopter was forced to land after running out of fuel and was not fired upon.

61. Ji Dong, *Unusual Times*, pp. 128–129. Wang Dongxing, *Memoirs of Wang Dongxing*, p. 2112, says Zhou Enlai told Wang Dongxing to go to the Great Hall of the People to report to Mao that Lin Biao had died in a plane crash, rather than Zhou reporting it to Mao himself.

62. Qiu Huizuo, *Memoirs of Qiu Huizuo*, p. 796.

63. Record of Gao Wenqian's interview with Ji Dengkui, quoted in Gao Wenqian, *Zhao Enlai's Later Years*, p. 358.

64. "Huang Chunguang and Qiu Luguang's Dialogue about '9-13,' July 20, 2011," *Jiyi (Remembrance)*, no. 75, September 13, 2011.

65. "CCP Central Committee Notice Regarding Lin Biao Betraying and Fleeing the Country," September 18, 1971, Central Committee Document No. 57 [1971].

66. Ding Sheng, *Hero in Hardship: The Memoirs of General Ding Sheng*, ed.

Jin Guang and Yu Ruxin, Hong Kong: Xingke'er chuban gongsi, 2008, p. 216.

67. "Material Written by Lin Liheng for the Central Commission on Discipline Inspection Regarding the Events of September 13," in *Looking Back at "9-13": Historical Fact and Analysis of the Lin Biao Incident*, ed. Yu Ruxin, Hong Kong: Xin shiji chubanshe, 2013, pp. 25–46.

68. Jiang Jian, "Unable to Bear Delving Deeply into History: Uncovering the Mystery of the Black Box in the '9-13 Incident,'" *Jiyi (Remembrance)*, no. 119, September 30, 2014.

23. CRITICIZING LIN BIAO—AS A LEFTIST OR RIGHTIST?

1. CCP Central Committee Documentary Research Room (ed.), *Chronology of Mao Zedong: 1949–1976*, vol. 6, p. 417.

2. *Manuscripts of Mao Zedong Since the Founding of the Country*, vol. 13, Zhongyang wenxian chubanshe, 1998, p. 334. On October 20, 1972, Liu's wife, Liu Shuqing, wrote a letter to Mao reporting that Liu Jianzhang had been restricted to three glasses of water per day in prison and was allowed only thirty minutes of exercise daily.

3. CCP Central Committee Documentary Research Room (ed.), *Chronology of Zhou Enlai*, vol. 2, p. 531.

4. CCP Central Committee Documentary Research Room (ed.), *Chronology of Mao Zedong: 1949–1976*, vol. 6, pp. 513–514.

5. CCP Central Committee Documentary Research Room (ed.), *Chronology of Zhou Enlai*, vol. 2, pp. 500–502.

6. Jin Chongji, ed., *Biography of Zhou Enlai*, Zhongyang wenxian chubanshe, 1998, p. 2017.

7. CCP Central Committee Documentary Research Room (ed.), *Chronology of Zhou Enlai*, vol. 2, p. 518.

8. CCP Central Committee Documentary Research Room (ed.), *Chronology of Zhou Enlai*, vol. 2, pp. 541–542.

9. CCP Central Committee Documentary Research Room (ed.), *Chronology of Zhou Enlai*, vol. 2, p. 507.

10. CCP Central Committee Documentary Research Room (ed.), *Chronology of Zhou Enlai*, vol. 2, p. 508.

11. CCP Central Committee Documentary Research Room (ed.), *Chronology of Zhou Enlai*, vol. 2, p. 521.

12. Zhou Peiyuan, "Learn from the Revolutionary Spirit of Premier Zhou," *Beijing Daily*, July 6, 1977.

13. Zhou Peiyuan, "Learn from the Revolutionary Spirit of Premier Zhou."

14. National Day editorial published in *People's Daily*, *Red Flag*, and *PLA Daily*, October 1, 1972.

15. Gao Wenqian, *Zhao Enlai's Later Years*, Mingjing chubanshe, 2004, 26th printing, pp. 389–390.

16. Wang Ruoshui, "The Transition from Criticizing 'Leftism' to Criticizing Rightism: Recalling the Disagreement over the Guiding Principle for Criticizing Lin in 1972," *Bainianchao*, no. 5, 1998.

17. The entire content of *People's Daily* criticizing anarchism, quoted in Wang Ruoshui, "The Transition from Criticizing 'Leftism' to Criticizing Rightism"; Li Dingzhong, "*People's Daily* Denounced Disastrous Anarchy," *Yanhuang Chunqiu*, no. 7, 2013.

18. The British writer Han Suyin, who was a friend of Zhou Enlai's and Deng Yingchao's, maintains this view. See Han Suyin, *Zhou Enlai and His World*, Zhongyang wenxian chubanshe, p. 512.

19. CCP Central Committee Documentary Research Room (ed.), *Chronology of Mao Zedong: 1949–1976*, vol. 6, p. 426.

20. Li Zhisui, *The Memoirs of Mao Zedong's Personal Physician*, Taiwan shibao wenhua chubanshe, p. 529; English edition, *The Private Life of Chairman Mao*, trans. Tai Hung-chao and ed. Anne F. Thurston, London: Chatto and Windus, 1994, pp. 551–552. Some informed sources are doubtful of what Li wrote in his book regarding Mao's remarks on major national affairs, because when Mao talked about politics, Li Zhisui wasn't present. However, what Li writes about Mao's health should be reliable.

21. Referring to Lin Biao's speech at the enlarged Politburo meeting on May 18, 1966.

22. Zhou Enlai, "Speech at the Central Committee's First Reporting Meeting on the Campaign to Criticize Lin," May 21, 1972.

23. Chen Xiaoya, "Mao Zedong's 'Letter to Jiang Qing': Genuine or Fake?," in *Retrying the Lin Biao Case*, vol. 2, ed. Ding Kaiwen, Mingjing chubanshe, 2004, pp. 614–620.

24. The author's conversation with Warren Sun at Peking University on October 25, 2013. Mr. Sun's special aptitude for textual research is highly regarded in historical circles.

25. Zhang Liangzuo, *Zhou Enlai's Last Ten Years: A Doctor's Memoirs*, Shanghai renmin chubanshe, 1998, pp. 295, 301.

26. Gao Wenqian, *Zhao Enlai's Later Years*, p. 378. *Biography of Zhou Enlai*, p. 2014, gives a different version, stating that on November 12, 1972, Mao wrote a memo on the report stating, "Should be treated as resting and conserving energy and not be considered critical."

27. Gao Wenqian, *Zhao Enlai's Later Years*, p. 375.

28. Zhou Enlai, "My Reflections on the Six Line Struggles During Our Party's New Democratic Revolution Phase," June 10, 1972, quoted in Gao Wenqian, *Zhao Enlai's Later Years*, p. 376.

29. CCP Central Committee Documentary Research Room (ed.), *Chronology of Zhou Enlai*, vol. 2, p. 531.

30. Gao Wenqian, *Zhao Enlai's Later Years*, p. 451.

31. Zhou Enlai's letter to comrades in the Foreign Ministry's party core group and Americas and Oceania Department, July 3, 1973, manuscript, quoted in Gao Wenqian, *Zhao Enlai's Later Years*, p. 452.

32. Jin Boxiong, "Why Zhou Enlai Was Denounced in 1973," *Yanhuang Chunqiu*, no. 2, 2012.

33. CCP Central Committee Documentary Research Room (ed.), *Chronology of Zhou Enlai*, vol. 2, p. 603.

34. CCP Central Committee Documentary Research Room (ed.), *Chronology of Zhou Enlai*, vol. 2, p. 604.

35. CCP Central Documentary Research Room, *Anthology of Documents from Ten Years of the Cultural Revolution*, vol. 2, quoted in Gao Wenqian, *Zhao Enlai's Later Years*, p. 454.

36. Record of Gao Wenqian's interview with Ji Dengkui, quoted in Gao Wenqian, *Zhao Enlai's Later Years*, p. 456.

37. CCP Central Committee Documentary Research Room (ed.), *Chronology of Zhou Enlai*, vol. 2, p. 604.

38. TN: See William Burr, ed., *The Kissinger Transcripts: The Top-Secret Talks with Beijing and Moscow*, New York: New Press, 1999, pp. 170–171.

39. Shi Yun and Li Danhui, *The Continuous Revolution That Was Difficult to Continue: From Criticizing Lin to Criticizing Deng*, Chinese University of Hong Kong Press, 2008, p. 180. TN: William Burr, *Kissinger Transcripts*, p. 173.

40. CCP Central Committee Documentary Research Room (ed.), *Chronology of Zhou Enlai*, vol. 2, p. 633.

41. TN: William Burr, *Kissinger Transcripts*, p. 183.

42. Jin Boxiong, "Why Zhou Enlai Was Denounced in 1973."

43. TN: William Burr, *Kissinger Transcripts*, pp. 203–204.

44. Shi Yun and Li Danhui, *Continuous Revolution*, p. 182.

45. Jin Boxiong, "Why Zhou Enlai Was Denounced in 1973."

46. Shi Yun and Li Danhui, *Continuous Revolution*, p. 183. Shi and Li base their record on documents relating to Sino-U.S. relations, including the record of conversations between Zhou Enlai and Henry Kissinger, which the United States declassified in early 1999. TN: William Burr, *Kissinger Transcripts*, pp. 210–211.

47. Record of Gao Wenqian's interview with Qiao Guanhua and Zhang Hanzhi, Gao Wenqian, *Zhao Enlai's Later Years*, pp. 463–464; *Chronology of Mao Zedong: 1949–1976*, vol. 6, p. 506.

48. Record of Gao Wenqian's interview with Qiao Guanhua and Zhang Hanzhi, Gao Wenqian, *Zhao Enlai's Later Years*, p. 465.

49. CCP Central Committee Documentary Research Room (ed.), *Chronology of Zhou Enlai*, vol. 2, p. 634.

50. Jin Boxiong, "Why Zhou Enlai Was Denounced in 1973."

51. Party historians claimed that there had been ten line struggles since the founding of the CCP with the following opposing parties: Chen Duxiu, Qu Qiubai, Li Lisan, Luo Zhanglong, Wang Ming, Zhang Guotao, Gao Gang, Peng Dehuai, Liu Shaoqi, and Lin Biao.

52. Record of Gao Wenqian's interview with Qiao Guanhua and Zhang Hanzhi, Gao Wenqian, *Zhao Enlai's Later Years*, p. 466.

53. Shi Yun and Li Danhui, *Continuous Revolution*, p. 175.

54. Zhou Bingde, *My Uncle, Zhou Enlai*, Renmin chubanshe, 2009, pp. 330–336.

55. Record of Gao Wenqian's interview with Ji Dengkui, quoted in Gao Wenqian, *Zhao Enlai's Later Years*, p. 472.

56. Mao Mao, *My Father, Deng Xiaoping: The Cultural Revolution Years*, Zhongyang wenxian chubanshe, 2000, p. 289.

57. CCP Central Committee Documentary Research Room (ed.), *Chronology of Mao Zedong: 1949–1976*, vol. 6, p. 512.

58. CCP Central Committee Documentary Research Room, *Biography of Mao Zedong: 1949–1976*, Zhongyang wenxian chubanshe, 2003, p. 1667.

59. Zhang Liangzuo, *Zhou Enlai's Last Ten Years*, p. 312.

60. Record of Gao Wenqian's interview with Qiao Guanhua and Zhang Hanzhi, Gao Wenqian, *Zhao Enlai's Later Years*, p. 474.

61. Gao Wenqian, *Zhao Enlai's Later Years*, p. 475.

62. Gao Wenqian, *Zhao Enlai's Later Years*, p. 475.

63. Material that Tang Wensheng and Wang Hairong wrote for Hua Guofeng on October 17, 1976, provided by the Central Committee trial leading group for the "two cases" (of the "Lin Biao and Jiang Qing counterrevolutionary cliques").

64. Xu Jingxian, *Xu Jingxian's Final Memoir*, Hong Kong: Xingke'er chuban youxian gongsi, 2013, p. 307.
65. Mao Mao, *My Father, Deng Xiaoping*, vol. 1, Zhongyang wenxian chubanshe, 1993, p. 318.
66. Zhu Zhongli, *Mao Zedong and Wang Jiaxiang in My Life*, Zhongyang dang-xiao chubanshe, 1995, p. 224.
67. Mao Mao, *My Father, Deng Xiaoping: The Cultural Revolution Years*, Zhong-yang wenxian chubanshe, 2000, pp. 44–45.
68. *Manuscripts of Mao Zedong Since the Founding of the Country*, vol. 13, p. 308.
69. CCP Central Committee Documentary Research Room (ed.), *Chronology of Zhou Enlai*, vol. 2, p. 644.
70. Gao Wenqian, *Zhao Enlai's Later Years*, p. 507.
71. CCP Central Committee Documentary Research Room (ed.), *Chronology of Mao Zedong: 1949–1976*, vol. 6, p. 523.
72. CCP Central Committee Documentary Research Room (ed.), *Chronology of Mao Zedong: 1949–1976*, vol. 6, p. 549.
73. Xu Jingxian, *The Ten-Year Dream*, Hong Kong: Shidai guoji chuban gongsi, 2003, pp. 291–292.
74. Mao Mao, *My Father, Deng Xiaoping: The Cultural Revolution Years*, p. 284.
75. Mao Yuanxin's conversation with Yan Changgui; see Yan Changgui, "Mao Yuanxin Again Speaks of Mao Zedong's Situation in 1976," *Yanhuang Chun-qiu*, no. 10, November 2012.
76. Wu De, as told to Zhu Shiyuan et al., *Wu De's Oral Account: A Chronicle of Ten Years of Trials and Hardships—Some of My Experiences Working in Beijing*, Dangdai Zhongguo chubanshe, 2004, pp. 110–111.
77. CCP Central Committee, "Resolution Regarding Historical Problems in the Party Since the Founding of the Country," June 27, 1981.
78. CCP Central Committee, "Resolution Regarding Historical Problems in the Party."
79. *Biography of Mao Zedong: 1949–1976*, pp. 1664–1665.

24. INTERNAL STRUGGLE DURING THE CAMPAIGN TO CRITICIZE LIN BIAO AND CONFUCIUS

1. Li Xun, *The Revolutionary Rebel Era: A History of Shanghai's Cultural Rev-olution Movement*, Hong Kong: Oxford University Press, 2015, pp. 1313–1315.
2. Xinhua News Agency reporter's investigation, "The Devastating Persecution of Educated Youth in the Eighteenth Regiment of the Fourth Division of the Yunnan Production-Construction Corps," *Galleys of Domestic Trends*, no. 241, ed. Xinhua News Agency, July 4, 1973. According to this report, more than one hundred young women were raped by military personnel in Yun-nan, and close to three hundred in Inner Mongolia.
3. CCP Central Committee Documentary Research Room (ed.), *Chronology of Zhou Enlai*, vol. 2, Zhongyang wenxian chubanshe, 1997, p. 649.
4. *Manuscripts of Mao Zedong Since the Founding of the Country*, vol. 13, Zhongyang wenxian chubanshe, p. 377.
5. Wang Sirui shares this view. See "Trial Analysis of the Leftist Spectrum in Today's China," *Modern China Studies* (Princeton University), no. 2, 2001.
6. Mr. Guo was Guo Moruo.
7. CCP Central Committee Documentary Research Room (ed.), *Chronology of Mao Zedong: 1949–1976*, vol. 6, Beijing: Zhongyang wenxian chubanshe, p. 485.

8. CCP Central Committee Documentary Research Room (ed.), *Chronology of Mao Zedong: 1949–1976*, vol. 6, p. 490.

9. CCP Central Committee Documentary Research Room (ed.), *Chronology of Mao Zedong: 1949–1976*, vol. 6, p. 500. Compared with the remarks by Mao communicated by Yao Wenyuan (see Song Yongyi et al., *Chinese Cultural Revolution Database*), the *Chronology* deleted the words "I'm also Qin Shihuang; Lin Biao berated me as Qin Shihuang."

10. Feng Youlan, "Twenty-Five Versified Historic Events (and Preface)," published in the September 14, 1974, edition of *Guangming Daily*.

11. Shi Yun and Li Danhui, *The Continuous Revolution That Was Difficult to Continue: From Criticizing Lin to Criticizing Deng*, Chinese University of Hong Kong Press, 2008, p. 345.

12. Wang Hui, *A Personal History of the Cultural Revolution in Tianjin*, self-published, 2011.

13. CCP Central Committee Documentary Research Room (ed.), *Chronology of Mao Zedong: 1949–1976*, vol. 6, p. 512.

14. Lao Tian, "Record of Conversations with People Who Experienced the Cultural Revolution."

15. Tan Qilong, *The Memoirs of Tan Qilong*, Zhonggong dangshi chubanshe, 2003, pp. 699–700.

16. Tan Qilong, *Memoirs of Tan Qilong*, p. 710.

17. Peng Chong (1915–2000) joined the CCP in 1934 and was a member of the Jiangsu Provincial Party Committee Secretariat when he was struck down at the outset of the Cultural Revolution. He was later reinstated, and prior to the CLCC campaign he was an alternate member of the Central Committee, vice-chairman of the Jiangsu Provincial Revolutionary Committee, and deputy party secretary of Jiangsu Province in charge of seizing production. Xu Jiatun (1916–2016) joined the CCP in 1938 and was a member of the Jiangsu Provincial Party Committee Secretariat when he was struck down at the outset of the Cultural Revolution. In 1969 he was reappointed vice-chairman of the provincial revolutionary committee, but had no real power.

18. In the two or three years after military control was imposed on Jiangsu, 350,000 of the province's urban residents were forced to settle in the countryside. In Nanjing alone, more than 130,000 people were sent to the villages. See Dong Guoqiang and Andrew G. Walder, "Nanjing's 'Second Cultural Revolution' of 1974," *China Quarterly*, no. 212, December 2012.

19. Dong Guoqiang and Andrew G. Walder, "Nanjing's 'Second Cultural Revolution' of 1974."

20. Dong Guoqiang and Andrew G. Walder, "Nanjing's 'Second Cultural Revolution' of 1974."

21. *Jiangsu Province Gazetteer: CCP Gazetteer*, Jiangsu renmin chubanshe, 2003, p. 320.

22. *Chronicle of Important Events in Jiangsu Province (1949–1985)*, Nanjing: Jiangsu renmin chubanshe, 1988, p. 329.

23. Dong Guoqiang and Andrew G. Walder, "Nanjing's 'Second Cultural Revolution' of 1974."

24. *Yudou County Gazetteer*, Xinhua chubanshe, chronology, p. 50; *Wanzai County Gazetteer*, Jiangxi renmin chubanshe, 1988, chronology, p. 31; *Dingnan County Gazetteer*, 1990, internally distributed, chronology, p. 37.

25. The material on Li Jiulian comes from Lao Gui, "The Whole Story of the Li Jiulian Case," *Southern Weekend*, November 24, 2005.

26. CCP Central Committee Secretariat transmission of "Report Outline of the State Planning Commission's Report to the Politburo Regarding the Present Industrial and Agricultural Production Problems," July 1, 1974.

27. Shi Yun and Li Danhui, *Continuous Revolution That Was Difficult to Continue*, p. 401.

28. Wang Hongwen's testimony at the Supreme Court trial of Jiang Qing, November 26, 1980.

29. CCP Central Committee Documentary Research Room (ed.), *Chronology of Mao Zedong: 1949–1976*, vol. 6, p. 554.

30. CCP Central Committee Documentary Research Room, *Biography of Mao Zedong: 1949–1976*, Zhongyang wenxian chubanshe, 2003, p. 1686.

31. The essays were actually resurrected by Mao in 1964. The general title of these nine essays was "Criticism of the Central Committee Line from September 1931 to January 1935." See *Manuscripts of Mao Zedong Since the Founding of the Country*, vol. 11, p. 49.

32. Chen Xilian's remarks on the crimes of the Gang of Four counterrevolutionary conspiratorial clique and the Central Committee's reports on the cases, August 16, 1980, quoted in Gao Wenqian, *Zhao Enlai's Later Years*, Mingjing chubanshe, 2004, 26th printing, p. 517.

33. Record of Mao Zedong's conversation with Politburo members in Beijing, July 17, 1974, quoted in Gao Wenqian, *Zhao Enlai's Later Years*, p. 519.

34. Gao Wenqian, *Zhao Enlai's Later Years*, p. 519.

35. CCP Central Committee Documentary Research Room (ed.), *Chronology of Mao Zedong: 1949–1976*, vol. 6, p. 579.

36. *Manuscripts of Mao Zedong Since the Founding of the Country*, vol. 13, p. 580.

37. Wu De, as told to Zhu Shiyuan et al., *Wu De's Oral Account: A Chronicle of Ten Years of Trials and Hardships—Some of My Experiences Working in Beijing*, Dangdai Zhongguo chubanshe, 2004, p. 160.

38. CCP Central Committee Documentary Research Room (ed.), *Chronology of Zhou Enlai*, vol. 2, p. 703. The meeting Wang Hongwen referred to was the enlarged Politburo meeting in December 1973 during which Zhou Enlai and Yi Jianying were denounced.

39. Mao Zedong, "Talk with Politburo Members in Beijing," May 3, 1975, a document provided by the secretariat of the Central Committee General Office, quoted in *Chinese Cultural Revolution Database*, ed. Song Yongyi et al., 3rd ed., Universities Service Centre for China Studies, Chinese University of Hong Kong Press, 2013. CCP Central Committee Documentary Research Room (ed.), *Chronology of Mao Zedong: 1949–1976*, vol. 6, pp. 582–584, also has this content.

40. CCP Central Archives Research Room, Jin Chongji, ed., *Biography of Zhou Enlai*, Zhongyang wenxian chubanshe, 1998, pp. 2130–2131.

41. CCP Central Committee Documentary Research Room (ed.), *Chronology of Zhou Enlai*, vol. 2, pp. 706–708.

42. This refers to what Mao said during his southern tour from mid-August to September 12, 1971: "We want to engage in Marxism, not revisionism; to be united, not divided; to be just and honorable, not scheming and intriguing."

43. CCP Central Committee Documentary Research Room (ed.), *Chronology of Zhou Enlai*, vol. 2, p. 709.

44. Record of the Politburo meeting criticizing the Gang of Four, May 27 and June 3, 1975, quoted in Shi Yun and Li Danhui, *Continuous Revolution That Was Difficult to Continue*, pp. 522–523.

45. CCP Central Committee Documentary Research Room (ed.), *Chronology of Deng Xiaoping: 1975–1997*, vol. 1, Zhongyang wenxian chubanshe, p. 53.

46. Wu De, *Wu De's Oral Account*, p. 162.

47. Record of Gao Wenqian's interview with Ji Dengkui, quoted in Gao Wenqian, *Zhao Enlai's Later Years*, p. 575.

25. FROM GENERAL OVERHAUL TO THE CAMPAIGN AGAINST DENG AND RIGHT-DEVIATING VERDICT-REVERSAL

1. TN: The Chinese term used here, *zhengdun*, can be translated in a number of ways, including "readjustment," "reorganization," "rectification," "consolidation," etc. Various works have provided different translations for Deng's actions and policies at this time. Given that Deng's policies incorporated both ideological and organizational elements, we have chosen to use the relatively ambiguous "overhaul" in this context.

2. Shi Yun and Li Danhui, *The Continuous Revolution That Was Difficult to Continue: From Criticizing Lin to Criticizing Deng*, Chinese University of Hong Kong Press, 2008, p. 531.

3. *Selected Works of Deng Xiaoping*, vol. 2, Renmin chubanshe, 1994, p. 9.

4. CCP Central Committee Documentary Research Room (ed.), *Chronology of Deng Xiaoping: 1975–1997*, vol. 1, Zhongyang wenxian chubanshe, 2004, pp. 59–60.

5. Xu Jingxian, *The Ten-Year Dream*, Hong Kong: Shidai guoji chuban gongsi, 2003, p. 373.

6. Mao Mao, *My Father, Deng Xiaoping: The Cultural Revolution Years*, Beijing: Zhongyang wenxian chubanshe, 2000, p. 376.

7. Mao Mao, *My Father, Deng Xiaoping: The Cultural Revolution Years*, pp. 352–353.

8. CCP Central Committee Documentary Research Room (ed.), *Chronology of Mao Zedong: 1949–1976*, vol. 6, Beijing: Zhongyang wenxian chubanshe, 2013, p. 619.

9. In *The Water Margin*, Chao Gai and Song Jiang are bandit leaders, and Gao Qiu, an evil official and general, is the chief villain.

10. CCP Central Committee Documentary Research Room (ed.), *Chronology of Mao Zedong: 1949–1976*, vol. 6, pp. 602–603.

11. CCP Central Committee Documentary Research Room (ed.), *Chronology of Mao Zedong: 1949–1976*, vol. 6, p. 604.

12. TN: In *The Water Margin*, Chao Gai dies before the Grand Assembly of the 108 heroes, but he continues to serve as a "spiritual guardian" to the outlaw band.

13. CCP Central Committee Documentary Research Room (ed.), *Chronology of Mao Zedong: 1949–1976*, vol. 6, p. 605.

14. An Jianshe, ed., *Zhou Enlai's Last Years: 1966–1976*, Zhongyang wenxian chubanshe, 1995, pp. 352–535.

15. Zhang Zuoliang, *Zhou Enlai's Last Ten Years: A Doctor's Recollections*, Shanghai renmin chubanshe, 1997, pp. 360–361. During the Cultural Revolution, when someone was struck down, an X was drawn through his name or over his face in photographs.

16. Gao Wenqian, "In the Last Days: Recalling the Seriously Ill and Hospitalized Comrade Zhou Enlai," in *History Pondered Here: A Record of 1966–1976*, ed. Zhou Ming, Beijing: Huaxia chubanshe, 1986, p. 79.

686 | NOTES TO PAGES 517–526

17. CCP Central Committee Documentary Research Room (ed.), *Chronology of Mao Zedong: 1949–1976*, vol. 6, p. 604.

18. CCP Central Committee Documentary Research Room (ed.), *Chronology of Mao Zedong: 1949–1976*, vol. 6, p. 610.

19. Liu Bing, *Years of Trials: Tsinghua 1964–1976*, Dangdai Zhongguo chubanshe, 2008, pp. 174–175.

20. Xu Jingxian, *Ten-Year Dream*, p. 377.

21. CCP Central Committee Documentary Research Room (ed.), *Chronology of Mao Zedong: 1949–1976*, vol. 6, p. 614.

22. CCP Central Committee Documentary Research Room (ed.), *Chronology of Mao Zedong: 1949–1976*, vol. 6, p. 614.

23. Wu De, as told to Zhu Shiyuan et al., *Wu De's Oral Account: A Chronicle of Ten Years of Trials and Hardships—Some of My Experiences Working in Beijing*, Dangdai Zhongguo chubanshe, 2004, p. 162.

24. Gao Wenqian, *Zhao Enlai's Later Years*, Mingjing chubanshe, 2004, 26th printing, p. 576.

25. CCP Central Committee Documentary Research Room (ed.), *Chronology of Mao Zedong: 1949–1976*, vol. 6, p. 619.

26. CCP Central Committee Documentary Research Room (ed.), *Chronology of Mao Zedong: 1949–1976*, vol. 6, p. 620.

27. What Mao Yuanxin told Ma Tianshui in the Jingxi Guesthouse while Deng was being denounced. Quoted in Xu Jingxian, *Ten-Year Dream*, p. 375.

28. CCP Central Committee Documentary Research Room (ed.), *Chronology of Mao Zedong: 1949–1976*, vol. 6, pp. 620–621.

29. CCP Central Committee Documentary Research Room (ed.), *Chronology of Mao Zedong: 1949–1976*, vol. 6, p. 621.

30. Ji Pomin, "In Office, Out of Office, Appointed and Dismissed: Listening to My Father Ji Dengkui Talk of the Past," Gongshiwang, October 14, 2013 10:25.

31. CCP Central Committee Documentary Research Room (ed.), *Chronology of Mao Zedong: 1949–1976*, vol. 6, p. 623.

32. CCP Central Committee Documentary Research Room (ed.), *Chronology of Mao Zedong: 1949–1976*, vol. 6, p. 624.

33. TN: Zhang Xun (1854–1923) was a Qing dynasty general who attempted to restore Puyi as emperor in the Manchu Restoration of 1917.

34. Li Xun, *The Revolutionary Rebel Era: A History of Shanghai's Cultural Revolution Movement*, Hong Kong: Oxford University Press, 2015, p. 1360.

35. Xiao Mu's conversation with Li Xun, quoted in Li Xun, *Revolutionary Rebel Era*, pp. 1361–1363.

36. CCP Central Committee Documentary Research Room (ed.), *Chronology of Mao Zedong: 1949–1976*, vol. 6, p. 625.

37. CCP Central Committee Documentary Research Room (ed.), *Chronology of Deng Xiaoping: 1975–1997*, vol. 2, p. 92, records that Deng Xiaoping received the delegation of journalists on September 5 but doesn't provide all of the content.

38. Record of interview with veteran revolutionary Wang Chun, wife of former vice-premier Ji Dengkui, published in *Weekend Journal*, no. 45, November 16, 2013.

39. CCP Central Committee's notice and appendices on transmitting "Main Points of Cautioning," November 26, 1975, Document No. 53 [1975].

40. CCP Central Committee Documentary Research Room (ed.), *Chronology of Deng Xiaoping: 1975–1997*, vol. 1, pp. 136–137.

41. Xu Jingxian, *Ten-Year Dream*, p. 381.
42. Xu Jingxian, *Ten-Year Dream*, p. 140.
43. Xu Jingxian, *Ten-Year Dream*, p. 145.
44. CCP Central Committee Documentary Research Room (ed.), *Chronology of Mao Zedong: 1949–1976*, vol. 6, pp. 634–635.
45. Yan Changgui, "Mao Yuanxin Again Speaks of Mao Zedong's Situation in 1976," *Yanhuang Chunqiu*, no. 10, November 2012.
46. Zhang Sheng, *Biography of Zhang Aiping: Emerging from Battle—a Dialogue Between Two Generations of Soldiers*, Zhongguo qingnian chubanshe, 2008, quoted in Li Lu, "Qian Xuesen, Distinguished by Wounding Words and Promoting the Great Leap Forward," *Humanities Reference*, no. 1, 2011.
47. Zhang Guangyou, *Indelible Memories: A Record of Major Events of the Republic*, Xinhua chubanshe, 2008, pp. 155–156.
48. Tang Qishan, born in 1931, was a railway worker who fought in the Korean War as an engine stoker. He joined the party in 1956. During the Cultural Revolution he was a rebel leader in Henan, and he served as party secretary of the Zhengzhou Railway Bureau, member of the provincial party committee standing committee, and party secretary of Zhengzhou, as well as in other positions. He was a member of the Ninth and Tenth Central Committees and a member of the standing committee of the Fourth National People's Congress.
49. TN: See chapter 18 for more on the factional conflict in Yunnan.
50. CCP Yunnan Provincial Party Committee Party History Research Room, ed., Record of Major Events in Yunnan's Cultural Revolution Movement, internal report, May 18, 2005.
51. Cao Chengyi, first draft, "Speaking of the Cultural Revolution with Mixed Feelings," ed. Chuan Yi, self-published, 2008, pp. 88–92.
52. Lao Tian, "Record of Conversations with People Who Experienced the Cultural Revolution (Mr. Xie)."
53. Cai Wenbin, "Zhao Ziyang in the Eyes of a Rebel Faction Member," *Zuotian* (*Yesterday*), no. 9, 2012.

26. THE APRIL FIFTH MOVEMENT

1. TN: English translations of these poems can be accessed at sites.google.com /site/babywords/mao-ze-dong-shi-ci-ying-yi-ben-gong36shou-han-ying-dui -zhao-translated-by-yan-xianyi, last accessed on October 26, 2017.
2. Bao Tong, formerly deputy director of the State Economic System Reform Commission, assisted Zhao Ziyang with political reforms. After the political turmoil in 1989, Bao spent several years in prison and has remained under house arrest since his release but publishes political commentaries in the overseas media.
3. CCP Central Committee Documentary Research Room (ed.), *Chronology of Mao Zedong* records Mao's diplomatic activities after Zhou Enlai died: On February 23 he met the U.S. president Richard Nixon, on March 17 he met a delegation from Laos, on April 20 he met with Vice-President Hosni Mubarak of Egypt, on April 30 he met with Prime Minister Robert Muldoon of New Zealand, on May 12 he met with Prime Minister Lee Kuan-yew of Singapore, and on May 27 he met with Prime Minister Zulfikar Ali Bhutto of Pakistan. He received no more foreign guests after that.

4. Liu Tiancheng, *The Memorable Time Thirty Years Ago: Commemorating the Thirtieth Anniversary of the "April 5th Movement."*

5. Lei Feng was a PLA soldier held up as an example for the entire country because of his love of helping others. He died in the line of duty at the age of twenty-two. Mao wrote the dedication "Learn from Comrade Lei Feng" on March 5, 1963, and March 5 was designated as the day when people all over China would learn from Lei Feng.

6. Yang Kaihui married Mao in 1920 and bore him three children before being arrested in October 1930 and executed in November. Two years before Yang lost her life, in 1928, Mao married He Zizhen. From 1928 to 1930, Mao led his army past the Yang family home near Changsha on two occasions without taking his wife and children with him. During the April Fifth Movement, mentions of Yang Kaihui were veiled criticisms of Mao's current wife, Jiang Qing.

7. The content for the Nanjing Incident is drawn from Wu Xueqing, "The Whole Story of the 'Nanjing Incident,'" *Bainianchao*, no. 8, 2002.

8. He Yuan, "Dust-Laden Memories: The 1976 'Qing Ming Incident' in Zhengzhou," October 7, 2005, Wuyouzhixiang website, wyzxsx.com.

9. Quoted in Song Yongyi et al., eds., *Chinese Cultural Revolution Database*, 3rd ed., Universities Service Centre for China Studies, Chinese University of Hong Kong Press, 2013, important heterodox documents from the Cultural Revolution. In this material, the quote "Thoroughly reform the socialist system, thoroughly improve the dictatorship of the proletariat" does not contain the word "thoroughly." However, the author clearly remembers the word "thoroughly" being included at that time.

10. Yin Hongbiao, *Footprints of the Lost*, Chinese University of Hong Kong Press, 2010, pp. 100–101.

11. Yin Hongbiao, *Footprints of the Lost*, pp. 101–109.

12. Song Yongyi et al., *Chinese Cultural Revolution Database*.

13. Wang Renzhou, a student at the Beijing Foreign Languages Institute with a contemplative bent, was expelled from school in 1964 as a "reactionary student" and sent to the countryside. The Ba River First Command Post was banned in February 1967 by the local authorities, and Wang was arrested. Released after the July 20, 1967, Wuhan Incident, he went home and organized a "new village" that put Mao's utopian vision into practice. Wang subsequently died in prison.

14. After Reform and Opening began, Yang Xiaokai went to the United States to study and became a famous economist. He died in Australia at the age of fifty.

15. Yin Hongbiao, *Footprints of the Lost*, pp. 433–434, 436.

16. Li Yizhe, "On a Socialist Democracy and Legal System," November 7, 1974, in Song Yongyi et al., *Chinese Cultural Revolution Database*.

17. Yin Hongbiao, *Footprints of the Lost*, pp. 396–404.

18. Yin Hongbiao, *Footprints of the Lost*, pp. 381–384.

19. Yin Hongbiao, "From the New Thought Trend to the New Class: Thought Trends and Criticism in Youth Society During the Cultural Revolution," in *The Cultural Revolution: Historical Truth and Collective Memory*, ed. Song Yongyi, Hong Kong: Tianyuan shuwu chubanshe, 2010, vol. 1, pp. 349–352.

20. Veteran cadres made up the main political force calling for restoration of the pre–Cultural Revolution social order. By 1980, this group had divided into the Chen Yun faction, which wanted restoration of the conditions preceding

1957, and the Deng Xiaoping faction, which wanted to establish market economy. Both insisted on the socialist road and the dictatorship of the proletariat.

21. Chen Ziming (1952–2014) was a political scientist and an activist in the Chinese democracy movement. As a participant in the 1976 April Fifth Movement, he became a representative of the masses at the square. Following the turmoil in Beijing in 1989, the authorities sentenced him to thirteen years in prison and an additional four years' deprivation of political rights for "conspiracy to subvert the government, and counterrevolutionary propaganda and incitement." During and after his imprisonment he published many political commentaries, which were published in twelve volumes as *Collected Works of Chen Ziming*.

22. Chen Ziming, *The Democracy Movement in China: Collected Works of Chen Ziming*, vol. 4, Hong Kong: Shijie huawen chuban jigou, 2010, p. 122.

23. Chen Ziming, *Democracy Movement in China*, pp. 140–141.

24. Wu Zhong, as told to Chen Chusan and Li Dazhen, "My Experience of the 1976 Tiananmen Incident," *Yanhuang Chunqiu*, no. 3, 2012.

25. CCP Central Committee Documentary Research Office, *Biography of Mao Zedong: 1949–1976*, vol. 2, Zhongyang wenxian chubanshe, 2003, p. 1768.

26. Wu Zhong, "My Experience of the 1976 Tiananmen Incident."

27. Chen Ziming, *Democracy Movement in China*, pp. 149–150.

28. Zhao Wentao, "Qing Ming 1976: I Acted as a Hatchet Man Under Orders."

29. Mao Mao, *My Father, Deng Xiaoping: The Cultural Revolution Years*, Zhongyang wenxian chubanshe, 2000, p. 469.

30. Shi Yizhi, "My Ten Years in the Public Security Ministry" (as related to his wife, Chen Feng, and according to his appeal material), internal document, 2002, p. 70.

31. In 1956, the Hungarian people carried out mass protests against autocracy. Subsequently, the CCP advised the Soviet Union to suppress them by military force. Imre Nagy, a senior Hungarian official who promoted democratic reform and served as president, was an activist in this movement and won public support. After the protests were suppressed, Nagy was executed. Prior to Reform and Opening, the CCP referred to the Hungarian Incident as a counterrevolutionary uprising.

32. Zhang Chunqiao's letter to his son, Zhang Maodi, April 18, 1976.

33. See Wang Wing'an, "The Handling of People Arrested in the Tiananmen Incident," *Qingkuang huibian*, no. 726, November 15, 1978. By November 1978, all 388 were released, except 3 who remained imprisoned on charges of arson and looting rather than as being counterrevolutionaries.

34. Mao Mao, *My Father, Deng Xiaoping: The Cultural Revolution Years*, p. 473.

35. CCP Central Committee Documentary Research Room (ed.), *Chronology of Mao Zedong: 1949–1976*, vol. 5, Beijing: Zhongyang wenxian chubanshe, 2013, p. 646.

36. Mao Mao, *My Father, Deng Xiaoping*, pp. 475–477, 482.

37. Bao Zunxin (1937–2007) became a pioneer of China's liberal and democratic thinking by editing the book series Toward the Future in the early 1980s. During the 1989 student movement, he and several other intellectuals went to Tiananmen Square and advised the students to end their hunger strike. He was subsequently jailed for five years as one of the "black hands" behind the movement, along with Chen Ziming, Wang Juntao, Liu Xiaobo, and others.

27. THE CURTAIN FALLS ON THE CULTURAL REVOLUTION

1. CCP Central Committee Documentary Research Office, *Biography of Mao Zedong: 1949–1976*, Zhongyang wenxian chubanshe, 2003, pp. 1774, 1776, 1777.
2. TN: Miki's party lost its majority in the Diet as a result of the election, after which Miki tendered his resignation and was succeeded in December 1976.
3. Lin Ke, Xu Tao, and Wu Xujun, *The Truth of History*, Zhongyang wenxian chubanshe, 1998, p. 154, quoted in *Biography of Mao Zedong: 1949–1976*, p. 1777.
4. Xinhua News Agency, *Galleys of Domestic Trends*, September 11, 1976.
5. Shi Yizhi, "My Ten Years in the Public Security Ministry" (as related to his wife, Chen Feng, and according to his appeal material), internal document, 2002, pp. 55, 63.
6. Qin Chu, "Chen Yonggui Talks About Hua Guofeng, Jiang Qing, and Hu Yaobang," *Historical Research*, no. 4, 2006.
7. Fan Shuo, *Ye Jianying in 1976*, Beijing: Zhongyang dangxiao chubanshe, 1995, pp. 259–262.
8. Li Xun, *The Revolutionary Rebel Era: A History of Shanghai's Cultural Revolution Movement*, Hong Kong: Oxford University Press, 2015, p. 1558.
9. Ding Sheng says that the letter written by Xu Shiyou's son, Xu Jianjun, was signed and sealed by Ding and Liao Hansheng and then sent to the Central Committee. Ding and Liao were the commander and political commissar of the Nanjing Military Region at that time. See Ding Sheng, *Hero in Hardship: The Memoirs of General Ding Sheng*, ed. Jin Guang and Yu Ruxin, Hong Kong: Xingke'er chuban gongsi, 2008, p. 252. The contents of the letter quoted here were related to this author by an informed person in the Xinhua News Agency at that time.
10. Sun Yuguo started out as the head of a frontier station in Heilongjiang, but after being declared a hero in the Battle of Zhenbao Island between China and the Soviet Union in March 1969, he was commended by Mao during the Ninth Party Congress and then rapidly rose through the ranks. In February 1974 he was named deputy commander of the Shenyang Military Region.
11. After the members of the Cultural Revolution faction in the central leadership were arrested in October, the Central Special Investigations Group asked the Tianjin municipal party committee to ascertain whether Zhang Chunqiao had been a traitor. Zhang had left Shanghai for Yan'an in 1937, and when passing through Jinan he had stayed at the home of the Jinan police bureau director, Zhao Fucheng, who was an agent for the Renaissance Society, a fascist organization within the Kuomintang. After 1949, Zhao Fucheng lived in Tianjin. Wang Hui, the head of the Tianjin municipal party committee secretariat who took part in the investigation, says that Zhao did not testify to Zhang being a traitor, but said, "I knew about Zhang, but Zhang didn't know about me." See Wang Hui, *A Personal History of the Cultural Revolution in Tianjin*, self-published, 2011, p. 254.
12. This was related to this author by a journalist at the Xinhua News Agency's Henan branch, Ji Shifa, and a veteran Xinhua editor, Xie Lifu.
13. Zhang Yaoci, *The Memoirs of Zhang Yaoci: The Days with Mao*, Zhonggong dangshi chubanshe, 2008.
14. Li Xun, *Revolutionary Rebel Era*, p. 1544.

15. Li Xun, *Revolutionary Rebel Era*, p. 1544.
16. Wang Zhongren, "The Whole Story Behind the Essay 'Handle Things According to the Fixed Policy,'" *Yanhuang Chunqiu*, no. 2, 2003.
17. It was subsequently proven that Jiang Qing was not a traitor.
18. Yao Jin, *A Hundred Evening Talks with Yao Yilin*, Zhongguo shangye chubanshe, 1998, p. 190.
19. My book *The Deng Xiaoping Era*, Zhongyang bianyi chubanshe, 1998, p. 92, describes Mao's criticism of Jiang Qing as "disappointment with unmet expectations," which drew criticism from the deputy director of the Central Propaganda Department, Liu Yunshan. Since then, many scholars have used this phrase.
20. Xiao Jinguang, *The Memoirs of Xiao Jinguang (Continued)*, Beijing: Jiefangjun chubanshe, 1984, pp. 351–352.
21. Fan Shuo, *Ye Jianying in 1976*, p. 274.
22. Nie Rongzhen, *The Memoirs of Nie Rongzhen*, vol. 2, Beijing: Jiefangjun chubanshe, 1995, p. 274.
23. Cheng Zhensheng, "Li Xiannian and the Smashing of the 'Gang of Four,'" *CCP Party History Research*, no. 1, 2002.
24. After retiring, Mao Yuanxin told this to Jiang Qing's former secretary, Yan Changgui. Yang Changgui told it to the author over dinner on December 21, 2007.
25. TN: Jin Zumin was a rebel organization leader and a member of the standing committee of the Shanghai municipal party committee.
26. Zhang Yaoci, *Memoirs of Zhang Yaoci*, pp. 270–271.
27. Zhang Yaoci, *Memoirs of Zhang Yaoci*, pp. 271–272.
28. Geng Biao joined the party in 1926 and was a high-ranking officer in the PLA. In 1950 he was transferred to the Foreign Ministry and was stationed at many embassies.
29. Li Pu and his wife, Shen Rong, spoke of this many times to the author.
30. Li Pu and Shen Rong spoke of this many times to the author.
31. TN: Chi Haotian was deputy political commissar of the Beijing Military Region at that time. He continued to rise in the ranks from then on and served as defense minister from 1993 to 2003, as well as being appointed to the Politburo.
32. Mao Mao, *My Father, Deng Xiaoping: The Cultural Revolution Years*, Zhongyang wenxian chubanshe, 2000, p. 523.
33. Shi Yun and Li Danhui, *The Continuous Revolution That Was Difficult to Continue: From Criticizing Lin to Criticizing Deng*, Chinese University of Hong Kong Press, 2008, p. 709.
34. Li Xun, *Revolutionary Rebel Era*, 2015, p. 1563.
35. Li Xun, *Revolutionary Rebel Era*, pp. 712, 713.
36. Li Xun, *Revolutionary Rebel Era*, p. 714.
37. Unless otherwise noted, the material on Shanghai's response to the October Coup is drawn from Li Xun, *Revolutionary Rebel Era*, pp. 1553–1593.
38. "Zhang Sizhi Reveals the Inside Story Behind the Trials of the Lin Biao, Jiang Qing Counterrevolutionary Clique," *Southern Metropolitan Daily*; Zhang Sizhi, as told to Yang Xiaoguang, "My Heterodox Defense in the Trial of the 'Gang of Four.'" Zhang Sizhi was designated the defense attorney for Jiang Qing, but Jiang Qing rejected him, so he subsequently became Li Zuopeng's defense lawyer.

39. Gao Wenqian, *Zhao Enlai's Later Years*, Mingjing chubanshe, 2004, 26th printing, p. 550.

40. Qiu Huizuo, *The Memoirs of Qiu Huizuo*, Hong Kong: Xinshiji chubanshe (New Century Press), 2011, p. 930.

41. "Zhang Sizhi Reveals the Inside Story," *Southern Metropolitan Daily*; Zhang Sizhi, "My Heterodox Defense."

28. CHINA'S FOREIGN RELATIONS DURING THE CULTURAL REVOLUTION

1. He Fang went to study at the Yan'an Anti-Japanese Military and Political College in 1938. In 1950 he joined the Foreign Ministry and served as head of the research office of the PRC embassy in the Soviet Union and also as deputy director of the Foreign Ministry General Office. From 1978 onward, he served as director of the Japan Research Institute of the Chinese Academy of Social Sciences and as deputy secretary-general of the State Council's Institute of International Studies. He is an honorary member of CASS.

2. When I asked He Fang to read and evaluate the initial draft of this chapter, his wife, Song Yimin, reported He Fang's words in her reply to me.

3. Wei Meiya, "Tracing the Entire Distribution of *Quotations from Chairman Mao*," *Yanhuang Chunqiu*, no. 8, 1993.

4. Huang Hua, "Absurd Foreign Affairs During the Cultural Revolution," Gongshiwang, December 5, 2014, 11:52, originally from Huang Hua, *Personally Experienced, Seen, and Heard*.

5. "Three freedoms and one contract" was "family plot, free markets, sole responsibility for profits and losses, and contracting production to households" among the peasants.

6. "Three appeasements and one reduction" was "appeasement toward imperialism, revisionism, and reactionaries in various countries, and reduced support for national liberation movements."

7. "Three capitulations and one extinguishing" was "capitulating to imperialism, revisionism, and reactionaries in various countries, and extinguishing the flames of the revolutionary people's movement."

8. Ma Jisen, *A True Record of the Foreign Ministry During the Cultural Revolution*, Chinese University of Hong Kong Press, 2003, pp. 312, 313.

9. *China Statistical Yearbook 1984*, p. 454.

10. *Lexicon of China's National Situation*, Zhongguo guoji guangbo chubanshe, 1991, p. 1208, quoted in Ma Jisen, *True Record of the Foreign Ministry*, p. 315.

11. *Lexicon of China's National Situation*, p. 295, quoted in Ma Jisen, *True Record of the Foreign Ministry*, p. 314.

12. Yang Rongjia, *Secrets of the Republic's Foreign Ministry*, Hong Kong: Dashan wenhua chubanshe, 2011, pp. 139–142.

13. Ne Win was Burma's president at the time.

14. TN: See chapter 15.

15. Yang Rongjia, *Secrets of the Republic's Foreign Ministry*, pp. 143–146.

16. TN: See chapter 15.

17. Huang Hua, "Absurd Foreign Affairs During the Cultural Revolution."

18. TN: See chapter 15.

19. CCP Central Committee Documentary Research Room (ed.), *Chronology of Mao Zedong: 1949–1976*, vol. 6, Beijing: Zhongyang wenxian chubanshe, 2013, pp. 113–114.

20. CCP Central Committee Documentary Research Room (ed.), *Chronology of Zhou Enlai*, vol. 2, Zhongyang wenxian chubanshe, 1997, pp. 183–184.

21. Ma Jisen, *True Record of the Foreign Ministry*, pp. 277–278.

22. CCP Central Committee Documentary Research Room (ed.), *Chronology of Mao Zedong: 1949–1976*, vol. 6, pp. 142–143. The Central Committee's International Liaison Department had published Anzai's views in a bulletin titled *Anzai et al. Believe That Japan Cannot Take the Road of the Villages Surrounding the Cities.*

23. CCP Central Committee Documentary Research Room (ed.), *Chronology of Mao Zedong: 1949–1976*, vol. 6, pp. 163–164.

24. CCP Central Committee Documentary Research Room (ed.), *Chronology of Mao Zedong: 1949–1976*, vol. 6, p. 237.

25. CCP Central Committee Documentary Research Room (ed.), *Chronology of Zhou Enlai*, vol. 2, pp. 395, 396.

26. Xie Yixian, ed., *History China's Foreign Affairs: People's Republic of China Period 1949–1979*, Henan renmin chubanshe, 1988, p. 392.

27. CCP Central Committee Documentary Research Room (ed.), *Chronology of Mao Zedong: 1949–1976*, vol. 5, p. 301.

28. Mao's conversation with Zhou Enlai, Ji Pengfei, and others on July 24, 1972, quoted in Li Danhui, "The Sino-Soviet Split and China's Foreign Relations During the Cultural Revolution Period," *Party History Research Materials*, no. 1, 1997.

29. CCP Central Committee Documentary Research Room, *Biography of Mao Zedong: 1949–1976*, Zhongyang wenxian chubanshe, 2003, p. 1619; Ma Jisen, *True Record of the Foreign Ministry*, p 298; CCP Central Committee Documentary Research Room (ed.), *Chronology of Zhou Enlai*, vol. 2, p. 338: Zhou "Here are three telegrams reporting on China's representative in Poland receiving the American ambassador. I suggest we wait for a bit to see everyone's reaction and then decide how to reply." Mao responded with the memo, "Act accordingly."

30. CCP Central Committee Documentary Research Room (ed.), *Chronology of Zhou Enlai*, vol. 2, p. 356.

31. Ma Jisen, *True Record of the Foreign Ministry*, p. 299.

32. *The Memoirs of Richard Nixon*, vol. 2, Shangwu yinshuguan, 1970, p. 230. Quoted in *Biography of Mao Zedong: 1949–1976*, p. 1620.

33. Qian Jiang, "The Whole Story of Ping-Pong Diplomacy," *The Diaoyutai Files: The Major Sino-U.S. Diplomatic Storm*, quoted in Ma Jisen, *True Record of the Foreign Ministry*, pp. 300–301.

34. Roderick MacFarquhar and Michael Schoenhals, *Mao's Last Revolution* (Chinese edition, trans. Guan Xin, proofreader Tang Shaojie), Hong Kong: Xinke'er chuban (Xianggang) youxian gongsi, 2009, p. 352. TN: English edition, Belknap Press of Harvard University Press, 2006, p. 347.

35. Shi Yun, Li Danhui, *The Continuous Revolution That Was Difficult to Continue: From Criticizing Lin to Criticizing Deng*, Chinese University of Hong Kong Press, 2008, pp. 81–82. TN: U.S. Department of State Archive, Foreign Relations, 1969–1976, Volume E-13, Documents on China, 1969–1972, Memorandum of Conversation, January 7, 1971, 2001-2009.state.gov/r/pa/ho/frus/nixon/e13/72530.htm.

36. TN: For the full text, see "Joint Statement Following Discussions with Leaders of the People's Republic of China," Office of the Historian, U.S. Department of State, history.state.gov/historicaldocuments/frus1969-76v17/d203.

37. Huang Hua, "Absurd Foreign Affairs During the Cultural Revolution."

38. TN: For a transcript of this conversation, see Office of the Historian, U.S. Department of State, Memorandum of Conversation, Beijing, February 17–18, 1973, history.state.gov/historicaldocuments/frus1969-76v18/d12.

39. CCP Central Committee Documentary Research Room (ed.), *Chronology of Mao Zedong: 1949–1976*, vol. 6, pp. 520–521. TN: Mao's concept of the three worlds was slightly different from that proposed by French scholar Alfred Sauvy in the early 1950s, which has been more widely adopted in the international community. See Zhou Taomo, "Ambivalent Alliance: Chinese Policy Toward Indonesia, 1960–1965," Woodrow Wilson International Center for Scholars, Cold War International History Project, Working Paper no. 67, p. 5, FN 12.

40. See Lenin's 1917 "Imperialism, the Highest Stage of Capitalism."

41. Deng Xiaoping, "Peace and Development Are the Two Significant Issues of the Modern World," *Selected Works of Deng Xiaoping*, vol. 3, Renmin chubanshe, 1993, pp. 104–105.

42. He Fang, *The Autobiography of He Fang: Reflections on the Road from Yan'an*, Hong Kong, Ming bao chubanshe, 2007, simplified character edition, self-printed in 2011, pp. 459–460.

29. REFORM AND OPENING UNDER THE BUREAUCRATIC SYSTEM

1. Hua Guofeng, "Carry Out Continuous Revolution Under the Dictatorship of the Proletariat to the End: Study Vol. 5 of Selected Works of Mao Zedong," *People's Daily*, May 1, 1977.

2. *People's Daily*, October 22, 1976.

3. *People's Daily*, October 23, 1976.

4. Dalian and Lüshun merged as Lüda on December 1, 1950. In 1981, Lüda was renamed Dalian, with Lüshunkou as a constituent district.

5. "Deng Xiaoping's Letter to Hua Guofeng, Ye Jianying, and the Party Central Committee," April 10, 1977.

6. "Completely and Accurately Understand Mao Zedong Thought," July 21, 1977, *Selected Works of Deng Xiaoping*, vol. 2, Renmin chubanshe, 1994, p. 42.

7. TN: "Song of the Torches," in Huang Xiang *A Bilingual Edition of Poetry Out of Communist China*, trans. Andrew J. Emerson, Edwin Mellen Press, 2004, p. 83.

8. Some of these publications included *April Fifth Forum, Today, Reference News for the Masses, Seeking Truth, Fertile Soil, Exploration, Beijing Spring*, and *Breaking Waves*, among many others.

9. Hu Yaobang, "Introduction to the Theoretical Conference," Central Documentary Research Room, ed., *Selection of Important Documents Since the Third Plenum*, Renmin chubanshe, 1982, pp. 46–60.

10. The "Nine Commentaries" referred to nine polemics published in *People's Daily* between September 1963 and July 1964 attacking the Soviet Union. These essays were written by a group organized by the Central Committee and vetted and finalized by Mao.

11. *People's Daily*, November 27, 1978; CCP Central Committee Documentary Research Room (ed.), *Chronology of Deng Xiaoping: 1975–1997*, vol. 1, Zhongyang wenxian chubanshe, pp. 436–437, records this conversation but

edits out this passage. TN: For an English language report on Deng's remarks, see *New York Times*, November 26, 1978.

12. Deng Liqun, *Twelve Springs and Summers (1975–1087)*, draft for soliciting opinions, 2005, pp. 206–207.

13. *Selected Works of Deng Xiaoping*, vol. 2, pp. 165–173.

14. During his southern tour in 1992, Deng Xiaoping said, "The essence of socialism is liberating productive force, developing productive force, abolishing exploitation, eliminating polarization, and ultimately achieving shared prosperity." He completely abandoned the textbook definition of socialism as characterized by public ownership of the means of production, planned economy, and distribution according to work done.

15. A Xinhua News Agency journalist who covered this story, Yang Kexian, told me in 2010 that Fu Yuehua's imprisonment was a case of injustice.

16. TN: For an official English translation of the interview, see "Answers to the Italian Journalist Oriana Fallaci, August 21 and 23, 1980," en.people.cn /dengxp/vol2/text/b1470.html (also in *Selected Works of Deng Xiaoping*).

17. Various volumes of *China Statistical Yearbook*, National Bureau of Statistics, ed., Zhongguo tongji chubanshe.

18. National Bureau of Statistics, *China Statistical Yearbook*, various years.

19. National Bureau of Statistics, *China Statistical Yearbook*, various years.

20. National Bureau of Statistics, *China Statistical Yearbook*, various years. There are discrepancies between the figures reported in one year and in the year before because figures in the subsequent year revise figures in the previous year. Here the figures provided in the subsequent year are used.

21. TN: The ranks from top down are ministry/department (*bu*), bureau (*ju, ting*), division (*chu*), and section (*ke*).

22. Figures obtained by the author while reporting on the State Commission for Public Sector Reform in 1990.

23. Figures obtained by the author while reporting on the State Commission for Public Sector Reform in 1990.

24. Extracted from National Bureau of Statistics, *China Statistical Summary*, various years.

25. Chen Yizi, *The Memoirs of Chen Yizi*, Hong Kong: Xinshiji chubanshe (New Century Press), 2013, pp. 294–295.

26. For the specifics on China's income disparity, see Yang Jisheng, *Analysis of Social Classes in Contemporary China*, Jiangxi gaoxiao chubanshe, 2013, pp. 59–84.

INDEX

A NOTE ABOUT THE AUTHOR

Yang Jisheng was born in 1940, joined the Chinese Communist Party in 1964, and worked for the Xinhua News Agency from January 1968 until his retirement in 2001. For fifteen years, he was a deputy editor at *Yanhuang Chunqiu* (*Chronicles of History*), an official journal that regularly skirted censorship with articles on controversial political topics. In 2015, he resigned under official pressure. For his groundbreaking work *Tombstone*, Yang won Sweden's Stieg Larsson prize for journalistic courage in 2015, and the Louis M. Lyons Award for Conscience and Integrity in Journalism, presented by the Nieman Fellows at Harvard University, in 2016. *Tombstone* also won the Manhattan Institute's 2013 Hayek Book Prize and the 2013 Lemkin Book Award from the Institute for the Study of Genocide. Yang Jisheng lives in Beijing with his wife and two children.

A NOTE ABOUT THE TRANSLATORS

Stacy Mosher learned Chinese in Hong Kong, where she lived for more than seventeen years. A longtime journalist, Mosher currently works as a translator and editor in Brooklyn, New York.

Guo Jian is a professor of English at the University of Wisconsin–Whitewater. Originally trained in the Chinese language and literature, Guo was on the Chinese faculty of Beijing Normal University until he came to the United States to study for his Ph.D. in English in the mid-1980s.